SIXTH EDITION

Residential Mortgage Lending

Principles and Practices

Thomas J. Pinkowish

President, REMOC Associates, LLC
www.remoc.com

President, Community Lending Associates, LLC
www.communitylendassoc.com

CENGAGE
Learning™

Australia • Brazil • Japan • Korea • Mexico • Singapore • Spain • United Kingdom • United States

CENGAGE Learning™

Residential Mortgage Lending: Principles and Practices, Sixth Edition
Thomas J. Pinkowish

Vice President/Editor-in-Chief: Dave Shaut

Acquisitions Editor: Sara Glassmeyer

Development Editor: Arlin Kauffman, LEAP Publishing Services

Sr. Marketing and Sales Manager: Mark Linton

Sr. Frontlist Buyer, Manufacturing: Charlene Taylor

Sr. Art Director: Pamela Galbreath

Content Project Management: PreMediaGlobal

Production Service: PreMediaGlobal

Copyeditor: PreMediaGlobal

Compositor: PreMediaGlobal

Internal Designer: PreMediaGlobal

Cover Designer: Chris Miller

Cover Image: Bethany Casey

For product information and technology assistance, contact us at **Cengage Learning Customer & Sales Support, 1-800-354-9706**

For permission to use material from this text or product, submit all requests online at **www.cengage.com/permissions** Further permissions questions can be emailed to **permissionrequest@cengage.com**

Library of Congress Control Number: 2011925555

ISBN-13: 978-0-324-78464-0

ISBN-10: 0-324-78464-3

Cengage Learning
5191 Natorp Boulevard
Mason, OH 45040
USA

Cengage Learning products are represented in Canada by Nelson Education, Ltd.

For your course and learning solutions, visit **academic.cengage.com**

Purchase any of our products at your local college store or at our preferred online store **www.cengagebrain.com**

Printed in the United States of America
1 2 3 4 5 6 7 15 14 13 12 11

CONTENTS

LIST OF FIGURES AND TABLES   ix

PREFACE   xv

PART **1**   **Principles**

CHAPTER **1**   **History of Mortgage Lending   1**
The Beginning   2
Roman Law   3
English Developments   3
American Developments   4
Government Intervention   8
Recent Residential Mortgage Lending   15
The 1980s: The Decade of Historic Change   16
The 1990s: A Shift in Policy, Boom Years,
and a Fundamental Change   17
2000–2010: The Rise and Fall of the Secondary
Mortgage Market   20

CHAPTER **2**   **Real Estate Law and Security Instruments   25**
English Common Law   27
Principles of Real Estate Law   28
Types of Ownership   33
Transfer of Land   35

Types of Deeds   36
Mortgage Law   38
U.S. Mortgage Law—Lien Theory vs. Title Theory   39
Foreclosure   43
Transfers of Mortgaged Real Estate   48
Changing a Mortgage   50

CHAPTER **3** **Role of Residential Mortgage Lending in the Economy**   53
Residential Mortgage Debt   54
Economic Stimulus of Housing   55
Importance of Savings to Housing   64
Capital and Mortgage Markets   65
Financial Intermediaries   70
Mortgage Lenders and the Primary Mortgage Market   71
Recent Trends in Mortgage Lending   73

CHAPTER **4** **The Mortgage Lenders**   77
Mortgage Bankers and Mortgage Brokers   82
Commercial Banks   92
Savings Institutions   95
Savings Banks (SBs)   99
Credit Unions   100
Primary Mortgage Market Risks   105

CHAPTER **5** **Secondary Mortgage Market**   111
Primary Markets and Secondary Markets   112
Economic Functions of the Secondary Mortgage Market   113
Mortgage-Backed Securities (MBSs)   114
Government National Mortgage Association (Ginnie Mae)   118
Participants in the Secondary Mortgage Market   123
The Government-Sponsored Enterprises: Fannie Mae
and Freddie Mac   124
Federal National Mortgage Association (Fannie Mae)   125
Ginnie Mae   133
Private Secondary Mortgage Market   134
Residential Lending and the Secondary Mortgage Markets   136
Post-Crisis Issues in the Secondary Mortgage Market   151

PART **2** **Programs**

CHAPTER **6** **Conventional Lending** 153
Evolution of the Standard Fixed-Rate, Fully-Amortizing
Mortgage 154
10-, 15-, 20-, or 40-Year Mortgages 157
Biweekly Mortgages 171
Conforming Mortgage Loans 174
Non-Conforming Mortgage Programs 177
Non-Prime (subprime) Mortgage Programs 179

CHAPTER **7** **Private Mortgage Insurance** 181
Why Is Private Mortgage Insurance so Important
in Today's Market? 182
How Does PMI Work? 189
Contracting with a Mortgage Insurance Company 194
MI Coverage Amount 194
Claims 196
Pool Insurance 196
The Mortgage Insurance Industry Today 198
Types of Reserves 202
"Piggyback" Loans—Self-Insurance? 202

CHAPTER **8** **Government Lending** 205
The Practice of Government Lending—Who Is the Lender? 206
Government Programs 208
Veterans Administration 227
U.S. Department of Agriculture 240

CHAPTER **9** **Construction Lending** 247
Construction Lending Basics 251
Construction Loan Programs 255
Construction Loan Origination 259

CHAPTER **10** **Home Equity Lending** 269
Home Equity Loan Program Design and Origination Practices 273
Closed-End Second Mortgages 277
Home Equity Line of Credit Programs 278
Marketing Home Equity Loans 288
Reverse Annuity Mortgages (RAMs) 289

PART **3** **Practices**

CHAPTER **11** **Compliance** 297
Fair Lending Regulations   300
Fair Housing Act   301
Equal Credit Opportunity Act   302
Fair Credit Reporting Act   307
Fair and Accurate Credit Transactions Act   308
Gramm-Leach-Bliley Financial Modernization Act of 1999   308
Truth in Lending Act (TILA)   311
MDIA and 2008 TILA Revisions/RESPA Final Rule   316
Real Estate Settlement Procedures Act (Regulation X)   325
Flood Disaster Protection Act (FDPA)   343
Homeowners Protection Act (HPA) of 1998   344
Home Mortgage Disclosure Act (HMDA)   347
Fair Debt Collection Practices Act   349
Community Reinvestment Act (CRA)   349
Secure and Fair Enforcement for Mortgage Licensing
Act of 2008   350
Dodd-Frank Wall Street Reform and Consumer Protection Act   351
Summary   357

CHAPTER **12** **Residential Mortgage Loan Origination and Processing** 359
Technology   361
Interview   362
Formal Application   364
Qualifying an Applicant   376
Supporting Documentation and Tax Returns   382
Credit History   387
Collateral   395
Other Compensating Factors   397
Final Check   397

CHAPTER **13** **Underwriting the Residential Mortgage Loan** 401
Underwriting by a Mortgage Lender   402
Underwriting Guidelines   404
Underwriting Areas of Review   410

Loan-to-Value Ratios   412
Capacity   414
Credit   419
Automated Underwriting Systems   424
Standard vs. Limited/Streamlined Documentations   425
The Underwriting Decision   430
Managing the Underwriting Function   434
Underwriting Guidelines and Loan Application Register   435
Discrimination and the Federal Government   435

CHAPTER **14**   **Residential Real Estate Appraisal**   **437**
The Residential Real Estate Appraisal Process   437
Completing the Residential Appraisal Report   442
Streamlined Appraisals and Automated Valuation Models   456

CHAPTER **15**   **Closing and Delivery; Quality Control and Fraud**   **463**
Federally Related Mortgage Loans   464
Steps in Closing a Residential Mortgage Loan   468
Documents Required for a Properly Closed First-Mortgage Loan   476
Conforming Documentation   476
Funding and Loan Delivery   490
Quality Control and Fraud Prevention   491

CHAPTER **16**   **Mortgage Loan Servicing and Administration**   **501**
Loan Servicing vs. Loan Administration   502
Servicing Responsibilities and Functions   504
Managing Delinquencies and Foreclosures   509
Loss Mitigation   514
Portfolio Management and Loan Administration   516
Alternatives to Servicing Residential Mortgage Loans   529

CHAPTER **17**   **Selling Residential Mortgage Loans**   **531**
Loan Sale Options   532
Which Mortgage Loans Are Sold?   535
Secondary Market Math   536
Pricing   539
Selling Loan Production to Investors   542
Investor Approval and Loan Commitments   543

Secondary Mortgage Market Commitments   545
Loan Delivery   548
Mortgage Pipeline Management   550

CHAPTER **18**   **Strategies for Generating Residential Loans**   **555**
The First Step—Focus on the Applicant   555
Requirements for a Successful Mortgage Lending Operation   561
Retail Loan Origination   568
Wholesale Loan Origination   573
Internet Lending   577

GLOSSARY   579
INDEX   589

LIST OF FIGURES AND TABLES

Chapter 1

FIGURE 1.1   Mortgage Originations and Interest Rates
FIGURE 1.2   Family Mortgage Originations
FIGURE 1.3   Market Share of Top 30 Originators and Servicers
FIGURE 1.4   Mortgage Product Mix 2003
FIGURE 1.5   Mortgage Product Mix 2006

Chapter 2

TABLE 2.1   State-by-state Comparison of Selected Aspects of Foreclosure

Chapter 3

FIGURE 3.1   U.S. Housing's Contribution to GDP
FIGURE 3.2   Spending by New Home Buyers in the First Year after Purchase
FIGURE 3.3   Metro and U.S. Home Price Changes 2009–2010
FIGURE 3.4   U.S. Single Family Housing Stock and Equity
FIGURE 3.5   U.S. Homeownership Rate
FIGURE 3.6   Projected Homeownership By Age Group 2010–2020
TABLE 3.1   Lower Interest Rates Make Housing More Affordable:
              Monthly Principal and Interest Payment on a 30-Year Mortgage
TABLE 3.2   New and Existing Home Sales 1990–2009
TABLE 3.3   Average Existing Home Price and Housing Inventory 2007–2010

Chapter 4

FIGURE 4.1   Comparison of Different Mortgage Bankers
FIGURE 4.2   Mortgage Loan Origination Agreement
FIGURE 4.3   Largest Residential Mortgage Originators 2009–2007

TABLE 4.1   U.S. Mortgage Debt Outstanding ($ in billions)

TABLE 4.2   Holders of 1–4 Family Mortgage Debt 2000–2010 ($ in billions)

TABLE 4.3   Commercial Bank Institutions

TABLE 4.4   Thrift Institutions by Charter Type

TABLE 4.5   Credit Union Data 2004–2009 ($ in millions)

TABLE 4.6   Credit Union First Mortgage Originations and Sales 1990–2010 ($ in billions)

Chapter 5

FIGURE 5.1   U.S. Outstanding Public and Private Bond Market Debt, 2010

TABLE 5.1   RMBS Share of Mortgage Debt Outstanding by Holder, 1980–2009

TABLE 5.2   Mortgage Related Securities Holdings by Investor Group

TABLE 5.3   Distribution of MBS Issuances by Issuer, 2000–2008

TABLE 5.4   GSE Volume and Share of Residential Mortgage Debt Outstanding, 1990–2009

TABLE 5.5   GSE Financial Performance, 2000–2009 ($ in billions)

TABLE 5.6   MPF®/MPP Outstanding, 2000–2010

TABLE 5.7   FHLB MBS Portfolio, 2010

TABLE 5.8   FHLB Advance Outstanding, 2005–2010

TABLE 5.9   Private Label MBS Issuance by Sector, 2000–2008

TABLE 5.10   1-4 Family Mortgage Originations and Securitizations

TABLE 5.11   1-4 Family MBS Issuances

TABLE 5.12   Market Share of Top 30 Originators and Servicers

TABLE 5.13   Loan Production—Average Income and Expense ($ per loan)

TABLE 5.14   Secondary Mortgage Market Originations, 2001–2009 ($ in billions)

TABLE 5.15   Historical Concentration of Top 25 Mortgage Originators

TABLE 5.16   Agency and Non-Prime Originations and Securitizations 2001–2006 ($ in billions)

TABLE 5.17   Top Subprime Originators, PLS Issuers, and Servicers, 2005–2006

TABLE 5.18   Subprime Mortgage Serious Delinquency Rate, 2008 (Percent)

Chapter 6

FIGURE 6.1   Adjustable-Rate Mortgage Loan Adjustment Notice

FIGURE 6.2   More About Indices

FIGURE 6.3   Composite APR Example

FIGURE 6.4   Adjustable Rate Note

FIGURE 6.5   ARM Examples

TABLE 6.1   Example of Term Loan Repayment versus Amortized Loan

TABLE 6.2   History of Fixed Rate vs. 1-Year Adjustable Rate Mortgages, 1984–2010

TABLE 6.3   Freddie Mac's 26th Annual Adjustable-Rate Mortgage Survey Treasury-Indexed ARM Features in January 2010

TABLE 6.4   FHFA Historical Conforming Loan Limits for Fannie Mae and Freddie Mac Loans

TABLE 6.5   Fannie Mae Standard Eligibility Requirements Matrix

Chapter 7

FIGURE 7.1   PMI Disclosure Form

FIGURE 7.2   Sample PMI Plans and Premiums

FIGURE 7.3   Sample Individual PMI Commitment/Certificate of Insurance

FIGURE 7.4   Mortgage Insurance Claims Settlement, 2008 ($ in billions)

FIGURE 7.5   Geographic Distribution of New Insurance, 2008 ($ in billions)

TABLE 7.1   Average Loan Amount: FHA, VA, PMI

TABLE 7.2   FHA/VA/PMI Loan Volume

TABLE 7.3   FHA/VA/PMI Origination Data, 1996–2009

TABLE 7.4   Comparision of FHA and PMI Premiums

TABLE 7.5   Standard and Minimum Required MI Coverage Levels

TABLE 7.6   Private Mortgage Insurance Company Activity (2008)

TABLE 7.7   Net Industry Risk/Capital ($ in thousands)

TABLE 7.8   Industry Assets and Reserves ($ in thousands)

Chapter 8

FIGURE 8.1   Important Notice to Homebuyers (HUD 92900-B)

FIGURE 8.2   Addendum to the URLA (HUD 92900-A)

FIGURE 8.3   Conditional Commitment/Direct Endorsed Underwriter Statement of Appraised Value (HUD 92800.5-B)

FIGURE 8.4   Loan Underwriting and Transmittal Summary (HUD 92900-LT)

FIGURE 8.5   Certificate of Eligibility

FIGURE 8.6   Sample Counseling Checklist for Military Homebuyers

FIGURE 8.7   Sample Department of Veteran Affairs Loan Analysis Form

FIGURE 8.8   Loan Guaranty Certificate

FIGURE 8.9   Request for Single Family Housing Loan Guarantee

TABLE 8.1   History of Increases in VA Maximum Guarantees

TABLE 8.2   VA Funding Fee Schedule (funding fee is based on the amount of down payment)

Chapter 9

FIGURE 9.1   Sample Construction Loan Advance Schedule

FIGURE 9.2   Sample Construction Program Description Letter

FIGURE 9.3   Inventory of Homes for Sale

FIGURE 9.4   Sample Cost Projection Worksheet

Chapter 10

FIGURE 10.1   Sample Home Equity Line of Credit Disclosure Statement

FIGURE 10.2   Sample Home Equity Line of Credit Periodic Statement

FIGURE 10.3   Sample Home Equity Loan Marketing Brochure

FIGURE 10.4   Comparison of Home Equity and Reverse Mortgage Features

FIGURE 10.5   Home Equity Conversion Mortgage Loan Comparison

FIGURE 10.6   Home Equity Conversion Mortgage Counseling Requirements

FIGURE 10.7   Key Reverse Mortgage Application Documents

FIGURE 10.8   Reverse Mortgage Origination Volume

TABLE 10.1   Consumer and Mortgage Loan Delinquency

TABLE 10.2   List of Documents Typically Required for Home Equity Loans—Closed-End Loans and Open-End Lines of Credit

TABLE 10.3   Traditional Home Equity Line of Credit Product

Chapter 11

FIGURE 11.1   The Equal Housing Opportunity Logo

FIGURE 11.2   Notice of Action Taken

FIGURE 11.3   Advanced ARM Disclosure Form

FIGURE 11.4   Sample Notice of Right to Rescission or Cancel Statement

FIGURE 11.5   Sample HUD Special Information Booklet

FIGURE 11.6   Servicing Disclosure Statement

FIGURE 11.7   Sample Good Faith Estimate Form

FIGURE 11.8   Sample HUD-1 Settlement Statement

FIGURE 11.9   Sample Flood Hazard Determination Form

FIGURE 11.10   Summary of Disclosure Requirements

TABLE 11.1   Reg Z Revisions Functional Impact

TABLE 11.2   RESPA Disclosure Requirement Summary

Chapter 12

FIGURE 12.1   Sample Uniform Residential Loan Application, Truth in Lending Disclosure, and Good Faith Estimate

FIGURE 12.2   Sample Qualification Worksheet

FIGURE 12.3   Sample Request for Verification of Employment (VOE)

FIGURE 12.4   Sample IRS Form 4506T

FIGURE 12.5   Sample Request for Verification of Deposit (VOD)

FIGURE 12.6   Sample Credit Report
FIGURE 12.7   First Mortgage Loan Documentation

Chapter 13

FIGURE 13.1   Pricing Adjustment Matrix
FIGURE 13.2   Postsettlement Delivery Fees
FIGURE 13.3   Calculation of the Total Debt Ratio
FIGURE 13.4   Primary Risk Assessment
FIGURE 13.5   Sample Underwriting Worksheet
FIGURE 13.6   Sample Underwriting Summary
TABLE 13.1   IRS Forms Documenting Income
TABLE 13.2   Credit Score and Underwriting Review Levels
TABLE 13.3   Collateral-related Characteristics of Property
TABLE 13.4   Assess Contributory Risk Factors

Chapter 14

FIGURE 14.1   Completing the Residential Appraisal Report
FIGURE 14.2   Sample Uniform Residential Appraisal Report
FIGURE 14.3   Sample Appraisal Review Checklist

Chapter 15

FIGURE 15.1   RESPA Fee Restrictions at Closing
FIGURE 15.2   Closing Costs By State, 2009–2010
FIGURE 15.3   Sample Commitment Letter
FIGURE 15.4   Sample Title Insurance Policy
FIGURE 15.5   First Mortgage Document Checklist
FIGURE 15.6   Fixed Adjustable Rate Rider
FIGURE 15.7   Sample Open-End Mortgage Deed
FIGURE 15.8   Sample Uniform Settlement Statement (HUD-1)
FIGURE 15.9   FBI Mortgage Fraud Warning
FIGURE 15.10   Fannie Mae Common Red Flags

Chapter 16

FIGURE 16.1   Serious Delinquency Rates, 1998–2009
FIGURE 16.2   Mortgage Delinquency Analyses
FIGURE 16.3   Sample Initial Escrow Account Disclosure Statement
FIGURE 16.4   Mortgage Servicing Values—Sample Servicing Released
                Premiums—November, 2010

TABLE 16.1   Organization of Mortgage-servicing Departments

TABLE 16.2   GSE Loss Mitigation Actions, 2008–2010

TABLE 16.3   Largest Residential Mortgage Servicers, 2010–2001–1993 ($ in millions)

TABLE 16.4   Mortgage Servicing Productivity

Chapter 17

FIGURE 17.1   Mortgage Application Lifecycle—Portfolio Loan

FIGURE 17.2   Mortgage Application Lifecycle—Secondary Market Loan

FIGURE 17.3   Hedge Cost

FIGURE 17.4   Secondary Mortgage Market and Trading Mortgage for Cash

FIGURE 17.5   Impact of Interest Rate Movement

FIGURE 17.6   Interest Rate and Price Risk

Chapter 18

FIGURE 18.1   Sample First Mortgage Loan Information Form

FIGURE 18.2   Sample Loan Tracking Summary

FIGURE 18.3   Mortgage Origination Channels, 1993–2006

FIGURE 18.4   Largest Lender Origination Channel Production 2008–2009

TABLE 18.1   Mortgage Origination Satisfaction Surveys, 2005–2010

TABLE 18.2   Example of Logical Pricing of Mortgage Rates (no-point option)

TABLE 18.3   1–4 Family Mortgage Originations, 1990–2010 ($ in billions)

TABLE 18.4   Online Mortgage Originations

PREFACE

Although the 6th edition of *Residential Mortgage Lending* is substantially re-worked and re-written, the basic purpose of this textbook remains the same as prior editions: to identify and explain the fundamentals of residential mortgage lending in as simple and concise a manner as possible. This goal becomes increasingly difficult as the industry becomes more complex and global, and as everything recently seems to take on monumental proportions—from record volume, profits, and homeownership rates to unsurpassed accounting scandals, fraud, and bankruptcies and bailouts.

The opening chapter begins with a catalogue of unprecedented changes and historically significant events which have occurred in the short space of ten years. They are worth repeating here—upfront—in the preface, as each item warrants a textbook in itself. Collectively, these past events help the reader understand today's dynamic environment for the mortgage lending industry and set the context going forward for its evolution from the series of monumental changes still to come:

- Record years in total annual residential mortgage origination volume of more than $3 trillion in 2003, 2005, and 2006—at least double the volume in any year prior to 2000.
- Dramatic yearly swings in total residential mortgage origination volume, with changes in volume exceeding $1 trillion per year in 2003, 2004, and 2008.
- 30-year record lows for fixed-rate mortgages (5.5 percent in 2003, then dropping further to 4.75 percent in 2009 and 4.5 percent in 2010).
- Homeownership at a historical high of 69 percent (2004), followed by a drop to its lowest level in a decade.
- Record low delinquency spiraling to the highest delinquency and foreclosure levels since the Great Depression over 70 years ago.

- Extensive use of online mortgage origination, automated underwriting systems, and other technological changes.
- Double the level of mortgage-backed securities (MBSs) outstanding to a peak of $7.6 trillion in 2009, and rapid decline to $3.1 trillion in 2010.
- Private Label Securities tripling to a peak of $3 trillion in 2007, then disappearing in 2008.
- An explosion of alternative, nonconforming, and subprime loan programs, then seeing those programs disappear in less than six months in 2008.
- Unprecedented levels of individual and collaborative mortgage fraud committed by all participants in the residential lending and secondary marketing industries.
- Increasing dominance of the mortgage banking strategy until 2007, replaced quickly by record origination levels for portfolio lenders in 2008.
- Revamping of the entire federal regulatory and examination structure for mortgage lending: extensive revisions to Truth in Lending and RESPA regulations; new SAFE Act licensing laws; reorganization of supervisory agency responsibilities and introduction of a new Consumer Finance Protection Bureau.

It would be understandable if the 6th edition of *Residential Mortgage Lending*, in a break from its five prior editions, focused only on the academic approach of placing industry events in historical context. But the long-standing purpose of this textbook, unlike many others with a number of mathematical formulas or legal citations, is to help the reader learn *how* to make a residential mortgage loan—not just explain *why* they were made. It is designed for both employees of mortgage lenders and college students studying real estate finance who want to supplement that study with practical residential mortgage-lending principles and practices. The SAFE Act of 2008 created a third audience for this textbook: mortgage loan originators who must meet federal- and state-mandated education requirements and need a comprehensive, practical reference.

This textbook is written assuming no prior knowledge of finance or any part of mortgage lending. It discusses each topic beginning with the fundamentals, then develops them to the point at which it is hoped the reader has a basic understanding of that topic. It is written for the student for academic study, as well as for a practitioner of mortgage lending who seeks to broaden his or her understanding of several other areas of the industry.

Recent events demonstrate painfully the hazards of not understanding how different areas of mortgage lending are connected. Subjects included in this book are pertinent to an independent mortgage broker or an employee of a mortgage banker, commercial bank, savings and loan association, credit union, or savings bank. Not every topic is applicable to every mortgage lender, nor will each one be of immediate interest to all readers. But each chapter is important.

Changes occur rapidly in this segment of the economy. An area in which a particular mortgage lender is not involved today may be where the growth and profit potential are tomorrow. All mortgage lenders should prepare for this growth and change by either employing suitably educated personnel or providing that education.

While explaining the fundamentals of residential mortgage lending, this textbook also examines the similarities and differences that exist among mortgage lenders and their business practices. Basically, therefore, this book is designed to fulfill the need of all mortgage lenders for a basic textbook to prepare new employees for the important job of helping to finance the evolving housing needs of the United States.

Finally, with this edition, I would like to acknowledge and thank Marshall Dennis. Marshall was the lead author in all five prior editions of *Residential Mortgage Lending, Principles and Practices*. His vision inspired the first edition in 1985, filling a void in the mortgage lending industry. Marshall's ability to convey the many aspects of this industry in a clear, logical manner has helped thousands of students and mortgage professionals expand their knowledge and understanding of its dynamics. Each subsequent edition gained popularity throughout the 1990s and 2000s in many universities and colleges nationwide. While each chapter in this edition required significant updating because of massive industry change, Marshall's work in several chapters forms the basis of the text.

Over the years, it has been this author's pleasure to work with Marshall, to learn from him, and to appreciate his dedication to the industry and its education—in texts as an author, in classrooms as a teacher, and in practice as a consultant. Marshall set a high standard for this text over twenty-five years ago. I'm honored to write the 6th edition and try to preserve the legacy he started, especially now when education is such a critical aspect of today's mortgage lending industry.

NEW AND UPDATED IN THE 6TH EDITION

As stated earlier, the 6th edition has been extensively re-worked: chapters re-organized; new topics and industry terms introduced; expanded discussion of subjects; updated information; and additional data provided.

Targeted Topical Sections/Chapter Re-organization

To keep faithful to the original goals of *Residential Mortgage Lending*, the author kept—but completely re-organized and updated—the chapters from the 5th edition. Now chapters are organized into three general categories of study:

Part 1: *Principles*

Part 2: *Programs*

Part 3: *Practices*

The new structure accomplishes several goals:

- allows the student to complete study in one area before moving onto the next
- builds from the basics to the actual practice of residential lending

- unites the more fundamental, academic areas of mortgage lending in a coherent order
- presents the explosion in mortgage programs in a more organized way
- concentrates the current practices of mortgage lending in one area for practitioners and advanced students

Enhanced Visual Learning

A second important enhancement contained throughout the 6th edition is the addition of over 84 new charts and graphs and updates to dozens of existing ones. These visually illustrate the dynamic activity of the industry and break up the summary discussion or data in the text, especially in the Principles section (chapters 1–5) dealing with history, economics, and secondary mortgage markets. Several key figures contain industry data throughout all the Program section (chapters 6–10) for conventional, PMI, government, construction, and home equity lending.

Comprehensive Lending Case Study

A third enhancement for this edition provides a better teaching tool for the Practices section (chapters 11–18). Included are updated disclosures and a more comprehensive case study for the practice of mortgage lending. Now students can view a unified set of origination, processing, underwriting, and closing forms which lenders actually use. Students can complete an actual analysis of "Ms. Green's" application as a classroom activity to help drive home the practical issues encountered in making an actual mortgage loan.

Additional Discussion Points

Additional "Discussion Points" were added in several chapters. These help students and instructors review relevant topics within that subject.

Chapter Introductions Revised

Extensive revisions to practically every chapter introduction will orient readers to important changes and fundamental dynamics within that chapter's subject area.

Mortgage Industry Data and Events Updated/Expanded

To keep the 6th edition current and relevant, each chapter includes up-to-date mortgage industry data and events from the date of the last revision, past the mortgage crisis, to the most recent year: 2010. Chapters now include expanded information to provide a more comprehensive picture of market changes.

Chapter Revisions

Several critically-important trends emerged and events occurred since the last edition. To reflect this activity, the 6th edition has been extensively re-worked: chapters re-organized; new topics and industry terms introduced; expanded discussion of subjects; updated information; and additional data provided. The following list highlights the 6th edition chapter changes:

Chapter 1—History of Mortgage Lending

Added new sections on The Rise and Fall of the Secondary Mortgage Market, 2000–2010, and The Role of Subprime Lending.

Topics updated include Deficit Reduction and Homeownership as a Political Goal; The 1990s: A Shift in Policy, Boom Years, and a Fundamental Change; Mortgage Market Activity, Federal Legislation after 2002; and Evolving Mortgage Lending Issues in the New Century.

New figures added on topics such as Mortgage Originations and Interest Rates 1977–2009; 1-4 Family Mortgage Originations; Market Share of Top 30 Originators and Servicers; Mortgage Product Mix for 2003; and Mortgage Product Mix for 2006.

Chapter 2—Real Estate Law and Security Instruments

Added discussion of state law trends and licensing activities.

Added new sections on mortgage modification and release of mortgage.

Updated figure on State-by-State Comparison of Selected Aspects of Foreclosure.

Chapter 3—Role of Residential Mortgage Lending in the Economy

Extensively restructured the chapter for better flow of topics.

Expanded discussion of economic factors in mortgage lending, demographics, home sales and prices, and the homeownership rate.

New figures added on topics such as economic history 2002–2010, U.S. Housing's Contribution to GDP, Average Existing Home Price and Housing Inventory 2007–2010, Metro and U.S. Home Price Changes 2009–2010, U.S. Single Family Housing Stock and Equity, U.S. Homeownership Rate, Projected Homeownership By Age Group 2010–2020.

Chapter 4—The Mortgage Lenders

Revised to include a more comprehensive discussion of lenders overall.

Added discussion of different roles of originators, lenders, holders, and servicers.

Added sections on Primary Mortgage Market Risks: Credit, Interest Rate, Prepayment, Liquidity, Portfolio, Collateral, and Compliance.

New figures added on U.S. Mortgage Debt Outstanding, Comparison of Different Mortgage Bankers.

Updated and expanded figures on Holders of 1–4 Family Mortgage Debt 2000–2010, Largest Residential Mortgage Originators, Commercial Banks, Thrift Institutions, and Credit Unions.

Chapter 5—Secondary Mortgage Market

Restructured chapter extensively to focus on secondary market activity, participants, and mortgage-backed securities.

Added new sections on Major Types of Residential Mortgage-Backed Securities, The Government-Sponsored Enterprises: Fannie Mae and Freddie Mac, GSE Business Overview, GSE Regulation, Residential Lending and the

Secondary Market, 1990s: Period of Secondary Market Growth, Mega-servicers and Mega-originators, 2000–2010: Part One—A Period of Expansion, 2000–2010: Part Two—Rapid Decline, 2008: Crisis in the Secondary Mortgage Market, and Post-Crisis Issues in the Secondary Mortgage Market.

Topics revised or updated include How Successful Have MBSs Been?, Types of Ginnie Mae MBSs, Private Issuers of MBSs, Importance of MBSs Today, Participants in the Secondary Mortgage Market, Fannie Mae, Freddie Mac, Secondary Market Operations, How Fannie Mae and Freddie Mac Finance Their Operations, Financing Mortgage Purchases, Fannie's and Freddie's Earnings, Competition Between the Major Players, The Federal Home Loan Banks, Private Secondary Mortgage Market, and Fraud in the Secondary Mortgage Market.

New figures added on RMBS Share of Mortgage Debt Outstanding by Holder 1980–2009, U.S. Outstanding Public and Private Bond Market Debt 2010, MBS Holdings by Investor Group, MBS Distribution By Issuer 2000–2008, GSE Volume and Share of Residential Mortgage Debt Outstanding 1990–2009, GSE Financial Performance 2000–2009, FHLB MPF Outstanding 2000–2010, FHLB MBS Portfolio, FHLB Advances Outstanding 2005–2010, Private Label Issues By Product 2000–2008, 1-4 Family Originations and Securitizations, 1-4 Family MBS Issuances, Market Share of Top 30 Originators and Servicers, Loan Production—Income and Expense, Secondary Market Originations 2001–2008, Historical Concentration of Top 25 Mortgage Originators, Agency and Non-Prime Originations and Securitizations, Top Subprime Originators, PLS Issuers, and Servicers 2005–2006, and Subprime Mortgage Serious Delinquency Rate 2008.

Chapter 6—Conventional Lending

Renamed and extensively restructured the Mortgage Instruments chapter to Conventional Lending to reflect current practices in mortgage lending.

New sections added include Mortgage Program Nomenclature and Definitions, Conventional vs. Government vs. Other, Conforming vs. Non-conforming, Non-traditional, Fully-indexed Accrual Rate, Hybrid ARMs, Conforming Mortgage Loans, Conforming Maximum Loan Amount, Fannie Mae and Freddie Mac Mortgage Programs, Maximum Loan-to-value Ratios for Standard Purchases, Mortgage Insurance Requirements and Credit Enhancement, Non-conforming Mortgage Programs, and Non-prime (Subprime) Mortgage Programs.

Topics revised or updated include Evolution of the Standard Fixed-Rate, Fully-Amortizing Mortgage, Direct Reduction Instrument, Mortgage Lenders' Dilemma, Alternative Mortgage Instruments, 1990 to 2010: Return of the Standard Fixed-Rate Fully-Amortizing Mortgage, 10-, 15-, 20-, or 40-yr Mortgages, Adjustable-Rate Mortgages (ARMs), Structure of an ARM: Adjustment Period, Index, Buydowns, Convertible Mortgages, Graduated Payment Mortgages (GPMs),

New or revised figures include Term Loan Repayment versus Amortized Loan, Treasury-Indexed ARM Features in January 2010, Mortgage Product Comparison—Fixed Rates, Other Types (Fixed Rate), Adjustable Rates, Other Types (ARMs), FHFA Conforming Loan Limits for Fannie Mae and Freddie Mac 1980–2010, and Fannie Mae Standard Eligibility Requirements Matrix.

Chapter 7—Private Mortgage Insurance

New sections added include The Beginning,1950s–1970s: The Rebirth of Private Mortgage Insurance, 2000 and Beyond: the Best of Times, the Worst of Times..., How Does PMI Work?, Financial Requirements and Strengths, and "Piggyback" Loans—Self-insurance?

Topics revised or updated include Why is Private Mortgage Insurance So Important in Today's Market?, The 1990s: Golden Years?, MI Coverage Amount, and Loan Quality and Portfolio Risk.

New or revised figures include Average Loan Amount: FHA, VA, PMI, FHA/VA/PMI Loan Volume, FHA/VA/PMI Origination Data 1996–2009, PMI Disclosure Form, PMI Plans and Premiums, Comparison of FHA and PMI Premiums, Master Policy, Individual PMI Commitment, Standard and Minimum Required MI Coverage Levels, Geographic Distribution of New Insurance, Private Mortgage Insurance Company Activity (2008), Net Industry Risk/Capital, and Industry Assets and Reserves.

Chapter 8—Government Lending

New sections added include The Practice of Government Lending—Who is the Lender?, FHA Loan Limits, Down Payment, Certificate of Reasonable Value, Property, Single Family—Homeownership Direct Loan Program, RHS Recent Changes.

Topics revised or updated include FHA Today, FHA Insurance, 203(b), Eligibility, Source of Funds, Qualifying Ratios, Automated Underwriting, Documentation, VA Program Today, Eligibility, Example, VA Down payment, Qualifying Ratios/Residual Income, Underwriting, Documentation, Rural Housing Services, RHS Single Family Programs—Section 502, Single Family—Home Loan Guarantee Program.

New or revised figures include Important Notice to Homebuyers, Addendum to the URLA, Conditional Commitment, Loan Underwriting Transmittal and Summary, Certificate of Eligibility, VA Funding Fee Schedule, VA Certificate of Eligibility, Counseling Checklist for Military Homebuyers, Loan Analysis, Loan Guarantee Certificate, Request for Single Family Housing Loan Guarantee.

Chapter 9—Construction Lending

Topics revised or updated include Housing Starts.

Chapter 10—Home Equity Lending

New sections include Home Equity Loan Program Design and Origination Practices, Loan Amount, Loan to Value, Home Equity Loan Processing, Qualifying Ratios, Disclosures, Loan Approval, No Closing Cost Programs, Reverse Annuity Mortgages (RAMs), Reverse Mortgage Amount and Funding, FHA Home Equity Conversion Mortgage, and Consumer Protection for Reverse Mortgages.

Topics revised or updated include Nomenclature and Types of Home Equity Loans, How Important Are Home Equity Loans to Lenders?, Appraisals,

Title Insurance or Title Search, Security Documentation, Closed-End Program Design, and Maximum Loan to Value.

New or revised figures include Home Equity Loans Outstanding 2003–2010, Consumer and Mortgage Loan Delinquency, List of Documents Typically Required for Home Equity Loans, Home Equity Line of Credit Disclosure Statement, Home Equity Loan Marketing Brochure, Comparison of Home Equity and Reverse Mortgage Features, Home Equity Conversion Mortgage Loan Comparison, Home Equity Conversion Mortgage Counseling Requirements, Key Reverse Mortgage Application Documents, and Reverse Mortgage Origination Volume.

Chapter 11—Compliance

Renamed, restructured, and extensively reorganized the Compliance chapter to reflect current emphasis and issues in mortgage lending.

New sections added include Fair Lending Regulations, Consumer Privacy Regulations, Consumer Protection Regulations, Discrimination, USA Patriot Act, FACT Act, Gramm-Leach-Bliley Financial Modernization Act of 1999, GLBA Definitions, Privacy Notice, Consumer's Right to "Opt Out", Telemarketing Sales Rule, "Do-Not-Call" Registry, TILA Scope, TILA Disclosures, MDIA and 2008 TILA Revisions / RESPA Final Rule, Disclosure Practices—for all *closed-end* mortgages secured by a consumer's principal *dwelling*, Required Lender Practices and Behavior, Advertising Practices—for all *closed-end* mortgages secured by a *dwelling*, Processing Practices—for all closed-end mortgages secured by a consumer's *principal dwelling*, Servicing Practices—for all closed-end loans secured by a consumer's *principal dwelling*, Mortgage Loan Programs—3 TILA Categories (as of 2009), RESPA Scope, Required Disclosures, Affiliated Business Relationship Disclosure, MDIA and HUD's RESPA Final Rule November 2008, RESPA Definitions, Escrow Rules and Requirements, Secure and Fair Enforcement for Mortgage Licensing Act of 2008, Federally Registered MLO Requirements, State Licensed MLO Requirements, Dodd-Frank Wall Street Reform and Consumer Protection Act, Title X, Title XIV, Timing, and Summary.

Topics revised or updated include Effects Test, Copy of the Appraisal, Adverse Action, Government Monitoring, Fair Credit Reporting Act, Truth in Lending Act (TILA), Finance Charge, Annual Percentage Rate (APR), Home Ownership and Equity Protection Act of 1994, Home Equity Loan Consumer Protection Act, Right to Rescind, Special Information Booklet, Servicing Disclosure Statement, Good Faith Estimate Form, HUD-1 Uniform Settlement Statement (HUD-1 or HUD-1A), Servicing Transfer Statement, Initial and Annual Escrow Statements, Escrow Surplus, Shortage, and Deficit, Home Mortgage Disclosure Act (HMDA), and Community Reinvestment Act (CRA).

New or revised figures include Notice of Action Taken, Sample Truth in Lending ARM Disclosure Form, REG X&Z Revisions /MDIA Disclosure/ Closing Timeline, Reg Z Revisions Functional Impact, Notice of Right to Rescission or Cancel Statement, RESPA Disclosure Requirement Summary, HUD Special Information Booklet, Servicing Disclosure Statement, Sample Good Faith Estimate Form, and Sample HUD-1 Settlement Statement.

Chapter 12—Residential Mortgage Loan Origination and Processing

New topics include Mortgage Loan Originator—SAFE Act, Other Application Compliance Issues, Telephone Applications, Electronic Applications, Supporting Documentation and Tax Returns, Public Assistance.

Topics revised or updated include Technology, Interview, Be Careful Not to Discourage a Formal Application, The Uniform Residential Loan Application and Uniform Documentation, Qualifying an Applicant, Loan Transaction and Program, Debt/Income Ratios, Self-Employment, Rental Income, Assets, Credit History, Credit Scores, Derogatory Items, Collateral, Other Compensating Factors, Final Check.

New or revised figures include Sample Uniform Residential Loan Application, Sample Request for Verification of Employment, Sample IRS Form 4506T, Sample Request for Verification of Deposit, Sample Credit Report, First Mortgage Loan Documentation.

Chapter 13—Underwriting the Residential Mortgage Loan

New topics include Risk-based Pricing Adjustments, NINA/SISA Programs, Managing the Underwriting Function, Fraud and Quality Control, and AUS and Comprehensive Risk Assessments.

Topics revised or updated include Analyzing Risk, Underwriting Guidelines, Use of Technology for Underwriting, Conflicting Objectives, Underwriting Areas of Review, Prequalification of Applicants, Loan Policy and Eligibility Issues, IRS and Sources of Income, Bankruptcy, Past Foreclosures or Deed in Lieu, Standard vs. Limited/Streamlined Documentation, Comprehensive Risk Assessment, and Discrimination and the Federal Government.

New or revised figures include Pricing Adjustment Matrix, Post Settlement Delivery Fees, IRS Forms Documenting Income, Credit Score and Underwriting Review Levels, Sample Underwriting Worksheet, and Sample Underwriting Summary.

Chapter 14—Residential Real Estate Appraisal

Restructured, and extensively reorganized the Appraisal chapter to reflect current issues in mortgage lending.

New topics include Uniform Appraisal Dataset and Uniform Collateral Data Portal, HVCC and Federal Reserve Final Rule—TILA Section 129E, and Regulatory Changes Affecting Appraisals.

Topics revised or updated include Uniform Residential Appraisal Report, Factors Affecting Market Value, Required Forms, Automated Valuation Models (AVMs), Use of Streamlined Appraisals and AVMs, and Hiring the Appraiser.

New or revised figures include Sample Uniform Residential Appraisal Report, and Sample Appraisal Review Checklist.

Chapter 15—Closing and Delivery; Quality Control and Fraud

Renamed and restructured the Closing chapter to reflect current emphasis and issues in mortgage lending.

New topics include Closing Costs, Conforming Documentation, Funding and Loan Delivery, Quality Control and Fraud Prevention, Mortgage Fraud, Mortgage Fraud Types, and Quality Control Programs Today.

Topics revised or updated include The Handling of Loan Closing, Insured Closings, and First Mortgage Checklist.

New or revised figures include RESPA Fee Restrictions at Closing, Closing Costs By State 2009–2010, Sample Commitment Letter, Sample Title Insurance Policy, First Mortgage Document Checklist, Sample Mortgage Note, Sample Open-End Mortgage Deed, Sample Uniform Settlement Statement (HUD-1), FBI Mortgage Fraud Warning, and Fannie Mae Common Red Flags.

Chapter 16—Mortgage Loan Servicing and Administration

New topics include Loan Servicing vs. Loan Administration.

Topics revised or updated include Welcoming Letter, Mortgage Payment Methods, Servicing Functions, Managing Delinquencies and Foreclosures, Reasons for Default, Telephone Contact, Two Months Delinquent, Curing Delinquencies, Loss Mitigation, Evolution of Loan Servicing, FASB Rules, Servicing Income, Servicing Profitability, A Profitability Squeeze with Each Refinance Wave, Cost of Servicing, Purchasing Servicing, Selling Servicing, and Subservicing.

New or updated figures include Serious Delinquency Rates 1998–2009, Mortgage Delinquency Analyses, GSE Loss Mitigation Activities 2008–2010, Largest Residential Mortgage Servicers 2010–2001–1993, Sample Initial Escrow Account Disclosure Statement, Servicing Productivity, and Cost of Servicing—Expenses.

Chapter 17—Selling Residential Mortgage Loans

Restructured, and extensively reorganized the Selling chapter to focus on the technical aspects of selling mortgage loans only.

New topics include Loan Sale Options and Secondary Market Math, When is a Mortgage Loan Sold?, Flow Basis or Pooling, Whole Loans or Participations, Recourse, "Seasoning" cures All?, Secondary Market Math, Risk-Based Pricing Adjustments, Loan Delivery, Documents Delivered to Secondary Market Investors, Fallout Risk, Delivery Risk, Investor Risk, Program Risk, Funding Risk, Repurchase Risk, and Price/Interest Rate Risk.

Topics revised or updated include Which Mortgage Loans are Sold?, Non-conforming Mortgages, Pricing, Strategic Options in Selling Mortgage Loans, Mortgage Banking Business Model, Direct Sales to Private Secondary Mortgage Market Entities, Selling Loan Production to Conduits for Packaging into MBSs, Investor Approval and Loan Commitments, Becoming an Approved Seller/Servicers, Mandatory Delivery Commitments, Best Efforts, Mortgage Pipeline Management, Liquidity Risk, Locking Rates at Application, Interest Rate Volatility, and Pipeline Reports.

New or updated figures include Mortgage Application Lifecycle—Portfolio Loan, Mortgage Application Lifecycle—Secondary Market Loan, Hedge Cost, Impact of Interest Rate Movement, and Interest Rate Risk.

Chapter 18—Strategies for Generating Residential Loans

New topics include Measuring Customer Satisfaction, Origination Channels, Purchase vs. Refinance Transactions, Refinances—Rates, Reputation, and Convenience.

Topics revised or updated include The First Step—Focus on the Applicant, The Most Effective "Tool" in Attracting Mortgage Applicants, Convenience for the Applicant, Consumer Stress in Applying for a Mortgage Loan, How Loyal are Mortgage Borrowers?, Requirements for a Successful Mortgage Lending Operation, Trained Personnel, Program Offerings, Competitive Pricing, Targeted Marketing, Loan Demand, Retail Loan Origination, Commission Loan Agents, FASB #91, Retail Branch Offices, Wholesale Loan Origination, Advantages and Disadvantages of Wholesale Lending, Mortgage Brokers and Loan Correspondents, Functions Performed, Yield Spread Premiums, What Motivates the Third-party Originator?, Fees and Premiums, Affinity Groups, Quality Control, Internet Lending.

New or updated figures include Mortgage Origination Satisfaction Surveys 2005–2010, Example of Logical Pricing of Mortgage Rates, Mortgage Origination Channels 1993–2006, 1-4 Family Mortgage Originations, 1990–2010, Largest Lender Origination Channel Productions 2008–2009, Online Mortgage Originations.

INSTRUCTIONAL SUPPORT

Instructors who adopt this book receive access to an online Instructor's Manual. Each chapter is supported with chapter overview and objectives, an outline of each chapter, True/False Quiz, multiple choice and short essay questions, as well as suggested answers to the discussion questions found at the end of each chapter in the text. Plus, there is a 100-question Final Exam with rationales.

Classroom PowerPoint® presentation slides also support each chapter outlining learning objectives, emphasizing key concepts and highlighting real world applications to help further engage learners and generate classroom discussion.

These instructional support materials are available online only to adopters from the text companion site www.cengage.com/realestate/pinkowish.

ACKNOWLEDGMENTS

A textbook of this scope is by necessity a team effort between writers and subject matter experts. Keeping all chapters current over the past year amidst unprecedented industry change was a lot like herding cats—major announcements occurred weekly if not monthly. I am deeply indebted to a number of experts for their valuable advice and assistance in preparing and updating this textbook. These individuals were most generous with their time and shared their many years of experience in mortgage lending.

Arlin Kauffman, Project Manager, provided valuable subject matter as well as publishing input throughout the process of writing, editing, and layout of the entire text.

Peter J. Taglia, CPA, CMB, Vice President, FTN Financial Capital Assets Corporation, Chicago, IL, assisted greatly with the two chapters on the secondary mortgage market and provided insightful comments.

MaryBeth Hickson, Account Manager, and MaryKay Scully, Director of Customer Education, Genworth Mortgage Insurance, Raleigh, NC, were invaluable in obtaining industry information for the private mortgage insurance chapter.

Theresa Ballard, Chief Executive Officer, BFO Solutions Incorporated, San Diego, CA, reviewed and edited the government lending chapter and provided an enormous amount of updated information on FHA, VA, and USDA loans.

Heidi Yanavich, assistant to the president, McCue Mortgage Company, New Britain, Connecticut, reviewed the chapter on government lending and provided valuable suggestions.

Brian P. Hedge, Assistant Vice President, Liberty Bank, Middletown, CT, reviewed the chapter on home equity lending and made many valuable suggestions.

Mark Burton, CSA, Mark A. Burton and Associates, Shelburne Falls, MA, authored the section on reverse mortgages.

Joseph Strilbyckij, Senior Account Executive, and Michele Streeto, Customer Support Specialist, Avantus, West Haven, Connecticut, provided the credit report and instructions on how it is to be read.

The following people from McCue Mortgage Company, New Britain, CT worked extensively to develop a detailed case study and sample forms for several chapters:

Heidi Yanavich, assistant to the president

Donna DeBenedetto, Vice President

Tammy Cote, Loan Analyst/Underwriter

Jutta Arena, Closing Administrator

Their support and timeliness is greatly appreciated!

Edmond R. Browne, Jr., Vice President, and Jon Anderson, Senior Underwriter, CATIC Financial, Inc., Rocky Hill, CT, for providing on a moment's notice a sample title insurance policy for the chapter on mortgage closing.

James MacCrate, MAI, CRE, ASA, MacCrate Associates LLC, New York, NY, reviewed and made valuable comments on the appraisal chapter.

Dale Robyn Siegel, President, Circle Mortgage Group, Harrison, NY, reviewed the chapter and provided valuable input on origination and processing.

Dr. Thomas J. Healy, CMB, President, Level1Loans, Ft. Lauderdale, FL, reviewed material and provided valuable insight in the chapter on loan administration.

David Minor, Executive Vice President, Graystone Solutions, Sudbury, MA, reviewed material and provided valuable insight in the chapter on loan administration.

Sharon Whitaker, Executive Vice President, and Dena Sclafani, Vice President, Lake Sunapee Bank, Newport, NH, provided valuable input on the strategies chapter.

Kit Harahan, Manager Information Services, Deanne Marino, Assistant to the Economist, Michael Mazur, Senior Manager, and Jim Chessen, Chief Economist, American Bankers Association, Washington, D.C., provided valuable industry data used in several chapters.

Steve Rick, Senior Economist, Credit Union National Association, Madison, WI, provided valuable industry data used in several chapters.

Deartra Todd, Senior Researcher, National Mortgage News, New York, NY, provided valuable industry data used in several chapters.

Angela Lynn, Joint Center for Housing Studies, Boston, MA, provided valuable research data used in several chapters.

Guy Cecala, Chief Executive Officer and Publisher, Inside Mortgage Finance Publications, Bethesda, MD, provided slides and information used in the history chapter.

Sonja Eveslage, Ph.D., President, elearn, Philadelphia, PA, Dean (Retired), Graduate School, Thomas Edison State College, Trenton, NJ, for valuable chapter review comments from an educational perspective.

I would also like to thank the associates of CFT, Center for Financial Training, and in particular Jeffrey Smith and Stacy Litke, for their invaluable input on the manuscript.

To my wife, Mary, who provided support and almost unlimited patience throughout this project.

For Alex: Ucz się ucz, bo nauka to do potęgi klucz

—Thomas J. Pinkowish

CHAPTER 1

History of Mortgage Lending

INTRODUCTION

Today's student or practitioner of residential mortgage lending may be hard pressed to keep pace with this rapidly changing business. This industry—so essential to our society and economy—typically evolves from year to year, if not month to month. Housing finance reflects the tastes, desires, and values of our nation, tempered by government policies and market realities.

The past ten years have been a sharp contrast to the steady evolution of this industry. The unprecedented, wholesale change in residential mortgage lending since 2000 is breathtaking—especially in the past five years. Here are some highlights:

- Total annual residential origination volume exceeded $2 trillion in 2001, for the first time in history, and was sustained at that level until 2007.

- Record years in total annual residential mortgage origination volume of more than $3 trillion in 2003, 2005, and 2006—at least double the volume in any year prior to 2000.

- Dramatic yearly swings in total residential mortgage origination volume—with changes in volume exceeding $1 trillion per year in 2003, 2004, and 2008.

- 30-year record lows for fixed-rate mortgages (5.5 percent in 2003, then dropping further to 4.75 percent in 2009 and 4.5 percent in 2010).

- Homeownership at a historical high of 69 percent (2004), followed by a drop to its lowest level in a decade, and the highest delinquency and foreclosure levels since the Great Depression 70 years ago.

- Extensive use of online mortgage origination, automated underwriting systems, and other technological changes.

- Double the level of mortgage-backed securities (MBSs) outstanding, from $3.2 trillion in 2000 to a peak of $7.6 trillion in 2009, and rapid fall to $3.1 trillion in 2010; private label $0.7 trillion to a peak of $3 trillion in 2007.

- Evolution of alternative types of mortgage instruments and non-conforming programs, then seeing those programs disappear in less than six months in 2008.

- Ever-increasing dominance of the mortgage banking strategy, followed quickly by record origination levels for portfolio/depository lenders.

- Revamping of the entire federal regulatory and examination structure for mortgage lending: extensive revisions to Truth in Lending and RESPA regulations; new SAFE Act licensing laws; reorganization of supervisory agency responsibilities and introduction of a new Consumer Finance Protection Bureau.

These developments could lead one to assume that all meaningful changes have occurred in only the past couple of years or so. That assumption would be wrong. Residential mortgage lending is, and always has been, a constantly changing part of our economic life and social history.

The basic concepts of mortgage lending developed over centuries, and the use of mortgages can be traced to the beginning of recorded history. Many of the complexities of today's residential mortgage lending system are the result of problems that existed not only half a century ago but hundreds of years ago as well. It is essential to understand this history to truly appreciate how and why residential mortgage lending works today.

THE BEGINNING

The underlying product in all real estate activities is land. Sociologists claim that the use of land, the desire to acquire it, and the need to regulate its transfer is among the fundamental reasons for the development of governments and laws. As government developed, it formulated laws that govern the ownership and use of land. Because of the importance of land in an agrarian society, it quickly was pledged as *security* to assure the performance of such obligations as debt repayment and the fulfillment of military service.

Evidence of transactions involving land as security exists in such ancient civilizations as Babylonia and Egypt. Many principles of mortgage lending—including the essential elements of naming the borrower, naming the lender, and describing the property—developed in those early civilizations. For example, the Egyptians were the first to use surveys to describe mortgaged land. The annual flooding of the Nile River, which often obliterated property markers, undoubtedly necessitated this practice.

During the period when Greek civilization was at its peak, temple leaders often loaned money with real estate as security. In fact, throughout history, organized religion maintained a strong interest in real estate and related activities.

ROMAN LAW

The Roman Empire developed mortgage lending to a high level of sophistication, beginning with the *fiducia*. This transaction was an actual transfer of possession and *title* to land. It was subject to an additional agreement that stated that if the borrower fulfilled the obligation, the land would *reconvey* back to the borrower. As Roman government became stronger and the law more clearly defined, a new concept of security called the *pignus* developed. No title transfer occurred. Instead, the land was "pawned." According to this concept, title and possession remained with the borrower, but the lender could take possession of the property at any time if it was deemed that a possibility of *default* existed.

The most important Roman development regarding mortgages, however, was the *hypotheca*, which was a pledge. The *hypotheca* is similar to the *lien* theory (described later) that exists in most states in this country today. The title remained with the borrower, who retained possession of the property. Only when an actual default occurred (a failure to perform on the part of the borrower) was the lender entitled to take possession of the land and its title.

As the Roman Empire receded in Europe during the Dark Ages, Germanic law introduced a new concept. A borrower was given the choice of fulfilling an obligation or losing the security. If the *mortgagor* defaulted, the *mortgagee* had to look exclusively to the property itself. This security system was called a *gage* in Germanic law: something was deposited for the performance of an agreement. As the Dark Ages continued and the governmental authority of Rome weakened to such a degree that lenders were not sure they would have support from central authorities in securing their debts, the *hypotheca* system decayed and died, and the more primitive concept of the *fiducia* returned.

ENGLISH DEVELOPMENTS

Later, in Europe, a new system of government and social structure—the feudal system—became widespread. The essential characteristic of the feudal system was the totality of the king's control. He was the owner of all lands, and he granted their use to certain lords in return for the lords' military fealty. Lords given the use of the land were permitted to continue on the land as long as they fulfilled their military obligation to the king. If this obligation was not fulfilled, or if the lord died, the use of the land was revoked and given to others. In this situation, land served as a security for the performance of an obligation—military service.

Along with the feudal system of land tenure, in 1066 William of Normandy introduced the Germanic system of the *gage* into early English law, following his successful invasion of England. The word *mortgage*, not found in English literature until after the Norman invasion, derives from the French words *mort*, meaning "dead" (the land was dead, since the mortgagor could not use or derive income from it), and *gage*, meaning "pledge." During the years after the Norman invasion, the Catholic Church established civil law in England. Church policy at this time stated that charging interest for money loaned was usury.

As the common law evolved in England, a gradual shift occurred from a concept of favoritism or protection of the *mortgagee* to favoritism or protection of the *mortgagor*. Finally, the common law reached a more balanced position. The realities of the economic and legal systems that existed at this early stage of mortgage development dictated the initial concept of mortgagee favoritism.

Mortgage lending was not a common occurrence during this period for two reasons: first, there was very little need for it; and second, no incentive to lend existed without the ability to collect interest. The mortgage lending that did occur was not for the purpose of providing funds to purchase real estate, but was usually provided to finance large purchases (such as a new mill or livestock) or perhaps to prepare a dowry for a daughter. Since lenders could not collect interest on these *loans*, they would take both title and possession of a designated portion of the borrower's land and thus be entitled to all rents and profits from it. When the obligation was fulfilled, title was reconveyed to the mortgagor. If the mortgagor defaulted, the mortgagee would permanently retain title and possession of the mortgaged land. The mortgagee was still entitled to expect performance of the underlying obligation.

During the fifteenth century, courts of *equity* allowed the mortgagor to perform the obligation, even after the required date, and redeem the property. This concept expanded, and by 1625 nearly all existing mortgage lending practices ended because a mortgagee never knew when a mortgagor might perform and thus redeem the property. To alleviate this problem, mortgagees petitioned the court for a decree requiring mortgagors to redeem the property within six months or lose the right to do so.

AMERICAN DEVELOPMENTS

Land development banks, borrowing primarily in Europe to finance their land purchases in the developing West, financed westward expansion in America following the Revolutionary War. Much of this land acquisition was speculative and eventually culminated in the bankruptcy of nearly all the land development banks. Thereafter, little if any real estate financing occurred on an organized basis until after the Civil War.

During the first 75 years of this country's history, most of the population lived on small farms whose ownership was passed down through families. Little need existed for mortgage lending in this society except for an occasional purchase of new land or for seed money. Primarily, family and friends provided the small amount of mortgage lending that did occur during this period. It is important to realize that until the 1920s, *individuals*—not financial institutions—comprised the largest category of mortgage lenders in the United States.

Thrift Institutions

The birth of various thrift institutions provided an opportunity for change in mortgage lending. The first thrift institution formed was a mutual savings bank, the Philadelphia Savings Fund Society, established in 1816. Of greater, long-term importance to mortgage lending is the organization of the first building society in the United States. Modeled after societies that existed in England and Scotland for 50 years, the Oxford Provident Building Association organized in 1831 in Frankfort, Pennsylvania. This association, like the ones that soon followed, existed only long enough for all of the organizers to obtain funds to purchase homes. Ironically, the first loan made by this association became delinquent, and another member of the association assumed the debt and took possession of the house. Later, other associations formed, providing a popular means of financing home purchases across the United States.

Even with these new financial institutions, mortgage lending was still not an important part of the economy in the first half of the nineteenth century. Rural families still lived on farms that met most of their requirements. No urgent need for savings existed. Away from the farm, there were few employment opportunities that provided excess cash for savings. In fact, the concept of saving was still new, and the number of active savers was very small. Then, as now, the impetus for mortgage lending was the inflow of savings to the institutions that would lend funds; thus, mortgage lending was infrequent.

Mortgage Companies

After the Civil War, the nation's expansion continued, and developments in mortgage lending resumed. Starting with a new westward expansion, which opened virgin lands for farming, a regular farm mortgage business developed in the predominantly rural Midwest. Many mortgage companies began in the Midwest, and it still has one of the heaviest concentrations of mortgage companies.

These companies did not originate mortgage loans for their own *portfolios*, as did the thrift institutions. Rather, these loans were for direct sale to wealthy individuals or to institutional investors such as life insurance companies. Most of these East Coast individuals and institutional *investors* needed local mortgage companies to originate loans for them. This need developed into the mortgage loan *correspondent* system.

The bulk of the mortgage business consisted of financing farms, usually with a prevailing loan-to-value ratio of 40 percent—occasionally 50 percent for a farm in a well-developed area. The loan term was short (less than five years), with interest payable semiannually and the *principal* paid at the end of the term. By 1900, outstanding farm mortgages originated by these mortgage companies totaled more than $4 billion.

During this period, the population's movement to urban areas increased, swelled by the ever-mounting numbers of immigrants. In 1892, the United States League of Savings Associations, a trade organization, formed in response to the expanding savings and loan industry. These institutions provided urban residents a place to save money and a source of funds to use in purchasing homes. Some S&L mortgages were repaid on an installment basis, not at the expiration of the term as were mortgages from other types of lenders.

Commercial Banks

Commercial banks made few real estate loans until the Civil War, when a sudden demand for loans to finance new farmsteads encouraged state-chartered commercial banks to make low-ratio farm mortgages. Except for a brief period, federally chartered commercial banks could not make real estate loans.

This competition from state-chartered banks eventually forced a change in federal banking law. In 1913, the Federal Reserve Act authorized federally chartered banks to lend money on real estate. This initial authorization limited mortgage loans to improved farms for a five-year term with the loan-to-value ratio of 50 percent. This authorization was extended in 1916 to include one-year loans on urban real estate.

Many changes occurred in both state and federal laws relating to the types and terms of mortgage loans made by commercial banks. Changes tended to lag behind advances made by other mortgage lenders. However, the commercial banks' contribution to mortgage lending is meaningful, especially in those areas of the country where they function as the principal mortgage lender.

Turn of the Century

During the 1870s to the early 1900s, a few *mortgage companies* in or near urban areas started to make loans on single-family houses. Initially, such loans constituted a very small percentage of their business, but they gradually grew to account for more and more total origination volume. The Farm Mortgage Bankers Association, a trade organization formed in 1914, changed its name in 1923 to the Mortgage Bankers Association of America to reflect the increasing emphasis on residential lending.

In the first two decades of the twentieth century, the typical loan made by a mortgage company on a single-family dwelling called for no more than a 50 percent loan-to-value ratio, with a three- to five-year mortgage term. There were no provisions for *amortization* of the loan, and interest was generally payable semiannually. The majority of these mortgages were renewed upon maturity, since few families had the money to retire the debt. The mortgage companies originating these mortgages charged the borrower from one to three percent of the amount of the loan as a fee. Upon renewal, they charged an additional one percent fee.

As the twentieth century progressed, thrift institutions—especially savings and loan associations—continued to expand. Savings banks, which had their greatest growth after the Civil War, remained principally in the New England states. But savings and loan institutions continued to grow and spread across the country. During this time, thrift institutions were originating short-term mortgage loans for their own portfolios.

All mortgage lenders participated in the real estate boom years of the 1920s. This was a period of unrestrained optimism. Most Americans believed growth and prosperity would continue forever. Real estate prices appreciated as much as 25 to 50 percent per year during the first half of the decade. Many lenders forgot their underwriting standards, believing that inflating prices would bail out any bad loan. As with any speculative period, the end came, and along with it, many personal fortunes dissipated.

Great Depression Era

The real estate boom of the 1920s began to show signs of weakening long before the stock market crash. By 1927, real estate values declined dramatically. Following the disastrous dive of the stock market in 1929, the entire economy of the United States was in danger of collapse. Real estate values plunged to less than half the level of the year before. The large-scale unemployment that followed the collapse of the stock market and the loss of economic vitality throughout the nation reduced the ability of both the individual borrower and the income property mortgagor to meet quarterly or semiannual interest payments.

Because periodic amortization of mortgages was not common, there was a six-month lag before an institutional investor realized a mortgage was in trouble. In addition, the various financial institutions were faced with a severe liquidity crisis that required them to sell vast real estate and mortgage holdings under very unfavorable conditions. This need to sell real estate holdings to obtain cash, coupled with a rise in foreclosures and tax sales, severely depressed an already crumbling real estate market. Many individual homeowners were threatened with property loss even if they retained their jobs, because when their five-year mortgages expired, many were unable to refinance their mortgages. Lenders were caught in the liquidity crisis and did not have the funds to lend.

Thrift institutions also experienced problems during this period, even though some of their mortgagors had installment-type mortgages. As many workers lost their jobs and unemployment reached 25 percent, the savings inflow to thrifts diminished drastically. All types of financial institutions began to fail, and as a result, savers withdrew funds and the liquidity crisis worsened for all lenders. In the early 1930s, many commercial banks and savings and loan institutions failed due to massive withdrawals of savings and the high foreclosure rate. By 1935, 20 percent of all mortgage assets were in the "real estate owned" category.

Second and third mortgagees, who needed to foreclose immediately in order to protect what little security they had, made the vast majority of all foreclosures during the 1930s. The highest number of foreclosures occurred from 1931 to 1935, averaging 250,000 each year. The increasing number of foreclosures, especially on family farms in the Midwest, forced the beginning of compulsory moratoria. In the Midwest, where economic deterioration was aggravated by the dust bowl storms, the cry for a moratorium reached the stage of near rebellion, and some violence occurred.

Reacting to the hysteria sweeping the farm belt and some of the larger cities, many mortgagees voluntarily instituted forbearance, some for as long as two years. The first law requiring a mortgage moratorium became effective in Iowa in February 1933. Over the next 18 months, 27 states enacted legislation suspending nearly all foreclosures. Most of the moratorium laws enacted during this period were intended to last for two years or less, although many were reenacted and allowed to continue as law until the early 1940s.

It is important to note that some foreclosures occurred when these laws were in effect. Whether or not to grant relief depended on the soundness of a debtor's fundamental economic position. If it was determined that a debtor would eventually lose the land anyway, then postponing the foreclosure or granting a moratorium was considered a waste of time and an injustice to the creditor. The moratoria of the early 1930s did not provide an actual solution to the underlying economic problems, but they did provide a respite during which the federal government could introduce some economic remedies and sooth public unrest.

GOVERNMENT INTERVENTION

In the early 1930s, the federal government realized that the drop in real estate values added to the growing depression of the entire economy, preventing its revitalization. Therefore, the government instituted a series of programs designed to help stabilize real estate values and, it was hoped, the entire economy. This period marked the beginning of a drastic reversal in previous governmental political philosophy, which had been generally laissez-faire. From this point on, the federal government assumed a more active role in residential housing and its finance.

Landmark Federal Legislation

Beginning in the last year of the Hoover administration, federal legislation usurped in large measure what previously was state-controlled real estate and mortgage lending activities.

The first legislation designed to meet the threat of the Depression created the Reconstruction Finance Corporation (RFC) in 1932, which, among other things, provided liquidity to commercial banks. Shortly thereafter, creation of the Federal Home Loan Bank (FHLB) provided a central credit facility to home finance institutions, primarily savings and loan institutions. The next major legislation, the Home Owners Loan Act (HOLA), in 1933 provided federal charters for savings and loan institutions. It also created the Home Owners Loan Corporation (HOLC) to provide emergency relief to homeowners by refinancing or purchasing defaulted mortgages. By enabling families to refinance balloon payment loans into amortizing ones, this program kept many tens of thousands of families from losing their homes in the 1930s. This reduced the massive number of foreclosures, helped stabilize the real estate market, and kept many lenders liquid.

One of the most far-reaching enactments of this period was the National Housing Act (1934), which created the Federal Housing Administration (FHA) and the Federal Savings and Loan Insurance Corporation (FSLIC). The FSLIC and the Federal Deposit Insurance Corporation (FDIC) were instrumental in encouraging depositors to return desperately needed deposits to financial institutions. FHA provided the framework and the impetus necessary for the development of a true national mortgage market. FHA either initiated or made popular many innovations in mortgage lending, such as mortgage insurance (MI) and the long-term, self-amortizing mortgage.

The Growth Era

A minimal amount of single-family housing construction occurred from 1926 to 1946 as a result of the Depression and World War II. However, the greatest boom in housing construction in the history of this country, and possibly the world, occurred from 1945 to 1955. Two government housing programs; the FHA and the Veterans Administration (VA), built-up demand for housing, and the liquid position of lenders were instrumental in this dramatic growth in housing.

At the end of the war, however, five million servicemen returned home, creating a tremendous demand for housing. The government, as part of its responsibility to returning veterans as well as a way of stimulating housing, passed the Servicemen's Readjustment Act (1944).

One of the major features of this act was a guaranty program that provided a desirable way of financing homes for veterans. The most distinguishing characteristic of this guaranty program (then and now) is no down payment requirement for eligible veterans. Under this program, veterans pay no mortgage insurance premiums; instead, the government absorbs the cost of the mortgage guaranty.

The highly liquid position of financial institutions was the second great impetus to the rapid expansion of single-family housing construction following World War II. In 1945, more than half of the assets of financial institutions were tied up in the no-risk but low-yield government securities that institutions were obligated to purchase during World War II. Postwar, these bonds could be converted into cash to fund mortgages, which provided a higher yield. Since the end of World War II, mortgages have been the largest user of long-term credit in the entire U.S. economy.

Housing Act of 1949

The Housing Act of 1949 is one of the most important pieces of social legislation passed in the last half of the twentieth century. It contained a national commitment to provide "a decent home and suitable living environment for every American family." Much of the legislative action in the housing and mortgage-lending field since then has been an attempt to fulfill this commendable but probably unrealistic goal.

The 1950s through early 1960s was a period of national optimism, economic growth, and, as far as mortgage lending is concerned, relative quiet in the legislative arena. This period of tranquility soon dissipated in the face of an onslaught of such national crises as political assassinations, civil rights demonstrations, urban blight, and the war in Vietnam.

Department of Housing and Urban Development

In 1965, a new cabinet-level department, the Department of Housing and Urban Development (HUD), was created by consolidating several federal housing agencies.. This change partially addressed the lack of adequate housing, a situation often associated with poverty. HUD became the focal point of much of the new legislation in upcoming years and assumed a dominant position in regulating real estate and mortgage lending.

The enactment of the Housing and Urban Development Act in 1968 started an avalanche of legislation and regulation that so changed mortgage lending. This was the first major legislation passed in the mortgage-lending field in more than a decade. The act committed the government to a goal of 26 million new housing starts in the next decade. At the time, many argued that this goal was impractical on fiscal and political grounds. However, the act introduced a new concept in government programs for residential real estate by adopting the principle of subsidizing interest rates.

These government subsidy programs, combined with national economic growth, stimulated housing production in 1972 to more than three million units—the highest ever. With political pressure to increase housing production, the inevitable problems developed almost immediately. Report of scandals in subsidized housing first appeared in 1971, involving FHA officials and some mortgage lenders. These scandals were followed by congressional investigations, which spotlighted the unforeseen high costs of these programs.

In January of 1973, President Richard Nixon ordered a freeze on all subsidy programs. This was partially lifted later, but only after a thorough review of government programs by a special task force created by HUD. This task force reviewed the history of government involvement in real estate and analyzed the impact of the various subsidy programs on housing. It concluded that the goal of providing homeownership for everyone was neither practical nor desirable when weighed against the cost.

The government's concept then changed from subsidizing homeownership to subsidizing rent. The Housing and Community Development Act (1974) formalized this change with the Section 8 program. This program allows low- and moderate-income families to choose the rental unit in the community in which they want to live, with the government subsidizing the amount of fair market rent that is in excess of 25 percent of the family's monthly income. This program provides assistance both to families who cannot afford the minimal housing expenses stipulated in prior programs and to families whose incomes are just over the maximum income limit to qualify for assistance in home purchasing.

Consumer Protection

A series of federal laws and regulations forever changed residential mortgage lending. These laws control residential mortgage lending to a great extent today. The Consumer Protection Act of 1968 was the first in this series. It helped redefine the concept of consumer protection regarding mortgage lending.

The federal government continues its goal to remove all inequities from residential mortgage lending. These actions have met with mostly good results, but occasionally inequities still appear. Later chapters throughout this book discuss these various pieces of federal legislation.

Role of Government

The government's role in the management of the nation's economy in general, and mortgage lending in particular, has been analyzed and debated many times—and undoubtedly it will continue. There is little argument that government, regardless of whether it is federal, state, or local, has an obligation to its citizens to provide adequate shelter for all—even if people cannot afford it themselves. This assistance comes in a variety of ways:

- rent assistance to temporarily help people with existing leases.
- mortgage assistance so people can purchase rather than rent.
- rent payment subsidies in certain employment or geographic areas.
- temporary housing shelters and other transitional homes.
- tax or other credits to construct low/moderate housing.

There are many arguments, though, regarding how to provide this basic necessity. Recently, some commentators suggest that excessive governmental interference results in fewer families being able to afford the average-priced home. That may be true, but most governmental laws and regulations have a commendable impact on real estate and mortgage lending. The Interstate Land Sales Full Disclosure Act (1968), which helped to prevent fraudulent land sales, is an obvious example. Many laws and regulations are necessitated by excesses and failures on the part of the lending community.

The contribution of some of these laws cannot be overstated. In fact, one governmental creation, the FHA, provided the framework for a modern, vibrant mortgage lending system that helped make this the best-housed nation in the world.

Following is a list of the more important federal legislative acts that impact residential mortgage lending:

1913–**Federal Reserve Act.** Established the Federal Reserve System and authorized federally chartered commercial banks to make real estate loans.

1916–**Federal Farm Loan Act.** Formed the Federal Land Bank Associations as units of the Federal Land Bank system, which was given authority to generate funds for loans to farmers via the sale of bonds.

1932–**Reconstruction Finance Act.** Created the Reconstruction Finance Corporation, designed to provide liquidity to commercial banks.

1932–**Federal Home Loan Bank Act.** Established the Federal Home Loan Bank Board and 12 regional banks to provide central credit facilities for home finance institutions that were members of the FHLB.

1932–**Home Owners Loan Act.** This act produced two results: (1) created the Home Owners Loan Corporation with authority to purchase defaulted home mortgages and to refinance as many as prudently feasible, and (2) provided the basic lending authority for federally chartered savings and loan associations.

1934–**National Housing Act.** Authorized the creation of the Federal Housing Administration and Federal Savings and Loan Insurance Corporation.

1938–**National Mortgage Association of Washington.** This governmental agency, soon renamed **Federal National Mortgage Association (FNMA),** authorized secondary mortgage market support for FHA mortgages.

1944–**Servicemen's Readjustment Act.** Established within the Veterans Administration a mortgage guarantee program for qualified veterans.

1949–**Housing Act.** Stated that the national housing goal was to provide "a decent home and suitable living environment for every American family." Consolidated past lending programs of the Farmers Home Administration.

1961–**Consolidated Farmers Home Administration Act.** Extended authority for the agency to make mortgage loans to nonfarmers in rural areas.

1965–**Housing and Urban Development Act.** Consolidated many federal housing agencies into the new Department of Housing and Urban Development, which was given expanded authority.

1966–**Interest Rate Adjustment Act.** Authorized the setting of maximum savings rates and the creation of a differential between the savings rates of commercial banks and thrift institutions.

1968–**Fair Housing Act.** Prohibited discrimination in real estate sales and mortgage lending based on race, color, national origin, or religion.

1968–**Interstate Land Sales Full Disclosure Act.** Required complete and full disclosure of all facts regarding interstate sale of real estate.

1968–**Consumer Credit Protection Act.** Contained Title I, better known as the Truth In Lending Act (TILA), which authorized the Federal Reserve Board to formulate regulations (Regulation Z) requiring advance disclosure of the amount and type of finance charge and a calculation of the *Annual Percentage Rate.* Title VI, better known as the Fair Credit Reporting Act, established disclosure requirements regarding the nature of credit information used in determining whether or not to grant a loan.

1968–**Housing and Urban Development Act.** This act put the existing Federal National Mortgage Association (FNMA) in private hands and authorized it to continue secondary mortgage market support. The act created a new government agency, the **Government National Mortgage Association (GNMA),** and authorized it to continue the FNMA special assistance function and guarantee mortgage-backed securities.

1969–**National Environmental Policy Act.** Required the preparation of an Environmental Impact Statement for the Council on Environmental Quality in order to determine the environmental impact of real estate development.

1970–**Emergency Home Finance Act.** Created a new secondary mortgage market participant, the **Federal Home Loan Mortgage Corporation**

(FHLMC), to provide secondary mortgage support for conventional mortgages originated by thrift institutions. The act also gave FNMA authority to purchase conventional mortgages in addition to FHA/VA.

1974–Flood Disaster Protection Act. Required the purchase of flood insurance for mortgage loans made in a flood hazard area.

1974–Real Estate Settlement Procedures Act (RESPA)—as amended in 1976, 1992, and 2008. Required mortgage lenders to provide mortgage borrowers with an advance disclosure of loan settlement costs and charges. Further, this act prohibited kickbacks to any person for referring business. The 1976 amendment required lenders to provide applicants with a Good Faith Estimate of Settlement Costs, a HUD booklet, and a Uniform Settlement Statement (HUD-1). The 1992 amendment extended RESPA to subordinate financing, effective 1993.

1974–Equal Credit Opportunity Act (ECOA)—as amended in 1976. Prohibited discrimination in lending on the basis of sex, marital status, age, race, color, national origin, religion, good faith reliance on consumer protection laws, or the fact that a borrower receives public assistance. In addition, if an application is rejected, the borrower must be notified of the reason for rejection within 30 days.

1975–Home Mortgage Disclosure Act (HMDA)—as amended in 1992. Required disclosure by most mortgage lenders of geographic distribution of loans in metropolitan statistical areas. The purpose was to establish lending patterns of lenders.

1976–RESPA amendment (*see* 1974).

1976–ECOA amendment (*see* 1974).

1978–Fair Lending Practices Regulations. These FHLB regulations required members to develop written underwriting standards, keep a loan registry, not deny loans because of age of dwelling or condition of neighborhood, and to direct advertising to all segments of the community.

1978–Community Reinvestment Act. This act required FSLIC-insured institutions to adopt a community reinvestment statement, which delineates the community in which they will invest; maintain a public comment file; and post a Community Reinvestment Act (CRA) notice.

1979–Housing and Community Development Amendments. This legislation exempted FHA-insured mortgages from state and local usury ceilings (Other concurrent legislation exempted VA and conventional mortgages).

1980–Depository Institutions Deregulation and Monetary Control Act. Extended the savings interest rate control and thrift institutions' one quarter of one percent differential for six years. Also extended the federal override of state usury ceilings on certain mortgages. Other changes included simplified truth in lending standards and eased lending restrictions, including geographical limitations, loan-to-value ratios, and treatment of single-family loans exceeding specified dollar amounts.

1980–Omnibus Reconciliation Act. Limited the issuance of tax-exempt housing mortgage revenue bonds.

1982–Garn-St. Germain Depository Institutions Act. Preempted state due-on-sale loan restrictions; mandated phase-out of interest rate differential by January 1, 1984; provided FSLIC and FDIC assistance for institutions with deficient net worth; and allowed S&Ls to make consumer, commercial, and agricultural loans.

1984–Deficit Reduction Act. Extended the tax exemption for qualified mortgage subsidy bonds; created new reporting procedures for mortgage interest.

1986–Tax Reform Act. Reduced top corporate tax rate from 46 to 34 percent; reduced taxable income bad debt deduction from 40 to 8 percent; provided for three-year carrybacks and 15-year carryforwards for savings institution net operating losses.

1987–Competitive Equality Banking Act. Set the FSLIC $10.8 billion recapitalization in motion, kept intact Savings Bank Life Insurance, and gave thrifts flexibility to form different types of holding companies.

1987–Housing and Community Development Act. Required that a notice of availability of counseling be given within 45 days of delinquency on single-family primary residence.

1989–Financial Institutions Reform, Recovery, and Enforcement Act (FIRREA). Restructured the regulatory framework by eliminating FHLBB and FSLIC; created the Office of Thrift Supervision (OTS) under the Treasury Department; enhanced FDIC to supervise safety and soundness of financial institutions, the Savings Institutions Insurance Fund, and the Bank Insurance Fund; created the Resolution Trust Corporation (RTC) to dispose of failed savings and loans; and established new capital standards for thrifts.

1992–RESPA amendment (*see* 1974). Coverage of RESPA is extended to subordinate financing.

1992—HMDA amendment (*see* 1975). Required mortgage companies and other nondepository institutions to comply with HMDA.

1994–Home Ownership and Equity Protection Act (HOEPA). Designed to provide protection to consumers from abusive practices involving high-cost home loans. Applies to so-called Section 32 loans.

1994–The Veterans Administration guarantees its 14 millionth home mortgage.

1997–Taxpayer Relief Act of 1997. Exempts from capital gains taxation gains of up to $500,000 on the sale of a home. It also reduces the top tax rate on capital gains from 28 to 20 percent.

1998–Homeowners Protection Act. Designed to protect people who buy homes using *private mortgage insurance (PMI)*. It allows for the cancellation of PMI in certain circumstances and ensures that borrowers are duly notified by the lenders of their right to cancel it when certain requirements have been met.

2008–Housing Economic and Recovery Act (HERA). Reformed Government-Sponsored Enterprise (GSE) regulation by establishing the Federal Housing Finance Agency (FHFA); modernized the Federal Housing

Administration (FHA); established the Hope for Homeowners program to help distressed homeowners; created the Secure And Fair Enforcement for Mortgage Licensing Act which established federal licensing requirements for mortgage loan originators; included the Mortgage Disclosure Improvement Act (MDIA) which coordinated revisions to Regulation Z (TILA) and Regulation X (RESPA); established housing preservation rules; revised housing tax incentives; revised Real Estate Investment Trust (REIT) tests and taxation.

2010–Dodd-Frank Wall Street Reform and Consumer Protection Act. Established the Bureau of Consumer Financial Protection to restructure consumer protection regulation; reformed the Federal Reserve's authority; established the Financial Stability Oversight Council to identify emerging systemic risks to the financial system; revised capital and leverage requirements for firms "too big to fail"; modified regulation of derivatives and hedge funds; established the Office of Credit Ratings to increase SEC oversight of Credit Rating Agencies; increased consumer protection in mortgage lending; revised mortgage-backed securities requirements; provides assistance to states and localities for neighborhood preservation and bridge loans and counseling to individuals for the effects of foreclosures.

RECENT RESIDENTIAL MORTGAGE LENDING

The most productive boom in real estate construction and financing in the United States occurred during the past 40 years. More housing units and other types of buildings have been constructed during this period than in all the years since this country was founded, as shown in Figure 1.1. While the housing boom changed the landscape of the American countryside, new office buildings, apartment complexes, and shopping centers provided the amenities

FIGURE **1.1** Mortgage Originations and Interest Rates

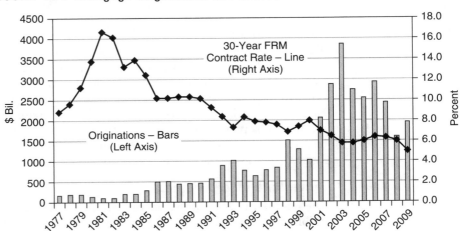

Source: MBA, Fannie Mae, Freddie Mac, Inside Mortgage Finance

and services needed by the families in these new homes. This boom can be credited to the availability of capital at a reasonable rate and the corresponding creation of the secondary mortgage market.

For example, in 1970 Fannie Mae (Federal National Mortgage Association) and Freddie Mac (Federal Home Loan Mortgage Corporation) were given expanded purchasing authority to provide secondary market facilities for conventional mortgages originated by savings and loan institutions.

In the 1970s, providing or stimulating housing for low- and moderate-income families was not the exclusive province of government at the federal level. Before 1960, the state of New York had the only state housing agency, but by 1975, nearly all states had some type of housing agency. Although some states have used tax-exempt bonds to raise revenue to lend to home-buyers at below-market interest rates, many have fulfilled their social responsibility by providing financing for multifamily units.

THE 1980S: THE DECADE OF HISTORIC CHANGE

The decade of the 1980s will be remembered as the time when the economy went through startling changes and, as a result, changed residential mortgage lending and mortgage lenders. This period witnessed positive developments such as the rapid growth of mortgage-backed securities, the evolution of alternative mortgage instruments, and, in general, more sources of needed capital. All of these positive developments, combined with much lower interest rates, resulted in one- to four-family originations of nearly $500 billion in both 1986 and 1987.

However, the decade also witnessed double-digit inflation, a major recession, a record high for the Dow Jones Industrial Average, and then a crash exceeding that of 1929. The decade ended with the near total collapse of the savings and loan industry and the related taxpayer bailout of the Federal Savings and Loan Insurance Corporation (FSLIC). All of these events produced drastic changes for the nation's economy in general and for mortgage lending in particular.

Federal Reserve and the Money Supply

The 1980s began with the nation's economy clearly running out of control. The Federal Reserve, responsible for managing and regulating interest rates and monetary supply, was forced in the fall of 1979 to bring about some order to the economy. Its fundamental decision was to stop attempting to regulate short-term interest rates and, instead, to exercise control over growth in the money supply. The theory was that control of the money supply would help reduce inflation, and that this in turn would decrease upward pressure on interest rates as investors decreased their need for inflation protection.

Prime Rate at 21½ Percent

The immediate result of this action was sharply higher interest rates. The most visible rate, the so-called prime rate, peaked at 21½ percent in 1981. Interest rates did come down fairly rapidly after that peak, partially as a result of the Federal Reserve action, but primarily because of a serious recession that followed this action. The recession that followed, at that time the worst since the Great Depression, resulted in unemployment exceeding 10 percent. This recession and the action of the Federal Reserve deflated the inflation balloon to the point at which inflation in the mid-1980s fell to about one percent per year before turning up modestly at the end of the decade. As a reaction to control over-inflation, the prime interest rate dropped sharply to 7½ percent by the spring of 1987 before turning up slightly.

With inflation under control and interest rates declining, the stock market rocketed to levels only dreamed of by the most optimistic of market watchers, as the Dow Jones Industrial Average hit a record of 2,722. Some market watchers were calling for 3000 by the end of the year, but what happened instead was a crash that exceeded the 1929 crash in *points*, but not percentage. A 508-point drop in the Dow Jones Industrial Average shocked Wall Street on October 19, 1987. A week later, the market dropped another 175. The sound heard around the world was the hard landing of other stock exchanges as they followed the lead of Wall Street.

The reasons for the crash of 1987 are many and varied, but the two principal ones cited are: 1) the market was simply overvalued, and 2) investors in the United States and abroad had lost faith in the ability of the U.S. government to control its huge deficit. The federal deficits for the second half of the 1980s averaged approximately $150 billion a year. These huge deficits turned the United States into the world's largest debtor nation, which owes hundreds of billions of dollars to foreigners. The impact of the crash of 1987 and the 1990–1991 recession chilled the home-purchasing plans of many Americans, and originations trailed off for the rest of the decade from the record years of 1986–1987.

Financial Institutions Reform, Recovery, and Enforcement Act (FIRREA)

By 1988, the problems of the savings and loan industry, which had been festering since the late 1970s, reached a climax. Speculative lending, negative earnings, low capital, and poor management characterized many savings and loan associations in the 1980s. These problems eventually culminated in many savings and loan associations' failures and the insolvency of the Federal Savings and Loan Insurance Corporation (FSLIC)—the deposit insurance fund for savings and loan associations.

The failure of the FSLIC precipitated a massive federal bailout of the insurance fund and the closing of hundreds of failed savings and loans. Financial Institutions Reform, Recovery, and Enforcement Act (FIRREA) mandated these changes in 1989. The cost of this federal bailout is projected to reach $400 billion to $500 billion over the life of the bonds sold to finance it.

THE 1990S: A SHIFT IN POLICY, BOOM YEARS, AND A FUNDAMENTAL CHANGE

The 1990s began with a recession that purged much of the spending excesses of the 1980s from the U.S. economy. Unemployment exceeded seven percent throughout the United States, but in some areas, especially New England and

California, unemployment exceeded 10 percent. As the Cold War ended with the fall of Communism throughout Europe, the American defense budget was cut and cut again, resulting in tens of thousands of Americans losing their jobs in defense-related industries.

With the economy in trouble and unemployment up, consumers stopped spending. This change in consumer attitudes toward spending, when combined with a drop in inflation, convinced the Federal Reserve to lower interest rates in the hope that this would stimulate businesses to expand and hire more workers.

At first, this drop in interest rates had another benefit: Americans jumped to refinance their home mortgages at the new low interest rates. A wave of refinancing during 1991 to 1993 allowed millions of Americans to refinance their home mortgages at interest rates that were the lowest in 20 years. During one period late in 1993, 30-year fixed-rate mortgages declined to less than seven percent. Thousands of American homeowners lowered their monthly payments and saved tens of billions of dollars in mortgage interest. Consumers spent much of this savings on consumer goods, thus helping to stimulate the economy in general.

In 1993, one- to four-family first mortgage originations reached the staggering level of $1.1 trillion. Approximately 55 percent of volume was from the refinancing of existing mortgages. This was the first time ever that refinancing exceeded purchase money mortgages for a whole year. An interesting sidebar to the surge in refinancing is that the overall quality of loans serviced improved as delinquencies hit a 20-year low in 1993, as shown in Figure 1.2.

Deficit Reduction and Homeownership as a Political Goal

During President Clinton's first year in office, the president and Congress agreed on a deficit reduction package that helped reduce the federal budget deficit gradually over a number of years. The financial markets reacted

FIGURE **1.2** Family Mortgage Originations

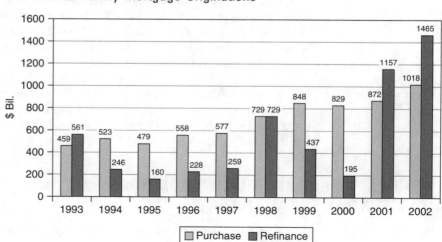

Source: HUD, MBA, Fannie Mae, Inside Mortgage Finance

positively to Congress finally making progress on deficit reduction, and, as a result, interest rates continued to decline throughout 1993. Interest rates bottomed in late 1993 at 20-year lows, and began a modest turn upward in 1994, led by Federal Reserve action designed to keep a lid on inflation.

The other significant change from Washington, D.C. was President Clinton's homeownership initiative. Increasing the homeownership rate now became a political issue and mandate. To achieve the homeownership goal created by the administration and Congress, the new policy mobilized Congress and federal regulatory, housing, and consumer protection agencies and placed numeric goals on the GSEs. The increase in homeownership improved the quality of life and created wealth for many households over the next decade. However, the financial and social consequences of this laudable political goal had unintended and disastrous consequences on the economy and personal finances when this cycle ended abruptly almost 15 years later.

Throughout the 1990s, real estate purchase activity continued strongly, but mortgage refinance volume was volatile: the refinance peaks and valleys in this decade were larger and lower. The impact on mortgage originators, servicers, and secondary market firms was severe at times. Large companies that hired hundreds of employees would in two or three years reduce their workforce by the same amount or more. The refinance activity would put some servicers out of business as their portfolio and servicing income disappeared almost overnight and they could not recoup the costs spent to acquire those loans.

The end of this decade saw the growth of foreign capital investing in mortgage-backed securities. As a result, Wall Street investment banks and other private entities increased their involvement as secondary market private conduits, and started to pose stiff competition to the market share of GSEs.

Fundamental shifts in both the secondary market and its resulting mortgage business strategy also started in the 1990s. Toward the end of the decade it became apparent that a large amount of capital from all over the world (many foreign governments) could be funneled into mortgage finance. This demand created more financial products, and Wall Street became more creative in how loans were designed, sold, and originated.

Total one- to four-family mortgages outstanding doubled throughout the 1990s, from less than $2.7 billion in 1990 to more than $5.2 billion in 2000. As mortgage origination numbers steadily increased throughout this period, businesses sought to grow market share to increase their operational efficiencies and profitability. The market share of the largest 30 mortgage originators and servicers shown in Figure 1.3 grew dramatically from 1994 to 1999: from less than 40 percent to roughly 60 percent. The mortgage servicing operation became a fundamental piece of origination strategy. Mortgage brokers now became central players in leveraging the origination numbers for mortgage banking operations. During refinance booms, large originators needed to expand their production quickly to meet portfolio run-off. Achieving this through mortgage brokers was less costly and quicker than hiring staff.

FIGURE **1.3** Market Share of Top 30 Originators and Servicers

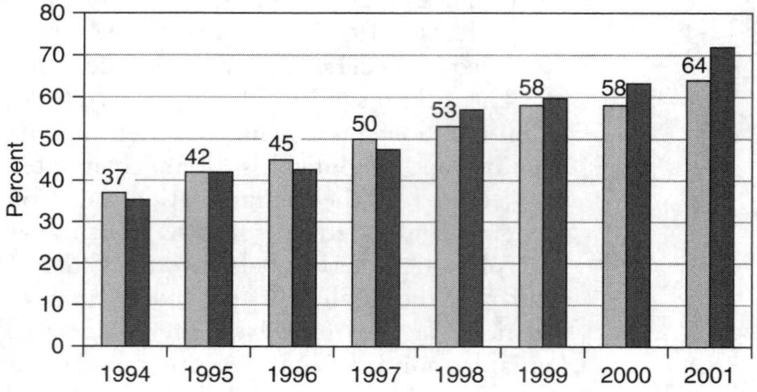

Source: Inside Mortgage Finance

2000–2010: THE RISE AND FALL OF THE SECONDARY MORTGAGE MARKET

What has become clear is that the original intent of home mortgage financing, government involvement, and the GSEs was lost as enormous amounts of capital were brought into secondary market conduits via Wall Street investment banks and other issuers of mortgage-backed and asset-backed securities.

The new century started out with the largest dollar amount of mortgage originations ever. A historically high $2 trillion in one- to four-family mortgage loans was originated in 2001 and 2002, only to be almost doubled in 2003 at $3.9 trillion. Originations remained at the incredible range of $3.3–$2.6 trillion for the next four years until 2008. Never before had originations reached such levels and certainly never for such an extended period.

One reason why so many homeowners refinanced during this period was decade-low interest rates. Many Americans refinanced to lower rates; others refinanced to pull out equity. Consumers greatly reduced the impact of the modest recession of 2001–2002 by spending the money obtained through cash-out refinances. However, refinance activity dropped from more than 74 percent of originations in 2004 to the 50 percent level from 2005 onwards as home purchase activity accelerated.

Another factor that fueled such a high, sustained volume was unprecedented home price appreciation in many real estate markets across the country. One result of these conditions was the increase in the U.S. homeownership rate to a record high of 69 percent in 2004, but at what cost?

Although mortgage originators profited greatly through the record origination volume, many mortgage servicers were hurt badly by the millions of mortgages that refinanced during the early years of the new century. These servicers purchased mortgage servicing rights, expecting the loans to remain on their books for a long enough period of time to make a profit on servicing those loans. This expectation was not borne out, as some consumers refinanced their mortgages two and three times within a three-year period. On the other hand, mortgage servicers may eventually benefit from these refinanced loans. New loans at lower rates typically experience longer durations, which results in a longer stream of servicing income; thus, the value of mortgage servicing portfolios increase.

Need for Additional Funds for Housing

For successive administrations, government policies, agencies, and rhetoric from politicians placed the housing market as the centerpiece of economic expansion. Also in the background was the continued political push from the prior decade to increase homeownership. These factors encouraged more expansive lending programs and policies and an expanding secondary mortgage market to fund it.

The two major secondary mortgage market players, Fannie Mae and Freddie Mac, projected that the following factors will lead to a need for increased mortgage financing in the first decade of the new century:

- 13 to 15 million more households in the first decade
- Homeownership rate increasing from 68 to 71 percent
- 14 million additional homeowners in the decade
- Homeownership growth for minorities (who trail the ownership rate for whites by 25 percent)
- 16 million new houses
- $16 trillion more in home loans (an average of $1.6 trillion each year)

The Role of Subprime Lending

It is important to note the change in loan products originated and their impact on mortgage lending during this decade. The economic growth outlook and strong economy enticed consumers to buy homes in earnest starting in 2003. Government policies and political mindset encouraged lenders to develop first-time homebuyer and other subprime programs to allow more applicants to qualify for homeownership. Secondary market conduits converted these higher-risk loans into private-label securities, funded by investment banks, national lenders, and foreign investors (See Chapter 5 – Secondary Mortgage Markets).

As a result, subprime lending increased rapidly from 2003 to 2006 as you can see in Figures 1.4 and 1.5. Conventional financing dropped from 62 percent to 34 percent of originations. Subprime, Alt A, and home equity loan production skyrocketed during this period - from 16 percent to 47 percent. Most subprime loans were originated by mortgage brokers and sent straight through Wall Street investment banks or national lenders into private-label securities. Fannie and Freddie Alt A programs (in reality, equally as subprime as many private-label loan programs) doubled in market share as well. Subprime home equity loans were combined with subprime first mortgages to bypass more stringent private mortgage insurance guidelines (See Chapter 6 – Conventional Lending).

In 2007 the subprime segment of the real estate and mortgage markets became unsustainable. Mortgage delinquency rose sharply, uncovering widespread fraud in many subprime applications and lenders. This caused a

FIGURE **1.4** Mortgage Product Mix 2003

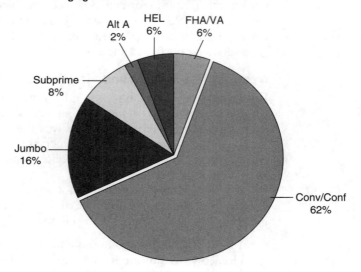

Source: Inside Mortgage Finance

massive decline in value of all mortgage-backed securities, shaking investor confidence and abruptly restricting mortgage funding. This helped cause the collapse in the mortgage and real estate markets, leading to the most severe economic recession in 80 years. Needless to say, none of the rosy GSE projections came to fruition by the end of the decade.

FIGURE **1.5** Mortgage Product Mix 2006

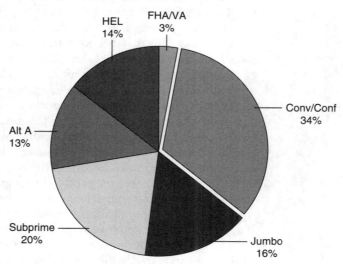

Source: Inside Mortgage Finance

In the wake of the mortgage and real estate market crisis, mortgage lending remains very restrictive and highly regulated. The federal government is directly involved in all segments of mortgage lending. Over 95 percent of loans conform to Fannie Mae, Freddie Mac, FHA, VA, and USDA guidelines. Many lenders feel they are in a "holding pattern": waiting for record levels of delinquency and foreclosures to subside, uncertain of how to implement recent regulatory changes, and unable to prepare for further wholesale changes to the regulatory landscape which are as yet unwritten.

Evolving Mortgage Lending Issues in the New Century

Putting aside the cyclical issues of economic recession, unemployment, and mortgage delinquency and foreclosure (which are all major issues in themselves), the residential mortgage lending industry still must grapple with several far-reaching issues as the second decade of the new century begins:

- How will the federal government redefine its role in mortgage finance in general as well as its role in the primary and secondary mortgage markets? Currently, the government is involved in at least 95 percent of originations via Fannie Mae, Freddie Mac, FHA, and VA. Clearly, this situation must change, but…
- What will Fannie and Freddie look like going forward?
  For two years, Congress and the present administration have not addressed the key question. Resolving their role is a first step in restoring stability in the mortgage lending arena.
- What will the new regulatory landscape look like, and how long will it take to be laid out?
  In a short period of time, the federal government put into play an unprecedented level of consumer compliance and regulatory legislation. In addition to the unknown impact that the many changes to RESPA, Truth In Lending, Mortgage Disclosure Improvement Act, and the SAFE Act will have on mortgage origination, the federal government initiated the restructuring of the entire regulatory system through the Dodd-Frank Wall Street Reform and Consumer Protection Act. Many key pieces of this new regulatory puzzle were left undefined; many others lack detail.
- How will the mortgage industry use technology to manage these changes?

From the consumers' standpoint, a major question that persists is: will the growth of online mortgage originations continue in this new mortgage-lending environment? Some experts project online mortgage originations to exceed 25 percent of all loans originated in the next few years, making this the fastest growing origination channel, but will this materialize amid the market and regulatory uncertainty? Many industry experts consider the use of technology the key to managing residential mortgage lending, from origination to servicing. The recession and housing market collapse spawned the development of many new technologies to detect fraud and improve quality control, manage and predict loan delinquency, and administer loan servicing and foreclosure portfolios.

DISCUSSION POINTS

1. Examine how the concept of private ownership of land has evolved since the days of the Egyptians.

2. How has the involvement of the federal government in real estate and mortgage lending allowed for growth in homeownership?

3. The Great Depression was the beginning of modern residential mortgage lending. Examine the changes that occurred during this period and their importance to modern mortgage lending.

4. The 1960–1970 period witnessed the enactment of many major consumer protection laws/regulations. How have these federal enactments changed the way in which residential mortgage lending is conducted?

5. What is the difference between the *title theory* and *lien theory* of mortgage lending? Which exists in your state?

6. What were two reasons for the stock market crash of 1987 and what was its impact on mortgage lending?

7. What role did subprime lending play in the mortgage industry events during 2000–2010?

Real Estate Law and Security Instruments

INTRODUCTION

Chapter 2 deals with real estate and mortgage law, how it developed under English common law and, finally, in the United States. This chapter is designed to provide reference material for the other chapters of the book. In addition, the second half of the chapter deals with the various forms of security instruments common to residential mortgage lending. Mortgage professionals should understand the purpose of the instruments, how they are constructed, and what clauses create legal rights and duties.

Possibly no other segment of the U.S. socioeconomic system is more involved with law than real estate and mortgage lending. Whether as a homeowner, a developer, or a financier, those involved with real estate and mortgage lending must understand the legal framework which defines real estate and protects the various rights and interests.

Law and real estate have been inseparable since the early days of the development of Anglo-American jurisprudence. This close relationship continues because of custom and the perception that real estate is normally an owner's most precious possession. However, this also has hindered the changes in real estate and mortgage lending concepts that are needed in an evolving society.

This chapter provides a fundamental review of how this relationship between law and real estate developed, and a discussion of the interests a person can have in real estate. It uses non-legal terminology as often as possible where the meaning or concept is not altered or affected in any way.

Each year state legislatures and county and municipal courts add laws and court cases to the body of real estate law, making it a more complex discipline to practice. The scope and subjects of state laws affecting mortgage lending vary greatly from state to state, but can include:

- Licensing of different types of lenders
- Advertising practices
- Application and rate lock-in requirements
- Mortgage servicing and escrows
- State housing agency mortgage program and servicing requirements

One recent trend seen in many states is enactment of more real estate law oriented toward consumer protection. There is a nationwide increase in laws providing consumers with more rights and protection against landlords and lenders. Some laws set standards for property owners to maintain the condition of properties in order to avoid neighborhood blight. Others add responsibilities for lenders during the foreclosure process. The aggregate effect of so much concurrent legal activity on so many fronts can actually restrict lending: it paralyzes regional and national lenders who must now comply with more regulations and adds a tremendous burden to local lenders who need to hire in the expertise needed to deal with these changes.

Municipal law deals more with zoning and building codes, which impact land use and the ways in which structures must be built. These laws vary tremendously from state to state. Even within a state, one can expect to find significant differences depending on the type of community, local customs, and changes in land use.

In light of the broad differences in state and local law, this review covers only the general principles of real estate law with no discussion of the unique features of any one state's law. In those situations in which there is a basic conflict in the general principles, the majority position is reviewed. Nevertheless, the laws of individual jurisdictions should be carefully determined. This is best accomplished by consulting a competent local attorney.

ENGLISH COMMON LAW

Real estate law throughout the United States, with few exceptions, is based almost entirely on the English common law, as it existed at the time of the American Revolutionary War. This system is based on a socioeconomic environment entirely different from that of the modern-day United States; nevertheless, most of our real estate law is derived from the common law and uses language that is hundreds of years old.

This common background has been modified as each jurisdiction's legislative changes, or as courts interpreted the law differently. Developments in real estate finance since 1776 have required new indigenous laws. As a result, the chief problem facing contemporary American real estate law is the existence of 51 jurisdictions (including the District of Columbia) with separate real estate laws—all based on an archaic system of law. A short review of the development of the common law is vital to an understanding of current real estate law.

Feudal System of Land Tenure

Before the Norman invasion of England in 1066, there was no well-developed system of land ownership in England. The family unit, rather than the individual, owned the land, and when the head of the household died, the new head of the household represented the ownership of the family in a particular piece of land. In 1066, when William the Conqueror invaded England, he imposed upon the English a European concept of land ownership called the "feudal system of land tenure," an economic, military, and political system of government that held that the king exclusively owned all land. The most valuable and important commodity in such a society was land. Land represented wealth, and all wealth came from the land. Money hardly existed, and barter was the means of exchange. Since the king owned all land, he had complete control over the country and the economy.

A king, of course, needed arms for protection of the realm. For this he depended on the loyalty, fidelity, and allegiance of the lords. In return for their allegiance and military service, the king allowed the lords to use the land, although no ownership was conveyed. The lords, in turn, allowed lesser lords to use portions of this land in return for a share of the profits and for swearing allegiance to them. Finally, these lesser lords allowed serfs, who were nothing more than slaves indentured to the land, to use the land in return for a promise of military service. In this pyramid of military allegiance, the serfs owed military service to the lesser lords, who in turn owed service to the lords, who swore allegiance to the king.

The right to own land didn't exist for many years, but one of the incidents of ownership, the ability to pass the use of land to heirs, produced a confrontation with King John in 1215. The result was the Magna Carta, which provided greater rights for the lords, including the right to pass the use of the land on to their sons. Land was passed on to sons only as a result of the doctrine of primogeniture, which dictated that the oldest male child had the right to inherit the land. This was desirable at the time, since it prevented estates from being broken up into smaller tracts and allowed for the development of landed gentry, which eventually developed the English society. Out of this society evolved the common law and, eventually, English real estate law. Although modified over the years, the feudal system survived until 1660, when it was abolished by law.

Allodial System

As contrasted with the feudal system, the **allodial system** recognizes that an owner of real estate has title irrespective of the sovereign and thus owes no duty, such as rent or the rendering of military service, to the sovereign. This system developed throughout the world with the exception of Western Europe and certain other areas where the feudal system remained.

The feudal system was an early part of the American land-ownership system in a few locations such as New York and Maryland. With those exceptions, the allodial system was paramount in America based on conquest, discovery, or purchase.

PRINCIPLES OF REAL ESTATE LAW

The first step in understanding the principles of real estate law is to define terms. **Real property** is land and everything permanently attached to it. Under the common law, and as a general rule today, this included ownership from the center of the earth, the surface, and up to the heavens. All other property is *personal property*. Real estate denotes both real property and the business of real estate, including financing.

Property can change from one classification to another fairly rapidly. For example, a tree standing in a forest is real property. When it is felled, it becomes personal property and, finally, after being made into lumber and becoming part of a house, it is real property again. The term **fixture** is used to describe a piece of personal property that has been attached in such a manner that it is now considered real property. This distinction is important, since title to real property is normally transferred by a deed, while personal property is transferred by a bill of sale.

Estate

When people talk about their legal ownership of land, they refer to the type of estate they have in real estate. This is as true in the United States as it was in England 500 years ago. An **estate** is defined as an interest in real property that is measured by its potential duration. There are two recognized classifications of estate in real property: *freehold* and *leasehold* (sometimes referred to as *nonfreehold*). The classification **freehold estate** is the highest form of interest possible in real property, as it involves all the rights in real property including use, passing the property to one's heirs, and selecting who is going to take it in a transfer. It is an estate of infinite duration, in that the *chain of title* could theoretically last forever. An example of a freehold estate is *fee simple absolute*.

On the other hand, the classification *leasehold estate* is an inferior interest in real property, because the owner of a leasehold interest has only the right of possession for a period of time. The owner of this interest does not have *seisin*, which is defined as the ability to pass title to one's heirs or assigns. An example of a leasehold estate is a tenant's interest in leased property.

Fee Simple Absolute

There has never been nor will there ever be complete ownership of land. Examples of the restraints or limitations on ownership of land include, among others, eminent domain, adverse possession, and easements. The greatest interest a person can have in real property is known as a *fee simple absolute*. Any owner of real property, whether it is a large corporation or John Doe, has a fee simple absolute if he possesses all possible rights to that piece of real property.

In order to explain a fee simple absolute, legal pedagogues use the "bundle of rights" concept. For example, assume that all rights (such as the right to sell, mortgage, and build on a piece of real property) are represented by "sticks" and are contained in this bundle of rights. If all of the sticks are present and the owner has all possible rights to the real property, then the bundle of rights is complete and is called a **fee simple absolute**. If a stick is missing, such as the right to use the property the way one wants, then the interest is less than a fee simple absolute.

Defeasible or Conditional Fee

A freehold estate, which is similar to a fee simple absolute but minus a stick (or a right) from the bundle of rights, is the *defeasible fee simple*. This is a freehold estate that could (but will not necessarily) last forever. An example of a defeasible fee simple occurs when conditions are placed on how the property may be used. Grantors of land may put any restrictions they desire on land use even after it has been conveyed. There are, of course, a few exceptions, such as those that are racially oriented. Grantors can always give less than the full interests they own in conveying land, but never more. They can give possession for any desired period of time, or for any specific use— for use only as a church, for example. If so conveyed, this creates a defeasible fee simple that could last forever, but it could also be terminated.

An example of a defeasible fee simple that would automatically end if a certain event occurs is when Adam grants land to an Anglican church on condition that the premises are used only for church purposes. The church has a defeasible fee simple that could last forever but will automatically end if the property ceases to be used for church purposes. When that happens, the title automatically reverts to Adam or Adam's heirs. This interest is classified as a fee simple since it could last forever if the property is always used for church purposes.

There are two legal types of defeasible fee simple: fee simple *subject to a condition subsequent* and fee simple *determinable*. The typical person involved in real estate does not need to know the distinction, but counsel for that person should. An example of a fee simple subject to a condition subsequent is when John conveys property to Janice as long as liquor is never sold on the premises. In this situation, the grantee Janice (the person to whom the land has been conveyed) has a fee simple, but it is subject to a condition subsequent in that if liquor is ever sold on the premises, the land will revert to the grantor (the one making the conveyances). The grantor must make an affirmative action for the property to revert, that is, reenter the property and sue to terminate the estate.

Most courts treat these two types basically the same. If forced to distinguish, courts attempt to find a fee on a condition subsequent in order that the grantor must reenter to terminate rather than have the estate terminate automatically.

Fee Tail

This type of estate originated from a desire in feudal England to keep land in whole parcels within the family. A **fee tail** is an estate of potentially infinite duration, but is inheritable only by the grantee's lineal descendants, such as children or grandchildren. To create a fee tail under the common law, it is necessary to state in the conveyance that the land transfers to Stephen and "the heirs of his body." This differed from the wording of any other common law transfer, which required only use of the term "and his heirs."

There are various types of fee tail. The **fee tail general** means the property is inheritable by the issue of the grantee. A **fee tail special** means the land is inheritable only by the issue of the grantee and a specifically named spouse (a conveyance to Robert and the heirs of his body, by his wife, Mary, would be an example). A fee tail general can specify whether the issue need be male or female, and there also is the possibility of a fee tail special, male or female. Although the fee tail is still allowed in some New England states, the practical effect of it has been abolished in all states today.

Life Estates

A **life estate** is a freehold estate like the fee simple absolute and others already mentioned, but it is not inheritable. Life estates can be either conventional (created by the grantor) or legal (created by operation of law). The creation of a life estate is a tool often used in estate planning, and is a fairly common interest in real estate. By the creation of a life estate, the life tenant (the one granted the right) has the use of real estate for a period of time measured by a human life. The human life used to measure the duration of the life estate may be that of another human life, but is most commonly measured by the life of the life tenant. An example is: Jennifer conveys a life estate to Benjamin for life, and as long as Benjamin is alive, Benjamin has the right to use the real estate, with certain exceptions, as if he owned it. The only incident of ownership that Benjamin lacks is the power to pass on a fee simple absolute. The right to sell or mortgage the interest is not expressly given, but a person could acquire only that which Benjamin had, which is the use of the land for a period measured by a life.

When Jennifer created this life estate, only a part of the complete interest was transferred. In other words, someone else was allowed to use the land for a period of time. However, at the expiration of that period of time, the remaining rights to the real estate are with the grantor. In the example given, in which Jennifer conveyed land to Benjamin for the duration of Benjamin's life, the land will revert to Jennifer (the grantor) or Jennifer's heirs upon the death of Benjamin (the life tenant) as no other conveyance was made.

When Jennifer created the life estate in Benjamin, the remainder could have been transferred in this way: Jennifer to Benjamin for life, and then to Neil. In this situation, Neil is the vested remainderman, because the grantor has transferred the remaining interest to Neil. The rights of Neil are vested irrespective of whether he survives the life tenant or not. If a vested remainderman does die before a life tenant, then the vested remainderman's heirs would inherit the fee interest.

On the other hand, a life estate can be created this way: Jennifer to Benjamin for Benjamin's life, and then to Neil if Neil is alive, in which case Neil must survive Benjamin to acquire any rights to the land. If Neil dies before Benjamin, the land reverts to the original owner. If it is impossible to determine at the time of the creation of the life estate who definitely will take the fee simple after the death of the life tenant, the remainderman is referred to as a contingent remainderman.

Another common example of this situation is: Jennifer to Benjamin for life, and then to Benjamin's children. Benjamin may not have any children; therefore, their interest is contingent upon their being born. To complicate it even further, the conveyance could read: Jennifer to Benjamin for Benjamin's life, and then to Benjamin's surviving children. The children, if any, must survive Benjamin before they can acquire any interest.

In summary, a conventional life estate is an interest which an individual has in real estate providing most of the incidences of ownership, with the exception of the ability to pass a fee simple absolute. The person who takes possession after the life tenant dies could be either the grantor, if the grantor did not convey the remainder, or it could be a third person who would be classified as either a contingent or a vested remainderman, depending on whether the identity can be determined precisely at the time of the creation of the life estate.

Legal Life Estates

In contrast with the conventional life estate, created intentionally by the grantor, a *legal life estate* is created by operation of the law. An example of a legal life estate is the right of dower. Dower was originally conceived to prevent a widow from being penniless during a period of English history when life insurance, welfare, and social security were unknown. Dower is a common law right of a widow still present in many jurisdictions. The equivalent right of the husband is curtesy, which has either been abolished or merged with dower in nearly all states.

Basically, the **right of dower** gives a wife, at her husband's death, a life estate in one third of the real estate owned by her husband during marriage. Generally, the widow has a choice of which real estate will be subject to her dower right, and this right is applicable to all real estate owned by the husband during the marriage, even if he had transferred it before death. In those states where this right exists, a wife's potential dower interest is extinguished if she executes a deed with her husband transferring the land to another.

In some states the right of dower has been abolished as unnecessary. The need for a right such as dower was eliminated in most states by the creation of a statutory right of each spouse to a minimum one-third share of the decedent's estate, and because of life insurance, social security, and other benefits.

Leasehold Estates (Nonfreehold Estates)

As mentioned earlier, the *leasehold estate* gives the owner the right to possession of real estate for a period of time. The actual duration may or may not be ascertainable at the beginning, but it does not carry with it the ability to pass title to the real estate. The owner of the land (the fee) has given up possession for a period of time, but retains the legal title to the real estate, and the owner (or heirs or assigns) will eventually retake possession. The legal term to describe the missing element in a leasehold estate is *seisin*.

Although the use of leases can be traced to the beginning of written history, the *leasehold estate* in England was originally used to circumvent the prohibition against lending money for interest, as any interest was usury under early church law. The person borrowing money would allow the lender to use some or all of the land for a period of time in lieu of interest. Therefore, under the common law, a leasehold was considered personal property, but now is considered an estate in real estate. A **lease**, which creates the leasehold estate, is a peculiar instrument in that it is both a conveyance giving the tenant possession for a period of time and a contract establishing rights and duties for the parties. The essential elements for a lease are:

- Name of landlord and tenant
- Agreement to lease
- Description of leased property
- Duration of lease
- Rental agreement
- Rights and duties of the parties
- Signature

A lease for a year or less may be verbal or in writing, but one for more than a year must be in writing. For the safety of both the landlord and tenant, all leases should be in writing. Most states have a 99-year limitation on a lease, although the vast majority of leases are for less than 10 years. The degree of complexity in leases increases from the relatively simple residential lease to the very complex shopping center lease. The type of tenancy acquired from a lease depends on whether the term is renewable and whether notice to terminate must be given by either party.

Additional Interests in Real Estate

In addition to the freehold and leasehold estates in real estate, there are certain other limited interests or rights to real estate. These include easements, profits, and covenants. These interests create a limited right to the real estate of another. A piece of real property subject to an easement, for instance, does not prevent it from being owned in fee simple absolute.

Easements

An **easement** is a nonpossessory interest in the real estate of another, giving the holder the right to a limited use of real estate. An example is the right to drive across the real estate of another to reach a highway. An easement is either *in gross* (a personal right) or *appurtenant* (belonging to whoever owns the benefited real estate). Most easements are expressed in writing, although they can be simply implied. The right of a gas company to install a gas line on a back property line is an example of an expressed easement appurtenant.

Covenants

Like the previous interests discussed, a *covenant* is an interest in the real estate of another. The difference between a covenant—a legal promise to do or not to do something—and other interests is that the former restricts or limits how the owner can use the real estate.

An example of a covenant is the requirement a farmer may put on the part of a farm being sold that the grantee use the real estate only for residential purposes. This interest is of benefit to the grantor because it allows control of the use of the real estate. Therefore, it is an interest in the real estate of another. This interest can be either in gross or appurtenant, although the term often used with covenants is *running with the land*. This interest should not be confused with a defeasible fee simple, since a breach of a covenant does not impact title—only damages or an injunction can be sought.

TYPES OF OWNERSHIP

Joint Tenancy

More than one person can own land. The most common type of joint or concurrent ownership is **joint tenancy**, which can exist between any two or more persons. Although joint tenants share a single title to the real estate, each owns an equal share of the whole. Joint tenancies are quite common, but a few states abolished or limited them for reasons that are discussed later. Most states allow the creation of a joint tenancy by simply referring to John and Sally as joint tenants. Other jurisdictions require reference to John and Sally as joint tenants with the right of survivorship. Only an affirmative action of the grantor creates this interest, not by operation of law.

The right of survivorship is the key concept of a joint tenancy. Upon the death of one of the joint tenants, all the decedent's interests in the real property terminate and the surviving joint tenant or tenants retain the ownership in the land. In other words, a joint tenancy is not an inheritable estate. Therefore, it does not pass through the estate of the decedent and does not pass to the heirs. Instead, it passes to or is possessed automatically by the surviving joint tenant.

For this reason, some states abolished—and most courts disfavor—joint tenancy because it automatically prevents property from flowing through the estate of an individual to the heirs. To create a joint tenancy, one must follow the strict statutory requirements of the respective state. To avoid the possibility that a court misunderstands a grantor's intention, a joint tenancy must use this phrase: to John and Sally as joint tenants with right of survivorship and not as tenants in common.

While there is a joint tenancy, an attachment of the portion of the whole belonging to any one of the joint tenants usually may satisfy that individual's legal debts. But the portion belonging to the other joint tenant(s) may not. Some states have laws that modify this approach if the joint tenants are husband and wife and the property in question is their home.

Although any joint tenant may sell or mortgage his or her interest (with some exceptions for married joint tenants), the joint tenancy terminates either by voluntary or by involuntary transfer. It is also terminated by the death of one of two joint tenants, but not by the death of one of more than two. The survivors in that case still have a joint tenancy among themselves.

Under the common law, both parties must acquire ownership to real estate at the same time for a joint tenancy to exist. Consequently, a husband who owns a property before marriage can't create a joint tenancy in it with his wife. One method devised to circumvent this requirement is the usage of a "straw man." For instance, the husband conveys title to his real estate to a friend or relative (the so-called straw man), who then transfers the title back to the husband and wife as joint tenants to satisfy the unit of time requirement.

Tenancy by the Entirety

A form of concurrent ownership much like joint tenancy is *tenancy by the entirety*, which is allowed in 20 states. It exists because of a vestige from the common law of some technical requirement for a joint tenancy, such as the unity of time, or because the state abolished joint tenancy. The primary difference between this form of ownership and the joint tenancy is that a tenancy by the entirety exists only between a legally married husband and wife; a joint tenancy exists between any two or more persons.

Another important feature of a tenancy by the entirety is that the interest of one of the parties cannot be attached for the legal debts of that person. Only a debt of both parties can become an attachment. For this reason, lenders in some states will require both a husband and wife to sign the mortgage note if the form of ownership of the real estate is to be as tenants by the entirety (even if only one has income). Many states allowing tenancy by the entirety presume that a conveyance to a husband and wife, silent as to the type of ownership, will be a tenancy by the entirety.

The surviving tenant becomes the sole owner like the surviving joint tenant, but this survivorship right stems from the concept that the husband and wife were one, so ownership was already with the survivor. Divorce or annulment will terminate this tenancy.

Tenants in Common

Tenancy in common is a concurrent estate with no right of survivorship. Therefore, when a person dies, the interest held in the real property passes through the estate. This interest can exist between any two or more individuals and, in effect, jointly gives them the rights and duties of a sole owner. Each of the cotenants is considered an owner of an undivided interest (not necessarily equal) in the whole property, and each has separate legal title, unlike joint tenants who share a single title. Courts of law look with favor on a tenancy in common, because a cotenant's share of ownership passes upon death to the heirs and is not forfeited. As contrasted with a joint tenancy or a tenancy by the entirety, a tenancy in common can arise by operation of law. For example, when a person dies *intestate* (without a will), heirs automatically inherit as tenants in common.

Any tenant in common can sell his or her interest, mortgage it, or have it attached for debts without destroying the joint interest. A grantee of a tenancy in common acquires only the percentage of the whole owned by the grantor. A tenancy in common is terminated by agreement between the parties or upon a petition to a court.

Community Property

Another form of concurrent ownership is *community property*. This is the law in nine states located primarily in the western part of the United States: AZ, CA, NM, NV, ID, WA, TX, WI, LA, and AK only if couples opt in. It derives from Spanish law originally and not English common law. Basically, the concept is that half of all property, personal and real, created during marriage belongs to each spouse. The underlying theory of this concept is that both have contributed to the creation of the family's wealth, whether or not both were gainfully employed.

Since each has equal interests, both must sign a mortgage note and security agreement. If a marriage terminates, each party should receive a one-half share. There are three exceptions to this rule:

- Property acquired from separate funds, such as a trust account
- Property acquired individually before the marriage
- Property inherited from another's estate

Tenancy in Partnership

The last form of concurrent ownership is *tenancy in partnership*. Under the common law, a partnership cannot own real estate in its partnership name. Therefore, one of the partners must own the real estate in his or her own name. This presents the possibility of fraud. The Uniform Partnership Act, as adopted by many states, provides that a partnership can own real property in its firm's name. Upon the death of a partner in a partnership, the surviving partner(s) is (are) vested with the share of the decedent or a percentage ownership of all property owned by the partnership. One partner's share of ownership may not necessarily be equal to that of another. It is quite common for partnerships to provide for a means of compensation for a deceased partner's estate, usually by insurance or a buy-sell agreement.

TRANSFER OF LAND

All title to real estate in the United States can be traced to one of three origins: conquest, discovery, or purchase. Today, title to real property can be transferred either voluntarily or involuntarily.

Voluntary Transfers

Most transfers of land are *voluntary* when a grantor intends to transfer title to land to a grantee by the use of a deed or possibly a will. Real estate that passes according to a will is also a voluntary conveyance, since it passes as the testator or the one making the will intended.

Involuntary Transfers

An **involuntary conveyance** occurs when a legal owner of real estate loses title contrary to the owner's intention. *Eminent domain* is one example. Any sovereign in the United States (federal, state, county, or city) and some quasi-public entities (such as the telephone company or gas line company) can exercise the right of eminent domain. This right is inherent in a sovereign and is not granted by a constitution, although it is limited by it. The two key elements are 1) it must be exercised for a valid public purpose or use, and 2) that it requires compensation paid to the legal owner.

Adverse possession is another example of involuntary transfer of title. The public policy behind the doctrine of adverse possession is to encourage land usage or to settle old claims to real property. Normally, a person who possesses the real property of another will hold that real estate for the legal owner's benefit. However, the one occupying the real property can acquire legal title if certain requirements are satisfied.

To claim title to real property by adverse possession, in most states the one occupying the real property must prove the following:

- Actual possession
- Hostile intent (to the possession of others)
- Notorious and open possession
- Exclusive and continuous possession
- Possession for a statutory period (ranges from 5 to 20 years)

Some states also require that the party claiming title by adverse possession base the claim on some written instrument—even if the instrument is not valid. Other states require the claimant to pay real estate taxes for the statutory period.

Another example of involuntary transfer includes foreclosure and subsequent sale if an owner of real estate defaults on a mortgage or other encumbrance, or does not pay property tax.

A final example of involuntary transfer occurs when a person dies *intestate*. In this situation the title to real property along with the personal property passes, not according to the dictates of the owner, but according to the statutes of that particular state. If the individual had no discernible heirs, the property would *escheat* (pass) to the state.

TYPES OF DEEDS

A **deed** is a legal instrument that transfers a grantor's interest. If a grantor has no actual interest in a particular piece of real estate, an executed deed will transfer nothing. In addition, a properly executed deed from a grantor who does have title but lacks legal capacity (the grantor is legally insane, for example) transfers nothing. *Abstracting* or checking the chain of title for defects can determine the validity of the title of the grantor.

Every state has a law known as a *statute of frauds,* which requires written transfers of real estate. Today, a deed does not require technical terms for transfer as long as it clearly shows the grantor's intention to transfer.

There are eight essential elements of a modern deed:

1. Grantor's name
2. Grantee's name
3. Description of real estate to be conveyed
4. Consideration (does not have to be actual amount paid)
5. Words of conveyance
6. Signature of grantor
7. Delivery and acceptances
8. Proper execution

There are three basic types of deeds; each has a specific purpose and function to perform. The least complicated is a *quitclaim deed*, which clears title to real estate. A person signing this deed makes no title guarantee. Instead, a grantor simply transfers whatever interest is owned, if any. This deed clears a cloud on the title caused by a widow having a potential right of dower. She would execute the deed, possibly for a fee, whereby she transfers whatever interest she has (in this case, dower), thus clearing the title.

A **general warranty deed** is the most common deed to transfer interest in real estate. With this deed, a grantor guarantees to a grantee that the title transferred is good against the whole world. This guarantee extends past the grantor to those in the chain of title. If a grantor refuses to use this deed, it may be an indication that the title is defective.

The **special warranty deed** is used in rare situations when a grantor wants to limit the guarantee. An executor of an estate would use this instrument to convey real estate to those specified in a will. By this deed, the grantor only guarantees that nothing was done to interfere with the title to the real estate while under the grantor's control and makes no guarantee about a decedent's claim to the real estate.

Recording

Transactions that create, transfer, or encumber an interest in real estate should be *recorded*. As in England centuries ago, the reason for recording is to prevent fraud. One example is when the owner of land would sell, possibly inadvertently, the same real estate to two or more innocent purchasers. Therefore, it was necessary to develop a system by which fraudulent transactions could be prevented. This was accomplished by devising a system of recording transactions affecting real estate.

To protect a buyer's interest, recording statutes require purchasers of real estate to record in the public land records the instrument by which they acquire the interest. Once an interest is recorded, any subsequent party (purchaser, lender, etc.) is considered to have either *constructive notice* or *actual knowledge* of the prior interest. The party gains actual knowledge when it checks the record. The act of recording gives constructive notice to the whole world that a party has acquired an interest in a particular real property.

An individual who wants to purchase real property has an obligation to check the record, usually in a county courthouse, to determine whether there have been any transactions involving that particular real estate. Therefore, any subsequent purchaser could not acquire the same interest.

If no transaction appears, an innocent purchaser acquiring an interest will be protected against the whole world, even against a prior purchaser. Every state has a "race statute" that dictates that the first of two innocent parties to record will be protected. If the party (the prior purchaser, for instance) who could have prevented a subsequent fraud by recording does not record, then that party will suffer the loss.

In summary, a prior purchaser is protected if a record is made, whether or not a subsequent purchaser checks the record. The same is true if there is actual notice. If A sold land to B, and B failed to record, and C, knowing of that transaction, buys the same land and records, B will be protected since C had actual notice of the transaction between A and B. If C did not have actual notice and recorded before B, C would be protected in any dispute between B and C.

MORTGAGE LAW

Historical Development

As used in the United States today, the mortgage is unique in many features, but its fundamentals are based on the common law as it has developed in England over the past 900 years. The classic common law mortgage, which evolved in England after the Norman invasion in 1066, was well developed and established by 1400. Basically, it was an actual *conveyance*—a title transfer—of real estate serving as security for a debt. For a conveyance to be effective under the common law, possession of that real estate actually had to pass, putting the mortgagee in possession of the real estate.

The instrument conveying the real estate title to the mortgagee contained a *defeasance clause* whereby the mortgagee's title was defeated if payment was made on the due date, called the *law day*. Originally, when title and possession were in the hands of the mortgagee, the mortgagee could retain all rents and profits generated by the land. This practice was established because a mortgagee could not charge interest on a loan; any interest was usury, which was illegal at this time. After this law changed and interest could be charged, the mortgagee was forced to credit all rents and profits to the mortgagor.

Early common law mortgages did not require any action on behalf of mortgagees to protect their rights if a mortgagor failed to perform. Since a conveyance had already been made, the mortgagee had title and possession. Thus, the only effect of the mortgagor's nonperformance was the termination of the possibility of reversion through the defeasance clause.

Equity of Redemption

The harsh result of a mortgagor not performing after the due date, even when not personally at fault, led mortgagors to petition the king for redress from an inequitable practice. Eventually, the courts of equity gave relief to mortgagors by allowing them the right to redeem their real estate through payment with interest of past-due debts. This was called the *equity of redemption*. By 1625, this practice had become so widespread that mortgagees were reluctant to lend money with real estate as security since they never knew when a mortgagor might elect to redeem the real estate. Mortgagees attempted to change this by inserting a clause in mortgages whereby the mortgagor agreed not to seek this redress. But courts of equity refused to allow the practice and would not enforce the clause. In order to restore an equitable balance, the courts began to decree that a mortgagor had a certain amount of time after default, usually six months, in which to redeem the real estate. If this were not done, the mortgagor's equity of redemption would be cancelled or foreclosed. This action soon became known as a foreclosure suit and is still used in some states today.

The equity of redemption should be contrasted with the statutory right of redemption, which is discussed in the next section dealing with American mortgage law.

U.S. MORTGAGE LAW—LIEN THEORY VS. TITLE THEORY

In U.S. law, the most important change from the common law relates to the concept of who actually owns the real estate that is serving as security for the performance of an obligation. The common law held that the mortgagee was the legal owner of the real estate while it served as security. This is known as **title theory**: the mortgagee holds title while the debt is outstanding and not in default. Twenty-two states (plus the District of Columbia) classify themselves as either intermediate or title theory states.

Shortly after the Revolutionary War, a New Jersey court held that a mortgagor did not lose title to real estate serving as security. The court's reasoning was that since the law already recognized the right of a mortgagor to redeem the real estate after default, the law had to accept a continuing ownership interest in the mortgagor. The court held that a mortgage created only a security interest for the mortgagee and that title should therefore remain with the mortgagor. This is known as **lien theory**: the mortgagor holds title while the debt is outstanding and not in default. This is the law in 28 states today.

All states recognize the mortgagor as the legal owner of the real estate. The principal difference between these two theories is in the manner of foreclosure. Currently, mortgagors are able to do as they please with mortgaged real estate as long as the activity does not interfere with the security interest of a mortgagee.

According to current law, any interest in real estate that can be sold can be mortgaged, including a fee simple, a life estate, or a lease. The determining factor is whether a mortgagee can be found willing to lend money with that particular interest as security.

Mortgage Debt: the Note

When a mortgage lender agrees to grant a loan secured by real estate, that lender first must negotiate and identify the terms under which funds will be borrowed, then consider the collateral. The *note* is the promise to pay. Either a promissory note or a bond evidences the debt secured by a mortgage. Normally, the mortgage and the note are separate documents, but in some jurisdictions they are combined.

The note should be negotiable so that the originating mortgagee can assign it. This is the normal practice today for most mortgage lenders. Both Fannie Mae and Freddie Mac have developed uniform notes which meet all legal requirements for each of the states. All mortgage lenders should use them since they contain well-conceived and tested language that protects the rights of both the borrower and lender.

Provisions of the Note

As mentioned, the uniform note provides protection for the various parties and also establishes important provisions such as what the interest rate is and how repayment will be made. Many provisions like this are not required by federal or state statutes, but follow common practice or are negotiated between the two parties—mostly to conform to secondary market standards. For example, the Fannie and Freddie interstate notes require that the first payment is due on the first of the month following a full month after closing (if a loan closed on May 15, the first payment would be due on July 1st).

Other important note items include:

- Original signatures of the borrowers
- All blanks are filled in and any corrections are initialed (no whiteouts)
- Clearly stated interest rate, payment schedule, and due dates
- Dates of note and mortgage match
- Appropriate uniform note used for each loan type (fixed rate, ARM, balloon, etc.)

The Security Interest

Lenders require collateral to secure the executed mortgage note. By obtaining a *security interest* in the real estate used for collateral, the lender has the right to use that collateral to recover losses from the note should the borrower not repay. In the United States, the security instrument used to accomplish this is either a *mortgage* or a *deed of trust* (sometimes called a trust deed or trust indenture). The purpose of each is to help create a lien on the real estate that the lender takes as security for the debt.

The Mortgage Instrument

The **mortgage instrument**, which creates the security interest in the real estate for the lender, does not have to appear in any particular legal form. There are no set requirements except that a mortgage instrument must be in writing. Any wording is sufficient that clearly indicates the purpose of the instrument, which is to create a security interest in described real estate for the benefit of a mortgagee. Today, most mortgage lenders use the Fannie Mae and Freddie Mac uniform mortgage instruments for their particular states.

Requirements for a Mortgage

If a conveyance is made to a mortgagee that appears to be a deed absolute but is actually intended to be a conveyance as security for a debt, all state courts have uniformly held that transaction to be a mortgage even if the defeasance clause is missing. On the other hand, if the parties agree in writing that money will be advanced, with the debt for those funds secured by a later mortgage, and a mortgage is not executed, the law holds that a creditor has a security interest in the real estate. This interest is called an equitable mortgage.

A valid mortgage instrument should include:

- Names of the mortgagor and mortgagee
- Words of conveyance or a mortgaging clause
- Amount of the debt
- Interest rate and terms of payment
- A repeat of the provisions of the promissory note or bond in some jurisdictions
- Detailed legal description of the real estate securing the debt (often Schedule "A")
- Clauses to protect the rights of the parties
- Date (same date as note)
- Signature of the mortgagor (and notarized, if required)
- Any requirements particular to that jurisdiction

Deed of Trust

The deed of trust was not known in the common law, so a state must first enact special enabling legislation for its use. It serves the same function and shares many features as a mortgage, but differs in two ways: title conveyance and foreclosure.

A mortgage is a two-party instrument between a mortgagor and a mortgagee, while a **deed of trust** is a three-party instrument between a borrower, a lender, and a third party, called a trustee. With a deed of trust, a borrower conveys title to a trustee who holds it until the obligation is satisfied, at which time title conveys back to the borrower. The title is held for the benefit of the lender.

Foreclosures for deeds of trust vs. mortgages is discussed later in this chapter.

Clauses to Protect the Rights of the Parties

The elements listed above comprise the foundation upon which a complete mortgage instrument is built. A mortgage instrument, such as the Fannie Mae and Freddie Mac uniform mortgage or deed of trust, contains clauses to solve many foreseeable problems. Of course, there are many types of mortgage clauses, but the most typical and important ones are the payment clause, the prepayment clause, and the acceleration clause.

Payment Clause

The most obvious clause in a mortgage is the one by which a mortgagor agrees to pay the obligation in an agreed-upon manner. The *mortgage payment clause* makes reference to the note or bond containing the terms and amount obligating the mortgagor. A separate clause may stipulate a covenant to pay taxes and hazard insurance (with a mortgage-payable clause) as they become due. However, this often is a part of the payment clause. A mortgagee may require the collection of funds for payment of property taxes and insurance as part of the mortgage payment. These funds are placed in an escrow fund and disbursed at appropriate times to the proper party.

Prepayment Clause

A **prepayment clause** typically imposes a penalty equal to a percentage of the principal balance if the borrower pays the note in full ahead of maturity (within the first two years of the note date on a 15- to 30-year term). Since 1979, residential mortgage loans sold to Fannie Mae or Freddie Mac prohibit enforcement of a prepayment penalty. Before that date, these clauses existed and were enforceable for portfolio and secondary market loans. A few portfolio lenders still use prepayment clauses on first mortgages, although it is more common for second mortgages or HELOCs. Such clauses are enforceable if allowed under federal and state law. Recent federal regulations prohibit their use on some first and second mortgage programs (*high cost* and *higher priced* mortgage loans, discussed in Chapter 11—Compliance).

Acceleration Clause

The **acceleration clause** is the most important clause in the entire mortgage for the protection of the mortgagee. It states that the mortgagee can accelerate the entire amount of the debt if the mortgagor defaults or breaches any stated covenant. Both the mortgage and the instrument that evidences the debt may include this clause. (Some states permit automatic acceleration clauses, but these should be avoided, if possible, because the mortgagee may have other more beneficial options for curing defaults or breaches.)

Default

Default is a violation by borrower or lender of one or more specified covenants in the note or mortgage. A borrower can default for reasons related to repayment of the debt or to the collateral. The most common defaults or breaches of covenants by a mortgagor that could trigger acceleration include:

- Failure to make the required payment when due
- Failure to pay taxes or insurance when due
- Failure to defend the property title from other interests (liens, judgments)
- Failure to maintain the property
- Committing waste (destructive use of property)

Some mortgagees have inserted clauses providing for acceleration if a mortgagor either further mortgages the secured real estate (*subordination clause*) or sells the real estate with the mortgage still attached. This clause ostensibly protects the mortgagee from a change in risk.

FORECLOSURE

After all attempts to cure a default fail, a mortgagee must move to foreclose and protect its investment. It is important for a lender to realize that when it forecloses a defaulted mortgage, it is fulfilling the covenants in the mortgage and performing its fiduciary responsibility to protect the funds loaned, which may be individual savings or investor funds.

Equitable Right of Redemption

Any time before a foreclosure sale or other disposition, a mortgagor or anyone claiming through the mortgagor, such as a spouse or junior lien holders, may exercise the *equitable right of redemption*. The mortgagor exercises this right by paying the mortgagee the outstanding balance plus interest and costs.

The first judicial method of cutting off a mortgagor's equity of redemption was known as *strict foreclosure*. If not redeemed within a set time, a court decree transferred the mortgagor's interest in the real estate to the mortgagee irrespective of any equity of the mortgagor in the property. This result was grossly unfair to the mortgagor. Therefore, a more balanced approach followed, which provided for selling the property to secure the debt. The proceeds of the sale went first to satisfy the mortgagee, then to other lien holders, and then to the mortgagor.

Methods of Foreclosure

The four modern methods of foreclosure, depending on the law of a state, are as follows:

1. Judicial proceeding
2. Power of sale
3. Strict foreclosure
4. Entry and possession

In most states that use deeds of trust there is no requirement for a foreclosure, with its time-consuming court proceedings. Instead, the trustee has the power of sale to satisfy the debt. Some states, however, require a foreclosure even if the financing vehicle is a deed of trust. Table 2.1 shows a state-by-state comparison of selected aspects of foreclosure. Regardless of the situation, there is always a requirement for a public notice of sale.

Judicial Proceeding

Most states provide for mortgage foreclosure through a court proceeding. This method best protects the interests of the various parties. The action is much like any other civil suit in that the case must be brought in a court

TABLE **2.1**
State-by-state Comparison of Selected Aspects of Foreclosure

State	Nature of Mortgage	Customary Security Instrument	Predominant Method of Foreclosure	Redemption Period (months)	Possession during Redemption
Alabama	Title	Mortgage	Power of sale	12	Purchaser
Alaska	Lien	Trust deed	Power of sale	None	N.A.
Arizona	Lien	Trust deed	Judicial	None	N.A.
Arkansas	Intermediate	Mortgage	Power of sale	12	Purchaser
California	Lien	Trust deed	Power of sale	None	N.A.
Colorado	Lien	Trust deed	Power of sale	2	Mortgagor
Connecticut	Intermediate	Mortgage	Strict foreclosure	None	N.A.
Delaware	Intermediate	Mortgage	Judicial	None	N.A.
Dist. of Columbia	Intermediate	Trust deed	Power of sale	None	N.A.
Florida	Lien	Mortgage	Judicial	None	N.A.
Georgia	Title	Security deed	Power of sale	None	N.A.
Hawaii	Title	Trust deed	Power of sale	None	N.A.
Idaho	Lien	Trust deed	Power of sale	None	N.A.
Illinois	Intermediate	Mortgage	Judicial	12	Mortgagor
Indiana	Lien	Mortgage	Judicial	3	Mortgagor
Iowa	Lien	Mortgage	Judicial	6	Mortgagor
Kansas	Lien	Mortgage	Judicial	12	Mortgagor
Kentucky	Lien	Mortgage	Judicial	None	N.A.
Louisiana	Lien	Mortgage	Judicial	None	N.A.
Maine	Title	Mortgage	Entry and possession	12	Mortgagor
Maryland	Title	Trust deed	Power of sale	None	N.A.
Massachusetts	Intermediate	Mortgage	Power of sale	None	N.A.
Michigan	Lien	Mortgage	Power of sale	6	Mortgagor
Minnesota	Lien	Mortgage	Power of sale	12	Mortgagor
Mississippi	Intermediate	Trust deed	Power of sale	None	N.A.

State	Theory	Security Instrument	Foreclosure Method	Redemption Period	Possession
Missouri	Intermediate	Trust deed	Power of sale	12	Mortgagor
Montana	Lien	Mortgage	Judicial	12	Mortgagor
Nebraska	Lien	Mortgage	Judicial	None	N.A.
Nevada	Lien	Mortgage	Power of sale	None	N.A.
New Hampshire	Title	Mortgage	Power of sale	None	N.A.
New Jersey	Intermediate	Mortgage	Judicial	None	N.A.
New Mexico	Lien	Mortgage	Judicial	1	Purchaser
New York	Lien	Mortgage	Judicial	None	N.A.
North Carolina	Intermediate	Trust deed	Power of sale	None	N.A.
North Dakota	Lien	Mortgage	Judicial	12	Mortgagor
Ohio	Intermediate	Mortgage	Judicial	None	N.A.
Oklahoma	Lien	Mortgage	Judicial	None	N.A.
Oregon	Lien	Trust deed	Power of sale	None	N.A.
Pennsylvania	Title	Mortgage	Judicial	None	N.A.
Rhode Island	Title	Mortgage	Power of sale	None	N.A.
South Carolina	Lien	Mortgage	Judicial	None	N.A.
South Dakota	Lien	Mortgage	Power of sale	12	Mortgagor
Tennessee	Title	Trust deed	Power of sale	None	N.A.
Texas	Lien	Trust deed	Power of sale	None	N.A.
Utah	Lien	Mortgage	Judicial	6	Mortgagor
Vermont	Intermediate	Mortgage	Strict foreclosure	6	Mortgagor
Virginia	Intermediate	Trust deed	Power of sale	None	N.A.
Washington	Lien	Mortgage	Judicial	12	Purchaser
West Virginia	Intermediate	Trust deed	Power of sale	None	N.A.
Wisconsin	Lien	Mortgage	Power of sale	None	N.A.
Wyoming	Lien	Mortgage	Power of sale	6	Mortgagor

Caveat. This chart lists only the customary form of security instrument used in each state and not all the forms that could be used. Therefore, it lists the method of foreclosure and period of redemption (if allowed) only for the customary form and not for all possible security instruments. The reader is further cautioned that many states have extensive qualifications and limitations on the period of redemption and for obtaining a delinquency judgment. Consult a local attorney for details.

Source: © 2012 Cengage Learning

with jurisdiction, either a circuit or district court of the state, where the real estate is located. This procedure requires a complaint naming the borrower, who is now the defendant—alleging that the defendant executed a mortgage with described real estate as security for a loan, and that a default has occurred. Further, the complaint alleges that the mortgagee has had to accelerate. The complaint will request foreclosure.

The defendant always has an opportunity to answer the allegations with any defenses available. For example, the defendant may attempt to prove one of the following:

- No mortgage existed
- The mortgage was satisfied
- No default occurred
- The interest rate was usurious

If the decision of the court is in favor of a mortgagee, the *decree of foreclosure* terminates the equitable right of redemption at the time of sale. A mortgagor loses all rights to the real property except the right to any excess proceeds from the sale after secured parties are paid. The exception is if a state has a statutory right of redemption. The court decree will order a sale and the manner for its execution. Many courts will include an upset price in the decree that is the acceptable minimum bid at the sale. The court usually designates the officer, such as a sheriff or referee, who will conduct the sale after giving the statutory notice of the sale. To encourage purchasers, a successful bidder acquires title to the property unencumbered by any interest except that of the mortgagor's statutory right of redemption, if allowed.

With one possible exception, anyone who can enter into a contract can purchase property at a foreclosure sale. Some states prevent a defaulting mortgagor from purchasing the real estate since the unencumbered title would cut off the rights of junior lien holders. Other states allow a mortgagor to repurchase at a foreclosure sale, but if the mortgagor does repurchase the property, all liens on the real estate prior to foreclosure reattach.

The key element in this form of foreclosure is that the sale must be accepted or confirmed by the court retaining jurisdiction. This requirement is for the protection of both the mortgagor and junior lien holders since a court will not approve a price that is unconscionably low.

Power of Sale

This method is sometimes called foreclosure by advertisement, since the clause creating a power of sale calls for an advertisement to give notice of the sale. This method is used primarily with deeds of trust, but it can be used with mortgages. The power to use this method rather than the more cumbersome judicial proceeding comes from a clause that is part of the securing instrument. The clause specifically explains how the sale will be carried out. This foreclosure method does not preclude a mortgagor's statutory right of redemption if it exists. Some states do not allow the right of redemption if the instrument is a deed of trust.

Foreclosure by advertisement procedures vary among the states. Therefore, lenders must use extreme care to ensure that they provide proper notice and that they fulfill all other requirements. Distribution of the sale proceeds is the same manner as in a judicial proceeding.

Strict Foreclosure

As mentioned earlier, this was the original method of foreclosure. It is still used in two states, CT and VT, that classify themselves as title theory states. The action involves a court of equity and requests a decree giving a mortgagor a period of time to exercise the equitable right of redemption or lose all rights to the property, with title vesting irrevocably in the mortgagee. When requesting this type of relief, a mortgagee must be able to prove all allegations just as it must in judicial proceedings.

Entry and Possession

Entry and possession is used only in Maine, Massachusetts, New Hampshire, and Rhode Island. After default, a mortgagee gives the mortgagor notice that it will take possession. If the mortgagor does not agree peacefully to relinquish possession, the mortgagee will have to use a judicial method. This "peaceful possession" must be witnessed and recorded. If the mortgagor does not redeem in the statutory period, title vests with the mortgagee.

Deed in Lieu

An alternative to foreclosure, which can be of benefit to both the mortgagor and mortgagee, is a *deed in lieu* situation. Here, the mortgagor executes a deed transferring the secured real estate to the mortgagee in lieu of foreclosure. The benefits to a mortgagor include not being subject to the embarrassment of a foreclosure suit or possibly being liable for a deficiency judgment. A mortgagee benefits by immediately acquiring title to the real estate for a quick sale, minimizing collection costs.

For a deed in lieu to be effective in transferring title, the existing mortgage liability of the mortgagor must be extinguished. If not, the transaction and deed will be considered as nothing more than a new security agreement.

The mortgagee must carefully consider the consequences of this alternative. If a mortgagee decides to take a deed in lieu of foreclosure, the rights of junior lien holders will not be extinguished. On the other hand, if a mortgagee forecloses, junior lien holders' rights are extinguished if not satisfied by the proceeds of the sale, but the mortgagor has the right of redemption, which can be of serious consequence to a mortgagee.

Statutory Right of Redemption

In addition to the equity of redemption discussed previously, about half the states provide another form of redemption right that begins to accrue to a mortgagor (or those claiming through the mortgagor) after foreclosure and sale. This right is called the **statutory right of redemption** because it only exists if created by statute. This redemption period ranges from six months to two years, depending on the state. Basically, this right allows a mortgagor who has had property sold at a foreclosure sale to "buy" back the property by paying to the purchaser the price the purchaser paid for the property plus back interest and all costs.

There are two reasons for a statutory right of redemption: 1) to provide a mortgagor with a chance to keep the real estate, and 2) to encourage bidders at foreclosure sales to bid the market value. The first is more important in agricultural states where a bad growing season can be followed by bumper crops. This right would provide a method for a mortgagor to keep the farm. This same reasoning applies in some income-property situations, but rarely in a residential case.

The second reason is equally important for all types of real estate since a bidder at a forced sale would more likely bid the true market value rather than chance later divestiture by the mortgagor.

The right of redemption currently has a limited impact on single-family transactions, since most of these transactions are a trust deed rather than a mortgage. In using a deed of trust there is generally no statutory right of redemption, as there is with a mortgage. This is one of the more important reasons why a mortgagee would use a deed of trust rather than a mortgage. The difference with a trust deed is that a grantor conveys all interest to the trustee at the creation of the transaction and consequently has nothing on which to base the redemption. Some states allow it, regardless of what the transaction is called, because if real estate secures a debt, then the transaction is a mortgage and all rights attach.

In many jurisdictions, a mortgagor has a period of time to redeem the property after default and foreclosure. If the right to redeem exists, this period varies from six months to two years, depending on state law. Even when the redemption right exists, it is seldom exercised since a mortgagor is more likely to sell the property before foreclosure if there is equity to protect.

Deficiency Judgments

A **deficiency judgment** is a court determination that the mortgagor, who has lost property by foreclosure, is liable for the difference between the sales price of the property at foreclosure and the amount owed (principal, interest, and foreclosure costs). Although most states still allow for deficiency judgments for residential mortgage loans, seldom do the courts render this judgment today. In about a dozen states, legislation has revoked the ability to get a deficiency judgment. In other states the deficiency judgment is limited to the difference between what the property sold for and the fair market value of the foreclosed property.

To a mortgagor, the advantage of a deed of trust is that a mortgagee does not have the right to a deficiency judgment.

TRANSFERS OF MORTGAGED REAL ESTATE

In all jurisdictions, whether the title or lien theory is followed, the mortgagor has the ability to transfer real estate that is serving as security for a debt, and has options on the method of transfer.

Free and Clear

The grantor (the one transferring) could transfer the land free and clear. This would occur if a mortgagor satisfied the obligation secured by the real estate and presumes that the mortgage could be prepaid. In such an event, the lender may require a prepayment penalty. Much mortgaged real estate sold today transfers in this manner, with the new owner obtaining new financing. The reason for this is inflation, which produces increased equity in real estate. The value of this equity is more than a purchaser would want to buy for cash. Therefore, a new purchaser normally would rather finance the purchase price than assume the mortgage and pay cash for the equity. During periods of exceedingly high interest rates, as occurred in 1979–1981, purchasers may desire to assume an existing lower interest rate mortgage and pay cash or use another financing technique for the equity.

In other free and clear situations, the existing mortgage documents contain a *due on sale clause*. This clause requires the mortgagor to satisfy the existing mortgage upon sale of the collateral, typically with the proceeds of the sale, before the lender releases the lien.

Subject to the Mortgage

The grantor could transfer the real estate subject to the mortgage, with the grantee (the one to whom the property is transferred) paying the grantor for any equity. If this occurs, the original mortgage remains effective and the personal liability of the original mortgagor to pay the mortgage continues, although the mortgage payment most likely will be made by the grantee from that point on. The grantee becomes the legal owner of the real estate after the sale, although it continues to serve as security for the original mortgage. The grantee assumes no personal liability for the original mortgage payment and could decide to abandon the real estate with no danger of contingent liability. If the grantee stops the mortgage payment and the mortgagee forecloses, the grantee loses only equity in the real estate, while the original mortgagor is liable for any amount of the obligation not satisfied by the sale of the mortgaged real estate.

Assumption of the Mortgage

The real estate could be transferred to the grantee, who would buy the grantor's equity and assume the mortgage. This is the most common manner in which real estate transfers with the existing mortgage remaining intact. Fannie and Freddie loan programs no longer allow assumptions; VA and FHA loan programs still allow them. In this situation, the grantee assumes personal liability for satisfying the mortgage debt, while the original mortgagor retains only secondary liability.

Recently, some mortgagees have inserted clauses into conventional mortgages to either prohibit the transfer of the mortgage or make the transfer conditional on the approval of the mortgagee. Other mortgagees, especially savings and loan institutions, have inserted due-on-sale clauses in conventional mortgages, which accelerate the entire debt if the real estate is sold with the mortgage still intact.

The stated rationale for such a clause is to protect the mortgagee's security interest by forcing the new mortgagor to meet the mortgagee's underwriting requirements. Often, however, the real reason is to force the grantee to assume an increase in the interest rate from the rate on the assumed mortgage to the higher current rate. The validity of these clauses evolved to the point at which many courts enforced the mortgagee's right to accelerate. Today, some states allow due-on-sale clauses while other states do not.

Many mortgagors, after selling the real estate to the grantee who assumes the mortgage, requested the mortgagee sign a *novation contract* that would end any secondary liability on the part of the original mortgagor. Many mortgagees agree to sign, but normally they require that the assuming grantee agree to an increase in the interest rate to the level of the prevailing rate.

CHANGING A MORTGAGE

Assignment of Mortgages

An **assignment of mortgage** is an instrument that transfers the interests and rights of a mortgagee to another entity. Many originators of mortgage loans, such as mortgage bankers, originate loans for sale to other investors. Any mortgage lender has the right to assign a mortgage, even if the mortgagor is unaware of the assignment.

The assignment of mortgage should be in writing and be recorded immediately to protect the investor from another assignment. At the time of assignment, the mortgagor may be required to sign an *estoppel certificate*. This is a statement by a mortgagor stating that there is a binding obligation not yet satisfied and that the mortgagor has no defenses against the mortgagee. An assigned mortgage has full effect and the mortgage payments may be made directly to the assignee or through the original mortgagee.

Mortgage Modification

At times the lender and borrower will negotiate and agree to change certain terms of the mortgage note or collateral, accomplished through a *modification agreement*. Examples include: a change in interest rate or payment, an advance to principal up to the original amount of the note, a partial release of real estate collateral (possibly in exchange for a large payment to reduce principal), or for a workout situation if the borrowers are having temporary difficulty making payments under the existing mortgage terms.

State laws and individual circumstances govern the exact manner in which the modification agreement must be completed. A change in the interest rate and payment on the note may require only the execution of a new note and may not require recording of a revised mortgage document. More complex modifications—especially those that involve a change in the collateral when multiple properties are secured by one mortgage—may require the recording of a revised mortgage instrument.

Recently, loan collection efforts place more emphasis on a loan workout approach rather than going straight to foreclosure. Borrowers with repayment difficulty may qualify for federal government or individual lender programs (discussed further in Chapter 16—Loan Administration). These programs may involve temporary or permanent modifications to the original terms. Whatever the specific agreement negotiated between the lender and borrower, the mortgage note and record security instrument must reflect these terms accurately and, if necessary, be recorded properly for that specific jurisdiction in which the property is located.

Release of Mortgage

The mortgage instrument must acknowledge and identify the debt it secures. When the entire debt is paid (satisfied), the note and the mortgage, which secures the debt, lose their effectiveness and no longer create a valid lien. A notice of full payment of a note and mortgage, sometimes called a **notice of satisfaction** or **release of mortgage**, is recorded when the debt is paid. The recording clears the cloud on the title created by the mortgage. Recent legislation requires prompt preparation and delivery of the release of mortgage, although most lenders charge the borrower a fee for its preparation (which rarely if ever is disclosed at application).

DISCUSSION POINTS

1. What is the term that is used in law to describe "the greatest interest a person can have in real estate"? Why is this interest not an absolute interest?
2. What is a conditional fee? Give an example of how this transaction could occur.
3. What is a legal life estate? Do these types of estates exist today?
4. What is the most common form of joint ownership today in the United States?
5. What are the essential elements of a deed that will allow for a valid transfer of real estate?
6. Identify the various means of mortgage foreclosure. Which exists in your state?

CHAPTER 3

Role of Residential Mortgage Lending in the Economy

INTRODUCTION

The importance of housing, and therefore residential mortgage lending, to the nation's economic health is unquestionable. The demand for new and existing homes depends greatly on employment and job growth, but it is often controlled by the availability of credit for home financing and by its cost. Several factors influence the availability of mortgage credit to consumers, among them: economic conditions, consumer demand, levels of interest rates, financial institution capital levels and delinquency rates, and funding sources.

Residential mortgage lending impacts the economy in four basic ways:

1. Enables consumer spending or investment by placing cash directly in their hands.
2. Provides investment in the vast housing market, which itself impacts the economy in multiple ways.
3. Maximizes the use of the money supply by converting funds on deposit into spendable dollars.
4. Increases foreign investment into the United States economy via secondary mortgage market purchases of mortgage-backed securities.

Since 2007, the federal government has played a dominant role in many areas of mortgage lending activity. Many would agree on the necessity of this activist role in the short term; however, government actions distort historic fundamentals and dynamics of mortgage lending and the economy, which will remain the focus of this chapter.

RESIDENTIAL MORTGAGE DEBT

At the end of 2002, outstanding single-family residential debt in the United States exceeded $6.4 trillion. This figure almost doubled in five years, peaking at more than $11.1 trillion in 2007. At the end of 2009, after a significant recession and "correction" (decrease) in housing values, total single family mortgages outstanding was more than $10.7 trillion.

The increase in number of homes and increase in home prices alone do not account for such a dramatic rise in total residential mortgage debt. Consumption of consumer goods and services accounts for much of the additional amount borrowed. While this helps drive the U.S. economy in the short term, it is a somewhat disturbing and unsustainable element that clouds the fundamental national housing picture for many economists and public policymakers.

Effect of Low Interest Rates

The low interest rates during this period (30-year rates reached a low of 5.75 percent in 2002) allowed record originations of more than $2 trillion in 2002. That record was eclipsed in three of the next five years, an astonishing level of activity. In 2009–2010 mortgage rates fell even further (4.25 percent—a record low not seen in 50 years). However, originations were not as high—a significant number of homeowners were unable to refinance or purchase because of the decline in home values, tighter credit standards, and adverse employment conditions.

Low interest rates lower the cost of owning a home and allow more people to become homeowners, increasing demand for housing as shown in Table 3.1. In response, the homeownership rate reached an all-time high of 69 percent in 2004. Lower mortgage payments also allow more homebuyers to purchase more expensive homes than they might otherwise afford, expanding housing demand to higher levels of housing and increasing home prices.

During this period, homeowners also had the opportunity to reduce their mortgage payments by refinancing, and to gain access to more of their accumulated home equity. In turn, this process pours money directly into the economy since it frees up consumers' resources for discretionary spending. Home equity lending—especially home equity lines of credit—help finance consumer goods and services when borrowers wish to repay these items over shorter terms.

TABLE **3.1**

Lower Interest Rates Make Housing More Affordable: Monthly Principal
and Interest Payment on a 30-Year Mortgage

Mortgage Amount	Interest Rate					
	4.5%	5.0%	5.5%	6.0%	6.5%	7.0%
$ 50,000	$ 253.34	$ 268.41	$ 283.89	$ 300.00	$ 316.00	$ 332.50
100,000	506.69	536.82	567.79	600.00	632.00	665.00
150,000	760.03	805.23	851.68	900.00	984.00	997.50
200,000	1,013.37	1,073.64	1,135.58	1,200.00	1,264.00	1,330.00
250,000	1,266.71	1,342.05	1,419.47	1,500.00	1,580.00	1,622.50
300,000	1,528.06	1,610.46	1,703.37	1,800.00	1,896.00	1,995.00
350,000	1,773.40	1,878.88	1,987.26	2,100.00	2,212.00	2,327.50

Source: © 2012 Cengage Learning

Consumer spending often increases dramatically when mortgage rates fall, although since the recent economic recession of 2007 other factors—like rising unemployment, job insecurity, and tightening of credit standards—have restricted lending and lowered consumer confidence. As a result, the nation has reduced its overall mortgage and debt levels.

ECONOMIC STIMULUS OF HOUSING

Housing and mortgage-lending activity stimulates the economy directly through the home sale transaction and indirectly through related purchases and expenditures that ripple through the economy after the sale. Economic commentators contend that from the time of the Great Depression the housing, construction, and related sectors (e.g., real estate sales, financing, home furnishing, taxes) are among the most important integrals of the engine that powers the United States economy. Economists conclude that housing and related sectors account for, on average, between 15 and 20 percent of the gross domestic product (GDP)—a measure of the nation's total output of goods and services. The amount and percentage varies with different business cycles and interest rate levels. According to the American Enterprise Institute for Public Policy (AEI), housing construction on average accounts for five percent of U.S. GDP (Figure 3.1), with spending on housing-related consumer goods adding another five percent. Residential housing investment adds another five to 10 percent to GDP growth as shown in Figure 3.1.

Although more than half of the 2002 record mortgage origination volume was for refinancing, nearly $1 trillion was for home purchases, a number that rose in subsequent years. The home purchase figure is important because it is estimated that homebuyers spend on average around $9,000 on home-related items within a year of purchase (Figure 3.2). According to Fannie

FIGURE **3.1** U.S. Housing's Contribution to GDP

	1970	1975	1980	1985	1990	1995	2000	2005	2009	2009Q1	2009Q2	2009Q3	2009Q4	2010Q1	2010Q2
Constant Dollars (2005, Billions)															
Gross Domestic Product	4,270	4,880	5,839	6,849	8,034	9,094	11,226	12,638	12,881	12,833	12,810	12,861	13,019	13,139	13,192
Gross private domestic investment	475	504	718	943	994	1,259	1,970	2,172	1,516	1,530	1,453	1,495	1,586	1,690	1,787
Residential Fixed Investment	248	256	310	384	386	456	580	775	343	353	334	342	342	331	351
Personal Consumption Expenditures	2,740	3,214	3,766	4,540	5,316	6,079	7,608	8,819	9,154	9,154	9,117	9,162	9,183	9,225	9,270
Housing Services	537	673	800	912	1,044	1,199	1,384	1,567	1,657	1,650	1,652	1,659	1,666	1,664	1,668
Residential Fixed Investment + Housing Services	785	929	1,110	1,296	1,430	1,656	1,964	2,342	2,000	2,003	1,986	2,002	2,008	1,995	2,019
Percentage of Real GDP															
Residential Fixed Investment	5.8	5.2	5.3	5.6	4.8	5.0	5.2	6.1	2.7	2.7	2.6	2.7	2.6	2.5	2.7
Housing Services	12.6	13.8	13.7	13.3	13.0	13.2	12.3	12.4	12.9	12.9	12.9	12.9	12.8	12.7	12.6
Residential Fixed Investment + Housing Services	18.4	19.0	19.0	18.9	17.8	18.2	17.5	18.5	15.5	15.6	15.5	15.6	15.4	15.2	15.3
Contribution to Real GDP Growth															
Gross Domestic Product Growth	0.2%	−0.2%	−0.3%	4.1%	1.9%	2.5%	4.1%	3.1%	−2.6%	−4.9%	−0.7%	1.6%	5.0%	3.7%	1.6%
Personal Consumption Expenditures	1.4%	1.4%	−0.2%	3.3%	1.3%	1.8%	3.4%	2.3%	−0.8%	−0.3%	−1.1%	1.4%	0.7%	1.3%	1.4%
Housing Services	0.4%	0.3%	0.4%	0.5%	0.2%	0.3%	0.4%	0.6%	0.1%	0.0%	0.1%	0.2%	0.2%	−0.1%	0.1%
Gross private domestic investment	−1.0%	−3.0%	−2.1%	−0.2%	−0.5%	0.5%	1.2%	0.9%	−3.2%	−6.8%	−2.3%	1.2%	2.7%	3.0%	2.8%
Residential Fixed Investment	−0.3%	−0.6%	−1.2%	0.1%	−0.4%	−0.1%	0.1%	0.4%	−0.7%	−1.2%	−0.5%	0.3%	0.0%	−0.3%	0.6%
Government expenditures and investment	−0.6%	0.5%	0.4%	1.4%	0.6%	0.1%	0.4%	0.1%	0.3%	−0.6%	1.2%	0.3%	−0.3%	−0.3%	0.9%
Net exports of goods and services	0.3%	0.9%	1.7%	−0.4%	0.4%	0.1%	−0.9%	−0.3%	1.1%	2.9%	1.5%	−1.4%	1.9%	−0.3%	−3.4%

Source: NAHB, U.S. Bureau of Economic Analysis.

© 2012 Cengage Learning

FIGURE **3.2** Spending by New Home Buyers in the First Year after Purchase

Property alterations	$ 3,194
Home furnishings	3,632
Appliances	2,079
Total Spending	8,905

Source: *Housing: The Key to Economic Recovery*, NABH Economics, 2002, page 4, from NAHB, Bureau of Labor Statistics Consumer Expenditure Survey.

Mae, purchasers of older homes spend nearly $7,000 in the first year as they make improvements. These expenditures help the overall economy by providing many jobs as well as tax receipts.

These factors increase as a result of new housing's economic stimulus:

- Consumption of raw materials for home construction (lumber, brick, wire, etc.)
- Wages earned by home builders that are spent on food, clothing, cars, furniture, and schooling, in addition to many other products and services
- Federal, state, and local taxes
- Fees earned by real estate professionals when the home is sold
- Interest earned by financial intermediaries on mortgage loans financing the construction and purchase of the home

The following National Association of Home Builders (NAHB, **www. nahb.com**) examples further illustrate the economic importance of housing:

- Housing construction, sales, and financing account for one out of every 12 jobs in the United States.
- In 2002, the economic impact of the construction of 1,000 single-family houses created:
  - nearly 1,800 man-years of employment
  - more than $80 million in wages
  - more than $42 million in federal, state, and local tax revenues

As is generally accepted, the ripple effect of a healthy home-building industry stimulates the entire economy, but can also depress it. The sharp drop in housing construction in 1989 and 1990 certainly contributed to the recession experienced in that time frame. Likewise, the substantial increase in housing construction in 1993–1994 contributed significantly to the economic revival of the mid–1990s. More recently, the strength of the housing sector during the recession of 2001–2002 is given much of the credit for that recession being shorter and less severe than other recessions. The strong economic expansion from 2002–2006 was driven by the housing sector, as was the downturn and recession from 2007–2010, ending almost two decades of reliance on the housing industry as the U.S. economy's main growth engine. See Chapter 9—Construction Lending, for additional discussion of housing and GDP.

TABLE **3.2**
New and Existing Home Sales 1990–2009

	New Homes	Existing Homes
1990	534,000	3,219,600
1995	667,000	3,888,000
2000	877,000	5,123,000
2001	908,000	5,258,000
2002	973,000	5,566,000
2003	1,086,000	6,100,000
2004	1,203,000	6,784,000
2005	1,283,000	7,072,000
2006	1,051,000	6,480,000
2007	776,000	5,652,000
2008	485,000	4,913,000
2009	375,000	5,156,000
2010	325,000(e)	4,430,000

Source: New home sales: U.S. Census Bureau, National Association of Home Builders; existing home sales: National Association of REALTORS®.

New and Existing Home Sales

The National Association of REALTORS® (**www.realtor.org**) reports annual and monthly existing and new home sales. In 2001, 5.25 million existing homes were sold, rising steadily and peaking at just over 7 million units in 2005. New single-family home construction increased from 0.9 million units in 2001, to peak in 2005 at 1.2 million units. Combined sales ranged from 6.5 million to more than 8.4 million during this period. These record years of combined home sales could only have occurred with a dynamic housing-financing system.

The opposite impact occurred when the recent mortgage crisis began. Although rates remained relatively low, lending credit standards tightened and many mortgage programs disappeared overnight. The housing market fell in all sectors of home sales starting in 2006, with new home sales dropping in 2009 (Table 3.2) to its lowest level in decades: just 375,000 units, with a lower level of 325,000 units projected for 2010. Combined home sales would have fallen further in 2009, but the federal government provided first-time homebuyers with an $8,000 one-time tax credit.

In addition to a drop in overall home construction and sales, the recent recession also impacted home prices. Table 3.3 shows how average U.S. home prices declined in three successive years, from $260,000 in 2007 to $216,900 in 2009. Home prices appear to stabilize in 2010 as the inventory

TABLE **3.3**

Average Existing Home Price and Housing Inventory 2007–2010

Year	Average Existing Home Price	Inventory / Mos. Supply	
2007	$266,000	3,974,000	8.9
2008	$242,700	3,700,000	10.4
2009	$216,900	3,283,000	8.8
2010	$218,700(e)	3,864,000(e)	10.5(e)

Source: National Association of REALTORS®.

of unsold homes declined, although the Federal Reserve projects a further decline economic conditions in 2011, which can impact the housing market.

The national housing market can differ greatly from regional and local markets in both strong and weak economic times. Even in the recent recession, considered the worst since the Great Depression, real estate markets vary. For example, from 2009–2010 in the Washington, D.C. metro area home prices increased 8 percent while the St. Louis metro area declined 10 percent. As a result, aggregate U.S. housing market information can be misleading for local and regional lenders as shown in Figure 3.3 on page 60.

The recent decline in U.S. home sales and prices was not a result of demographics or higher interest rates, but instead shows the importance of a stable financing system to housing activity and the economy. Once lenders feel comfortable in the new regulatory and political environment, and home financing gains a stable platform, economic conditions and the underlying demographics should drive the housing market once again.

Economic and Social Value of Housing

According to the Federal Reserve, the market value of all homes owned by U.S. households grew to a record $10 trillion in 2000, and doubled to more than $22.6 trillion by 2006. The market value of housing on a national basis plummeted 27 percent or more in just two years, to $16.4 trillion in 1Q2009, and rebounded slightly to more than $17 trillion as of 2Q2010. Certainly, some areas of the country did not experience as much volatility as others. But the extended level of price volatility for so much of the nation for such a long period is unprecedented.

As a result, on a national basis the owners' equity as a percentage of household real estate now stands at 40 percent, down from the 2006 peak of almost 60 percent. To place these large numbers in some perspective, according to the AEI, this drop in equity is almost equal to wiping out the total amount of retirement and pension savings held by 78 million baby boomers between the ages of 44 and 62 See Figure 3-4 on page 61.

FIGURE **3.3** Metro and U.S. Home Price Changes 2009–2010

#	MSA	Median Price		% Change from 1 Year Ago	
		Oct-09	Oct-10	Price	Sales
1	Atlanta	122,900	109,900	−10.6%	−22.2%
2	Baltimore	244,600	245,500	0.4%	−29.6%
3	Boston	330,100	349,500	5.9%	−27.8%
4	Cincinnati	128,800	125,400	−2.6%	−37.2%
5	Dallas-Fort Worth	142,700	146,300	2.5%	−30.2%
6	Houston	149,500	151,400	1.3%	−22.6%
7	Indianapolis	115,500	122,500	6.1%	−34.3%
8	Kansas City	139,300	140,900	1.1%	−36.6%
9	Miami-Ft. Lauderdale	214,600	210,200	−2.1%	−17.3%
10	Minneapolis-St. Paul	169,000	170,000	0.6%	−40.7%
11	New Orleans	158,000	165,200	4.6%	−36.5%
12	New York-Northern New Jersey-Long Island	378,800	390,900	3.2%	−26.7%
13	Philadelphia	n/a	n/a	n/a	n/a
14	Phoenix	142,100	135,500	−4.6%	−19.7%
15	Portland	241,700	229,900	−4.9%	−34.6%
16	San Antonio	142,300	150,500	5.8%	−24.3%
17	San Diego	378,500	384,600	1.6%	−21.6%
18	St. Louis	130,600	117,300	−10.2%	−38.4%
19	Washington, DC	302,400	327,700	8.4%	−23.9%
20	U.S.	172,000	171,100	−0.5%	−28.0%

*All data reported herein is unadjusted for seasonality.
**NOTE: There may be differences between this data and locally reported data because of differences in geographic coverage area and housing types.
©2010 NATIONAL ASSOCIATION OF REALTORS®

U.S. Homeownership Rate

Residential mortgage lending, in addition to being an important part of our nation's economy, also allows for the fulfillment of certain sociological demands and political goals, principal among them obtaining the "American Dream" of owning a home. According to an Urban Land Institute study, historically, the homeownership rate remained within a 45–48 percent level from 1900 to 1930. After WWII this level increased to the low-60 percent level in 1960, where it remained for over 30 years.

The homeownership rate first exceeded 64 percent in the 1990s. Assisted by low interest rates, low unemployment, and accommodating government policies, homeownership reached a historic high of 69.2 percent in 2004 according to the U.S. Census Bureau. Homeownership among minority groups improved as well, with Hispanic and Latino (49.5%) homeownership recording the highest increase of at least 20 percent from 1994 to 2005, and Native (58.2%) and African (48.2%) Americans both recording increases of almost 14 percent.

FIGURE **3.4** U.S. Single Family Housing Stock and Equity

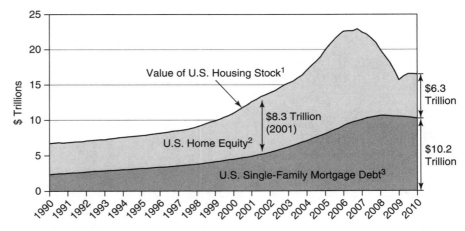

[1] Value of U.S. Housing Stock: Federal Reserve Board's Flow of Funds Accounts, June 10, 2010, Table B.100 (line #49). This figure includes homes with and without underlying mortgages.

[2] U.S. home equity is the difference between the value of the U.S. housing stock and the amount of U.S. single-family mortgage debt.

[3] U.S. single-family Mortgage Debt Outstanding: Federal Reserve Board's Flow of Funds Accounts, June 10, 2010, Table L.100 (Line #26).

Source: Freddie Mac, Federal Reserve Board's Flow of Funds Accounts.

The homeownership rate declined with the 2007 economic recession, with many recent first-time homebuyers owning little or no equity suffering the most through foreclosure. In 2010, this rate dropped to 66.9 percent, the lowest level in more than ten years, but still equal to most other developed countries. Federal homeowner assistance programs now attempt to correct this public policy imbalance, but at a significant cost. Additionally, since 2008 the federal government now backs or guarantees more than 90 percent of all new mortgage loans. To a large extent, over the past two decades the federal government's policies and programs that emphasized home buying but not sustained homeownership and its lax GSE oversight helped create this situation.

Belatedly, in 2010 the federal government formally recognized via announcements from HUD and both senate banking and house finance committee chairs what many economists and industry leaders cautioned for years: promoting the dream of homeownership (for short-term political gain) without considering its sustainability (affordability, ongoing costs, and responsibilities) can have dangerous, long-term consequences for consumers and the economy.

Research by the Urban Land Institute and Harvard University predicts that, although 1.25 to 1.5 million new households will form annually in the next decade, the homeownership rate (Figure 3.5) will continue to decline, perhaps back to the 60–64 percent level seen during the 1960s–1990s. Flat or declining incomes and constrained credit flows will cause more prime homebuyers to rent longer instead of purchasing.

FIGURE **3.5** U.S. Homeownership Rate

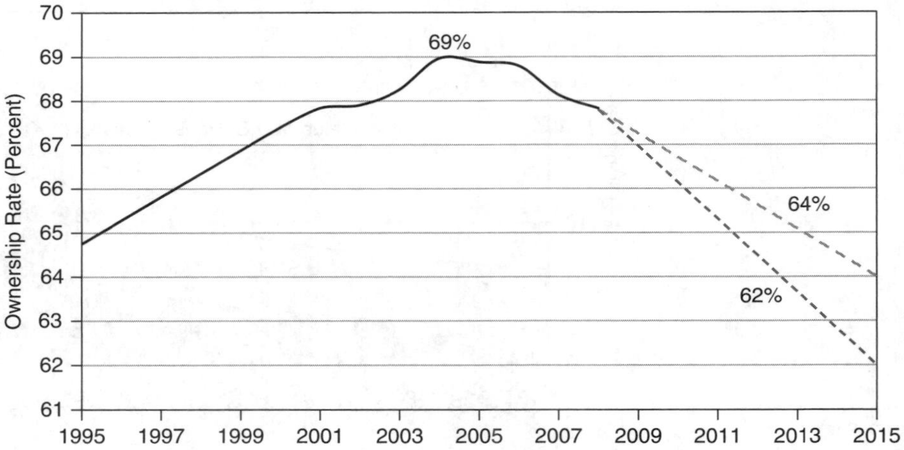

Source: © 2012 Cengage Learning

Demographic Forces in Housing

Demographic forces in the long term will increase or lower housing demand. Couples reaching their home-buying years, new immigrants, and certain minority groups increase demand for housing. These groups are expected to form new households at a rate of more than one million per year for the next decade. Financing this demand for housing will challenge the housing finance system, but will also provide an opportunity for growth in residential mortgage lending.

On the other hand, as a large segment of baby boomers mature and become "empty nesters," their housing needs change and impact the demand for larger (three- or four-bedroom) housing. As a demographic group, they will either downsize their residences or leave the homeownership market.

A 2010 Urban Land Institute study, *Housing in America: The Next Decade* (**http://www.uli.org/~/media/Documents/ResearchAndPublications/ Fellows/McIlwain/HousinginAmerica.ashx**), identifies four post-recessionary demographic trends that will impact housing demand in the next decade:

1. Older baby boomers (ages 55–64) totaling 26 million, may stay closer to family members instead of moving to the Sun Belt and will want smaller housing longer before moving to retirement living communities.
2. Younger baby boomers (ages 46–54) totaling 52 million, due to lasting impacts of the housing crisis, will defer the purchase of larger or more expensive homes.
3. Generation Y (late teens to early 30s) 83 million will remain in rental units longer and tend to move to more urban areas.
4. Immigrants comprising 40 million people will tend to cluster around inner suburbs instead of urban areas. Current housing prices may need to fall further to allow many in this group and Generation Y group to enter into the homeownership market.

FIGURE **3.6** Projected Homeownership By Age Group 2010–2020

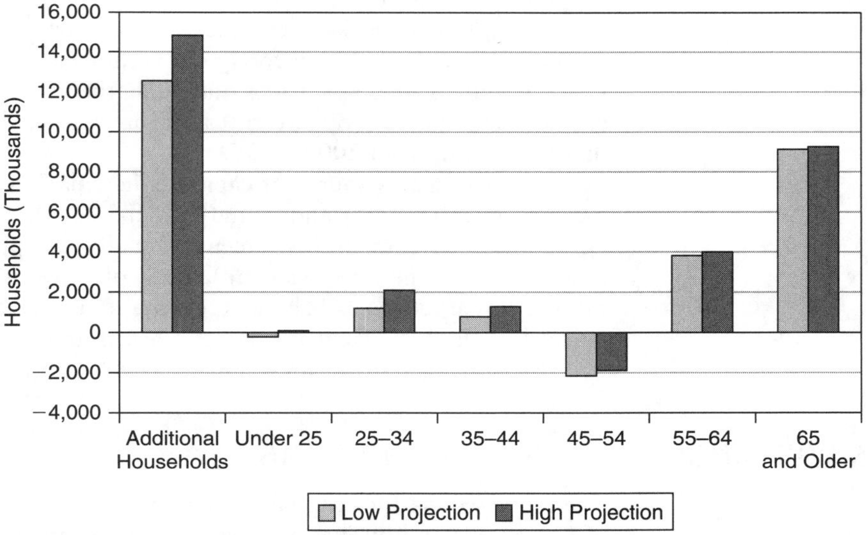

Source: Urban Land Institute, Housing in America; Harvard Joint Center for Housing Studies, The State of the Nation's Housing 2009.

Although housing and homeownership are in transition (Figure 3.6) after the recent housing crisis and recession, our society benefits in the long-term from sustainable homeownership by all groups of people. People who have their own home have a more substantial stake in their community and our nation's society, with many resulting benefits.

Capital Formation

The common requisite for all residential mortgage lenders, whether depository institutions or not, is the accumulation of sufficient savings to produce the capital needed for mortgage loans. Unless financial intermediaries have access to sufficient savings, capital shortages result and credit restraints occur that affect all mortgage lenders, often with disastrous results. This has been the situation periodically in U.S. economic history, and as a result, during those periods housing starts and sales of existing homes have dropped dramatically.

Secondary mortgage markets can assist housing somewhat during these periods of credit restraint by tapping the capital markets, but they cannot solve the basic problem of a lack of savings inflow to primary market mortgage lenders.

Shortage of capital is not always the reason for falloffs in housing starts. The dramatic falloff in housing starts in 1989 to 1991 was not the result of a shortage of capital for housing, but rather a sharp drop in consumer confidence because of the Gulf War and a spreading recession.

Recently, the impact of the United States housing and mortgage finance markets expanded well beyond our shores. Foreign investment in the U.S. mortgage markets grew significantly since 2000, peaking in 2008 at $1.3 trillion invested in GSE corporate debt and mortgage-backed securities

($800 billion in Asia alone), according to the U.S. Treasury. This represents 25 percent of GSE debt.

The mortgage-backed securities (MBS) market now plays a large role in the global economy. Many foreign governments, companies, and individuals invest heavily in these securities and value them similar to U.S. Treasury obligations. The increase of foreign capital investment helped the U.S. mortgage market expand from 2000–2006.

One risk in this source of capital is its volatility. Shaken by the dramatic increase in mortgage fraud found in MBS—both privately-issued and GSE-agency issued—foreign investment virtually disappeared suddenly (as did much of the domestic investment). Lack of investor confidence in secondary mortgage market issues helped accelerate housing's collapse starting in 2007. Since then the U.S. Treasury has purchased approximately the same amount of MBS to replace these funds and stabilize that market.

IMPORTANCE OF SAVINGS TO HOUSING

The funds required for capital formation are derived primarily from the savings of individuals and businesses. This process of capital formation produces most of the capital used by the various segments of our economy. **Business savings** are defined as retained earnings and capital consumption allowances. They exceed personal savings by a substantial amount. However, the savings generated by individuals—either as deposits at financial institutions or as reserves in whole life insurance policies—account for the majority of the funds used for residential mortgage lending, as high as 90 percent, but lower since 2000.

The recent influx of capital going into the secondary mortgage market from outside of the United States helped to expand the pool of funds available for mortgage lending and supplement savings as a source of funding, but it is more volatile and does not change this fundamental dynamic.

Savings Rates

There is a strong link between personal savings dollars and funding for residential mortgage lending. Since the end of World War II, the personal savings rate ranged from the current low of about zero to a high of about nine percent of disposable income. In recent years, according to the U.S. Bureau of Economic Analysis, the personal savings rate ranged from just over one percent in 2005 to more than five percent from the fourth quarter of 2008 to 2010.

These savings provide (except for brief periods of disintermediation) borrowers with needed funds at reasonable rates. Through this process, the percentage of Americans who own the homes in which they live reached an all-time high in 2004, but proved unsustainable and declined slightly with the 2007 recession.

Savings inflows are not constant, which can affect the availability of mortgage funds. The savings function must compete with food, shelter, clothing, transportation, recreation, and other real or perceived demands for an individual's after-tax income. Individuals who save are usually motivated by such desires as accumulating funds for retirement, future security, and major purchases such as a home or a college education.

Decline in the Savings Rate

The savings rate declines as a result of different factors: low rates of interest paid on savings, taxation of interest earned, reliance on home equity and/or retirement and pension funds, and cultural change from saving to spending on consumer goods and services.

Another reason for previous declines in savings rates has been inflation psychology. During the high inflation period of the early 1980s, many sophisticated individuals realized it was more prudent to borrow than to save. They rationalized that it made sense to borrow money now for immediate consumption and then pay back the money later with deflated dollars. That psychology, as it spread to many Americans in the early 1980s, led to a period of **disintermediation**—withdrawal from financial intermediaries of more money than was being deposited. During this period, capital was very short, and, as a result, interest rates were very high for residential mortgage loans.

Recently, the savings rate for the average American decreased to nearly zero. During double digit increases in the stock market and home prices, many Americans felt financially comfortable because of gains in the value of their investment portfolios or the equity in their homes.

Since 2005, the recent increase in the savings rate is due to several factors:

- Tendency of aging population to save more and borrow less
- Erosion of confidence in the economy
- Lack of alternatives (e.g., stock market too volatile)
- Price depreciation for consumer goods and real estate

Changes in the economy directly influence savings in many ways. For example, if the business cycle is down and unemployment increases, individuals may increase savings because of uncertainty about their employment. The result could be a savings inflow, which theoretically should cause interest rates to decline as more dollars chase less demand. On the other hand, with a downturn in the business cycle and an increase in unemployment, those who are unemployed may have to withdraw savings for living expenses. If the economy is expanding and rates increase, savings may also accumulate because the demand for funds could reach a point at which high interest rates attract more savings.

For a period of time during the late 1970s and early 1980s, depository institutions could not attract savings during periods of high interest because of regulatory limits on the interest rate paid to savers. Since the early 1980s, savings and loan rates have been deregulated and now move with the market.

CAPITAL AND MORTGAGE MARKETS

The U.S economy financial market consists of the capital markets and the money markets. These two markets compete with each other for funds. The basic difference between the two markets is the maturity of the financial instruments. Money market instruments (U.S. Treasury bills, corporate commercial paper, etc.) mature in less than one year. Capital markets, on the other hand, are markets for long-term obligations.

The mortgage market is only part of the complete capital market. Within the capital market, a specific demand for funds (e.g., mortgages) must compete with other instruments, such as corporate bonds. The price of money equals the interest rate offered or paid—the rate of return a user of funds expects to pay or earn.

Users of Credit

In today's economic environment, the demand for credit comes from three sectors:

1. Business demand
2. Consumer demand
3. Government demand

Businesses demand credit for financing inventory, accounts receivable, plant expansion and modernization, and occasionally for research and development. The magnitude of business loan demand is normally tied to the economic cycle. Business normally looks to commercial banks to provide needed capital, usually at the prime rate (or lower in some cases). If a business's credit rating is high enough, that business may look to sell commercial paper.

The economic cycle and employment also impacts consumer demand. During a high interest rate environment, many consumers cannot qualify for a loan, thus demand falls off. When unemployment increases, consumers worry about income and tend to decrease borrowing. Consumer credit finances the purchase of automobiles, furniture, clothing, and other durable and nondurable goods. In addition, consumer credit includes funds to purchase residential real estate (or to refinance existing home mortgages).

Finally, all levels of government experienced insatiable appetites for borrowed funds from the late 1970s to the present time. These borrowed funds (Treasury and agency bonds) primarily finance the federal government's deficits, in addition to other local needs such as mortgage revenue bonds. The government's fiscal policy establishes spending and taxing levels and controls the amount of borrowing by the federal government. Regrettably, for all users of credit, the fiscal policy of the federal government for decades continues to spend more money than it collects. Since the 1980s the level ranged mostly from a surplus to a $400 billion deficit, twice exceeding that range. In 2008 the federal deficit *tripled* to more than $1.4 trillion dollars and remains at that level.

Interest Rates

If the demand for available funds is high, the price for these funds (the interest rate) will probably be high as well. Therefore, the price of money is subject to supply and demand like any other commodity. For example, if the federal government borrows extensively to fund its deficits, it increases the demand for funds, and all else being equal will increase mortgage interest rates.

Competition for Funds

As a general rule, any users of credit can obtain needed funds if they are willing to pay the price (interest rate) for those funds. But, when all users of credit are competing for funds at the same time, other factors come into play and some users are in an unfavorable position.

For example, if business demand for credit is high and business is willing to pay a price equal to that offered by mortgages, funds would generally flow to bonds to the detriment of mortgage lending. The preference for corporate debt lies in the unique characteristics of mortgage debt. Mortgage debt requires a higher yield because of the longer maturity, lack of uniformity in real estate laws, lower liquidity, and the problems and delays of foreclosure. Inflation and supply and demand for funds are the most important factors in the rise and fall of interest rates. Another factor is the degree of risk inherent in a mortgage loan or a bond offering. Of course, if the other major consumers of capital—the various levels of government—are also active in the capital markets, their activity puts pressure on interest rates as well.

Public Debt versus Private Debt

When any government—federal, state, or local—spends more money than it collects, it must borrow in the same markets in which other users of credit borrow. This includes issuers of corporate bonds and homebuyers. In this manner, government competes with other users of credit for the limited capital available. The federal government in particular has been in a severe deficit position for the past few decades, a condition that many economists believe was the basic cause of the persistent inflation of the early 1980s. This inflation and the continuing credit demands of the federal government resulted in high interest rates, which played havoc in both the money markets and the capital markets. As a result, all users of credit suffered during this period.

The federal government has the legal authority to get as much money as it demands. Therefore, unless available credit is expanding at a rate that allows for the accommodation of all users of credit, excessive federal borrowing will have a crowding-out effect on less creditworthy borrowers.

For a few years in the late 1990s and early 2000s, the federal government actually ran a surplus. The result of this rare surplus was that interest rates in general plummeted and long-term residential mortgage rates reached levels not seen in decades.

In the past five years, federal government deficits increased tremendously. This raises concerns about the overall level of interest rates in the long term. Since 2008, however, to keep mortgage interest rates low the federal government became an active buyer of mortgages by purchasing over $1.25 trillion in GSE MBS (See Chapter 5—Secondary Mortgage Markets).

Monetary Policy and Interest Rates

Another important element in determining interest rates is monetary policy. The Federal Reserve Bank implements the government's *monetary policy* by using the supply of money to control interest rates and economic activity.

The administrative branch and legislative branches of the U.S. government impose taxes, borrow, and spend money as part of its fiscal policy to help stimulate or slow economic growth. Both monetary and fiscal policies need to work in concert to be effective.

Thus, when the Federal Reserve needs to stimulate the economy, it increases the supply of money. The fiscal policy of the federal government often forces the Federal Reserve to act in an attempt to moderate the impact of federal borrowing on the nation's economy.

Another major impact that residential mortgage lending has on the economy is its effect on the "velocity" of money—the number of times a year each dollar is spent in the economy. Mortgage loans convert personal savings on deposit in financial institutions into funds for other consumers to use elsewhere without adding more money into the economy, which can negatively impact other fiscal and monetary policy actions.

The Federal Reserve Bank System

In addition to its banking functions, the Federal Reserve Bank is responsible for controlling the nation's credit system through financial institutions. The Federal Reserve uses several methods to manage this responsibility:

- *Reserve requirements.* An increase in the amount of money a member institution must have in its reserve account results in less money available for lending. Conversely, if the Federal Reserve lowers the reserve requirement, this will increase the amount of money available and make credit easier to obtain.
- *Open-market operations.* This commonly used method allows the Federal Reserve to decrease the supply of money by selling Treasury securities on the open market. The securities are paid for by checks drawn on commercial banks. This decreases the banks' reserves, therefore reducing the amount of funds that can be loaned. If the Federal Reserve intends to increase the supply of money, it buys the securities by issuing a check drawn upon itself.
- *Fed funds target—intended federal funds rate.* Open-market operations (purchases and sales of U.S. Treasury and federal agency securities) are the Federal Reserve's principal tool for implementing monetary policy. The short-term objective for open-market operations is specified by the Federal Open Market Committee (FOMC). This objective can be a desired quantity of reserves or a desired price (the federal funds rate). The *federal funds rate* is the overnight interest rate at which depository institutions lend balances at the Federal Reserve to other depository institutions.
- *Discount rate.* The Federal Reserve operates a service of discounting (paying less than par) commercial paper from member institutions. By discounting, the Federal Reserve provides funds that can be loaned. Increasing the *discount rate* (considered to be the interest rate that a member institution pays the Federal Reserve) makes it more expensive for an institution to borrow to obtain necessary reserves. Consequently, the interest rate a member institution must then charge a borrower increases.

If the discount rate is lowered, borrowing is easier for a financial institution and the interest rate charged to a borrower could be lowered. Although the discount window was long ago superseded by open-market operations as the most important tool of monetary policy, it still has a complementary role in the day-to-day implementation of policy. The discount window functions as a safety valve in relieving pressures in reserve markets; in circumstances in which extensions of credit can help relieve liquidity strains in the banking system, the window also helps to assure the basic stability of financial markets more generally.

The ability of the Federal Reserve to influence the economy was very evident during the first two years of the new century. During 2001 and 2002, the Federal Reserve cut the fed funds target rate twelve times, trying to stimulate an economy slowed by the twin forces of recession and the terrorist attacks of September 11, 2001 (**http://www.ny.frb.org/markets/omo/dmm/historical/fedfunds/ff.cfm**).

The last reduction, in November 2002, took the fed funds target rate to 1.25 percent, the lowest since 1961. As the economy grew, the fed funds rate increased gradually and typically in 0.25 percent increments to 5.25 percent in June 2006, where it remained until September 2007. From that point fears of a recession influenced monetary policy and the fed funds rate dropped five percent in just over one year in aggressive 0.5 to 0.75 percent increments. In December 2008, the fed funds target rate dropped from 1.0 percent to 0–0.25 percent, where it remained through September 2010.

Countercyclical Nature of Real Estate

During periods of high demand for credit (normally, the apex of an economic cycle), the capital markets are usually unable to satisfy the combined demands for credit of individuals, government, and business. Mortgage lending usually suffers during such periods because each increase in the price of money, as indicated by the interest rate, means fewer potential homebuyers will qualify for a mortgage. In some situations in the past, mortgage interest rates have been forced up against a state's usury ceiling. Because real estate in general and mortgage lending in particular are the losers in a credit crunch, they have often been classified as countercyclical. The development of the secondary mortgage market has eased this situation by obtaining funding from the capital markets for housing during periods of high credit demand.

The counter-cyclicality of real estate means that real estate activity, and consequently mortgage lending, usually expands when the general business cycle is down and credit demand is low. The normal situation when the economic cycle is down is lower interest rates in general, which allow more borrowers to qualify for a mortgage loan. Conversely, as the economy begins to improve and demand for credit from other users increases, real estate activity begins to slow down as interest rates increase. This somewhat simplified explanation demonstrates the direct relationship between the availability of credit and real estate activity.

FINANCIAL INTERMEDIARIES

The more modern and clearly more descriptive term, *financial intermediaries*, describes that classification of economic units previously called financial institutions. Their principal economic function is to serve as the middleman—the intermediary—between the saver and the borrower. Both saver and borrower benefit from this arrangement. The saver, as is explained later, is able to earn a higher return on savings, while the borrower can obtain needed funds at a more reasonable rate.

The term *financial intermediaries* includes these major economic units, among others:

- Commercial banks
- Savings and loan institutions
- Mortgage companies
- Credit unions
- Mutual savings banks
- Life insurance companies
- Finance companies
- Investment companies
- Pension funds
- Money market funds
- Stockbrokers

Financial intermediaries are essential to the entire economy, but are especially crucial to mortgage lending, since they lend much of the funds required by homebuyers, and accumulate those funds almost exclusively from individual savers. The characteristics of these lenders are examined later, but let us first examine how savers benefit from using these intermediaries.

How Savers Benefit

When dealing with financial intermediaries, the benefits to savers are a higher yield, safety, and diversification. Others, such as economies of scale, variety of maturities, and specialization, are not. Higher yields result from the increased level of knowledge and experience intermediaries have over the average saver. The experts know where, how, and when to make safe, profitable investments. Safety is derived both from federal deposit insurance and from the informed investment decisions of the experts. Diversification is also an element of safety that, for a smaller saver, can be reached without sacrificing yield only through the use of an intermediary.

How Mortgage Borrowers Benefit

The cost to a consumer in need of a mortgage loan is made lower by dealing with an intermediary. Instead of having to solicit many savers for funds, this mortgage borrower need only deal with one financial intermediary, which has been able to pool the funds of many savers. The benefit to savers in this arrangement is a higher yield, since a part of the saved cost of borrowing can be passed on to them while borrowers also benefit from this economy of scale. Each saver has different objectives in mind for savings deposited. Since financial intermediaries can also lend to borrowers with differing needs and for differing maturities, the match is beneficial to both parties. Finally, since many financial intermediaries specialize in a selected type of lending, they can provide that type of lending more cheaply than competitors, with a resulting benefit to both saver and borrower. An example of this type of specialization is thrift institutions and single-family mortgage lending.

Gross Profit Spread

Financial intermediaries are able to fulfill their important economic function by operating on a spread between their cost of funds (generally, the interest on savings of individuals) and their portfolio yield (the interest earned on loans outstanding). The typical spread changes with market conditions and interest rate levels.

As a general rule, in the 1980s and 1990s savings institutions sought a gross profit spread of two or three percent (200 or 300 *basis points*). As an example, if the average interest rate paid by a savings bank on all savings deposits is five percent, the average portfolio yield must be between seven and eight percent for that institution to be profitable. Assuming an operating expense ratio of one percent, this leaves the institution with a one- to two-percent net interest margin (NIM) on their savings and lending activities, a common measure of their core profit before taxes.

When rates dropped and mortgage demand increased, competition among lenders lowered the gross profit spread. Today, mortgage lenders typically target two percent (200 basis points) for NIM.

Interest Rate Risk

One primary economic danger for financial intermediaries that are portfolio lenders, such as some credit unions and savings institutions, is that interest rates will begin a rapid increase. The financial institution then must match the rising rates on savings deposits in order to retain its deposits. It then must lend these funds out at what should be an increased mortgage rate.

The problem is that even with the increased interest rate on current mortgage production, the entire mortgage portfolio may not have a sufficient yield to generate a profitable spread. Thus, a typical institution currently lending at 100 to 125 basis points above its cost of funds may not impact the portfolio yield enough to create a profitable spread; in fact, it may even be negative, as it was for savings institutions during the high interest rate period of 1981 to 1983. Additionally, when rates rise, mortgage demand falls, reducing the market for these higher yielding mortgage loans.

MORTGAGE LENDERS AND THE PRIMARY MORTGAGE MARKET

The primary economic function of a residential mortgage lender is to lend money for the purchase or refinance of residences of all types in the primary mortgage market. This would include single-family detached, condominiums, cooperative housing, and two- to four-family housing. These loans are secured by either a first or second mortgage. The primary mortgage market is that market in which funds are loaned (credit extended) directly to a borrower.

Financial intermediaries usually involved in the residential primary mortgage market include the following:

- Mortgage bankers
- Mortgage brokers
- Commercial banks
- Savings and loan institutions
- Savings banks
- Credit unions
- Housing finance agencies

These mortgage lenders, along with a few nontraditional mortgage lenders (such as General Motors Acceptance Corporation), originate nearly all residential mortgage loans each year. Some of these mortgage lenders also hold mortgages in their own portfolios.

The primary market differs from the secondary mortgage market, in which mortgages originated in the primary market are bought and sold. The secondary mortgage market is discussed in detail in Chapter 5—Secondary Mortgage Market.

All the institutions listed above can participate in the secondary market. Others, such as mortgage bankers, must sell all of their originations to other lenders or into the secondary mortgage market. Some of these same lenders are also very active in commercial mortgage lending.

Funding for Mortgage Debt

Lenders obtain the money for residential mortgage loans from the following sources:

- Funds deposited by savers
- Funds borrowed from other financial intermediaries
- Sale of commercial paper (short-term *promissory note*)
- Proceeds from the sale of mortgage loans

Normally, all of the residential mortgage lenders are active on a day-to-day basis in the primary market, but during some stages of the economic cycle, one or more may temporarily drop out. When this occurs, it is usually because of the high cost of funds to lend. By bringing together borrowers and savers from different economic sectors and geographic locations, mortgage lenders as financial intermediaries contribute to a more efficient allocation of the economy's resources. The mortgage lenders are discussed individually in detail in Chapter 4—The Mortgage Lenders.

Mortgage Investors

In addition to mortgage lenders that hold mortgage debt in their own portfolios, a number of other financial intermediaries are important holders of mortgage debt. These intermediaries hold only residential mortgage debt (either individual loans or mortgage-backed securities); they do not originate any loans. Classified as mortgage investors, they include the following:

- Federal National Mortgage Association (Fannie Mae)
- Federal Home Loan Mortgage Corporation (Freddie Mac)
- Federal Home Loan banks
- Retirement and pension funds
- Other federal agencies
- State housing agencies
- Life insurance companies
- United States government
- Foreign governments (central banks) and financial institutions
- Individuals

These investors acquire the mortgage debt they hold either directly from the mortgage lenders that originated them or through the operation of the secondary mortgage market. Some participants in the primary mortgage market will, on occasion, also buy loans from other originators because they believe they can acquire mortgage loans and/or servicing rights cheaper this way. For a discussion of the secondary mortgage market, see Chapter 11—Secondary Mortgage Market.

RECENT TRENDS IN MORTGAGE LENDING

Residential mortgage lending continues to evolve rapidly. More changes are occurring now than at any other time since the 1930s. These changes affect the following factors:

- Who the lenders are in the primary market
- How residential loans are originated
- How technology is used to enhance profits
- How funds for mortgages are generated
- How interest rates are calculated
- How mortgages are sold and securitized
- How mortgages are serviced and by whom
- How borrowers are qualified
- Who the mortgage investors are in the secondary markets

This text discusses several of these changes and trends. The most meaningful changes in residential mortgage lending over the past 10 years include the following:

- Demise of thrifts as the dominant originator of residential debt and the rise of the mortgage banker
- Widespread use of mortgage-backed securities to access the capital markets for additional funds for residential loans
- Adoption of alternative mortgage instruments by financial intermediaries to spread the risk of mortgage lending
- Explosion of refinance activity because of low interest rates and the resulting runoff of servicing

- Federal government's active role in primary and secondary mortgage markets
- Expansion of modification and other workout scenarios for distressed borrowers

Mortgage Revenue Bonds (MRBs)

Prior to 1978, state housing finance agencies were the only government entities using tax-exempt MRBs to provide financing for mortgage borrowers. Their normal method of financing was to borrow money and then provide below-market rate loans to low- and moderate-income groups.

The concept behind using tax-exempt MRBs for financing is quite simple. An issuer, whether state or city, is able to sell its tax-exempt bonds in the capital market with an interest rate substantially below taxable bonds because of the tax savings to investors. This money is then channeled through various mortgage lenders to mortgage borrowers. As a result of this low-cost borrowing, mortgagors often can obtain a loan two or three percentage points below the conventional market rate.

The various state programs in past years caused little reaction as they attempted to help the low- and moderate-income groups, but when new programs developed that were designed to assist middle-income groups, the concern of many segments of society was vocalized. The Mortgage Subsidy Bond Act (1981) resulted from this rising concern. This act severely restricts the use of tax-exempt MRBs issued by state and local housing authorities. It limits eligibility of buyers and imposes purchase price ceilings and limitations on states' annual volumes.

Mortgage Credit Certificates (MCCs)

The law extending authority for mortgage revenue bonds also provided state and local governments with an alternative to MRBs with which to assist first-time homebuyers. This alternative provides for the issuance of MCCs to qualified homebuyers, allowing them a nonrefundable tax credit of from 10 to 50 percent (as determined by the state or local government) of the interest paid on home mortgage indebtedness. MCCs are limited to first-time homebuyers having a joint income below the local area median income, and to the purchase of homes whose *acquisition costs* do not exceed 90 percent of the local average purchase price. The MCC concept is an attempt to ensure that the entire amount of the subsidy, in the form of tax credits, flows directly to first-time homebuyers and not partially to others. Congress perceived that MRBs had a part of the subsidy flowing to tax-exempt investors and intermediaries, in addition to the homebuyer. The MCC provides the same subsidy or more as the MRB to first-time homebuyers, and at a reduced revenue loss to the federal tax coffers. This subsidy is meant to complement the mortgage interest deduction that provides greater benefits to higher-income homebuyers and little or no benefit to low- and middle-income taxpayers.

Under the law, state and local governments have the choice of issuing MRBs or MCCs, or a combination of both. The aggregate annual amount of MCCs issued by a state may not exceed 20 percent of the authorized MRB volume for the state. The state's MRB volume is determined by an average of originations over the past three years or $200 million, whichever is greater.

Builder Bonds

Builder bonds are being used frequently today as a means whereby builders can access the capital markets directly in order to obtain the funds needed by the purchasers of their homes. To builders, the obvious benefit of this financing technique is that they can sell more houses than they could otherwise. This is true even during those periods of the economic cycle when some of the traditional lenders are out of the market because of a lack of savings inflow. A builder (or group of builders) will use a mortgage banker or a similar organization to take local applications, underwrite the loan, and provide loan servicing.

As important as this direct access to the capital market is, another aspect is more important to some builders. The use of builder bonds to finance the purchase of houses allows a builder to report house sales on an installment basis for tax purposes and thus be able to defer most of the income tax until later years. The reason is that since the mortgage payments are spread out over 20 years or more, the house is paid for over that same period. Taxes are paid according to the amount of profit earned each year.

Builder bonds are mortgage-backed securities that are backed either by the individual mortgages on houses sold or by Government National Mortgage Association (Ginnie Mae) certificates purchased for the purpose of serving as collateral for a builder bond. For an extensive discussion of mortgage-backed securities, see Chapter 5—Secondary Mortgage Market.

DISCUSSION POINTS

1. Real estate and mortgage lending are a major part of the American economy. Examine and explain the magnitude of their involvement in the economy.
2. Real estate and mortgage lending are significantly impacted by changes in the economy, especially interest rates. What was the impact on mortgage lending of the dramatic drop in interest rates in 2001–2002? Why did interest rates drop so much?
3. What is the difference between financial intermediaries, mortgage lenders, and mortgage investors?
4. How does "the Fed" attempt to manage the economy? What tools are most important?
5. As a general rule, where does the money for residential mortgage lending come from?
6. How do demographic forces impact real estate and the mortgage markets?

CHAPTER 4

The Mortgage Lenders

INTRODUCTION

This chapter examines the types of mortgage lenders involved in the origination of residential mortgage loans in the primary mortgage market and the different roles they may play in this process. To understand the present market and its lenders, one must appreciate the various social, economic, and legislative events which shaped the current primary and secondary mortgage markets, the organization of the players active in them, and the different roles that the government plays as a lender and a regulator.

Historically, the mortgage originator, lender, and servicer was one entity—either a private lender or a bank. As the United States developed, the residential mortgage finance industry became more complex. Mortgage investors came into the picture, playing a larger and larger role in financing mortgage loans. Today, these specialized functions are often performed by different entities.

It is important to distinguish between these roles of mortgage loan *originators*, *lenders*, *holders,* and *servicers*. An originator of mortgage debt takes the application and may process it partially or completely. The mortgage *lender* approves the application, provides the funding, and normally controls the loan closing. The *holder* of that mortgage debt is the entity who keeps the mortgage note after closing (frequently this is not the same entity as the loan *servicer*).

In many cases the original lender—the entity that funded and closed the mortgage loan—neither took the application nor kept it in its mortgage loan portfolio, so it is not the "final" holder of that mortgage loan. Additionally, the holder of mortgage debt often may sell it to another entity before the loan is paid off (often transferring its servicing in the process).

For example, mortgage brokers never fund the applications they take—they must find a lender to approve and fund the loan. Mortgage bankers must sell all of the loans they originate or obtain from brokers. On the other hand, many (but not all) local thrifts, credit unions, and small commercial banks will originate, lend, and hold their mortgages.

Along this line, the term *financial intermediary* applies to all residential mortgage originators, even though not all mortgage lenders are depository institutions. For example, mortgage bankers, who originate about half of all residential mortgage loans each year, are financial intermediaries but not depository institutions—they do not accept deposits from consumers or businesses. Instead, mortgage bankers obtain funds for residential mortgage lending by borrowing from other financial institutions or through the sale of commercial paper.

However, another term, *mortgage loan originator (MLO)*, as a result of the Secure And Fair Enforcement for Mortgage Licensing Act of 2008 (SAFE Act) now has a very specific legal meaning. It applies to individuals only and will not be used in this chapter as a general industry term. (A *MLO* is either federally registered or state licensed; each class has different SAFE Act requirements outlined further in Chapter 11—Compliance.)

When a loan moves from the original lender to another holder of the loan (an investor), it becomes part of net overall secondary market activity (see Chapters 5 and 17). So while the final holder of mortgage debt may not be the original lender, in aggregate it represents the eventual source of funds that drives the mortgage finance market at that time.

Holders of Residential Debt

As of 2010, the Federal Reserve reports more than $10.7 trillion of one- to four-family mortgage debt outstanding, as shown in Table 4.1. This represents 76 percent of all mortgage debt on all property, a fairly consistent percentage since 2000.

TABLE **4.1**

U.S. Mortgage Debt Outstanding ($ in billions)

Mortgage Type	2000	2001	2002	2003	2004	2005	2006	2007	2008	2009	1Q 2010
Total Mortgage Debt	$6,785	$7,474	$8,353	$9,377	$10,637	$12,073	$13,470	$14,533	$14,263	$14,341	$14,200
Home (1-4 Family)	$5,119	$5650	$6,382	$7,240	$8,268	$9,382	$10,456	$11,166	$11,071	$10,859	$10,749
Multifamily Residential	$404	$446	$485	$557	$604	$667	$707	$790	$841	$849	$852
Commercial	$1,171	$1,282	$1,393	$1,497	$1,669	$1,920	$2,199	$2,465	$2,582	$2,494	$2,461
Farm	$91	$96	$103	$83	$96	$105	$108	$113	$130	$139	$138

Source: © 2012 Cengage Learning

In today's highly sophisticated and segmented residential mortgage lending market, holders of mortgage debt fall into several broad categories: private lenders, financial intermediaries, financial institutions, government agencies and GSEs, and secondary market investors. See Table 4.2.

Before the Great Depression, wealthy individuals made up the largest classification of holders of residential debt (private lenders). Private lenders lend their own funds directly to the borrower, and range widely in sophistication. In this category falls the true "family sale," where a parent sells the family homestead to a descendent and is repaid by either an informal arrangement or by a formal loan secured by a lien on the property. Also in this category are wealthy individuals or real estate investors who provide debt directly to borrowers. Although individuals today still hold $111 billion of residential mortgage debt, this represents just over one percent of the total amount outstanding. Financial intermediaries originate and fund residential mortgage loans using money "borrowed" from depositors or from other financial intermediaries. Normally they retain the mortgage loans in their own portfolios; they make up the second largest sector of mortgage holders with over $3.3 trillion dollars.

If, on the other hand, the financial intermediary sells mortgage loans to other financial institutions or the secondary market, the purchaser of the loans or the mortgage-backed security itself is classified as the holder of residential mortgage debt. Secondary market investors hold by far the largest amount of mortgage debt, totaling more than $7.2 trillion.

Federal, state, and local governments hold a small amount of mortgage debt, approximately $121 billion. This number reflects the normal market activity of some government lending programs, described in detail in Chapter 8, but not the full activity of FHA, VA, and other programs where the government provides credit enhancement but is not the primary lender.

However, since 2008 when the federal government placed Fannie and Freddie into conservatorship, their large holdings of mortgage-backed securities technically have increased federal government mortgage holdings to more than $4.8 *trillion* dollars in GSE-owned mortgage loans and securities. This

TABLE **4.2**
Holders of 1–4 Family Mortgage Debt 2000–2010 ($ in billions)

Holder	2000	2001	2002	2003	2004	2005	2006	2007	2008	2009	1Q2010	% of Total 1-4 Family Mortgages
Total Mortgages	$5,119	$5,650	$6,382	$7,240	$8,268	$9,382	$10,456	$11,166	$11,071	$10,859	$10,749	
Home Equity	$407	$436	$501	$594	$776	$915	$1,066	$1,131	$1,114	$1,032	$1,013	9%
Secondary Market Total Investors	$3,028	$3,430	$3,860	$4,473	$4,953	$5,664	$6,460	$7,087	$7,234	$7,272	$7,215	67%
Financial Intermediaries Total	$2,619	$2,791	$2,982	$2,543	$3,066	$3,456	$3,738	$3,845	$3,605	$3,355	$3,302	31%
Government Total	$85	$83	$79	$82	$86	$91	$98	$104	$104	$120	$121	1%
Private Total	$117	$128	$135	$142	$164	$172	$152	$131	$128	$114	$111	1%
Financial Intermediaries												
Commercial Bank	$965	$1,024	$1,222	$1,360	$1,582	$1,792	$2,082	$2,211	$2,249	$2,260	$2,221	21%
Savings Institutions	$594	$621	$632	$703	$874	$954	$868	$879	$666	$449	$445	4%
Finance Companies	$187	$210	$286	$320	$422	$490	$538	$473	$375	$328	$317	3%
Credit Unions	$125	$141	$159	$160	$188	$220	$250	$282	$315	$318	$319	3%
	12%	11%	10%	10%	11%	10%	8%	8%	6%	4%	4%	
Government												
State & Local Government	$67	$66	$63	$68	$72	$78	$85	$90	$88	$98	$99	1%
Federal Government	$18	$17	$16	$14	$14	$13	$13	$14	$16	$22	$23	0%

Secondary Market Investors											% of Total HE Loans
GSE - Portfolio	$210	$233	$282	$519	$509	$454	$458	$448	$457	$439	$4,751	44%
Agency and GSE Pools	$2,426	$2,749	$3,064	$3,234	$3,277	$3,446	$3,740	$4,372	$4,864	$5,267	$984	9%
ABS Issues	$378	$434	$489	$666	$1,049	$1,622	$2,141	$2,174	$1,861	$1,527	$1,440	13%
REIT	$9	$9	$20	$37	$103	$127	$104	$79	$37	$28	$29	0%
Other	$5	$5	$5	$17	$15	$15	$17	$14	$15	$11	$11	0%
Private												
Household	$87	$95	$100	$106	$113	$118	$103	$91	$91	$83	$81	1%
Nonfinancial Corporate Business	$21	$23	$25	$26	$40	$41	$36	$25	$21	$16	$15	0%
Nonfarm Non-corporate Business	$9	$10	$10	$10	$11	$13	$13	$15	$16	$15	$15	0%
Home Equity Loans (included in Total 1-4 Family Mortages)												
Commercial Bank	$235	$259	$303	$366	$484	$549	$654	$692	$776	$762	$751	74%
Savings Institutions	$73	$78	$79	$96	$121	$152	$138	$181	$120	$80	$78	8%
Credit Unions	$41	$45	$48	$52	$64	$76	$87	$94	$99	$95	$92	9%
Finance Companies	$49	$45	$56	$64	$84	$98	$108	$95	$75	$66	$63	6%
ABS Issues	$10	$13	$16	$16	$23	$40	$80	$69	$45	$30	$28	3%

Source: Federal Reserve 06/10
© 2010 Community Lending Associates, LLC
www.communitylendassoc.com

makes the federal government the leading holder of mortgage debt (45 percent market share), transforming its role dramatically—a situation most economists and policy makers agree is untenable and at the same time very difficult to change.

Industry consolidation is another critical feature of mortgage debt that has developed in the past ten years. A recent, very comprehensive study by the OCC and OTS analyzed the mortgage servicing portfolios of only eleven institutions: nine banks and two thrifts. Their servicing portfolios totaled more than $6 trillion across 34 million loans—over 64 percent of first-lien mortgage loans outstanding! At least 90 percent were loans serviced for other secondary market investors. The study illustrates how pervasively the mortgage banking business model dominates the residential mortgage lending landscape. It also illustrates the unprecedented level of government involvement and systemic risk present today in the overall mortgage industry, impacting originators, lenders, holders, and servicers. Some industry experts argue it is easier to regulate fewer organizations to curb abuses. Others argue against this approach. In reality, the size and complexity of these organizations (i.e., Fannie Mae, Freddie Mac, Countrywide) impede effective regulation and present too much industry concentration risk—"too big to fail".

MORTGAGE BANKERS AND MORTGAGE BROKERS

Mortgage bankers and mortgage brokers typically originate approximately 60 percent of all residential mortgage loans each year. In addition, mortgage bankers service approximately 70 percent of the $13 trillion in outstanding residential mortgage debt. Both of these figures represent major growth in the 1990s and early 2000s.

A mortgage company is usually identified as a mortgage banker, but may actually be a mortgage broker or part of a financial intermediary (such as Bank of America or General Motors). The term *mortgage banker* is somewhat misleading, as it implies that this lender is a depository—like a financial institution. As mentioned earlier, mortgage bankers lend with borrowed money and do not accept deposits, but are classified as intermediaries because they serve as financial bridges between borrowers and lenders.

The term "mortgage banker" can also be confusing as it sometimes is used generally to describe all participants involved in the mortgage banking process—mortgage brokers, correspondent lenders, wholesale lenders, mortgage companies, mortgage servicers, and mortgage subservicers. These different participants often perform specific secondary market functions as shown in Figure 4.1.

Mortgage Brokers (Not to Be Confused with Mortgage Bankers)

According to the U.S Bureau of Labor Statistics, the number of mortgage brokers peaked at about 500,000 in 2006, the height of subprime and private investor origination. During their boom years of 2001–2007, brokers were involved in more than 60 percent of all mortgage originations. Since then,

FIGURE 4.1 Comparison of Different Mortgage Bankers

Type	Function(s)	Funding Source(s)	Income Source(s)	Ownership
Mortgage Broker	Originate applications Do not approve loans Rarely close loans Rarely fund loans Sell all loans Do not pool loans Do not service loans	None Line of credit	Origination fees Yield spread premium	Independent
Correspondent Lender	Originate applications May approve loans Close loans Fund via borrowed funds Sell all loans May pool closed loans Do not service loans	Line of credit	Origination fees Yield spread premium Mortgage servicing right	Independent Financial institution subsidiary CUSO
Mortgage Company	Originate applications May approve loans Close loans Fund via borrowed funds Sell all loans May pool closed loans May issue MBS May service loans, buy/sell servicing	Line of credit	Origination fees Yield spread premium Mortgage servicing right Servicing fee Sale of servicing	Independent Financial institution subsidiary CUSO
Wholesale Lender	Do not originate applications May approve loans Close loans Fund via borrowed funds Sell all loans May pool closed loans May issue MBS Service loans, sell servicing	Line of credit	Yield spread premium Mortgage servicing right Servicing fee Sale of servicing	Independent Financial institution subsidiary
Government Sponsored Entity (GSE)	Do not originate applications Approve loans Do not close loans Purchase and sell closed loans Pool closed loans Issue MBS Do not service loans	Line of credit Stock issue Bond issue	Yield spread premium Guarantee fee	Fannie Mae Freddie Mac Ginnie Mae Farmer Mac
Financial Institution	Originate applications May approve loans Close loans Fund via deposits or borrowed funds May portfolio or sell loans May pool closed loans Service loans, sell servicing	Deposits Borrowed funds Mortgage servicing right	Origination fee Interest on loan Yield spread premium Credit Union Servicing fee Sale of servicing	Commercial Bank Savings and Loan Association Savings Bank
Mortgage Servicer	Service loans Buy and sell servicing	Line of credit	Servicing fee Mortgage servicing right Sale of servicing	Independent Financial institution subsidiary CUSO
Mortgage Subservicer	Service loans	Line of credit	Servicing fee	Independent CUSO

their numbers dropped quickly, to fewer than 250,000 in early 2010—less than half.

This decline is partially as a result of the collapse in the private investor segment of the mortgage market and partially because of more restrictive mortgage broker licensing requirements in the SAFE Act of 2008. How *much* of an impact from stricter licensing renewal requirements will become clearer at the end of 2010, but it is likely that the number of active mortgage brokers will continue to drop throughout 2010. For more information on mortgage brokers, see the National Association of Mortgage Brokers Web site at **www.namb.org.**

Rightly or wrongly, mortgage brokers shared with Wall Street the majority of the blame for the recent mortgage crisis. Despite hostile treatment from Congress, the media, and many lenders, mortgage brokers still serve an important, beneficial, and vital role in mortgage origination, and are major producers of residential mortgage loans in the marketplace. In a typical mortgage transaction involving a mortgage broker, the broker takes the loan application from a consumer and then receives a commission for providing it to another mortgage lender (often called a wholesale lender). The mortgage broker may also process the application, but the lender typically approves, closes, and funds it. After the loan closes, the mortgage broker has no continuing responsibility. In some situations, the mortgage broker will close the loan in its own name but immediately sell it to a lender (and release the servicing to that lender also. See Chapter 16—Mortgage Loan Servicing and Administration—for a discussion of this activity).

The mortgage broker acts as an independent contractor in providing such services as counseling the borrower, taking the loan application, ordering verifications, processing and reviewing credit, performing preliminary underwriting, and preparing the application package for approval or denial by the lender. With the mortgage broker fulfilling these functions, it allows lenders to cut origination costs and thus improve profits. Viewed another way, mortgage brokers help lenders offer lower loan rates due to their minimal overhead and setup costs.

Recent wording in RESPA and the SAFE Act expand the broker's responsibilities to act as an agent for the applicants as well as the lender. From the consumer's standpoint, the mortgage broker's mission is to find a loan that best suits the applicant's financial circumstances, needs, and goals. A broker maintains relationships with several lenders and has knowledge of their many programs, so he is in a position to match the consumer with the best lender.

Mortgage Broker Fees

Mortgage brokers receive fees from consumers and lenders. Is this legal? Federal law (RESPA—see Chapter 11—Compliance) allows mortgage originators and settlement service providers to charge fees, as long as they are reasonable, for services, goods, or facilities actually provided. New RESPA regulations also describe in more detail the *how*s and *when*s for these origination and settlement service fees and their disclosure to the applicant. The newly-revised HUD forms, the Good Faith Estimate, and HUD-1/HUD-1A Settlement Statements provide detailed information on these fees.

Mortgage brokers provide the same RESPA-defined *loan origination services* to consumers as do retail mortgage originators (such as commercial banks or mortgage banks), for which they charge an *origination fee*. Loan origination services include counseling the consumer on the loan process, taking the loan application, providing disclosures, ordering the credit report and appraisal, and collecting the necessary documents. Mortgage brokers may charge the consumer processing or other origination fees, which can total a thousand dollars or more. RESPA and GSE changes limit some of their services.

Mortgage brokers also earn a fee from the lender. The broker provides separate and distinct services to a lender than those it provides to a consumer. These include marketing the lender's products, and assembling and delivering the completed loan package. Historically, wholesale lenders have paid mortgage brokers a *yield spread premium* or *service release premium* (see Chapter 17—Selling Loans). These fees represent payment for the projected return to the investor for the loan, and the projected income the servicer will receive from the investor for servicing the loan. However, the payment of YSP and SRP has come under regulatory scrutiny. Proposed regulatory changes forbid compensation based on interest rate and other risk-based characteristics. Other proposals would limit the amount of compensation as well. Mortgage brokers typically do not receive compensation from the lender (from 0.25 to 2.0 percent or more of the loan amount) unless the loan closes. Thus, the broker has the ultimate incentive to provide the best possible customer service to the consumer.

Mortgage Bankers (Not to Be Confused with Mortgage Brokers)

Like mortgage brokers, mortgage *bankers* sell all of the mortgages they originate (or purchase from others, such as mortgage brokers). However, mortgage bankers may approve, close, and fund loans. Often they continue to service them after the sale. Many states have separate licensing requirement for mortgage brokers and mortgage bankers, reflecting the different services they provide to the consumer and investor. The primary trade association representing mortgage bankers is the Mortgage Bankers Association of America (MBA, **www.mbaa.org**), which provides legislation lobbying and valuable market research and economic data.

The number of independent mortgage bankers is actually quite small (only a few hundred). The majority of mortgage bankers are geographically located in traditional capital-deficit areas such as the South and West. These mortgage bankers continue to render a valuable service to both borrowers and mortgage investors by moving funds for mortgages from capital-surplus areas to areas where insufficient capital exists to meet the needs of homebuyers.

FIGURE **4.2** Mortgage Loan Origination Agreement

You, *Thomas Stavola/Susan Stavola* agree to enter into this Mortgage Loan Origination Agreement with **NORTHFIELD MORTGAGE COMPANY (NMC)** as an independent contractor to apply for a residential mortgage loan from a participating lender with which we from time to time contract upon such terms and conditions as you may request or a lender may require. You inquired into mortgage financing with **NMC** on June 18, 2003. We are licensed as a "**Mortgage Broker**" under the Laws of the State of Florida.

Section 1. Nature of Relationship. In connection with this mortgage loan:
- We are acting as an independent contractor and not as your agent.
- We will enter into separate independent contract agreements with various lenders.
- While we seek to assist you in meeting your financial needs, we do not distribute the products of all lenders or investors in the market and cannot guarantee the lowest price or best terms available in the market.

Section 2. Our Compensation. The lenders whose loan products we distribute generally provide their loan products to us at a wholesale rate.
- The retail price we offer you—your interest rate, total points, and fees—will include our compensation.
- In some cases, either you or the lender may pay us all of our compensation.
- Alternatively, both you and the lender may pay us a portion of our compensation. For example, in some cases, if you would rather pay a lower interest rate, you may pay higher upfront points and fees.
- Also, in some cases, if you would rather pay less upfront, you may be able to pay some or all of our compensation indirectly through a higher interest rate, in which case we will be paid directly by the lender.

We also may be paid by the lender based on (i) the value of the Mortgage Loan or related servicing rights in the market place, or (ii) other services, goods, or facilities performed or provided by us to the lender. By signing below, the mortgage loan originator and mortgage loan applicant(s) acknowledge receipt of a copy of this signed Agreement.

_____*Iamm Fiducia*_____ Date __6/18/03__   _____*Thomas Stavola*_____ Date __6/18/03__
Mortgage Loan Originator   **Applicant**

                                              _____*Susan Stavola*_____ Date __6/18/03__
                                              Applicant

Source: © 2012 Cengage Learning

Many financial institutions implement a mortgage-banking strategy in different forms: a secondary market operation in the mortgage department, a separate secondary market department, and/or a mortgage bank subsidiary. Today, commercial banks and savings institutions own many of the largest mortgage-banking companies. For the past several years, between six and eight of the largest have been associated with depository institutions, while only one or two of the ten largest mortgage originators are independent mortgage banking companies.

Figure 4.3 illustrates the large influence of the ten largest mortgage originators. They represent between 55-71 percent of total mortgage originations from 2007-2009. Ony two of the ten largest originators are independent mortgage banks. It also illustrates how volatile mortgage origination volume has been since the "mortgage meltdown" crisis in 2007:

- seven of the ten largest experienced a decline in volume of over 25 percent from 2007-2008.
- three of the ten largest experienced an increase in volume of over 100 percent from 2008-2009.
- eight of the ten largest experienced a change in volume of over 25 percent from 2008-2009. Also indicative of this recent volatility is that four of the ten largest mortgage originators in 2007 suffered losses so severe that they were unable to operate independently.

Not a Portfolio Lender

Because mortgage bankers do not intentionally hold mortgages for their own portfolio, they originate residential mortgage loans with the intent of selling the loans to mortgage investors, either directly or through a secondary mortgage market conduit. On occasion, a mortgage banker may originate a "mistake" that cannot be sold as a conforming loan to an established investor. When this happens, the mortgage banker usually sells the loan to another investor at a *discount* rather than hold on to it.

Many mortgage bankers also service loans for investors. A servicing portfolio can be a good source of income, but only if the mortgage banker meets stringent secondary market servicing requirements and controls its servicing costs.

Development of Mortgage Bankers

Mortgage companies, later called mortgage bankers, developed to fulfill a need for farm financing in the second half of the nineteenth century. Following the Civil War, the opening of new farmland in the Ohio Valley and further west required an infusion of credit from the capital-surplus areas of New England. Originally, a few real estate agents, attorneys, and some commercial bankers made mortgage loans and then sold them to wealthy individuals or institutions in the East. This practice grew until farm mortgage lending specialists developed and formed the first mortgage companies. At the turn of the twentieth century, approximately 200 mortgage companies existed. They originated farm mortgages with the 50 percent loan-to-value, interest-only loans, and with five-year maturities.

Following World War I, the migration from farms to the developing urban areas accelerated. At this time, a few of the more aggressive mortgage companies began to make single-family mortgage loans. This new type of loan was similar to the farm mortgages made by mortgage companies for the previous 50 years in regard to loan-to-value ratios and term. These non-amortizing mortgages, which normally required refinancing at the expiration

FIGURE **4.3** Largest Residential Mortgage Originators 2009–2007

Company Name	2009 Total Volume (dollar)	Market Share	Volume Change 2008–2009	Company Name	2008 Total Volume (dollar)	Market Share	Volume Change 2007–2008	Company Name	2007 Total Volume (dollar)	Market Share
Wells Fargo & Company	$427,211	22.0%	80%	Wells Fargo & Company	$237,160	14.8%	−13%	*Countrywide	$408,234	16.7%
Bank of America	$391,318	20.2%	115%	Chase	$187,142	11.7%	−11%	Wells Fargo & Company	$271,932	11.1%
Chase	$155,770	8.0%	−17%	Bank of America	$182,213	11.4%	−4%	Chase	$210,201	8.6%
CitiMortgage, Inc.	$81,253	4.2%	−30%	CitiMortgage, Inc.	$115,386	8.6%	−68%	CitiMortgage, Inc.	$197,965	8.1%
Ally Bank/Residential Capital, LLC (GMAC)	$64,731	3.3%	13%	Ally Bank/Residential Capital, LLC (GMAC)	$57,333	7.2%	−42%	Bank of America	$189,213	7.7%
U.S. Bank Home Mortgage	$55,572	2.9%	62%	SunTrust Bank	$37,246	3.6%	−40%	*Washington Mutual, Inc.	$142,151	5.8%
SunTrust Bank	$50,462	2.6%	35%	U.S. Bank Home Mortgage	$34,256	3.2%	−48%	*Wachovia Bank, N.A.	$99,218	4.1%
Provident Funding Associates	$37,825	2.0%	160%	PHH Mortgage	$33,919	2.5%	−72%	Ally Bank/Residential Capital, LLC (GMAC)	$95,483	3.9%
PHH Mortgage	$37,564	1.9%	11%	Provident Funding Associates	$14,529	2.3%	−37%	*OneWest Bank/IndyMac	$76,979	3.1%
MetLife Home Loans	$37,242	1.9%	547%	MetLife Home Loans	$5,757	2.2%	−25%	SunTrust Bank	$59,404	2.4%
Total - Largest 10 Originators	**$1,338,948**	**69.0%**			**$904,941**	**56.6%**			**$1,750,780**	**71.4%**

Source: Mortgagestats.com
© 2010 Community Lending Associates, LLC
www.communitylendassoc.com
*No longer operates independently

of the term, were the principal reason why a large number of families lost their homes in the Depression of the 1930s. The liquidity crisis prevented financial institutions and many individuals from refinancing mortgage loans as they rolled over and the lender foreclosed.

Government Programs

In the early 1930s, the federal government implemented several acts and programs to stabilize the economy and declining real estate values. These are described in Chapter 1—History, but in particular, the Home Owners Loan Corporation (HOLC) in 1933 allowed all lenders, including mortgage bankers, to exchange defaulted mortgages for government bonds. This program helped save many family homes—and mortgage companies—and helped stabilize the real estate market, as HOLC restructured mortgages and put them on an amortizing basis.

Beginning of Modern Mortgage-Lending Standards

The Federal Housing Administration (FHA), created in 1934, provided the main stimulus to the formation of the modern mortgage banker. FHA established minimum standards for both the borrower and the real estate before it would insure a mortgage loan. FHA minimum standards prompted life insurance companies to seek permission from state insurance commissioners to make out-of-state loans with higher loan-to-value ratios and longer terms. State regulatory authorities eventually agreed to the request, and mortgage bankers soon began originating FHA-insured mortgages for sale to life insurance companies.

FHA adopted the HOLC practice of offering amortizing mortgage loans to assist borrowers in budgeting mortgage payments. Amortizing loans require a servicer to collect the monthly principal and interest and forward the payment to an investor. This requirement for servicing was the linchpin that allowed mortgage bankers to become the dominant originators of FHA-insured mortgage loans. Their dominant position in regard to FHA-insured mortgage loans remains constant even to the present time.

After World War II, Congress created another government mortgage program—the Veterans Administration (VA) guaranteed loan. Mortgage bankers quickly became the dominant originator of this type of loan, also. Mortgage bankers originated, sold, and serviced FHA-insured and VA-guaranteed mortgages for the Federal National Mortgage Association (now called Fannie Mae), which bought only FHA and **VA mortgages** until the early 1970s.

Modern Mortgage Bankers

The evolution of mortgage bankers produced a modern financial intermediary capable of adapting to changes in economic and marketplace conditions. For instance, in 2001, the top five mortgage companies originated nearly 38 percent of one- to four-family mortgage loans produced either by direct origination, wholesale, or via their correspondent system. When viewed from the perspective of direct retail origination, these five major players originated about 13 percent of total one- to four-family originations.

The modern mortgage banker earns most of its revenue from four main sources:

1. Origination fees charged to applicants
2. *Servicing fees* paid by investors
3. Marketing difference between interest rate on underlying mortgage and yield required by *commitment (yield spread premium)*
4. *Warehousing* difference between interest rates on funds borrowed and loaned

Today, some mortgage bankers have dual capabilities—single-family housing and income property origination—while other companies specialize in only one type of property. The modern mortgage banker performs some or all of the following functions:

- Originates, processes, underwrites, and closes all types of residential mortgage loans
- Arranges construction financing
- Warehouses closed residential mortgage loans
- Sells residential loans, either as *whole loans* or participations
- Sells to private investors or secondary mortgage market
- Pools residential mortgages into mortgage-backed securities
- Services the loans after sale

Organization and Regulation

Unlike other mortgage lenders, mortgage bankers are not chartered by either a state or the federal government, but instead are licensed by each state in which they originate or service loans. State licensing laws (in addition to SAFE Act standards) include requirements for a branch or location, bonding and/or net worth, and minimum education. Mortgage bankers are also unique in that they are not subject to direct regulation or supervision by any federal agency.

If a mortgage banker is an FHA-approved lender, VA-approved lender, or an approved seller/servicer for Fannie Mae or Freddie Mac, it is subject to periodic audits by those entities. HUD has attempted to exercise some control over mortgage bankers by issuing regulations governing several areas of concern, among them the way a mortgagee handles delinquency problems with a mortgagor. During the early 1980s, when merger activity between commercial banks and mortgage bankers was common, the Federal Reserve exercised some control by requiring approval prior to an ownership change.

Financing the Mortgage Banker

Mortgage bankers finance their lending activity differently than most other deposit-based residential mortgage lenders. Since they have no deposit funds to lend to mortgagors, a mortgage banker finances its loan activity by either the sale of commercial paper or by drawing on a line of credit with another lender—usually a commercial bank.

Historically, the latter was the primary way of obtaining funds. Commercial paper is a short-term debt instrument with a maximum term of 180 to 270 days, which carries a fixed rate of interest for a fixed term. Mortgage bankers use this alternative during those periods in the economic cycle when the rate for commercial paper is lower than the prime rate.

Sale of Commercial Paper

In addition to a lower cost of borrowing, the use of commercial paper removes the need for **compensating balances**—funds left on deposit with a commercial bank to provide an additional incentive to lend funds. If a commercial bank lends its support to the commercial paper of a mortgage banker by backing it with an irrevocable letter of credit, the bank will require a fee and some compensating balances. On the other hand, commercial paper sold under the name of a holding company of a mortgage banker requires no compensating balances. This alternative requires that the parent company have an acceptable credit rating. Market volatility is one problem with selling commercial paper. During periods of tight money, only mortgage companies with the highest credit ratings can obtain high-cost funds.

Line of Credit and Warehousing

The most popular alternative that mortgage bankers use for obtaining funds to lend to residential mortgagors is accessing a line of credit with a commercial bank. This process is usually a part of a unique function performed by mortgage bankers—warehousing. *Warehousing* refers to when mortgage bankers hold mortgages in the "warehouse" on a short-term basis, pending sale to an investor. These warehoused mortgage loans also serve as security for the revolving line of credit at a commercial bank.

This method finances the mortgage banker's loans to borrowers and the mortgage banker's inventory of closed residential loans. The mortgage banker repays the commercial bank's line of credit from the proceeds of periodic sales of mortgages to investors. Warehousing aptly describes the flow of closed mortgages into a mortgage banker that is then used to secure the bank loan. Some closed mortgages remain for 30 to 90 days in the warehouse until the mortgage banker sells a group, or *pool*, of mortgages to an investor, typically in million-dollar units.

Warehouse lines attract commercial banks because they are short term and normally involve little risk. The risk is minimal because the residential mortgage loans serving as collateral are usually presold to an investor who is obligated to purchase by a commitment. Commercial banks usually require that compensating balances, typically 20 percent of the maximum line of credit, support this line of credit. These required compensating balances might consist of tax and insurance escrows collected by the mortgage banker and deposited with the lending bank until needed.

Recently, commercial banks issuing lines of credit and mortgage banking borrowers experienced *investor risk*. The lender/investor would disappear overnight, leaving the mortgage banker the problem of funding a loan with nowhere to place it. This in turn caused mortgage bankers to fold, and left many consumers unable to complete their financing.

Mortgage Banking Today

Whether performed by an independent mortgage banker or another type of mortgage lender, the "mortgage-banking strategy" is the predominant and preferred strategy for originating residential mortgage loans, minimizing risk, and growing a servicing portfolio. Chapter 17—Selling describes this strategy further. In recent years, mortgage bankers originate (one way or another) at least 50 percent of residential mortgage loans. Other lenders, such as commercial banks and savings institutions, also follow the same strategy of originating loans, selling them, and growing a servicing portfolio.

COMMERCIAL BANKS

A **commercial bank** is a private financial institution organized to accumulate funds primarily through time and demand deposits, and to make these funds available to finance the nation's commerce and industry.

Commercial banks have the second largest number of institutions behind credit unions, but their numbers have declined significantly in the last 20 years, as shown in Table 4.3.

Although the number of banks dropped 40 percent over this period, the number of branches increased by that amount, and the total assets increased more than 350 percent, evidence of the intense pressure for industry consolidation. The assets of all commercial banks are more than twice those of all savings and loans, savings banks, and credit unions combined.

Since deregulation in the early 1980s, commercial banks replaced thrifts as the largest originators of one- to four-family mortgages behind only mortgage bankers. They are also first in origination of income property loans and construction mortgages.

Over the past 20 years, commercial banks expanded their real estate finance operations from what were mostly short-term mortgage loans to include many long-term mortgage loan products. As a result, commercial banks now hold more one- to four-family mortgage loans than any other classification of financial institution, increasing *600 percent* from $351 billion in 1989 to more than $2.1 trillion in 2009. Only mortgage pools have a larger dollar amount in one- to four-family mortgage loans.

TABLE **4.3**
Commercial Bank Institutions

Year	Banks	Branches	Total Assets (trillions)	Total 1-4 Family Mortgages (trillions)
1989	12,715	48,458	$3.3	$0.35
1999	8,582	64,330	$5.7	$0.84
2009	6,839	83,320	$11.8	$2.1

Note: In 2009, State-chartered commercial banks numbered 5,378, with $3.5 trillion in assets, and $526 billion in one- to four-family residential loans.
Source: FDIC

Historical Development

Except for a one-year period following the enactment of the National Bank Act of 1863, federally chartered commercial banks were not allowed to make real estate loans until 1913. During the period from 1863 to 1913, state-chartered banks thrived, as they were able to make real estate loans. Then in 1913, the Federal Reserve Act provided the authorization for federally chartered commercial banks to make mortgage loans. The typical mortgage loan provided by banks during this early period was similar to those made by other lenders: a 50 percent loan-to-value ratio for a five-year term, with the principal payable at the end of the term and with interest payable semiannually.

Commercial banks in the 1930s were in a position similar to that of other financial institutions—lacking liquidity—and consequently many failed. (In fact, the number of commercial banks decreased during this period from more than 30,000 to about 16,000.) President Franklin D. Roosevelt enacted many new federal laws affecting the economy early in his first term. The Federal Deposit Insurance Corporation (FDIC), authorized by the Banking Act of 1933, restored confidence in commercial banks and encouraged badly needed funds to flow back into bank vaults to provide liquidity for new loans. In 2006, the Federal Deposit Insurance Reform Act merged the two insurance funds, the Bank Insurance Fund (BIF) and the Savings Association Insurance Fund (SAIF) into a single Deposit Insurance Fund (DIF). In 2008 the Emergency Economic Stablilization Act (EESA) increased the maximum amount of insurance for deposits in all federally-insured banks and savings institutions from $100,000 to $250,000.

Organization and Regulation

Either the federal government (through the comptroller of the currency) or a state banking agency approves charters for commercial banks. State-chartered banks outnumber federally chartered banks by almost four to one, although federally-chartered banks hold three times the amount of assets. State-chartered banks may be members of the Federal Reserve System; however, all federally-chartered commercial banks must be members.

Commercial banks try to maintain a balance in the maturity of their source of funds and their loan portfolio. Bank funds are primarily short term and derived from passbook savings and deposits in checking accounts. Because of the short-term maturity of their funds, long-term lending is risky for banks. Most commercial banks focus on short-term commercial and industrial loans for a better match between the maturity of assets (loans) and liabilities (deposits).

When commercial loan demand is high, practically all commercial bank funds flow to meet that demand, and mortgage loans are neglected unless the bank actively participates in the secondary mortgage market. During those periods in the business cycle when loan demand is low, banks place excess funds in real estate debt—either directly in loans or indirectly in mortgage-backed securities.

Mortgage Lending Activity

Larger commercial banks, as a general rule, are different from other major mortgage lenders. Their balance sheets and culture are not organized toward residential mortgage lending. As stated previously, many handle mortgage lending through wholly-owned mortgage banking subsidiaries. On the other hand, banks located in smaller, more rural areas are more inclined toward residential mortgage lending. As a whole, banks increased their real estate lending activity (both residential and income property) by about 50 percent from 1984 to 1992. The growth since then has been as strong. One reason for this shift in emphasis is the capital requirements (50 percent risk weight) for single-family mortgage loans, which are half that required for commercial and industrial loans (100 percent risk weight). Put another way, a commercial bank needs twice the capital to make commercial and industrial loans as needed for single-family mortgage lending.

Real estate financing activity has been very profitable to banks during certain phases of the business cycle. But it has also been very damaging to banks at times, because some of the mortgage loans that were made probably should not have been. In the second half of the 1980s, banks made a major move into real estate. For example, during 1988 to 1990, Citicorp was the largest originator of mortgage debt in this country. However, for some of the banks, this recent experience with real estate lending was not profitable. Many bank failures of the late 1980s and early 1990s, according to FDIC, were the result of poor real estate lending by the banks.

Currently, commercial banks make all types of mortgage loans, but often construction loans on residential and income properties comprise a large percentage of mortgage financing activity. Banks normally classify them as ordinary commercial loans, not real estate loans. The interest rate is generally two to five points above the prime rate, depending on the borrower. The yield and short term (6 to 36 months) make these loans better matched to the bank's source of funds (See Chapter 9—Construction Lending).

Federal Reserve Regulations

The Board of Governors of the Federal Reserve Bank issues regulations affecting real estate lending activity by member banks. A state agency and state laws govern state-chartered banks. These regulations usually are similar to those of the Federal Reserve. Current Federal Reserve regulations allow loans up to 90 percent of value with an amortization of up to 30 years. A bank can lend up to 70 percent of its deposits or 100 percent of capital and surplus, whichever is greater. Commercial banks may have up to 10 percent of real estate loan units in a "basket," or nonconforming classification. Regulations allow leasehold loans if the lease extends at least ten years past the date of full amortization.

The mortgage-lending activity of commercial banks is more diverse than that of other lenders. Banks not only engage in both government and conventional residential mortgage lending, but also are the largest income-property lender. They are the largest mortgage lender for construction loans, and they help finance other lenders, especially mortgage bankers, by issuing lines of credit allowing for the warehousing of loans.

Commercial banks, like other mortgage lenders, originate residential mortgage loans for their own portfolio and for sale to others.

Also, like other lenders, banks purchase mortgages originated by others—mortgage brokers and other financial intermediaries. Additionally, banks invest—some heavily—in GSE and private label mortgage-backed securities. Since 2006, both of these strategies experienced higher than normal delinquency and loss in value than in prior decades due to increased fraud, a decline in property values, and an increase in delinquency.

SAVINGS INSTITUTIONS

The historical role of savings institutions (sometimes called thrift institutions) in the nation's economy is to pool savings of individuals for investment, primarily in residential mortgages. The term *savings institution* here includes several forms of organization: both federal- or state-chartered savings and loans (S&Ls) or savings banks (SBs), which can be either stock- or mutually-owned associations, and either an individual or holding company. Although they may be named differently in some states (e.g., homestead associations, mutual savings banks, building and loans, cooperatives), the role of the savings institution remains the same today.

Historically, thrifts were the largest lender and originator of mortgage debt. Thrifts easily held 40–45 percent of all mortgage debt until the 1980s, when their prominence in residential lending began its decline. Savings institutions have had great difficulty remaining competitive with the mortgage banking model since the hyperinflation period of the early 1980s, however they still originate a significant volume of first and second mortgage loans each year. Thrifts are no longer the largest holder (commercial banks overtook them in 1992), and they are no longer the largest originator each year (mortgage bankers and commercial bankers are both larger). By 1991 the percentage dropped to less than 20 percent, and went below 10 percent in 2002. The dollar amount of one- to four-family mortgage debt held in thrift portfolios peaked in 2005 at $954 billion, but declined steadily to $445 billion, or four percent of outstanding loans in 2009.

Savings institutions still operate in all 50 states, but since 1970 when about 4,700 existed, their numbers have decreased significantly. At year-end 2000, approximately 1,500 (with about 20,000 branches) remained, with total assets of approximately $1.2 trillion, which is the same size as year-end 1985. Although total assets remains above $1 trillion at the start of 2010, approximately 780 thrifts remain. That number is expected to decline further because the federal government does not allow new mutual thrift charters, and stock conversions make them targets for commercial bank takeovers.

Historical Development

From the founding of the first association in 1831 (Oxford Provident Building Association in Frankfort, Pennsylvania), S&Ls spread across the United States and provided funds for the housing growth of the nation. For example, S&Ls provided much of the institutional financing of urban homes for middle-income Americans before the 1930s. Although the number of S&Ls peaked in 1927 at more than 12,000, their contribution to housing finance has been controversial ever since.

The 1930s were years of dramatic change for S&Ls. More than half of those in existence failed during this decade, and more than 25 percent of S&L mortgage assets were in default. As discussed earlier under Commercial Banks, the major problem for all lenders during the 1930s was a lack of liquidity. In addition to the legislation described previously, Congress created the Federal Home Loan Bank (FHLB) system in July 1932 to help address the liquidity problem.

The FHLB provides liquidity during periods of credit restraint for member S&Ls, and serves the industry in the way that the Federal Reserve System serves the needs of commercial banks. The law created 12 regional banks, one to serve each geographic area. The enactment of the Financial Institutions Reform, Recovery and Enforcement Act (FIRREA) in 1989 stripped away many of the functions of the FHLBs.

Another important step toward the development of the modern S&L occurred with the creation of the Federal Savings and Loan Insurance Corporation (FSLIC), as authorized by Title IV of the National Housing Act of 1934. This vital step helped restore consumer faith in the safety of S&Ls deposits and it paved the way for new deposits needed to make new mortgage loans. As mentioned in the Commercial Bank section, since 2006, deposits in savings institutions are insured by the DIF. Under EESA, in 2008 the insured amount increased up to $250,000.

An Institution in Trouble

The 20 years before the enactment of FIRREA (1989) contained periods of highs and lows for S&Ls. The 1970s witnessed steady growth in total assets and profitability, but during the 1980s, the S&L industry struggled for survival. The collapse of many S&Ls and of their insurance fund (FSLIC), with the resulting federal bailout, has been debated in many forums. The experts agree that the primary reason for the eventual collapse of S&Ls was the low-yielding, fixed-rate mortgages of the early 1980s, which, when combined with high inflation, created a negative spread between the cost of funds and the portfolio yield.

The S&L industry attempted to solve this problem by seeking and winning federal government/regulatory approval for deregulation of depository institutions, in addition to creative accounting changes that differed from GAAP (generally accepted accounting principles). Further, S&Ls lobbied for and received regulatory permission to expand their activity into high-yield/high-risk lending. All of these changes occurred without increased supervision. For a few years, these changes allowed S&Ls to improve their bottom line. But these changes proved to be the undoing of many struggling S&Ls.

The Tax Reform Act of 1986 was most likely the beginning of the end. This act eliminated many of the tax benefits from real estate that had made real estate such an attractive investment. As a result of these tax law changes, builders and developers found they could not sell their properties, and many S&Ls that had financed these properties had to take them back. Earnings were once again under pressure, and regulators were starting to look very carefully at earnings and loan portfolios. What they saw was a disaster developing: the S&L industry lost $20 billion in 1989 alone.

The National Association of Realtors sums up the problem this way, "Deregulation and new investment powers made financial and managerial demands that most thrift executives had not contemplated. Speculative investments, a regulatory system which failed to exercise controls, basic mismanagement, and an unprecedented level of fraud and abuse perpetrated by many thrift executives resulted in the inevitable legislative backlash." That legislative backlash was FIRREA, which is estimated to cost the American taxpayer up to $400 billion over the life of the bonds sold to finance the S&L bailout.

Organization and Regulation

The enactment of FIRREA in 1989 completely changed the regulation of savings institutions. FIRREA restructured the regulatory framework by abolishing the Federal Home Loan Bank Board (but not the Federal Home Loan Banks) and FSLIC. FSLIC insurance of deposits was replaced with the Savings Associations Insurance Fund (SAIF), a part of FDIC. The Office of Thrift Supervision (OTS), under the Treasury Department, replaced the role of the FHLBB as regulator.

State-chartered savings banks were non-OTS-regulated savings institutions. Their regulators include their state banking authority and the FDIC. FDIC was given extensive new powers to ensure the safety and soundness of financial institutions (but not credit unions), and was given the supervision of separate S&L (SAIF) and bank deposit insurance funds (BIF). Finally, FIRREA created the Resolution Trust Corporation (RTC) to dispose of failed S&Ls and their assets.

From 1989–2010, the Office of Thrift Supervision served as the primary regulator of all federally chartered—and many state-chartered—savings and loan associations and holding companies. At year-end 2009, it supervised 780 institutions with assets of $1 trillion, and 452 thrift holding companies with U.S. based assets of approximately $5.5 trillion.

The 2010 financial reform legislation preserved the thrift charter for existing institutions, but revised their regulatory oversight. Congress once again completely changed regulation of thrifts through the Dodd-Frank Wall Street Reform and Consumer Protection Act of 2010. As a result, the OTS will merge into the OCC, which will supervise federal thrifts. The FDIC will supervise state-chartered thrifts, and the Federal Reserve will regulate thrift holding companies and their non-depository subsidiaries.

Although many in Congress have long wanted to consolidate financial institution oversight, the OTS restructuring (Table 4.4) is a reaction to the failure and government bailout of three large OTS-supervised thrift bank/bank subsidiaries:

1. Washington Mutual
2. IndyMac
3. AIG

These failures, along with those of the Wall Street firms Lehman Brothers, Merrill Lynch, and Bear Stearns (and later the GSEs Fannie Mae and Freddie Mac), caused panic in financial and credit markets worldwide in 2007 and 2008, and provided the political impetus to reform Wall Street as well with this same Act.

Savings Institutions Today

Over the years, savings institutions have loaned hundreds of billions of dollars to millions of borrowers for home purchases. In the early 1980s when the problem at savings institutions multiplied, their share of originations decreased and never rebounded. Despite the recent thrift failures since 2007, savings institutions remain a major source of mortgage money. The surviving institutions (approximately 780) still place greater emphasis on residential mortgage lending and less on commercial lending, as their balance sheets and culture have always centered on real estate lending.

Today, many savings institutions participate actively in the secondary mortgage market, both as buyers and as sellers. Beginning in 1987, savings institutions often were net sellers of mortgages in the secondary mortgage

TABLE **4.4**
Thrift Institutions by Charter Type

| | | OTS-Regulated Savings Institutions | | | | | |
| | | Federal Charter | | State Charter | | | Grand Total |
Non-OTS-Regulated Savings Institutions		Stock	Mutual	Stock	Mutual	Total	
1985	352	385	1,364	710	815	3,274	3,626
1990	456	684	825	347	503	2,359	2,815
1995	593	744	431	101	161	1,437	2,030
2000	522	607	309	46	106	1,068	1,590
2005	524	504	268	20	71	863	1,387
2009	470	458	243	13	51	780	1,250

Source: OTS, ABA.
© 2010 Community Lending Associates, LLC
www.communitylendassoc.com

market. For example, in 2001, these institutions originated $398 billion in one- to four-family mortgage loans, and sold $403 billion. This development is significant in that it demonstrates a change in lending philosophy from one dominated by local concerns to one affected and shaped by the nation's economy. Many savings institutions formed mortgage-banking subsidiaries to originate all types of loans for sale into the secondary mortgage market. During the 1990s and 2000s, for example, Washington Mutual's mortgage company grew to be at times the nation's largest originator and servicer of mortgage loans.

Because of their historical local focus and previously existing legal limitations on their lending area, many savings institutions did not become involved in either FHA-insured or VA-guaranteed mortgages. Instead, savings institution deposits were invested in local conventional mortgages originated either for savings institutions' own portfolios or for sale. Today, in response to the marketplace, many savings institutions originate all types of residential loans, including government and second mortgages.

SAVINGS BANKS (SBs)

Savings banks often are categorized as commercial banks, and sometimes as savings institutions. Many are more active in commercial banking than "traditional" savings institutions. Many are state-chartered and have mutual ownership like savings and loan associations. Although a savings bank has some of the characteristics of both, it is actually a unique thrift institution.

Historical Development

Like the first savings and loan, the first savings bank was founded in Pennsylvania. The Philadelphia Savings Fund Society (now called Meritor Savings Bank), the nation's largest savings bank, began in 1816. It was followed in 1817 by the Provident Institute for Savings in Boston.

Unlike the early building societies, these institutions encouraged savings by the small wage earner, who had been virtually ignored by the other financial institutions. Savings banks were well received and began to spread throughout the New England states. By 1875, the number of SBs had reached a peak of 674. The SB concept never spread far from its origins, though, most likely due to the development of S&Ls, which encouraged savings and housing, and the development of savings accounts at commercial banks. Today, most of the approximately 400 remaining state-chartered savings banks are located mainly in the Northeast in each state from Pennsylvania to Maine, but are also located in Wisconsin, Illinois, Indiana, Ohio, Maryland, Delaware, North Carolina, South Carolina, Georgia, Louisiana, Texas, Oregon, Washington, and Alaska.

Organization and Regulation

Until the early 1980s, all savings banks were mutual organizations and as such had no stockholders. Beginning in the early 1980s, many savings banks realized that they needed additional capital if they were going to be able to compete in the new, deregulated environment. Today, about half of the savings banks are stock institutions, and the trend appears to be in the direction of more mutuals converting to stock.

If an SB remains a mutual organization, all depositors share ownership and it is managed by a self-perpetuating board of trustees, usually made up of prominent local business leaders. If the SB is a stock organization, then a board of directors manages it, representing the bank's stockholders who own the bank.

In 1979, changes in federal law allowed savings banks to be federally chartered. Before this time, all SBs were state chartered. The majority of SBs is still state chartered, but that may change as federal law evolves regarding capital requirements and portfolio structure. Since the vast majority of SBs is chartered by various states, the regulations that govern their operations vary from state to state. State regulations establish guidelines for deposits, reserves, and the extent of mortgage lending allowed, as well as maximum loan amounts, loan terms, and loan-to-value ratios. These limits are usually similar to those of S&Ls and are governed to a great extent by what the markets require, especially the secondary mortgage market. Like other financial intermediaries, FDIC insures all SB deposits up to a $250,000 maximum.

Mortgage-Lending Activity

Savings banks differ somewhat from S&Ls in that they were never encouraged by regulators to invest a set amount of money in mortgages. At the end of 2001, SBs had 50 percent of their assets in mortgage loans. This level ranges between 40 and 70 percent from year-to-year, with major exceptions at each end, depending on the individual bank's strategic plan. Savings banks have had the authority to make other types of loans longer than S&Ls, and today most make consumer loans and commercial loans. Other assets include corporate stocks and bonds, U.S. Treasury and federal agency obligations, and state and local debt obligations.

In the current mortgage market, SBs originate both conventional and FHA/VA mortgages for their own portfolios. Since the majority of SBs are located in capital-surplus areas, and therefore have more funds than are demanded locally, some purchase low-risk FHA/VA and conventional mortgages from other mortgage lenders, particularly mortgage bankers, in capital-short areas of the country. Recently, many purchased mortgage-backed securities and, like other financial intermediaries, have sustained significant losses in value of these investments.

CREDIT UNIONS

A credit union is a specialized financial institution, however, in recent years their business practices mirror traditional savings institutions and commercial banks. Credit unions are one of the fastest-growing financial intermediaries in the U.S. economy as shown in Table 4-5. Currently, credit unions serve nearly 30 percent of all Americans, up from 25 percent in 2002. In the last five years, total assets increased more than 35 percent while the number of credit unions dropped 16 percent, following the same consolidation trend found in banks and thrifts.

At the end of 2009, the approximately 7,500 credit unions served 90 million members and held nearly $900 billion in assets. Much of this growth comes from significant change in credit union strategy—from a common bond charter to a community charter. Traditionally, credit unions represented a specific employer, industry, or community group. To expand market share, many credit unions changed to a community charter, which allows a very general "bond." The NCUA streamlined this process as recently as December 2009, to make conversion easier. In another departure from traditional credit union industry, many now are active in commercial lending and deposit gathering. For decades, credit unions focused on serving individual needs and not those of the business community.

The largest credit union is the Navy Federal Credit Union, which is—by charter—a traditional, single-sponsor credit union. The sponsor evolved from serving only Naval employees in D.C. in 1933 to serving Department of Defense employees worldwide. In the last ten years, it grew from less than 2.1 million members and assets of $16 billion, to presently serving more than 3.4 million members with assets of at least $40 billion.

Loan performance in the credit union industry now mirrors banks and thrifts. In the past five years, credit union industry total loans and assets increased equally, but the mortgage portfolio increased at least 67 percent, and home equity loans more than 49 percent. Unfortunately, during this same period credit union net worth and loan delinquency suffered like other depositories. Net worth declined 10 percent, and delinquencies increased by at least 150 percent, exaggerated by poorly performing business loans.

Credit union mortgage activity has been a wild card of sorts. For several years, credit union industry trade groups have emphasized growth in mortgage lending. Both the Credit Union National Association (CUNA) and American Credit Union Mortgage Association (ACUMA) actively support more credit union involvement in mortgage lending, developing products, training, and strategic partnerships with real estate finance vendors and realtor associations. ACUMA several years ago targeted a goal for credit unions: 10 percent market share of total mortgage originations in ten years. Despite this concerted effort and an increase in total mortgage lending, credit unions until 2006 remained in the 2 percent range. In a mortgage market favoring most depositories during 2008–2010, credit union market share increased 57 percent in 2008 to 4.4 percent, peaked at 4.8 percent in 2009, and then receded to 4.0 percent in the first half of 2010. Overall, both large, multibillion dollar and small traditional credit unions increased production during this period. Whether or not this represents a new sustainable level for the industry remains to be seen, as during this period large commercial banks, which account for the majority of bank mortgage lending, restricted their lending because of liquidity concerns.

TABLE 4.5
Credit Union Data 2004–2009 ($ in millions)

	Dec-04	% Change 04-05	Dec-05	% Change 05-06	Dec-06	% Change 06-07	Dec-07	% Change 07-08	Dec-08	% Change 08-09	Dec-09	Change 2004–2009
Number of Credit Unions Reporting	9,014	-3.54	8,695	-3.83	8,362	-3.12	8,101	-3.64	7,806	-3.23	7,554	-16%
Number of Members	83,564,678	1.13	84,506,880	1.48	85,753,540	1.26	86,824,354	2.03	88,587,610	1.52	89,931,442	8%
Total Assets	$646,970	4.9	$678,665	4.61	$709,949	6.16	$754,990	7.43	$811,117	9.08	$884,757	37%
Total Loans	$414,265	10.61	$458,237	7.88	$494,335	6.66	$528,555	7.08	$565,996	1.14	$572,439	38%
1st Mortgage Real Estate Loans	$130,095	11.54	$145,108	10.04	$159,682	12.79	$181,622	14.5	$207,965	4.39	$217,100	67%
Other Real Estate Loans	$62,018	18.36	$73,405	15.03	$84,437	8.24	$91,302	5.74	$96,545	-4.27	$92,418	49%
Mortgage Loans-to-Total Loans	46%		48%		49%		52%		54%		54%	
Mortgage Loans-to-Total Assets	30%		32%		34%		36%		38%		35%	
Net Worth Ratio	10.96%		11.24%		11.54%		11.41%		10.61%		9.91%	-10%
Delinquency Ratio	0.72%		0.73%		0.68%		0.93%		1.38%		1.82%	153%
Net Charge-Off Ratio	0.53%		0.54%		0.45%		0.51%		0.85%		1.21%	128%

Source: NCUA
© 2010 REMOC Associates, LLC
www.remoc.com

Historical Development

Credit unions began in Germany during the middle of the nineteenth century. The principal objective of the founders of the credit union movement was to combat usurious rates at banks and to provide consumers with an opportunity to borrow at reasonable rates. The first credit union in the United States was organized in New Hampshire in 1908. Credit unions were chartered under state law only until the Federal Credit Union Act was passed in 1934.

Slowly, the various states enacted enabling legislation until, in 1969, the number of credit unions in the United States peaked at 23,876. Since then, the number of credit unions has declined fairly rapidly to less than 10,000, as many smaller credit unions merged into larger ones.

Credit unions operate somewhat differently than other thrift institutions. After providing for operating expenses and reserves, credit unions return their earnings to their members. Credit unions pay, on average, about 80 basis points more in dividends than competitors' savings products. This is one of the primary reasons for their popularity. Unlike banks and thrifts, credit unions do not pay federal and most state income taxes, a source of contention between credit unions and all other depositories. This competitive advantage lowers credit union operating costs by about 50 basis points.

Organization and Regulation

All credit unions are mutual organizations and, as such, are directed by a board of directors elected by the membership. The members of the board are all volunteers except in situations in which one member from management serves on the board. Management (excluding the board) and employees of credit unions are paid.

Approximately 50 percent of credit unions are chartered by the federal government and, as a result, are regulated by the National Credit Union Administration (NCUA). State-chartered credit unions are regulated by the state and usually have greater leeway in what they may do and how they do it. The National Credit Union Share Insurance Fund (NCUSIF), with the amount of deposit insurance the same as FDIC deposit insurance, insures nearly all credit unions. A small percentage of a credit union is insured privately. Recent, significant losses in the credit union industry forced these funds to increase their insurance assessments dramatically, straining hundreds of remaining credit unions nationwide.

Many state-chartered credit unions have had the authority to make real estate loans since the early 1930s, but federally chartered credit unions acquired that right only in 1978. One recent problem for credit unions is a decline in consumer lending in general and automobile loans in particular, a result of increased competition from automobile manufacturers and other financial intermediaries. In the face of this increased competition and the resulting sea of liquidity, credit unions turned to mortgage lending in earnest in the 1980s. Of course, the tax law changes introduced in 1986 encouraged still other credit unions to enter into mortgage lending.

TABLE **4.6**

Credit Union First Mortgage Originations and Sales 1990–2010 ($ in billions)

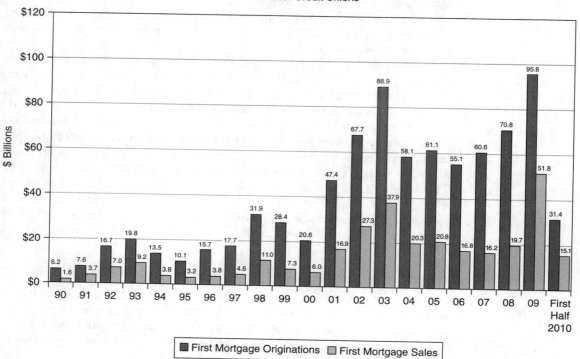

Source: CUNA

Mortgage-Lending Activity

By the end of 2001, credit union mortgage loans totaled at least $60 billion and comprised 40 percent of credit union loans outstanding, a tremendous increase from 6.4 percent of credit union loans outstanding in 1984. According to the data compiled by NCUA, 50 percent of all credit unions offered first-mortgage loans at the end of 2001, and nearly all credit unions with assets over $50 million offered these loans. First-mortgage loans originated were approximately $47 billion, which represents about 2 percent of total first-mortgage originations.

Credit union mortgage (see Table 4-6) loan portfolios continued to increase—tripling from 2001 to 2004. Such an increase transformed the balance sheet and risk profile for credit unions, which historically were weighted toward short-term consumer loans.

In response to this growth, starting in 2003 the NCUA issued several Letters to Credit Unions to highlight the increased interest rate and other risks inherent in mortgage lending.

Mortgage portfolio growth continued to outpace asset growth, and continued a sharp increase of more than 60 percent, to at least $309 billion in 2009. They now comprise 50 percent or more of credit union loans and at least 30 percent of total assets nationwide, with a greater emphasis on first mortgage loans rather than shorter-term home equity loans.

More worrying for the NCUA, the growth in credit union mortgage portfolios occurred during an extended market for fixed rate mortgages. Fixed rate mortgages comprised approximately 60 percent of the credit unions' mortgage portfolios in 1995. This percentage increased over the past fifteen years to almost 80 percent of the $319 billion credit union mortgage portfolio in 2009. Thus, market share growth in credit union mortgage lending is largely through fixed rate mortgages, exposing the industry to a significant level of long-term interest rate risk in the process.

As with most new entrants to residential mortgage lending, credit unions first originated mostly for their own portfolios. A major change for credit unions in the 1990s was that their products became more standardized and, hence, more easily sold to regular secondary market outlets or specialized ones, such as CUNA Mortgage (a trade association/mortgage company that purchases loans only from credit unions). According to CUNA studies, from 1994 to 2008, credit unions generally sold between 25–30 percent of mortgage originations. In 2009 and 2010, both the volume and level of secondary market sales doubled. Some credit unions still chose not to sell mortgages, probably as a result of their excess liquidity.

As an industry, credit union mortgage lending continues to evolve and grow in sophistication. Activities expanded to increased sales of mortgages into the secondary mortgage market, more diverse loan products, and the use of Credit Union Service Organizations (CUSOs) to originate, sell, and/or service credit union mortgage loans. CUSOs are companies owned by one or more credit unions, and they provide services common to those owners and other credit unions. Unfortunately, quality control and fraud became issues in several CUSOs and resulted in severe, high profile losses to many credit unions. However, many credit unions across the country were able to participate in mortgage lending at a more sophisticated level using the CUSO strategy. CUSOs now have SAFE Act licensing issues to resolve, as the NCUA rules that their employees are not credit union employees and must be state licensed. Additionally, RESPA changes may impact or curtail the connection between shared origination responsibilities between credit union and CUSO employees.

PRIMARY MORTGAGE MARKET RISKS

The primary mortgage market involves the borrower and the original lender holding the note as an investment. Through the years, mortgage lenders have learned that an investment in a residential mortgage loan contains several risks, which can be as simple as credit risk (i.e., a borrower cannot or will not repay the loan) or as complex as interest rate risk (i.e., the cost of funding a loan exceeds the yield on the loan). Portfolio lenders must manage the following risks:

- Credit risk
- Interest rate risk
- Prepayment risk
- Liquidity risk
- Portfolio risk
- Collateral risk
- Compliance risk

In addition to the economic functions performed by the secondary mortgage market, selling loans and servicing helps mortgage lenders manage many of these risks. But these activities present other risks as well, described in Chapter 5—Secondary Market, Chapter 16—Loan Administration, and Chapter 17—Selling Loans. Chapter 13—Underwriting discusses credit risk in detail.

Interest Rate Risk

Interest rate risk refers to changes in market rates compared to the note rate. For secondary market transactions, the period of time (for the lender) is limited to the time the borrower locks the rate and the originator sells the loan. For a portfolio loan the period extends to the life of the loan because the lender continually funds the amount outstanding. Funding costs can change with market rates.

The most popular mortgage product is the 30-year, fixed-rate note. However, mortgage lenders do not have a matching 30-year funding source, exposing the noteholder to changes in market interest rates on the funding side while their interest income from the mortgage note never changes.

Depository institutions fund most of their mortgage loan portfolio using short- and long-term deposits, with the maximum term for any deposit generally being five years. Thus, if a depository institution retained 30-year, fixed-rate mortgages in its portfolio and funded them with five-year deposits, it runs the risk that the cost of the deposits could eventually exceed the yield on the mortgages. This was exactly what happened to savings and loans in the early 1980s when, for a couple of years, the cost of funds was higher than the yield on the mortgage portfolio.

Depositories also manage interest rate risk by borrowing from the Federal Home Loan Bank or Federal Reserve, often matching the amount, rate, and term to a specific mortgage product or marketing initiative.

Interest rate risk forced many originators into the secondary mortgage market. Selling some or all mortgage loans to investors transfers the interest rate risk to them or to the investors in mortgage-backed securities. However, originating loans to sell concentrates the interest rate risk into the mortgage pipeline area, described further in Chapter 17—Selling Loans.

Prepayment Risk

Of course, most 30-year mortgages do not last 30 years. Over the past 50 years, the average life of a 30-year, fixed-rate mortgage has never been higher than **twelve** years (during periods of high interest rates) and often no more than five years (during periods of lower interest rates and high refinance volume). In the last **twenty** years, the average life of a 30-year, fixed-rate mortgage has been between three and eight years, depending on the lender.

Prepayment risk derives from mortgage borrowers paying more than the scheduled principal and interest—the exact amount that mortgage notes require to amortize the loans over the full terms. This activity benefits borrowers because it pays off loans quicker, but prepayments force mortgage lenders to reinvest the prepayment funds unexpectedly.

Most prepayment activity occurs when interest rates fall and borrowers refinance existing loans. During periods of low rates, such as occurred in 2001–2002, more than half of the one- to four-family mortgage loans originated were refinances; in 2009–2010, with 30-year lows and a slow purchase market, this level passed 70 percent. Portfolio lenders must reinvest refinanced loan funds into lower-rate mortgages or other lower-yielding investments (reinvestment risk). Selling mortgage loans to investors transfers this risk to the investors.

Liquidity Risk

Liquidity risk includes a number of issues. In high-volume periods, it means finding funding for the new mortgages. In secondary market transactions, it may mean that loans do not meet the requirements of the secondary market or private investors, and cannot be sold without taking large losses. Having mortgage loans that cannot be readily converted into cash presents a mortgage investor with a major problem that can lead to serious consequences, as witnessed by some savings and loan associations in the 1980s for underwriting, and different types of lenders in 2009 and 2010 for fraud.

Liquidity risk also refers to the different cash flows from long-term mortgage loans. For example, the cash flow of a five-year automobile loan is quite different from the cash flow of a 30-year mortgage loan. Financial institutions that retain both loans in their portfolios must manage their liquidity needs in consideration of the slower cash flow of principal from long-term investments.

Collateral Risk

Collateral risk involves changes in the value or marketability of the underlying loan collateral. Inadequate collateral exposes the lender to additional loss in case of default, or can be a source of liability if the property presents a danger or hazard to the public.

Normally, this risk impacts a lender only when there is a default and foreclosure. Real estate values rose consistently since the 1950s, with very few periods of market decline ranging from 5 percent to 20 percent annually and lasting from two to four years. More frequent are situations where the subject property suffers damage, or improper construction requires extensive reworking or destruction before completion of the property. This impacts marketability, as the property may require several months of work (and thousands of dollars) before it can be sold.

Compliance Risk

Mortgage lenders always have the responsibility and legal obligation to comply with all applicable laws. Today, lenders must contend with increasingly complex regulations and more lender liability. Additionally, lenders assume liability for vendor work, third-party originations, and secondary market guidelines, when applicable. Violations can subject the lender and even employees to fines, civil money penalties, and cease and desist orders. More thorough compliance information is in Chapter 11—Compliance.

Portfolio Risk

Simply put, portfolio risk means the change in size, composition, and value of the mortgage portfolio. The portfolio size changes when new loan origination (or loans purchased) does not equal scheduled repayments and prepayments. The portfolio lender then needs to find more funding or reinvest unanticipated cash. As described above, prepayments from heavy refinance periods can reduce the portfolio's size. Strong home purchase markets, like in the early 2000s, grow portfolios quickly and stress the lender's sources of funding.

The portfolio composition changes when the amount of different loan products, purpose, and borrowers change. Originating many ARM vs. fixed-rate loans over time will change a portfolio. During refinance booms, the size of the portfolio may remain even, but the ARM loans are replaced with fixed-rate loans. Adding many loans to first-time homebuyers who change homes in a few years may shorten the expected loan life. These changes can impact current and future interest income from the portfolio.

Before a portfolio lender can manage risks effectively, it first must establish the value of its loan portfolio and *mark-to-market* those assets it identifies as being in the portfolio long-term (not loans to be sold in less than one year). A portfolio's mark-to-market value basically reflects what all the loans are worth right now in today's market. Determining this is a complicated financial procedure that must be performed regularly and is subject to the lender's regulatory scrutiny. The value includes several areas of consideration, each with assumptions that have varying levels of objectivity: credit quality, interest rate/yield, payment type and frequency, repricing amount and date, contractual and projected maturity, delinquency, and local/regional/national economic and financial considerations.

Since the 1980s, mortgage rates have been less volatile (changing less than two percent annually) and declined in a relatively steady fashion over **twenty** years. Since mid–2002, they remained under 6.5 percent. However, at different times over this period the exact opposite problem affected portfolio lenders (and MBS investors): a sudden decrease in rates resulted in massive prepayments. Portfolio lenders needed to replace higher-yielding loans with lower-yielding ones, or see their portfolios disappear completely. Investors who paid a certain price for loans (or the right to service them) never realized the anticipated income from those purchases.

Many economists believe that we are at the bottom of the interest rate cycle (in the five percent range for a 30-year, fixed-rate mortgage), increasing the upside risk. Today, all mortgage lenders (financial institutions and mortgage bankers) are still very sensitive to interest rate changes.

Some Exclusive Portfolio Lenders Remain

The most common residential mortgage-lending strategy today involves selling some or all of current production. Some mortgage lenders will continue to portfolio loans. Some local credit unions, thrifts, and commercial banks have valid reasons for keeping some or all of the mortgages in their portfolios. These community-oriented lenders often have trouble putting all of their deposits to work, so they keep many of their mortgages in portfolio to put that excess liquidity to work. (Of course, as described above, these mortgages should still be saleable so that if a need ever develops, the loans can be sold.)

Asset/Liability Management

Mortgage lenders that maintain a significant loan portfolio have ways to protect themselves against the risks inherent in this strategy. **Asset/liability management (ALM)**, as it relates to residential mortgage lending, refers to how a mortgage lender will fund the mortgage loans it closes and sells, or closes and will keep, in portfolio long-term. For mortgage bankers, ALM is normally straightforward (but not necessarily easy): fund the loans with the company line of credit, make sure the line available can support the volume originated and projected to close, and account for and cover interest rate expense and other funding fees. A significant drop in loan portfolio value can impact the amount of capital that the lender must maintain to continue to operate.

For portfolio lenders it is much more complicated, as the funding source is deposits. Depositories must match funding sources/costs (deposit amounts outstanding/projected and deposit yield paid/projected) to funding needs (loan principal outstanding/projected and loan yield received/projected). ALM typically struggles with how to lengthen the maturity of liabilities (deposits and certificates) and shortening the maturity of assets (e.g., when the mortgages will reprice) and/or indexing the interest rates on those assets. The desired change on the liability side can be achieved by obtaining more core deposits (low- or no-interest checking), longer terms for certificates of deposit, and possibly by borrowing from a Federal Home Loan Bank. In regard to assets, a portfolio lender often tries to originate as many variable-rate loans (both first and equity loans) as possible. These suggested changes will help all lenders, but especially those mortgage lenders that opt for portfolio lending.

As mentioned earlier, the principal danger to portfolio lenders is a sudden, significant, sustained increase or decrease in interest rates. A rise in rates will reduce loan prepayments and decrease the net interest margin between loan income and deposit interest paid. A drop in rates will increase prepayments but increase the net interest margin. Better asset/liability management can minimize these dangers, but not eliminate them completely.

DISCUSSION POINTS

1. Explain which mortgage lenders are most important in residential mortgage lending as originators, and which as investors.

2. Discuss the major difference between mortgage brokers/bankers and portfolio lenders.

3. The mortgage broker is a major originator of residential mortgages. Examine the inherent conflict a mortgage broker faces when originating a mortgage loan.

4. Why are mortgage bankers tied so closely to commercial banks?

5. Which mortgage lender originates the majority of FHA/VA mortgage loans? Why is this the case?

6. How has the number and organization of mortgage lenders changed over the past ten years?

CHAPTER 5

Secondary Mortgage Market

INTRODUCTION

This chapter examines the role that the secondary mortgage market plays in residential mortgage lending and the economy, reviews the major players in that market and their participation, and explains the characteristics of its main investment vehicle : the mortgage-backed security.

For more than 60 years—since Fannie Mae became independent from Ginnie Mae in 1950—loans closed and sold in the conventional secondary market provided financing for millions of Americans who otherwise could not qualify, and funding for lenders who otherwise could not lend. Over this time, secondary mortgage market efficiencies in pricing and securitization resulted in lower interest rates and real savings for millions of homeowners as well.

The years 2001–2010 saw arguably the most significant period of change in the secondary mortgage markets: its dramatic rise, fall, and collapse. The secondary market activity doubled its volume, peaked, and would have all but disappeared if not for the active support of the U.S. government. Hundreds of firms and thousands of workers entered the mortgage market and then left abruptly. Billions of dollars in new capital were invested in the secondary market and lost almost overnight, along with several major players. Many non-conforming mortgage programs appeared and then disappeared quickly. Delinquency skyrocketed from near-record lows to unprecedented levels in just a few years. These unprecedented events deserve an entire textbook for a complete explanation and analysis. This chapter places highlights of that period in historical context.

In the aftermath of the mortgage crisis of 2008, mortgage fraud, loan delinquency, and the massive economic disruption have damaged the effectiveness and integrity of the secondary mortgage market. However, the long-term benefits of the secondary mortgage market to consumers, lenders, and investors are unquestionable. The task ahead for regulators, GSEs, and industry professionals is to restore this function so that the secondary mortgage market can continue to bring benefits to consumers and businesses.

PRIMARY MARKETS AND SECONDARY MARKETS

The distinction between the primary and secondary mortgage markets is not always clear, especially today with so many originations being funded from sources other than deposits at financial intermediaries. However, most authorities agree that a primary mortgage market exists when a lender extends mortgage funds directly to a borrower.

In contrast, a secondary mortgage market transaction does not involve the borrower directly. A secondary market exists when the lender sells a mortgage loan to an investor. The sale of a single loan is a *whole loan* sale; many loans at once is called a *pooled loan* sale. Often loans are pooled together and used as collateral to create a security (a *securitized loan* transaction).

A basic secondary market transaction creates two assets:

1. A sold loan
2. A *mortgage servicing right* (MSR)—the right to service the sold loan

The key concept here is that the sold loan and the MSR are two independent assets. A mortgage loan can be sold at closing, immediately after, or at some point in the future from the lender's portfolio (*seasoned*). The same options apply with the mortgage servicing right (MSR). The act of servicing a sold loan generates servicing fee income paid by the investor to service their loan.

The most common secondary market transaction occurs when a mortgage originator sells a mortgage to one of the government-sponsored enterprises. The GSEs are prohibited from servicing loans, so the seller has several options:

- Sell the loan; keep servicing it, and earn a servicing fee.
- Sell the loan; sell the servicing to another GSE-approved servicer.
- Sell the loan; keep the servicing right (MSR), and hire a subservicer to perform the servicing.

The process of secondary marketing involves the buying and selling of mortgages—either one loan at a time or in pools—and the rights to service them, *mortgage servicing rights* (MSRs). The same origination process occurs when a lender originates the mortgage for its own portfolio, for direct sale to an investor, or for selling the loan into a security as a pool of loans. However, a secondary market sale involves a few additional steps:

- Negotiating the price at and manner by which the loan will be sold.
- Packaging the loan documents for delivery to the investor.
- Funding of the sold loan by the investor.
- Transferring the loan servicing to a servicer (this only occurs if the lender selling the loan does not retain the right to service that loan).
- Monthly reporting and remittance of sold loan payments to the investor.

All subsequent sales of loans (from one investor to another) are also secondary market transactions. Secondary marketing may occur as part of the normal course of business for a mortgage lender, or utilized only during periods of credit restraints. Finally, it is important to note that a large segment of the secondary market activity involves the sale of large pools of loan servicing—sale of MSRs, and not the sale of the loan—from one servicer to another.

ECONOMIC FUNCTIONS OF THE SECONDARY MORTGAGE MARKET

The secondary mortgage market performs these four important economic functions:

1. *Provides market liquidity*—Any originator, portfolio lender, or investor can buy or sell mortgage loans in the market *quickly and at any time* (assuming the mortgages are of sufficient investment quality). This allows a lender who sells mortgage loans to meet any immediate needs for cash (e.g., to meet deposit withdrawals, to fund other loans, or to satisfy other demands). Many investors who have not traditionally invested in residential mortgage loans (such as pension funds and trust accounts or foreign governments) are more likely to invest knowing that a ready market exists if they are forced to liquidate their holdings.

2. *Moderates the cyclical flow of mortgage capital*—During periods of general capital shortage, the regional funds available for residential mortgages can become scarce. Local interest rates may rise in response to this and real estate activity slows down. The shortage can occur from adverse economic conditions or from high loan demand. Any institution operating in the secondary market can purchase existing mortgages directly from a region's local primary mortgage lenders—or purchase securities backed by mortgages in that region. Either way provides additional funds to that region for additional mortgages. This availability of capital for mortgages helps to lessen the countercyclical nature of real estate.

3. *Assists the flow of capital from surplus areas to deficit areas*—The operations of the secondary market allow the transfer of capital from an investor in a capital-surplus area (for example, a regional lender in

New England), to invest in mortgages originated in a capital-deficit area (such as a mortgage in the South or West). Normally, capital-surplus areas are the developed, slower-growing areas of the country—local lenders are able to meet the needs of the local, stable real estate markets. Capital-deficit areas are those with more rapid development or population expansion—the demand for housing credit exceeds the supply of capital created locally by the savings of individuals.

4. *Decreases the geographical spread in interest rates and allows for portfolio diversification*—The increased access to capital for mortgage loans moderates the geographical differences in mortgage interest rates. Capital flows to areas of high loan demand faster, thus pressuring rates downward. In addition, geographical risk (e.g., a large industry closing) is spread to more investors, thus lessening its effect. In theory, consumers benefit from lower rates overall.

Another important (and somewhat economic) benefit that the secondary market provides is the concept of standardization of loan documentation and investment vehicles. This helps make a more uniform loan product for sale on the secondary market, which results in a security for investors that behaves in a more consistent manner. Standardization eventually generates economies of scale in the origination, servicing sides, and investment area of the business. In theory, this lowers the costs to consumers as well.

Finally, selling mortgage loans in the secondary market usually allows an originator to increase mortgage originations without additional business capital, which can lead to an increase in profits. As a lender sells mortgage loans, it can originate more mortgages with the proceeds of the sale and repeat the cycle again, leveraging its existing level of resources and capital.

MORTGAGE-BACKED SECURITIES (MBSs)

Before one can appreciate the dynamics of the secondary mortgage market and the players involved, one must understand the purpose, evolution, and mechanics of the mortgage-backed security—the foundation upon which the secondary mortgage market is built. (Secondary market servicing and MSRs are discussed in more detail in Chapter 16—Loan Administration.)

The basic concept behind MBSs is simple: to provide a way for more capital to flow into housing. Disintermediation among the traditional mortgage lenders in the late 1960s and early 1970s resulted in a shortage of capital for housing, and focused attention on the need to develop additional sources of finance (see Chapter 3—Role of Residential Mortgage Lending in the Economy). These additional sources were from nontraditional mortgage lenders (i.e., those institutions that traditionally had not invested in mortgages) such as pension funds, retirement systems, life insurance companies, and trusts, among others. The challenge was to provide a way for these nontraditional mortgage lenders to get involved in residential mortgage financing. The answer was mortgage-backed securities.

Why Were Nontraditional Investors Afraid of Mortgages?

Nontraditional mortgage investors were not interested in residential mortgage debt before MBSs because of the cumbersome nature of mortgage investments and the high cost for each transaction. As a potential investment, a mortgage loan presents the following drawbacks:

- Diverse state real estate and mortgage laws (e.g., foreclosure, redemption)
- Lack of liquidity (ability to sell quickly) of mortgages
- Lack of day-to-day evaluation of mortgages
- Monthly repayment of principal and interest that required monthly reinvestment decisions
- Unknown maturity (possibility of sudden repayment from sale of home or refinance)

The alternative to mortgages were government and corporate bonds with little default risk, substantially lower administrative expenses, and fewer state-related differences to worry about, so it is not surprising that most investors had little interest in mortgages before MBSs.

What was needed was a way to make mortgage debt a more attractive investment for more investors. The tool used was an instrument that investors were already familiar with—a *capital market security*. An MBS successfully turns distinct, individual mortgage debt into a standardized capital market instrument easily understood by investors and readily traded in capital markets.

Some large mortgage insurance companies that sold participation bonds to the general public used this concept in the 1920s. Neither these mortgage insurance companies nor the bonds they guaranteed survived the Great Depression. Because of the severity of the losses caused by these bonds, mortgage-backed securities were dormant for nearly 50 years.

How Successful Have MBSs Been?

In 1970, the traditional mortgage lenders (not including mortgage companies that sold all their originations) held 78 percent of the outstanding residential mortgage debt in portfolio as loans. By 1995, half of total mortgage debt was in the form of residential mortgage-backed securities (RMBSs or MBSs), and it remains above that percentage. In most years, mortgage loan securitizations comprise 40–60 percent of total mortgage loan originations. RMBSs (Table 5.1) now constitute the largest classification of residential debt, with at least $3 trillion outstanding at the end of 2002 and almost $7 trillion outstanding at the end of 2009.

The MBS structure is also the largest classification of ANY debt in the United States, exceeding U.S. Treasury and corporate debt. See Figure 5.1.

Holders of residential MBSs now span the globe. They include federal, state, and foreign governments and central banks, financial institutions, various funds (pension, mutual, and hedge), and insurance companies. See Table 5.2.

TABLE 5.1
RMBS Share of Mortgage Debt Outstanding by Holder, 1980–2009

Total 1-4 Family Mortgage Debt and RMBS Outstanding

	Residential Mortgage Debt Outstanding	Total Residential MBS Outstanding	Percentage RMBS / Mortgage Debt	Fannie Mae MBS	Freddie Mac MBS	Ginnie Mae MBS	Private Issue MBS	Percent GSE RMBS / Mortgage Debt	Percent Ginnie Mae RMBS / Mortgage Debt	Percent Private RMBS / Mortgage Debt
1980	$969,000	$125,000	13%	$0	$13,000	$92,000	$4,000	1%	9%	0%
1985	$1,533,000	$407,000	27%	$54,000	$100,000	$207,000	$24,000	10%	14%	2%
1990	$2,647,000	$1,046,000	40%	$291,000	$308,000	$392,000	$55,000	23%	15%	2%
1995	$3,510,000	$1,771,000	50%	$570,000	$512,000	$461,000	$228,000	31%	13%	6%
2000	$5,508,600	$2,925,458	53%	$1,016,398	$816,602	$592,624	$499,834	33%	11%	9%
2005	$10,042,500	$5,041,619	50%	$1,753,708	$1,294,521	$371,484	$1,621,906	30%	4%	16%
2009	$11,683,100	$6,731,081	58%	$2,547,733	$1,829,199	$836,761	$1,517,388	37%	7%	13%

Note: Dollars in millions

Sources: RMBS Outstanding data: Federal Reserve, FHFA, Ginnie Mae, Freddie Mac, Fannie Mae; Mortgage Debt Outstanding: Federal Reserve, Freddie Mac, Fannie Mae
© Community Lending Associates, LLC
www.communitylendassoc.com

FIGURE **5.1** U.S. Outstanding Public and Private Bond Market Debt for 2010

Outstanding Public and Private Bond Market Debt – $35.3 Trillion

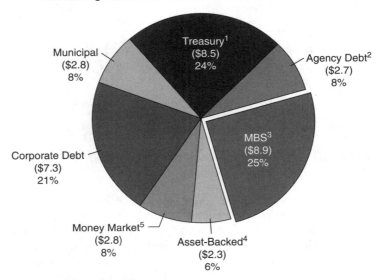

[1] Interest-bearing marketable public debt.

[2] Includes Freddie Mac, Fannie Mae, Federal Home Loan Banks, Farmer Mac, the Farm Credit System, and federal budget agencies (e.g. TVA).

[3] MBS include Ginnie Mae, Fannie Mae and Freddie Mac mortgage-backed securities and CMOs, CMBS and private-label MBS/CMOs.

[4] Includes auto, credit card, home equity loans, manufacturing, student loan and other. CDOs of ABS are included.

[5] Includes commercial paper, bankers acceptances and large time deposits.

Note: Percentages may not add up to 100% due to rounding.

Source: Freddie Mac Securities Industry and Financial Markets Association as of June 30, 2010.

TABLE **5.2**
Mortgage Related Securities Holdings by Investor Group

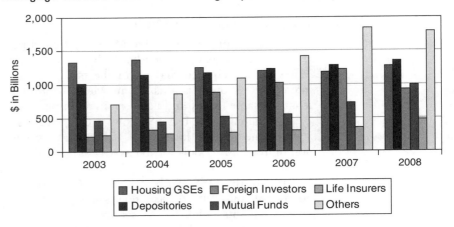

Source: FHFA, Federal Reserve Bank.

Major Types of Residential Mortgage-Backed Securities

There are three major categories for RMBSs, divided by issuer:

Issuer	Type of MBS	Mortgage Programs
1. Government	Ginnie Mae	FHA/VA/FmHA
2. GSE	Conventional MBS/PC	Fannie Mae/Freddie Mac Conforming
3. Private institution	Private Label Security (PLS)	Non-conforming

GOVERNMENT NATIONAL MORTGAGE ASSOCIATION (GINNIE MAE)

Historically, the revival of the MBSs starts with the Government National Mortgage Association (GNMA), or as it is called, Ginnie Mae. Ginnie Mae was not the first to use mortgage-backed securities. Many financial institutions and individual investors lost considerable money with prior MBS instruments in the 1920s and 1930s because the issuer failed. The success of Ginnie Mae MBSs comes from the federal government providing a credit enhancement as a guarantor of the instrument.

The way a Ginnie Mae MBS works is as follows: First, an issuer, most often a mortgage banker or lender, seeks a commitment from Ginnie Mae to guarantee a pool of acceptable FHA, Farmers Home Administration (FmHA), or VA mortgages. Once it receives the Ginnie Mae guarantee, the lender issues its MBS, backed by this pool. The issuer then places the mortgages in a custodian account as collateral for a Ginnie Mae guaranteed security.

This MBS is sold to investors through a securities dealer based on the guarantee that the issuer will pay all principal and interest due even if not collected. The issuer's guarantee is backed by Ginnie Mae, which is backed by the full faith and credit of the federal government.

Types of Ginnie Mae MBSs

The face rate of a Ginnie Mae MBS is 50 basis points less than the coupon rate of the mortgages underlying the security. Originally, all Ginnie Mae MBSs issued required that all of the mortgages in the pool have the same interest rate (now issued as Ginnie Mae I MBS). Ginnie Mae I MBS must be from the same lender and have a minimum pool size of $1 million.

The Ginnie Mae II MBS allows a 0.5 percent spread in loan rates (unless it was issued before July 2003). Single lender pools must be at least $1 million; multi-lender pools can be as low as $250,000.

If the loans pooled in the MBS have a coupon rate of 6 percent, then the face rate of the MBS will be 50 basis points less, or 5.5 percent. The 50 basis points are split, with 6 basis points going to Ginnie Mae as a guaranty fee, 19 basis points going to the servicer as the mandatory minimum servicing fee (lowered from 44 basis points in July 2003), and 25 basis points going to the servicer as excess servicing fee. These fees are to compensate the following:

- The servicer, for its risk in making monthly payments to investors even if principal and interest were not collected from the borrower.
- Ginnie Mae, for its guarantee, backing up the servicer.

Over the years, Ginnie Mae guaranteed more than $2.8 trillion in MBSs, involving at least 35 million borrowers. By the end of 2002, nearly $650 billion Ginnie Mae MBSs of all types were outstanding. This level dropped in subsequent years to a low of $373 billion in 2005, as more appealing subprime mortgage programs replaced the demand for FHA and VA product. When many subprime mortgage programs disappeared in 2007/2008, demand for FHA/VA products grew dramatically, increasing Ginnie Mae MBS outstanding to $836 billion. Ginnie Mae issues rose to more than $400 billion government-guaranteed new issues in 2010.

Until 2010, Ginnie Mae would not issue a guarantee until the security contained a certain number of loans. This structure favored larger lenders (for example, Bank of America and Wells Fargo issued 55 percent of all Ginnie Mae securities in 2009). In July 2010, Ginnie Mae allowed lenders to securitize individual loans—a major shift in focus. This new policy allows small lenders to issue Ginnie Mae securities directly instead of selling to larger lenders who aggregate the loans before securitizing them. Ginnie Mae now has at least 300 approved single-family issuers participating in its programs.

Conventional MBSs

A conventional MBS (sometimes called an agency MBS for the GSEs) contains only conventional mortgages (either fixed-rate or adjustable-rate, but not mixed together) that may or may not have private mortgage insurance. Generally, the issuer of a conventional MBS may remit payments to investors in one of two ways: *scheduled/scheduled* or *actual/actual*.

Scheduled/scheduled remittance means that the issuer (through its servicer) pays the scheduled principal and interest, and any principal prepayments, to investors on a specific date of the month, and may pay principal prepayments in the following month. Since mortgagors typically pay their mortgages on or about the first of the month, this delay in payment in effect results in a slight decrease in yield to an investor. However, this float can be very profitable to issuers based on the amount of MBSs they have issued.

In an **actual/actual remittance** arrangement, the issuer (again, through its servicer) pays all payments received to investors several times throughout the month. The result is a higher effective yield for the investor and a smaller float for the issuer.

Issuers of Conventional MBSs

Freddie Mac issued the first conventional MBSs in 1971 when it sold participation certificates (PCs) backed by conventional loans purchased from savings and loan associations. Today, Freddie Mac issues PCs using loans purchased from any mortgage lender.

Prior to being under conservatorship by the federal government, the Freddie Mac guarantee on its PCs technically was not a federal guarantee; thus, there has always been a slight increase in the yield to investors when compared to Ginnie Mae securities. At the end of 2002, nearly $1 trillion of Freddie Mac PCs was outstanding, (ten to thirty basis points) increasing to $1.4 trillion in 2009.

Fannie Mae was a decade behind Freddie Mac in issuing its first MBS in October 1981, but in the mid-1990s surpassed its primary competitor. Fannie Mae backs MBSs consisting of either conventional or FHA/VA mortgages. By the end of 2002, Fannie Mae had more than $1 trillion in MBSs outstanding, increasing to $2.4 trillion in 2009.

In 1987, Fannie Mae introduced a new concept with its Fannie Majors program, under which mortgage originators could combine their mortgage loans into a multiple-lender MBS. The lender received back a portion of the larger MBS equal to the principal amount of mortgages it had contributed to the pool. This process provided the benefits of geographical diversification to small lenders, and lower-volume pooling requirements. Lenders can do one loan at a time in Majors, as contrasted with needing at least $1 million to do a single-issue MBS.

Both Fannie Mae and Freddie Mac can issue only MBSs backed by mortgages (fixed-rate or adjustable-rate) with a principal balance below their conforming loan limit. This limit rose dramatically in the last 20 years, from $187,450 in 1990, to $417,000 in 2010. Jumbo loans above that limit are non-conforming and in privately issued securities.

Private Issuers of MBSs

Private label MBS securities (PLSs) originally were issued mainly by mortgage companies. For the last 20 years, a growing percentage of new PLS issues come from Wall Street companies and large financial institutions. While PLS works in the same manner as conforming MBS, the guarantee relies on private issuer and the loans involved typically do not conform to Fannie or Freddie guidelines in any of the following: amount, product (usually ARM, interest only, or payment option), underwriting, property, or documentation.

In the 1990s through 2007, Countrywide was the largest independent mortgage company and at times the largest originator of loans and PLS, alternating in this role with mortgage banking subsidiaries of Wells Fargo, Bank of America, and Washington Mutual.

Some private MBSs are sponsored by or affiliated with private mortgage insurance companies that use the conduit concept. A conduit works by channeling the originations of a number of traditional mortgage originators into a single security. Investors find this more attractive because the mortgage pool has more diverse economic and geographical risk. Mortgage insurance companies are interested in sponsoring these conduits because they have the opportunity to provide both primary mortgage insurance for individual loans and pool insurance on the overall pool of loans. The pool insurance enhances the credit quality of the underlying loans. See Chapter 7—Private Mortgage Insurance, for more detailed information on pool insurance.

Normally, PLS represent 10 to 20 percent of MBSs annually, with nearly $550 billion outstanding at year-end 2000. As the demand increased for subprime and non-conforming mortgage programs, the private issues funding them dominated the market in 2004-2007. Private label securities exceeded 50 percent of all securitizations in 2005-2006, with new issues exceeding $1 trillion. Since the mortgage crisis, 2009/2010 PLS new issues have been under 10 percent of all new MBS issues. See Table 5.3.

Conceptual Problems with MBSs

Mortgage-backed securities have accomplished what they were designed to do. They have allowed more dollars to flow into housing. But they are not a perfect solution. Disregarding the recent credit-related events (which one hopes will be a unique period in mortgage lending), there are still basic, conceptual problems with MBSs.

Probably the most significant is their irregular cash flow. This refers not to regular monthly cash flows, but to prepayments. The biggest problem with prepayments is that they usually come at the worst time, from an investor's perspective. Mortgagors tend to prepay more when interest rates fall—exactly when an investor wants to lock in a yield. On the other hand, when interest rates are going up and an investor would welcome prepayments (to reinvest these extra funds at a higher yield), prepayments fall off.

Call protection is another problem casting a shadow on MBSs. The issue of call protection is also tied into monthly cash flow of principal and interest for some investors. Many investors would like to have an issuer reinvest the cash flow rather than have it flow through. In other words, if an investor puts money out at 6 percent and then interest rates drop, the investor will get the monthly payment of principal and interest, but it probably cannot reinvest it at 6 percent. In this situation, an investor would like some

TABLE **5.3**

Distribution of MBS Issuances by Issuer, 2000–2008

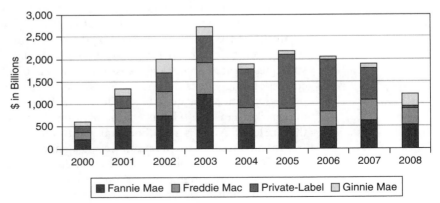

Sources: Inside Mortgage Finance Publications and Federal Housing Finance Agency

protection on its yield. The problem is that providing active management of an investment trust for mortgages in order to protect yield would incur some tax liabilities.

In addition to reinvestment and prepayment risks (already discussed), there are three other items to keep in mind when discussing conceptual problems of MBSs:

- The market price could change, although that's a risk with any type of commodity subject to market price.
- Credit risk of the security issuer (and the servicer) can also impact liquidity and price of MBSs. Historically this risk has been low, but at different times (1981–1982, 2000–2002, 2006–2010) questions surfaced about the ability of some security issuers and servicers to make required payments if mortgagors default. Most recently this risk extended to companies (AIG, for example) that provide credit enhancement to a subprime MBS.
- A liquidity risk exists, which concerns the ability to resell a security. There is little or no liquidity risk with Ginnie Mae, Freddie Mac, or Fannie Mae because of their real or perceived link with the federal government. But private-labeled MBSs are subject to liquidity risk until the marketplace has fully accepted the integrity of the issuer.

Importance of MBS Today

Over the past 30 years, MBSs have been important tools for mortgage lenders and secondary mortgage market players. The use of MBSs increased the total amount of housing financed. Further, MBSs are important to financial institutions because of regulatory capital requirements. MBSs are considered safer than most of the other investments that an institution can have in its portfolio, so their capital requirements are lower than for most other investments. In fact, since Ginnie Mae MBSs carry the "full faith and credit of the U.S. government," their capital requirements are the same as for Treasury securities: zero. GSE MBSs carry a lower capital requirement than for whole loans.

As a result of these lower capital requirements, many financial institutions securitize some of their residential mortgage portfolio. Others hold a significant MBS portfolio as part of their investments, either as a long-term strategy or to make up for a lower loan demand than was planned. These strategies created some serious issues during 2007–2009 as MBS ratings and corresponding values declined sharply. MBS price deterioration began in subprime securities, but quickly spread to AAA/Agency rated MBS as the housing market crashed. However, for at least 25 years, an investment strategy that included MBSs served financial institutions well.

In an attempt to maintain credit quality, the 2010 Dodd-Frank Wall Street Reform and Consumer Protection Act requires federal regulators to set risk-retention requirements for non-agency MBSs by April 15, 2011, with implementation to occur within one year of issuance. It is intended that these regulations be crafted on an interagency basis for uniformity and to preserve the marketability of the underlying securities.

The first agency to do so, the FDIC, created two categories of MBS: GSE and non-GSE, effective in January 2011. The non-GSE category requires the issuer to maintain a five percent risk-retention interest in the security. This "holdback" is intended to keep issuers of some MBSs more interested in the long-term performance of the loans securitized. There is also a "safe harbor" provision that gives investors some protection should the issuing depository fail. These rules do not apply to GSE-issued MBSs (specifically, Fannie, Freddie, Ginnie).

Mortgage economists project one- to four-family residential mortgage originations to average a trillion dollars annually for the next few years. Some economists have predicted that outstanding single-family mortgage debt will continue a slow decline that started in 2007. This level of mortgage financing cannot be met by traditional sources of capital. Mortgage-backed securities (MBSs) provide one of the few ways to meet this demand by attracting more capital from the investment sector into the lending sector.

PARTICIPANTS IN THE SECONDARY MORTGAGE MARKET

Although the mortgage-backed security forms the basis of the secondary mortgage market, the entire industry encompasses much more activity than just issuing of this security. At the broadest level, secondary market participants fall into three organizational categories: federal and state governments, financial institutions, and private investors. Years ago their activities were fairly segmented; today it is important to realize that participants from all three categories are involved in all aspects of mortgage lending and secondary marketing, including origination, as described below.

Often, larger secondary market participants are involved in different secondary market activities at once: originating and funding loans, selling loans, purchasing loans, servicing loans, selling servicing to others. Other participants specialize in one or two areas of secondary market activity; they can be national in scope or have fewer than five employees.

The major participants and their secondary market participation include:

- Federal government (through agencies and government-sponsored enterprises), which:
  - packages and sells conforming loans as a conduit
  - issues mortgage-backed securities and bonds
  - invests in mortgage-backed securities and bonds
  - occasionally originates loans directly with the consumer
- State governments (through housing finance agencies), which:
  - purchase agency-approved loans as a conduit
  - issue mortgage-backed securities and bonds
  - invest in mortgage-backed securities and bonds
  - occasionally originate loans directly with the consumer
- Financial institutions (deposit-based), which:
  - originate, fund, and portfolio loans
  - package and sell loans to GSEs or directly to investors as a conduit

- issue mortgage-backed securities and bonds
- invest in mortgage-backed securities
- service loans held in portfolio and sold to others

- Financial institutions (mortgage bankers), which:
  - originate and fund loans, holding them briefly in portfolio until sold
  - package and sell loans to GSEs or directly to investors as a conduit
  - issue mortgage-backed securities and bonds
  - service loans sold to others

- Private investors, which:
  - package and sell conforming and non-conforming loans as a conduit
  - issue mortgage-backed and asset-backed securities
  - invest in mortgage-backed securities

- Small or independent mortgage brokers, who:
  - originate loans and deliver to other lenders for a fee

- Financial institutions (mortgage servicers), which:
  - service loans sold to others

Also review Figure 4.1, Comparison of Different Mortgage Bankers, on page 83.

Federal Government Participants

The federal government's largest players in the secondary mortgage market are the so-called government-sponsored enterprises (GSEs). As mentioned earlier, the GSEs include the following entities:

- Fannie Mae (initially named the Federal National Mortgage Corporation)
- Freddie Mac (initially named the Federal Home Loan Mortgage Corporation)

In addition to these two GSEs, two other players are federally-related:

- Ginnie Mae (initially named the Government National Mortgage Association), a federal corporation under HUD
- Federal Home Loan Banks (offering the Mortgage Partnership Finance program, or MPF) which are regional cooperative banks, created by Congress and now regulated by the Federal Housing Finance Agency

All four of these organizations are sometimes referred to as the "government-sponsored" secondary mortgage market to distinguish them from the private secondary mortgage market.

THE GOVERNMENT-SPONSORED ENTERPRISES: FANNIE MAE AND FREDDIE MAC

Fannie Mae and Freddie Mac are the players most often associated with the secondary market as they fulfill their fundamental role in the U.S. housing finance system by linking the local mortgage market and the global capital market.

These government-sponsored enterprises (GSEs) are so identified because the federal government was involved in their creation. Both GSEs became private corporations until 2008. For decades, the importance of the GSE classification is that the debts of the GSEs were often treated in the marketplace as "United States agency" securities, even though neither one technically was part of the federal government. Since the marketplace equates GSE debt securities as agency debt backed by the U.S. government, this debt is sold at lower rates than similar corporate debt. These private corporations enjoyed a market advantage during this period. As mentioned earlier, their rapid erosion in capital forced the U.S. government to assume control of them in September 2008.

These two GSEs are also described as conduits since they purchase loans from many originators and then pool these loans into mortgage-backed securities. (Other private investors also purchase loans for their own portfolios or package them into mortgage-backed securities that are insured privately.) Since 2000, the GSEs (Table 5.4) securitize approximately 30 to 55 percent of the one- to four-family mortgage loans originated each year. For example, in 2001 they securitized a combined $1.3 trillion of the $2.0 trillion total origination in each of those years, with their combined figure peaking at $1.8 trillion of $3.9 trillion originated in 2003. In 2009 their volume declined more than 50 percent, to $787 billion of almost $2 trillion in originations.

Fannie Mae and Freddie Mac not only securitize mortgage loans, they are also meaningful holders of mortgage debt and are often referred to as mortgage investors. An example of the magnitude of these two players is that their combined holding of residential debt (whole loans and mortgage-backed securities) has increased from 36 percent in 1980 to more than 70 percent currently. Over the years, their mortgage investment portfolio provided significant income; however, in 2009 credit and REO losses totaled more than $73 billion for Fannie Mae and $29 billion for Freddie Mac.

The significant advantage that Fannie Mae and Freddie Mac enjoy in secondary mortgage market transactions is the result of the magnitude of their secondary activities and their GSE status. To a great degree, these two GSEs have established the various standards (documentation, underwriting, loan to value, etc.) for first-mortgage loans. Their advantages have served thus far to prevent any significant penetration by other entities into the secondary market for conforming mortgages. After the federal government intervened in 2008, GSE market share exceeded 72 percent of all origination.

FEDERAL NATIONAL MORTGAGE ASSOCIATION (FANNIE MAE)

Any discussion of the secondary mortgage markets must start with the Federal National Mortgage Association, generally referred to as "Fannie Mae," historically the most active participant in the secondary mortgage market. In 2001, Fannie Mae was the largest holder of residential mortgage debt in the world (more than $705 billion), and at year-end 2009, maintained a mortgage portfolio of $386 billion.

TABLE **5.4**
GSE Volume and Share of Residential Mortgage Debt Outstanding, 1990–2009

| | Residential Mortgage Debt | | GSE Share of Residential Mortgage Debt | | | | | |
| | | | GSE Net MBS Outstanding | | | GSE Retained Mortgage Portfolios | | |
	Residential Mortgage Debt Outstanding	GSE Total Activity%	Total	Fannie Mae	Freddie Mac	Total	Fannie Mae	Freddie Mac
1990	$2,893,700	26%	$604,434	$288,075	$316,359	$138,486	$116,628	$21,858
1995	$3,719,300	36%	$972,275	$513,230	$459,045	$360,935	$253,511	$107,424
2000	$5,508,600	41%	$1,282,823	$706,722	$576,101	$1,002,420	$610,122	$392,298
2005	$10,042,500	40%	$2,573,118	$1,598,918	$974,200	$1,448,235	$737,889	$710,346
2009	$11,683,100	47%	$3,928,056	$2,432,789	$1,495,267	$1,524,524	$769,252	$755,272

Note: Dollars in millions except where noted; retained mortgage portfolio totals are inclusive of consolidations.

Sources: Retained Mortgage Portfolio data: Enterprise financial statements, 1994–2009; Net MBS Outstanding data: FHFA 2008 Annual Report to Congress, Enterprise 2009 financial statements; Mortgage Debt Outstanding: Federal Reserve Board's Flow of Funds Accounts of the United States, Annual Flows and Outstandings, March 11, 2010; FHFA
© 2010 Community Lending Associates, LLC
www.communitylendassoc.com

Fannie Mae is also the largest purchaser of mortgages each year. In 2009, Fannie Mae purchased nearly $824 billion, about 40 percent of all loans produced that year. This massive amount of money allowed more than three million Americans to purchase or refinance a home during that year.

Prior to 2008, Fannie Mae was a congressionally chartered, shareholder-owned, privately managed corporation. At its peak, it was the fifth largest corporation in the United States. Currently, Fannie Mae purchases residential mortgages from 2,600 or more originators across the United States, including mortgage bankers, commercial banks, thrifts, housing finance agencies, and credit unions.

Fannie Mae's Beginnings and Separation from Ginnie Mae

The importance of an effective secondary market has been recognized since 1924, when a bill was introduced in Congress to establish a system of national home loan banks that could purchase first mortgages. The legislation failed to become law. The first federal attempt to establish and assist a national mortgage market was the Reconstruction Finance Corporation (RFC), created in 1935 and followed in 1938 by a wholly-owned subsidiary, the National Mortgage Association of Washington, soon renamed the Federal National Mortgage Association.

In 1950, Fannie Mae was transferred to the Department of Housing and Urban Development (HUD) and was later partitioned into two separate corporations by an amendment to the Housing and Urban Development Act of 1968. This was done to permit the "new" Fannie Mae to more actively support the mortgage market outside the federal budget. The new entity, named the Government National Mortgage Association, remained in HUD and retained the special assistance and loan liquidation functions of the old Fannie Mae. Ginnie Mae is discussed in greater detail in a later section.

The new Fannie Mae Corporation was to be basically private, though some regulatory control remained with HUD. In addition, Fannie Mae retained a $2.25 billion line of credit with the U.S. Treasury (which remained unused until the recent mortgage crisis in 2007). It also retained the Federal National Mortgage Association's name as well as the assets and responsibilities for secondary market operations. Until its take-over in 2008 by the federal government, the corporation was run by an 18-member board of directors, consisting of 13 selected by stockholders and 5 appointed by the president of the United States.

From its beginning until 1970, Fannie Mae purchased only FHA/VA mortgages that were originated predominantly by mortgage bankers. In 1970, Congress (in the same bill that created the Federal Home Loan Mortgage Corporation) authorized Fannie Mae to purchase conventional mortgages. The first conventional mortgages were purchased in 1971, and today, Fannie Mae purchases more conventional mortgages than any other type of mortgage loan.

Federal Home Loan Mortgage Corporation (Freddie Mac)

The second major player in the so-called organized secondary mortgage market is the Federal Home Loan Mortgage Corporation, also known as Freddie

Mac. The Emergency Home Finance Act of 1970, in addition to giving Fannie Mae the power to purchase conventional mortgages, authorized the establishment of a new secondary market player. Because it was originally a government-sponsored enterprise, it carries the GSE designation. This player was originally intended to provide secondary market facilities for members of the Federal Home Loan Bank System, which meant savings and loan associations. The corporation's initial capital was from the sale of $100 million of nonvoting common shares to the 12 district Federal Home Loan Banks (FHLBs). The charter of Freddie Mac has been modified to include all mortgage lenders; therefore, any originator of mortgage loans that meets the financial and experience qualifications of Freddie Mac may sell to this GSE.

Freddie Mac was a publicly owned corporation similar to Fannie Mae and listed on the New York Stock Exchange with 60 million shares outstanding. Prior to its take-over by the federal government in 2008, Freddie Mac's management was structured identically to Fannie Mae's.

Freddie Mac's enabling legislation in 1970 authorized it to request that the FHLB guarantee Freddie Mac's debts or help it raise funds. This authorization remains unused. Although Freddie Mac was not formally a part of the federal government (unlike Fannie Mae), its ties to the FHLB led investors to classify it as a quasi-governmental agency. As a result, its debt offerings, like Fannie Mae, sold at governmental or near-governmental rates.

In 1992, Freddie Mac made a major strategic decision to begin adding loans to its own portfolio. This action allows Freddie Mac to have the same strategic alternatives available as Fannie Mae during periods of interest rate volatility. For a few years in the early 2000s, Freddie Mac became the largest purchaser of conventional loans, securitizing or purchasing mortgages for more than 50 million homes. In 2001, Freddie Mac purchased approximately $475 billion worth of mortgages from various lenders. More than 5,000 lenders were approved to do business with Freddie Mac. It managed a residential mortgage portfolio of approximately $508 billion at that time. For years this area of investment provided revenue to Freddie Mac, but—like Fannie Mae—recently became a source of significant losses. Fulfilling its secondary mortgage market function in addition to its purchases, Freddie Mac issued nearly $450 billion in original issue mortgage securities in 2009.

Secondary Market Operations

Fannie Mae and Freddie Mac, like other institutions in the secondary mortgage market, make extensive changes in their programs and in the way they operate in an attempt to adapt to changing economic conditions. These changes occur often, even monthly; therefore, any discussion of the GSE's current programs runs the risk of becoming dated quickly. Recognizing that risk, a text without at least an overview of current practices and programs of Fannie and Freddie would appear to diminish the importance of these major players in the secondary mortgage market.

Fannie and Freddie purchase mortgages only from Approved Seller/Servicers that have obtained delivery commitments. To become a GSE-Approved Seller/Servicer, a lender must have a minimum net worth of $2.5 million.

They also require an appropriate level of experience on a lender's part and will periodically review the volume of loan originations and amount of serviced loans. The GSEs want assurance that a lender's quality control system contains written procedures, identifies discrepancies, and takes corrective action.

An approved Seller/Servicer will check online or call to receive current quotes on yield requirements. If a lender decides to obtain a commitment, it provides its identification number and the type and amount of loan(s) the lender wants to sell and the delivery period desired. The Web site/operator confirms the commitment over the Internet/phone, and emails/mails two copies of the written contract to the lender. When received, the lender must sign and return the contract within 24 hours. The yield to the GSE is the net yield; that is, it does not include the lender's servicing fee.

The GSEs also offer **master commitments**, which allow a mortgage seller the opportunity to sell mortgages over a specified period of time that typically covers six to twelve months. Once a seller decides to deliver a specified amount of mortgages to the GSE in accordance with the master commitment, a separate purchase contract is executed for the specific delivery and sale.

How Fannie Mae and Freddie Mac Finance Their Operations

Fannie and Freddie finance their secondary market operations by tapping the private capital markets using short-, medium-, and long-term obligations. Currently, the largest portion of the debt is short-term. At times, they use callable debentures for funding, providing some interest rate protection. Purchasers of GSE debentures include international concerns (largest purchasers), pension funds, local governments, and individuals.

Financing Mortgage Purchases

Fannie Mae and Freddie Mac buy and sell mortgage loans on a constant basis. The GSEs finance most of their mortgage purchases with the sale of guaranteed mortgage securities—MBSs for Fannie Mae; mortgage participation certificates (PCs) for Freddie Mac. Mortgages financed in this way are referred to as the *sold portfolio*.

The GSEs fund some loans purchased for their portfolios by selling debt securities in the capital market.

Fannie and Freddie's Earnings

Although the GSEs produce revenue from three sources, the first two are by far the most important:

1. *Net interest income /trust management income*: The spread between their borrowing costs and the yield on their mortgage investments. This includes the net float benefit or loss, which is the difference between interest earned and interest paid on cash flows generated by the sold portfolio held by the GSEs (Table 5.5) pending remittance to investors. The float arises because of inherent timing differences between the remittance of principal and interest payments to the GSEs by mortgage servicers and the pass-through of such payments to security holders.

TABLE **5.5**

GSE Financial Performance, 2000–2009 ($ in billions)

Year	Fannie Mae Guaranty Income	Freddie Mac Guaranty Income	Fannie Mae Net Interest Income	Freddie Mac Net Interest Income	Fannie Mae Credit Income/ Expenses	Freddie Mac Credit Income/ Expenses
2000	1.4	1.5	5.7	2.8	–0.1	–0.1
2005	3.9	1.4	11.5	5.4	–0.4	0.1
2009	7.2	3	14.5	17	–73.5	–29.8

Source: FHFA, Fannie Mae, Freddie Mac

© 2010 Community Lending Associates, LLC

www.communitylendassoc.com

2. *Guaranty fees:* The management and fees charged for providing a guaranty that the principal and interest will be paid to investors holding their PCs/MBSs on a timely basis. This consists of the fee income or effective spread earned on the corporation's sold portfolio. The effective spread is the difference between the effective interest rate received on sold mortgages and the effective rate paid to the holders of mortgage securities.

3. *Fee income:* From financial and information services such as the issuance of Real Estate Mortgage Investment Conduits (**REMIC**).

Competition between the Major Players

Just as competition in the primary mortgage market is intense, so is competition in the secondary market. The two GSEs compete intensely and directly with each other year in and year out, although certain requirements (such as the conforming loan limit) are the same for both. As discussed above, Fannie Mae and Freddie Mac are now structured similarly and have basically the same business plan. Mortgage lenders should be approved to do business with both of these corporations since, at any given time, the product mix, price, or services rendered may be better at one than the other. Lenders may take advantage of pricing differences on a daily basis for improved loan sale executions.

At the present time, Fannie Mae and Freddie Mac appear to have the secondary market, for all practical purposes, to themselves. But it is important to understand that these two players purchase on average about 40 to 70 percent of the one- to four-family mortgage debt originated each year. That amount may equal about 65 to 90 percent of the loans actually sold into the secondary market. Therefore, other private entities are buying mortgage loans either for their portfolios or so they can issue mortgage-backed securities.

The Federal Home Loan Banks

The most recent government entrants into the action of buying mortgage loans are the various Federal Home Loan Banks (FHLBs). Like Fannie and Freddie, the FHLBs are GSEs, but are privately capitalized and act as cooperatives (unlike Fannie and Freddie stock, which trades publicly). In 1997, the Federal Home Loan Bank of Chicago became the newest entrant into the secondary mortgage market when it purchased from LaSalle Bank a loan used to fund the purchase of a home in Chicago, thus initiating the Mortgage Partnership Finance (MPF) program. Other Federal Home Loan Banks soon joined the FHLB of Chicago. An FHLB member institution approved to sell loans under the MPF program is known as a Participating Financial Institution (PFI), and includes local commercial banks, thrifts, credit unions, and insurance companies.

The MPF program was created to give local mortgage lenders new options when selling first-mortgage loans. Before 1997 and the introduction of the MPF program, local lenders could either retain first mortgages in their portfolios or sell them to the GSEs, following their underwriting guidelines. The MPF program provided a new concept whereby the credit underwriting and origination expertise of a local lender is combined with the funding and hedging advantages that an FHLB has as a governmental agency. When a loan is sold through the MPF, the lender/PFI still retains a percentage of the credit risk of their MPF loans, and transfers the interest rate and prepayment risks to the FHLB. The PFI is paid a credit enhancement fee for its credit expertise rather than being charged a guarantee fee when loans are securitized with Fannie Mae and Freddie Mac.

The PFI/lender can use its own underwriting guidelines to originate, but each loan submitted through MPF receives a Credit Enhancement rating through its AUS based on the risk factors present and resulting potential for loss. Potential losses are separated into different layers: PMI (if applicable), FHLB First Loss Account, PFI/lender loss. Because each lender shares in the credit risk with the FHLB, the local lender has ultimate control over the underwriting of loans it originates.

Since its inception in 1997, MPF programs have expanded to include funding through MPF Xtra and certain government programs (FHA and USDA RHS), while adding mortgage servicing options to give PFI/lenders even more secondary market alternatives.

At the end of 2002, 300 PFIs purchased nearly $60 billion. At the end of 2007, the MPF program had funded more than one million loans totaling at least $166 billion, and sold nearly $40 billion conventional and FHA/VA mortgage loans under the Mortgage Partnership Finance program.

While the MPF program enjoyed great success in its first decade, some FHLBs have experienced significant losses in 2008–2010 due to interest rate risk hedging, like many other portfolios containing mortgage-backed securities. After peaking in years 2003 and 2004 at $114 billion in outstanding MPF loans, the level dropped almost 50 percent to $67 billion in mid-2010. In 2010, only the following FHLBs were actively offering the "original" MPF Credit Enhanced programs: Boston, Des Moines, New York, Pittsburgh, and Topeka, but the MPF continues to be an excellent secondary marketing outlet for its members. See Table 5.6.

The FHLB (Table 5.7) also purchases and holds agency and non-agency MBSs. FHLB banks held more than $440 billion in MBSs prior to the mortgage crisis. In 2010, approximately $150 billion of FHLB investments were

TABLE **5.6**
MPF®/MPP Outstanding, 2000–2010

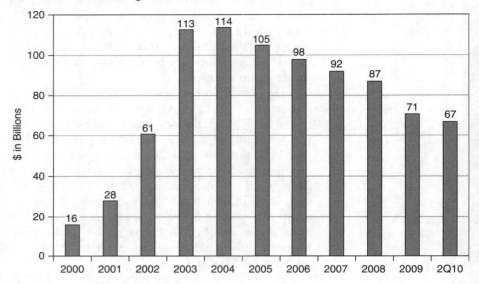

Source: Combined Financial Reports–subject to rounding
FHLBanks, Office of Finance

TABLE **5.7**
FHLB MBS Portfolio, 2010

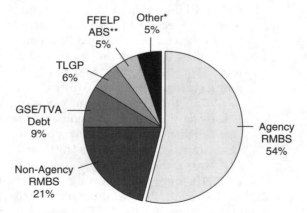

MBS and Other Securities
$195 Billion

* Includes US Treasuries, state/local housing agency obligations,
GNMA, SBA. Agency & Non-Agency CMBS, & home equity &
manufactured housing loans
** Federal Family Education Loan Program - guaranteed by a
guarantee agency and re-insured by the US Dept. of Education

Source: 2Q 2010 Combined Financial Report–Based on carrying value, and subject to rounding
FHLBanks, Office of Finance.

TABLE **5.8**
FHLB Advances Outstanding, 2005–2010

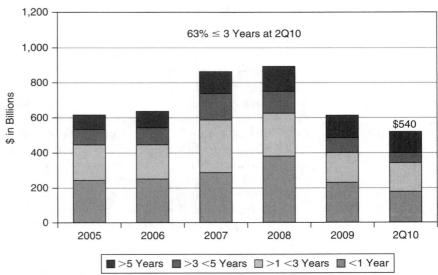

Secured Loans to Members

63% ≤ 3 Years at 2Q10

$540

■ >5 Years ■ >3 <5 Years ☐ >1 <3 Years ■ <1 Year

At 2Q10, 74% were fixed rate and 26% were variable rate

Source: 2Q 2010 Combined Financial Report–based on par value, excludes amortizing advances &
adjustments
FHLBanks, Office of Finance

in agency and non-agency MBSs, accounting for 75 percent of total investments.

The third way that the FHLB provides liquidity to the secondary market is through advances to member institutions. FHLB advances are secured loans at favorable rates. The majority is short-term (less than three years). They help large and small mortgage lenders fund loans before selling them.

This liquidity source is particularly important during sudden refinance booms, and was critical in the recent housing crisis, when private funding disappeared overnight. From 2006–2008, FHLB (Table 5.8) short-term advances spiked from $641 billion to $929 billion. This amount has declined almost 35 percent, to $540 billion in mid-2010, as market liquidity returned. Approximately 50 percent of advances are secured by first mortgage loans; another 17 percent are secured by HELOCs and home equity loans.

GINNIE MAE

In contrast to the GSEs, Ginnie Mae is an actual federal agency under the Department of Housing and Urban Development and thus carries the "full faith and credit of the federal government."

Ginnie Mae currently does not purchase mortgage loans the way Fannie Mae and Freddie Mac do. Instead, Ginnie Mae provides a mechanism for lenders to sell FHA/VA mortgages into the secondary mortgage market by wrapping its government guarantee around mortgage-backed securities backed by FHA/VA mortgages.

GSE Regulation

The Federal Housing Enterprises Financial Safety and Soundness Act of 1992 created a regulatory oversight structure for both GSEs. The U.S. Department of Housing and Urban Development (HUD) kept its oversight responsibilities for the housing mission of the GSEs. Safety and soundness regulation was vested in the Office of Federal Housing Enterprise Oversight (OFHEO). The OFHEO was within HUD, but operated independently of the secretary of HUD. OFHEO had the responsibility of monitoring and enforcing safety and soundness standards for both Fannie Mae and Freddie Mac. Over the years, several OFHEO recommendations to Congress were not acted upon, which later became significant.

Risk-based capital standards require the GSEs to be able to withstand 10 years of extreme and sustained credit and interest rate fluctuation without exhausting their capital bases. Until 2007, both GSEs were considered well capitalized, with excess capital above regulatory requirements. GSE capital eroded suddenly when the sudden collapse of the real estate and secondary mortgage markets exposed hundreds of billions of dollars in GSE investments in subprime MBSs to the same market losses experienced worldwide by other subprime MBS investors.

Congress finally realized the inadequacy of existing GSE regulation. In response to the crisis now unfolding, it reformed GSE and Federal Home Loan Bank regulation with the Housing and Economic Recovery Act of 2008. This act created a new regulator for Fannie Mae and Freddie Mac and the Federal Home Loan Banks, the Federal Housing Finance Agency (FHFA). The FHFA combined the OFHEO, FHFB, and elements of HUD, which supervised the GSEs. FHFA now reports to Congress annually on all GSE activity.

PRIVATE SECONDARY MORTGAGE MARKET

Oftentimes, when the term *secondary mortgage market* is used, mortgage lenders automatically think of Fannie Mae or Freddie Mac or Ginnie Mae. But at other times, a thriving private secondary mortgage market exists, which involves the following players:

- Wall Street investment banks
- Commercial banks
- Thrifts: Savings banks and savings and loan associations
- Life insurance companies
- Pension funds
- Private conduits
- GSEs (Fannie Mae, Freddie Mac, FHLB)—as investors

Since the secondary market's growth in the 1980s, Fannie Mae and Freddie Mac account for between 50 and 90 percent of secondary mortgage market issues annually, and Ginnie Mae five to 20 percent. In the last 20 years, five to 20 percent of secondary market issues were in the form of private label securities (PLSs). This level rose dramatically in 2004, peaking at 38 percent in 2005 and 2006 just before the mortgage crisis. See Table 5.9.

Some reasons for the growth of the private secondary mortgage market include:

- deregulation, and a shift in political sentiment to less government
- government-related agencies borrowing in the capital markets at the same time excessive federal deficits drive up interest rates and thus crowd out some other borrowers
- perception of unfair competition, as government-related agencies borrow more cheaply than private companies
- growth of primary and secondary mortgage markets providing profit opportunities for private entities
- increased demand for less restrictive non-conforming and subprime lending programs verses "outdated" GSE and government (FHA/VA) programs

TABLE **5.9**

Private Label MBS Issuance by Sector, 2000–2008

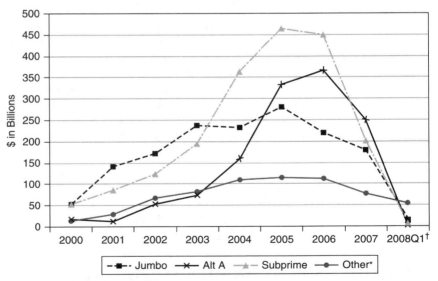

*All other MBS issuance includes MBS backed by second-lien mortgages and MBS backed by resecuritized loans from other MBS.
†Estimated annual volume based on quarterly activity.

Source: OFHEO, Inside Mortgage Finance Publications

- development and growing acceptance of asset-backed securities and other creative financing and credit enhancement tools
- international demand for mortgage-backed securities

Private entities are most active in non-conforming mortgage loan programs. At first, they developed the secondary market for conforming jumbo loans—loans that exceed the set statutory loan limit above which Fannie Mae and Freddie Mac can purchase mortgages but otherwise meet conventional guidelines. Private investors, as a general rule, did not compete with Fannie and Freddie on loans below that loan limit because government-related agencies have a substantial pricing advantage with volume efficiencies, their lower cost of funds, and their government guarantee (perceived or real).

Private issuers also developed other non-conforming loan programs that included one or more higher risk factors (subprime): low or no down payment, delinquent credit, high debt/income ratios, and low or no documentation of income and/or assets. Wall Street investment banks, large commercial banks, and large mortgage companies developed these programs and pricing models using credit enhancements or other "creative" financial instruments to offset the additional risks that these loans present. The validity of many of these pricing models would prove to be grossly inaccurate.

These higher-yielding PLSs attracted investors from all over the world (including U.S. GSEs) and brought billions of dollars into the U.S. mortgage market. With plenty of investor interest, the level of non-conforming mortgages originated and sold in the secondary market grew steadily beginning in the late 1990s.

In the early 2000s, GSEs sought to participate more actively in this subprime market as issuers, but were prohibited by their regulator. Instead, GSEs indirectly participated in the market by purchasing billions of dollars in PLS for their investment portfolios.

In the period of 2005–2007, fraud and other credit risk issues surfaced with the quality of the underlying mortgages in these securities, sparking the mortgage crisis. As a result, funding for PLSs of non-conforming loans dropped precipitously and remains almost non-existent, reducing this market to less than five percent of its activity just two years before. Four main factors keep the private sector of the secondary market at a standstill:

1. Dominance of GSEs via federal government intervention and an explicit guarantee
2. Increasingly restrictive regulations for private-issue MBS
3. Limited liquidity of PLS investors from the economic recession
4. Residual investor lack of confidence and trust in PLS

RESIDENTIAL LENDING AND THE SECONDARY MORTGAGE MARKETS

One important reason for the sharp increase in real estate lending activity since the end of World War II has been the demand for and the supply of mortgage money at reasonable rates. The demand for housing credit resulted from pent-up housing needs, population growth, demographic changes, and the migration of many people from one area of the country to another—for employment opportunities, for retirement, or quality of life issues. Capital accessed through the various mortgage-backed investment instruments created by the secondary mortgage market helped provide the funds for these housing demands and was essential for continued economic growth.

Before 1961, the only originating lender concerned with selling loans was the mortgage banker, and that was the result of necessity. Practically all other mortgage lenders at that time were portfolio lenders and thus were not concerned with selling loans. In 1961, savings and loan institutions were authorized by their regulators to buy and sell whole loans originated outside their normal lending area. Now that the major originators of residential mortgages could participate more fully, selling mortgage loans became more common.

The Depository Institutions Deregulation and Monetary Control Act (1980) completed the evolution. It revised federal lending regulations to the extent that any federally chartered thrift institution could buy and sell whole loans or participations under the exact terms as if originating such a loan.

During periods of tight money or credit restraints, such as existed in the 1970s and 1980s, the capital available through the secondary market provided the funding needed for a large portion of residential lending. In particular, the use of mortgage-backed securities enabled a direct path of needed funds from the capital markets to the mortgage markets.

Secondary mortgage market activity grew and expanded in complexity throughout the 1980s and 1990s. As a result, it attracted different types of participants. Several business strategies evolved. As secondary market activity grew, its significance to both the United States and global economies also increased.

1990s: Period of Secondary Market Growth

Marketing of residential mortgages and the activity of the secondary mortgage market have taken on new importance since the near disaster faced by thrifts in the early 1980s. Other lenders, including commercial banks and some credit unions, became sellers in the 1980s and 1990s as originations exceeded their ability to portfolio loans, and secondary market efficiencies made it more practical to do so.

As a result, the secondary market effectively brought in additional capital to fund growing mortgage demand nationwide. Total residential mortgage debt doubled during the 1990s, increasing from $2.6 trillion in 1990 to $5.2 trillion in 2000. Outstanding MBS increased steadily during the same period and almost tripled, rising from approximately $1 trillion in 1990 to almost $3 trillion in 2000.

With respect to current production, secondary mortgage market issues soon exceeded total primary market volume from a few years earlier. In the first half of the 1990s, for example, for every four mortgage loans originated in the primary market, approximately three were sold into the various secondary mortgage market outlets. This activity indicates a greater acceptance of the MBS instrument by more investors, and more efficient operation of lenders to match this demand. See Table 5.10.

TABLE **5.10**
1-4 Family Mortgage Originations and Securitizations

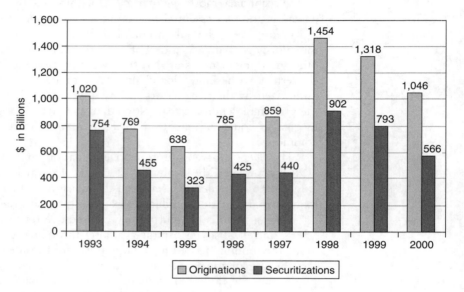

Source: MBA, Fannie Mae

© 2010 Community Lending Associates, LLC

www.communitylendassoc.com

Mortgage originations were more volatile throughout the decade compared to prior decades. Securitizations in all sectors (GSE, government, private) mirrored the large swings in loan demand, an indication that a larger, diverse range of investors was developing to fund these different types of securities issued. See Table 5.11.

Mega-servicers and Mega-originators

The 1990s also saw the maturation of a business strategy that saw limited success the decade before the formation of mega-servicers and mega-originators. See Table 5.12. The larger servicers grew ten-fold from the 1980s to the 1990s, as the total amount of mortgage servicing kept increasing. Data processing issues that plagued large servicers now appeared manageable, resulting in further growth of mega-servicers from single- to double-digit market share nationwide. More efficient processing and secondary marketing allowed mega-originators to double production in one year to another. By the end of the decade, the top 25 servicers and originators essentially doubled their national market share to more than 60 and 70 percent, respectively.

What made this strategy successful? Income from mortgage servicing can have a profound impact on mortgage origination volume. The servicing strategy relies on the following dynamic: collect approximately 25 basis points in servicing income (0.25 percent) on the outstanding balance of a loan, minimize the cost to service that loan by generating operational efficiencies through size of the total portfolio, then use the net income generated in servicing to offset origination expense.

TABLE **5.11**
1-4 Family MBS Issuances

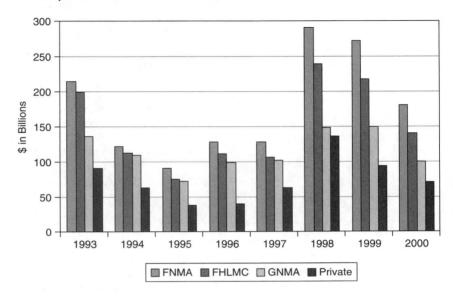

Source: MBA, Fannie Mae
© 2010 Community Lending Associates, LLC
www.communitylendassoc.com

TABLE **5.12**
Market Share of Top 30 Originators and Servicers

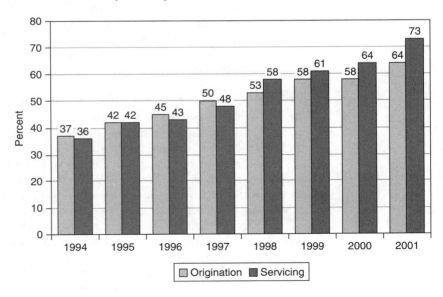

Source: Inside Mortage Finance
© 2010 Community Lending Associates, LLC
www.communitylendassoc.com

While servicing income remains constant (as long as the loan remains on the books), servicing costs vary widely. Cost of servicing depends on many factors, such as refinances/prepayments, delinquency, escrows, and loan product. However, lenders who both originate and service often use the net servicing income to offset origination costs. The Mortgage Bankers Association (MBA) publishes an annual Mortgage Bankers Performance Report that includes origination and servicing data. The average cost per loan per year varies widely from year to year and servicer to servicer (from $35–$225 per loan per year).

For example, a servicer with an average loan size of $100,000 and an average cost of $75 per loan per year would have the following net income:

$$\$10,000,000,000 \text{ loans serviced} \times 0.0025 = \$25,000,000$$
$$\text{(servicing fee)} \qquad \text{gross income}$$
$$100,000 \text{ loans} \times \$75 \text{ (cost to service} = \$7,500,000$$
$$\text{each loan)} \qquad \text{gross expense}$$
$$\text{Net Income} = \$17,500,000$$

The MBA's annual Mortgage Bankers Performance Reports also reveal wide ranges in costs to originate, again depending on a variety of factors: type of transaction, loan products, volume, *"pull-through rates"* (closed/sold loans divided by total applications), secondary market sales, yield-spread, and servicing-released premiums.

Mega-originators with large servicing portfolios rely on net servicing income to offset origination losses. To maintain a constant flow of volume and servicing level, mega-originators may sell a loan at par or even slightly below par to stay "in the market."

The key to the "mega" strategy is to maintain a stable servicing volume through diverse market conditions. To offset servicing portfolio runoff in high refinance periods or very active purchase markets, a large servicer may supplement its retail loan production with third-party originations. See Table 5.13. The small originators or brokers relied on other origination fees to make up the difference for the low yield spread premium paid by mega-originators.

2000–2010: Part One—A Period of Expansion

The first ten years of the new millennium saw rapid expansion, decline disruption, and restructuring in the secondary mortgage market—clearly the most volatile period since its inception.

In the first part of this period, Fannie Mae and Freddie Mac (GSE) securitizations doubled in two years, and the size of their own mortgage investment portfolios grew to unprecedented levels. Private label securitizations (PLSs) also increased dramatically—at least 900 percent from 2001 to its peak in 2005. Although GSE securitization was still four times that of private label issues, PLSs were to play a dominant role in secondary market events after the turn of the century. See Table 5.14.

Total secondary mortgage market transactions for 2001 were approximately $1.3 trillion, a figure higher than total originations in the primary market for any year before 1998. Volume more than tripled by 2003, to $2.7 trillion, its peak,

TABLE **5.13**

Loan Production—Average Income and Expense ($ per loan)

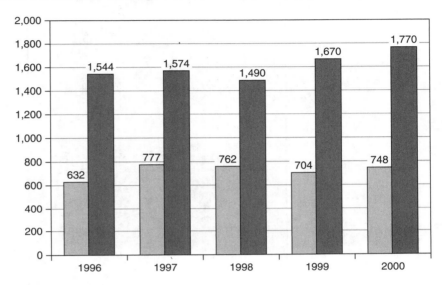

Source: MBA's 2001 Cost Study

© 2010 Community Lending Associates, LLC

www.communitylendassoc.com

reflecting the increase in lending programs available and the growing number of different lenders and origination channels involved.

By 2005, one- to four-family mortgage debt doubled again from 1998—more than triple the amount just fifteen years earlier—totaling more than $9.1 trillion in mortgage debt outstanding. Secondary mortgage market outstanding balances continued to increase to almost $7 trillion, a level at which it has remained since 2007.

This expansionary period at the start of the new century also saw new players enter the secondary market and existing ones shift strategies in all fields: origination, servicing, and investment. Improved technology leveraged the capacities of individual workers and entire companies. New and small companies could specialize and quickly gain access to certain market segments; large companies sought to dominate larger markets. Mortgage production departments—now operating at double the volume than in the 1990s—were meeting this higher level of demand more efficiently than in the prior decade.

Mega-servicers and mega-originators continued to grow and increase market share (and at the same time increase the industry's concentration risk). By 2010, the top three servicers (Bank of America, Wells Fargo, Chase) managed more than $5.3 trillion in mortgage debt of $10.7 trillion outstanding—a 50 percent market share. Bank of America alone services more than 10 million mortgage loans totaling $2.1 trillion (20 percent market share). Wells Fargo services $1.8 trillion (17 percent market share). The ten largest servicers handle at least 70 percent of all mortgage loans.

TABLE **5.14**
Secondary Mortgage Market Originations, 2001–2009 ($ in billions)

Year	Total Mortgage Originations	Total Secondary Originations	Secondary Issues% of Total Mtg Originations	GSE-Issued Securities% of Total Mtg Originations	PLS% of Total Mtg Originations	GSE-Issued Securities	GSE% of Total Secondary	Private Label Securities (PLS)	PLS% of Total Secondary	Refinance/ Purchase
2001	2,243	$1,063	47%	44%	3%	$997	94%	$66	6%	57%
2002	2,854	$1,450	51%	47%	4%	$1,329	92%	$121	8%	62%
2003	3,812	$2,074	54%	48%	6%	$1,839	89%	$235	11%	66%
2004	2,773	$1,332	48%	32%	16%	$900	68%	$432	32%	53%
2005	3,003	$1,453	48%	30%	18%	$900	62%	$553	38%	50%
2006	2,730	$1,309	48%	32%	16%	$879	67%	$430	33%	49%
2007	2,306	$1,116	48%	44%	5%	$1,012	91%	$104	9%	51%
2008	1,508	$787	52%	52%	0%	$787	100%	$0	0%	52%
2009	1,815	$1,750	96%	94%	3%	$1,700	97%	$50	3%	67%

Sources: FHFA, Fannie Mae, Freddie Mac, CoreLogic, LLC, MBA.

© 2010 Community Lending Associates, LLC

www.communitylendassoc.com

A similar dynamic occurred on the origination side. In 2007, the top five mortgage originators (Countrywide, Wells Fargo, Chase, Bank of America, and Citi) originated a total of $1.2 trillion—more than 50 percent of total originations. See Table 5.15 for a list of the Top 25 Mortgage Originators. Mortgage brokers played a vital role in feeding mega-originators. Increased competition to originate loans resulted in reduced income from loan sales, but higher origination fee income.

In addition to the mega-originator/mega-servicer dynamic, the period of 2001–2007 (Table 5.16) saw a rapid increase in the origination of Alt A and subprime mortgage products. PLS volume in subprime, jumbo, and Alt-A programs increased almost ten times in five years. From 2000–2007, funding from foreign investors tripled to represent more than 18 percent of PLS investment.

The mega-originator/servicer business model applied here, too, with a concentration of originators specializing in these products. Four of the top five mortgage originators in 2007 were also top ten subprime originators, PLS issuers, and servicers as shown in Table 5.17.

2000–2010: Part Two—Rapid Decline

Sadly, the secondary mortgage market collapse was just as abrupt as its rise, and the impact of its decline more severe, helping to push the United States economy into its worst economic period in 70 years. The scope of financial loss and its effects shook economies worldwide.

TABLE **5.15**

Historical Concentration of Top 25 Mortgage Originators

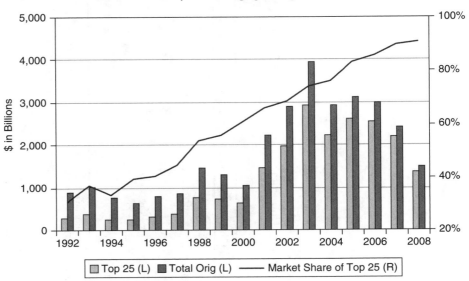

Source: FHFA, Inside Mortgage Finance Publications

TABLE **5.16**
Agency and Non-Prime Originations and Securitizations, 2001–2006 ($ in billions)

Year	Sub-prime			Alt-A			Jumbo			Agency		
	Origination	Issuance	Ratio	Origination	Issuance	Ratio	Origination	Issuance	Ratio	Origination	Issuance	Ratio
2001	$190.00	$87.10	46%	$60.00	$11.40	19%	$430.00	$142.20	33%	$1,433.00	$1,087.60	76%
2002	$231.00	$122.70	53%	$68.00	$53.50	79%	$576.00	$171.50	30%	$1,898.00	$1,442.60	76%
2003	$335.00	$195.00	58%	$85.00	$74.10	87%	$655.00	$237.50	36%	$2,690.00	$2,130.90	79%
2004	$540.00	$362.63	67%	$200.00	$158.60	79%	$515.00	$233.40	45%	$1,345.00	$1,018.60	76%
2005	$625.00	$465.00	74%	$380.00	$332.30	87%	$570.00	$280.70	49%	$1,180.00	$964.80	82%
2006	$600.00	$448.60	75%	$400.00	$365.70	91%	$480.00	$219.00	46%	$1,040.00	$904.60	87%

Notes: Jumbo origination includes non-agency prime. Agency origination includes conventional/conforming and FHA/VA loans. Agency issuance GNMA, FHLMC, and FNMA. Figures are in billions of USD.

Source: Federal Reserve Bank of New York, Inside Mortgage Finance (2007).

TABLE **5.17**

Top Subprime Originators, PLS Issuers, and Servicers, 2005–2006

		Top Subprime Mortgage Originators			
		2006		2005	
Rank	Lender	Volume ($b)	Share (%)	Volume ($b)	%Change
1	HSBC	$52.8	8.8%	$58.6	−9.9%
2	New Century Financial	$51.6	8.6%	$52.7	−2.1%
3	Countrywide	$40.6	6.8%	$44.6	−9.1%
4	CitiGroup	$38.0	6.3%	$20.5	85.5%
5	WMC Mortgage	$33.2	5.5%	$31.8	4.3%
6	Fremont	$32.3	5.4%	$36.2	−10.9%
7	Ameriquest Mortgage	$29.5	4.9%	$75.6	−61.0%
8	Option One	$28.8	4.8%	$40.3	−28.6%
9	Wells Fargo	$27.9	4.6%	$30.3	−8.1%
10	First Franklin	$27.7	4.6%	$29.3	−5.7%
	Top 25	$543.2	90.5%	$604.9	−10.2%
	Total	$600.0	100.0%	$664.0	−9.8%

		Top Subprime MBS Issuers			
		2006		2005	
Rank	Lender	Volume ($b)	Share (%)	Volume ($b)	%Change
1	Countrywide	$38.5	8.6%	$38.1	1.1%
2	New Century	$33.9	7.6%	$32.4	4.8%
3	Option One	$31.3	7.0%	$27.2	15.1%
4	Fremont	$29.8	6.6%	$19.4	53.9%
5	Washington Mutual	$28.8	6.4%	$18.5	65.1%
6	First Franklin	$28.3	6.3%	$19.4	45.7%
7	Residential Funding Corp	$25.9	5.8%	$28.7	−9.5%
8	Lehman Brothers	$24.4	5.4%	$35.3	−30.7%
9	WMC Mortgage	$21.6	4.8%	$19.6	10.5%
10	Ameriquest	$21.4	4.8%	$54.2	−60.5%
	Top 25	$427.6	95.3%	$417.6	2.4%
	Total	$448.6	100.0%	$508.0	−11.7%

TABLE **5.17** (*Continued*)

		2006		2005	
Rank	Lender	Volume ($b)	Share (%)	Volume ($b)	%Change
1	Countrywide	$119.1	9.6%	$120.6	1.3%
2	JP MorganChase	$83.8	6.8%	$67.8	23.6%
3	CitiGroup	$80.1	6.5%	$47.3	39.8%
4	Option One	$69.0	5.6%	$79.5	−13.2%
5	Ameriquest	$60.0	4.8%	$75.4	−20.4%
6	Ocwen Financial Corp	$52.2	4.2%	$42.0	24.2%
7	Wells Fargo	$51.3	4.1%	$44.7	14.8%
8	Homecomings Financial	$49.5	4.0%	$55.2	−10.4%
9	HSBC	$49.5	4.0%	$43.8	13.0%
10	Litton Loan Servicing	$47.0	4.0%	$42.0	16.7%
	Top 30	$1,105.7	89.2%	$1,057.8	4.5%
	Total	$1,240	100.0%	$1,200	3.3%

Top Subprime Mortgage Servicers

Source: Federal Reserve Bank of NY, Inside Mortgage Finance (2007)

GSE volume fell from a peak of more than $2 trillion in 2003 to less than $800 million in 2008. In the same period, the PLS market literally disappeared as well: from $900 billion to just $300 *million*. As a result, major financial investment banks failed and hundreds of secondary market lenders disappeared. Many foreign governments, private and institutional investors, and financial markets around the world that profited from its rise suffered greater losses when it fell.

Rapidly rising delinquency in recently originated MBSs caused those investments to decline in value, and investor funding for new issues to disappear. Fannie Mae alone saw its non-performing loans increase from $14 billion in 2005 to $119 billion in 2008. GSE losses spiked in their MBS holdings and loan portfolio, causing Fannie Mae to end the year with a net worth deficit of $15 billion; Freddie Mac's net worth deficit was at least $30 billion.

PLS loan performance was worse, compared to GSE production. MBA delinquency surveys show a rapid rise in subprime serious delinquency (Table 5.18) to unprecedented levels:

1Q2006	6%
1Q2007	8%
1Q2008	16%
1Q2009	25%
1Q2010	30%

TABLE **5.18**

Subprime Mortgage Serious Delinquency Rate, 2008 (Percent)

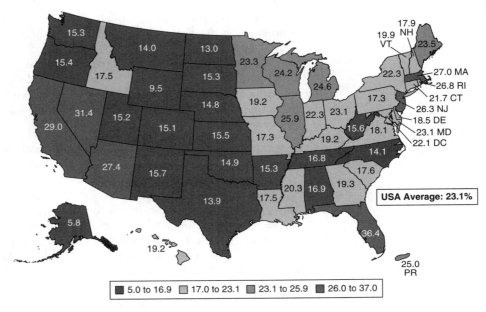

Source: FHFA, Mortgage Bankers Association

The difference in GSE vs. PLS loan delinquency came as no surprise to most industry professionals. An FHFA study of $10.6 trillion in mortgage loans originated from 2001–2008 compared risk features of both, and revealed the following significant underwriting differences:

Risk Factor	GSE	PLS
FICO < 620	5%	32%
LTV > 80%	18%	34%
ARM	12%	30%
Total Loans Reviewed (trillions)	$8.6	$2.0
Delinquency (90+ days)—Fixed	5%	20%
Delinquency (90+ days)—ARM	10%	30%

As loan delinquency rose during 2005–2007, further loan-level investigation uncovered severe deficiencies throughout the entire secondary mortgage market system of origination and securitization. These deficiencies include:

- undetected mortgage fraud committed by all parties directly and indirectly involved in residential lending transactions: consumers, realtors, originators, processors, underwriters, closers, appraisers, closing agents, lenders, secondary market managers, quality control analysts, credit rating agencies, etc.

- poor secondary market pricing models by GSEs, private conduits, and government agencies that did not adequately reflect the risks involved in many underwriting guidelines or loan product features
- lax or inadequate regulation of companies originating loans for secondary market sales who were unable to repurchase deficient closed loans
- neglect on the part of credit rating agencies that awarded prime or near-prime ratings on many security issues, but did not complete due diligence properly, or at all

These systemic deficiencies shook the financial markets worldwide during 2007. As mortgage delinquencies on MBSs rose, the values of mortgage-backed securities fell. Values then plummeted upon discovery of widespread loan fraud, ineffective loan quality control, and poor securities credit rating systems in both private and GSE issues. In cases of fraud and underwriting errors, private issuers, GSEs, and Ginnie Mae increased the buyback option in their master commitments with their originators. Many capitalized originators (i.e., brokers and mortgage companies) could not handle the buyback orders and went out of business, while others lost their secondary market outlets for active loan programs.

In 2007, worried investors stopped investing in secondary mortgage market transactions, and funding for many mortgage programs disappeared. With the housing market declining and the U.S. economy stalling in a recession, a liquidity crisis loomed.

2008: Crisis in the Secondary Mortgage Market

The United States government took unprecedented, aggressive actions, starting in 2008, to stabilize and support the mortgage-backed securities market and the secondary market GSEs. Two large investment banks heavily involved in the secondary mortgage market failed (Bear Stearns and Lehman Brothers), as did a major insurer of mortgage-related securities (AIG), requiring hundreds of billions of dollars of government intervention and assistance. The Housing and Economic Recovery Act of 2008 authorized the U.S. Treasury to actively purchase the GSEs' debt, equity, and mortgage-backed-securities (MBSs). The FHLB regulator authorized those banks to double their MBS holdings overall to 600 percent of capital, with holdings over 300 percent required to be in GSE-sponsored MBS and Ginnie Mae. As a result, the federal government became the most active purchaser of GSE MBSs, and at one point held in its portfolio more than *$1.4 trillion* in GSE-issued mortgage-backed securities.

The secondary mortgage market shifted fundamentally in September 2008, when the U.S. government placed in conservatorship the two GSEs, Fannie Mae and Freddie Mac, to avoid further deterioration of their financial condition and destabilization of the U.S. housing and financial markets. The technical impact of these actions and events that unfolded during this dynamic period is still being studied, and their long-term effects are not completely understood.

Although securitizations fell almost 30 percent from 2007 to 2008, the level of GSE-issued MBSs held steady, Ginnie Mae MBSs increased, and PLS funding disappeared—falling from more than $670 billion in 2007 to $45 billion in 2008.

In 2009, mortgage delinquency almost doubled for Fannie Mae, to $216 billion, with at least five percent of its portfolio seriously delinquent (over 90 days past due). Freddie Mac experienced similar increases in seriously delinquent loans (3.9 percent), as did FHA (9.4 percent) and VA (5.5 percent) programs, as did many private investor programs throughout the industry, according to the MBA.

Total originations in 2009 increased more than 30 percent, to reach $2.0 trillion, due to historically low rates and an active year for refinances. GSE- and government-issued MBSs increased to $5.3 trillion outstanding and 95 percent of 2009 securitizations, with FHA/VA activity increasing to 25 percent of originations. PLS did not rebound and remained at three percent of all MBS volume, with very limited funding for subprime and jumbo programs extending since late 2007.

Despite a good year in new securitization issues, the GSEs suffered another year of losses due to continued decline in the values of MBS holdings and poor performance in their loan portfolios. At year-end 2009, Fannie Mae lost $74 billion; Freddie Mac lost at least $22 billion.

Fraud in the Secondary Mortgage Market

One would be naïve to think that lending fraud is a recent phenomenon. Although fraud in secondary market transactions is not common, it does happen. Sadly, a series of major events since 2000 impacted an essential element of lending and of securities trading: the element of trust.

The first major incident occurred in 2003 when a massive accounting scandal surfaced involving Freddie Mac, which later paid fines totaling more than $175 million and a settlement to shareholders of $410 million. In 2004, accounting irregularities were uncovered at Fannie Mae, which later paid a fine of $400 million. These irresponsible actions were totally within the control of senior executives at the GSEs, who separately paid more than $50 million in fines and penalties.

These events damaged the integrity of these two organizations. Investors worldwide rely upon their reputations and their position as the foundation of the secondary mortgage market for which billions of dollars trade annually. In retrospect, they seem to foreshadow how the entire secondary market process had been tainted by greed for individual profit or gain.

The second major area where trust was violated occurred throughout the lending and securitization process. Although mortgage fraud is always present in a small percentage of primary and secondary mortgage market transactions, its prevalence increased dramatically during this period, mainly in the less regulated sectors involving mortgage brokers and private investors. The national media reported at least weekly a flow of fraudulent acts either initiated or aided by origination personnel and lenders, and continued on by issuers of securities and their rating agencies. Vendors and "rings" of organized fraudsters conspired to cheat borrowers, lenders, or investors out of millions of dollars in several fraud schemes nationwide.

Rising delinquencies helped alert the industry to the scope of the problem, as they sparked unprecedented efforts to detect and contain both transactional and systemic fraud. Still, the discovery of such widespread occurrences damaged the integrity of the entire secondary market process.

A third, final area of mistrust occurred by companies and individuals knowingly engaging in predatory lending practices as part of their normal business operations, causing further erosion of trust in the mortgage lending industry. Entire businesses encouraged repeated refinancing, which provided no benefit to the consumer but generated fees for the company. They also placed borrowers in subprime loan programs to receive higher compensation, when the borrower qualified for better terms. Other lenders steered consumers into risky loan products with the intent of acquiring the property through loan default.

How can one measure or quantify the short-term and long-term effects of these events or its duration? How do you "calculate" and compensate for the emotional and social trauma that delinquency and foreclosure brings to individuals and families who were victims of fraud and predatory lending? What is appropriate punishment for individuals who used the secondary mortgage market mechanism as a stage for their criminal activity? What steps are necessary to restore trust in the system and prevent another occurrence?

In 2010, the FBI investigated more than 3,000 mortgage fraud cases nationwide, which is more than double the number from just two years earlier. Mortgage fraud takes many forms in both the origination and secondary market environment, explained in more detail in Chapter 15. Although GSE, government, and private issuers attempt to address this problem through their underwriting and servicing guidelines and requirements, certain types of fraud remain difficult to address. From the secondary mortgage market perspective, the biggest fraud concerns are systemic ones:

- third-party originations, where the lender does not have complete control over the origination process
- credit rating agency due diligence and when examining the underlying loans in the MBS
- strength of the guarantee of the institution issuing the private-label security

After widespread fraud issues were exposed in 2004–2007, the major players in the secondary market (Fannie, Freddie, FHA) raised the industry standards for pre-closing quality control and post-closing due diligence. They also increased lender/originator liability in the representations and warranties areas of secondary market written commitment.

Many state regulators increased bond and net worth requirements for state-licensed lenders and originators. Federal and state government agencies also passed several rules and regulations (described in more detail in Chapter 11—Compliance), increased consumer protection, and improved overall quality of secondary market transactions, which included these changes:

- increase licensing requirements for mortgage loan originators and mortgage lenders
- permanently ban from the industry those who commit a financial felony
- strengthen the independence of the appraisal function
- modify and restrict the compensation structure involved when originating loans and securities in secondary market

Over time, these combined steps will help rebuild investor confidence in the entire secondary mortgage market mechanism.

POST-CRISIS ISSUES IN THE SECONDARY MORTGAGE MARKET

Restoring the integrity of the secondary mortgage market is a huge concern. Other important secondary market issues resulting from the recent crisis include: more restrictive underwriting guidelines, elimination or restriction in third-party origination, a revision in GSE guarantee fees, compensation and risk retention throughout the secondary market process, and resolution or restructure of the GSEs.

More restrictive guidelines on several risk features of loans purchased by the GSEs resulted in an increase in loan quality from prior years. Average LTV was lower, credit scores were higher, and fewer loans had risk layering characteristics (see Underwriting—Chapter 13). GSEs also increased risk-based pricing fees nationwide for the following risk characteristics, in effect making future borrowers pay for past underwriting and pricing mistakes: credit scores, cash out refinance LTVs, and subordinate financing.

As a result of the higher loan quality, GSE guaranty fees declined in 2009 from 25 to 22 basis points to reflect the higher quality and longer loan life expected, but only a few lenders will benefit from them. More favorable pricing applies to the largest lenders, leaving hundreds of small-to-medium sized lenders at a market disadvantage. Industry experts will argue that this situation represents an unfair advantage for large lenders, since the federal government controls the two GSEs and they hold a monopoly of more than 70 percent of annual originations. The GSEs get most of their volume from the top ten sellers. This scenario may discriminate against all but twenty or thirty companies nationwide.

In May 2010, HUD announced it would no longer accept loans directly from brokers; Fannie Mae and Freddie Mac in policy and practice increased the responsibility of approved sellers for loans they do not originate directly.

Additionally, regulatory changes in 2010 discontinue compensating originators differently for high-risk loans and hold lenders and MBS issuers more accountable for loan performance after the sale of the loan or security. The Federal Reserve updated Truth in Lending to restrict payment of yield-spread premiums and limit payment based on volume only (see Chapter 11—Compliance).

The Dodd – Frank Wall Street Reform and Consumer Protection Act requires issuers of non-GSE/government-backed MBSs to keep a percentage of the security on reserve in case of poor performance (described in more detail earlier in this chapter). Dodd-Frank also requires that mortgage banking subsidiaries and affiliates of federally chartered banks and thrifts now be subject to state compliance laws and licensing requirements. Dodd-Frank will have a large impact on the secondary market going forward as well, as many specific regulations in other areas are yet to be determined.

Clearly, these policy changes on guarantee fees, broker/third-party origination, and originator compensation/risk retention have the effect of restricting business practices for many lenders and reducing the choices that consumers have in obtaining mortgage financing. Their long-term impact on market competition for lenders, and impact on mortgage pricing for consumers, is unknown.

Despite the recent mortgage and housing crisis, secondary market activity still provides the foundation for residential mortgage lending in this country. It is so critical to housing finance, the federal government already has invested more than $148 billion to support its two giant pillars, Fannie Mae and Freddie Mac. The Federal Housing Finance Agency estimates total support to re-capitalize and re-establish the GSEs will cost $224–$360 billion; an S&P estimate places this number around $700 billion.

Most industry and economic experts agree that a viable secondary mortgage market plays a central role in housing financing and the economy. The secondary mortgage market—and the exit strategy for the government's dominant role in subsidizing it—is at the center of the current debate on financial reform. Resolving its future may be one of the most critical financial and economic issues our country faces in the next decade.

DISCUSSION POINTS

1. What economic functions are performed by the secondary mortgage market?
2. Identify the major players in the secondary market and their specific roles.
3. What types of mortgage loans will Fannie Mae and Freddie Mac buy?
4. What factors helped cause the secondary mortgage market crisis in 2008?
5. What are credit enhancements? Why are they important in today's market?
6. What does *recourse* mean? How can a lender avoid this risk?
7. What are mortgage-backed securities? Why are they so important?
8. What are the important differences between GSE-issued and privately-issued MBSs?

CHAPTER 6

Conventional Lending

INTRODUCTION

The recent explosion of different mortgage programs changed the industry and the way consumers finance a home. One reason for the growth over the past 20 years is an overall increase in housing demand and along with it the variety of financing situations involved. Additionally, in the last 15 years, the number and different types of secondary mortgage market investors has grown, bringing more capital to different areas of the housing finance market. This combination allowed lenders to develop financing programs in many different areas, from first-time homebuyers to consumers with prior credit difficulties to real estate investors to families moving to a larger, more expensive home. More mortgage programs helped increase national homeownership levels and enable more consumers to realize their dreams—concrete financial, social, and personal gains for the country and for individuals.

However, having so many mortgage programs came at a cost to some people as well. Mortgage delinquency rose not from normal financial hardships, but from borrowers having the wrong mortgage program for their financial situation or from not understanding their mortgage program. While industry experts can debate the reasons for these shortcomings, clearly there are many more, complex mortgage programs available today than 20 years ago. As a result, there is more confusion among lending personnel, consumers, and even regulators as to exactly how all these mortgage programs work and the different terms used to describe them.

Today's mortgage origination personnel face a more difficult task to explain clearly the many financing choices available to consumers and the benefits and drawbacks of each program. This chapter explains the various definitions and terms commonly used in conventional lending (often incorrectly), describes their significant features, and points out their pros and cons for different consumers.

EVOLUTION OF THE STANDARD FIXED-RATE, FULLY-AMORTIZING MORTGAGE

Before the Great Depression of the 1930s, most homes were financed by a term mortgage with the entire principal due at the end (or term) of the loan. It was normal practice for one of these loans to be rolled over into another loan at the end of the term, typically five years. However, as a result of this practice, many homeowners lost their homes during the economic emergency of the early 1930s because traditional lenders faced liquidity issues and were unable to refinance these mortgages as they came due.

As a means of addressing the national wave of foreclosures, the Home Owners Loan Corporation (HOLC), a federal agency, began exchanging government bonds for defaulted mortgages. If HOLC determined that a loan it received was basically sound and in default only because of the liquidity crisis, that loan was reconstituted as a 20-year loan with a self-amortizing monthly payment of principal and interest. This became the standard fixed-rate mortgage, which was used almost exclusively until recently, and which allowed this nation to have such a high ownership rate.

Direct Reduction Instrument

During the period between the Great Depression and the early 1980s, practically all residential real estate loan transactions used a fixed-rate, monthly amortizing mortgage instrument. Equal monthly payments for the term of the loan reduce the amount owed by first paying interest accrued on the loan since the last payment and then using the remainder of the payment to reduce principal. Two most important features of the standard fixed-rate mortgage are the regular, periodic reduction of principal, and that the borrower knows exactly how much is due each month.

The direct reduction of principal allows for a considerable savings in the total amount of interest a borrower would have to pay if interest were calculated on the entire amount of principal, as occurs with a term loan. As noted earlier, term loans allow for no principal repayment during the term—only periodic interest payments, with the entire principal due at the end of the term (a *balloon payment*).

Table 6.1 demonstrates the savings to a borrower using an amortized loan as opposed to a term loan:

TABLE **6.1**
Example of Term Loan Repayment versus Amortized Loan

Example: $100,000 loan at 6% interest for 30 years. Term loan pays interest only monthly; amortized loan pays principal and interest monthly

	Term Loan					Amortized Loan			
Year	Monthly Payment	Total Interest Paid	Total Principal Paid	Total of All Payments	Year	Monthly Payment	Total Interest Paid	Total Principal Paid	Total of All Payments
1	$500.00	$6,000.00	$0.00	$6,000.00	1	$599.55	$5,966.59	$1,228.01	$7,194.60
10	$500.00	$60,000.00	$0.00	$60,000.00	10	$599.55	$55,631.79	$16,314.28	$71,946.07
20	$500.00	$60,000.00	$0.00	$120,000.00	20	$599.55	$97,895.71	$45,996.41	$143,892.12
30	$500.00*	$60,000.00	$100,000.00	$280,000.00	30	$599.55	$115,838.19	$100,000.00	$215,838.19

*plus one final $100,000.00 payment of principal

Source: Bankrate.com Amortization Table

This mortgage instrument served both borrower and lender well from the 1930s until the middle 1970s. Over decades, these institutions built up loan portfolios of 20- to 30-year mortgages worth hundreds of billions of dollars. With rates set by the federal government, they borrowed money at 5 or 5.5 percent and loaned it out to homebuyers at 7 or 7.5 percent. The 150- to 250-basis-point spread between these lenders' cost of funds and the yield on their portfolios covered all operating expenses and included an attractive profit. As home prices and loan amounts increased, the 30-year mortgage loan replaced the 20-year mortgage loan as the industry standard.

Mortgage Lenders' Dilemma

During the late 1970s and early 1980s, rapid increases in inflation and federal deregulation of deposit and loan rates doubled most mortgage lenders' cost of funds in just a period of months, outpacing their ability to add higher yielding mortgage loans for income.

Many portfolio lenders were now faced with a negative spread of over 100 basis points. As a direct result of these unforeseeable events, many lending institutions were forced to close their doors or to merge with other institutions. This forced all mortgage lenders to re-examine how they would lend on mortgages in the future.

Alternative Mortgage Instruments

The surviving mortgage lenders began to offer a number of *alternative mortgage instruments* in addition to the standard fixed-rate amortizing mortgage. Alternative mortgage instruments in this context are basically any loan program that is not a 30-year, fixed rate, monthly payment, regular amortizing mortgage. They differ by allowing either:

- a periodic adjustment in the loan interest rate (not fixed rate)
- a payment that:
  - is irregular or does not occur monthly
  - does not fully amortize the loan balance by the end of the loan term

These different features can be very important to a lender during a changing financial environment, helping it manage the different risks involved in long-term lending at a fixed interest rate.

The **adjustable rate mortgage** effectively shares the interest rate risk between lender and borrower. Many different programs have evolved with different adjustment periods, interest rates, and payment caps, which limit the changes and indices upon which the interest rate is adjusted.

A **balloon payment** (from pre-Depression years) limits the lender's fixed interest rate risk to a five- or seven-year term and keeps the borrower's payment low by calculating the required payment based on a thirty-year amortization. Other balloon payment loans have an *interest-only* payment (IO), which lowers the monthly payment for the borrower marginally, but extends the interest rate risk of the full principal balance to the loan's maturity date for the lender.

1990 to 2010: Return of the Standard Fixed-rate Fully-amortizing Mortgage

Many lenders vowed that they would never again originate and portfolio fixed-rate, fully-amortizing mortgages after the disaster of the early 1980s. These same lenders were forced to change their minds when mortgage fixed rates tumbled in the late 1980s and extended their general decline over the past 30 years, dropping to 40- and 60-year lows. During different interest rate spikes since 1980, consumers selected alternative mortgage instruments for as many as 60 percent of all new residential mortgage loan originations. More recently, with fixed rates dipping into the low four percent range, more than 80 percent of new originations are fixed-rate mortgages of varying maturities. If rates do move up significantly, consumers will again be interested in the various alternative mortgage instruments.

10-, 15-, 20-, OR 40-YEAR MORTGAGES

Until recently, most American homeowners had become conditioned to making monthly mortgage payments on a 30-year mortgage. However, in the last 15 years many baby boomers refinanced their existing 30-year mortgages (as a result of the unprecedented drop in long-term mortgage rates) with 10-, 15-, or 20-year mortgages in order to finish paying their mortgages upon retirement. With the decline in rates, many homeowners were able to keep the same monthly principal and interest payment and reduce the term, resulting in a substantial savings on total interest paid over the term of the mortgage loan. On the other hand, a 40-year mortgage lowers the monthly payment and effectively allows the consumer to borrow more.

Sharing the Risk

In order for residential mortgage lenders to remain active in the mortgage market on a daily basis, they must have ways of meeting interest rate shifts in a profitable manner. Some mortgage lenders have solved the problem by selling some or all of the fixed-rate mortgages they originate. Other portfolio lenders have decided they can obtain a greater spread between their cost of funds and portfolio yield by retaining the fixed-rate mortgages with their higher initial yield in their mortgage portfolios.

During periods of interest rate volatility, mortgage lenders offer mortgage borrowers *adjustable-rate mortgages* (ARMs) at more attractive rates than their fixed rate mortgage to protect themselves from interest rate risk. All mortgage lenders should develop strategies that allow future lending activity to produce a sufficient spread between their cost of funds and their portfolio yield so they can cover the following:

- cost of funds/interest expenses
- cost of loan processing
- operating expenses
- reasonable profit

In the past, many mortgage lenders borrowed short and loaned long by using market-sensitive savings to finance 20- to 30-year mortgages. With the bitter lesson of the 1980s behind them, most lenders are more sophisticated and learned how better to match the maturity of their liabilities with their assets. Today, portfolio lenders use certificates of deposit and FHLB advances to lock in their cost of funds for a longer period for better asset/liability management.

Mortgage Program Nomenclature and Definitions

Many different types of alternative mortgage instruments have evolved since the first type was used in California in the early 1970s. The terms "fixed rate" and "alternative instrument" simply describe the *mortgage instrument*—the mortgage note or debt instrument—used for the terms of repayment (see Chapter 2—Real Estate Law). There is a higher level of complexity involved in mortgage lending today. To explain all the features involved now for a particular mortgage loan requires we use the term "**mortgage program**," which describes the entire package of required underwriting guidelines and restrictions in addition to the instrument involved. The term "*mortgage product*" is used inconsistently throughout the industry either in place of mortgage program or mortgage instrument. The following sections discuss the more common mortgage programs offered today, using the current industry nomenclature and categories.

Conventional vs. Government vs. Other

The first box of the first section of the GSE's industry standard application, the Uniform Residential Loan Application (Fannie Mae Form 1003/Freddie Mac Form 65), describes the most basic criteria for distinguishing the different types of mortgage programs.

A **government mortgage** is one intended for one of several federal or state government-sponsored programs: Federal Housing Agency (FHA), Veteran's Administration (VA), USDA/Rural Housing (RHS)/Farmer's Home Administration (FmHA), or state agency (see Chapter 8—Government Lending, for a full description of these programs.)

"*Other*" mortgage programs include land, construction, home equity, or reverse (*home equity conversion*) mortgage program (see Chapters 9—Construction Lending, and 10—Home Equity Lending).

A *conventional mortgage* can be either conforming or non-conforming, and includes many different mortgage programs. It acts as more of an umbrella category that includes everything that is *not* a "government-sponsored" or "other" program. Sometimes "conventional" and "conforming" terms are used interchangeably, but that is inaccurate as the conforming category includes non-conforming and portfolio mortgage loans.

Conforming vs. Non-conforming

A **conforming mortgage** loan is one that meets all the GSE eligibility and underwriting guidelines (Fannie Mae and Freddie Mac only). This category includes a myriad of first and second mortgage programs and debt instruments. The term "conforming loan" does not describe risk—"prime" vs. "subprime" describes risk. A common misconception is that all conforming loan programs are "prime" (and non-conforming loan programs are "subprime"). Many conforming loan programs are considered subprime because of their higher risk features, but are still eligible for sale to the GSEs.

A **non-conforming mortgage** loan does not meet GSE guidelines and is ineligible for sale to Fannie Mae or Freddie Mac. It takes only one feature to make a loan non-conforming (i.e., a jumbo loan, which exceeds the GSEs' authorized loan limit), so non-conforming mortgages may appear exactly like conforming ones except for that one feature. Non-conforming mortgages typically include jumbo, unique alternative instrument, and sub-prime/non-prime mortgage programs. What constitutes a "subprime" loan has evolved over the last 15 years, and the industry is using the term "non-prime" more frequently instead. When used properly and understood fully by sophisticated consumers, subprime/non-prime products provide real benefits to many borrowers over standard or conforming ones. Partial blame for the mortgage crisis falls on how these riskier non-conforming and subprime loans were marketed to consumers and how secondary mortgage market investors compensated mortgage originators for them. Regulators tried over time to come to grips with an appropriate definition for and way to regulate these higher-risk loans. Interagency statements issued in 1999, 2001, and 2007 each expanded the definition and included more and more risk features.

Non-traditional

As used today, this term is a bit of a misnomer. The SAFE Act (see Chapter 11—Compliance) defines a *non-traditional mortgage loan* as any loan that is not a 30-year fixed rate loan. As discussed above, the 30-year fixed rate loan evolved relatively recently from other, more "traditional" mortgage loans. Also, under this definition a fixed rate, 30-year term, interest only payment, 97 percent loan-to-value, no income/no asset verification, credit repair mortgage program would be considered "traditional" under the SAFE Act definition, but not by the industry. The SAFE Act definition should only be used in the context of education requirements for licensed mortgage loan originators and should not be used in outside that context. Instead, the federal Interagency Guidance on Nontraditional Mortgage Products and CSBS-AARMR-NACCA Guidances on Nontraditional Mortgage Products, issued in 2005 and 2006, provide a more practical definition: all mortgage products (except HELOCs) allowing the deferment of principal and/or interest payments (i.e., payment option ARMs). They also provide lenders with direction on how to design, originate, and manage these products and programs. One can argue this definition still does not reflect fully what a non-traditional loan program entails.

Adjustable-Rate Mortgages (ARMs)

The most popular form of alternative mortgage instrument is the adjustable-rate mortgage (ARM), or as it sometimes called, a variable-rate mortgage loan. Over the past 25 years, the percentage of residential mortgage loans

TABLE **6.2**
History of Fixed Rate vs. 1-Year Adjustable Rate Mortgages, 1984–2010

	30-Year Fixed Contract Rate	1-Year ARM Contract Rate	ARM Share of Originations %	Contract Rate Differential
1984	13.88%	11.51%	61%	2.4%
1985	12.43%	10.05%	50%	2.4%
1986	10.19%	8.43%	31%	1.8%
1987	10.21%	7.83%	43%	2.4%
1988	10.34%	7.90%	58%	2.4%
1989	10.32%	8.80%	39%	1.5%
1990	10.13%	8.36%	28%	1.8%
1991	9.25%	7.09%	23%	2.2%
1992	8.39%	5.62%	20%	2.8%
1993	7.31%	4.58%	20%	2.7%
1994	8.38%	5.36%	39%	3.0%
1995	7.93%	6.06%	33%	1.9%
1996	7.81%	5.67%	27%	2.1%
1997	7.60%	5.61%	22%	2.0%
1998	6.94%	5.58%	12%	1.4%
1999	7.44%	5.99%	22%	1.5%
2000	8.05%	7.04%	25%	1.0%
2001	6.97%	5.82%	15%	1.2%
2002	6.54%	4.62%	17%(e)	1.9%
2003	5.83%	3.76%	15%(e)	2.1%
2004	5.84%	3.90%	33%	1.9%
2005	5.87%	4.49%	31%(e)	1.4%
2006	6.41%	5.54%	25%(e)	0.9%
2007	6.34%	5.56%	19%(e)	0.8%
2008	6.03%	5.17%	8%(e)	0.9%
2009	5.04%	4.70%	5%(e)	0.3%
2010	4.69%	3.78%	6%(e)	0.9%

Source: Freddie Mac Primary Mortgage Market Survey

© 2010 Community Lending Associates, LLC

that were ARMs exceeded 35 percent when interest rates were high, and dropped below 25 percent when interest rates were low. An ARM is perceived as an alternative mortgage instrument that allows the interest rate to adjust periodically to some predetermined index, with the payment increasing or decreasing accordingly.

ARM programs, common around the world, were first used in this country in the early 1970s by state-chartered savings and loan institutions in California. These thrifts initially had only qualified success with these programs. Many borrowers rejected the early ARMs because they were afraid that their interest rates would increase rapidly, and thus they continued to select fixed-rate mortgages.

ARMS became more popular with borrowers only after mortgage lenders began putting *caps*—limits—on how much interest rates could adjust each year and over the life of the loan. With this basic consumer concern met, lenders then developed different ARM programs using indices that better matched their funding and at times gave the consumers the benefit of a lower initial and recurring rate. The most recent refinement in ARM programs is the hybrid ARM, which comprises most originations today. This program gives consumers even more interest rate and payment protection up front. Since the turn of the century, the hybrid ARM grew in popularity with lenders and borrowers and now account for much of ARM volume annually.

Mortgage interest rates are one of the most important factors affecting housing affordability. Typically, as interest rates decline, fewer people select adjustable-rate mortgages. ARMs become more popular when it appears that rates are at a current peak and will decline for an extended period.

ARM volume also increases during active real estate markets. Depending on its structure, an ARM program can allow a purchaser to qualify for a larger mortgage and, hence, a more expensive home.

Structure of an ARM: Adjustment Period

The interval at which the interest rate and payment can change is called the **adjustment period**. The most common ARM adjustment periods are the one-year, three-year, five-year, and seven-year adjustment periods. Therefore, an ARM with a one-year adjustment period is called a one-year ARM. As a general rule, the shorter the ARM adjustment period, the lower the initial interest rate. See Figure 6.1.

The one-year ARM often is the most popular of the various ARMs offered, but occasionally the three-year has more originations. The one-year ARM usually has the lowest interest rate of all the various ARMs. It also places the highest level of interest rate risk on the borrower.

Index

The concept behind an ARM is that it will produce an interest rate that moves as interest rates in general move, thus providing the lender or investor some protection against interest rate risk. In order to accomplish this, the interest rate for the ARM is tied to an *index*. A good ARM index is independent (beyond the control of the lender) and recognizable (based on a marketable financial instrument). The three most common indices used for mortgage ARMS are:

1. COFI—a general cost of funds (e.g., the 11th District of the Federal Home Loan Bank)

FIGURE **6.1** Adjustable-Rate Mortgage Loan Adjustment Notice

Borrower: _John L. Lewis_ Date: _April 3, 2011_
Loan Number: _#42668_

This notice is to inform you of:

__x__ An adjustment to your interest rate with a corresponding adjustment to your payment.
_____ An adjustment to your interest rate without a corresponding adjustment to your payment.
The interest rate on your loan with _First National Bank of Missoula_ secured by a mortgage on property located at 53 Flathead St., Missoula, Montana is scheduled to be adjusted on May 1, 2011. The index on which your interest rate is based is "One year Treasury adjusted to a constant maturity" as found in Federal Reserve publication H-15.

You should be aware of the following interest rate adjustment information concerning your Adjustable Rate Mortgage Loan.

1. Your new interest rate will be _7.00%_ , which is based on an index value of _4.25%_.

2. Your previous rate was _6.75%,_ which was based on an index value of _4.00%._

3. Your loan has a _2%_ annual cap and a _6%_ lifetime cap. The initial interest rate on your loan was _5%_. The maximum interest rate on this loan can be _11%_.

4. Your new payment will be _$1,545.89._

5. Your new loan balance is _$135,989.90._

If you have any questions about this notice, please contact:

George Mitchell, Loan Officer
First National Bank of Missoula
_800-123-3456_

© REMOC ASSOCIATES, LLC.

2. Treasury—a treasury security with a similar period of maturity (e.g., a three-year ARM indexed to the three-year treasury). The most common index is the one-year treasury bill (adjusted to a constant maturity)
3. LIBOR—the London Interbank Offering Rate (a base rate at which banks lend to each other). The Prime rate is another example of this type, but it is used more for commercial lending and for HELOC adjustments

These indices (see Figure 6.2) can be tracked using the Federal Reserve Board's statistical release H.15 (found at **www.federalreserve.gov**).

FIGURE **6.2** More About Indices

Treasury indices. Most ARM loans use one of the various Treasury indices. The *One-Year Treasury Index* is the most common index in the eastern United States. It is based on the "constant maturity" of all outstanding federal obligations with a year or less to maturity. The *Three-Year Treasury Index* (used for a 3/3 ARM) is based on all federal obligations with three years or less to maturity.

COFI—Cost of Funds Index. The Eleventh District Cost of Funds is the most prevalent index in the western United States. The COFI, which is a weighted monthly average, has been published since 1981 by the San Francisco Federal Home Loan Bank (the Eleventh District). This index is considered a trailing index since it measures existing liabilities at member institutions.

LIBOR—London Interbank Offered Rate. LIBOR is the rate on dollar-denominated deposits, also known as Eurodollars, traded between banks in London. The index is quoted for one-, three-, and six-month periods and for one-year periods.

Margin

To calculate the borrower's ARM interest rate, lenders add to the index rate another figure called the **margin**. The margin originally corresponded to a lender's operating expenses, but it is now market driven. Recently, margins have ranged between 200 and 300 basis points, with an average of about 275 basis points (0.275%). This is an important number for a consumer to establish before entering into any ARM transaction. Once the margin is established, it is set for the life of the loan.

$$\text{Index Rate} + \text{Margin} = \text{ARM Interest Rate}$$

Interest Rate Caps

Interest rate caps place a limit on the amount the interest rate can increase or decrease. In December 1987, Truth-in-Lending required that all ARM loans must have an interest rate ceiling (but no floor). Most ARMs today have other caps. The introduction of caps made the ARM acceptable to most consumers. Three common types of interest rate caps used today are:

1. *Periodic cap*, which limits the interest rate increase (or decrease) from one adjustment period to the next. One or two percent caps are the most common.
2. *Lifetime cap*, which limits the interest rate increase (or decrease) over the life of the loan. Five or six percent caps are the most common.
3. *Initial adjustment cap*, used more with hybrid ARMS. This cap applies only to the first time the interest rate adjusts. For example, with a 5/1 ARM this cap applies to the 5th year of the loan only for the first adjustment. Afterward, in years 6-30 the periodic and lifetime caps apply.

A few ARMs have payment caps that limit the monthly payment increase at each adjustment period, usually a certain percentage of the previous payment. A recent payment cap used is 7.5 percent, meaning that the payment cannot increase more than that percentage amount each adjustment period.

Payment caps are less popular because they can produce *negative amortization* (deferred interest). This occurs when the monthly mortgage payment isn't sufficient to pay all the interest due on the mortgage, thus the mortgage balance is increasing, not decreasing. Truth in Lending Act restricts the use of negative amortization loans. These loans may not be saleable in the secondary mortgage market because of investors' concerns that these mortgages have increased risk of delinquency.

Fully-indexed accrual rate

A fully-indexed interest rate (FIR) or fully-indexed accrual rate (FIAR) is the interest rate resulting from adding the margin to the index (prior to the influence of any caps). Often the first year or offering rate for ARMs—the interest rate advertised and at which the borrower closes—is not the FIR; it is market-driven.

Discounts

In order to make an ARM loan attractive to more consumers, most lenders lower the initial interest rate (and thus the payment rate) from the FIR. This initial rate is called a **discounted rate** and may be 200 basis points or more below the FIR. If the rate is 300 basis points or more, the rate is called a **teaser rate**. Mortgage borrowers should be wary of teaser rates, as they often require large loan fees or have larger-than-normal margins.

Mortgage lenders must be careful that they make the correct annual percentage rate (APR) disclosure when offering a discounted ARM. The correct annual percentage rate disclosure for a discounted ARM is a composite APR. A **composite APR** reflects the initial payment rate and the rate that would have resulted from the use of the full index (as it existed at closing) for the remaining term. See Figure 6.3.

Spread

Offering a discounted ARM is important to a lender if that lender wants to originate ARMs (Figure 6.4). There must be enough of a difference between the rate at which the fixed-rate mortgage is offered and the rate at which the ARM is offered. If no meaningful difference exists, few borrowers will select an ARM because those borrowers would be taking on the risk of interest rates increasing. Lenders in effect compensate borrowers for this added risk by making the initial payment rate of an ARM attractive as compared to the fixed-rate mortgage. See Figure 6.5 for some ARM examples.

FIGURE **6.3** Composite APR Example

Local Savings Bank offers its one-year ARM at an initial payment rate of 3.50 percent even though the full indexed accrual rate called for a rate of 5.00 percent. In order to correctly disclose the APR, the bank will use a composite APR that reflects the 3.50 percent rate for a year and the 5.00 percent rate for the remaining term.

FIGURE **6.4** Adjustable Rate Note

MIN: 100017000000112614

FIXED/ADJUSTABLE RATE NOTE

(LIBOR One-Year Index (As Published In *The Wall Street Journal*)—Rate Caps)

THIS NOTE PROVIDES FOR A CHANGE IN MY FIXED INTEREST RATE TO AN ADJUSTABLE INTEREST RATE. THIS NOTE LIMITS THE AMOUNT MY ADJUSTABLE INTEREST RATE CAN CHANGE AT ANY ONE TIME AND THE MAXIMUM RATE I MUST PAY.

March 28, 2011	FAIRFIELD	Connecticut
[Date]	[City]	[State]

1144 REEF ROAD
FAIRFIELD, CT 06824

[Property Address]

1. BORROWER'S PROMISE TO PAY

In return for a loan that I have received, I promise to pay U.S. $**180,000.00**   (this amount is called "Principal"), plus interest, to the order of Lender. Lender is **THE McCUE MORTGAGE COMPANY**

I will make all payments under this Note in the form of cash, check or money order.

I understand that Lender may transfer this Note. Lender or anyone who takes this Note by transfer and who is entitled to receive payments under this Note is called the "Note Holder."

2. INTEREST

Interest will be charged on unpaid principal until the full amount of Principal has been paid. I will pay interest at a yearly rate of **3.7500**%. The interest rate I will pay may change in accordance with Section 4 of this Note.

The interest rate required by this Section 2 and Section 4 of this Note is the rate I will pay both before and after any default described in Section 7(B) of this Note.

3. PAYMENTS

(A) Time and Place of Payments

I will pay principal and interest by making a payment every month.

I will make my monthly payments on the first day of each month beginning on   **May 01, 2011**   . I will make these payments every month until I have paid all of the principal and interest and any other charges described below that I may owe under this Note. Each monthly payment will be applied as of its scheduled due date and will be applied to interest before Principal. If, on   **April 01, 2041**   , I still owe amounts under this Note, I will pay those amounts in full on that date, which is called the "Maturity Date."

I will make my monthly payments at **ONE LIBERTY SQUARE, NEW BRITAIN, CT 06050**

or at a different place if required by the Note Holder.

(B) Amount of My Initial Monthly Payments

Each of my initial monthly payments will be in the amount of U.S. $**833.61**   . This amount may change.

(C) Monthly Payment Changes

Changes in my monthly payment will reflect changes in the unpaid principal of my loan and in the interest rate that I must pay. The Note Holder will determine my new interest rate and the changed amount of my monthly payment in accordance with Section 4 of this Note.

MULTISTATE FIXED/ADJUSTABLE RATE NOTE—WSJ One-Year LIBOR—Single Family—**Fannie Mae Uniform Instrument**   Form 3528 6/01

MULTISTATE
ITEM 7524L1 (060409)

GreatDocs®
(Page 1 of 5)

MFCD7524

00125224

FIGURE **6.4** (*Continued*)

4. ADJUSTABLE INTEREST RATE AND MONTHLY PAYMENT CHANGES

(A) Change Dates

The initial fixed interest rate I will pay will change to an adjustable interest rate on the first day of **April 2016** , and the adjustable interest rate I will pay may change on that day every 12th month thereafter. The date on which my initial fixed interest rate changes to an adjustable interest rate, and each date on which my adjustable interest rate could change is called a "Change Date."

(B) The Index

Beginning with the first Change Date, my adjustable interest rate will be based on an Index. The "Index" is the average of interbank offered rates for one-year U.S. dollar-denominated deposits in the London market ("LIBOR"), as published in *The Wall Street Journal*. The most recent Index figure available as of the date 45 days before each Change Date is called the "Current Index."

If the Index is no longer available, the Note Holder will choose a new index that is based upon comparable information. The Note Holder will give me notice of this choice.

(C) Calculation of Changes

Before each Change Date, the Note Holder will calculate my new interest rate by adding **Two and One Quarter** percentage points (**2.2500**%) to the Current Index. The Note Holder will then round the result of this addition to the nearest one-eighth of one percentage point (0.125%). Subject to the limits stated in Section 4(D) below, this rounded amount will be my new interest rate until the next Change Date.

The Note Holder will then determine the amount of the monthly payment that would be sufficient to repay the unpaid principal that I am expected to owe at the Change Date in full on the Maturity Date at my new interest rate in substantially equal payments. The result of this calculation will be the new amount of my monthly payment.

(D) Limits on Interest Rate Changes

The interest rate I am required to pay at the first Change Date will not be greater than **8.7500**% or less than **2.2500**%. Thereafter, my adjustable interest rate will never be increased or decreased on any single Change Date by more than two percentage points from the rate of interest I have been paying for the preceding 12 months. My interest rate will never be greater than **8.7500**%.

(E) Effective Date of Changes

My new interest rate will become effective on each Change Date. I will pay the amount of my new monthly payment beginning on the first monthly payment date after the Change Date until the amount of my monthly payment changes again.

(F) Notice of Changes

The Note Holder will deliver or mail to me a notice of any changes in my initial fixed interest rate to an adjustable interest rate and of any changes in my adjustable interest rate before the effective date of any change. The notice will include the amount of my monthly payment, any information required by law to be given to me and also the title and telephone number of a person who will answer any question I may have regarding the notice.

5. BORROWER'S RIGHT TO PREPAY

I have the right to make payments of Principal at any time before they are due. A payment of Principal only is known as a "Prepayment." When I make a Prepayment, I will tell the Note Holder in writing that I am doing so. I may not designate a payment as a Prepayment if I have not made all the monthly payments due under this Note.

I may make a full Prepayment or partial Prepayments without paying any Prepayment charge. The Note Holder will use my Prepayments to reduce the amount of Principal that I owe under this Note. However, the Note Holder may apply my Prepayment to the accrued and unpaid interest on the Prepayment amount before applying my Prepayment to reduce the Principal amount of this Note. If I make a partial Prepayment, there will be no changes in the due dates of my monthly payments unless the Note Holder agrees in writing to those changes. My partial Prepayment may reduce the amount of my monthly payments after the first Change Date following my partial Prepayment. However, any reduction due to my partial Prepayment may be offset by an interest rate increase.

6. LOAN CHARGES

If a law, which applies to this loan and which sets maximum loan charges, is finally interpreted so that the interest or other loan charges collected or to be collected in connection with this loan exceed the permitted limits, then: (a) any such loan charge shall be reduced by the amount necessary to reduce the charge to the permitted limit; and (b) any sums already collected from

MULTISTATE FIXED/ADJUSTABLE RATE NOTE—WSJ One-Year LIBOR—Single Family—Fannie Mae Uniform Instrument   Form 3528 6/01

MULTISTATE
ITEM 7524L2 (060409)
MFCD7524

GreatDocs®
(Page 2 of 5)
00125224

FIGURE **6.5** ARM Examples

Index	5.69%	Annual Adjustment Cap	2%
Margin	2.75%	Lifetime Adjustment Cap	6%
Discount	1.75%	30-Year Fixed Rate	7.85%

Example 1: Calculate the fully indexed rate:

Index	5.69%
+ Margin	2.75%
Fully Indexed Rate	8.44%

Example 2: Calculate the initial rate:

Index	5.69%
+ Margin	2.75%
− Discount	1.75%
Initial Rate	6.69%

Example 3: Calculate maximum rate after first adjustment:

Initial Rate	6.69%
Annual Adj. Cap	2.00%
Maximum Rate	8.69%

Example 4: Calculate the fully indexed rate when no change occurs from first year:

Index	5.69%
+ Margin	2.75%
Fully Indexed Rate	8.44%

Thus, payment rate could only increase to 8.44%.

Example 5: Calculate the maximum rate (lifetime) for this loan:

Initial Rate	6.69%
+ 6% Lifetime Cap	6.00%
Maximum Rate	12.69%

This spread is usually from 200 to 300 basis points below that at which the fixed-rate mortgage is offered. As interest rates for all types of residential mortgages increase, the amount of spread between the fixed-rate and ARM rate typically decreases, since consumers expect rates to drop in the future.

The risk to a borrower with an ARM at a discounted rate is that the payment rate may still go up at the adjustment period, even if the index does not.

In order to protect consumers, Congress passed an amendment to Regulation Z (truth-in-lending) requiring lenders to provide the following information to consumers who inquire about or who apply for ARM loans:

- the interest rate ceiling
- CHARM booklet (Consumer Handbook on Adjustable Rate Mortgages) explaining ARMs
- 15-year historical example of how rates would have changed with this loan
- worst-case example, assuming a $10,000 loan

ARM Programs
Hybrid ARMs

Hybrid ARMs programs represent the most recent evolution of this type of mortgage instrument, and have dominated the market for the past ten years. The program draws on features of fixed rate and ARM programs, hence the "hybrid." The traditional ARM program used regular adjustment intervals throughout the term of the loan: one-year ARM was adjusted every year; three-year ARM was adjusted every three years, etc.

In contrast, the hybrid ARM extends the initial adjustment period (in effect, "fixing" the rate like a fixed-rate loan) for an extended period before changing to a one-year ARM. The most popular hybrids are 3/1 ARMs (fixed rate/payment for three years, then adjusted annually for 27 years for a 30-year loan) and 5/1 ARMs (fixed rate/payment for five years, then adjusted annually for 25 years for a 30-year loan).

Both a hybrid and traditional ARM may have the same interest rate for the first adjustment period. But it is important to note that after the initial period, the loan programs behave very differently. The number of adjustment periods for a hybrid ARM exceeds the number for a traditional ARM. For example, a 3/1 hybrid ARM has 26 rate adjustment periods (annually after 36 monthly payments: from the start of the fourth year until the last year after 346 payments). A traditional 3/3 ARM adjusts nine times (every third year after 36 payments).

Other hybrid ARM programs offered include 7/1 and 10/1 ARMs as shown in Table 6.3. The longer the initial period, the closer the initial rate is to a standard 30-year fixed rate mortgage. At times the initial rate for a 7/1 or 10/1 hybrid ARM will exceed the 30-year fixed rate. This pricing spread implies that lenders are fairly certain that interest rates will decline shortly and for an extended period.

Buydowns

Sometimes a seller or builder will pay a lender so that a borrower can get a lower initial rate or have a lower initial payment. A transaction of this type is called a **buydown**, which became popular during the extremely high interest rate period of the early 1980s. Buydown mortgage programs address the issue of affordability of housing, and not the issue of protecting lenders' relative yields. Although market interest rates cannot be changed (the market dictates what they will be), the effective rate to a homebuyer can be changed by "buying down" the market rate to a rate that will allow a potential homebuyer to qualify for a loan. While the borrower pays a lower interest rate than a standard ARM, the lender in effect receives the same interest rate in total—just from a different source.

A buydown occurs when a builder, home seller, parent of a buyer, or homebuyer prepays a portion of the interest that a lender will earn over the life of the loan. This one-time nonrefundable payment is either paid directly to the lender in one lump sum or put into an interest-earning account that a lender debits monthly to subsidize the reduced monthly payment.

TABLE **6.3**

Freddie Mac's 26th Annual Adjustable-Rate Mortgage Survey
Treasury-Indexed ARM Features in January 2010

	1-Year ARMs		3-Year ARMs		Longer Initial-Period Hybrid ARMs		
	Conforming	Jumbo	3/1	3/3	5/1	7/1	10/1
Loan Terms			– – – Percentage Points – – –				
Underlying Index Rate	0.42	0.42	0.42	1.62	0.42	0.42	0.42
Margin	2.75	2.74	2.74	2.78	2.74	2.73	2.73
Fully-Indexed Rate	3.17	3.16	3.16	4.40	3.16	3.15	3.15
Initial Year's Discount	−1.14	−1.82	−1.19	−0.35	−1.31	−1.88	−2.17
Initial Interest Rate	4.31	4.98	4.35	4.75	4.47	5.03	5.32
Fees and Points	0.6	0.5	0.7	0.8	0.6	0.7	0.5
Fixed-Adjustable Rate Spread	0.78	0.11	0.74	0.34	0.62	0.06	-0.23
Product Availability (percent of lenders)	23%	23%	62%	7%	84%	55%	24%

The sample is limited to ARMs indexed to either the 1-year or the 3-year constant maturity Treasury (CMT) yields. Data were collected from 117 ARM lenders during the week ending January 7, 2010. The 3-year, 5-year, 7-year, and 10-year ARM results are limited to conforming loans for prime borrowers. The initial discount is based on the value of the weekly average 1-year or 3-year CMT yield for the comparable week ending January 7, 2010. The "Fixed-Adjustable Rate Spread" is the average interest rate on a 30-year conventional conforming fixed-rate mortgage, less the initial rate on the ARM using Freddie Mac's Primary Mortgage Market Survey®.
Source: Freddie Mac

This arrangement reduces the borrower's mortgage payments for a temporary period—usually one to five years—or permanently. The buydown can be structured in many ways; for example, a reduced monthly payment could increase once or yearly, or remain constant over the life of the loan.

This benefit allows many more families to qualify for a mortgage loan. Often, the lender will use the reduced rate and payment, rather than the FIAR payment, to qualify applicants. Secondary market guidelines and federal regulations now require that certain ARM programs use the FIAR for qualification.

Convertible Mortgages

A **convertible mortgage** program attempts to combine the best features of the fixed-rate and the adjustable-rate mortgage. Sometimes called a convertible ARM, it allows a borrower to start out with the lower payment rate that makes ARMs attractive. Later, under certain conditions the borrower can elect to convert the existing ARM to a fixed-rate mortgage.

The time frame within which to convert depends on the mortgage instrument, but most instruments allow the borrower to convert anytime after the 13th month and until the 60th month. Typically, the borrower pays a small fee—say, $250 to $500.

At first glance, the ability to convert may not appear to be of great value to a borrower since a borrower can always refinance to a new fixed-rate mortgage. The problem with that strategy is that the cost of refinancing can amount to many thousands of dollars, negating some or all of the benefit.

A convertible ARM may have interest rates 25 to 50 basis points more than a normal ARM. The convertible ARM makes sense to a borrower if the borrower expects interest rates to drop over the next couple of years. If that occurs, the borrower will benefit from the lower ARM interest rate initially and, after converting, will benefit by locking in a fixed interest rate for the remainder of the mortgage term.

When would a borrower choose this convertible ARM over a normal ARM or a fixed-rate mortgage? It depends mostly on whether the borrower can qualify for a fixed-rate mortgage. In addition, a borrower must decide whether the spread between the mortgage alternatives makes one more attractive than another.

Two-Step, or Reset, Mortgages

Two-step mortgage programs share the same features as convertible mortgages. A two-step mortgage program provides a borrower with the certainty of a fixed-rate mortgage for a period of time (usually five or seven years), and then the rate adjusts to a new fixed rate (indexed to the 10-year Treasury, weekly average) with the payment remaining at that rate for the remaining 25 or 23 years. The advantage to the consumer is that this mortgage starts out low (lower than a 30-year fixed-rate mortgage) and remains at that low rate for five or seven years, with typically a 6 percent adjustment cap. If a consumer plans to stay in the home for only five or seven years, or will otherwise refinance soon after, they benefit from the lower rate.

Graduated Payment Mortgages (GPMs)

The GPM is a program that was specifically designed to provide borrowers with an opportunity to match their expected increase in income with a mortgage payment that is initially low but increases yearly. This approach helps qualify more potential homeowners for mortgages. Many otherwise qualified potential homeowners are unable to qualify for a standard fixed-rate mortgage because their current income is not sufficient; however, if their conservatively estimated future income could be factored in, they could qualify.

GPMs do not address the issue of sheltering lenders from interest rate shifts. The interest rate and the term of the loan are set before closing, as with a standard fixed-rate mortgage. The difference is that the initial monthly payment begins at a lower level than it would with a standard mortgage. The result is monthly payments that are not sufficient to fully amortize the loan. Since the payments do not fully amortize the loan, the borrower, in effect, is borrowing the difference between the payment being made and the interest actually due. The amount of accrued but unpaid interest is added to the outstanding principal amount. Through this negative amortization, the outstanding principal balance actually increases for a period of time rather than decreases, as with a standard mortgage.

In the following year or years, the monthly payment increases to a predetermined rate, say, 7.5 percent or lower, with additional increases occurring each year for a set number of years. Depending on the plan selected, as the yearly increases occur at some point, the monthly payments equal or exceed the payment under a standard mortgage. At that point, negative amortization stops, but the payment increases continue until they reach a level that fully amortizes the outstanding balance over the remaining years of the loan.

From the example, two important points emerge. If borrower income does not increase at the anticipated rate, the burden of the scheduled mortgage payment increases may result in a default. The second point is that a GPM increases the total amount of interest paid. This is the result of the negative amortization during the early years of the mortgage when principal is increasing, rather than decreasing as with a fully-amortizing mortgage program.

BIWEEKLY MORTGAGES

Developed during the middle of the 1980s, the biweekly mortgage is a popular instrument that some homeowners use for shortening the life of their mortgage debt and saving on the total interest paid over the life of the mortgage. A **biweekly mortgage** is a fixed-rate, level-payment, fully amortizing mortgage that requires the borrower to make payments every two weeks rather than monthly—for a total of 26 payments a year. Each biweekly payment is exactly half the amount that would be payable under a comparable monthly-payment mortgage. Thus, the 26 biweekly payments are equivalent to 13 monthly payments a year. The benefits to consumers of such a payment schedule include the following:

- A payment schedule that fits the budget of those who are paid on a weekly or biweekly basis
- More frequent payment schedule substantially reduces the total interest paid over the life of the loan
- The life of the loan is meaningfully shortened

The biweekly payment schedule reduces the principal balance earlier—twice a month—and by a larger amount over the course of the year with the extra payment as compared to the standard monthly payment loan. Because the principal is paid off faster, the loan matures in a shorter length of time and accrues less interest overall.

The biweekly payment is calculated on a 30-year *amortization schedule* at the market rate that typically is between one eighth to one half percent lower than for a regular 30-year mortgage.

There are few negative aspects of the biweekly mortgage as far as the borrower is concerned. These negative aspects mainly center on coordinating the mortgage payment with the borrower's payday. Lenders make this process easier for borrowers by setting up checking accounts that are debited automatically every 14 days for the mortgage payment. Many borrowers have their paychecks deposited directly into these checking accounts, thus making the payment process even easier. Of larger concern, however, is how well the biweekly payment schedule matches the borrowers' income. The biweekly mortgage is best suited to borrowers receiving regular income—typically salary earners. Consumers with very cyclical incomes (i.e. retail, commission, high bonus/low salary) need to manage their cash flow carefully and make sure they save enough during their high income periods so that funds are on deposit for payments during their low income periods.

The major negative aspect as far as lenders are concerned is the increased cost associated with processing and calculating the increased number of payments. More sophisticated computer processing systems minimize this internally, but most of the cost is associated with customer service issues when funds are not available.

Biweekly mortgages use simple interest—based on 365 days a year rather than 360 days as with regular monthly mortgages. A lender must have the capacity to reamortize the loan after each payment.

The underwriting requirements for a biweekly mortgage are the same as for any other mortgage, except that the biweekly principal and interest payment is adjusted to the equivalent monthly payment to qualify applicants. Fannie Mae and Freddie Mac have developed uniform biweekly notes and payment riders. Each buys 15- and 30-year biweekly mortgages through its Standard Commitment Window and will consider 10- and 20-year biweekly mortgages on a negotiated basis.

Mortgage Product Comparison—Fixed Rates

Product	Features	Pros/Cons
• Fixed Rate (FRM)	Interest Rate and Payment do not change. Regular Fully-Amortizing Monthly Payment. Terms of 10/15/20/25/30/40 yrs.	Stable interest rate and payment. Best for fixed-income borrowers. Best for low-risk tolerance borrowers. May prepay when rates decline. May payoff early when rates decline.
• Balloon Payment (5/30, 10/30, 15/30)	Interest Rate does not change. Partially-Amortizing Monthly Payment. Large final payment at end of term. Terms of 3/5/7/10/15/20 yrs.	Stable interest rate and payment. Best for borrowers with equity. Best to minimize monthly payment. May prepay when rates decline. May payoff early when rates decline. Risk increases as balloon decreases.
• Buydown, Graduated Payment (3/2/1, 2/1)	Interest Rate does not change. Payment changes in initial years. Fully-Amortizing Monthly Payment. Regular Terms (10-40 yrs.)	Stable interest rate Payment changes in regular intervals. Best for low cash borrowers. Minimizes initial payment. Risk of increased payments later. May payoff early when rates decline.

(continued)

Mortgage Product Comparison—Other Types ("Fixed Rates")

Product	Features	Pros/Cons
• Construction Only/ Construction-Perm	Separate Loan Advance and Loan Repayment Terms. Fixed Rate for Construction Period. ARM or Fixed for Repayment Period. Interest-only payment during Construction Phase. Regular Amortizing Monthly Payments in Repayment Phase.	Riskiest loan transaction and product. Collateral being built/financed. Possible Construction and Cashflow issues. Allows custom home for borrower. Best for borrowers with equity, liquid assets. Best to minimize monthly payment.
• Bi-weekly Payment	Usually Interest Rate and Payment do not change. Auto Payment made every 2 weeks. Fully-Amortizing Monthly Payment. Extra payment yearly vs. Fixed. Terms of 15/20/30/40 yrs.	Stable, regular payments. Automatic payment. Payment schedule speeds amortization (12 yr v 15 yr; 23yr v 30 yr). Best for stable income borrowers. May payoff early when rates decline.
• Reverse	Lien on property for full amount. Principal advanced in regular monthly installments.	Lengthy origination process. Not fully understood or accepted in market place. Best for low liquidity borrowers with equity.

Mortgage Product Comparison—Adjustable Rates

Product	Features	Pros/Cons
• Adjustable Rate (ARM, VRM) (1/1,3/3, 5/5,) (1-,2-, 6-month)	Interest Rate and Payment can change. Regular rate review periods. Fully-Amortizing Monthly Payment. Terms of 10/15/20/25/30/ 40 yrs.	Interest rate and payment can change. Review period and lifetime caps. Best for increasing-income borrowers. Best for mod/high-risk tolerance borrowers. May payoff early when rates decline.

(continued)

• Hybrid ARM (3/1, 5/1, 7/1, 10/1)	Interest rate and Payment can change. Initial fixed rate/payment period then 1-yr ARM. Fully Amortizing Monthly Payment.	Same Features as Above. Offers some rate/payment stability.
• Option ARM (IO)	Same Features as Above... PLUS... Borrower selects regular or interest-only payment. Interest Rate does not change. Usually Amortizing Monthly Payment.	Offers greatest flexibility for borrower. Best for borrowers with equity, liquid assets (sophisticated borrower). Best to minimize monthly payment. May prepay when rates decline. May payoff early when rates decline. Risk increases with flexibility. Negative amortization possible.

Mortgage Product Comparison—Other Types ("ARMs")

Product	Features	Pros/Cons
• Convertible ARM	Same Features as ARM. Option to fix rate/payment in years 3, 4, 5 only.	Offers stability to borrowers. Rates usually higher than market for ARMs (at origination) and fixed (at conversion).
• 2-Step (5/25, 7/23)	Same as Fixed Rate with 1 Interest Rate/Payment adjustment only. Fully Amortizing Monthly Payment.	Offers stability to borrowers. Rates usually higher than market for ARMs (at origination) and fixed (at conversion).

CONFORMING MORTGAGE LOANS

A conforming loan is one that meets Fannie Mae or Freddie Mac standard program eligibility and underwriting guidelines as shown in Table 6.4. Underwriting issues (described more fully in Chapter 13—Underwriting) deal more "within" the loan file: qualifying the applicants and subject property.

Eligibility issues deal more with the design or restrictions of the loan program itself: maximum loan amount and loan-to-value, type of transaction and property, mortgage insurance coverage, mortgage instruments and documentation used, etc.

TABLE **6.4**
FHFA Historical Conforming Loan Limits for Fannie Mae and Freddie Mac Loans

	Continental United States only; Alaska and Hawaii limits are higher						
Year	1 Unit	2 Units	3 Units	4 Units	Second Mortgage	5-yr Increase	Annual Increase
1980	$93,750	$120,000	$145,000	$180,000	N/A		
1985	$115,300	$147,500	$178,200	$221,500	$57,650	23%	
1990	$187,450	$239,750	$289,750	$360,150	$93,725	63%	
1995	$203,150	$259,850	$314,100	$390,400	$101,575	8%	
2000	$252,700	$323,400	$390,900	$485,800	$126,350	24%	
2001	$275,000	$351,950	$425,400	$528,700	$137,500		9%
2002	$300,700	$384,900	$465,200	$578,150	$150,350		9%
2003	$322,700	$413,100	$499,300	$620,500	$161,350		7%
2004	$333,700	$427,150	$516,300	$641,650	$166,850		3%
2005	$359,650	$460,400	$556,500	$691,600	$179,825	42%	8%
2006-2011	$417,000	$533,850	$645,300	$801,950	$208,500	16%	
2008-2011 HC	$729,750	$934,200	$1,129,250	$1,403,400	$208,500		

Loan limits decreased once since 1980: 1989-1990

Permanent limits determined by HERA of 2008

American Recovery and Reinvestment Act of 2009 determine county limits

Source: FHFA

© Community Lending Associates, LLC

Conforming Maximum Loan Amount

The GSEs can purchase loans that are within their maximum loan amount, set annually by their regulator, the FHFA. Any loan exceeding this maximum is by definition a **jumbo loan**, even if it is conforming in all other ways.

Fannie Mae and Freddie Mac Mortgage Programs

The two GSEs offer dozens of standard purchase and negotiated purchase programs. These numerous conforming programs are in constant state of revision. For the most current eligibility parameters, visit either the Fannie Mae or Freddie Mac Web sites, or contact an appropriate representative.

https://www.efanniemae.com/sf/refmaterials/eligibility/
http://www.freddiemac.com/singlefamily/mortgages/

The following is an example of Freddie Mac's eligible loan programs, organized by Loan Type:

Fixed-Rate Mortgages
- 15-, 20-, and 30-year fixed-rate mortgages
- Affordable Merit Rate® mortgages
- Alt 97

- A-minus mortgages
- Cash-out refinance mortgages
- Condominium unit mortgages/streamlined condo review
- Construction conversion mortgages
- Financed permanent buydown mortgages
- Freddie Mac-owned streamlined refinance mortgages
- Initial Interest^{SM} fixed-rate mortgages
- Investment property mortgages
- Loans with secondary financing
- Manufactured homes
- Mortgages for two- to four-unit properties
- Mortgages for newly constructed homes
- Mortgages with temporary subsidy buydown plans
- Newly built home mortgages
- No cash-out refinance mortgages
- Relief Refinance Mortgages^{SM}—same servicer
- Relief Refinance Mortgages—open access
- Renovation mortgages
- Rural Housing Service Section 502 leveraged seconds
- Seller-owned modified mortgages
- Super conforming mortgages

Adjustable-Rate Mortgages
- A-minus mortgages
- Cash-out refinance mortgage
- CMT-indexed ARMs
- Cost-of-Funds Indexed (COFI) rate-capped ARMs
- Financed permanent buydown mortgages
- Freddie Mac-owned streamlined refinance mortgages
- Home Possible® 97 mortgages
- Initial Interest^{SM} ARMs
- Investment property mortgages
- LIBOR-indexed ARMs
- Loans with secondary financing
- Manufactured homes
- Mortgages for two- to four-unit properties
- Mortgages with temporary subsidy buydown plans
- No cash-out refinance mortgages
- Relief Refinance Mortgages—same servicer
- Relief Refinance Mortgages—open access
- Seller-owned converted mortgages
- Seller-owned modified mortgages
- Super conforming mortgages

Balloon/Reset Mortgages
- Balloon/reset mortgages (five- and seven-year)
- A-minus mortgages
- Cash-out refinance mortgages
- Freddie Mac-owned streamlined refinance mortgages

- Investment property mortgages
- Loans with secondary financing
- Mortgages for two- to four-unit properties
- Mortgages with temporary subsidy buydown plans
- No cash-out refinance mortgages
- Seller-owned modified mortgages

Government-sponsored Offerings
- FHA 203 (k) rehabilitation mortgages
- Guaranteed rural housing mortgages
- HUD-guaranteed Section 184 Native American mortgages
- RHS leveraged seconds
- Veterans Affairs (VA) mortgages

The GSEs also offer multifamily (5–20 units) and cooperative programs.

Maximum Loan-to-Value Ratios for Standard Purchases

The following maximum loan-to-value ratios currently apply to the GSE's standard purchases:

- 95 percent for fixed-rate mortgages if owner-occupied principal residence
- 90 percent for adjustable-rate if owner-occupied principal residence
- 90 percent for fixed- and adjustable-rate on owner-occupied refinances
- 80 percent for investment properties and second homes

See Table 6.5 for more information about maximum loan-to-value ratios.

Mortgage Insurance Requirements and Credit Enhancement

GSEs are required by their charter from the federal government to obtain mortgage insurance on all mortgage loans if the loan-to-value (LTV) ratio at the time of purchase is greater than 80 percent. In the past, this meant that mortgage insurance or guaranty was required for all loans if the LTV was greater than 80 percent. Today, both GSEs will purchase loans with more than 80 percent LTV without mortgage insurance or guaranty if another form of "credit enhancement" is available. This could take the form of pool insurance on a large group of mortgage loans or recourse arrangements whereby the seller agrees to repurchase loans that become delinquent. Credit enhancements are becoming a large part of the business for both GSEs. For instance, 33 percent of Fannie Mae's total mortgage purchases in 2001 were credit enhanced.

NON-CONFORMING MORTGAGE PROGRAMS

Non-conforming mortgage programs, as described above, do not meet standard GSE program eligibility and/or underwriting guidelines. This impacts their marketability—meaning, the loans would not have as many willing buyers as GSE loans or receive the best price if sold on the secondary market. However, not all non-conforming mortgage programs are subprime (nonprime). In fact, non-conforming loan programs often are of an even higher quality (lower risk) than standard GSE loans. For example, jumbo loan

TABLE 6.5
Fannie Mae Standard Eligibility Requirements Matrix

Standard Eligibility Requirements
Maximum Allowable LTV Ratios and Minimum Credit Scores
Manual Underwriting, Fully Amortizing Loans
(Excludes MyCommunityMortgage®, HomeStyle® Renovation, Refi Plus™, High-Balance Mortgages)

Transaction Type[1,2]	Number of Units	Maximum LTV/CLTV[3]/HCLTV	Minimum Credit Score[4]
Principal Residence			
Purchase	1 Unit	95/95/95%	660 if > 75%
Limited Cash-Out Refinance	No Co-ops		620 if ≤ 75%
(LCOR)	1 Unit Co-op[5]	Purchase: 95%/NA/NA	660 if > 75%
		LCOR: 90%/NA/NA	620 if ≤ 75%
	2 Units	80/80/80%	660 if > 75%
			640 if ≤ 75%
	3–4 Units	75/75/75%	660
Cash-Out Refinance	1 Unit	85/85/85%	680 if > 75%
	No Co-ops		620 if ≤ 75%
	1 Unit Co-op[5]	85%/NA/NA	680 if > 75%
			620 if ≤ 75%
	2 Units	75/75/75%	680
	3–4 Units	75/75/75%	680
Second Home[6]			
Purchase	1 Unit	90/90/90%	680 if > 75%
Limited Cash-Out Refinance	No Co-ops		620 if ≤ 75%
	1 Unit Co-op[5]	Purchase: 90%/NA/NA	680 if > 75%
		LCOR: 75%/NA/NA	620 if ≤ 75%
Cash-Out Refinance	1 Unit	75/75/75%	680
	No Co-ops		
Investment Property[6,7]			
Purchase	1 Unit	85/85/85%	680 if > 75%
			620 if ≤ 75%
	2 Units	75/75/75%	660
	3–4 Units	75/75/75%	660
Limited Cash-Out Refinance	1 Unit	75/75/75%	640
	2 Units	75/75/75%	680
	3–4 Units	75/75/75%	680
Cash-Out Refinance	1 Unit	75/75/75%	700
	2 Units	70/70/70%	680
	3–4 Units	70/70/70%	680

Bolded fields indicate an update from previous version of document. References to LTV ratios include LTV, CLTV, and HCLTV ratios.

[1] If the property was purchased within the prior six months, the borrower is ineligible for a cash-out transaction. If the property was listed for sale in the past six months, the LTV ratios for a cash-out transaction are limited to 70% (or maximum allowed if less than 70%, such as for manufactured homes). If the transaction is a single-closing construction-to-permanent loan, and the credit or appraisal documents exceed standard guidelines, then the LTV ratios are limited to 70%. If the borrower is unable to demonstrate an acceptable continuity of obligation, the maximum LTV ratio may be limited. Refer to the Continuity of Obligation topic in the *Selling Guide* for specific requirements.

[2] The maximum allowable LTV ratios in this chart may not apply to certain mortgage loans secured by properties in condo projects in Florida. Refer to the *Selling Guide*, Chapter B4-2, Project Standards, for additional information.

[3] The CLTV may be up to 105% only if the mortgage is part of a Community Seconds® transaction.

[4] Minimum credit score requirements are for mortgage loans underwritten outside of DU and do not apply to loan casefiles underwritten with DU or mortgage loans where the borrowers are relying solely on nontraditional credit to qualify. The minimum credit score must be based on the highest of LTV, CLTV, or HCLTV, as applicable. Fannie Mae will allow accommodations to the credit score based on the underwriter's comprehensive risk assessment. Regardless of the documented circumstances or offsetting contributory risk factors, the minimum credit score may not be lower than 620 or 40 points below the minimum required, whichever is higher. See additional information in the *Selling Guide* for borrowers without credit scores or with credit scores impacted by erroneous data. Borrowers using employment-related assets as qualifying income are not eligible for the 40 point credit score flexibility. Refer to the Other Sources of Income topic in the *Selling Guide* for specific requirements.

[5] No subordinate financing permitted on cooperative share loans.

[6] Borrowers who own five to ten financed properties are subject to the following additional eligibility requirements:
- Second home: purchase - 75/75/75% LTV/CLTV/HCLTV and limited cash-out refinance - 70/70/70% LTV/CLTV/HCLTV
- Investment property: purchase - 1 unit 75/75/75%, 2 - 4 units 70/70/70%; limited cash-out refinance - 1 - 4 units 70/70/70% LTV/CLTV/HCLTV
- 720 minimum credit score
- Cash-out refinance transactions are not permitted.

[7] Units in a cooperative project are not permitted as investment properties.

Source: © 2010 Fannie Mae. Trademarks of Fannie Mae. September 20, 2010.

programs or portfolio loan programs often have higher credit score or property thresholds. The point is: a non-conforming label is not necessarily a higher-risk/subprime label.

NON-PRIME (SUBPRIME) MORTGAGE PROGRAMS

What is subprime mortgage lending? Unfortunately, there is no common industry definition. It was a question federal regulators and the industry have been chasing as the mortgage market kept introducing new programs throughout the late 1990s and up until the mortgage crisis unfolded. Unfortunately, confusion between the terms subprime, conforming, and conventional delayed increased supervision and management of these loan programs and growing portfolios.

The simple answer is that subprime (now referred to as non-prime) is all mortgage lending that is not prime! Prime lending follows *standard* GSE guidelines (Fannie and Freddie). Non-prime loan programs do not meet prime (GSE standard) programs for one or more of the following risk factors:

- Credit history
- Loan-to-value or down payment amount
- Income source or stability
- Asset source or stability
- Property type, characteristics, or condition
- Loan terms or instrument
- Underwriting documentation

Note that the list of risk factors goes beyond just borrower characteristics.

Non-prime loan programs include conforming loans—loans that meet GSE guidelines. For example, the following GSE programs include one or more elevated risk factors: Alt A/A-, Expanded Approval, and affordable housing programs. These programs became popular in the early to mid-2000s as the GSE tried to capture some of the growing non-prime market. Congress prevented further direct GSE lending in non-prime, but unfortunately the GSEs then merely invested in privately-issued non-prime MBSs and experienced heavy losses on them.

The first Interagency Statement on Subprime Mortgage Lending in 1999 provided lenders with some direction on how to manage subprime mortgages, but these were defined using only borrower characteristics (delinquent credit history). Later interagency statements and Guidelines, in 2001 and 2005–2007, expanded this definition to include limited or no-documentation requirements and loan product characteristics: discount ARMs (300 or more basis points) and short initial rate periods (i.e., 2/28 ARM programs). By this time the agencies realized they should have been focusing on individual risk elements, risk layering, and overall risk, instead of just delinquent credit or some ARM loans or the sponsor of the loan program.

Today, regulations for non-prime mortgage programs require verification of applicants' income, an assessment of whether or not the applicant can make the mortgage payment, and direction on what payment should be used to qualify. They also require a higher level of communication with the applicants, warning them of the risks involved with that particular non-prime program. Additionally, regulations require that lenders have more effective monitoring and control systems in place for originating non-prime applications and servicing these loans. GSE requirements mirror the high level of federal regulatory scrutiny now present in this area of mortgage lending.

The Dodd-Frank Act also proposes several rules which will require certain disclosures and restrict features in some loan programs, depending on the level risk characteristics present. These proposals may impact loan program design, as well as all the subsequent phases of originatin and servicing. See Chapter 11—Compliance for a summary of Dodd-Frank Act proposals.

DISCUSSION POINTS

1. Discuss how the standard fixed-rate mortgage developed in the United States and why it was an important tool for reviving real estate and mortgage lending after the Great Depression.

2. Explain why a self-amortizing (direct reduction) mortgage can save a mortgage borrower a substantial amount of interest over a term loan.

3. Discuss the differences between conventional and conforming mortgage programs.

4. Identify and discuss the components of an adjustable-rate mortgage.

5. What must a mortgage lender do to attract consumers to an adjustable-rate mortgage when fixed-rate mortgages are attractively priced?

6. What makes a mortgage loan "subprime" and what are some of the benefits and challenges in this area of lending? How do they differ from "non-prime" mortgages?

7. What is the difference between an eligibility issue and an underwriting guideline?

8. Explain the difference between mortgage instruments, programs, and products.

CHAPTER 7

Private Mortgage Insurance

INTRODUCTION

This chapter explains how private mortgage insurance (PMI) works, its role in residential lending, and which factors helped it gain so much ground in the mortgage insurance business. Mortgage insurance is one form of *credit enhancement* that protects a lender from loan loss. An *endorsement* is one form of credit enhancement—as in the Veteran's Administration programs, which reimburse lenders for losses on loans to eligible borrowers. A *guarantee* is the second form of credit enhancement—as in the USDA Rural Housing Services guarantee. Chapter 8—Government Lending—describes these programs and FHA (mentioned below) in greater detail.

The third type of credit enhancement, mortgage insurance (MI), pays a lender for an agreed upon amount, should a loan loss occur. Any insurance serves to spread the economic risk or loss from a particular hazard over a large group—that is, the insured group. There are three types of mortgage insurance:

- Private—individual corporations who specialize in this insurance
- Government—Federal Housing Agency or state agency
- Self—an individual lender "self-insures" a mortgage

Like other forms of credit enhancements, PMI enables lenders to approve a loan that they otherwise might be prohibited from making. Specifically, PMI allows lenders to make high loan-to-value mortgage loans (80–95, even 97 percent). Private mortgage insurance allows lenders to meet regulatory requirements which, as a general rule, prohibit lenders from making a mortgage loan with a loan-to-value exceeding 80 percent without some form of mortgage insurance. For example, Fannie Mae's and Freddie Mac's charter prohibits them from buying a residential mortgage loan with a loan-to-value greater than 80 percent unless the loan is insured, guaranteed, or has some other type of credit enhancement.

In addition to insuring individual loans, PMI companies also insure pools of loans for individual lenders, investors, and government agencies. Pool insurance may improve the rating of the underlying mortgage-backed security. In this way, PMI assists lenders and investors.

For consumers, PMI enables the purchase of homes with a smaller down payment, purchase of higher-priced homes, or refinancing of existing homes when they have little equity.

FHA/VA/PMI credit-enhanced loans averaged approximately 22.5 percent of total originations in the last twenty years, according to FHFA (Federal Housing Finance Agency, www.fhfa.gov). During this period, PMI market share of insured mortgages increased steadily, becoming the dominant form of mortgage credit enhancement over government-sponsored programs.

WHY IS PRIVATE MORTGAGE INSURANCE SO IMPORTANT IN TODAY'S MARKET?

PMI assists many potential homebuyers who do not have the 20 percent down payment and who do not qualify for either FHA or VA loans. According to the FHFA House Price Index (HPI), home prices nationally increased at least two percent annually from 1991–2007. From 1997 to 2005, the annual rate of appreciation nationally increased steadily from four percent to 11 percent, making it more difficult for many consumers to save a large enough down payment. Throughout this period, MI programs with down payments as low as five percent and even three percent allowed many consumers to remain in the home purchase market even when home prices increased more than their savings.

Compared to government programs, PMI allowed many families to participate in the home purchase market during this twenty-year period of home price appreciation. From 1997–2003 when total originations increased, PMI *tripled* its dollar volume as shown in Table 7.1. In comparison, government-insured/endorsements only doubled in volume. According to MICA (Mortgage Insurance Companies of America, www.privatemi.com), the average PMI loan

TABLE **7.1**
Average Loan Amount: FHA, VA, PMI

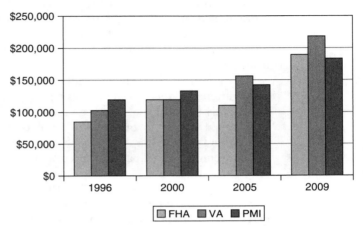

Source: FHFA, MICA, FFIEC

© Community Lending Associates, LLC

www.communitylendassoc.com

amount during roughly the same period rose significantly—from $118,000 to $156,000—reflecting the increase in housing prices and GSE loan limits. Clearly, PMI enabled more consumers to participate in a broader segment of the real estate market than government-insured/endorsed programs.

Starting in 2007, housing values dropped significantly in many areas of the country. In 2008 and 2009, the FHFA HPI showed a four percent decline nationally, with much higher depreciation in some regions. Consumers who before were unable to participate in homeownership at the higher price level because of an insufficient down payment now may be able to afford a home with the assistance of PMI. Consumers who purchased homes recently without needing PMI now may have little equity left in that same home. They may need PMI in order to refinance to a lower rate—as will many other existing homeowners with hybrid ARM loan programs (See Chapter 6—Conventional Lending) who wish to refinance into less risky fixed rate programs at historically low rates.

Private Mortgage Insurance History and Evolution

Before examining current government and private mortgage programs, a brief review of the historical development of mortgage insurance will be helpful in order to gain an understanding of present practices.

The Beginning

Early title insurance companies began mortgage insurance in the 1890s by insuring the repayment of mortgages in addition to the validity of titles. The first statutory law providing for this type of insurance was enacted in New York State in 1904.

The social and demographic changes that emerged in the United States after 1900 (particularly following World War I) led mortgage lending into a more important position in the U.S. economy. As mortgage lending became more prevalent and important, mortgage insurance became more accepted and desired. Because of this increased interest, title insurance companies became involved in providing this financial service as a no-cost add-on to title insurance.

The residential mortgage-lending and title insurance business was practiced differently then from the way it is practiced today. It was customary during this period for a mortgage company to exchange a new mortgage for a defaulted one or to buy back a troubled loan sold to an investor. As the real estate boom of the 1920s continued, this custom gave way to the actual guaranteeing of principal and interest by a new entity—the mortgage guaranty company.

During their peak years (1925–1932), as many as 50 companies were in operation, located primarily in the state of New York. These companies prospered by originating and selling mortgages with a guarantee to institutional investors or to individual investors as mortgage participation bonds. The units sold to individual investors were usually in $500 or $1,000 denominations. Yield and apparent safety made the units very attractive. A trustee would hold the mortgages and be responsible for foreclosure if any default in payment occurred. The prevailing viewpoint during this period was that real estate values would continue to appreciate, and, if any lax underwriting or appraising occurred, the resulting questionable mortgage would be saved by inflation. This optimism affected the investing public. Large portions of accumulated savings were invested in mortgage bonds issued by apparently successful mortgage guaranty companies.

Due to the general optimism about the economy and the laissez-faire attitude of the government, these mortgage guaranty companies were virtually unregulated. Lack of regulation often led to poor underwriting, self-dealing, fraud, and ultimately to a lack of adequate reserves to meet any meaningful emergency.

Even before the stock market crash of 1929, the real estate industry was in serious trouble. Real estate values started to drop and foreclosures resulted, which further depressed values. It was inevitable that these companies would not survive the bank holiday declared by President Roosevelt in March 1933. Institutional investors lost many billions of dollars, with similarly tragic results for private investors because of the failure of these companies.

The collapse left such an ugly mark on the real estate finance industry that private mortgage insurance did not reappear for almost 25 years.

1950s–1970s: The Rebirth of Private Mortgage Insurance

Following the failures of mortgage insurance during the Great Depression, private mortgage insurance companies (PMIs, or simply, MIs) returned in 1957 after a lapse of a quarter of a century. The first of the "reborn" mortgage insurance companies was the Mortgage Guaranty Insurance Corporation (MGIC), organized in 1957 under a Wisconsin state law enacted in

1956. Several additional companies followed. A strong regulatory structure was necessary to ensure that MI companies were stable and committed to the industry.

In the early years of rebirth, MI programs were not as dominant as the government insurance programs, which were generally the first choice of consumers who qualified for them. MI companies offered an alternative to the successful VA and FHA mortgage insurance programs, for which many consumers and some properties were ineligible.

Of great importance to the rapid growth of MI was the Emergency Home Finance Act (1970). This act first authorized Fannie Mae and Freddie Mac to purchase loans with less than 20 percent down payment, as long as the loans had MI, which was required on these loans to reduce the lender's exposure down to 75 percent of loan-to-value (using the lesser of sales price or appraisal).

High-ratio conventional mortgages became increasingly popular in the 1970s, as home prices appreciated steadily and the 20 percent down payment eluded more and more potential borrowers. Once these mortgages could trade in the secondary market, more mortgage lenders (in particular, savings associations) offered them. Today, Fannie Mae, Freddie Mac, and other secondary market participants purchase high-LTV loans regularly with MI, and with many different insurance programs and levels of coverage (see Chapter 5— Secondary Mortgage Market, for a discussion of credit enhancements).

The 1980s: Difficult Years

Until the early 1980s, the MI process worked well, and all parties to the transaction benefited. In the 1980s, the economic recession impacted jobs and housing values. The MI industry suffered spectacular losses, with $5 billion paid out in claims to policyholders. Dramatic increases in inflation and interest rates resulted in a general slowing of property appreciation in most areas and significant property depreciation in entire regions of the country. As a result, many homeowners could not sell their properties and pay off their mortgages to avoid foreclosure. Lenders who foreclosed faced the same situation. This poor real estate market, combined with the popularity and expansion of 95 percent loan-to-value lending in the years immediately preceding that economic recession and coupled with exotic ARM loan programs, significantly raised delinquency and foreclosure rates nationwide. Soon to follow were sharp increases in the claims incidence for MI.

Many MI companies discovered, to their financial disappointment, that the claims levels on loans written in the early 1980s were five or six times that of loans written in the 1970s. (Delinquency and claims on loans originated in the early 1990s were higher than preceding years as well, but not as severe.) As a result of these staggering losses to the MI companies, confrontations developed between MI companies and mortgage lenders over questionable origination and servicing practices. The Mortgage Insurance Companies of America (MICA) estimates that during this period, five out of every 1,000 lender policyholders were denied claims because of some irregularities.

The decade ended with the MI industry paying claims to mortgage lenders in the billions of dollars. Such large payouts are strong evidence of the value of mortgage insurance during periods of economic downturn and deflation in housing values. If MI companies had not absorbed these losses, lenders would have had to suffer the losses, with the resulting economic chaos. As it turned out, the losses were too much for some MI companies, and they either stopped writing new business or merged with larger, better-capitalized MI companies.

The 1990s: Golden Years?

A comparison of FHA/VA/PMI loan volume for 1990 through 2009, as shown in Table 7.2, reveals some of the dynamics of "today's" mortgage insurance. It is important to note that volume for all three credit enhancement sources reacted to economic changes in generally the same way, but with some differences and some exceptions.

The MI companies benefited tremendously during the economic expansion of the 1990s, a welcome period after the painful 1980s. Although current business and financial performance for MI companies was stellar, the MI companies had learned a painful lesson during the 1980s. In the 1990s they developed programs that would hedge the potentially negative effects of a poor home purchase market.

From 1990 to 2000, home purchase activity remained consistent and grew steadily as strong economic conditions sustained the consumer confidence

TABLE **7.2**
FHA/VA/PMI Loan Volume

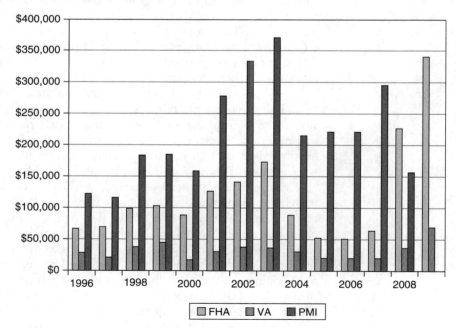

Source: FHFA, MICA

© 2010 Community Lending Associates, LLC

www.communitylendassoc.com

level needed to commit to such a large purchase. Although overall purchase activity did not decline, mortgage insurance activity declined sharply in 1994 and 1999, as increases in interest rates impacted the first-time home purchase market disproportionately to overall housing activity.

Although these three sources of mortgage credit enhancement increased and decreased in unison (mostly) during these economic turning points, the severity and duration of increase/decrease differed. This illustrates the differences in these types of insurance. From 1990 to 2009, both FHA and private mortgage insurance volume were more volatile compared to the more consistent (although lower) VA volume. This is largely a result of the restrictive eligibility requirement for the VA program versus more of the general public being eligible for FHA and PMI programs. Changes in interest rates have less impact on VA mortgage volume compared to FHA and PMI programs.

FHA is more restrictive than PMI as well because of its loan limits. FHA determines a maximum loan amount in each county of the country for one-, two-, three-, and four-unit properties. Although the highest single-family amount in 2010 is approximately $729,750, in most areas of the country the limit is around $271,050. This amount is approximately 65 percent of the 2010 Fannie Mae/Freddie Mac loan limit, which excludes many loan transactions that are eligible for PMI. This also explains why the average-size loan insured by PMI is higher than that by FHA. Chapter 8—Government Lending, discusses FHA, VA, and USDA programs in detail.

PMI volume became quite volatile starting in 1996. It rose dramatically to 62 percent of the mortgage insurance market (higher in later years). The loan limits alone do not explain this change. During this period PMI companies implemented new insurance programs that work in conjunction with less stringent automated underwriting guidelines from Fannie Mae and Freddie Mac, while the FHA program remained relatively constant. PMI developed additional programs which increased insured LTV to 97 percent, then insured 100 percent, and even 103 percent LTV! Many of these new programs only recently (in 2007) encountered a strong recession, so they are either greatly restricted or not available today.

Additional reasons for the rebirth of the MI companies and their impressive growth since the 1950s include the following:

- Extensive use of the secondary market by mortgage bankers
- Eligibility of MI loans for secondary mortgage market sale
- Government-sponsored enterprise (**GSE**) requirement that loans greater than 80 percent LTV must have MI
- Relatively slow loan processing with state/federal government programs
- Lower loan limits for FHA mortgages
- Increase in high-LTV conventional lending

2000 and Beyond: The Best of Times, the Worst of Times ...

From 2000–2007, PMI accounted for 59–76 percent of the dollar volume of *insured* mortgage originations—more than twice the level of FHA and VA. This is quite an accomplishment for a segment of the industry that disappeared from the 1930s until 1957. However, from 2008–2010 in the aftermath of the mortgage crisis the dollar amount and percentage of PMI dropped precipitously to 38 percent of insured originations. FHA increased significantly during this period, almost doubling the amount of coverage from prior years.

During the mortgage and housing crisis of 2008–2009, more restrictive underwriting and decreasing property values adversely impacted PMI volume, causing PMI volume to drop below government-insured/endorsed volume for the first time since 1990. Table 7.3 shows the PMI origination data for the past 14 years. According to MICA, new MI certificate volume fell sharply and steadily to 10 percent of its 2007 level.

During this period, PMI-loan delinquency increased significantly (as did overall loan delinquency). MI companies paid more than $15 billion in claims, and MI company capital dropped to dangerous levels. Many companies project one to two years, until 2012, to work out most of their insurance default issues. MI companies recently have contested more claims than in prior years, citing lender and/or borrower fraud as the main reason for refusing to pay claims.

On the positive side, in 2010, MI companies began curing more delinquencies than they received for the first time since 2007, helping to lower their level of exposure. Perhaps aided by the federal government's tax

TABLE **7.3**
FHA/VA/PMI Origination Data, 1996–2009

Year	FHA Dollar	FHA% of Total ($)	VA Dollar	VA% of Total ($)	PMI Dollar	PMI% of Total ($)	New PMI Approved Number	PMI Approval Rate	PMI Dollar Outstanding
1996	$71,617	31%	$33,358	14%	$126,972	55%	1,068,707	78%	$513,240
1997	$74,243	33%	$26,874	12%	$120,896	54%	974,298	77%	$546,133
1998	$103,165	31%	$42,584	13%	$187,437	56%	1,473,344	74%	$559,445
1999	$108,106	31%	$49,580	14%	$188,871	54%	1,455,354	83%	$598,515
2000	$93,110	33%	$22,208	8%	$163,136	59%	1,236,214	76%	$650,073
2001	$131,240	29%	$35,443	8%	$282,506	63%	2,035,546	73%	$698,316
2002	$145,053	28%	$41,945	8%	$337,053	64%	2,305,709	76%	$733,279
2003	$176,947	30%	$40,546	7%	$375,700	63%	2,464,973	80%	$619,029
2004	$93,660	27%	$35,310	10%	$219,043	63%	1,708,972	95%	$609,196
2005	$57,527	19%	$24,884	8%	$225,024	73%	1,579,593	97%	$615,082
2006	$55,277	18%	$24,461	8%	$226,076	74%	1,444,330	96%	$668,399
2007	$68,426	17%	$25,157	6%	$300,052	76%	1,979,074	95%	$819,812
2008	$231,526	53%	$40,582	9%	$162,219	37%	971,595	84%	$952,196
2009	$344,865	69%	$74,025	15%	$80,797	16%	442,224	75%	$863,448

Source: FHFA, VA, MICA

© 2010 REMOC Associates, LLC

www.remoc.com

incentive for first-time homebuyers, new certificate volume doubled from its lowest levels, but still remains well below its peak levels.

HOW DOES PMI WORK?

Mortgage insurance provides a financial guarantee to a mortgage lender in return for a fee (a premium), usually paid by the borrower. The lender submits an application to a PMI company. If approved and the loan closes, the servicer establishes a PMI escrow similar to a tax escrow, and remits these funds to the PMI company. Generally, the amount paid is the original loan amount multiplied by the initial or annual premium (i.e., $100,000 \times 1.15\% = \$1,150$).

In 1998, the Homeowners Protection Act required disclosures and cancellation guidelines for lenders on loans with PMI (FHA has similar requirements). It also provides borrowers with an option to cancel PMI if the loan's LTV drops below 78% or 80%, depending on if it is automatic termination or borrower requested termination. Figure 7.1, PMI Disclosure Form, and Chapter 11—Compliance, further describe these requirements.

FIGURE **7.1** PMI Disclosure Form

Private Mortgage Insurance Disclosure
Northland Mortgage Company

Borrower Name: Lisa Dennis Valvo
Address: 1190 North Benson Drive
Hollywood, Illinois 60062
Account Number: 1234567

You are required to maintain private mortgage insurance in connection with the above referenced mortgage loan. Private mortgage insurance protects lenders and others against financial loss in the event borrowers default on their loans. Mortgage insurance enables you to purchase a home with a downpayment of less than 20 percent, which might otherwise not be possible.

Under certain circumstances, the federal Homeowners Protection Act of 1998 gives you the right to cancel private mortgage insurance or requires that such insurance automatically terminate. This disclosure describes those circumstances. Also enclosed is an amortization schedule that shows the principal and interest due on your mortgage loan and the remaining balance after each scheduled payment.

Requesting Cancellation of Private Mortgage Insurance

You have the right to request that private mortgage insurance be canceled on or after:

(a) (See attached amortization schedule) 04/04/10, which is the date the principal balance of your mortgage loan is first *scheduled* to reach 80 percent of the original value of the property securing the loan; or

FIGURE **7.1** (*Continued*)

(b) The date 04/04/10 when the principal balance of your loan *actually* reaches 80 percent of the original value of the property.

"Original value" means the lesser of the contract sales price of the property or the appraised value of the property at the time the loan is closed.

Private mortgage insurance on your loan will be canceled only if all of the following conditions are met:

(a) You submit a written request for cancellation;

(b) You have a good payment history (meaning, no payments 60 or more days past due within two years and no payment 30 or more days past due within one year of the cancellation date); and

(c) We receive, if requested and at your expense, evidence satisfactory to the holder of your loan that the value of the property has not declined below its original value, and certification that there are no subordinate liens on the property.

Automatic Termination

When you are current on your loan payments, the mortgage insurance on your loan will automatically terminate on the date the principal balance of your loan is first *scheduled* to reach 78 percent of the original value of the property. That date is 06/01/11 (see attached amortization schedule). If you are not current on your loan payments as of that date, the private mortgage insurance will automatically terminate only when you become current.

High-Risk Loans

The rights to cancellation and automatic termination described above do not apply to certain loans that may present a higher risk of default. As your loan is not designated a "high-risk" loan, the cancellation and automatic termination provisions described above do apply to your loan.

I/we acknowledge having received, read, and understood this Initial Disclosure for fixed-rate mortgage; or it has been thoroughly explained to me/us.

_____   _____

Lisa Dennis-Valvo   Date

You should consult your attorney with respect to this act.

Source: © 2010 REMOC Associates, LLC

Over the years, PMI companies developed several different payment plans. The basic trade-off is between the upfront premium (paid at closing) and the monthly premium (escrowed for and paid with the regular monthly mortgage payment). See Figure 7.2. Also, like Fannie and Freddie and other secondary market investors, MI companies now utilize risk-based premium pricing. The largest adjustments are credit-related, but risk factors influence the final premium charged to the borrower.

FIGURE **7.2** Sample PMI Plans and Premiums

Genworth Financial ☀.

NATIONAL RATES

May 3, 2010

Genworth Mortgage Insurance Corporation
Genworth Residential Mortgage Assurance Corporation

RATE NOTES

Find Rates Fast

Use our *Rate Finder* to compare products, loan types, terms and payments. Visit **mortgageinsurance.genworth.com.**

MI PRODUCTS

Monthly Premium MI is a payment option which features a coverage term of one month; premiums are remitted monthly. The premium rate shown is the annualized first year and renewal premium rate. The premium to be remitted monthly is determined by multiplying the annualized premium rate by the loan amount and dividing that amount by 12.

Zero Monthly Premium MI is a payment option which features monthly premium rates with no initial premium required at closing.

Level Annual Premium MI is a payment option which features a coverage term of twelve months; premiums are remitted annually. The Level Annual option features one identical rate for both first year and renewal premiums. The 1st year premiums may be financed into the loan amount.

Single Premium MI provides coverage until the loan amortizes to 78% of the original value, unless previously cancelled. Premiums are earned in accordance with North Carolina insurance statutes using the *Earnings Schedules.*

> **Earnings Schedule:** Refer to our *Earnings Schedules* in the *Rates and Guidelines* section of **mortgageinsurance.genworth.com.**

> **Five Year Refund Period** provides refunds according to the refund schedule (5160144) in the event of a cancellation within the first 60 months of the loan, or at any time, if a refund is required under the Homeowners Protection Act of 1998.

> **Financed Premium:** Refer to our *Underwriting Guidelines* for details.

Split Premium MI is a payment option that features lower monthly rates combined with an upfront premium due at closing. The upfront premium may be financed into the loan amount. Rates are nonrefundable.

LOAN TYPE DEFINITIONS

Fixed Mortgages feature level payments for the first five years of the loan term. All acceptable plans must (1) fully amortize over a maximum of 40 years, (2) have the initial payment rate equal to or greater than the initial accrual rate, and (3) have no temporary buydowns, rate concessions or the potential

for negative amortization during the first five years. Also included, 2% Graduated Payment Mortgages whose annual payment increases are limited to 2%.

ARMs with Annual Caps of 1% or Less (Includes Temporary Buydowns) feature payment changes, or the potential for payment changes, and have effective annual interest rate caps of 1% during the first three years of the mortgage. Examples of eligible loans include: 3-year ARMs with 3% cap or less on first adjustment; 2-year ARMs with 3% cap or less on first adjustment; 1-year and 6-month ARMs with 1% or less effective annual interest rate caps; blended ARM/fixed instruments; and buydowns.

ARMs with Annual Caps Greater Than 1% feature payment changes, or the potential for payment changes, and have effective annual interest rate caps greater than 1% during the first three years of the mortgage. Mortgages featuring scheduled negative amortization or potential negative amortization during the first five years are included.

Non-Fixed Payment Loans: Feature payment changes or the potential for payment changes during the first five years of the mortgage. Loans featuring negative amortization are not eligible for insurance.

LOAN TERM DEFINITIONS

30 Year: Fully amortize over a period greater than twenty-five years and no greater than forty years.

≤ 25 Year: Fully amortize over a maximum of twenty-five years.

RENEWAL PREMIUMS DEFINITIONS
For level renewals:
- The renewal premium rate is applied to the original loan balance for years 1 through 10.
- For years 11 through term, the rate is reduced to 0.20% or remains the same if the rate is less than 0.20%.
- Premium adjustments do not apply to the 11th year rate through term.

For amortized renewals:
- The renewal premium rate is applied annually to the outstanding loan balance as of the anniversary date of the loan for years 1 through term.

PREMIUM ADJUSTMENT RULES
Rate Floor of .15% applies. If original rate is below .15%, then discounts are not effective. If the rate is reduced to less than .20% after the discount is applied, the renewal rate will remain the same.

Multiple Discounts: Multiple discounts may not be applied.

ADDITIONAL NOTES
Non-Refundable Rates: A lower premium rate applies in lieu of a premium refund when coverage is cancelled. No premium will be refunded when coverage is cancelled, unless cancelled under the Homeowners Protection Act of 1998.

NEGATIVE AMORTIZATION NOT PERMITTED.

Relocation Loans: To qualify for relocation rates, the loan must meet agency guidelines for employee relocation mortgages as found in our underwriting guidelines.

Nontraditional Credit: Use Nontraditional rates.

Counseling Saver: Refer to our *Underwriting Guidelines* for details.

Underwriting Guidelines: Refer to our *Underwriting Guidelines* to determine loan eligibility. Properties located in some markets may be subject to Genworth's *Geographic Guidelines.* Refer to *Standard Guidelines for Property and Appraisals* section for more details.

Investor Coverage: As with all programs, check directly with your investor for specific coverage requirements.

For additional rates, coverages, or a refund schedule: Visit our website at **mortgageinsurance.genworth.com** and access our *Rate Finder* or select *Rates & Guidelines.* Or call the ActionCenter® at 800 444.5664 or your local underwriting office.

RATES MAY NOT BE AVAILABLE OR APPROVED IN ALL STATES. RATES ARE BASED ON PROPERTY LOCATION.

5961474.0510

Nontraditional Credit: Use nontraditional rates.

FIGURE **7.2** (*Continued*)

Genworth Financial ☼. | **NATIONAL RATES**

May 3, 2010
Genworth Mortgage Insurance Corporation
Genworth Residential Mortgage Assurance Corporation

MONTHLY PREMIUM MI & ZERO MONTHLY PREMIUM MI

30 Year Term		FIXED *Level payments for the first 5 years*			ARMs *With annual caps of 1% or less includes temporary buydowns*			ARMs *With annual caps greater than 1%*		
		CREDIT SCORE			CREDIT SCORE			CREDIT SCORE		
LTV	Coverage	700+	680-699**	Nontraditional	700+	680-699**	Nontraditional	700+	680-699**	Nontraditional
97%*- 95.01%	35%	1.15%	1.53%	—	1.34%	1.71%	—	1.41%	1.90%	—
	30	1.03	1.35	—	1.20	1.51	—	1.26	1.67	—
	26	.93	1.19	—	1.08	1.33	—	1.14	1.47	—
	25	.90	1.14	—	1.04	1.28	—	1.10	1.41	—
	20	.76	.97	—	.88	1.08	—	.93	1.20	—
	18	.75	.90	—	.82	1.00	—	.87	1.12	—
95%- 90.01%	35	1.06	1.37	1.37%	1.21	1.53	1.53%	1.25	1.70	1.70%
	30	.94	1.20	1.20	1.04	1.34	1.34	1.08	1.49	1.49
	25	.84	1.08	1.08	.90	1.21	1.21	.94	1.34	1.34
	20	.75	.90	.90	.80	1.01	1.01	.84	1.12	1.12
	18	.74	.85	.85	.79	.93	.93	.82	1.05	1.05
	16	.72	.79	.79	.77	.85	.85	.79	.98	.98
90%- 85.01%	35	.75	.75	1.05	.92	.92	1.18	.96	.96	1.30
	30	.69	.69	.88	.84	.84	.99	.89	.89	1.09
	25	.62	.62	.76	.73	.73	.85	.78	.78	.94
	20	.52	.52	.67	.59	.59	.75	.64	.64	.83
	17	.49	.49	.61	.56	.56	.68	.61	.61	.76
	12	.44	.44	.52	.45	.45	.58	.50	.50	.64
85%- & Below	30	.57	.57	.75	.67	.67	.84	.71	.71	.93
	25	.48	.48	.69	.55	.55	.77	.59	.59	.86
	20	.45	.45	.65	.51	.51	.73	.55	.55	.81
	17	.43	.43	.58	.44	.44	.65	.49	.49	.72
	12	.38	.38	.44	.39	.39	.49	.44	.44	.55
	6	.34	.34	.38	.36	.36	.43	.40	.40	.47

*Rates for LTV 97 - 95.01% are only available for loans meeting Genworth's Affordable Housing Guidelines.

**Rates shown for LTV > 90% and credit scores < 700 are nonstandard rates.

Nontraditional Credit: Use nontraditional rates.

AGENCY COVERAGE LEVELS

▓ Standard Coverage Levels for 26 - 40 year fixed and all non-fixed mortgages

░ Charter Level Coverages for MyCommunity Mortgage® & HomePossible®

PREMIUM ADJUSTMENT SYSTEM			
Cash Out Refinance	+.20%	Rate/Term Refinance	+.10
Condominium	+.10	Refundable Premium	+.01
Cooperative Unit	+.10	Relocation Loan***:	
Counseling Saver	-.05	LTV ≤ 85%	-.07%
Level Annual Premium (Refundable)	-.04	LTV 85.01% - 90%	-.10
Loan Amount > $417,000	+.25	LTV ≥ 90.01%	-.12
Manufactured Housing	+.20	Second Home	+.14
Primary 2 Unit	+.25	Term ≤ 25 years	-.11

***No discount available with LTV > 90% and credit score < 700.

One benefit of PMI vs. FHA is that PMI offers plans with no upfront premium, which FHA requires. For example, for a loan amount of $100,000 at 95 percent LTV, FHA would charge one percent ($1,000 paid at closing) and $95.83 on a monthly basis. PMI would have no cost at closing (a real benefit for many first-time homebuyers), but the monthly premium for that plan ($95.83) would equal that of FHA. Overall, the five-year total with a PMI plan would cost the borrower $5,749.80, and the five-year total with an FHA plan would be $6,749.80, an additional cost of $1,000. At lower LTVs, the PMI plan is between $1,800 and $4,600 less than the comparable FHA plan shown in Table 7.4.

Depending on the plan selected, the MI premium can add approximately 0.75 percent to the APR at a 95 percent loan-to-value, the highest cost level. FHA insurance at the same level will add approximately 1.0 percent to the APR. At lower LTV levels PMI compares favorably to FHA by about:

- 0.5% lower APR at 90%
- 0.625% lower APR at 85%
- 0.75% lower APR at 80%

TABLE **7.4**
Comparison of FHA and PMI Premiums

Loan-to-value		Fixed Rate Loan Amount $100,000			
		Initial Premium	Monthly Premium	Total Cost (5 yrs)	PMI vs. FHA
95.01–96.5%	FHA	$1,000.	$95.83	$6,749.80	
		1.00%	1.15%		
	PMI	$0.	$98.83	$5,749.80	−$1,000.00
		0%	1.15%		
90.01–95%	FHA	$1,000.	$91.67	$6,500.20	
		1.00%	1.10%		
	PMI	$0.	$78.33	$4,699.80	−$1,800.40
		0%	0.94%		
85.01–90%	FHA	$1,000.	$91.67	$6,500.20	
		1.00%	1.10%		
	PMI	$0.	$51.67	$3,100.20	−$3,400.00
		0%	0.62%		
<85%	FHA	$1,000.	$91.67	$6,500.20	
		1.00%	1.10%		
	PMI	$0.	$31.67	$1,900.20	−$4,600.00
		0%	0.38%		

NOTE: FHA premiums effective 04/18/11; PMI premiums may change then, too.

Source: Reprinted with permission of Genworth Financial Rates & Comparisons Tool

It is important to emphasize that the borrower pays for mortgage insurance *to protect the lender only*. MI comes into play only if the loan becomes delinquent and the lender suffers a loss. The lender (and servicer) agrees to follow certain servicing and collection procedures to keep the PMI valid.

CONTRACTING WITH A MORTGAGE INSURANCE COMPANY

In order to do business together, a mortgage insurance company must first approve a lender and issue it a *master policy*. The approval process is similar to doing business with Fannie and Freddie, FHA and VA. MI companies review the lender's experience in originating and servicing first-mortgage loans, in addition to their financial strength. This screening process may include conducting interviews with the lender's mortgage-processing, underwriting, and servicing staff, as well as management. The MI companies want to ensure that the loans they will be insuring have been originated in a thorough and professional manner. They also wish to establish that the servicing lender has the experience to manage the ongoing insurance policy requirements.

Once the MI company issues a master policy to an approved lender, it will then review mortgage application packages submitted by its lender client (similar to Fannie or Freddie or any other investor). The MI company completes its review within a day or two of receipt and, if approved, issues individual insurance commitments *to the lender*.

According to MICA numbers, the approval percentage of applications submitted to PMI companies can vary significantly. For example, from 2007 to 2009, approval percentage dropped from 95 percent to 62 percent. Over the past 15 years, it reached a high of 97 percent in 2005 and a low of 73 percent in 2001. During this period, there were six years in which the approvals were in the 70th percentile, four years in the 80th percentile, and four years in the 90th percentile.

MI COVERAGE AMOUNT

For many years, secondary market mortgage insurance requirements fell into one standard MI program. With the addition of their automated underwriting and "expanded" (subprime) programs, Fannie Mae and Freddie Mac now allow different MI coverage levels in addition to the standard MI program. Table 7.5 lists typical standard and minimum coverage levels required by Fannie Mae and Freddie Mac for 30-year, fixed-rate primary residence mortgage loans (subject to change).

While on the surface it appears that consumers benefit from this reduced coverage, Fannie Mae and Freddie Mac adjust their pricing to reflect this increased risk, and will impose a Loan Level Pricing Adjustment (LLPA). For loans with less than standard MI coverage, Fannie Mae and Freddie Mac charge a fee ranging from an additional 0.125 percent to 1.75 percent—even higher for credit scores lower than 680. In this way, the GSE (and investors who receive some of this premium) in effect "self-insure" a percentage of these high-LTV loans and charge the lender (and therefore the consumer).

FIGURE **7.3** Sample Individual PMI Commitment/Certificate of Insurance

Genworth Financial ☀️℠

Attn: TEST CUSTOMER

From: GENWORTH MORTGAGE INSURANCE CORPORATION

CONTACT NUMBER: 800-444-5664

Date: 04/23/2010

COMMITMENT/CERTIFICATE OF INSURANCE
PLEASE VERIFY THAT ALL INFORMATION ON THIS COMMITMENT/CERTIFICATE MEETS YOUR REQUIREMENTS PRIOR TO REMITTING PREMIUM.

In consideration of the premium hereinafter set forth and in reliance upon the statements made in the application the, Company hereby issues this Commitment and Certificate of Insurance for the mortgage loan herein described subject to the terms and conditions of your Master Policy identified below, and subject to any Special Conditions that may be set forth below.

TERM OF COVERAGE STD/1 MONTH	EXPIRATION DATE 08/21/2010	EFFECTIVE DATE 04/23/2010	MASTER POLICY NUMBER B222225VGP	COMMITMENT NUMBER **6300187519**

INSURED'S NAME AND ADDRESS:	BORROWER NAME AND PROPERTY ADDRESS:
TESTING ORG. NUMBER TEST PLEASE CALL ACTION CTR @ 800-444-5664 RALEIGH NC 27615-0000	TEST BORROWER TEST CO-BORROWER 1 TEST ROAD TEST CITY GA 30332-0000

LOAN TYPE FIXED RATE/FIXED PAYMENT	INSURED AMOUNT 150,000	SALES PRICE 160,000	APPRAISED VALUE 177,000	TERM OF LOAN 360 MONTHS	COVERAGE TOP 30%
LTV/OCCUPANCY 95/PRIMARY	INITIAL PREMIUM RATE .95000000	RENEWAL RATE .95000000	RENEWAL TYPE MONTHLY-LEVEL	INITIAL PREMIUM 118.75	INITIAL TOTAL DUE 118.75

PREMIUM SCHEDULE • PREMIUMS ON THIS COMMITMENT MUST BE REMITTED MONTHLY IN ACCORDANCE WITH MASTER POLICY ENDORSEMENT FOR GENWORTH MORTGAGE INSURANCE .9500% x ORIG LOAN AMT x 1/12 (EFF MO RATE = .07916700%) FOR MOS 1–120, THEREAFTER AT .2000% x ORIG LOAN AMT x 1/12 (EFF MO RATE = .01666600%).

REFUNDABLE PREMIUM IF CANCELLED   FIXED RATE - EASY MONTHLY

SPECIAL CONDITIONS •
– UNDERWRITTEN AND APPROVED BY GENWORTH SUBJECT TO LOAN FILE TERMS AND CONDITIONS ABOVE. CHANGES TO LOAN FILE REQUIRE RESUBMISSION TO GENWORTH.
– Genworth has purchased job loss protection from 3rd party on this loan.
Coverage subject to all terms and conditions of policy & related certificate.

* * ACTIVATION INSTRUCTIONS * *
Please provide loan closing date and servicing information in the boxes below. Mail form and Initial Total Due (if any) to:
GENWORTH MORTGAGE INSURANCE CORP.
PO BOX 277197
ATLANTA   GA 30384-7197
You will be billed once Genworth receives your Initial Total Due and loan closing date.
* *
* Insurance will not be in force until
* Genworth receives the Initial Total Due
* and loan closing date.
* *

CALCULATION ASSUMES A TERM FROM CLOSING OF 360 MONTHS USING INITIAL PRINCIPAL AND INTEREST PAYMENT.

SERVICING TRANSFER DATA *(complete only if servicing has been transferred):*

New Servicer's Name (Please print): _____

New Servicer's Loan Number: _____

Address: _____

City: _____   State: _____   Zip: _____

New Servicer's Contact: _____   Phone Number: (_____)_____-_____

Instructions to Lenders: Insurance coverage as set forth above shall become effective as of the loan closing date or such later date as mutually agreed to by you and the Company. Any revision or modification of the terms and conditions as set forth in this Commitment/Certificate, or failure to satisfy any Special Conditions specified above, without prior written consent of the Company, or any material change in circumstance occurring before coverage becomes effective resulting in the failure of the loan to qualify for insurance will invalidate this Commitment/Certificate and the related insurance coverage.

Insured's Certification: By tender of premium, or in case of "Zero Monthly" mortgage insurance, by submission of the date on which the referenced loan has closed, the Original Insured accepts the Company's offer set forth above and represents and certifies that the above Loan transaction has been consummated, in accordance with the loan documents provided to the Company by the Insured and the Original Insured understands and acknowledges that this Loan is covered by and subject to the terms and conditions of the Policy.

LENDER'S LOAN NUMBER 3800017806	LOAN CLOSING DATE	PREMIUM REMITTED	DATE OF SIGNATURE	AUTHORIZED REPRESENTATIVE OF LENDER

CC(12/96)

TELEPHONE NUMBER

[signature] PRESIDENT   *[signature]* SECRETARY   *[signature]* AUTHORIZED REPRESENTATIVE

Source: Reprinted with Permission of Genworth Financial

TABLE **7.5**

Standard and Minimum Required MI Coverage Levels

LTV	Standard Coverage (%)	Minimum Coverage (%)
80.01–85 LTV	12%*	6%
85.01–90 LTV	25*	12
90.01–95 LTV	30*	16
95.01–97.LTV	35*	18

*Any plan below Standard requires an MI Loan Level Pricing Adjustment (LLPA)

Source: FFIEC

In certain situations, lenders may require more extensive coverage, even lower than the normal 75 percent coverage, for certain loan products and in certain geographical areas. Many state-sponsored mortgage programs require MI (or FHA) coverage on high-LTV loans and, in some cases, on all loans regardless of LTV.

CLAIMS

Because mortgage lending is a business that has risk, defaults by mortgage borrowers occur even in the best of times. When a default is not cured (usually through the sale of the home and the subsequent payoff of the mortgage), a claim on a mortgage insurance company could result. Claims are settled in three ways:

1. The MI company pays the lender an insurance settlement equal to the percentage of loan coverage specified in the policy. The lender keeps its loan collection and collateral responsibilities.
2. At its option, the mortgage insurance company pays the lender the entire loan amount and all amounts outstanding, and then takes over the loan completely, assuming all responsibility for collections and collateral:
   a. The MI company may choose to counsel and work with the borrower directly until the loan is current and performing again.
   b. If not, the MI company would take title to the property and sell it to offset the amount paid to the lender. Figure 7.4 is an example of an MI Disclosure.

POOL INSURANCE

With the explosion of subprime lending on the secondary market through private investors and through Fannie Mae and Freddie Mac, MI companies began to insure pools of mortgages. These mortgages are not necessarily greater than 80 percent LTV, but instead may present some other greater

FIGURE **7.4** Mortgage Insurance Claims Settlement, 2008 ($ in billions)

Assume a home appraised at $100,000 is purchased with a 10 percent down
payment at a fixed rate of 8 percent interest for 30 years. Default has occurred and
a claim against the mortgage insurance company is filed. The lender obtained
25 percent coverage.

Principal balance	$88,500
Accumulated interest from default at 8 percent	*3,300*
	$91,800
Attorney fees—3 percent	$2,754
Property taxes	700
Hazard insurance	250
Preservation of property	250
Statutory disbursements	+*100*
	$95,854
Escrow funds	(350)
Claim Total	$95,504
Percentage with coverage	×*0.25*
Payoff to lender	$23,876

As an alternative approach, the mortgage insurance company could pay the claim off
($95,504), take title to the property, and sell it. Assuming property sold for $85,000:

Sales price	$85,000
Less 6 percent sale commission	– 5,100
Less expenses	– 1,000
Less carrying cost of money	– *2,000*
	$76,900
Payoff to lender	95,504
Proceeds of sale	*76,900*
Net loss to MI company	$18,604

Source: FFIEC

risk than traditional "investment quality" secondary market loans (for example,
lower credit scores, no income verification). The MI company insures the entire
pool of loans to improve them to investment grade. With this form of credit
enhancement, they make their way into private-label securities. Usually, the
pool insurance reduces both investor and MI company exposure to a certain percentage of the original pool loan amount negotiated, typically five to 25 percent.

This source of MI business has grown appreciably in recent years, but not
all eight MI companies actively participate. MI companies began reporting this
volume separately in the third quarter of 2001. According to MICA, pool
insurance accounted for 12 percent of the total insurance originated in that
period. From 2005–2008, the height of the mortgage and housing boom, the
level of new pool insurance swung widely, starting at approximately $500 billion,
doubling to $1.1 trillion in 2006, then declining to $270 billion in 2008. Overall,
pool insurance remained in the $6.5 to $8.5 trillion range.

THE MORTGAGE INSURANCE INDUSTRY TODAY

Evolving MI Business

After nearly half of a century of progress and service, mortgage insurance companies have recently evolved into one of the more innovative members of the real estate finance business. In addition to insuring mortgage loans of all types, these companies also offer the following products and services:

- Serve as intermediaries between mortgage loan originators and investors
- Maintain extensive involvement in private mortgage-backed securities
- Operate conduits to pool and sell privately insured mortgage-backed securities
- Provide contract underwriting during periods of peak origination
- Assist in the portfolio restructuring of lenders
- Offer cutting-edge technology products and services
- Develop innovative affordable housing programs
- Educate lenders in origination and quality control, and counsel consumers

These logical extensions of the mortgage insurance business assisted in the tremendous growth of MI companies recently. For example, MI companies deliver their insurance products through satellite underwriting offices across the country, and employ a significant sales force that regularly calls on lenders. From this delivery structure, MI companies bring together originators and investors to facilitate secondary market transactions. MI companies often provide secondary market assistance (and other services) free or at a reduced fee, with the hope that these services will result in additional insurance business for the MI company.

Loan Quality and Portfolio Risk

Any discussion of MI necessarily involves the subjects of mortgage loan quality and risk. Mortgage lenders, investors, and regulators are very interested in the quality of mortgage loans, but for mortgage insurers it is critical. A mortgage insurance company analyzes the different risks in a loan (or portfolio), and charges a premium based on that risk. In contrast to lenders and investors who have portfolios with a mix of loan-to-values, the *entire* portfolio of loans insured by MI companies has high loan-to-values: 80 percent and higher. As a result, the first party to lose money in a default and foreclosure situation is the mortgage insurance company with exposure. MI companies are most sensitive to changes in collateral values, as that asset often becomes the only way to recover the claim payments made to a lender with an insured loan.

To help manage risk, MI companies diversify their portfolios in other ways. Although all LTVs in their portfolios are above 80 percent, MI companies mix in different levels from 80–95 percent LTV. A 95 percent LTV loan has different risk characteristics and performs much differently than an 85 percent LTV loan.

MI companies spread their portfolio risk over a large geographic area (unlike a local lender, with a much higher geographic concentration). Because the national economy is a combination of numerous local economies, MI companies will not be overly exposed to any one area in economic decline. For example, in 2008, the MI industry managed concentration risk by insuring loans in the following manner: West 27 percent; South 35 percent; Midwest 21 percent; Northeast 17 percent (source: MICA). These percentages do not vary much over time (less than 10 percent in a region), but will change in response to growing or contracting real estate markets and economies as shown in Figure 7.5.

To make matters worse, MI companies have had to deal with another risk: home price depreciation. According to FHFA, after an extended increase in home prices, since 2007 they have fallen nationwide at an average of four percent in 2008 and 2009, with much larger declines (up to 20 percent) depending on the region. So MI companies have on average lost more on each loan going into foreclosure.

Geographic distribution of high-LTV loans does not eliminate all MI portfolio risk. The delinquency and foreclosure rates increased significantly in 2007, creating losses on more loans for MI companies.

Mortgage insurance volume is tied to the home purchase market, and generally rises and falls with it. Understanding this market provides an understanding of the mortgage insurance industry. More specifically, the *first-time* home purchase market has a closer impact on MI activity, as these borrowers have not accumulated 20 percent equity from prior homeownership. Typically, first-time homeowners at the beginning of their income-earning years have not accumulated investments or retirement funds, and have other consumer debt. They

FIGURE **7.5** Geographic Distribution of New Insurance, 2008 ($ in billions)

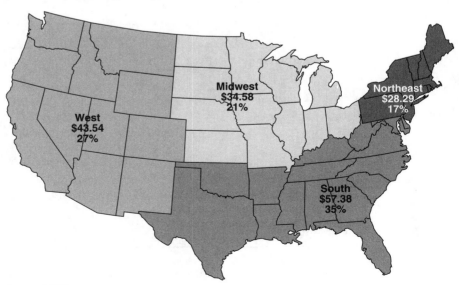

Source: MICA

are more sensitive to affordability and interest rate levels, and present a higher risk to a lender, as compared to middle-age borrowers with more accumulated wealth and more stable income from a longer employment history.

The Federal Financial Institutions Examination Council (FFIEC), HUD, other regulators, and community groups are interested in affordable housing and lending to low/moderate-income areas. The FFIEC compiles PMI activity by census tracts via information reported for the Home Mortgage Disclosure Act. PMI, FHA, and VA use this information to monitor their effectiveness in this area of mortgage lending (see Table 7.6). This information can be obtained online at **www.ffiec.gov/hmda/mica.htm**.

Because they manage portfolios with several of these high risk characteristics, MI companies keep their focus on maintaining quality loan originations and servicing. Adding to the difficulty is the distance of the MI company from the parties directly involved in the transaction. As a result, MI companies actively provide education and training for lenders to identify fraud and improve the quality of loan production.

TABLE **7.6**
Private Mortgage Insurance Company Activity (2008)

Private MI Company	Market Share Percentage
Mortgage Guaranty Insurance Corporation Milwaukee, WI	25%
PMI Mortgage Insurance Co. San Francisco, CA	11
Radian Mortgage Assurance Company Philadelphia, PA	15
Genworth Financial Raleigh, NC	20
United Guaranty Corporation Greensboro, NC	12
Republic Mortgage Insurance Company Winston-Salem, NC	11
Triad Guaranty Insurance Corporation* Winston-Salem, NC	2
Essent Guaranty, Inc.** Radnor, PA	0

*Triad stopped writing new policies July 15, 2008
**Essent obtained approval to write new policies in 2009 and GSE approval in 2010
Source: FFIEC

Financial Requirements and Strengths

Strong regulatory control coupled with sound actuarial reserves, two elements missing in the old mortgage insurance business, is now present with the new MI. The laws of the state in which MI companies are organized, as well as the states in which they do business, carefully regulate all mortgage insurance companies. The regulating entity is normally the state insurance commission or department. The specific regulations vary by state, but generally provide that a MI company can insure first liens on one- to four-family residences that do not exceed 95 percent of fair market value.

Authority has been expanded to include the various alternative mortgage instruments. Before a mortgage insurance company can begin insuring loans, it must meet minimum limits for paid-in capital and surplus. Then its insurance exposure is limited to 25 times the value of its capital, surplus, and contingency reserves. In other words, MI companies set aside one dollar of capital for every 25 dollars of risk they insure. **Insured risk** is defined as the percentage share of each loan that is actually covered by the individual insurance policy.

Rating agencies, such as Moody's, Fitch, and Standard & Poor's, also rate mortgage insurance companies on their financial strength and performance.

MI companies have suffered enormous losses, starting in 2007, partly a result from the general economic recession, partly from insuring subprime and alternative loan programs from private conduits, and partly from insuring other high risk loan programs from GSEs (Alt A and Expanded Approval) and state housing finance agencies. These high-risk loan programs (see Table 7.7) included different risk characteristics: low or no documentation, low and no down payment, lower credit scores, higher debt-to-income ratios. MI companies have endured the worst period in mortgage lending since the Great Depression, demonstrating the strength of the regulatory requirement structure and individual MI company management.

TABLE **7.7**
Net Industry Risk/Capital ($ in thousands)

	1997	2000	2005	2008
Net primary risk in force	$122,036,185	$139,481,548	$141,278,085	$219,015,800
Net pool risk in force	$5,502,172	$8,298,755	$8,714,852	$8,713,900
Total Net Risk in Force	$127,538,357	$147,780,302	$158,017,883	$227,729,700
Policyholders surplus	$2,378,366	$3,689,362	$5,645,758	$4,848,589
Contingency reserve	$5,151,672	$9,501,271	$11,197,751	$7,127,809
Total Capital	$7,530,038	$13,190,663	$16,843,509	$11,976,399
Risk-to-Capital Ratio	16.94	11.20	8.91	19.01

Source: MICA

TABLE **7.8**

Industry Assets and Reserves ($ in thousands)

	1997	2000	2005	2008
Admitted assets	$10,528,316	$16,149,811	$20,243,363	$27,313,994
Unearned reserve premium	$572,598	$503,098	$444,138	$913,979
Loss reserve	$3,478,716	$1,923,089	$2,158,579	$13,400,525
Contingency reserve	$5,151,672	$9,501,271	$11,197,751	$7,127,809

Source: MICA

TYPES OF RESERVES

Mortgage insurance companies must maintain three types of reserves. See Table 7.8:

1. *Unearned premium reserve*: Premiums received but unearned for the term of a policy are placed in this reserve.
2. *Loss reserve*: This reserve is established for losses or potential losses on a case-by-case basis as the company learns of defaults and foreclosures.
3. *Contingency reserve*: This is a special reserve required by law to protect mortgage lenders against the type of catastrophic loss that can occur in severe economic periods. Half of each premium dollar received goes into this reserve and cannot be used by a mortgage insurance company for 10 years, unless losses in a calendar year exceed 35 percent of earned premiums and the insurance commissioner of the state in which the insurer is domiciled concurs in the withdrawal.

"PIGGYBACK" LOANS—SELF-INSURANCE?

Another significant reason for the recent decline in PMI volume was the increasing popularity of *piggyback loans*. These structured transactions feature multiple loans: a first mortgage and a second mortgage (or HELOC) combined (or piggybacked). The lender closes both loans at the same time, but limits the exposure of the first mortgage to less than 80 percent loan-to-value, which eliminates the need for mortgage insurance. Assuming other requirements are satisfied, this transaction is eligible for sale to either Fannie Mae or Freddie Mac, or a private investor. The consumer avoids the cost of the PMI premium, but often pays a higher interest rate to the lender for the subordinate financing. In this way the lender effectively "self-insures" the two loans, and the higher interest rate is similar to an insurance premium.

For example, a mortgage lender would be willing to put together a 75 percent first mortgage loan, and at the same time, create a 15 percent second (equity) mortgage. The combined loan-to-value is 90 percent, but the borrower avoids the purchase of mortgage insurance. The *combined* loan-to-value of 90 percent in this transaction is not the deciding factor in whether or not mortgage insurance is required—*individual loan exposure* determines this.

The logic behind this approach is that a lender could make a 75 or 80 percent LTV today (with no mortgage insurance), and the borrower could come back a month later and obtain a 10 or 15 percent with no requirement for mortgage insurance (in some cases, borrowers may obtain loans with a combined LTV of 100 percent!). Thus, what difference does a month make? The exposure for both the borrower and lender is the same.

More mortgage lenders now offer this approach to high loan-to-value financing. They may sell the first mortgage into the secondary market and retain the second mortgage in their portfolio (or sell it to some investor other than Fannie Mae or Freddie Mac). By utilizing the piggyback loan structure, mortgage lenders limit their risk, and consumers can save money by avoiding mortgage insurance premiums.

While this form of creative financing makes sense for many consumers, unfortunately it became a method for some dishonest originators to get a purchase deal to closing. Many originators abused this method during the explosion in mortgage volume starting in the year 2000. SMR Research Corporation estimates that piggyback loans increased from 20 percent to 40 percent of home purchase mortgage dollars from 2001 to 2004. During this same period, PMI market share of all mortgage dollars fell from 12.8 percent to 8.5 percent.

DISCUSSION POINTS

1. How is private mortgage insurance (PMI) different from government insurance and guaranty programs?
2. Explain the recent growth of PMI compared to government-sponsored programs.
3. What is pool insurance, and how is it used?
4. How have PMI companies performed in the 1980s? In the 1990s? In the 2000s? Why the difference?
5. Discuss how PMI impacts the housing market and the secondary mortgage market.
6. What different methods of PMI premium payment exist and how do you calculate them?
7. What are the benefits and drawbacks of PMI vs. government insurance vs. self-insurance programs?

CHAPTER 8

Government Lending

INTRODUCTION

As described in the beginning of Chapter 7—Private Mortgage Insurance, there are three types of credit enhancement in mortgage lending: endorsements, guarantees, and insurances. Government credit enhancements allow lenders to approve riskier loans than they otherwise could, enabling more people to qualify for financing. Additionally, these enhancements serve to direct more mortgage funds into areas not traditionally served by private institutions or lenders.

Overall, government lending disperses risks and makes mortgage investments more attractive to mortgage investors. The federal government offers all three types of credit enhancement through different mortgage programs and agencies:

- Federal Housing Administration (FHA) insurance
- Veterans Administration (VA) endorsement
- USDA Rural Housing Services (RHS) guarantee

Government programs provide a social benefit by allowing for more people to purchase homes, refinance their existing homes, or improve existing housing stock. Government programs effectively reach targeted segments of the population and geographical areas—either by intent or by effect. For example, VA programs benefit military veterans; non-veterans are ineligible. FHA programs benefit many low- and moderate-income families, but there are no income limits excluding consumers with higher incomes. USDA programs require that the property be in a rural area, excluding consumers in urban and suburban areas.

Most industry professionals agree on the social and economic benefits of these programs. But there has been a high cost. Government programs historically experience twice the level of delinquency of conventional financing. According to the Mortgage Bankers Association National Delinquency Survey, the delinquency rate for FHA loans (13.15 percent) and VA loans (7.96 percent) still exceeded prime loans (6.17 percent) as of December 2009, despite the recent historic increase in non-government loans.

Government loan programs are complex and more difficult to administrate than conventional programs. The many requirements apply to both the origination and the servicing of these loans. If a lender or servicer fails to comply, it may make the loan ineligible for the government program. Then the lender assumes full liability.

Recently, mortgage fraud persists at what appears to be higher levels than in the conforming market.

Since the renaissance of FHA and VA programs, and the reclassification of Fannie Mae and Freddie Mac as part of the federal government (again), government lending technically now accounts for more than 95 percent of mortgage volume. Clearly, this is an unsustainable situation. The future of these GSEs is not certain. But the role they play will be critical to the practice of residential mortgage lending.

The level and involvement of government lending increases and decreases periodically. It plays a critical role in lending when economic conditions deteriorate or when a persistent or perceived need goes unmet by private sector lenders. The question that has been raised again and again since the 1930s is: "How active and dominant a role should government lending play in residential mortgage finance?" Can the private sector more effectively or more efficiently serve those areas now assisted by government programs?

THE PRACTICE OF GOVERNMENT LENDING—WHO IS THE LENDER?

It is important to stress that, with minor exceptions, the federal government is never the *lender* in these above-referenced programs (FHA, VA, USDA, Fannie Mae, Freddie Mac, FHLB). The private sector is. The private sector sets the interest rates, provides the mortgage funds, originates, processes, approves, closes, and services these "government" loans. The government agency responsible for the program maintains an administrative role throughout the lending process and will step in to provide either the insurance, endorsement, or guarantee, should the lender suffer a loss on the loan.

Before offering a government program, a lender must apply for and be approved by the appropriate agency in a process similar to receiving approval status from Fannie Mae or Freddie Mac. Once approved, the lender can begin originating. Both FHA and VA offer qualified lenders a Direct Endorsement (FHA) and Automatic Authority (VA) status. A DE- or AA-approved lender can originate, underwrite, and close its government loans before sending them to either FHA or VA for review and final approval. This streamlines the process tremendously, and many lenders operate in this manner. Most government loan origination today is done via the DE/AA-approved method.

Often, lenders who obtain one government approval continue on to offer additional programs. The originating lender often finds it more manageable to run a government processing, underwriting, and closing operation separate and parallel to a conventional origination team because of the special requirements involved. Lenders with DE/AA status are especially careful to comply with all requirements, because they will be responsible for the loan if an error occurs.

In addition to these three main federal government programs listed above, other important forms of government lending exist:

- GSE-sponsored programs through Fannie Mae and Freddie Mac
- Federal Home Loan Bank (FHLB)
- State Housing agencies
- State economic development and/or municipal grants and assistance

Chapter 5—Secondary Markets, discusses GSE and FHLB activity in detail. As with the FHA, VA, and USDA programs, the federal government rarely is the lender. However, government lending at the state and municipal level plays a significant role in meeting the specific needs of their respective markets. These programs take on many different forms and variations too broad to discuss in this text. However, many government programs at this level target a type of borrower, property, or geographic or economic area:

- First-time homebuyers or low/moderate income borrowers
- Urban or rural areas, or low/moderate census tracts
- Multi-family, affordable housing, or property rehabilitation

Unlike most federal programs, the state and municipal entity involved is often the lender that funds the loans. The private sector—if involved at all—helps in and is compensated for origination, processing, closing, and servicing. Approval or denial remains with the state or municipal entity.

In general, state agencies fund their programs via the issuance of a state agency bond. Because of their tax-exempt status and high rating, these bonds pay a below-market interest rate to investors. This allows the state agencies to turn these funds into mortgage loans to consumers at or below market rates.

GOVERNMENT PROGRAMS

Federal Housing Authority (FHA)

Immediately following the stock market crash, there was much debate on the proper roles of the government in the nation's economy and housing markets. Many in Congress urged action; others were against it. Most, however, agreed that government action would benefit real estate by helping put a floor under real estate prices. Those in favor of stimulation reasoned that expanding waves from a healthy real estate industry would have a multiplier effect on the remainder of a depressed economy.

The National Housing Act (1934) contains provisions to help stimulate the construction industry. The act created the Federal Housing Administration (FHA) to encourage lenders to make real estate mortgages again by providing government-backed mortgage insurance as protection.

Title I of this law provides insurance, initially free, to lenders who would loan money for home improvements and repairs. Title II established a Mutual Mortgage Insurance Fund, funded by premiums paid by mortgagors. This fund paid any claims submitted by the protected lenders.

Initially, the mortgagor paid an annual *mortgage insurance premium* (MIP) of one-half of one percent, based on the original amount. This insurance premium has changed through the years.

The current FHA premium for one- to four-family homes includes an *upfront* premium (UFMIP) as well as an annual premium that the borrower pays monthly. The upfront premium can be paid at closing, or is often financed.

Now a part of the Department of Housing and Urban Development (HUD), FHA has other insurance programs, each designed to meet a specific need. But the Mutual Mortgage Insurance Fund remains the largest and most important.

Early Opposition

Initially, the legislation to establish FHA was faced with opposition from some thrift institutions against the federal government getting involved in housing. Even after enactment, FHA did not meet with great acceptance among financial centers, since many felt that mortgage insurance as a concept was discredited, or felt strongly that government should not get involved in what was basically a private enterprise.

History, however, has proved this to be a shortsighted belief, especially in view of the many changes for which FHA has paved the way in real estate finance. As an example, FHA insurance has allowed for the development of a national mortgage market by providing for the transferability, and thus the liquidity, of mortgage instruments. The FHA-insured mortgage was attractive to many investors because it established property and borrower standards with a corresponding reduction in risk.

The FHA mortgage insurance program allowed life insurance companies to justify a successful request to state insurance commissioners to purchase loans with higher loan-to-value ratios and with lower down payments. The program also gave them the opportunity to lend across the nation. With this new authorization, life insurance companies could lend in those areas of the country that desperately needed capital. Subsequently, they could receive a higher yield than what was previously available in the capital surplus area of New England, where most of the major life insurance companies were located. Mortgage companies were the principal intermediaries for moving this capital from capital surplus areas to capital deficit areas by originating mortgages with FHA insurance and then selling them to life insurance companies.

Mortgage Lending Industry Benefits Derived from FHA

One of the primary reasons for the increase in homeownership—from about 40 percent of all homes occupied in 1930 to the 60-plus percent that has held since the 1960s, according to the U.S. Census Bureau—is the innovation provided by FHA that led to the following:

- More liberal underwriting criteria
- Established property and borrower lending standards
- Reintroduced mortgage insurance
- Self-amortizing mortgage loans
- Higher loan-to-value ratios
- Longer mortgage terms

These factors contributed to a more diverse lending market with more programs and practices, including a rebirth of private mortgage insurance.

Although any mortgage originator can take FHA-insured mortgage applications, they must channel them through an approved FHA lender. Historically, about 75 percent of all FHA mortgages are originated by mortgage brokers. Initially, this high percentage of origination was due to the local lending philosophy of the other mortgage lenders and the correspondent system that developed between mortgage bankers and life insurance companies. Most FHA-insured mortgages are still originated by mortgage bankers and brokers, but recently third-party origination has come under much scrutiny because of fraud.

FHA Today

FHA offers a myriad of housing services and mortgage programs today. Mortgage programs include:

- Section 203(b) Insured Mortgage
- Section 203(k) Rehabilitation Mortgage
- Title I Home Improvements
- Energy Efficient Mortgage
- Section 255 Home Equity Conversion
- Section 248 Indian Reservations and Other Lands
- Section 203(h) Insured Mortgage for Disaster Victims

FHA and its various insurance programs have been in existence for more than 75 years, and have insured 35 million homes at a mortgage volume of about $2 trillion, according to a Congressional Research Survey Report for Congress (by Bruce E. Foote). FHA targets households that otherwise would have difficulty obtaining mortgages. FHA reports that during 2009, its programs insured 1,947,158 loans, of which 995,695 were initial purchase endorsements. Of these purchase endorsements, 781,789 were loans made to first-time homebuyers, and 233,120 loans were made to minority first-time homebuyers.

Although FHA's single family housing programs have made substantial contributions to increase the national homeownership rate, its market share declined over the last 20 years. FHA market share then increased dramatically during the recent housing and mortgage crisis starting in 2007, providing valuable funding during a critical time.

Throughout its history, FHA's innovations influenced residential mortgage lending programs and practice. Not all of these have been smooth. FHA's role continues in this manner, however, as it continues to advance policies and implement initiatives to serve target constituencies and maintain financial viability. FHA's Web site reflects this, and contains a broad scope of information for consumers, lenders, homebuyers, builders, real estate brokers, servicers, nonprofits, and others: http://portal.hud.gov/portal/page/portal/HUD/federal_housing_administration.

Current initiatives include:

Loss Mitigation Tools

FHA assists homeowners facing financial difficulties to remain in their homes via increased access to its loss mitigation programs. In the past, loss mitigation was not available to a borrower after foreclosure was initiated because of unreimbursed costs and legal fees. Effective August 2008, FHA allows mortgagees to incorporate legal fees and foreclosure costs related to a canceled foreclosure action into either the partial claim or loan modification.

In addition, under the FHA-Home Affordable Modification Program (FHA-HAMP) the maximum partial claim amount increased from 12 months of monthly mortgage payments to 30 percent of the unpaid principal balance (UPB). The new claim amount, commonly referred to as super partial, is converted into an interest-free second lien—due at sale, refinance, or maturity. To qualify a loan for the super partial program, a lender had to prove that all other loss mitigation options, including special forbearance, mortgage modification, and original partial claim tools, were not viable methods to prevent default. As a result of conditions and new FHA initiatives, FHA reports that participation in the loss mitigation program increased from 68,755 cases in 2002 to 134,544 cases in 2009.

HOPE for Homeowners (H4H)

Title IV of HERA authorized H4H. The goal of the program is to help distressed homeowners refinance their mortgages into safer and sustainable FHA-insured mortgages by writing down the principal of the loan amount to an affordable level. Initially, the federal government estimated that approximately 400,000 households would benefit from the program. H4H has not been cost-effective for many FHA lenders. According to FHA, as of December 2008, lenders had only placed 312 loans into the program.

As a result, Congress amended the program twice to address its challenges. Under the Helping Families Save Their Home Act, Congress revised the role of the Board of Directors (making it advisory in its capacity), reduced the costs to borrowers, and made it easier for lenders to offer the program. FHA has worked to reintroduce the H4H program in fiscal year 2010.

Green Initiative

Introduced in 2008, Section 2123 of the HERA increased the maximum additional amount that can be added to an FHA insured mortgage for energy-efficient improvements, also known as Energy Efficient Mortgages (EEMs). The maximum dollar amount of cost-effective energy improvements that may be added to the mortgage increased to the lesser of:

Five percent of the value of the property

115 percent of the median area price of a single family dwelling

150 percent of the conforming Freddie Mac limit

Lender Insurance (LI)

This initiative, started in 2006, allows high-performing mortgagees to endorse FHA loans without a pre-endorsement review by FHA. LI saves lenders time and money during the loan process. During 2009, loans endorsed under LI accounted for approximately 70 percent of FHA-insured mortgages.

FHA Modernization

Implemented in 2008, FHA modernization streamlined the insurance process and made FHA products more attractive to lenders and consumers alike. Changes in the programs include more favorable loan terms with higher loan limits, extended repayment time, and flexible down payment options.

Additional Single Family Improvements

Program enhancements to improve all stages of the single family mortgage insurance process:

- Re-engineering and Integration Single Family Housing:
  Such efforts assist FHA to: comply with federal legislation, address identified audit weaknesses, improve overall monitoring and oversight, and adhere to HUD's Enterprise Architecture Framework. The goal is to simplify systems administration, reduce costs, and provide flexible and adaptable business processes.
- Overall Risk Management:
  FHA uses monitoring tools—such as a Risk-Based Targeting Model (RBTM), Post Endorsement Technical Review Process (PETR), and Appraiser Watch—to monitor program performance and oversight of lenders, Management & Marketing (M&M) contractors, and appraisers. In addition, FHA revised its delinquency rate reporting standards and took corrective action against problem lenders, underwriters, and appraisers. In 2009, FHA removed 2,382 appraisers from its roster. FHA now monitors and will mitigate the risk of new market and economic conditions on its programs and future liabilities. For example, FHASecure and the Hope for Homeowners program will increase the number of higher risk borrowers, which may affect future liabilities.
- Fraud and Identity Theft:
  In response to the rising volume of mortgage business and a general increase in the number of mortgage fraud cases, FHA increased its fraud

detection efforts. FHA now trains industry partners in fraud detection and increased fraud detection techniques, such as automated valuation for verifying appraisals and income. These tools allow FHA to review consumer, application, and property aspects of origination through automated checks and analysis of multiple data sources. For example, lenders can now use FHA Connection to validate Social Security Numbers (SSN) through other governmental agencies.

FHA Insurance

The FHA insurance premium is comprised of two components: an upfront premium paid at closing and an annual premium. Premiums change periodically and were most recently revised in October, 2010.

The upfront premium (UFMIP) varies by program or transaction:

- Purchase money mortgages and full credit refinance = 1.00 percent
- Streamline refinance (all types) = 1.00 percent
- HOPE for Homeowners (delinquent mortgages) = 2.0 percent
- Home equity conversion mortgages = 2.0 percent

For traditional purchase and refinance products, the borrower pays the annual premium in monthly installments, and the servicer remits this to FHA annually. The amount charged is based on the initial loan-to-value ratio and the mortgage term according to the following schedule:

LTV	Annual for Loans > 15 years	LTV	Annual for loans ≤ 15 years
≤ 95	1.10%	≤ 90	0.25%
> 95	1.15%	> 90	0.50%

In 2001, FHA's mortgage insurance mirrored changes in PMI insurance, which under certain conditions provided for automatic amortization cancellation or borrower-requested cancellation. Amortized cancellation occurs once the unpaid principal balance, excluding the financed upfront MIP, reaches 78 percent of the lower of the initial sales price or appraised value based on the initial amortization schedule. FHA determines when the mortgage reaches the amortized 78 percent loan-to-value threshold based on the initial note rate and the loan-to-value information. FHA discloses to the consumer the date that the mortgage insurance will automatically end, as well as the amortized loan balance.

Section 203(b)

The most important FHA program for residential lending is Section 203(b). The maximum term is 30 years, and the loan is assumable (with some limitations) with no prepayment penalty to a qualified borrower.

The insurance premiums, maximum loan amount, and other program requirements change periodically. Typically, the FHA issues changes through *Mortgagee Letters* (MLs). In recent years the number of program changes has increased dramatically, and it is imperative that mortgage lenders and originators keep current with the many changes occurring with all FHA loans. The following FHA Handbook Portal Web site directs you to the most current information contained in FHA Handbooks, MLs, and other resources: http://www.fhaoutreach.gov/FHAHandbook/prod/index.asp.

FHA Loan Limits

FHA loan limits are quite complicated even when compared to other government programs. The American Recovery and Reinvestment Act of 2009 (ARRA) increased FHA loan limits to bring the program more in line with the GSEs and the real estate market.

Under ARRA, the revised FHA loan limits for 2009 incorporate rules from the Economic Stimulus Act of 2008 (ESA) and the Housing and Economic Recovery Act of 2008 (HERA). The loan limits set under ESA introduced to FHA a maximum high cost limit (the national ceiling) of 175 percent of the national conforming limit ($729,750 in the continental U.S.).

Under HERA, the national conforming loan limit remains at $417,000 for FY 2011. The Federal Housing Finance Agency (FHFA) determines the new loan limits. HERA also sets the one-unit mortgage limit for any given area at 115 percent of the median house price. These rules and other exceptions are covered in several FHA-issued MLs: 2008-06, 2008-36, 2009-07, 2009-50 and 2010-40.

FHA loans are subject to a floor as well as a ceiling, or maximum loan amount. The floor limits establish maximum loan amounts in certain Metropolitan Statistical Areas (MSAs). The limit does not set a minimum loan amount. Both loan limits are established according to the state and county in which the property is located.

FLOOR LOAN LIMIT	
One Unit	$271,050
Two Units	$347,050
Three Units	$419,400
Four Units	$521,250
"HIGH COST" LOAN LIMIT	
One Unit	$729,750
Two Units	$934,200
Three Units	$1,129,250
Four Units	$1,403,400

These limits are in effect through December 31, 2011.

Eligibility

In addition to normal and FHA-specific underwriting requirements, FHA requires that applicants not be listed on HUD's Limited Denial of Participation (LDP) or the General Services Administration (GSA) List of Parties Excluded from Federal Procurement or Non-procurement Programs.

Applicants who are currently delinquent on any federal debt (VA-guaranteed loan, federal student loan, Title I loan, SMA loan, or federal taxes) are not eligible for an FHA-insured loan until such delinquency is brought current, paid off, or has had a satisfactory repayment plan approved in writing from the federal agency involved.

Lenders must also check HUD's Credit Alert Interactive Voice Response System (CAIVRS) to screen applicants who currently have FHA-insured loans in default or prior claims paid (within the past three years) by FHA. An applicant whose name and Social Security number shows up during this screening is ineligible for a FHA-insured loan. Exceptions may be made by contacting FHA in some cases, such as divorce, assumption, or bankruptcy situations.

Down Payment

Unlike conforming loans, this amount can be cash, grant, or a gift from a relative. In 2009, the minimum down payment required under the FHA mortgage program increased to 3.5 percent (formerly 3.0 percent). Another change scheduled for 2010 ties the maximum down payment to the applicant's credit score. FHA will require a minimum down payment of 10 percent for an applicant with a credit score under 580. An applicant with a credit score below 500 is not eligible for a FHA-insured mortgage.

The maximum loan amount calculation is similar to a secondary market loan:

1. Multiply the lesser of the sales price or appraised value (plus or minus any adjustments for repairs, or seller/financing concessions) by 96.5 percent to calculate the maximum base mortgage amount. The base loan amount cannot exceed the maximum County Loan Limit established by FHA.
2. Calculate the required Up Front Mortgage Insurance Premium (UFMIP). Determine if the applicant will finance this amount or pay in cash. If the amount will be financed, add the UFMIP to the base loan amount (rounded to the nearest dollar) to reflect the total loan amount. The total loan amount can exceed the maximum County Loan Limit established by FHA.

 EXAMPLE

Mr. and Mrs. O. K. Byrne want to purchase a home with a sales price of $135,000.

The applicant's minimum investment is $4,725 ($135,000 × 3.5 percent).
The maximum base mortgage is $130,275 ($135,000 × 96.5 percent).
The UFMIP is - $1302.75 ($130,275 × 1.00 percent).
The total loan amount is $131,577($130,275 + $1,302).
75 cents is paid in cash as a closing cost.

Source of Funds

FHA does not require the applicant to provide a minimum investment from his or her own savings, a major difference from conventional lending. All down payment and closing costs can be gifted, as long as the donor has no relationship to or interest in the real estate transaction and is an acceptable source, which includes:

- A relative
- A close friend whose relationship can be clearly explained
- An employer
- A labor union
- A charitable organization
- A governmental agency or public entity that has a program providing homeownership assistance to:
  - Low- and moderate-income families
  - First-time homebuyers
  - A close friend with a clearly defined and documented interest in the applicant

Other down payment assistance programs have all but been eliminated. FHA does not allow gifts to pay off:

- Installment loans
- Credit cards
- Collections
- Judgments
- Similar debts

FHA currently allows seller contributions toward the mortgage insurance premium, closing costs, prepaid items, and escrows in an amount not to exceed six percent of the property's selling price. FHA previously established a Homeownership Bridal Registry Account to encourage young couples to save for homeownership. The account, which is not limited to newlyweds, allows cash gifts from friends and relatives to be deposited, and then when the applicant purchases a new home, the funds from the lender-supervised account would be available and documented as gift funds.

Income and Employment

FHA calculates qualifying income similar to conventional lending, but more emphasis is placed on the applicant's income stability than on job stability. If the lender can document continuity of stable income, FHA allows a much more liberal look at applicants with gaps in employment, frequent job changes, and so forth.

Credit/Liabilities

Historically, FHA's view of credit, credit reestablishment, and credit history has been and continues to be more liberal than conventional lending. FHA requires acceptable explanations that clearly establish whether derogatory credit was due to extenuating circumstances or poor financial management; however, the time and amount of reestablished credit tends to be shorter than that required by Fannie Mae or Freddie Mac.

FHA is more conservative than conventional underwriting regarding liabilities with less than 10 months remaining. In these situations, the debt should be included in the qualifying ratios if it affects the applicant's ability to pay the mortgage during the months immediately after loan closing. Underwriters look closely at this type of situation to determine whether the applicant will have limited or no cash assets after closing.

Qualifying Ratios

Again, FHA debt/income ratios are more liberal compared to those for the standard secondary market. A lender can expand beyond FHA's ratios of 31 percent for housing debt/income and 43 percent for total debt/income if it can establish the presence of compensating factors justifying the loan approval with higher ratios. Some acceptable compensating factors include:

- Applicant has made a large down payment (10 percent or more) toward the purchase of the property.
- Minimal increase in current to proposed housing expense (less than 100 percent).
- Substantial cash reserves.
- Conservative use of credit, ability to save, and a history of devoting a large portion of monthly income to rent and/or housing debts.

Processing

Processing has become more uniform between the conventional and government sectors during the past decade. Still, FHA-insured loans have issues particular to themselves. FHA no longer requires a face-to-face interview with potential applicants, but in all cases they must have the option for a face-to-face interview.

Automated Underwriting

Surprisingly in the forefront of technology in 1996, FHA joined forces with Freddie Mac to pilot an automated underwriting system. FHA later approved a configuration for Fannie Mae's Desktop Underwriter as well. FHA's AUS system is referred to as Technology Open to Approved Lenders (TOTAL) mortgage scorecard. The system evaluates several loan application elements, including:

- Income
- Credit history
- Cash reserves
- Mortgage loan

FHA requires all transactions to be scored through TOTAL Mortgage Scorecard except for Streamlined. It provides an underwriting recommendation with one of two outcomes: either the credit and capacity are acceptable, or the loan application must be referred to an individual underwriter. TOTAL does not evaluate property acceptability; an individual underwriter must review each appraisal.

Like conventional lending, FHA's automated underwriting system has stretched income, ratio, and credit guidelines beyond traditionally accepted standards, resulting in homeownership opportunities for many millions of American families. Unfortunately, FHA delinquency historically has been well above conforming programs as well.

Documentation

FHA-insured loans require several additional documents during origination and underwriting:

- *Important Notice to Homebuyers (HUD 92900-B)*: This is a multifaceted disclosure advising applicants regarding the setting of their interest rate and points, fraudulent practices, and the possible refund of mortgage insurance premiums. See Figure 8.1 on page 218.
- *Addendum to the URLA (HUD 92900-a)*: This is the application for FHA insurance as shown in Figure 8.2 on page 220. Applicants sign page two at application, and then again at closing along with page four. Page one is signed by the Lender at the time of application and again at closing. The Lender also executes page four at the time of closing. Page three is completed and signed by the Underwriter when the loan is approved. In September 2010, FHA modified form 92900-A to capture the following information:
  1. Loan Origination Company
  2. Loan Origination Tax ID
  3. NMLS ID of Loan Origination Company
- *Social Security number*: All applicants on FHA-insured mortgages must provide evidence of their Social Security numbers. Acceptable documentation is a copy of a Social Security card, pay stub, driver's license, or IRS form W2.
- *Real Estate Certification*: The certification attests that the Sales Contract is the entire agreement, and there are no other agreements. The certification must be signed by all buyers, sellers, builders, selling agents, and brokers involved in the transaction.
- *"For Your Protection: Get a Home Inspection" (HUD 92564-CN)*: This brochure informs homebuyers of the availability and importance of getting an independent home inspection. It also clarifies the differences between an appraisal and a home inspection, and stresses the importance of radon testing. Lenders must provide the document to the homebuyer at first contact or no later than the time of initial application. No signature is required.
- *Amendatory clause to the real estate contract*: This amendment states that the applicants understand that if the appraised value comes in under the contracted sales price, they are no longer bound by the contract and are entitled to a full refund of any deposit monies. It is used when the appraised value has not been disclosed to the applicant prior to signing the sales contract.
- *Conditional Commitment/Direct Endorsed Underwriter Statement of Appraised Value (HUD 92800.5-B)*: In addition to a full URAR and additional certifications by an approved appraiser, FHA requires that all properties have this form completed by a direct endorsement underwriter. It states the property value, and lists any conditions or repairs that are required prior to closing. See Figure 8.3 on page 224.

FIGURE **8.1** Important Notice to Homebuyers (HUD 92900-B)

Important Notice to Homebuyers	**U.S. Department of Housing and Urban Development** Office of Housing - Federal Housing Commissioner	OMB Approval No. 2502-0059 (Expires 11/30/2010)

You must read this entire document at the time you apply for the loan. Return one copy to lender as proof of notification and keep one copy for your records.

Condition of Property

The property you are buying is not HUD/FHA approved and HUD/FHA does not warrant the condition or the value of the property. An appraisal will be performed to estimate the value of the property, but this appraisal does not guarantee that the house is free of defects. You should inspect the property yourself very carefully or hire a professional inspection service to inspect the property for you.

Interest Rate and Discount Points

HUD does not regulate the interest rate or the discount points that may be paid by you or the seller or other third party. You should shop around to be sure you are satisfied with the loan terms offered and with the service reputation of the lender you have chosen.

The interest rate, any discount points and the length of time the lender will honor the loan terms are all negotiated between you and the lender.

The seller can pay the discount points, or a portion thereof, if you and the seller agree to such an arrangement.

Lenders may agree to guarantee or "lock-in" the loan terms for a definite period of time (i.e., 15, 30, 60 days, etc.) or may permit your loan to be determined by future market conditions, also known as "floating". Lenders may require a fee to lock in the interest rate or the terms of the loan, but must provide a written agreement covering a minimum of 15 days before the anticipated closing. Your agreement with the lender will determine the degree, if any, that the interest rate and discount points may rise before closing.

If the lender determines you are eligible for the mortgage, your agreement with the seller may require you to complete the transaction or lose your deposit on the property.

Don't Commit Loan Fraud

It is important for you to understand that you are required to provide complete and accurate information when applying for a mortgage loan.

Do not falsify information about your income or assets.

Disclose all loans and debts (including money that may have been borrowed to make the downpayment).

Do not provide false letters-of-credit, cash-on-hand statements, gift letters or sweat equity letters.

Do not accept funds to be used for your downpayment from any other party (seller, real estate salesperson, builder, etc.).

Do not falsely certify that a property will be used for your primary residence when you are actually going to use it as a rental property.

Do not act as a "strawbuyer" (somebody who purchases a property for another person and then transfers title of the property to that person), nor should you give that person personal or credit information for them to use in any such scheme.

Do not apply for a loan by assuming the identity of another person.

Do not sign an incomplete or blank document; that is, one missing the name and address of the recipient and/or other important identifying information.

Penalties for Loan Fraud: Federal laws provide severe penalties for fraud, misrepresentation, or conspiracy to influence wrongly the issuance of mortgage insurance by HUD. You can be subject to a possible prison term and fine of up to $10,000 for providing false information. Additionally, you could be prohibited from obtaining a HUD-insured loan for an indefinite period.

Report Loan Fraud: If you are aware of any fraud in HUD programs or if an individual tries to persuade you to make false statements on a loan application, you should report the matter by calling your nearest HUD office or the HUD Regional Inspector General, or call the HUD Hotline on 1 (800) 347-3735.

Warning: It is a crime to knowingly make false statements to the United States Government on this or any similar form. Penalties upon conviction can include a fine and imprisonment. For details see: Title 18 U.S. Code Section 1001 and Section 1010.

Discrimination

If you believe you have been subject to discrimination because of race, color, religion, sex, handicap, familial status, or national origin, you should call HUD's Fair Housing & Equal Opportunity Complaint Hotline: 1 (800) 669-9777.

FIGURE **8.1** (*Continued*)

About Prepayment

This notice is to advise you of the requirements that must be followed to accomplish a prepayment of your mortgage, and to prevent accrual of any interest after the date of prepayment.

You may prepay any or all of the outstanding indebtedness due under your mortgage at any time, without penalty. However, to avoid the accrual of interest on any prepayment, the prepayment must be received on the installment due date (the first day of the month) if the lender stated this policy in its response to a request for a payoff figure.

Otherwise, you may be required to pay interest on the amount prepaid through the end of the month. The lender can refuse to accept prepayment on any date other than the installment due date.

FHA Mortgage Insurance Information

Who may be eligible for a refund?

Premium Refund: You may be eligible for a refund of a portion of the insurance premium if you paid an upfront mortgage insurance premium at settlement and are refinancing with another FHA mortgage.

Review your settlement papers or check with your mortgage company to determine if you paid an upfront premium.

Exceptions:

Assumptions: When a FHA insured loan is assumed the insurance remains in force (the seller receives no refund). The owner(s) of the property at the time the insurance is terminated is entitled to any refund.

FHA-to-FHA Refinance: When a FHA insured loan is refinanced, the refund from the old premium may be applied toward the upfront premium required for the new loan.

How are Refunds Determined?

The FHA Commissioner determines how much of the upfront premium is refunded when loans are terminated. Refunds are based on the number of months the loan is insured.

Monthly Insurance Premiums

If you paid an upfront mortgage insurance premium, you will also be charged a monthly mortgage insurance premium until the loan-to-value of your mortgage reaches 78 percent of the initial sales price or appraised value of your home, whichever was lower (provided that premiums are paid for at least five years). You will reach the 78 percent loan-to-value threshold in one of two ways: Through normal amortization as you make your monthly payments, or by paying additional principal on the mortgage. Your lender can advise you on when the mortgage will reach the 78 percent loan-to-value threshold. If you were not charged an upfront premium, you will pay the monthly premium for the life of the mortgage.

Important: The rules governing the eligibility for premium refunds are based on the financial status of the FHA insurance fund and are subject to change.

SI USTED HABLA ESPANOL Y TIENE DIFICULTAD LEYENDO O HABLANDO INGLES, POR FAVOR LLAME A ESTE NUMERO TELEFONICO 800.697.6967.

You, the borrower(s), must be certain that you understand the transaction. Seek professional advice if you are uncertain.

Acknowledgment: I acknowledge that I have read and received a copy of this notice at the time of loan application. This notice does not constitute a contract or binding agreement. It is designed to provide current HUD/FHA policy regarding refunds.

Signature & Date: Signature & Date:

X_____   X_____

Signature & Date: Signature & Date:

X_____   X_____

Source: www.HUD.gov

FIGURE **8.2** Addendum to the URLA (HUD 92900-A)

HUD/VA Addendum to Uniform Residential Loan Application

OMB Approval No.   VA: 2900-0144
HUD: 2502-0059 (expires 11/30/2010)

Part I - Identifying Information (mark the type of application)	2. Agency Case No: (include any suffix)	3. Lender's Case No.	4. Section of the Act (for HUD cases)
1. ☐ VA Application for Home Loan Guaranty ☑ HUD/FHA Application for Insurance under the National Housing Act	352-1234567-703	NJ123405	203(b)

5. Borrower's Name & Present Address (include zip code)	7. Loan Amount (include the UFMIP if for HUD or Funding Fee if for VA)	8. Interest Rate	9. Proposed Maturity
NORMAL A. HOMEBUYER WIFEY A. HOMEBUYER 123 RENTAL AVE ELSEWHERE, NJ 00123	$ 365,493.00	4.750 %	30 yrs. mos.

6. Property Address (including name of subdivision, lot & block no. & zip code)	10. Discount Amount (only if borrower is permitted to pay)	11. Amount of Up Front Premium	12a. Amount of Monthly Premium	12b.Term of Monthly Premium
431 ENDLESS ROAD SOMEWHERE, NJ 00123	$ 3,618.75	$ 271.41/mo.		120 months

13. Lender's I.D. Code	14. Sponsor/Agent I.D. Code
57111100005	87000011116

15. Lender's Name & Address (include zip code)	16. Name & Address of Sponsor/Agent
BASIC MORTGAGE BROKER 452 BROKER AVE. SOMEWHERE, NJ 00123 **Type or Print all entries clearly**	ANY MORTGAGE BANKER 322 MBS AVE. SOMEWHERE, NJ 00123
	17. Lender's Telephone Number 609-788-9100

VA: The veteran and the lender hereby apply to the Secretary of Veterans Affairs for Guaranty of the loan described here under Section 3710, Chapter 37, Title 38, United States Code, to the full extent permitted by the veteran's entitlement and severally agree that the Regulations promulgated pursuant to Chapter 37, and in effect on the date of the loan shall govern the rights, duties, and liabilities of the parties.

18. First Time Homebuyer?	19. VA Only: Title will be Vested in:	20. Purpose of Loan (blocks 9 - 12 are for VA loans only)	
a. ☑ Yes b. ☐ No	☐ Veteran ☐ Veteran & Spouse ☐ Other (Specify):	1) ☑ Purchase Existing Home Previously Occupied 2) ☐ Finance Improvements to Existing Property 3) ☐ Refinance (Refi.) 4) ☐ Purchase New Condo. Unit 5) ☐ Purchase Existing Condo. Unit 6) ☐ Purchase Existing Home Not Previously Occupied	7) ☐ Construct Home (proceeds to be paid out during construction) 8) ☐ Finance Co-op Purchase 9) ☐ Purchase Permanently Sited Manufactured Home 10) ☐ Purchase Permanently Sited Manufactured Home & Lot 11) ☐ Refi. Permanently Sited Manufactured Home to Buy Lot 12) ☐ Refi. Permanently Sited Manufactured Home/Lot Loan

Part II - Lender's Certification

21. The undersigned lender makes the following certifications to induce the Department of Veterans Affairs to issue a certificate of commitment to guarantee the subject loan or a Loan Guaranty Certificate under Title 38, U. S. Code, or to induce the Department of Housing and Urban Development - Federal Housing Commissioner to issue a firm commitment for mortgage insurance or a Mortgage Insurance Certificate under the National Housing Act.

A. The loan terms furnished in the Uniform Residential Loan Application and this Addendum are true, accurate and complete.

B. The information contained in the Uniform Residential Loan Application and this Addendum was obtained directly from the borrower by an employee of the undersigned lender or its duly authorized agent and is true to the best of the lender's knowledge and belief.

C. The credit report submitted on the subject borrower (and co-borrower, if any) was ordered by the undersigned lender or its duly authorized agent directly from the credit bureau which prepared the report and was received directly from said credit bureau.

D. The verification of employment and verification of deposits were requested and received by the lender or its duly authorized agent without passing through the hands of any third persons and are true to the best of the lender's knowledge and belief.

E. The Uniform Residential Loan Application and this Addendum were signed by the borrower after all sections were completed.

F. This proposed loan to the named borrower meets the income and credit requirements of the governing law in the judgment of the undersigned.

G. To the best of my knowledge and belief, I and my firm and its principals: **(1)** are not presently debarred, suspended, proposed for debarment, declared ineligible, or voluntarily excluded from covered transactions by any Federal department or agency; **(2)** have not, within a three-year period preceding this proposal, been convicted of or had a civil judgment rendered against them for (a) commission of fraud or a criminal offense in connection with obtaining, attempting to obtain, or performing a public (Federal, State or local) transaction or contract under a public transaction; (b) violation of Federal or State antitrust statutes or commission of embezzlement, theft, forgery, bribery, falsification or destruction of records, making false statements, or receiving stolen property; **(3)** are not presently indicted for or otherwise criminally or civilly charged by a governmental entity (Federal, State or local) with commission of any of the offenses enumerated in paragraph G(2) of this certification; and **(4)** have not, within a three-year period preceding this application/proposal, had one or more public transactions (Federal, State or local) terminated for cause or default.

Items "H" through "J" are to be completed as applicable for VA loans only.

H. The names and functions of any duly authorized agents who developed on behalf of the lender any of the information or supporting credit data submitted are as follows:

Name & Address	Function (e.g., obtained information on the Uniform Residential Loan Application, ordered credit report, verifications of employment, deposits, etc.)

If no agent is shown above, the undersigned lender affirmatively certifies that all information and supporting credit data were obtained directly by the lender.

I. The undersigned lender understands and agrees that it is responsible for the omissions, errors, or acts of agents identified in item H as to the functions with which they are identified

J. The proposed loan conforms otherwise with the applicable provisions of Title 38, U.S. Code, and of the regulations concerning guaranty or insurance of loans to veterans.

Signature of Officer of Lender	Title of Officer of Lender DIRECTOR	Date (mm/dd/yyyy) 3/1/2011

Part III - Notices to Borrowers. Public reporting burden for this collection of information is estimated to average 6 minutes per response, including the time for reviewing instructions, searching existing data sources, gathering and maintaining the data needed, and completing and reviewing the collection of information. This agency may not conduct or sponsor, and a person is not required to respond to, a collection information unless that collection displays a valid OMB control number can be located on the OMB Internet page at http://www.whitehouse.gov/omb/library/OMBINV.LIST.OF.AGENCIES.html#LIST_OF_AGENCIES. **Privacy Act Information.** The information requested on the Uniform Residential Loan Application and this Addendum is authorized by 38 U.S.C. 3710 (if for DVA) and 12 U.S.C. 1701 et seq. (if for HUD/FHA). The Debt Collection Act of 1982, Pub. Law 97-365, and HUD's Housing and Community Development Act of 1987, 42 U.S.C. 3543, require persons applying for a federally insured or guaranteed loan to furnish his/her social security number (SSN). You must provide all the requested information, including your SSN. HUD and/or VA may conduct a computer match to verify the information you provide. HUD and/or VA may disclose certain information to Federal, State, and local agencies when relevant to civil, criminal, or regulatory investigations and prosecutions. It will not otherwise be disclosed or released outside of HUD or VA, except as required and permitted by law. The information will be used to determine whether you qualify as a mortgagor. Any disclosure of information outside VA or HUD/FHA will be made only as permitted by law. Failure to provide any of the requested information, including SSN, may

Calyx Form - fhavaa1.frm (09/10)	page 1	form HUD-92900-A (09/2010) VA Form 26-1802a

FIGURE **8.2** (*Continued*)

Case No: 352-1234567-703

result in disapproval of your loan application. This is notice to you as required by the Right to Financial Privacy Act of 1978 that VA or HUD/FHA has a right of access to financial records held by financial institutions in connection with the consideration or administration of assistance to you. Financial records involving your transaction will be available to VA and HUD/FHA without further notice or authorization but will not be disclosed or released by this institution to another Government Agency or Department without your consent except as required or permitted by law. Caution. Delinquencies, defaults, foreclosures and abuses of mortgage loans involving programs of the Federal Government can be costly and detrimental to your credit, now and in the future. The lender in this transaction, its agents and assigns as well as the Federal Government, its agencies, agents and assigns, are authorized to take any and all of the following actions in the event loan payments become delinquent on the mortgage loan described in the attached application: (1) Report your name and account information to a credit bureau; (2) Assess additional interest and penalty charges for the period of time that payment is not made; (3) Assess charges to cover additional administrative costs incurred by the Government to service your account; (4) Offset amounts owed to you under other Federal programs; (5) Refer your account to a private attorney, collection agency or mortgage servicing agency to collect the amount due, foreclose the mortgage, sell the property and seek judgment against you for any deficiency; (6) Refer your account to the Department of Justice for litigation in the courts; (7) If you are a current or retired Federal employee, take action to offset your salary, or civil service retirement benefits; (8) Refer your debt to the Internal Revenue Service for offset against any amount owed to you as an income tax refund; and (9) Report any resulting written-off debt of yours to the Internal Revenue Service as your taxable income. All of these actions can and will be used to recover any debts owed when it is determined to be in the interest of the lender and/or the Federal Government to do so.

Part IV - Borrower Consent for Social Security Administration to Verify Social Security Number

I authorize the Social Security Administration to verify my Social Security number to the Lender identified in this document and HUD/FHA, through a computer match conducted by HUD/FHA.

I understand that my consent allows no additional information from my Social Security records to be provided to the Lender, and HUD/FHA and that verification of my Social Security number does not constitute confirmation of my identity. I also understand that my Social Security number may not be used for any other purpose than the one stated above, including resale or redisclosure to other parties. The only other redisclosure permitted by this authorization is for review purposes to ensure that HUD/FHA complies with SSA's consent requirements.

I am the individual to whom the Social Security number was issued or that person's legal guardian. I declare and affirm under the penalty of perjury that the information contained herein is true and correct. I know that if I make any representation that I know is false to obtain information from Social Security records, I could be punished by a fine or imprisonment or both.

This consent is valid for 180 days from the date signed, unless indicated otherwise by the individual(s) named in this loan application.

Read consent carefully. Review accuracy of social security number(s) and birth dates provided on this application.

Signature(s) of Borrower(s)	Date signed	Signature(s) of Co-Borrower(s)	Date signed
	/ /		/ /

Part V - Borrower Certification

22. Complete the following for a HUD/FHA Mortgage

22 a. Do you own or have you sold **other** real estate within the past 60 months on which there was a HUD / FHA mortgage? ☐ Yes ☑ No | Is it to be sold? ☐ Yes ☐ No | 22 b. Sales Price $ | 22 c. Original Mortgage Amt $

22 d. Address

22 e. If the dwelling to be covered by this mortgage is to be rented, is it a part of, adjacent or contiguous to any project subdivision or group of concentrated rental properties involving eight or more dwelling units in which you have any financial interest? ☐ Yes ☐ No If "Yes" give details.

22 f. Do you own more than four dwellings? ☐ Yes ☐ No If "Yes" submit form HUD-92561.

23. Complete for VA - Guaranteed Mortgage. Have you ever had a VA home loan? ☐ Yes ☐ No

24. Applicable for Both VA & HUD. As a home loan borrower, you will be legally obligated to make the mortgage payments called for by your mortgage loan contract. The fact that you dispose of your property after the loan has been made **will not relieve you of liability for making these payments. Payment of the loan in full is ordinarily the way liability on a mortgage note is ended.** Some home buyers have the mistaken impression that if they sell their homes when they move to another locality, or dispose of it for any other reasons, they are no longer liable for the mortgage payments and that liability for these payments is solely that of the new owners. Even though the new owners may agree in writing to assume liability for your mortgage payments, this assumption agreement will not relieve you from liability to the holder of the note which you signed when you obtained the loan to buy the property. Unless you are able to sell the property to a buyer who is acceptable to VA or to HUD/FHA and who will assume the payment of your obligation to the lender, you will not be relieved from liability to repay any claim which VA or HUD/FHA may be required to pay your lender on account of default in your loan payments. **The amount of any such claim payment will be a debt owed by you to the Federal Government.** This debt will be the object of established collection procedures.

25. I, the Undersigned Borrower(s) Certify that:

(1) I have read and understand the foregoing concerning my liability on the loan and Part III Notices to Borrowers.

(2) **Occupancy:** (for VA only -- mark the applicable box)
☐ **(a)** I now actually occupy the above-described property as my home or intend to move into and occupy said property as my home within a reasonable period of time or intend to reoccupy it after the completion of major alterations, repairs or improvements.

☐ **(b)** My spouse is on active military duty and in his or her absence, I occupy or intend to occupy the property securing this loan as my home.

☐ **(c)** I previously occupied the property securing this loan as my home. (for interest rate reductions)

☐ **(d)** While my spouse was on active military duty and unable to occupy the property securing this loan, I previously occupied the property that is securing this loan as my home. (for interest rate reduction loans)

Note: If box 2b or 2d is checked, the veteran's spouse must also sign below.

(3) Mark the applicable box (not applicable for Home Improvement or Refinancing Loan) I have been informed that ($3,925.00) is:
☐ the reasonable value of the property as determined by VA or;
☑ the statement of appraised value as determined by HUD/FHA.

Note: If the contract price or cost exceeds the VA "Reasonable Value" or HUD/FHA "Statement of Appraised Value" mark either item (a) or item (b), whichever is applicable.

☐ **(a)** I was aware of this valuation when I signed my contract and I have paid or will pay in cash from my own resources at or prior to loan closing a sum equal to the difference between the contract purchase price or cost and the VA or HUD/FHA established value.

I do not and will not have outstanding after loan closing any unpaid contractual obligation on account of such cash payment;

☐ **(b)** I was not aware of this valuation when I signed my contract but have elected to complete the transaction at the contract purchase price or cost. I have paid or will pay in cash from my own resources at or prior to loan closing a sum equal to the difference between contract purchase price or cost and the VA or HUD/FHA established value. I do not and will not have outstanding after loan closing any unpaid contractual obligation on account of such cash payment.

(4) Neither I, nor anyone authorized to act for me, will refuse to sell or rent, after the making of a bona fide offer, or refuse to negotiate for the sale or rental of, or otherwise make unavailable or deny the dwelling or property covered by his/her loan to any person because of race, color, religion, sex, handicap, familial status or national origin. I recognize that any restrictive covenant on this property relating to race, color, religion, sex, handicap, familial status or national origin is illegal and void and civil action for preventive relief may be brought by the Attorney General of the United States in any appropriate U.S. District Court against any person responsible for the violation of the applicable law.

(5) All information in this application is given for the purpose of obtaining a loan to be insured under the National Housing Act or guaranteed by the Department of Veterans Affairs and the information in the Uniform Residential Loan Application and this Addendum is true and complete to the best of my knowledge and belief. Verification may be obtained from any source named herein.

(6) **For HUD Only** (for properties constructed prior to 1978) I have received information on lead paint poisoning. ☑ Yes ☐ Not Applicable

(7) I am aware that neither HUD/FHA nor VA **warrants the condition or value of the property.**

Signature(s) of Borrower(s) -- **Do not sign** unless this application is fully completed. Read the certifications carefully & review accuracy of this application.

Signature(s) of Borrower(s)	Date signed	Signature(s) of Co-Borrower(s)	Date signed
X	/ /	X	/ /

(Borrowers Must Sign Both Parts IV & V) Federal statutes provide severe penalties for any fraud, intentional misrepresentation, or criminal connivance or conspiracy purposed to influence the issuance of any guaranty or insurance by the VA Secretary or the HUD/FHA Commissioner.

Calyx Form - fhavaa2.frm (09/10)

form HUD-92900-A (09/2010)
VA Form 26-1802a

FIGURE **8.2** (*Continued*)

Direct Endorsement Approval for a HUD/FHA-Insured Mortgage

U.S. Department of Housing and Urban Development

Part I - Identifying Information (mark the type of application)	2. Agency Case No. (include any suffix)	3. Lender's Case No.	4. Section of the Act (for HUD cases)
1. ☒ HUD/FHA Application for Insurance under the National Housing Act	3521234567-703	NJ123405	203B

5. Borrower's Name & Present Address (include zip code)		
NORMAL A. HOMEBUYER WIFEY A. HOMEBUYER 123 RENTAL AVE., SOMEWHERE, NJ 00123		

7. Loan Amount (include the UFMIP)	8. Interest Rate	9. Proposed Maturity
$ 365,493.00	4.75 %	30 yrs. 0 mos.

6. Property Address (including name of subdivision, lot & block no. & zip code)

431 ENDLESS ROAD
SOMEWHERE, NJ 00123

10. Discount Amount (only if borrower is permitted to pay)	11. Amount of Up Front Premium	12a. Amount of Monthly Premium	12b. Term of Monthly Premium
0	$ 3,618.75	$ 271 / mo.	120 months

13. Lender's I.D. Code	14. Sponsor / Agent I.D. Code
57111100005	87000011116

15. Lender's Name & Address (include zip code)	16. Name & Address of Sponsor / Agent
BASIC MORTGAGE BROKER 452 BROKER AVE. SOMEWHERE, NJ 00123	ANY MORTGAGE BANKER 322 MBS AVE. SOMEWHERE, NJ 00123

17. Lender's Telephone Number

(609) 788-9100

Type or Print all entries clearly

Sponsored Originations	Name of Loan Origination Company BASIC MORTGAGE BROKER	Tax ID of Loan Origination Company 00-1234567	NMLS ID of Loan Origination Company 0987786

☒ **Approved:** Approved subject to the additional conditions stated below, if any.

Date Mortgage Approved	1/1/2011	Date Approval Expires	02/28/2011

☐ Modified & Approved as follows:	Loan Amount (include UFMIP) $	Interest Rate %	Proposed Maturity Yrs. Mos	Monthly Payment $	Amount of Up Front Premium $	Amount of Monthly Premium $	Term of Monthly Premium months

Additional Conditions:

☐ If this is proposed construction, the builder has certified compliance with HUD requirements on form HUD-92541.

☐ If this is new construction, the lender certifies that the property is 100% complete (both on site and off site improvements) **and** the property meets HUD's minimum property standards and local building codes.

☐ Form HUD-92544, Builder's Warranty is required.

☐ The property has a 10-year warranty.

☐ Owner-Occupancy **Not** required (item (b) of the Borrower's Certificate does not apply).

☐ The mortgage is a high loan-to-value ratio for non-occupant mortgagor in military.

☐ Other: (specify)

☒ This mortgage was rated as an "accept" or "approve" by FHA's Total Mortgage Scorecard. As such, the undersigned representative of the mortgagee certifies to the integrity of the data supplied by the lender used to determine the quality of the loan, that a Direct Endorsement Underwriter reviewed the appraisal (if applicable) and further certifies that this mortgage is eligible for HUD mortgage insurance under the Direct Endorsement program. I hereby make all certifications required for this mortgage as set forth in HUD Handbook 4000.4

Mortgagee Representative___*Darla Underwriter ZFHA 1/1/2011*___

☐ This mortgage was rated as a "refer" by a FHA's Total Mortgage Scorecard, and/or was manually underwritten by a Direct Endorsement underwriter. As such, the undersigned Direct Endorsement underwriter certifies that I have personally reviewed the appraisal report (if applicable), credit application, and all associated documents and have used due diligence in underwriting this mortgage. I find that this mortgage is eligible for HUD mortgage insurance under the Direct Endorsement program and I hereby make all certifications required for this mortgage as set forth in HUD Handbook 4000.4

Direct Endorsement Underwriter _____   DE's CHUMS ID Number _____

The Mortgagee, its owners, officers, employees or directors ☐ do ☒ do not **have a financial interest in or a relationship, by affiliation or ownership, with the builder or seller involved in this transaction.**

form **HUD-92900-A** (09/2010)
VA Form 26-1802a

FIGURE **8.2** (*Continued*)

Borrower's Certificate:

The undersigned certifies that:

(a) I will not have outstanding any other unpaid obligations contracted in connection with the mortgage transaction or the purchase of the said property except obligations which are secured by property or collateral owned by me independently of the said mortgaged property, or obligations approved by the Commissioner;

(b) One of the undersigned intends to occupy the subject property, (note: this item does not apply if owner-occupancy is not required by the commitment);

(c) All charges and fees collected from me as shown in the settlement statement have been paid by my own funds, and no other charges have been or will be paid by me in respect to this transaction;

(d) Neither I, nor anyone authorized to act for me, will refuse to sell or rent, after the making of a bona fide offer, or refuse to negotiate for the sale or rental of or otherwise make unavailable or deny the dwelling or property covered by this loan to any person because of race, color, religion, sex, handicap, familial status or national origin. I recognize that any restrictive covenant on this property relating to race, color, religion, sex, handicap, familial status or national origin is illegal and void and any such covenant is hereby specifically disclaimed. I understand that civil action for preventative relief may be brought by the Attorney General of the United States in any appropriate U.S. District Court against any person responsible for a violation of this certificate.

Borrower'(s) Signature(s) & Date

Lender's Certificate:

The undersigned certifies that to the best of its knowledge:

(a) The statements made in its application for insurance and in this Certificate are true and correct;

(b) The conditions listed above or appearing in any outstanding commitment issued under the above case number have been fulfilled;

(c) Complete disbursement of the loan has been made to the borrower, or to his/her creditors for his/her account and with his/her consent;

(d) The security instrument has been recorded and is a good and valid first lien on the property described;

(e) No charge has been made to or paid by the borrower except as permitted under HUD regulations;

(f) The copies of the credit and security instruments which are submitted herewith are true and exact copies as executed and filed for record;

(g) It has not paid any kickbacks, fee or consideration of any type, directly or indirectly, to any party in connection with this transaction except as permitted under HUD regulations and administrative instructions.

I, the undersigned, as authorized representative of
mortgagee at this time of closing of this mortgage loan, certify that I have personally reviewed the mortgage loan documents, closing statements, application for insurance endorsement, and all accompanying documents. I hereby make all certifications required for this mortgage as set forth in HUD Handbook 4000.4.

Lender's Name ANY MORTGAGE BANKER		**Note:** If the approval is executed by an agent in the name of lender, the agent must enter the lender's code number and type.	
Title of Lender's Officer DIRECTOR			
		Code Number (5 digits)	Type
Signature of Lender's Officer	Date 03/01/2011		

form HUD-92900-A (09/2010)
VA Form 26-1802a

FIGURE **8.3** Conditional Commitment/Direct Endorsed Underwriter Statement of Appraised Value (HUD 92800.5-B)

Conditional Commitment
Direct Endorsement
Statement of Appraised Value

U.S. Department of Housing
and Urban Development
Office of Housing
Federal Housing Commissioner

OMB Approval No. 2502-0494
(exp. 01/31/2011)

General Commitment Conditions

1. Maximum Mortgage Amount and Term:
(a) Occupant Mortgagors: Mortgage amount and terms assume satisfactory owner-occupant mortgagor(s). They may be changed depending upon the rating of borrower, his/her income and credit.
(b) Changes: The Commissioner or Direct Endorsement (DE) Underwriter may, after reviewing pertinent information, change the mortgage amount and term.

2. Approval of Borrower: A determination for approval will be based upon receipt of acceptable application for mortgage credit analysis.

3. Validity Period: This document expires six months from the issue date in the case of an "existing" house or not more than twelve months from its date for "proposed" construction, or 203K rehabilitation loan. A shorter period may be imposed by HUD for proposed construction.

All cases are classified as "existing" or "proposed" for the purpose of determining expiration date. Accordingly a house, even though still under construction, may be classified as an existing house if it was not approved by HUD, VA, or a DE Lender prior to beginning of constction. Lower loan-to-value ratios will be applied unless construction exhibits are certified by builder as meeting applicable codes and HUD requirements and are covered by a HUD approved insured 10-year protection (warranty) plan.

4. Cancellation: This document may be cancelled after 60 days from the date of issuance if construction has not started.

5. Property Standards: All construction, repairs, or alterations proposed in the application or on the construction exhibits returned herewith must equal or exceed applicable codes and HUD requirements.

Information: The estimates of fire insurance and taxes are furnished for mortgagee's and mortgagor's information. They must be used to prepare the Addendum to the Uniform Residential Loan Application, form HUD-92900-A, when a firm commitment is desired.

Commitment Terms

[✓] Conditional Commitment for Mortgage Insurance under the National Housing Act, Sec. 203b

[ ] See below

By: DARLA UNDERWRITER JA01

Lender ID 57111100005
Sponsor/Agent
87000011116
Mortgagee
ANY MORTGAGE BANKER
322 MBS AVE.
SOMEWHERE, NJ 00123

Action Date 01/01/2011
FHA Case No. 352-1234567-703
INST Case Ref. No.

Est. Value of Prop. $ 392,500

Property Address: 431 ENDLESS ROAD
SOMEWHERE, NJ 00123

[✓] Existing [ ] Proposed
(see gen. cond. 3)

Commitment Issued 12/01/2010
Commitment Expires 03/01/2011
Improved Living
Area 2432 Sq. Ft.

Monthly Expense Estimate
Fire Insurance ..... $ 80.75
Taxes .... $ 701.42
Condo. Com. Exp.$ 0.00
Total.................... $ 1,051.67

Specific Commitment Conditions (Applicable when checked)

HUD's commitment to insure a mortgage on this property is dependent on the completion of the conditions listed below.
HUD Does Not Guarantee the work done to comply with the conditions.

Estimated Remaining Economic Life of this property is **40** years.
This property [✓] is, [ ] is not eligible for maximum financing (high loan-to-value ratio mortgage).

[ ] Manufactured Housing

[ ] **Assurance of Completion:** If the required repairs cannot be completed prior to submission of closing papers, Form HUD-92300 made in the amount of $ (or such additional amount as the lender desires) may be established as the means to ensure completion.

[ ] See indicated additional items on attached:
[ ] See the following additional conditions on the back:

FIGURE **8.3** (*Continued*)

Public reporting burden for this collection of information is estimated to average seven minutes per response, including the time for reviewing instructions, searching existing data sources, gathering and main- taining the data needed, and completing and reviewing the collection of information. This information is required to obtain benefits. HUD may not collect this information, and you are not required to complete this form, unless it displays a currently valid OMB control number.

Section 203 of the National Housing Act authorizes the Secretary of the Department of Housing and Urban

Development to insure mortgages on appraisal and commitment/direct endorsement statement of appraised value on a designated property. This form serves as the application for individual "proposed construction" and "existing construction" properties.

The Conditional Commitment / Direct Endorsement Statement of Appraised Value (Form HUD-92800.5B) sets forththe terms upon which the commitment/direct endorsement statement of appraised value is made and the specific conditions that must be met before HUD can endorse a Firm Commitment for Mortgage Insurance.

Responses to the collection of information are required to obtain mortgage insurance. Information contained in these collections will be used only for the purpose of determining the eligibility of a property for mortgage insurance. The information is considered confidential. While no assurances of confidentiality are pledged to respondents, HUD generally discloses this data only in response to a Freedom of Information request.

Specific Commitment Conditions (Applicable when indicated on the front of this form)

B. **Proposed Construction:** The builder or mortgagee must notify the assigned Fee Inspector as appropriate (see items 11, 12, and 13 below).

C. **Warranty:** Form HUD-92544 is required on all new construction and shall be executed between the builder and the purchaser.

D. **Section 223:** This commitment is issued pursuant to Section 223(e).

E. **Health Authority Approval:** Submit local health authority approval (on a form or letter) indicating the individual water supply and/or sewage disposal system is acceptable.

F. **Reserved.**

G. **Prefabricator's Certificate:** The Lender shall provide a prefabrication certificate as required by the related engineering bulletin.

H. **Termite Control:** (Proposed Construction) If soil poisioning is used, the builder shall complete form HUD-92052, Termite Soil Treatment Guarantee, and transmit a copy to HUD or the Direct Endorsement Underwriter. The Mortgagee will deliver the original and a copy to the mortgagor at closing.

4. **Flood Insurance Requirement:** This property is located in a special flood hazard area and must be covered by flood insurance in accordance with HUD regulation 24 CFR 203.16a.

5. **Carpet Identification:** (as listed in Certified Products Directory) Manufacturer recommended maintenance program must be provided to the homebuyer.

6. **Termite Control** (Existing Construction): A recognized termite control operator shall furnish certification using form NCPA-1, or State-mandated form, that the house and other

structures within the legal boundaries of the property indicate no evidence of active termite infestation.

7. **Code Enforcement:** The lender shall submit a statement from the public authority that the property meets local code requirements. If the mortgage on the property is to be insured under Section 221(d)(2), a code compliance inspection is required.

8. **Repairs:** The lender shall notify the original appraiser upon completion of required repairs, unless otherwise instructed.

9. **Lender's Certificate of Completion:** The lender shall furnish a certificate that required repairs have been examined and were satisfactorily completed.

10 **Manufacturers Warranties** must be provided to the homebuyer covering heating/cooling systems, hot water heaters, ranges, etc.

11. **Initial Inspection** (2 working days) is requested before the "beginning of construction" with forms in place.

12. **Frame Inspection** (1 working day) is requested when the building is enclosed and framing, plumbing, heating, electrical, and insulation is complete and visible.

13. **Final Inspection** is requested when construction is completed and the property ready for occupancy.

14. **Insulation Certificate** must be posted in a conspicuous location in the dwelling.

15. **The Insured Protection Plan Warranty Agreement** shall be executed between the builder and the homebuyer.

16. The lender shall furnish a certificate of occupancy or letter of acceptance from the local building authority.

Source: Reprinted with permission of BFO Solutions, Incorporated www.fhaoutreach.gov/FHAHandbook/prod/index.asp
© 2010 Community Lending Associates, LLC

- *Loan Underwriting and Transmittal Summary (HUD 92900-LT)*: This form simplifies disclosure of loan-level information and replaces the Mortgage Credit Analysis Worksheet (MCAW 92900-WS). It is similar to the Fannie Mae 1008. An underwriter who signs this form is approving the loan application for FHA mortgage insurance. See Figure 8.4 Transmittal Summary on page 226.

FIGURE **8.4** Loan Underwriting and Transmittal Summary (HUD 92900-LT)

FHA Loan Underwriting and Transmittal Summary
See back of page for Public Burden and Sensitive Information statements

U.S Department of Housing and Urban Development
Office of Housing Federal Housing Commissioner

OBM Approval No. 2502 - 0059
expires (11/30/2010)

Borrower and Property Information

FHA Case No. 352-1234567-703   SOA 203b

Borrower Name NORMAL A HOMEBUYER	SSN 001-00-1234
Co-Borrower Name WIFEY A. HOMEBUYER	SSN 001-11-4321
Property Address 431 ENDLESS ROAD SOMEWHERE, NJ 00123	

Property Type (Check only 1)
- [✓] 1 unit
- [ ] 2 units
- [ ] 3 - 4 units
- [ ] Condominium
- [ ] Co-op
- [ ] Manufactured Housing

Additional Property Information
Sales Price $ 375,000
Appraised Value $ 392,500

Property Rights
- [✓] Fee Simple
- [ ] Leasehold

Construction
- [✓] Existing
- [ ] Proposed
- [ ] New (less than 1 year)

Mortgage Information

Amortization Type (Check only 1)
- [✓] Fixed-Rate-Monthly Payments
- [ ] ARM 1_, 3_, 5_, 7_, or 10_ yr
- ARM Index _____
- ARM Margin _____ %
- [ ] Int. Rate Buydown

Loan Information
Mortgage w/o UFMIP	$	361,875
Total UFMIP	$	3,618
Mortgage w/ UFMIP	$	365,493
Interest Rate		4.750 %
Qualifying Rate		4.750 %
(1 Yr. ARM)		
Loan Term (in months)		360

Loan Purpose (Check all that apply)
- [✓] Purchase
- [ ] No Cash-Out Refinance
- [ ] Cash-Out Refinance
- [ ] Streamline Refinance
- [ ] w/appraisal
- [ ] w/o appraisal
- [ ] Construction-to-Permanent
- [ ] Energy Efficient Mortgage
- [ ] Building On Own Land
- [ ] HUD REO
- [ ] 203(k)
- [ ] Other

Secondary Financing
Source/EIN
- [ ] Gov't [ ] NP [ ] Family
- [ ] Other _____
Amount of Secondary Financing
$ _____

Gifts Seller Funded DAP [N]
1.) Source/EIN RELATIVE-PARENT
- [ ] Gov't [ ] NP [✓] Family
- [ ] Other _____
Amount of Gift $ 5,000.00
2.) Source/EIN _____
- [ ] Gov't [ ] NP [ ] Family
- [ ] Other _____
Amount of Gift $ _____

Underwriting Information

Monthly Income	Borrower	Co-Borrower	Total
Base Income	$ 6,231.88	$ 8,750.00	$ 14,981.88
Other Income	$	$	$
Net Rental Income	$	$	$
Total Income	$ 6,231.88	$ 8,750.00	$ 14,981.88

Debts & Obligations	Monthly	Unpaid Balance
Total Installment debt	$ 1,316.00	$ 76,653.00
Child Support	$	$
Negative Rental Cash Flow	$	$
All other monthly payments	$ 180.00	$ 38,652.00
Total Fixed Payment	$ 4,437.29	

Borrower Funds to Close
Required	$ 14,450.00
Verified Assets	$ 14,498.00
Closing Costs	$ 1,326.00
Source of Funds	CHECKING/SAVING/GIFT
No. of Months in Reserves	
Seller Contribution	2.133 %

Underwriter Comments
Verified assets include Gift

Proposed Monthly Payments
Borrowers Primary Residence
First Mortgage P&I	$ 1,887.71
Monthly MIP	$ 271.41
HOA Fees	$ 0.00
Lease/Ground Rent	$ 0.00
Second Mortgage P&I	$
Hazard Insurance	$ 80.75
Taxes & Special Assessments	$ 701.42
Total Mortgage Payment	$ 2,941.29

Qualifying Ratios
LTV	96.500 %
CLTV (if 2nd permitted)	96.500 %
Mortgage Payment-to-income	19.632 %
Total Fixed Payment-to-Income	29.618 %

	Borrower	Co-Borrower
CAIVRS #	A123456789	A987654321
LDP/GSA	[✓] yes [ ] no	[✓] yes [ ] no

Underwriter's signature & date (if required)	CHUMS ID #
X 1/1/2011	ZFHA

Risk Assessment
Scored by TOTAL? [✓] yes [ ] no   Risk Class [ ] A/A or [ ] Refer
CHUMS ID # for Reviewer of appraisal   JA01
(Required for loans scored by TOTAL with risk class A/A or loans where the appraisal and credit reviews are performed by different underwriters.)

Calyx form - fhatransum1.frm (8/2008)   form HUD-92900-LT (05/2008)

VETERANS ADMINISTRATION

VA-Guaranteed Loans

As a gesture to returning World War II veterans, Congress enacted the Servicemen's Readjustment Act (1944), which authorized the Veterans Administration (VA) to provide several benefits to eligible veterans. Included was the authority to guarantee mortgage loans made by lenders to eligible active and retired military personnel and their spouses. (For simplicity, this chapter uses the term *veteran* to include all the different categories of people eligible to participate in the VA program.) The guaranteed loan program, now administered by the Department of Veterans Affairs, no longer represents a large segment of originations each year, but still serves the needs of many veterans. The following VA Web site includes extensive information for veterans and lenders on the VA Loan Guaranty Home Loan Program (see http://www.benefits.va.gov/homeloans).

VA Program Today

The percentage of total residential originations that were VA guaranteed has slowly increased. Recent Congressional committee testimony indicates that since inception through 2009, VA guaranteed more than 18.7 million mortgages, totaling more than one trillion dollars. According to FHFA, in 2009, VA originated $191.4 million in loans, serving 325,673 veterans. Since 1990, VA volume remained in a more consistent range than FHA volume.

The VA program differs from conventional lending in several ways, the most significant ones being: the VA guarantee, applicant eligibility and entitlement, down payment amount and source, the certificate of reasonable value, and the residual income calculation.

VA Guarantee

The *VA guarantee* authorizes the Veteran's Administration to reimburse the lender for a percentage of its loss after foreclosure on a VA loan. Without it, lenders would be prohibited by their regulators from providing credit under such favorable terms to the borrower.

The original amount that VA guaranteed was the lesser of the first 50 percent of the loan amount or $2,000. This increased through the years to the current loan entitlement of $60,000 for purchase, new construction, and Interest Rate Reduction Refinancing Loans (IRRRL). A veteran who has full entitlement and no down payment can borrow four times this amount, or $240,000. Table 8.1 shows the history of VA maximum guarantees dating all the way back to 1940. Regular refinance transactions are limited to an entitlement of $36,000, or $144,000 loan amount.

Additionally, Ginnie Mae will purchase VA-guaranteed loans up to $962,500.00, including the financed VA funding fee, but the cash down payment plus the guarantee must equal at least 25 percent of the sales price or certificate of reasonable value (CRV), whichever is less.

TABLE **8.1**

History of Increases in VA Maximum Guarantees

Change Date	Increased to (dollars)
September 16, 1940	$4,000.00
April 20, 1950	7,500.00
May 7, 1968	12,500.00
January 1, 1975	17,500.00
January 1, 1978	25,000.00
October 7, 1980	27,500.00
February 1, 1988	36,000.00
January 1, 1990	46,000.00*
October 13, 1994	50,750.00*
December 28, 2001	60,000.00*

*Only available on purchases when the loan amount is in excess of $144,000—otherwise, the maximum guarantee is $36,000.
Source: REMOC Associates, LLC
© 2010 REMOC Associates, LLC
www.remoc.com

Eligibility

The VA loan guarantee is not available to veterans only. It is also available to qualified persons related to the military defined as:

- current or former armed service personnel
- active duty personnel
- National Guard reservists
- unremarried surviving spouses of veterans whose deaths were caused by a service-related injury or ailment
- spouses of members of the armed services who have either been missing in action or prisoner of war for more than 90 days

Only the VA can determine and authorize a person's eligibility for home loan benefits. The VA Web site has detailed information on eligibility for active military personnel, veterans, and spouses (http://www.homeloans.va.gov/elig2.htm). Again, this chapter uses the term "veteran" to mean all of these categories of eligible people.

A person who believes he or she is eligible for a VA-guaranteed loan must apply to the VA for a Certificate of Eligibility (CE) that establishes eligibility and the amount of the guarantee available (See Figure 8.5 on page 235). Alternatively, he or she may apply online at http://www.homeloans.va.gov/pdf/veteran_registration_coe.pdf.

Restoration of Veteran's Entitlement

The 1974 law that increased the maximum guarantee to $17,500 also provided for restoration of veterans' entitlement. Prior to this change, once a veteran used his entitlement, it could not be restored. The 1974 law provided for partial and, in some situations, full restoration of benefits. This change was partially motivated by Congress's desire to stimulate housing during that economic downturn. A veteran's entitlement may be restored if the following conditions can be met:

- Real estate was sold for reasons of health or condemnation
- Real estate was destroyed by fire or a natural hazard
- Loan was paid in full

The veteran obtains a release of liability form to restore his eligibility. A veteran's entitlement is restored to the extent that it was not used.

 EXAMPLE

A veteran purchased a home in January 1993 for $150,000. The maximum entitlement at that time was $46,000. This veteran wants to purchase another home today for $200,000 using the remaining entitlement.

$150,000 loan amount on first home

$\times 0.60$

$90,000 amount of entitlement used

The amount of guarantee used exceeds the amount available, but the amount is 50 percent of the purchase price, which exceeds the 25 percent required by a lender.

Maximum loan available now is established by subtracting the entitlement used from the current entitlement: $60,000 current entitlement minus $46,000 entitlement used, multiplied by four, equals $140,000 remaining entitlement; thus, the veteran may qualify for a $56,000 maximum loan with no down payment. In this case, the veteran will have to put $36,000 down ($200,000 price − $56,000 maximum loan = $144,000 divided by 25 percent down payment = $36,000).

VA Down Payment

Originally, this program was designed to allow veterans to buy homes with no money down—a major difference between VA and all other programs (except USDA Rural Housing). The VA program still operates on that concept, although a veteran now must pay a *funding fee* (Table 8.2), which is the guarantee or MI premium. A down payment might be required if the loan amount exceeds a certain limit. A veteran with a service-related disability acknowledged by the Veterans Administration is exempt from the funding fee. The funding fee schedule is based on the amount of down payment.

Currently, a qualified veteran (or any other eligible person) can buy a home costing up to $240,000 without a down payment financed by a mortgage guaranteed by the VA. The current maximum guarantee ($60,000) is the reason why lenders will accept no down payment financing. Although a lender provides a $240,000 mortgage, only $180,000 ($240,000 − $60,000 = $180,000), or

TABLE **8.2**

VA Funding Fee Schedule (funding fee is based on the amount of down payment)

(%)	First-Time User (%)	Multiple User (%)	Nat'l Guard First Time User (%)	Nat'l Guard Multiple User (%)
Purchase down payment **0–<5%**	2.15%	3.30%	2.40%	3.30%
Purchase down payment **5%–<10**	1.50	1.50	1.75	1.75
Purchase down payment **10% or more**	1.25	1.25	1.50	1.50
Interest Rate Reduction Refi (IRRR)	.50	.50	.50	.50
Cash Out Refi	2.15	3.3	2.4	3.3

Source: VA Pamphlet 26-7, Lender's Handbook, Revised April 10, 2009

75 percent of the loan amount, is made with any risk. If foreclosure becomes necessary, the real estate should bring at least the $180,000 that the lender had at risk. This amount, combined with the $60,000 guarantee, should make the lender whole.

If a veteran wants to buy a home appraised at more than $240,000, a lender would typically require a down payment equal to 25 percent of the amount in excess of $240,000. This keeps the loan within the 75 percent loan-to-value ratio and fully eligible for the VA guarantee.

Source of Funds

Because the Veterans Administration program does not require a down payment, there is less emphasis on source of funds. All gifts, grants, and normal sources of savings are allowed for a down payment, but lenders must verify all funds used for down payment and/or closing costs.

The seller is permitted to pay any closing costs, the VA funding fee, prepaid, or escrows; however, seller concessions are limited to four percent of the reasonable value as stated by the VA.

Credit/Liabilities

The VA program requires lenders to check FHA's Credit Alert Interactive Voice Response System (CAIVRS) to screen for applicants with FHA-insured loans in default or prior claim paid (within the past three years) by FHA. An applicant whose name and Social Security number appears during this screening may be ineligible for a VA Guaranty.

Because of the nature of risk associated with a no down payment loan, the VA program's credit standards are relatively strict. If the credit report shows delinquency, the applicant must have reestablished his credit, documented by a credit report showing a 12-month history of "as agreed" payments for all accounts. All delinquent credit explanations must be documented and make perfect sense.

Like the FHA program, the VA program will include in the qualifying ratio an applicant's personal or installment loan with less than 10 months remaining—if these obligations might cause a severe impact on the applicant's resources for any period of time.

> *Example*: A $300 monthly auto loan payment with a remaining balance of $1,500, even though it should be paid out in 5 months, is considered significant. The payment amount is large enough to impact the family's resources during the first and most critical months of homeownership.

The underwriter must determine whether or not the debts and obligations that do not fit the description of "significant" should be given any weight in the analysis, as they may impact the applicant's ability to provide for family living expenses.

Lenders must consider job related expenses, including costs for child care, significant commuting costs, and any other direct or incidental costs associated with the applicant's (or spouse's) employment.

An eligible married applicant in a non-community property state may obtain the loan in his or her name only. However, in community property states, lenders must consider the spouse's debts and obligations even if the eligible applicant wishes to obtain the loan in his or her name only.

Income and Employment

The VA closely follows conventional underwriting guidelines when considering a veteran's employment history and the income used to qualify. There are a few additional regulations required, starting with the veteran's pay stubs. While certified copies are accepted, the VA prefers that the loan package include at least one original pay stub/Leave and Earnings Statement (LES) for each applicant. In addition, active duty military personnel whose tour ends within one year of a home purchase must state their intention and plans to reenlist, and must obtain their commanding officers' written statements verifying whether they are eligible to reenlist *or* they must provide written evidence of commitment or contract for a new job in a similar or the same field.

If rental income is used to qualify when purchasing a two- to four-family house, the veteran must show evidence of six months' worth of reserves and a two-year history of property management, including the collection of rents. Income from a non-subject rental property may be used to offset the mortgage debt of that same property.

One significant difference between conventional underwriting and VA underwriting is the eligibility of a non-spouse co-applicant. It is possible to have a co-applicant that is not the spouse of the veteran, however the terms are limited. When there is a non-spouse, non-veteran co-applicant, the guaranty will be based on the veteran's portion of the loan only. The guaranty cannot cover the non-veteran's part of the loan. Lenders may require a higher down payment in order to cover the risk on the unguaranteed non-veteran's portion of the loan. The application must be underwritten by the VA, as delegated underwriting is not allowed.

The VA allows verifiable nontaxable and tax-free income to be grossed up.

Qualifying Ratios/Residual Income

The VA program calculates underwriting debt-to-income ratios differently than conventional or FHA programs. The VA program does not utilize a housing debt-to-income ratio. It uses only a total debt-to-income ratio of 41 percent, which includes the monthly PITI of the subject property and all of the veteran's debts.

Lenders can exceed the 41 percent ratio if the veteran's monthly housing debt does not increase more than 20 percent with the transaction, but the increase must be reasonable based on the other strengths and merits of the loan. If the housing expense increase exceeds 20 percent and the ratio exceeds 41 percent, the loan must have a minimum of two compensating factors justifying the underwriting decision.

In addition to the debt-to-income ratio, VA loan applicants must also pass the residual income test. Residual income is the amount of net income remaining (after deduction of debts and obligations and monthly shelter expenses) to cover family living expenses such as food, health care, clothing, and gasoline

The veteran's gross income is reduced by:

- federal, state, and local taxes that apply
- the monthly housing (PITI)
- a fee for heat, utilities, and maintenance
- all debt

The remaining income (residual income) must be equal to or more than a minimum amount published by the VA. The minimum amount required is based on data supplied in the Consumer Expenditures Survey (CES) published by the Department of Labor's Bureau of Labor Statistics. It varies according to loan size, family size, and geographical region of the country.

Processing

Processing a VA loan still differs from other loan programs, both conventional and other government-backed. In the past, the Veterans Administration was not unlike other military offices with an abundance of paperwork and procedures. Today, VA has automated many steps of the loan process, from obtaining the Certificate of Eligibility to issuance of the Loan Guaranty. Today, the VA underwrites less than one percent of the loans originated; more than 99 percent of new loans are underwritten by the Lender under a Direct Endorsed arrangement similar to FHA.

Certificate of Reasonable Value

The appraisal process for VA loans differs from conforming mortgage lending. VA requires an appraisal completed by a VA-approved appraiser to establish the "reasonable value" of the real estate. Based upon that appraisal (or the sales price, if lower), the VA issues a certificate of reasonable value (CRV) to the lender. The maximum guarantee is based on the loan amount. The maximum loan amount is based on the CRV, not the appraisal. The CRV may differ from the appraisal in value or conditions required prior to closing.

In 1987, Congress authorized the Lender Appraisal Processing Program (LAPP). This program allows the lenders with automatic underwriting approval authority to make value determinations. The appraisal must be reviewed by a Staff Appraisal Reviewer (SAR). When reviewing an appraisal, the SAR will make different assessments:

- Is the appraisal complete?
- Does the appraisal conform to industry practices and/or other VA requirements?
- Is the property value reasonable?

After his assessment, the SAR will send a written notice to the buyer with any conditions and requirements for the loan.

Underwriting

Overall, the Veterans Administration program is relatively conservative when qualifying a veteran for a mortgage loan. Stricter guidelines are understandable, as many VA loans have no down payment and, therefore, are very high risk.

Delegated underwriting authority is given only to lenders who are approved for automatic processing or who are being supervised by a lender who is approved. All other lenders must submit their loan files directly to the VA for prior approval. Various other circumstances also require prior approval, such as:

- Joint loans—two veterans, where each is using his/her own Entitlement
- Loans to veterans in receipt of a VA non-service-connected pension
- Interest Rate Reduction Refinancing Loans (IRRRLs) made to refinance delinquent VA loans
- Manufactured homes (except when the manufactured home is permanently affixed to the lot and considered real estate under state law), unless the lender has been separately approved for this purpose
- Cooperative loans
- Unsecured loans, or loans secured by less than a first lien
- Supplemental loans

Automated Underwriting

In 1998, the Veterans Administration approved the use of automated underwriting in conjunction with VA-guaranteed loans. AU started through Freddie Mac's Loan Prospector system, but it now is available through Fannie Mae's Desktop Underwriter as well. Any AU system a lender uses can evaluate the risk associated with an application and only recommend levels of documentation based on that risk; it does not supply a loan approval or rejection. The

VA warns lenders to be cautious when using an automated underwriting system: the final decision still stays with the lender. The lender is also fully responsible for meeting the VA's lending and eligibility criteria.

Documentation

In addition to the standard origination forms used for conventional lending, VA loans require the following documentation:

- *Interest Rate and Discount Disclosure Statement*: This form basically educates the veteran/applicant about interest rates and points, **rate locks**, and the consequences that rate changes could have on an already-approved loan.
- *VA Addendum to the URAR (VA form 26-1802a)*: This two-page form is the veteran's application for the VA guarantee (also used with an FHA loan).
- *VA Certificate of Eligibility*: This is the only form to verify eligibility for the Lender. It can now be generated online through ACE (Automated Certificate of Eligibility). See Figure 8.5.
- *Request for a Certificate of Eligibility for VA Home Loan Benefits (VA 26-1880)*: When it is necessary to manually order a Certificate of Eligibility, the veteran completes this form, outlining his or her military service data and any previous VA loan data. Then it is sent to VA's Winston-Salem, North Carolina Eligibility Center to request a copy of the veteran's most recent Certificate of Eligibility.
- *Military Discharge Papers (VA DD214)*: This is the most common type of proof of service and has been issued to veterans discharged from all branches of service since January 1, 1950. These forms are required when the veteran has been out of the military for less than two years. The discharge papers help document a full two-year employment history and are also used to order a Certificate of Eligibility manually.
- *Statement of Service*: The Statement is used for individuals currently on regular active duty who have not been previously discharged from active duty service. The form is completed and signed by, or at the direction of, an appropriate official. The statement must provide the veteran's date of entry on active duty and the duration of any time lost. If the veteran remains on active Selected Reserve duty, the Statement of Service should be from the veteran's unit commanding officer and should cite the length of time the veteran has served with the reserve unit.
- *Leave and Earnings Statement (LES)*: If the applicant is on active duty, is a reservist, or is in the National Guard, this form is used to show earnings, dates in service, and position. It is the military's equivalent of a pay stub.
- *Child Care affidavit or statement*: This form is required when the veteran has any minor children who require child care. The form states who is responsible for the child's daily care and what the monthly or weekly expense of that care is. This amount is used as a monthly debt in underwriting.

FIGURE **8.5** Certificate of Eligibility

VA **Department of Veterans Affairs**

CERTIFICATE OF ELIGIBILITY

FOR LOAN GUARANTY BENEFITS

REFERENCE NUMBER 25205

NAME OF VETERAN **IMA VETERAN**

SERVICE NUMBER
SOCIAL SECURITY NUMBER **XXX-XX-6762**

ENTITLEMENT CODE **05** BRANCH OF SERVICE **Air Force**

Prior Loans charged to entitlement					
VA Loan Number	State	Loan Amount	Date of Loan	Entitlement Charged	Status

THIS VETERAN'S BASIC ENTITLEMENT IS $36,000*
TOTAL ENTITLEMENT CHARGED TO PREVIOUS VA LOANS IS $0*

The veteran is eligible for the benefits of Chapter 37, Title 38, U.S. Code, subject to any condition(s) cited below. Basic entitlement for veterans who have not previously used home loan benefits is $36,000. Additional entitlement is available for most loans in excess of $144,000. In such cases, the entitlement amount is 25% of the VA loan limit for the county where the property is located. VA county loan limits are adjusted annually, and the current limits are available at www.homeloans.va.gov.

Issued By: Ura Veteran		Date: August 05, 2010

CONDITIONS

Subsequent Use Funding Fee- Entitlement code of '5' indicates previously used entitlement has been restored. The veteran must pay a subsequent use funding fee on any future loan unless veteran is exempt.

Source: Reprinted with permission of BFO Solutions, Incorporated www.benefits.va.gov.homeloans/

- *Verification of VA Benefit-Related Indebtedness (VA 26-8937)*: This document is required only if the veteran is receiving VA disability benefits or if the veteran would be entitled to VA disability benefits except for the receipt of retirement pay, has received VA disability benefits in the past, or the applicant is a surviving spouse of a veteran who died during active duty or as a result of a service-related disability. The form is submitted to the VA during the processing of the loan file to verify how much, if any, indebtedness the veteran has to the VA.
- *Counseling Checklist for Military Homebuyers (VA 26-0592)*: This document (Figure 8.6) is required for active-duty military. This form notifies the applicant of the responsibilities and potential difficulties of

homeownership in the face of serving in the military, and must be signed by the applicants and lender.

- *VA Amendatory Clause*: This is a clause in the sales contract that is required to be signed by both the veteran and the sellers. It states that they understand that if the Statement of Reasonable Value is less than the agreed upon sale price, the veteran is not bound by the contract and may be entitled to a full refund of any deposit monies.
- *VA Request for Determination of Reasonable Value (real estate) (VA 26-1805)*: This is the order form for an appraisal, and the VA's review of said appraisal and determination of value. This form *must* be typed, not handwritten.
- *LAPP Notice of Value (NOV)*: This form lists any special requirements or conditions applicable to the property. For cases processed under LAPP, the SAR must send to the veteran the NOV and a copy of the reviewed appraisal report within five business days.
- *Loan Analysis (VA 26-6393)*: This form (Figure 8.7) is the Veterans Administration's version of a Loan Summary (FNMA 1008), and summarizes the veteran's income, debt, ratio calculation, loan terms, etc.
- *Loan Guarantee Certificate (VA 26-1899)*: This form provides evidence of VA's approval of the application and loan guarantee to the lender for the named veteran. See Figure 8.8.

Assumptions

Unlike most conventional loans, a VA-guaranteed loan can be assumed without an increase in the mortgage interest rate. This feature makes homes with a VA guarantee more attractive to purchasers, especially during periods of rising interest rates. The purchaser does not have to be a veteran, although they must be judged to be a creditworthy applicant. As mentioned, the existing loan's interest rate and terms do not change, but the VA charges the assumptor a modest funding fee equal to 0.05 percent of the outstanding loan balance.

VA No-Bids

The VA's normal way of handling foreclosures changed in the late 1980s, to the detriment of mortgage lenders. Before this change, the VA would acquire the title to foreclosed property after the foreclosure sale for an amount up to the guarantee. The VA would then market the foreclosed property, hoping to recoup as much of the guarantee amount as possible. The VA learned that in many cases it actually lost more money by taking title to the property and attempting to sell it.

As a result, the VA now requires an appraisal before the foreclosure sale. If that appraisal indicates a value that will produce a loss to the VA greater than its guarantee, the VA issues "nonspecific" bidding instructions. The effect of this "no-bid" is that the servicer acquires the property at foreclosure and must market the property itself. The VA will provide no more than the maximum amount of its guarantee.

FIGURE **8.6** Sample Counseling Checklist for Military Homebuyers

 **Department of Veterans Affairs**

COUNSELING CHECKLIST FOR MILITARY HOMEBUYERS

1. Failure on the part of a borrower on active duty to disclose that he/she expects to leave the area within 12 months due to transfer orders or completion of his/her enlistment period may constitute "bad faith." If your loan is foreclosed under circumstances which include such bad faith, you may be required to repay VA for any loss suffered by the Government under the guaranty. (In ANY case in which VA suffers a loss under the guaranty, the loss must be repaid before your loan benefits can be restored to use in obtaining another VA loan.)

2. Although real estate values have historically risen in most areas, there is no assurance that the property for which you are seeking financing will increase in value or even retain its present value.

3. It is possible that you may encounter difficulty in selling your house, recovering your investment or making any profit, particularly if there is an active new home market in the area.

4. Receiving military orders for a permanent change of duty station or an unexpected early discharge due to a reduction in force will not relieve you of your obligation to make your mortgage payments on the first of each month.

5. "Letting the house go back" is **NOT** an acceptable option. A decision to do so may be considered "bad faith". A foreclosure will result in a bad credit record, a possible debt you will owe the government and difficulty in getting more credit in the future.

6. If unexpected circumstances lead to difficulty in making your payments, contact your mortgage company promptly. It will be easier to resolve any problems if you act quickly and be open and honest with the mortgage company.

7. **YOUR VA LOAN MAY NOT BE ASSUMED WITHOUT THE PRIOR APPROVAL OF VA OR YOUR LENDER**.

8. **DO NOT BE MISLED!** VA does not guarantee the **CONDITION** of the house which you are buying, whether it is new or previously occupied. VA guarantees only the **LOAN.** You may talk to many people when you are in the process of buying a house. Particularly with a previously occupied house, you may pick up the impression along the way that you need not be overly concerned about any needed repairs or hidden defects since VA will be sure to find them and require them to be repaired. This is **NOT TRUE!** In every case, ultimately, it is your responsibility to be an informed buyer and to assure yourself that what you are buying is satisfactory to you in all respects. Remember, VA guarantees only the loan - **NOT** the condition.

9. If you have any doubts about the condition of the house which you are buying, it is in your best interest to seek expert advice before you legally commit yourself in a purchase agreement. Particularly with a previously occupied house, most sellers and their real estate agents are willing to permit you, at your expense, to arrange for an inspection by a qualified residential inspection service. Also, most sellers and agents are willing to negotiate with you concerning what repairs are to be included in the purchase agreement. Steps of this kind can prevent many later problems, disagreements, and major disappointments.

10. Proper maintenance is the best way to protect your home and improve the chance that its value will increase.

11. If you are buying a previously owned house, you should look into making energy efficient improvements. You can add up to $6,000 to your VA loan to have energy efficient improvements installed. Consult your lender or the local VA office.

I HEREBY CERTIFY THAT the lender has counseled me and I fully understand the counseling items set forth above.

_____   _____
(Borrower's Signature)   (Date)

I HEREBY CERTIFY THAT the borrower has been counseled regarding the counseling items set forth above.

_____   _____
(Lender's Signature)   (Date)

VA Form
JUN 1995   **26-0592**   EXISTING STOCK OF VA FORM 26-0592, JUL 1990, WILL
                            BE USED.

Source: Reprinted with permission of BFO Solutions, Incorporated www.benefits.va.gov.homeloans/
© 2010 Community Lending Associates, LLC

FIGURE **8.7** Sample Department of Veteran Affairs Loan Analysis Form

OMB Control No. 2900-0523
Respondent Burden: 30 minutes

| ▼A Department of Veterans Affairs | LOAN ANALYSIS | LOAN NUMBER 72-72-6-2345678 |

PRIVACY ACT INFORMATION: The VA will not disclose information collected on this form to any source other than what has been authorized under the Privacy Act of 1974 or Title 5, Code of Federal Regulations 1.526 for routine uses as (i.e., the record of an individual who is covered by this system may be disclosed to a member of Congress or staff person acting for the member when the request is made on behalf of the individual) identified in the VA system of records, 55VA26, Loan Guaranty Home, Condominium and Manufactured Home Loan Applicant Records, Specially Adapted Housing Applicant Records, and Vendee Loan Applicant Records - VA, published in the Federal Register. Your obligation to respond is required in order to determine the veteran's qualifications for the loan.

RESPONDENT BURDEN: This information is needed to help determine a veteran's qualifications for a VA guaranteed loan. Title 38, USC, section 3710 authorizes collection of this information. We estimate that you will need an average of 30 minutes to review the instructions, find the information, and complete this form. VA cannot conduct or sponsor a collection of information unless a valid OMB control number is displayed. You are not required to respond to a collection of information if this number is not displayed. Valid OMB control numbers can be located on the OMB Internet Page at: **www.whitehouse.gov/omb/library/OMBINV.VA.EPA.html#VA.** If desired, you can call 1-800-827-1000 to get information on where to send comments or suggestions about this form.

SECTION A - LOAN DATA

1. NAME OF BORROWER	2. AMOUNT OF LOAN	3. CASH DOWN PAYMENT ON PURCHASE PRICE
IMA HERO	$ 195,237.00	$ 0.00

SECTION B - BORROWER'S PERSONAL AND FINANCIAL STATUS

4. APPLICANT'S AGE	5. OCCUPATION OF APPLICANT	6. NUMBER OF YEARS AT PRESENT EMPLOYMENT	7. LIQUID ASSETS (Cash, savings, bonds, etc.)	8. CURRENT MONTHLY HOUSING EXPENSE
46	E7	22	$ 4,000.00	$ 2,163.00

9. UTILITIES INCLUDED	10. SPOUSE'S AGE	11. OCCUPATION OF SPOUSE	12. NUMBER OF YEARS AT PRESENT EMPLOYMENT	13. AGE OF DEPENDENTS
☐ YES ☒ NO	35	N/A		0

NOTE: ROUND ALL DOLLAR AMOUNTS BELOW TO NEAREST WHOLE DOLLAR

SECTION C- ESTIMATED MONTHLY SHELTER EXPENSES (This Property)

SECTION D - DEBTS AND OBLIGATIONS (Itemize and indicate by (✓) which debts considered in Section E, Line 40) (If additional space is needed please use reverse or attach a separate sheet)

	ITEMS	AMOUNT		ITEMS	(✓)	MO. PAYMENT	UNPAID BAL.
14.	TERM OF LOAN: 30 YRS.		22.	PENTAGON FCU	✔	$ 223.00	$ 2,539.00
15.	MORTGAGE PAYMENT (Principal and Interest) @ 4.50 %	$ 978.22	23.	NFCU	✔	15.00	342.00
			24.	USAA FSB	✔	15.00	288.00
16.	REALTY TAXES	269.25	25.				
17.	HAZARD INSURANCE	65.00	26.				
18.	SPECIAL ASSESSMENTS		27.				
19.	MAINTENANCE & UTILITIES	215.00	28.				
20.	OTHER (HOA, Condo fees, etc.)		29.	JOB RELATED EXPENSE (e.g., child care)			
21.	TOTAL	$ 1,527.47	30.	TOTAL		$ 253.00	$ 3,169.00

SECTION E - MONTHLY INCOME AND DEDUCTIONS

	ITEMS	SPOUSE	BORROWER	TOTAL
31.	GROSS SALARY OR EARNINGS FROM EMPLOYMENT		4,131.30	4,131.30
32.		FEDERAL INCOME TAX	$	597.67	
33.		STATE INCOME TAX		382.92	
34.	DEDUCTIONS	RETIREMENT OR SOCIAL SECURITY		316.04	
35.		OTHER (Specify)			
36.		TOTAL DEDUCTIONS	$	$ 1,296.63	$ 1,296.63
37.	NET TAKE-HOME PAY		2,834.67	2,834.67
38.	PENSION, COMPENSATION OR OTHER NET INCOME (Specify) BAH, Clothing, Subsistanc		2,667.87	2,667.87
39.	TOTAL (Sum of lines 37 and 38)	$	$ 5,502.54	$ 5,502.54
40.	LESS THOSE OBLIGATIONS LISTED IN SECTION D WHICH SHOULD BE DEDUCTED FROM INCOME			253.00
41.	TOTAL NET EFFECTIVE INCOME			$ 5,249.54
42.	LESS ESTIMATED MONTHLY SHELTER EXPENSE (Line 21)			1,527.47
43.	BALANCE AVAILABLE FOR FAMILY SUPPORT		GUIDELINE $ 738.00	$ 3,722.07
44.	RATIO (Sum of Items 15, 16, 17, 18, 20 and 40 ÷ sum of Items 31 and 38)			0.23 %

45. PAST CREDIT RECORD	46. DOES LOAN MEET VA CREDIT STANDARDS? (Give reasons for decision under "Remarks," if necessary, e.g., borderline case)
☒ SATISFACTORY ☐ UNSATISFACTORY	☒ YES ☐ NO

47. REMARKS (Use reverse or attach a separate sheet, if necessary)

CAIVR# A3408494163

DU APPROVED/ELIGIBLE MID SCORE 637   ⊞

CRV DATA (VA USE)

| 48A. VALUE 189,000.00 | 48B. EXPIRATION DATE 02/26/2011 | 48C. ECONOMIC LIFE 30 YRS. |

SECTION F - DISPOSITION OF APPLICATION AND UNDERWRITER CERTIFICATION

☒ Recommend that the application be approved since it meets all requirements of Chapter 37, Title 38, U.S. Code and applicable VA Regulations and directives.

☐ Recommend that the application be disapproved for the reasons stated under "Remarks" above.

The undersigned underwriter certifies that he/she personally reviewed and approved this loan. (Loan was closed on the automatic basis.)

49. DATE 09/26/2010	50. SIGNATURE OF EXAMINER/UNDERWRITER

51. FINAL ACTION	52. DATE 09/29/2010	53. SIGNATURE AND TITLE OF APPROVING OFFICIAL
☒ APPROVE APPLICATION ☐ REJECT APPLICATION		Betsy Underwriter

VA FORM SEP 2006 **26-6393**

EXISTING STOCKS OF VA FORM 26-6393, OCT 2005, WILL BE USED.

Source: Reprinted with permission of BFO Solutions, Incorporated www.benefits.va.gov.homeloans/
© 2010 Community Lending Associates, LLC

FIGURE **8.8** Loan Guaranty Certificate

Department of Veterans Affairs

UNITED STATES OF AMERICA
LOAN GUARANTY CERTIFICATE

ISSUED TO:

SAMPLE VA LENDER

123 LOAN AVENUE

SOMEWHERE, US 22501

Loan Number	Date Of Loan	Amount Of Loan	Guaranty Amount	Percent Guaranteed
72-72-6-1234567	09/24/2010	$195,237.00	$48,809.00	25.00%

CERTIFICATION TO FINANCIAL INSTITUTION

This is to certify that, in this case, the Department of Veterans Affairs (VA) has complied with the applicable provisions of the Right to Financial Privacy Act of 1978, title xi of Public Law 95-630. Pursuant to section 113(h)(2) of the Act, no further certification shall be required for subsequent access by the Department of Veterans Affairs, Loan Guaranty Service or Division to financial records on this loan during the term of the loan guaranty.

This is to certify that pursuant to chapter 37, title 38, U.S.C., as amended, and the regulations effective thereunder on the date of this certificate, the indebtedness outstanding from time to time under the loan identified herein is guaranteed in the following amount(s):

Full Name(s) Of Veteran(s)	Amount Of Loan	Entitlement Charged	Date Of Guaranty
IMA VETERAN	$195,237.00	$48,809.00	11/08/2010

DATE OF THIS
CERTIFICATE _____ 11/08/2010 _____

ISSUING
OFFICE _____ Electronic Guaranty _____

Upon full satisfaction of this loan by payment or otherwise, this certificate must be appropriately endorsed and signed, and returned to VA pursuant to 38 CFR 36.4218 or 36.4333. Check the appropriate box to show the reason for the termination for VA's guaranty liability.

PAID-IN-FULL   CLAIM PAID

VA Form 26-1899
JAN 2008

U.S. DEPARTMENT OF AGRICULTURE

Rural Housing Services (RHS)

The Rural Housing Service (RHS) is an agency of the U.S. Department of Agriculture (USDA). It offers a wide range of programs under the USDA's Rural Development mission. Residential lending falls under the Housing and Community Facilities Programs (HCFP). Additional information about the program can be located at the following website: http://www.rurdev.usda.gov/LP_Subject_HousingAndCommunityAssistance.html

RHS Single Family Programs—Section 502

Unlike FHA and VA, Rural Housing Service will lend directly to the consumer if no local lender is available. Nationally, the vast majority of residential volume comes from approved lenders. An annual publication in the *Federal Register* entitled "The Notice of Funding Availability" (NOFA) describes types of funding available and provides a contact in each state for application submission. http://www.rurdev.usda.gov/RD_NOFAs.html

RHS Single Family assistance targets low- to moderate-income families in rural areas. The RHS has a mandate to direct approximately 40 percent of its loan funding to assist very low income households. Its assistance comes in the following forms:

- Direct loans made and serviced by the USDA
- Loan guarantees of loans made by banks and other lenders
- Grants to individuals or organizations

RHS Single Family programs provide the following:

- Assistance to tenants and developers of multifamily housing
- Community facilities
- Farm labor housing
- Funding for housing rehabilitation and preservation
- Financing for individual homeownership and construction

Additional information on the RHS Single Family Programs (loans and grants) can be found at the following website.

- http://www.rurdev.usda.gov/HSF_SFH.html

Two popular single-family programs under Section 502 are the Rural Housing Guaranteed Loan (RHGL) and the Rural Housing Direct Loan (RHDL). Each program has different terms and eligibility criteria for applicants, but basically the same criteria for properties.

Property

Eligible properties must be in a rural area. A RHS-defined *rural area* includes open country and places with a population of 10,000 or less. Small towns and cities with between 10,000 and 25,000 residents may be eligible if they are in closer proximity to metropolitan areas.

Houses must be modest in design, cost, and size. A property must also meet the Voluntary National Model Building Code adopted by the state within which it is located, as well as RHS thermal and site standards.

Manufactured housing is eligible for the RHDL program if it is permanently installed, and meets HUD's Manufactured Housing Construction and Safety Standards and RHS thermal and site standards. Existing manufactured housing is not eligible for the RHGL program unless it is an REO (real estate owned) of, or is currently financed by, an RHS direct or guarantee loan.

Single Family—Homeownership Direct Loan Program

In the Homeownership Direct Loan Program (HDLP), the RHS funds the loan directly to consumers, often at below market interest rates. The HCFP sets the interest rate for the program; however, RHS may include a payment assistance subsidy to lower the individual borrowers' effective interest rate to as low as one percent.

Because many RHS applicants may not qualify for conventional lending programs, the HDLP enables many more families who would otherwise be excluded to enjoy the benefits of homeownership.

Often, income levels in rural and very rural areas are well below the national average, so HDLP loan terms vary with the applicant's level of income and purpose of the loan. Sometimes the loan is structured with a payment subsidy. To structure loan terms, RHS uses the following income definitions based on the *area median income* (AMI) for the community involved:

- *Moderate income*: between 80 and 100 percent of AMI
- *Low income*: between 50 and 80 percent of AMI
- *Very low income*: 50 percent or below AMI

The loan terms are for up to 33 years, and can extend up to 38 years for those with income below 60 percent AMI. More information is available at http://www.rurdev.usda.gov/HAD-Direct_Housing_Loans.html.

Single Family—Home Loan Guarantee Program (SFHLGP)

In the RHS SFLGP (Figure 8.9), the RHS guarantees an eligible mortgage loan made by a lender to a consumer. In the event of default, RHS pays the lender. An individual or family must apply through an approved lender. The individual lender sets the interest rate. SFLGP loans can be sold to various secondary market conduits, including Freddie Mac, Fannie Mae, Ginnie Mae, and many state housing finance agencies.

The SFHLGP program assists low- to moderate-income families, and allows a household income of up to 115 percent of AMI. The family must have a reasonable credit history.

The loan purpose can be to purchase or to repair a home. RHS SFHLG loans are for a 30-year term only. No down payment is required, but underwriting debt-to-income ratios of 29/41 are strictly adhered to.

FIGURE **8.9** Request for Single Family Housing Loan Guarantee

Committed to the future of rural communities

USDA Single Family Housing Guaranteed Loan Program

Form RD 1980-21 "Request for Single Family Housing Loan Guarantee"
Revised October 2010

Form RD 1980-21 must be complete with accurate loan information and the signatures of <u>both</u> the approved lender and the applicant(s) before submission to Rural Development (RD) to request a Conditional Commitment for Loan Note Guarantee.

Side annotation (left): Enter the "Approved Lender" that has an approved Form RD 1980-16 (Lender Agreement) on file with the Agency.

Side annotation (left): Identify "Third Party Originator" if applicable. TPO's are not required to be approved lenders.

Side annotation (left): Ethnicity and Race must be selected by the lender if not provided by the applicant(s).

Side annotation (left): Enter the representative FICO score.

Side annotation (left): Utilize an additional Form RD 1980-21 when more than 2 applicants apply.

Side annotation (left): List each eligible cost that will be <u>financed</u> into the loan.

Side annotation (left): The online Form RD 1980-21 calculates the total request via auto-sum.

Side annotation (right): Enter the 9 digit Federal Tax Identification Number (TIN) of the approved lender. This # is also on the Lender Agreement.

Side annotation (right): Enter the loan reference number assigned by the lender.

Side annotation (right): Indicate the method and date utilized for calculating the interest rate.

Side annotation (right): Confirm if the interest rate is locked or floating.

Form RD 1980-21
(Rev. 10-10)

UNITED STATES DEPARTMENT OF AGRICULTURE
RURAL DEVELOPMENT
RURAL HOUSING SERVICE

Form Approved
OMB No. 0575-0078

REQUEST FOR SINGLE FAMILY HOUSING LOAN GUARANTEE

Approved Lender: _____ Approved Lender Tax ID No.: _____

Contact: _____ Approved Lender E-Mail: _____

Phone Number: _____ Fax Number: _____

Third Party Originator (TPO): _____ TPO Tax ID No: _____

USDA Application Number: _____ Lender Loan Reference Number: _____

Please issue a Conditional Commitment for Single Family Housing Loan Guarantee in the following case:

Applicant Information (Please complete, circle, or mark as appropriate)	Co-Applicant Information (Please complete, circle, or mark as appropriate)
Name: _____	Name: _____
SSN: _____ Date of Birth: _____	SSN: _____ Date of Birth: _____
U.S. Citizen: ☐ Yes ☐ No	U.S. Citizen: ☐ Yes ☐ No
Permanent Resident/Qualified Alien: ☐ Yes ☐ No	Permanent Resident/Qualified Alien: ☐ Yes ☐ No
Veteran: ☐ Yes ☐ No Disabled: ☐ Yes ☐ No	Veteran: ☐ Yes ☐ No Disabled: ☐ Yes ☐ No
Gender: ☐ M ☐ F First Time Homebuyer ☐ Yes ☐ No	Gender: ☐ M ☐ F First Time Homebuyer ☐ Yes ☐ No
Ethnicity: (Check only One Box) ☐ Hispanic or Latino ☐ Not Hispanic or Latino	Ethnicity: (Check only One Box) ☐ Hispanic or Latino ☐ Not Hispanic or Latino
(Check as many boxes as applicable) Race: ☐ American Indian or Alaska Native ☐ Asian ☐ Black or African American ☐ Native Hawaiian or Other Pacific Islander ☐ White	(Check as many boxes as applicable) Race: ☐ American Indian or Alaska Native ☐ Asian ☐ Black or African American ☐ Native Hawaiian or Other Pacific Islander ☐ White
Marital Status: ☐ Married ☐ Separated ☐ Unmarried	Marital Status: ☐ Married ☐ Separated ☐ Unmarried
The applicant ☐ has ☐ does not have a relationship with any current Rural Development employee.	The co-applicant ☐ has ☐ does not have a relationship with any current Rural Development employee.
Applicant's Credit Score: _____ ☐ No Score	Co-Applicant's Credit Score: _____ ☐ No Score

ANY ADDITIONAL APPLICANTS MUST BE FULLY DOCUMENTED ON A SEPARATE FORM.

Property Address: _____

City, State, Zip Code: _____   County: _____

Is this a Refinance Loan? ☐ No ☐ Yes   If Yes, refinanced loan is an RD Single Family Housing ☐ Guaranteed Loan ☐ Direct Loan

1. Number of persons in the household: _____ Number of dependants under Age 18 or Full-time Students: _____
2a. The current annual income for the household is: $_____ 2b. The current adjusted income for the household is: $_____
3. PITI ratio: _____ TOTAL DEBT ratio: _____
4. We propose to loan $_____ for 30 years at _____ % per annum with payments (P&I) of $_____ per month.
5. The interest rate is based on the ☐ Fannie Mae on ____/____/____ (required).
   ☐ The interest rate is locked in until ____/____/____
   ☐ The interest rate will float until loan closing (documentation of lock date will be required w/ loan closing report).
   NOTE: If the interest rate increases at loan closing, the loan must be re-underwritten and this document must be recertified.
6. The applicant understands that Rural Development approval of guarantee is required and is subject to the availability of funds.
7. The applicant is unable to secure the necessary conventional credit without a Rural Development guarantee upon reasonable rates, terms, and conditions in which the applicant could reasonably be expected to fulfill.
8. Loan funds will be used for the following purpose(s):

Purchase / Refinance Amt: _____	$_____
Financed Loan Closing Costs: _____	$_____
Repairs/Other: _____	$_____
Guarantee Fee: _____	$_____
Total Request: _____	$_____

According to the Paperwork Reduction Act of 1995, an agency may not conduct or sponsor, and a person is not required to respond to, a collection of information unless it displays a valid OMB control number. The valid OMB control number for this information collection is 0575-0078. The time required to complete this information collection is estimated to average 30 minutes per response, including the time for reviewing instructions, searching existing data sources, gathering and maintaining the data needed, and completing and reviewing the collection of information.

Page 1 of 4

FIGURE **8.9** (*Continued*)

An authorized representative of the approved lender must execute the lender certification.

Certifications

Approved Lender Certification

In order to induce the Agency to issue the requested guarantee, we certify that we have originated and underwritten the loan in compliance with all Agency loan requirements. This form contains or is supplemented with all information required by 7 C.F.R. § 1980.353(c).

_____   _____
Lender's Authorized Representative Signature / Title   Date

_____
Name of Authorized Representative

_____
Title/Company

Applicant(s) Acknowledgments and Certifications

Applicants must read all terms under "Acknowledgments and Certifications." If agreed, they must execute their certification.

CERTIFICATION: As the applicant, I certify to the best of my knowledge and belief; (1) I am not presently debarred, suspended, declared ineligible, or voluntarily excluded from covered transactions by any Federal department or agency; (2) I have not within a three year period preceding this proposal been convicted or had a civil judgment rendered against me for commission of fraud or a criminal offense in connection with obtaining, attempting to obtain, or performing a public (Federal, state, or local) transaction or contract under a public transaction; or commission of embezzlement, theft, forgery, bribery, falsification, or destruction of records, making false statement, or receiving stolen property; (3) I do not have an outstanding judgment lien on any property for a debt in favor of the United States which was obtained in any Federal court other than the United States Tax Court; and (4) I am not delinquent on any outstanding debt to the Federal Government (excluding any Federal Tax debt).

The "Debt Collection and Improvement Act" (DCIA) statement is now in bold to emphasize the importance of this acknowledgment.

I (we) certify and acknowledge that if the Agency pays a loss claim on the requested loan to the lender, I (we) will reimburse the Agency for that amount. If I (we) do not, the Agency will use all remedies available to it, including those under the Debt Collection Improvement Act, to recover on the Federal debt directly from me (us). The Agency's right to collect is independent of the lender's right to collect under the guaranteed note and will not be affected by any release by the lender of my (our) obligation to repay the loan. Any Agency collection under this paragraph will not be shared with the lender.

I AM (WE ARE) unable to provide the housing I (we) need on my (our) own account, and I am (we are) unable to secure the credit necessary for this purpose from other sources upon terms and conditions which I (we) can reasonably fulfill. I (we) certify that the statements made by me (us) in this application are true, complete and correct to the best of my (our) knowledge and belief and are made in good faith to obtain a loan.

Warning: Section 1001 of Title 18, United States Code provides: "Whoever, in any matter within the jurisdiction of any Department or Agency of the United States knowingly and willfully falsifies, conceals or covers up by any trick, scheme, or device a material fact, or makes any false, fictitious or fraudulent statements or representations, or makes or uses any false writing or document knowing the same to contain any false, fictitious or fraudulent statement or entry, shall be fined under this title or imprisoned not more than five years, or both."

Each of the undersigned hereby acknowledges having read page three and four of this document as it relates to information regarding the PRIVACY ACT and a NOTIFICATION TO APPLICANT ON USE OF FINANCIAL INFORMATION FROM FINANCIAL INSTITUTION.

Print the applicant's name.

_____   _____   _____
Print Applicant's Name   Applicant's Signature   Date

_____   _____   _____
Print Co-Applicant's Name   Co Applicant's Signature   Date

Page 2 of 4

DCIA Note: *When an applicant signs Form RD 1980-21, they acknowledge that if a loss payment is paid by the Agency, they are responsible for reimbursing the Agency for the amount of loss paid. Release of liability from the lender does not release them from liability from the Federal government.*

Signature Note: *Original Signatures are not required to be submitted to Rural Development. Rural Development accepts fax, email, photocopy, and scanned documents.*

FIGURE **8.9** (*Continued*)

NOTICE TO APPLICANT REGARDING PRIVACY ACT INFORMATION

The information requested on this form is authorized to be collected by the Rural Housing Service (RHS), Rural Business Cooperative Services (RBS), Rural Utilities Service (RUS) ("the agency") by title V of the Housing Act of 1949, as amended (42 U.S.C. 1471 et seq.) or by the Consolidated Farm and Rural Development Act (7 U.S.C. 1921 et seq.), or by other laws administered by RHS, RBS or RUS.

Disclosure of information requested is voluntary. However, failure to disclose certain items of information requested, including your Social Security Number or Federal Identification Number, may result in a delay in the processing of an application or its rejection. Information provided may be used outside of the agency for the following purposes:

1. When a record on its face, or in conjunction with other records, indicates a violation or potential violation of law, whether civil, criminal or regulatory in nature, and whether arising by general statute or particular program statute, or by regulation, rule, or order issued pursuant thereto, disclosure may be made to the appropriate agency, whether federal, foreign, state, local, or tribal, or other public authority responsible for enforcing, investigating or prosecuting such violation or charged with enforcing or implementing the statute, or rule, regulation, or order issued pursuant thereto, if the information disclosed is relevant to any enforcement, regulatory, investigative, or prosecute responsibility of the receiving entity.

2. A record from this system of records may be disclosed to a Member of Congress or to a Congressional staff member in response to an inquiry of the Congressional office made at the written request of the constituent about whom the record is maintained.

3. Rural Development will provide information from this system to the U.S. Department of Treasury and to other Federal agencies maintaining debt servicing centers, in connection with overdue debts, in order to participate in the Treasury Offset Program as required by the Debt Collection Improvement Act, Pub. L. 104-134, Section 31001.

4. Disclosure of the name, home address, and information concerning default on loan repayment when the default involves a security interest in tribal allotted or trust land. Pursuant to Cranston-Gonzales National Affordable Housing Act of 1990 (42 U.S.C. 12701 et seq.), liquidation may be pursued only after offering to transfer the account to an eligible tribal member, the tribe, or the Indian Housing Authority serving the tribe(s).

5. Referral of names, home addresses, social security numbers, and financial information to a collection or servicing contractor, financial institution, or a local, state, or federal agency, when Rural Development determines such referral is appropriate for servicing or collecting the borrower's account or has provided for in contracts with servicing or collection agencies.

6. It shall be a routine use of the records in this system of records to disclose them in a proceeding before a court or adjudicative body, when: (a) the agency or any component thereof; or (b) any employee of the agency in his or her official capacity, or (c) any employee of the agency in his or her individual capacity where the agency has agreed to represent the employee; or (d) the United States is a party to litigation or has an interest in such litigation, and by careful review, the agency determines that the records are both relevant and necessary to the litigation, provided; however, that in each case, the agency determines that disclosure of the records is a use of the information contained in the records that is compatible with the purpose for which the agency collected the records.

7. Referral of name, home address, and financial information for selected borrowers to financial consultants, advisors, lending institutions, packagers, agents, and private or commercial credit sources, when the agency determines such referral is appropriate to encourage the borrower to refinance their RHS indebtedness as required by title V of the Housing Act of 1949, as amended (42 U.S.C. 147 1) or to assist the borrower on the sale of the property.

8. Referral of legally enforceable debts to the Department of the Treasury, Internal Revenue Service (IRS), to be offset against any tax refund that may become due the debtor for the tax year in which the referral is made, in accordance with the IRS regulations and under the authority contained in 31 U.S.C. 3720A.

9. Referral of information regarding indebtedness to the Defense Manpower Data Center, Department of Defense, and the United States Postal Service for the purpose of conducting computer matching programs to identify and locate individuals receiving Federal salary or benefit payments and who are delinquent in their repayment of debts owed to the U.S. Government under certain programs administered by the agency in order to collect debt under the provisions of the Debt Collection Act of 1982 (5 U.S.C. 5514) by voluntary repayment, administrative or salary offset procedures, or by collection agencies.

10. Referral of names, home addresses, and financial information to lending institutions when Rural Development determines the individual may be financially capable of qualifying for credit with or without a guarantee.

11. Disclosure of names, home addresses, social security numbers, and financial information to lending institutions that have a lien against the same property as the agency for the purpose of the collection of the debt by Rural Development or the other lender. These loans can be under the direct and guaranteed loan programs.

12. Referral to private attorneys under contract with either the agency or with the Department of Justice for the purpose of foreclosure and possession actions and, collection of past due accounts in connection with the agency.

13. It shall be a routine use of the records in this system of records to disclose them to the Department of Justice when: (a) the agency or any component thereof; or (b) any employee of the agency in his or her official capacity; or (c) the United States Government, is a party to litigation or has an interest in such litigation, and by careful review, the agency determines that the records are both relevant and necessary to the litigation and the use of such records by the Department of Justice is therefore deemed by the agency to be for a purpose that is compatible with the purpose for which the agency collected the records.

14. Referral of names, home addresses, social security numbers, and financial information to the Department of Housing and Urban Development (HUD) as a record of location utilized by Federal agencies for an automatic credit prescreening system.

15. Referral of names, home addresses, social security numbers, and financial information to the Department of Labor, state wage information collection agencies, and other federal, state, and local agencies, as well as those responsible for verifying information furnished to qualify for federal benefits, to conduct wage and benefit matching through manual or automated means, for the purpose of determining compliance with federal regulations and appropriate servicing actions against those not entitled to program benefits, including possible recovery of improper benefits.

16. Referral of names, home addresses, and financial information to financial consultants, advisors, or underwriters, when Rural Development determines such referral is appropriate for developing packaging and marketing strategies involving the sale of Rural Development loan assets.

17. Rural Development, in accordance with 31 U.S.C. 3711 (e)(5), will provide to consumer reporting agencies or commercial reporting agencies information from this system indicating that an individual is responsible for a claim that is current.

18. Referral of names, home and work addresses, home telephone numbers, social security numbers, and financial information to escrow agents (which also could include attorneys and title companies) selected by applicant or borrower for the purpose of closing the loan.

Page 3 of 4

Note: *Applicants must read the "Notice to Applicant Regarding Privacy Act Information" prior to executing the certification on page two. The Privacy Act is page three of Form RD 1980-21.*

FIGURE **8.9** (*Continued*)

NOTIFICATION TO APPLICANT ON USE OF FINANCIAL INFORMATION FROM FINANCIAL INSTITUTION

Pursuant to Title XI, section 1113(h) of Public Law 95-630, your application for a government loan or loan guaranty authorizes the Agency, in connection with the assistance you seek, to obtain financial information about you contained in financial institutions. No further notice of subsequent access to this information shall be provided during the term of the loan or loan guaranty.

As a general rule, financial records obtained pursuant to this authority may be used only for the purpose for which they were originally obtained. However, they may be transferred to another Agency or department if the transfer is to facilitate a lawful proceeding, investigation, examination, or inspection directed at the financial institution in possession of the records (or another legal entity not a customer). The records may also be transferred and used (1) by counsel representing a government authority in a civil action arising from a government loan, loan guaranty, or loan insurance agreement; and (2) by the Government to process, service or foreclose a loan or to collect on an indebtedness to the Government resulting from a customer's default.

The Agency reserves the right to give notice of a potential civil, criminal, or regulatory violation indicated by the financial records to any other agency or department of the Government with jurisdiction over that violation. Such agency or department may then seek access to the records in any lawful manner.

Page 4 of 4

Note: *Applicants must receive and review the "Notification to Applicant On Use of Financial Information From Financial Institution" prior to executing the certification on page two. This notice is page four of Form RD 1980-21.*

TIPS FOR SUCCESS:
- Applicants **cannot** execute a blank Form RD 1980-21.
- All data fields must be completed. Form RD 1980-21 must be executed by an approved lender's representative and all applicants.
- Interest rates that are "floating to close" will require supporting documentation to confirm the date of the rate lock, to ensure compliance with RD Instruction 1980-D, section 1980.320.

http://www.rurdev.usda.gov/regs/forms/1980-21.pdf

RHS charges the lender a one-time guarantee fee that is either paid by the borrower at closing or financed. The FY 2011 guarantee fees are:

- 3.5 percent of the loan amount for purchase transactions; 103.5 percent LTV maximum
- 1.0 percent of the loan amount for refinance transactions; 101.0 percent LTV maximum

After the onetime fee is either paid or financed, there is no other recurring monthly expense charged for guaranteeing the loan.

The following example from the RHS Web site illustrates how the SFHLG program calculates LTV and the guarantee fee:

Purchase Price $175,000

Appraised Value $190,000

There is a $15,000 difference between the appraisal and the purchase price; however, the borrowers only want to finance $10,305 in closing costs plus the USDA fee.

Purchase Price $175,000 + $10,305 closing costs = Loan Amount $185,305

Loan Amount $185,305 divided by .9650 = Total Loan Amount $192,025.91

Subtract Total Loan Amount - $192,025.91 from Loan Amount $185,305 = $6,720.91

Total Loan Amount $192,025.91 × 3.5% = $6,720.91

More information is available at: http://www.rurdev.usda.gov/HAD-Guaranteed_Housing_Loans.html

RHS Recent Changes

In 2010, the RHS program was the subject of much Congressional debate. The Rural Housing Improvement Act of 2010 and RHS enacted several changes (included above):

- increase the guarantee fee to 3.5 percent
- allow an annual fee of no more than 0.5 percent a year on the balance of the loan.
- lenders may set an interest rate for a SFHGLP loan that either does not exceed the Lender's published rate for VA first mortgage loans with no discount points or does not exceed the current Fannie Mae posted yield for 90-day delivery (Actual/Actual), plus six tenths of 1 percent for 30 year fixed rate conventional loans, rounded up to the nearest one quarter of 1 percent.
- allow the Secretary of Agriculture in certain circumstances to recoup funds it pays in a claim under the RHS guarantee if the original lender did not comply with SFHGLP requirements.

The intent of these proposals is to create a more uniform, simpler standard for interest rates under the SFHGLP and to improve loan quality to reduce unnecessary losses.

DISCUSSION POINTS

1. Discuss the positive and negative ways in which government-sponsored mortgage programs impact housing.
2. How is mortgage insurance (FHA or PMI) different from a mortgage guarantee (VA or USDA)?
3. Why has FHA mortgage lending increased so dramatically in recent years?
4. How do FHA mortgage programs differ from conventional mortgage programs?
5. How do VA-guaranteed programs work?
6. What program eligibility issues and restrictions does the VA impose?
7. What eligibility issues and restrictions do USDA RHS programs have?

CHAPTER 9

Construction Lending

INTRODUCTION

This chapter provides an overview on the financing of residential one- to four-family home construction, the special risks associated with this line of business, who provides this type of financing, and how it is done. It cannot discuss in detail the many issues specific to state and local law and customs: zoning requirements, building codes, legal documentation, and title insurance requirements. The chapter does point out when these items require special consideration compared to conventional mortgage financing.

As discussed to some extent in Chapter 3—Role of Residential Mortgage Lending in the Economy, single-family residential construction comprises one of the most significant elements of the U.S. economy, directly accounting for approximately four to six percent, annually, of the U.S. economy over the past 20 years. According to the U.S. Dept. of Commerce, in 2000 residential construction totaled $580 billion, or four percent. At the height of the recent home building boom in 2005, this figure peaked at more than three times that amount: $775 billion, or six percent of the economy. Then, new home building activity declined 33 percent from 2005 to 2009, to $343 billion.

Lenders also restricted residential construction underwriting requirements and/or funding during this time. Many stopped lending entirely, especially those relying on capital from other companies to fund the projects. During this period, more lenders relied on the FHA 203(k) program, which recently is less restrictive and cumbersome, but still is quite involved compared to private institution programs.

The National Association of Home Builders (NAHB) reports that more than six million people are directly involved in construction, materials, and other construction resources. Despite these large numbers, the majority of firms producing new homes is family owned and produces fewer than 25 homes per year. The typical home builder company decreased in size. In 2009, the average home builder employed an average of 7.5 people, and built 17 homes annually for approximately $1.36 million.

Millions more are involved in jobs related to construction. In their most recent study of 2009, NAHB estimates that construction of 100 single family homes and 100 rental apartments in a typical metro area generates:

	Single Family	Multi-family
Construction and related jobs	324	122
Local income	$21 million	$7.9 million
Tax revenue	$2.2 million	$827,000

(Local, state, and federal)

Additionally, the annual recurring impacts are:

100 Single family units	$3.1 million in local income
	$742,000 in taxes and other local government revenue
	53 new local jobs
100 rental units	$2.1 million in local income
	$395,000 in taxes and other local government revenue
	32 new local jobs

Source: National Association of Home Builders (NAHB), **www.nahb.com**

Housing Starts

Every month, the financial markets watch closely the numbers released for building permits issued and *housing starts*—leading indicators for the economy. To determine housing starts, the U.S. Census surveys recent holders of building permits nationally to see if they actually started construction. Typically, 90 percent do so within two months of obtaining a permit.

There are more than 110 million housing units in the United States, whose value doubled from 1990 to 2000, doubled *again* from 2000 to 2005, and then dropped more than 30 percent from 2006 to 2010. Despite these wide changes in value, the volume of new housing stock has been relatively stable for this period, with some notable exceptions during economic boom and bust years.

According to the U.S. Census, for 15 of the past 30 years (1979–2009) the U.S economy had approximately 1.0 to 1.3 million new single-family housing starts. In eight of those years, the volume was higher, with 2005 being the peak at 1,715,800 single-family starts. In seven of the years, the volume was less than one million single-family starts, with the lowest two years being the most recent (2008 totaled 622,000; in 2009 it plunged further to only 445,000). During the same period, 160,000 to 350,000 multifamily starts occurred each year. During the recessions of 1980–1982 and 1990–1992, total housing starts dipped below 900,000. In the most recent recession starting in 2007, total new single-family housing starts dropped dramatically from one of its highest levels of 1.7 million in 2005 to a low of 550,000 in 2009, according to Freddie Mac's economic research.

As can be seen from the U.S. Census Bureau 2000 Census information, residential construction involves more than single-family units. Multi-family units and mobile homes account for almost 34 percent of all housing. It is also important to recognize that U.S. housing stock is replenished at approximately 15 to 20 percent per decade. As one might imagine, the age of housing stock varies significantly from older, colonial states along the East Coast to recent "boom" areas, such as Phoenix, Arizona. Although each year has significant swings in production, residential construction proceeds at a fairly steady pace over time, driving the U.S. economy.

Multiplier Effect

It's not only actual home construction that impacts the economy to such a large degree, but it is also the multiplier effect housing has on the economy. Purchases of other goods associated with new home construction comprise a significant amount of consumer spending, which is the largest single element of the U.S. economy.

According to NAHB, buyers of newly built homes on average spend $8,900 in housing-related purchases within 12 months—twice the amount spent by buyers of existing homes. Consumers fill their homes with durable and nondurable goods: furnishings, alterations, appliances, lighting fixtures, cabinets and woodworking, plumbing, flooring, lawn and garden items, and so forth. One trip through a Home Depot or Wal-Mart demonstrates the full economic impact of building and moving into a new home. See Chapter 2—Role of Residential Mortgage Lending in the Economy.

Who Does Construction Loans?

All types of mortgage lenders participate in construction lending: commercial and national banks, thrifts and community banks, credit unions, and mortgage companies. According to the Federal Reserve, from 1990 to 2005 construction loans typically accounted for 1.1 to 1.4 percent of all outstanding one- to four-family mortgage debt. Precise figures are not available because one- to four-family construction lending is not reported as a separate category and is excluded from HMDA data, but in 2001, residential construction lending totaled approximately $260 billion for those lenders regulated by the FDIC and the OTS. FDIC-regulated lenders extended the majority of the money, with almost $232 billion in residential construction and land development loans provided.

Almost 86 percent of 436 community banks that completed a 1997 survey by America's Community Bankers (**www.acbanker.org**) reported participating in residential construction lending. The highest percentage group was the local lenders that had between $100 million and $500 million in assets.

Why does so much more residential construction lending take place in small to medium-sized institutions rather than nationwide lenders? Unlike conventional mortgage financing, construction lending is extremely specific to an area, so it is less of a commodity. Lenders must develop their operations to match the restrictions, limitations, and procedures imposed by the state, county, city/town, neighborhood, and even parcel in their lending areas. Large lenders lose their advantage in lower production to serve numerous residential construction markets.

Developing a large secondary market for residential construction loans has been very difficult. This is partly a result of the dynamic of the residential construction project, and partly a result of the lack of uniformity in process and procedure, since so many smaller lenders perform construction lending in an independent fashion tailored to their specific regions.

Why Lenders Do Construction Loans

Despite the difficulties and risks involved, construction lending provides several benefits to a lender and the communities it serves. Construction loans:

- Earn a higher interest rate and provide excellent fee income, which, given the short maturity of one year or less, are usually reflective of current market rates and result in a significantly higher yield than first-mortgage lending.
- Fill a product and market niche and reach different segments within an institution's marketing area, such as small builders and other individuals who will build the home.
- Facilitate the expansion, renewal, and renovation of local housing stock. This increases the number and condition of homes, which increases the market for mortgage loans and produces economic growth.

A secondary benefit derived from construction lending is the economic stimulus to local suppliers, businesses, and industries whose products and services are tied directly to home construction—the multiplier effect described previously. This includes professionals and laborers throughout the process: architect, surveyor, excavator and landscaper, concrete pourer, carpenter, framer, mason, roofer, drywall contractor, electrician, plumber, floor installer, cabinet maker, appliance supplier, interior decorator, and all the materials these people use during construction.

Finally, construction lending enables the relationship-oriented lender (typically, the small bank, thrift, or credit union) to solidify its connection to the customer and compete more effectively against the transaction-oriented lender (typically, regional or national lenders or mortgage bankers). Transaction-oriented lenders usually avoid very involved, or hands-on, loan products, and mortgage bankers cannot fund loans for long construction periods before selling them on the secondary market.

Larger mortgage bankers are an exception to this general statement. Many now offer correspondent construction programs. These are nationwide lenders (such as GMAC) that, because of their large size, offer programs in most states and can fund the construction period before selling the loan on the secondary market. Often, large lenders will focus on big residential construction projects (100+ units) and at times become an equity investor as well as financer. The larger project size makes their portfolio easier to manage, and holding equity gives them more control in the project.

A Fannie Mae program developed in 1999 helped develop and standardize the secondary market for the construction-permanent loan product. However, in August 2009, Fannie Mae announced that it will be retiring its HomeStyle® Construction-to-Permanent program due to lack of sufficient volume and increased operational costs and risks. This illustrates the overall difficulty of managing a construction lending program through all economic conditions, and highlights the need for strong controls throughout the process.

CONSTRUCTION LENDING BASICS

Construction lending differs from permanent financing in two basic ways: funding and collateral. As a result, a construction lender's policies, programs, and practices reflect the procedural changes and unique risks associated with this type of lending. Local lenders typically allow more flexibility than nationwide lenders do.

The most obvious situation in which a borrower would request construction financing is for building a new home on a vacant building lot. Although building a new home is a complicated and time-consuming project, it can save consumers thousands of dollars and at the same time tailor the design to their specific taste.

Another situation for a construction loan is the "home improvement project gone wild." Often, large home improvement projects mirror the time frame and expense of a new home project. If the scope and expense of a home renovation is large enough, a construction loan may be the most appropriate method of financing.

Advances or Draws

Unlike a normal first-mortgage purchase or refinance transaction, at a construction loan closing the lender disburses to the borrower only a portion of the loan funds. Each disbursement is called an **advance** or **draw**. After closing, the borrowers receive additional construction advances according to a schedule that is determined ahead of time by the lender.

The timing and amounts of these advances vary with each lender, but in general, each advance matches the progress on the home. During the construction phase, the relationship of loan advances to the extent of home construction is extremely important to monitor. The lender makes the final advance, thereby disbursing the full loan amount, only upon completion of construction. As a result, the borrower must rely more on liquid assets (cash) to keep the project going between these advances.

Collateral

The second way in which construction and permanent lending differ is that for construction lending only a portion of the loan collateral exists at the time of closing. This poses a challenge for the lender. If the borrower defaults with insufficient collateral securing the loan, the lender faces an enormous risk. The lender may need to contribute additional funds to complete the project before selling it in order to recover the defaulted loan amount. Lender and borrower must work together—and share the risk—to complete the project on which the loan is based. Managing this relationship successfully is the key to construction lending.

Construction lending involves other questions and issues: What if the borrower needs additional funds to complete the project? Can the borrower afford to build and pay for the project? What if the house is not worth the projected value? What if the house is not built correctly or does not conform to zoning? How good is the builder? What if something else goes wrong?

Construction Loan versus Permanent Loan

Construction lending requires special loan products that match the dynamics of these transactions. Loan structure differs from conventional loan products in three ways: term, repayment, and disbursement.

Term

The loan term is the first decision a lender must make when developing its construction loan program and product. *Term*, in this context, does not mean "time," but "phase." A lender and home builder must first determine exactly what they want to finance in home construction: the construction phase only, or the construction phase *and* the amortized repayment phase (the payback) of the loan.

A typical construction period generally lasts 6 to 12 months, depending on the type of house being built, overall construction activity, and weather. If the lender also finances the permanent financing phase of the loan, that phase is normally 15 to 30 years.

Phases of Disbursements

The second area in which a construction loan differs from permanent financing is in the phases of disbursement of funds. Many construction lenders advance less than 20 percent of the total loan amount at closing, with additional funds disbursed later in the construction phase. After the borrower completes a stage of construction, the lender (or an agent) inspects the property, then disburses an amount that reflects the work completed. To avoid daily, small disbursements, the lenders allow up to four or five construction advances. If the project is unusually large or complex, more advances may occur.

All construction loans, whether or not they end at the construction phase or continue through repayment of the permanent financing, have this disbursement schedule in common. This differs from first-mortgage loans, which advance the full loan amount at closing to either purchase or refinance the subject property.

Schedule of Disbursements

No universal schedule would apply to all areas of the country, since construction differs widely as a result of geography and climate, zoning, economic factors, and the laborers' work schedules. But notice how the schedule of disbursements mirrors the construction activity on the house and matches funding to the expenses involved.

The use of an advance schedule allows the lender to monitor the progress of construction and its risk exposure. For administrative consistency, a lender assigns each advance a percentage of the total loan amount. Within that advance, each specific stage of construction is also assigned a percentage of the loan amount. This allows lenders (and borrowers) to "mix and match" the funds disbursed to the actual level of completion the lender sees when inspecting the property for an advance. Following a schedule insures that the lender has sufficient collateral to cover the amount advanced.

Figure 9.1 is a sample advance schedule showing a typical format in which loan funds are disbursed to the borrower. Many lenders follow a similar schedule, but use an advance schedule which more closely mirrors the manner in which residential construction occurs in that area.

Repayment

The final area in which a construction loan differs from permanent financing is in its repayment. As discussed earlier, the borrower receives funds over time, so the principal balance changes during the construction phase. During this time, the lender normally requires non-amortizing, interest-only payments, and only on the advanced loan amount, instead of requiring a principal and interest payment based on the full loan amount as in conventional financing. In this way, the borrower pays interest only on the money used. Interest-only payments lower the borrower's debt burden during the construction phase so the borrower can dedicate more liquid assets to the construction of the home.

Who Is the General Contractor: Builder or Borrower?

Before offering its construction loan program, a lender must first decide who it will allow to perform the construction: an individual borrower or a builder. This decision is critical for a lender, since project management falls squarely in the hands of the person responsible for the construction and directly affects loan repayment.

FIGURE **9.1** Sample Construction Loan Advance Schedule

Construction Disbursement Schedule

Each line item should be completed and inspected before issuing funds:

1. First Advance—33%
   - 10% Foundation
   - 23% Frame, Sheathing, and Roof
2. Second Advance—33%
   - 3% Rough grading
   - 3% Rough plumbing
   - 2% Rough electric
   - 4% Rough heating
   - 5% Exterior walls and trim, windows, and doors installed
   - 1% Exterior prime coat of paint
   - 5% Interior walls complete
   - 3% Water supply connected
   - 3% Sewer system connected
   - 4% Cellar floor installed
3. Third Advance—34%
   - 4% Plumbing complete
   - 2% Electrical complete
   - 4% Heating complete
   - 1% Exterior paint complete
   - 2% Bathroom(s) complete
   - 8% Interior trim complete
   - 5% Floors complete
   - 4% Interior painting complete
   - 4% Kitchen cabinets complete
4. Final Advance—2% of loan amount or minimum of $2,000

The Final Advance is disbursed after the lender receives a satisfactory Certificate of Occupancy, final survey, and as is appraisal inspection.

Source: REMOC Associates, LLC
www.remoc.com

In building a new home, many consumers wish to manage the construction project themselves. If a consumer becomes the *general contractor* (GC), he is responsible for seeing that the work is completed according to code, according to plans and specs, and is approved by the town. The general contractor deals with all workers, town, zoning, material providers, and so forth, and must manage the schedule and order of work and delivery of materials on-site. This is an enormous responsibility for the average consumer, who may have other obligations such as work and family.

Not all lenders will allow an "amateur" consumer to be the GC. Some lenders require a licensed builder to be the GC. Normally, lenders with this policy will not select the builder or officially recommend a particular builder for the consumer. But as a result of past experience, a lender may decide to not work with certain builders.

CONSTRUCTION LOAN PROGRAMS

Lenders active in residential construction lending often develop different programs, so they are not as uniform as with permanent financing developed by the GSEs in the secondary market. Which program is best for an applicant depends on how each suits the particular transaction, borrower preference, and the lender's business strategy. According to recent data from FDIC, the following is true of lenders participating in single-family construction:

- 80 percent use a variable-rate feature based on prime
- 48 percent require more than 10 percent in cash available
- 97 percent require an LTV of less than 85 percent

Residential construction lending programs fall into three main categories, depending on the product or the borrower:

- Construction only (with two closings)
- Construction/permanent (with one closing)
- Builder speculative construction

As long as the construction loan is considered temporary financing, it does not have to meet the onerous RESPA changes for good faith estimates and closing costs. The following supervisory LTV limits apply to those institutions regulated by the Federal Financial Examination Council (FFIEC) agencies, which includes the Federal Reserve BOG, FDIC, OCC, OTS, and NCUA:

- Raw land: 65 percent
- Land development: 75 percent
- Commercial or Multifamily development: 80 percent
- One- to four-family family residential development: 85 percent (a higher LTV is allowed with proper credit enhancements)

Construction Only (With Two Closings)

In this program, the lender finances only the construction phase, so financing is for one purpose only: to complete the home. There is no extended repayment feature for the permanent financing. Typically, the loan term is six to twelve months and calls for monthly interest-only payments on the loan amount outstanding (not the full loan amount). The loan then repays with one balloon payment for the full outstanding balance and interest due. This can occur either at the end of the loan term or within a specified time from when the loan becomes fully advanced (typically 30 or 60 days), whichever occurs first.

Since the full amount of the loan is due with that one balloon payment, it is not an amortizing loan. The borrower must obtain separate financing, if needed, to pay off the construction loan. It is the borrower's responsibility either to have sufficient liquid assets or to find other financing to pay off the construction loan.

The construction-only program places more emphasis on the short-term aspects of the project—the value of the finished collateral (the house) and the present financial condition of the borrower—rather than on the ongoing repayment ability of the borrower.

Construction-Permanent (With One Closing)

This program begins like the preceding one, but then adds a repayment phase similar to permanent financing, with principal and interest amortization over a 15- to 30-year term. As described previously, the borrower receives principal advances during the construction phase, but then the loan automatically converts to the permanent loan phase. This phase begins when the loan is fully advanced or at the end of the construction phase, again usually within six to twelve months.

With a construction-permanent program, the borrowers go through the application, processing, approval, and closing process only once. Like the construction-only program, the lender advances funds according to a predetermined schedule. Once the home is complete, the documents detail the manner in which the repayment of the loan occurs: interest rate on the loan, monthly payment, start date of loan, and maturity date. The exact terms of repayment may be set either before the loan closes or upon completion of the construction phase. Since only one application, processing, approval, and closing covers everything, both lenders and consumers find this loan program more convenient and less costly.

However, construction-permanent financing presents additional underwriting and financial risks for both the lender and consumer. Unlike the construction-only program, with construction-permanent financing more emphasis is placed on the long-term aspects of the financial transaction. These include the present financial condition of the borrower, the ongoing ability of the borrower to repay the loan, and the value of the collateral. In addition, both the lender and borrower share the financial interest rate risk of setting the terms for a 15- to 30-year repayment period anywhere from 90 days to one year in advance.

Builder Speculation Homes

A third construction lending program involves lending to a builder and not to the occupant of the new home. This home is being built on "speculation" (sometimes called a **spec home**) to be sold upon completion. The builder may or may not have a signed contract of sale for the home when construction financing begins.

Like the construction-only program, this program finances only the construction phase, has a loan term of six to twelve months, and requires monthly interest-only payments on the loan amount outstanding. The loan repays with one balloon payment.

The difference here is the source of repayment. The borrower and lender rely more on proceeds from the sale of the house to pay the debt and less on ongoing cash flow or profit of the builder–borrower. The reality is that the lender is somewhat an investor in the home, as is the builder. Like the construction-only program, the short-term aspects of the project and the value of the finished collateral (the house) are more significant to the lender than the repayment ability of any particular borrower.

In addition, lending to a builder can present more risk than lending to a consumer. If the builder is a partnership, LLC, or corporation (not a sole proprietor), then the lender can only look to the assets of the company in the case of default. The lender must require the borrower to pledge personal assets if needed to offset this risk.

Construction Loans for Rehabilitation

Construction loans also finance the extensive rehabilitation of older or damaged homes. These projects can be riskier and more complicated than building a new home, partly because of the amount and the difficult nature of the work involved. In addition, the total cost and time can change dramatically once the project begins (and everyone has committed resources).

Normally, it is more difficult to assess and rehab an existing dwelling than it is to build a new one. Rather than "starting from scratch," as in new home construction, rehab projects must first demolish or expose significant sections of the existing dwelling. This may either cause more damage in the process or uncover new areas needing rehabilitation—either way, it means more work and, therefore, more (unbudgeted) time, money, or financing to complete the project. Only after going through this process does the real scope of the renovation project become clear.

Also, the type of work required is often of a higher or specialized level of craftsmanship, so fewer people possess the skills or experience required for the project. This can result in a higher hourly expense for skilled labor and longer delays to get the right craftsman on-site.

As a result of these difficulties, the borrower embarking on the rehabilitation project faces more difficult challenges in budgeting and cash flow, as well as more constraints on time, material, and labor. Simpler remodeling or home improvement projects do not require the involved financing structure of a construction loan. Less-involved projects that require less time and work, such as adding a room or remodeling a kitchen, may be financed better using a second mortgage or home equity line of credit.

Construction Lending Drawbacks for the Leader

Lenders may earn a higher return on construction loans, but they also incur higher costs. This type of lending requires additional time and training for originators, processors, underwriters, and closers. Construction loans require the lender to commit more capital reserves—100 percent vs. 50 percent for permanent financing. After closing, the loans require constant management until final disbursement of all funds. During this time, lenders must monitor exposure on each account, inspect construction progress, and calculate the amount of each disbursement.

If default and foreclosure occurs, the lender is in an extremely difficult position. A partly built home cannot be sold "as is." It requires that the lender provide additional time and funds to complete the project. If the project has many unique or custom features, it may not be as valued by others as the original borrowers. Once completed, the house must appraise for what it cost to build and must be sold in a housing market that is as favorable as when the loan was made. Economic downturns in 1986 and 2007 illustrate the extremes of collateral and market risks in construction lending.

Construction Loan Management

For these reasons, it is imperative that lenders closely manage their residential construction-lending program by monitoring the status of each loan regularly. A prudent practice is to review weekly the following for individual loans and the entire construction loan portfolio collectively:

- Repayment history
- Stage of construction
- Mechanic's lien waiver documentation
- Percent of total loan advanced
- Advance history
- Date and amount of the last advance
- Time remaining in the construction phase of the loan

In addition to this "office" review, it would be ideal (but impractical) for a lender to visit on-site all construction projects weekly. Instead, in practice, each construction advance request provides the lender an opportunity to inspect the collateral and compare the level of construction to the loan amount remaining. In most situations, this level of inspection ensures that the loan has sufficient collateral and that the project progresses in a satisfactory manner.

Another source of concern is when the lender receives no construction advance requests on a loan for a period of time. This may indicate simply that the borrower is using cash to avoid paying interest, or it may indicate a serious problem that will result in default. Perhaps the builder has encountered a major problem, or work has otherwise been delayed because of shortages, materials, zoning issues, or nonpayment of subcontractors.

Whatever the reason, when a project falls behind schedule, the lender must quickly determine a resolution to the situation, as the construction period is set at loan closing and may end before the borrower completes the project. Depending on the situation, the lender may extend the construction period, provide additional financing, or foreclose and take possession of the property and all materials on it. Maintaining proper documentation and strict controls will save the lender thousands, minimize losses, and resolve situations more quickly.

Mechanic's Liens

One can imagine the complications that arise in worst-case scenarios for construction loans. Anyone who performs work on the financed property and who is not paid has the right to place a **mechanic's lien** on that property to secure his claim for payment. In most states a mechanic's lien takes priority over the first mortgage—even if it is filed after loan closing—putting the lender in second or third position if more than one party is not paid. To minimize this risk, lenders should require signed lien waivers for each phase of construction before disbursing funds.

Operational Issues

Aside from program design, pricing, and underwriting considerations, when designing a construction-lending program, the lender must consider the following operational items separately from conventional financing:

- Creating closing documents, since standard secondary market documents alone do not work for this type of lending
- Selecting closing attorneys/agents based on their construction expertise, particularly when using customized documents
- Selecting appraisers based on their construction experience
- Selecting or updating of the loan-servicing system to handle construction advances and other manual transactions
- Determining whether or not the same area will handle the construction, conversion, and permanent phase of the loan
- Developing an in-house loan-tracking system or purchase of an outside system
- Developing policies and procedures for all areas of origination, servicing, and collections
- Training origination, servicing, and collection staff

CONSTRUCTION LOAN ORIGINATION

Construction loan origination is more involved than permanent loan financing for both the lender and the applicant. These differences are significant, and must be fully understood by both the lender and the applicant.

Application

Prior to actual application for a construction loan, the loan officer often must educate applicants by informing them of the difficulty and unpredictability of the construction process—even if the applicants hire a builder as general contractor. At application, lenders can use the standard secondary market forms for the application and verifications, but they will need nonstandard forms and to provide more information as well.

The loan officer should obtain as much information as possible on the actual construction of the home. Many lenders have a checklist for a consumer who plans to build a home. It details the required documentation, depending on the type of house, property, and local zoning and building codes. This information includes any and all of the following items (some of which may not be available at application):

- Building plans and specifications
- Plot plan and site survey
- Building permit
- Builder's license and liability insurance
- Inspections for water, well, perk, and so forth
- Material list and cost estimates
- Contracts for materials and work to be performed
- Payment receipts for materials purchased and work performed

From what is usually a sizeable package of documentation, the construction loan officer must make a reasonable estimate of what it will cost to construct the home, including all large items such as labor, cement, lumber, roofing, windows, and floors—down to the cost of paint, nails, and duct tape. The construction loan officer is able to do this based on experience/understanding of what it costs to build a particular type of house in that geographical location. Normally, builders have this information better organized than do consumers acting as general contractors.

Instead of using the term **purchase price**, which implies one set, known amount, construction lending may use the term **acquisition cost** if the applicants need to purchase the lot, or **cost to construct** if the applicants already own the land. In any event, once this cost is determined, the loan officer can then concentrate on qualifying the applicants.

Cash Flow Analysis

Of particular importance in qualifying applicants for construction lending is the cash flow analysis. Some applicants may have a satisfactory credit history and earn enough income to support repayment of the debt, but may not have enough savings required to meet the demands of home construction. The construction loan officer will then match the lender's advance schedule to the construction project. This means calculating the timing and amount of funds needed for each phase of construction, then reviewing when the lender will advance funds to replenish the borrower's liquid assets.

Another area the loan officer should assess is how well prepared the applicants appear to be to handle such a complicated project. Construction delays and unanticipated problems arise over the course of a project, resulting in additional expense. Lenders typically require applicants to have in reserve an additional 10 percent of the projected cost to construct in order to meet cost overruns.

Lenders should at this time also provide a detailed description of their particular construction loan program(s). This description should cover the following:

• Required documentation to be supplied by applicants
• Interest rate, points, and fees
• Loan terms—construction period and repayment period
• Loan payment—timing and amount
• Loan advance schedule—manner and requirements
• Underwriting guidelines
• Property requirements
• Acquisition cost/cost to construct
• Construction and builder documentation (See Figure 9.2)

While lending regulations do not require all these items, lender and applicants must understand how the complex construction loan process works, and what is needed. Following is a sample construction program description letter.

FIGURE **9.2** Sample Construction Program Description Letter

Construction Program Information

Thank you for choosing us for your construction financing needs. We provide the following information to assist you in understanding our program and to answer questions you may have. Please contact a loan officer for additional information or to set up an appointment.

1. The Application Process—What do I need to do?

We need the following information to begin processing your construction loan application:

- A. Completed mortgage application
- B. Construction contract
- C. Building plans and specifications
- D. Lender's builder questionnaire
- E. Lender's construction cash flow worksheet
- F. Lender's advance schedule
- G. Application and origination fee
- H. Supplemental construction cost estimate
- I. Construction program information
- J. Verification of income, assets, and liabilities

2. Inspections and Construction Loan Advances—How do they work?

- A. Land advances

We will advance part of the land value at the closing under the following conditions:

1. For land that you own free and clear for over 1 year, up to 50 percent of the appraised value, but no more than the lesser of $100,000.00 or 40 percent of the loan amount.
2. For land that you are purchasing, up to 75 percent of the lesser of the sales price or appraised value, but no more than the lesser of $100,000.00 or 40 percent of the loan amount.

- B. Construction advances

At application you will receive a Construction Loan Advance Schedule that breaks down your advances into percentages. You should budget your funds since the money provided in the mortgage will be only a percentage of the funds required for each advance.

You should discuss the advance schedule with your builder to avoid any misunderstandings or delays in the construction. If any funds are advanced against the land, the remaining funds of loan amount are computed against the reduced amount. You should demonstrate that sufficient funds are available to complete the construction with this schedule.

- C. Inspections

Lender employees or a fee inspector will inspect the property before authorizing an advance. All inspections should be scheduled 5 days prior to the advance.

Please note that inspectors are neither engineers nor architects and should not be relied on to evaluate material or workmanship.

- D. Final inspection

Lender will hold back at the greater of $2,000.00 or 2 percent of the loan amount. These funds will be advanced on completion of the property and receipt of lien waivers, final inspection report, final survey, and Certificate of Occupancy.

3. Contractor Requirements

You should select an established contractor to build your home. The Lender will require the completion and review of a Builder Questionnaire, but it is up to you to check the builder's references and reputation. Lender takes no responsibility for the builder's ability or reputation.

4. Closing Requirements—What will I need?

- A. All required building permits
- B. Builder's risk insurance
- C. Flood insurance, if applicable
- D. Certified survey with proposed foundation, well, septic, driveway, and other improvements

Please sign and date below acknowledging that you have received and understand our requirements.

_____   _____
Name   Date

Source: REMOC Associates, LLC
www.remoc.com

Depending on how the loan product is structured, adjustable-rate mortgage regulations may apply. If the interest rate can change at any time during the construction period, at conversion, or during the repayment period, the loan officer may need to provide ARM disclosures.

Processing

From a lender's perspective, the major differences in processing between conventional first-mortgage lending and construction lending deal with: the cost to construct, the appraisal, and verifications. Often the loan officer does not receive complete cost estimates for all phases of construction. It is the processor's job to help follow up and track down the remaining pieces of information to develop a complete construction estimate. Once this is complete, the lender can order an appraisal report.

The processor sends along with the appraisal request all information collected for the cost to construct to give the appraiser the most accurate picture of what the house will look like. Since there is no house yet (or it is partially complete), the appraiser must work from plans and specs (and whatever else he or she can find to estimate the value of the property). Instead of completing the appraisal report as is, the appraiser will complete it "subject to plans and specifications." Upon completion of the house at a later date, the appraiser must return to determine whether the actual property built is what was appraised originally, and then certify its value.

Because cash flow is such an important element in construction, the processor must be careful to obtain an accurate snapshot of the applicants' deposits. Verifications and deposit statements must be closely dated, since applicants often move funds around to consolidate them for the project. Some lenders also obtain information on the builder or the applicant if he or she is the general contractor. This would verify whether that person is licensed to perform this function and has insurance for people working on the site, and it may include personal or business financial statements for the builder. If the application gets delayed or the closing is not set for a few months, the lender may need to recertify the file, obtain a new credit report, and resend verifications.

Underwriting

As mentioned previously, residential construction lending differs from conventional first-mortgage lending in liquidity risk and collateral risk, where underwriters must place special consideration. In addition to the prudent guidelines discussed in Chapter 7—Underwriting the Residential Mortgage Loan, construction loan underwriters require additional skills in the following areas: determining the cost to construct, cash flow analysis, and reviewing property appraisals.

Local and national economic conditions have a large influence on underwriting guidelines for local and regional lenders. Lenders will increase the rate or points, lower LTV ceilings, increase cash reserve requirements, or otherwise restrict construction lending when any or all of the following negative economic indicators occur: an extended increase in inventory of unsold

FIGURE **9.3** Inventory of Homes for Sale

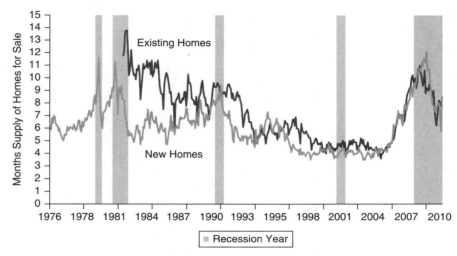

Source: Freddie Mac, U.S. Census Bureau, National Association of REALTORS(r)

homes, a significant layoff in the area, a sudden or extended increase or decrease in home prices, a rise in interest rates. Figure 9.3 shows Inventory Home Sales 1976-2010.

Cost to Construct

For an underwriter to successfully review a construction loan application, he or she must be familiar with all stages of construction and relative costs involved for typical houses in the area. Land and labor costs vary widely across the United States, and certain areas present unique construction challenges, such as ledges or swamps. An experienced underwriter knows the area's general costs from reviewing many applications, and will review the present applicants' estimates with this store of knowledge as a reference. The underwriter must be able to determine whether the cost estimate prepared by the applicants is realistic or whether it has omitted any significant items. Many lenders request the original signed estimates from suppliers and laborers to verify actual costs.

To assist in this step, lenders develop a checklist (see Figure 9.4) of items that mirrors their advance schedule, but includes more specific information at each step of the construction process—estimates for labor, materials, appliances, and so forth. Some construction lenders require labor and material costs to be separated. A sample cost projection worksheet follows.

Cash Flow Analysis

Once the underwriter verifies the actual cost to construct, the next step is to compare the costs to the construction loan advance schedule. This calculation determines the actual construction cost from loan advance to loan advance. Finally, the underwriter compares the amounts needed to how much verified cash the applicants have on deposit.

FIGURE **9.4** Sample Cost Projection Worksheet

Construction Cost Projection Worksheet

Estimate

1. Land acquisition
2. Land clearing
3. Excavation
4. Concrete—labor and materials
5. Waterproofing
6. Drains
7. Driveway—labor and materials
8. Septic—design, labor, and materials
9. Water hookup/well drilling
10. Pump and installation
11. Modular home sales price
12. Framing and trim—labor and materials
13. Doors—labor and materials
14. Windows—labor and materials
15. Siding—labor and materias
16. Roofing—labor and materials
17. Gutters and leaders
18. Interior stairs and railings
19. Fireplace and chimney—labor and materials
20. Flashing
21. Electrical Hookup and temporary service
22. Electrical—labor and materials
23. Telephone—prewire and jacks
24. Plumbing—labor and materials
25. Insulation—labor and materials
26. Plasterboard and taping—labor and materials
27. Heating—labor and materials
28. Deck/Porch—labor and materials
29. Flooring—labor and materials
30. Linoleum and tile—labor and materials
31. Carpeting—labor and materials
32. Exterior walls, walks, steps—labor and materials
33. Painting—Exterior
34. Painting—Interior
35. Garage and cellar doors
36. Appliances
37. Electrical fixtures
38. Bathroom accessories
39. Cabinets, vanities, amenities
40. Mirrors
41. Landscaping
42. Upgrades—Interior
43. Upgrades—Exterior
44. Upgrades—Fixtures
45. Upgrades—Other

Total Projected Costs	$
10% Cost Overrun Estimate	$
Total Needed	$

Source: REMOC Associates, LLC
www.remoc.com

This analysis is critical to the success of the construction project. The essence of cash flow analysis is to ensure that the applicants are the main supporters of the construction project and the lender is not. Do the applicants have enough liquid assets to get them through all stages of construction? What happens if excavation runs over or the contractor must dig several wells before one passes inspection? Are there sufficient funds—between the applicant's funds and the construction advances—to allow the project to progress from construction advance to advance, even with some additional costs?

Although the applicants may have excellent debt/income ratios, they may have insufficient funds to complete the next stage in construction. This undermines the entire project and would leave the lender in a difficult position. For this reason, many lenders require applicants to have an extra 10 to 15 percent above the estimated cost to construct to allow for unanticipated cost overruns and upgrades. At different times, the lender may increase this requirement to 20 or even 25 percent.

Property Appraisal

The underwriter has several concerns when reviewing the appraisal report:

- Is the subject property appraised the same lot and structure as detailed in the construction cost estimates submitted to the lender?
- How will the market value and market appeal support the cost to construct and the proposed property?
- What does the market for new homes look like and how much new construction activity is in the neighborhood and region?

As stated earlier, appraisals for new construction are completed using plans and specifications. This sometimes makes locating the subject property difficult, as well as projecting what it will look like once built. Appraisers use standard values for estimating construction costs, usually obtained from cost estimates such as Marshall and Swift, local builders, and the appraiser's prior files. The appraiser must explain in the appraisal report any substantial changes to these objective reference sources.

Ideally, the appraiser will include at least one newly constructed home to establish the current value of new construction in that area. If the proposed home is a modular home, log cabin, or other structure that may be somewhat unique to the neighborhood, the appraiser must try to use a comparable of similar type.

The underwriter must compare the dimensions and characteristics of the house described in the appraisal to the information submitted in the loan application file. Another consideration is how well the proposed property conforms to the neighborhood. Finally, the underwriter should note how the change in land use and built-up rate may affect property value, especially if the subject property is part of a larger development.

The appraiser completes the report "per plans and specifications," and the loan closes with this appraisal report. After closing—but before the final construction loan advance—the appraiser must recertify the property value on an "as is" basis. This recertification of value requires the appraiser to reinspect the property upon completion of the house, and after the town issues a **Certificate of Occupancy**.

Closing

Unlike conventional mortgage financing, in construction lending not all loan funds are advanced at closing. The underwriter determines the amount disbursed at closing, based on total loan amount, LTV, the stage of construction, and what has been paid to date.

Either prior to or at closing, the lender should require the following documents unique to a newly constructed house:

- Survey
- Building permit
- Builder license
- Builder liability/builder's risk insurance
- Mechanic's lien waivers for all completed work
- Applicable town inspections/approval for all completed work
- Title insurance endorsements for construction

Application Process—Builder

If the applicant is a builder, the lender may require the following documents for a commercial application package:

- Dunn & Bradstreet report (equivalent to a business credit report)
- Tax returns
- Recent personal and corporate financial statements
- Complete schedule of all real estate work in progress
- Trade references/suppliers

To evaluate the builder, the lender really performs more of a commercial loan analysis than a consumer analysis. Briefly, the lender evaluates the following characteristics of the builder:

- *Capacity*: Does the builder have the experience, management expertise, staffing, and finances to handle this project? A builder questionnaire asks a series of questions to help evaluate this.
- *Credit*: What has the builder's repayment history been? The lender builds a main credit file that includes references from:
  - Dunn & Bradstreet
  - Credit reports
  - Trade creditors/suppliers
  - Local building supply organizations
  - Bonding company
  - Building departments
  - Other lenders
- *Experience*: In addition, the lender may do the following:
  - Visit past and current projects/historical experience
  - Talk to prior customers

While lending directly to a builder is more of a commercial loan transaction, many small- to medium-sized lenders handle these applications in the residential mortgage area because it is most familiar with real estate.

Loan Administration and Funding

Once a residential construction loan closes, the lender must pay particular attention to its administration during the construction phase. Usually, a separate department or person handles these loans. It is imperative that the lender constantly communicates with the borrower and builder, and serve their funding needs by processing advance requests promptly.

In order to advance funds the lender must inspect the property, using either a qualified employee or an outside appraiser, and document the exact stage of construction. Once this has been established, the applicant must provide the applicable mechanic's lien waivers and receipts for payment to contractors, suppliers, and others. The lender determines the amount of the advance based on the loan amount and the preceding documentation.

As mentioned previously, the lender must notify the borrower of loan expiration dates, and track progress of construction with these dates in mind. A lender (or borrower or builder) cannot always control construction delays; unfortunate events are part of the risk of lending. But it is critical that the lender keep accurate documentation during the construction phase in case a problem occurs and the lender needs to evaluate this situation for modification, delinquency, and so forth.

Before issuing the final advance, the lender must obtain the following documents:

- Completion certificate
- Recertification of value
- Certificate of Occupancy/temporary Certificate of Occupancy
- Complete mechanic's lien waivers

At that time, the loan either matures or goes into repayment, depending on the loan documents.

DISCUSSION POINTS

1. Why do lenders participate in residential construction lending?
2. How are construction loans structured?
3. What are the benefits and drawbacks for both the lender and borrower in using "two-closing" loan products? What are the benefits and drawbacks of "one-closing" products?
4. How do construction loans differ from first-mortgage, home improvement, or home equity loans?
5. What should a lender review when managing a construction loan portfolio?
6. Explain the construction and funding process.

CHAPTER 10

Home Equity Lending

INTRODUCTION

This chapter examines in detail the various types of home equity loan programs that consumers can obtain using their home as security. Included in this category are Reverse Annuity Mortgages (RAMs), or reverse mortgage programs, a growing but less conventional form of home equity loan that allows senior citizens to convert the equity in their home to obtain funds.

Traditional home equity loan programs are popular with the American consumer; nearly 30 percent of homeowners have one. From 1990–2000, home equity loans represented seven to nine percent of all mortgages outstanding. That level rose to a range of nine to eleven percent from 2000–2010, according to Federal Reserve data. However, the total dollar amount outstanding since 1990 increased fourfold—from $233 billion to more than $921 billion, with most of this increase (at least $500 billion) occurring since 2000.

Mortgage lenders are very interested in these loan programs because they are typically made to the best credits in our society, and the loans are often variable rate.

Nomenclature and Types of Home Equity Loans

Home equity loan programs are referred to by many names and have different characteristics. No one name or single description applies to all. Examples of different home equity loan types include:

- Second mortgage
- Home equity line of credit

- Home improvement loan
- "Piggyback" mortgage

Home equity loans often are referred to as second mortgages because they are commonly in a secondary lien (or junior lien) position. On the other hand, some borrowers have a home equity loan, but do not have a first mortgage; thus, the "second mortgage" is in a first-lien position. A home improvement (HI) loan is another name often used, which it relates more specifically to the loan purpose. However, some lenders retain the "home improvement" name but do not secure the loan, so it is not a lien at all.

Perhaps the most common feature shared by home equity loan programs is their purpose. Consumers use them for larger, intermediate-term, non-business financing needs—typically not to purchase a home (or refinance the original mortgage used to purchase the home). But even this attempt at classification has an exception. As discussed in Chapter 7—Private Mortgage Insurance, lenders developed the "piggyback" second mortgage to complete home purchase financing and avoid PMI.

Home equity loans can be either closed-end or open-end. Closed-end junior lien loans are the traditional second mortgages. Some lenders call them home equity loans. Open-end junior liens are home equity lines of credit (HELOCs). Regulatory agencies tend to use this classification because of the difference in risk exposure that each category presents: amortizing debt vs. revolving line. According to FDIC and CUNA figures, more than $218 billion in (closed-end) second mortgages and $703 billion in HELOCs were outstanding at year-end 2009.

One type of home equity loan program that this chapter does not discuss is the one that exceeds the appraised value of a person's home (>100% LTV). These types of home equity loans are often a workout loan used by a creditor to convert an unsecured consumer loan into a secured one. Most traditional mortgage lenders do not engage in this type of mortgage lending, leaving it to finance companies. Another related loan program is an automobile loan that is also recorded as a mortgage loan so that the borrower can deduct the interest on his or her tax return. This is not a true mortgage loan program and is not discussed in this chapter.

Consumer Loans or Mortgage Loans?

The consumer loan industry is diverse and very competitive, with banks (30–50 percent), finance companies (10–20 percent), and credit unions (10 percent) having the largest market share among lenders nationally. Some lenders treat home equity loans as consumer loans because, to a great extent, they have replaced many types of consumer loans and finance many consumer-purpose needs. Other lenders consider these loans to be mortgage loans because they are secured by real estate. Although it does not make a great deal of difference which department handles these loans, as long as they are administered correctly, traditionally they have been considered mortgage loans.

How Important Are Home Equity Loans to Lenders?

Many lenders consider these loans to be as important as first-mortgage loans. One reason is the high credit standard of borrowers using them. The Consumer Bankers Association (*2001 Home Equity Study*) found that the average FICO score for home equity borrowers was a high 715. Another startling fact about home equity loans is that nearly 60 percent of all consumer credit (excluding credit cards) granted in the United States each year is in the form of home equity loans.

Home equity loans are excellent tools for asset/liability management, primarily because many are variable rate. Additionally, the term and average loan life is shorter than first mortgage loans, further reducing interest rate exposure.

Finally, when analyzed over a 25-year period, home equity loans are among the safest loans a lender can make. Of all the major loan types, the home equity line of credit has the lowest rate of delinquency, normally below one percent. During the recent economic recession, the delinquency rate for all mortgage loans increased rapidly from three percent to eleven percent from 2007–2010, surpassing consumer loans for the first time in the fourth quarter of 2008.

During this period, home equity loan delinquency maintained a stable but elevated level of four percent, and HELOCs declined from a historic high of 2.12 percent in the third quarter of 2009. It is also important to compare home equity delinquency to other consumer loan delinquency rates, as many homeowners use them to finance similar purchases. Home equity loan delinquency actually decreased in the first quarter of 2010, but first mortgage loans and all consumer loans continued to rise, as shown in Table 10.1.

Consumers' Choice

Home equity loans are very popular with consumers for a number of reasons. Probably the most important reason is that the interest on the loan (with some limitations) can be deducted on the borrower's income tax return. In fact, the modern home equity loan market really began to thrive after the 1986 tax law change, which phased out the deduction of interest for consumer loans. Basically (with a few limitations), up to $100,000 in home equity loan interest can be deducted as long as the loan does not exceed the original purchase price of the home.

Consumers also like the convenience of home equity loans, especially home equity lines of credit, because they can write themselves a loan (up to the maximum line) at any time. This takes away the uncertainty that many consumers feel when applying for a loan.

Home equity loans should experience dramatic growth in future years, after the extended periods of low interest rates of 2002–2003, 2005–2006, and 2008–2010 when 30-year fixed-rate mortgages were offered for as low as 4.5–5.5 percent. Once consumers have locked in a low rate on their first mortgages, they are hesitant to refinance them when they need additional funds. Instead, they will keep their first mortgage and turn to a home equity loan for additional funds.

TABLE 10.1
Consumer and Mortgage Loan Delinquency

Loan Type	1q2010	4q2009	3q2009	2q2009	1q2009	4q2008	3q2008	2q2008	1q2008	4q2007	1q2006	Prior 20 yrs
ABA Data—300 banks; 30-day delinquency												
All Consumer	2.98%	3.19%	3.23%	3.35%	3.23%	3.22%	2.90%	2.68%	2.62%	2.65%		
Home Equity	4.12%	4.32%	4.30%	4.01%	3.52%	3.03%	2.63%	2.56%	2.34%	2.39%		
HELOC	1.81%	2.04%	2.12%	2.02%	1.89%	1.46%	1.15%	1.08%	1.10%	0.96%		
Home Improvement	1.40%	1.63%	1.64%	1.72%	1.46%	1.75%	1.63%	1.49%	1.78%	1.81%		
Personal Loan	3.61%	3.63%	3.74%	3.90%	3.47%	2.88%	2.69%	2.67%	2.55%	2.48%		
Credit Card	3.88%	4.39%	4.77%	5.01%	4.75%	4.52%	4.20%	4.54%	4.51%	4.38%		
Direct Auto	1.79%	1.94%	2.04%	2.46%	3.01%	2.03%	1.71%	1.77%	1.92%	1.90%		
Indirect Auto	3.03%	3.15%	3.15%	3.26%	3.42%	3.53%	3.25%	3.07%	3.09%	3.13%		
Mobile Home	3.65%	3.41%	3.63%	3.53%	3.70%	2.96%	3.08%	3.03%	3.22%	2.92%		
RV	1.58%	1.44%	1.64%	1.72%	1.52%	1.38%	1.27%	1.07%	1.11%	1.08%		
Marine	1.93%	1.63%	2.21%	2.28%	2.04%	2.35%	1.82%	1.54%	1.75%	1.57%		
Federal Reserve Data—all banks; 30-day delinquency												
All Consumer	4.65%	4.61%	4.73%	4.82%	4.67%	4.27%	3.73%	3.55%	3.49%	3.41%		normally 3-4%
All Residential Mortgage	11.29%	10.14%	9.63%	8.72%	7.87%	6.59%	5.23%	4.40%	3.70%	3.07%		normally 1-3%
Total Loans and Leases	7.36%	7.16%	6.96%	6.43%	5.63%	4.71%	3.72%	3.34%	2.86%	2.46%		normally 2-5%
CUNA Data—U.S. credit unions; 60+ day delinquency, % of ALL loans outstanding												
All consumer	1.45%	1.67%	1.55%	1.55%	1.51%	1.57%	1.33%	1.19%	1.14%	1.22%		
All First Mortgage	2.24%	2.12%	1.93%	1.70%	1.46%	1.26%	1.00%	0.78%	0.68%	0.64%		
All Other Mortgage (Home Equity)	1.58%	1.61%	1.52%	1.43%	1.21%	1.06%	0.86%	0.78%	0.74%	0.73%		
Credit Card	1.90%	2.06%	2.03%	1.98%	1.99%	1.88%	1.64%	1.41%	1.35%	1.34%		

Source: ABA, Federal Reserve, CUNA
© 2010 REMOC Associates, LLC

If the new borrower is refinancing and has sufficient equity, some mortgage lenders will automatically approve that borrower for a home equity loan when they approve that borrower for a first-mortgage loan. All mortgage lenders should consider this strategy since it allows them to make a home equity loan at little or no additional expense.

HOME EQUITY LOAN PROGRAM DESIGN AND ORIGINATION PRACTICES

A lender will often originate, process, underwrite, and close both types of home equity loans (closed-end and open-end) using the same procedures, even though they have different structures. For example, typically the same personnel originates, processes, underwrites, and closes both loan types. Both closed- and open-end home equity loan programs use the same documentation, except for different compliance requirements. Often a lender will use the same verification, collateral valuation, and title search methods for both.

Loan Amount

A lender's different home equity loan programs often share the same minimum and maximum loan amounts. Limiting these amounts helps distinguish these programs from their consumer and first mortgage programs.

Depending on the average home value and who pays closing costs, a minimum loan amount of $5,000 to $50,000 can be found at different lenders in different parts of the country. At the $5,000–10,000 minimum range, the lender is concerned about generating enough interest income to offset their higher origination costs when compared to an unsecured or auto loan. At the $25,000–50,000 range, the lender typically is offering preferred terms: lower initial rate, lower margin, no closing costs, etc.

Loan to Value

Closed- and open-end home equity loans often share the same loan-to-value limits for a lender. Many lenders have developed complex matrices with minimum and maximum loan amounts tied to maximum LTV's and even minimum credit score ranges. Competition drove maximum LTV's to 90 percent and above for some lenders in the late 1990s until the mid-2000s. Today, a maximum 80 percent LTV is the norm again in most areas of the country.

Types of Collateral

Both the closed-end loans and open-end lines of credit are usually secured by a person's single-family dwelling. Initially, all home equity loans were so secured. Recently, the type of collateral that lenders accept has begun to evolve. Many lenders today will accept condominiums and cooperatives as well as second and vacation homes as collateral, but some will do so at either a higher interest rate or lower LTV. A few lenders allow the use of residential rental property as collateral. If non-rental property is used as collateral, it will usually be at a higher interest rate and lower LTV.

Home Equity Loan Processing

However, there are more differences from lender to lender when processing and underwriting home equity loans than there are for first-mortgage loans. Although home equity loans can be sold in the secondary market, few are, because lenders very much prefer to keep these loans in their own portfolios. As a result, most lenders do not attempt to follow standard secondary market guidelines when making these loans.

For example, instead of using the Verification of Employment to verify income and employment, many lenders use the consumer's pay stub (covering 30 days) for such verification, or even a verbal verification. A borrower then signs at closing an affidavit stating that he or she is still employed. Often, lenders do not verify liquid assets disclosed, but will use a recent deposit statement if needed.

Lenders use a typical consumer credit report (costing a dollar or two), not the more expensive Residential Mortgage Credit Report. In order to underwrite and process home equity loans quickly, most mortgage lenders use credit scores or a combination of credit scores and personal judgments to approve loan applications. Some lenders automatically approve applicants with high scores. And as stated earlier, some lenders limit the LTV or loan amount based on the credit score.

Appraisals

Rather than use a full-blown appraisal, home equity lenders will use tax assessments, existing appraisals if not dated, or a drive-by appraisal or an automated valuation model (AVM) if any new appraisal is actually needed. Some lenders make the loan without an appraisal if the loan-to-value ratio is perceived to be low (say, below 60 percent).

Qualifying Ratios

For all debts, including the home equity loan, most lenders use a 42 percent debt-to-income ratio although some allow this ratio to be as high as 50 percent. Although this ratio is higher than the one used for first mortgages, its use is justified by the credit standards of the typical home equity borrower and their very low delinquency rates.

Although the debt-to-income ratio often is the same for both loan types, the proposed payment used to qualify differs. Lenders base the proposed payment for a HELOC application on the minimum payment necessary to repay the maximum draw on the line. Some lenders use an amortizing payment; others use an interest-only payment. Others still use a higher interest rate than at application to calculate the proposed payment. The proposed payment for a closed-end second mortgage typically is an amortizing one, so lenders use that payment to qualify an applicant.

Disclosures

One major difference in processing closed-end vs. open-end home equity loans comes in the compliance area. HELOCs have specific documentation required. Closed-end second mortgages now have increased RESPA requirements for

Good Faith Estimate of fees and closing costs; along with the new mandatory waiting periods should loan terms change. Chapter 11—Compliance, discusses these complex requirements in more detail.

Loan Approval

Home equity loans need a quicker turnaround time than first mortgage loans. This dynamic is driven by the consumer, who often needs the loan to finance an unanticipated purchase in days rather than weeks: auto repair, home repair, auto purchase, appliance purchase, etc. Lenders often implement the strategy of producing the fastest processing and decision making to remain competitive. Because these are relatively simple loans to underwrite and process, home equity applications can be approved at the main office, a regional office, or a branch. Depending on the size of a mortgage lender, many allow the branches, if they are properly staffed, to handle these loans.

Closing Home Equity Loans

The lender typically closes its own home equity loans internally. Doing so saves the lender the cost of an attorney or title company. A competent loan officer, with minimal training, can handle the closing of these loans. Additionally, home equity loans often have less closing documentation—especially if the same lender holds the first mortgage (which has a full title search and current hazard insurance policy). A good practice for lenders is to use a Notary to verify signatures and identity at closing, just like with first mortgage closings.

Title Insurance or Title Search?

Many lenders do not require title insurance for a home equity loan if the first mortgage has title insurance. In this case, the lender simply has a "title update" or search done, which involves a professional checking the public record for additional security interest filings on the subject property. Other lenders require title insurance only if the home equity is in a first-lien position or if the loan amount exceeds a certain dollar amount (say, $25,000).

No Closing Cost Programs

Lenders often have the same requirements for closed- and open-end home equity programs where the consumer does not pay closing costs. In these programs, the lender must absorb these costs and price the loan correctly, while maintaining its loan quality. The previous sections outline some alternatives to more expensive credit report, appraisal, and title insurance. Other fees that a lender would absorb include flood and tax determinations, and recording fees.

Again, for most lenders, all of these fees add up to $200 or $300. Many lenders protect themselves against the risk that the consumers may refinance or pay off the loan in a few months. The lender will require that the consumer sign an affidavit at closing that states the consumer will pay back the closing costs paid by the lender if he or she refinances the loan with another lender within two years. Again, lenders must ensure that these types of closed-end, no closing cost programs meet new RESPA guidelines.

Security Documentation

Lenders normally develop home equity loan documents themselves. The secondary market does have a security form and note that can be used for closed-end second mortgages, but not a form for open-end loans. Many mortgage forms companies can supply the required documents, as shown in Table 10.2, or a lender can request these documents from a local attorney. It is critical that a lender be very careful in developing these documents because each state has unique laws governing home equity loans and each lender may have different loan terms.

TABLE **10.2**

List of Documents Typically Required for Home Equity Loans—Closed-End Loans and Open-End Lines of Credit

	Closed-End Loans	Open-End Lines of Credit
Any state disclosures	x	x
Application	x	x
ARM disclosures	x	
Closed-end mortgage	x	
Closed-end note	x	
Commitment letter	x	x
Credit report	x	x
First mortgagee letter	x	x
Good Faith Estimate of Closing Costs	x	
Hazard insurance with loss payee	x	x
HUD-1A	x	
Initial HELOC disclosure		x
Notice of Right to Appraisal	x	x
Notice of Right to Rescission	x	x
Open-end mortgage		x
Open-end note		x
Payoff letters (if needed)	x	x
Pay stub (income verification)	x	x
Privacy Notice	x	x
Property valuation (appraisal, AVM, etc.)	x	x
Standard flood determination	x	x
Title search (or title insurance)	x	x
Truth in Lending Disclosure	x	
Underwriting worksheet	x	x
When Your Home Is on the Line		x

Source: REMOC Associates, LLC
© 2010 REMOC Associates, LLC

Keys to Success

Because the competition for home equity loans is so intense, lenders must be aggressive in two areas if they want to attract consumers for their loans. The two keys to success for a lender's home equity loans are product design and marketing. **Product design** refers to how the loan product is structured, including maximum loan amount and LTV/CLTV, the interest rate and fees, required monthly payment, loan advance and repayment periods, and term.

Marketing simply means that lenders have to use as many means as practical to communicate why their home equity loans are better than those of the competition. Both areas (discussed in more detail later) are equally important, and usually one without the other leads to low acceptance by consumers.

CLOSED-END SECOND MORTGAGES

The so-called traditional home equity loan, often called a second mortgage, is a closed-end loan whereby the borrower is approved for a certain dollar amount that is advanced all at once and is repaid on an amortized basis over a fixed term. This loan is called closed-end because, as payments are made, those funds cannot automatically be re-advanced and borrowed again under the same loan.

These loans have been around for centuries, although not all depository institutions could make these loans until fairly recently. For many years, the largest suppliers of these loans were finance companies. During the Great Depression, many of the real estate loans that became delinquent were second mortgages.

Because of the high delinquency rate on these early second mortgages, lenders were very hesitant to grant these loans for many years. But the market for these loans changed dramatically after the 1986 tax law change that phased out consumer credit deductions. Today, all classifications of mortgage lenders offer this loan.

In today's society, when consumers want to buy an automobile, take an extended vacation, or repay outstanding credit card debt, they often turn to home equity loans. The closed-end second mortgage is attractive to a segment of society that wants the discipline of being required to make a principal and interest payment every month and to others who want the security of a fixed interest rate.

Closed-End Second as a Fixed-Rate Product

A closed-end second mortgage can be either fixed rate or variable rate. Most lenders (approximately 75 percent) offer the loan as a fixed-rate product to distinguish it from the variable-rate home equity line of credit. Since a line of credit is usually variable rate, the closed-end loan serves those consumers who want a fixed-rate product.

Closed-End Program Design

Because the closed-end loan has been around for a long time, the product is well developed. Most lenders offer basically the same program as other lenders, the only difference being the interest rate, loan-to-value ratio, or the type of real estate offered as security. To repeat, the characteristics of this loan are as follows:

- It is a closed-end loan
- The entire loan is advanced at one time
- It is for a fixed period of time
- Payment is sufficient for the loan to be self-amortizing

Lenders offer closed-end loan programs with five- and ten-year terms, with many now offering 15- and 20-year terms. Of course, these loans legally can be for any period of time up to the maximum term for a mortgage under state law. Many lenders charge consumers closing costs for these loans, although some lenders are starting to pick up some or all of these costs, often including a prepayment penalty—equal to the closing costs—in the first two or three years.

Perhaps because they are so established, closed-end home equity loan programs are perceived as identical from lender to lender. But today, these loan programs can differ significantly with each lender. Although they receive less fanfare than their cousins, the home equity lines of credit, home equity loan programs can generate good volume for lenders with the proper targeted marketing plan.

HOME EQUITY LINE OF CREDIT PROGRAMS

In direct contrast to the closed-end home equity loan program, the home equity line of credit (HELOC) program has been the "new" product (they are almost thirty years old) with which lenders have been very inventive. Because the competition for HELOC loans is so intense, lenders should review the terms and features of their HELOC programs at least annually to ensure that they are still attractive to consumers.

Some mortgage lenders entice consumers to their HELOC program by offering various incentives, such as free airline or event tickets, or no closing costs. A few lenders were even "buying" balances (transfer $20,000, get a 50-basis-point bonus, which equals $100 paid at closing).

HELOCs Should Use Variable Rates

Some features of a HELOC, such as the type of interest calculation, should not differ from one lender to another. Practically all lenders offer the HELOC with a variable rate. It really does not make sense for a lender to allow consumers to borrow funds in the future at a rate that is fixed today. Interest rates in general could skyrocket two or three years in the future, and to allow a consumer to borrow money at that time, at rates set two or three years in the past, is not advisable.

A growing practice among lenders is to convert part of the line of credit from a variable to a fixed rate. These lenders allow the consumer to lock in—at a fixed rate—a portion of the line, often for a single advance. For example, if a consumer with a $50,000 line of credit buys a $25,000 automobile and uses the HELOC to pay for it, the lender could allow that particular $25,000 advance to carry a fixed rate, while the rest of the line remains variable rate. Treating part of the line at one rate while the remainder of the line is variable requires a sophisticated data-processing system.

Index and Margin

Similar to ARM first mortgage loans, the lender calculates a HELOC interest rate by adding the index and margin together, adjusting for any caps involved. The index that most lenders use (greater than 85 percent) is the average prime rate as reported in the *Wall Street Journal* and other newspapers. Other indices used include the three- and six-month Treasury bill yields. A lender should not use its own internal cost of funds as an index; in fact, many lenders are prohibited from using this index.

Some lenders have considered other indices because they believe the prime rate is too volatile. The prime rate often remained unchanged for years, and remained in the 3.5 percent to 7.5 percent range for decades. However, as monetary policy became more active, the prime rate changed more frequently and more widely.

Just look at its ten-year history, starting in 2000: The prime rate moved from a high of 9.5 percent in December 2000, to a low of 4.5 percent in December 2001; it increased steadily almost four percent to peak at 8.25 percent in June 2006, then in two years declined five percent to its current level of 3.25 percent, where it has been for more than two years, since December 2008.

The prime rate can indeed be volatile, although it has also been stable for years at a time. Despite its volatility, the general public is accustomed to using it as the index for HELOCs, so lenders should continue to do so.

The amount of the margin used to calculate the interest rate depends on what the lender wants the interest rate to be. When HELOCs were first introduced, they started at a "prime plus" pricing level: prime plus 0.25 percent; prime plus 0.5 percent. For many lenders, competition drove this level to where the margin today is zero or a negative figure. If a lender wants to advertise that its HELOC has a rate of 50 basis points below prime, the documentation for the loan will have to state that the margin is minus 50 basis points.

Introductory Rate

The vast majority of mortgage lenders believe that they must offer the consumer a low introductory rate, or, as it is sometimes called, a "teaser rate," to initially attract them. Lenders have offered promotional rates of 50 to 100 basis points below the regular or fully adjusted rate, and for a 30-, 60-, 90-, or 120-day period. A few lenders actually apply the introductory rate for a full year. A review of local competitors can help determine how long the introductory rate should last in order to be attractive in the local market.

Tier Rates

The interest rate for a HELOC loan is often the same for loans up to 80 percent loan-to-value. But the rate may be different for loans with higher loan-to-value ratio. Other features that can produce a different, or tier, interest rate include the following:

- Collateral type
- Credit risk (measured by credit score)
- Loan amount

The following is a complex example of how a lender might apply a tiered rate:

Prime rate (3.25%) + 0.5% (660 credit score) + 0.5% (85% LTV) + 0.5% (second home) = 4.75% initial rate.

Maximum Loan to Value

When the HELOC first became popular after the 1986 tax law change, most lenders offered this loan with a maximum loan-to-value (LTV) ratio of 80 percent, meaning that the maximum LTV for all mortgage debt secured by the real estate could not exceed 80 percent. Thus, if a property was appraised at $100,000 and had a $60,000 first mortgage, the maximum HELOC could be only $20,000.

As competition for these loans increased, lenders began offering higher and higher maximum LTVs for HELOCs and closed-end home equity loans. During the late 1990s and early 2000s, competition drove lenders to offer the HELOC at higher LTVs than the then-less-risky, closed-end loan. At that time, most lenders offered 90 percent LTV of appraised value. Today, practically all lenders have lowered their maximums to 80 percent or less, depending on other loan and economic characteristics.

Lenders taking higher LTV risk often limit other loan terms severely. Lenders may still advertise that they will lend up to 90 or 100 percent of appraised value, but few applicants will qualify. Lenders adopting these—and other—deceptive or misleading practices know that they will receive many inquiries, and a good number of those will turn into applications and closed loans at lower LTVs.

Term

Practically all HELOCs consist of two periods: a draw period and a repayment period. A few lenders offer these two periods as one concurrent period, but this type of HELOC (Figure 10.1) is disappearing fast as consumers select loans with the two separate periods. The **draw period** is that time within which a consumer can draw on the line of credit. This draw period usually ranges from five to ten years, although it can be for any period up to the maximum period allowed for a mortgage loan in a particular state. During this period, a consumer can draw on the line up to the amount he is approved for and, as he repays that advance, he can draw that amount again, as well as any unused amount in the line. When the draw period ends, the ability to draw on the line ends. Any amount that is owed at this point is either due as a balloon payment or, more commonly, is repaid over the course of the repayment period.

FIGURE **10.1** Sample Home Equity Line of Credit Disclosure Statement

LIBERTY
BANK

Supplement to Important Terms of our
Home Equity Credit Line Account

This supplement contains important information about our Home Equity Credit Line Accounts. Please read this supplement carefully and keep a copy for your records.

1. **Variable-Rate Feature:** Liberty Bank offers two different types of Home Equity Credit Line Accounts, as follows:

• **HELOC up to $24,999 Program:** We offer credit limits from $10,000 to $24,999 with a monthly variable-rate feature where the Annual Percentage Rate is adjusted each Billing Cycle to equal the index described in the accompanying **"Important Terms of our Home Equity Credit Line Account"** (**"Important Terms"**) plus a margin. Ask us for the amount of our current margin. The total loan-to-value ratio ("LTV") under this Home Equity Credit Line program (taking into account any mortgage loan that may be ahead of our Home Equity Credit Line mortgage and also the Home Equity Credit Line credit limit) cannot be more than 80 percent of the estimated market value of your home as of the date we open the account if your first mortgage lien is with Liberty Bank and 70% if your first mortgage lien is with another lender. We sometimes refer to this Home Equity Credit Line program in this Supplement as the **"HELOC up to $24,999 Program."** Under this HELOC up to $24,999 **Program**, your Annual Percentage Rate (corresponding to the periodic rate) and minimum monthly payment may change once each Billing Cycle, as the value of the index changes.

• **BreakFree**[SM] **Program:** We offer credit limits from $25,000 to $450,000 with a monthly variable-rate feature where the Annual Percentage Rate is adjusted each Billing Cycle to equal the index described in the accompanying **"Important Terms"** plus a margin. We sometimes refer to this Home Equity Credit Line program in this Supplement as the **"BreakFree**[SM] **Program."** Ask us for the amount of the margin that we currently add to the index under this BreakFree[SM] program. Under this BreakFree[SM] program, your Annual Percentage Rate (corresponding to the periodic rate) and minimum monthly payment may change once each Billing Cycle, as the value of the index changes.

Minimum Interest Rate for the BreakFree[SM] **Program:** Under the BreakFree[SM] program, the **ANNUAL PERCENTAGE RATE** cannot decrease to less than 3.00%. (We call this the "lifetime floor.")

• **Maximum interest rate for all programs:** Under each of the two Home Equity Credit Line programs described above, the **ANNUAL PERCENTAGE RATE** cannot increase to more than 18%. Apart from this "lifetime cap," and apart from the "lifetime floor" (which applies only to the BreakFree[SM] program), there is no limit on the amount by which the rate can change during any one-year period.

Automatic Payment Deduction Feature: The regular margin we would normally add to the index under the Breakfree[SM] program may be decreased by ¼ of one percentage point (0.25%) if you agree to have your minimum monthly payments automatically deducted each Billing Cycle from a Liberty Bank checking (or savings)account acceptable to Liberty Bank (an "eligible deposit account") when the Breakfree[SM] Account is opened. (We sometimes call such automatic minimum monthly payments the "automatic payment deduction" feature.) For example, if the regular margin we would normally add to the index under the Breakfree[SM] program was 49/100 of one percentage point (0.49%), we may agree to decrease this margin by ¼ of 1% (0.25%) to 24/100 of one percentage point (0.24%) if you agree to the automatic payment deduction feature when the Breakfree[SM] Account is opened. In such a case, if the automatic payment deduction feature ends for any reason (whether because you or we choose to end the feature, or because you or we closed the deposit account from which the automatic payments were deducted), the margin we would add to the index under this Breakfree[SM] program would increase by ¼ of one percentage point (0.25%) in the next Billing Cycle (to equal the regular margin we would have normally added to the index, if you had not agreed to the automatic payment deduction feature when the Breakfree[SM] Account was opened), and would remain at that higher (regular) margin until all amounts owed under the Breakfree[SM] Account are paid in full and the Account is closed. Therefore, if you choose the automatic payment deduction feature when the Breakfree[SM] Account is

FIGURE **10.1** (*Continued*)

LIBERTY
BANK

opened, your Annual Percentage Rate(corresponding to the periodic rate) may increase by as much as ¼ of one percentage point (0.25%) in the Billing Cycle after the automatic payment deduction feature ends, even if the index does not increase. If the Annual Percentage Rate increases (whether because the index increases or because the margin we add to the index increases),the minimum monthly payment may also increase.

2.   **Additional Information about the BreakFree**[SM] **program:** The total loan-to-value ratio ("LTV") under the BreakFree[SM] program (taking into account any mortgage loan that may be ahead of our Home Equity Credit Line mortgage and also the Home Equity Credit Line credit limit) cannot be more than 80 percent of the estimated market value of your home as of the date we open the account if your first mortgage lien is with Liberty Bank and 70% if your first mortgage lien is with another lender.

3. **Minimum Payment Examples:**
• **HELOC up to $24,999 Program:** If you took one single $10,000 advance at the beginning of the Draw Period, at an **ANNUAL PERCENTAGE RATE** of 4.50% (the index value as of July 30, 2010 plus a margin of 1.25 percentage point[1]), you would make:
    118 minimum payments of $36.99 each during the Draw Period; and
    122 minimum payments ranging from $118.96 to $85.61 during the Final Period.

Breakfree[SM] **program (without Liberty Bank automatic payment deduction**): If you took one single $10,000 advance at the beginning of the Draw Period, at an **ANNUAL PERCENTAGE RATE** of 3.74% (the index value as of July 30, 2010 plus a margin of .49 percentage points[2] you would make:
    118 minimum payments of $30.74 each During the Draw Period; and
    122 minimum payments ranging from $112.71 to $ 84.99 during the Final Period.

Breakfree[SM] **program (with Liberty Bank automatic payment deduction):** If you took one single $10,000 advance at the beginning of the Draw Period, at an **ANNUAL**

PERCENTAGE RATE of 3.49% (the index value as of July 30, 2010 plus a margin of .24 percentage points[3] you would make:
    118 minimum payments of $28.68 Each during the Draw Period; and
    122 minimum payments ranging From $110.65 to $84.79 during The Final Period.

4. **Maximum Payment Examples:**
• If you took one single $10,000 advance at the beginning of the Draw Period, at the maximum 18% **ANNUAL PERCENTAGE RATE**, the minimum monthly payment would be $147.95 during the Draw Period. If you had an outstanding balance of $10,000 at the beginning of the Final Period, at the maximum 18% **ANNUAL PERCENTAGE RATE**, the minimum monthly payment at the beginning of the Final Period would be $229.92.
The maximum 18% **ANNUAL PERCENTAGE RATE** could be reached as early as the start of the second Billing Cycle of the Draw Period and could also be reached as early as the start of the Final Period.

5.   **Historical Example:** The table on the following page shows how the Annual Percentage Rate and minimum monthly payments would have changed based on changes in the index over the last 15 years, for each of our two different Home Equity Credit Line programs. The index values are from the Wall Street Journal most recently published on the last business day of July of each year. While only one payment amount per year is shown, payments would have varied slightly during each year of the Final Period. Years 1996 through 2005 show the Annual Percentage Rate and the minimum monthly payments during the Draw Period. Years 2006 through 2010 show the Annual Percentage Rate and one of the minimum monthly payments during the first five years of the Final Period.
        For both loan programs, the table assumes one single $10,000 advance taken at the beginning of the Draw Period and that until 2004 the balance remained at exactly $10,000. The table also assumes that no additional loan advances were taken, that only the minimum payments were made, and that the index and Annual Percentage Rate remained constant during each year. The table does not necessarily indicate how the index or your payments will change in the future.

MEMBER
FDIC
Equal Housing Lender

FIGURE **10.1** (*Continued*)

LIBERTY
BANK

	Year	Index	HELOC up to $24,999 Program		BreakFree℠ Program	
			Annual Percentage Rate[4]	Minimum Monthly Payment (a)	Annual Percentage Rate[5]	Minimum Monthly Payment (a)
Draw Period	1996	8.25	9.50	$78.08	8.74	$71.84
	1997	8.50	9.75	$80.14	8.99	$73.89
	1998	8.50	9.75	$80.14	8.99	$73.89
	1999	8.00	9.25	$76.03	8.49	$69.78
	2000	9.50	10.75	$88.36	9.99	$82.11
	2001	6.75	8.00	$65.75	7.24	$59.51
	2002	4.75	6.00	$49.32	5.24	$43.07
	2003	4.00	5.25	$43.15	4.49	$36.90
	2004	4.25	5.50	$45.21	4.74	$38.96
	2005	6.25	7.50	$61.64	6.74	$55.40
Final Period (a)	2006	8.25	9.50	$158.77	8.74	$152.63
	2007	8.25	9.50	$151.09	8.74	$145.56
	2008	5.00	6.25	$122.39	5.49	$117.48
	2009	3.25	4.50	$107.44	3.74	$103.14
	2010	3.25	4.50	$103.80	3.74	$100.11

(a) This table does not show the remaining payments over the last 5 years of the term of the account which would result in the repayment of the entire principal balance.

---

1 This is a margin we have used recently in the HELOC up to $24,999 program. Ask us for the amount of our current margin.
2 This is a regular Breakfree℠ margin we have used recently in the BreakFree℠ program. Ask us for the amount of the margin we currently add to the Index under the BreakFree℠ program.
3 This margin is ¼ of one percentage point (0.25%) lower than a regular Breakfree℠ margin we have used recently, and reflects the lower margin that may be available if you agree to the automatic payment deduction feature when the Breakfree℠ Account is opened.
4 This reflects a 1.25% margin we have used recently in the HELOC up to $24,999 Program. Ask us for the amount of our current margin.
5 This reflects a (.49%) regular Breakfree℠ margin we have used recently in the BreakFree℠ program. Ask us for the amount of the margin we currently add to the index under the BreakFree℠ program.
This Historical Example assumes that no automatic deduction feature had been agreed to when the Breakfree℠ Account was opened.

 MEMBER FDIC

Source: Reprinted with permission of Liberty Bank
© 2010 Liberty Bank

The **repayment period** is that period of time, usually 10 to 15 years, when the borrower must repay all money owed at the end of the draw period. The payment during the repayment period is principal and interest, thus it is a fully amortized loan. The interest rate during the repayment period can be either fixed or variable. Thus, if a borrower owes $10,000 at the end of the draw period and the repayment period is 15 years, the $10,000 would be divided by 180 repay periods and the principal payment would be $55.56 per period. The interest payment that is combined with the principal payment would depend on whether the HELOC is fixed or variable, and the rate of interest at the time the payment was calculated.

Payment Method

Lenders have many options for how to establish the consumer's minimum monthly payment during the draw period. It is important to realize that consumers may make any payment they choose as long as it is at least the minimum. Consumers may pay off the entire balance with their first payment, if they so select. The biggest decision a lender has to make concerns the amount that will be required as a minimum payment—principal and interest, or interest only. A majority of lenders requires some principal reduction each month, and the current sentiment with regulators supports this. Examiners will review with increased scrutiny those HELOC programs with interest-only payments for the full term of the loan.

Interest-Only Payments

The vast majority of lenders (more than 75 percent) offer interest-only payments, but only during the draw period. During the repayment period, the loan is self-amortizing, with principal and interest due each month.

The reason why so many lenders have converted to interest-only is consumer-driven—to advertise a lower monthly payment. A substantial difference exists between an interest-only payment and one that requires principal payments during the draw period. Many lenders have an 18-percent-maximum interest rate on their HELOCs. To avoid the possibility of negative amortization, they require a monthly payment that produces enough to add up to 18 percent interest if necessary. For example, if a borrower owes $10,000, the monthly payment with a principal reduction requires a minimum payment of 1.5 percent of the loan amount, or, in this case, $150, to always collect enough money to meet an interest rate of 18 percent ($10,000 × 18 percent = $1,800, or 12 monthly payments of $150).

If a competing lender offers interest-only payments, and the interest rate on its HELOC is six percent, the difference of $100 in the minimum monthly payment ($10,000 × six percent = $600 divided by 12 months = $50 monthly payment) is so obvious that most consumers will go to the competitor.

Other Payment Methods

Some lenders amortize the amount owed over the remaining life of the loan (draw period and repayment period) to establish the minimum payment.

A few lenders use a payment calculation method whereby the amount of the payment is established by a range of outstanding debt. For example, if the balance is between $1,000 and $3,000, the minimum payment is $75. Consumers often are not attracted to this type of payment calculation.

Whichever way a lender establishes the payment, it should establish a minimum payment plus whatever else it intends to collect. For example, the minimum payment may be $50 or interest only, whichever is greater.

Adjustment Periods

The **adjustment period** refers to how often the interest rate can change. Most lenders have a monthly adjustment period, with a few using a daily period. HELOC lenders should strive to use an adjustment period that is at least monthly. An adjustment period longer than one month diminishes the asset/liability advantage of this type of variable-rate loan.

Methods of Access

Mortgage lenders devised many ways for consumers to access their lines of credit, as shown in Table 10.3. Today, the most common way is by check. A rapidly increasing method of access for borrowers is by plastic, either credit card or debit card. This method could be the major access method in the future, since it is so convenient for the consumer. A little more than one third of lenders already offer this access method, but only about 10 percent of consumers are currently using the card method.

Other access methods for HELOC include the following:

- Overdraft protection for regular checking
- Telephone transfer to regular checking
- Personal withdrawal
- Automated teller machines (ATMs)

Closing Costs and Other Fees

As discussed earlier, lenders offer a no closing cost HELOC to get consumers to consider their HELOC over that of another. This practice is so common that the lender that tries to pass on some of the closing costs to the consumer has a hard time in the marketplace. Depending on the state, closing costs for a HELOC loan generally run between $200 and $300. Of course, if a state or locality charges a mortgage tax, the cost is much higher.

Annual Fee

The only other fee that lenders sometimes charge consumers is an annual fee for keeping the line open. This fee typically is $25 to $50 per year. The basic concept behind these fees is that if a consumer is not going to use the line, the consumer will not pay the fee, and thus the lender can close the line.

Periodic Statement

Truth in Lending requires mortgage lenders with a HELOC product to send out a periodic statement to each HELOC borrower. Basically, the statement

TABLE **10.3**

Traditional Home Equity Line of Credit Product

Feature	Typical Arrangement
Index for interest calculation	Average prime rate
Margin for interest calculation	Zero to minus 50 basis points
Introductory rate	Zero to minus 100 basis points below fully adjusted rate
Frequency of adjustment	Monthly
Draw period	5 or 10 years
Repayment period	10 or 15 years
Closing fees	$0
Annual fees	$50
Maximum loan-to-value	80 percent in most markets; 90 percent in some markets
Caps on annual increases	None
Maximum line	$100,000 is average, but some lenders have no limits
Minimum line	$10,000
Payment (monthly)	Draw period: $50 or interest only, whichever is greater
	Repayment period: $50 or principal and interest, whichever is greater
Access method	Check or credit card
Security	Primary residence; some lenders have added second homes and rentals
Underwriting	
• Debt ratio	40–45 percent
• Employment/income	Pay stub (tax returns if self-employed)
• Credit report	Consumer credit report
• Data to establish value	Tax assessment, existing appraisal, drive-by appraisal
• Title	Title search usually; insurance if needed
• Flood determination	Always
• Hazard insurance	Always
Payment due date	Anytime, often twentieth of month

looks like a credit card statement that many consumers receive in the mail each month. The statement must be mailed or delivered for each billing cycle (but at least quarterly) in which a loan has a balance of more than $1 or on which a finance charge has been imposed.

This statement must be mailed at least 14 days prior to any payment date or the end of any time period required to be disclosed in order for the consumer to avoid an additional finance or other charge. For this reason, many lenders have decided to make the payment date for HELOC different from other mortgage loans. Often the day selected is the twentieth of the month.

FIGURE **10.2** Sample Home Equity Line of Credit Periodic Statement

LIBERTY
BANK
MORTGAGE CORPORATION

```
********************************
* MINIMUM PAYMENT      241.10 *
* Payment Due Date   05/17/10 *
********************************

1    THOMAS J PINKOWISH

                         Statement Date:    04/23/10
                         Account Number:    65

                          AMOUNT REMITTED: $_____
[ ] Check here to payoff and close out credit line account.

      Please return this payment stub with your payment.
      Please make checks or money orders payable To: Liberty Bank

***************** Home Equity Credit Line      6510      *********************

Date_Eff-Dt_Description_____Amount_____Balance__

03/23        Previous Balance ------------------------------------  53,870.43
04/12        Regular Payment                        500.00-         53,370.43
04/19        Check Number      1013              20,000.00          73,370.43
04/23        Finance Charge                         241.10          73,611.53


Account Summary                      Payment Summary
--------------                       ---------------
Previous Statement       03/23/10    Amount Past Due            .00
Previous Balance        53,870.43    Principal                 .00
+ Advances & Debits     20,000.00    Finance Charge         241.10
- Payments & Credits       500.00    Other Charges             .00
+ ** Finance Charge **     241.10    Fees                      .00
+ Late Charges                .00    Insurance                 .00
New Balance             73,611.53    Late Charges              .00
Credit Limit            75,000.00    Amount Over Limit         .00

Credit Available         1,629.57    Minimum Payment        241.10

Finance Charge Summary
----------------------
            Principal      Int     Periodic   # Of    Finance
Eff-Dt_____Balance_____Rate_____Rate_____Days_____Charges
03/24      53,664.02     5.000%   .01369863%  19      139.67
04/12      53,370.43     5.000%   .01369863%  07       51.18
04/19      73,370.43     5.000%   .01369863%  05       50.25
                                              ----    ---------
                                              31       241.10


** ANNUAL PERCENTAGE RATE ** 5.000     Periodic Rate May Vary

Year To Date Interest        891.61
```

Member FDIC   315 Main Street, Middletown, Connecticut 06457   Equal Housing Lender

The periodic statement (Figure 10.2) must contain the following information:

- Balance outstanding at the beginning of the billing cycle.
- Identification of each credit transaction, including amount, date, and so forth.

- Any credit to the account during the billing cycle, including the amount and date.
- The periodic rate used to compute the finance charge, along with the range of balances to which it applies and the corresponding APR.
- Balance to which a periodic rate was applied and any explanation as to how the balance was determined.
- Amount of any finance charge added to an account during the billing cycle, using the term *finance charge* and itemizing the components of the finance charge.
- APR equivalent to the total finance charge imposed during the billing cycle.
- Amounts, itemized and identified by type, of any charge other than finance charges debited to the account.
- Closing date of the billing cycle and the outstanding balance on that date.
- Date by which the new balance may be paid to avoid additional finance charges.
- Address for notification of billing errors.

MARKETING HOME EQUITY LOANS

As mentioned earlier in this chapter, the two keys for success in home equity lending are the loan program design and marketing. This section discusses some of the techniques and tools that mortgage lenders have used that have resulted in successful marketing of these loans.

Marketing Plan

Probably the first requirement for successful marketing of any loan program is that the lender has a marketing plan for it. One part of this plan should examine the medium to be used for advertising the program, while another part will provide a realistic budget to allow for success. The Consumer Bankers Association, in its yearly home equity study, concludes that lenders spend between $50 and $90 in marketing and advertising costs per home equity loan actually made.

Understanding Your Market

An essential part of a marketing plan for a home equity loan program is to understand what the competition is offering. Many lenders make the mistake of assuming that they have to be concerned only with what local lenders are offering as home equity loans. Of course, that is important, but these lenders must also consider what the national lenders are offering. Because these loans are so attractive, many national lenders (Bank of America, Citicorp, Chase, Wells Fargo) have attractive home equity products that are offered across the United States. These lenders will solicit directly all of the best credits in each locality. Local lenders must understand what the national lenders are offering and have a loan product that is comparable.

Types of Media Used

Mortgage lenders have many options for getting the story of their home equity loans out to the public. Most lenders use some combination of the following media:

- Statement stuffers
- Newspapers
- Direct mail
- Radio
- Telemarketing
- Television
- Billboards
- Internet
- Magazines

Lenders often find that the effectiveness of the various media falls approximately in the order of this list. It is interesting to note that statement stuffers are one of the most effective, but also one of the least expensive media. Newspapers are also effective but are quite expensive. Direct-mail pieces are effective for many lenders, but are also quite expensive. Billboards are not generally effective except in some specific geographical areas where a large volume of traffic passes the billboard locations. Internet usage and effectiveness varies greatly from lender to lender. An example of a HELOC marketing brochure can be found in Figure 10.3.

Other tools that lenders use for marketing inside their places of business include the following:

- Banners in the branch offices
- "Tents" at teller windows
- Displays at loan officer desks
- Video displays
- Brochures
- Internet/Intranet Kiosks

REVERSE ANNUITY MORTGAGES (RAMS)

The RAM, or *reverse mortgage*, as shown in Figure 10.4, is designed to enable older retired homeowners who are likely to be on fixed incomes to use the equity in their homes as a source of supplemental income while still retaining ownership. Reverse mortgage programs have been in the market for nearly 50 years, although they have only become popularized since the late 1990s. Legend has it that the first reverse mortgage was originated in 1961, by a savings and loan association in Deering, Maine, to help one senior citizen. In the intervening 50 years, reverse mortgages have remained a largely misunderstood niche product.

The reverse mortgage allows a homeowner to access the built-up equity—converting it to cash payments—while still owning the property. Unlike conventional mortgage programs, this loan type is considered to be "in reverse"

FIGURE **10.3** Sample Home Equity Loan Marketing Brochure

>> HOME EQUITY OPTIONS

With a variety of flexible, easy-to-apply-for, and easy-to-use home equity loan and credit line options, we have one that is right for you. Use a home equity loan or a home equity credit line to put the equity in your home to work to pay for college tuition, home improvements, debt consolidation, a dream vacation, or almost any other purpose you choose.

In addition to our really low rates on home equity loans and credit lines, there are no application fees and no closing costs. Low monthly payments make it easy for you to budget. Visit any Liberty branch today or apply by phone at (888) 570-0773, or apply online at www.liberty-bank.com.

WHY A HOME EQUITY LOAN OR LINE OVER ANOTHER TYPE OF LOAN?
>> Lower interest rate than most credit cards or unsecured personal loans
>> Interest may be tax-deductible (consult your tax advisor)
>> Money can be used for a wide variety of purposes
>> Borrow up to 80 percent of the equity in your home (depending on your circumstances)

To get more information or to apply for a home equity credit line or loan, call us at (888) 570-0773, and we'll take your application over the phone or visit www.liberty-bank.com and apply online.

WHAT'S THE DIFFERENCE BETWEEN A HOME EQUITY LOAN AND A HOME EQUITY CREDIT LINE?

Home Equity Loan:*
>> You borrow a specific amount
>> The fixed interest rate never goes up
>> Monthly or biweekly payments are fixed for the life of the loan, so you know how much to budget
>> The loan is paid back over a fixed period of time
>> No application fee
>> No closing costs or annual fees

Home Equity Credit Line:*
>> You borrow only what you need, when you need it
>> Write checks for any amount from $100 up to your credit limit
>> Funds are available whenever you need them, for the term of your advance period
>> Variable interest rate with cap
>> You owe nothing until you access your line
>> No application fee or closing costs

*Trust review fees may apply

Flexible options. Easy to use. Easy to apply for.

WWW.LIBERTY-BANK.COM

Source: Reprinted with permission of Liberty Bank
© 2010 Liberty Bank

because it makes payments *to* a homeowner, rather than the other way around. Instead of the loan balance declining over time, building up home-owner equity, a reverse mortgage balance increases over time, reducing the homeowner's equity. Reverse mortgages are, essentially, negative amortization loans.

A lender's security for a RAM is the same as with a standard mortgage: the home itself. If the homeowner (or owners) dies before the term, the estate may be liable for the debt. Of course, if the house is sold before death, the debt must be paid off. If the homeowner (or owners) is still alive when the loan comes to term, a new RAM can be created, assuming that the property has appreciated. The proceeds from the new RAM first repay the old one, and the difference purchases a new annuity for the homeowner.

FIGURE **10.4** Comparison of Home Equity and Reverse Mortgage Features

Reverse Mortgages	Home Equity Loans
No Monthly Payment	Monthly Payment Required
Payments to a borrower may be for a defined term or for life	N/A
Line of credit grows at the effective accrual rate	Line of credit does not grow
No credit requirements	Credit score required
No income requirements	Debt ratio qualification required
No foreclosure during life if covenants are followed	Property foreclosed for loan default
Higher closing costs	Lower closing costs

Source: Reprinted with permission of Mark A. Burton and Associates
© 2010 REMOC Associates, LLC

Reverse Mortgage Amount and Funding

Depending on the program, borrowers may receive proceeds from their reverse mortgage in several ways:

- One lump-sum distribution
- Monthly payments for the remainder of the borrower(s) life
- Monthly payment based on a defined term
- Line of credit
- Combination of cash, monthly payments, and credit line

These amounts are determined by several factors, including the youngest borrower's age, current levels of interest rates, the value of the home, and the amount of any liens that need to be paid off by the reverse mortgage.

Reverse mortgage programs almost always have a minimum age requirement for all borrowers on the note, most often 62 years. Whether or not a reverse mortgage will be of benefit to an older homeowner is dependent upon that homeowner's specific circumstances. The younger the homeowner, the less money he or she may receive because of the longer period of negative amortization before he or she leaves the home. Conversely, the older the homeowner, the greater the proceeds will be.

The interest rate at which the loan accrues affects the proceeds: higher rates cause the loan to negatively amortize more quickly, and vice versa for lower rates. Simply put, circumstances that cause a loan to accrue for a longer period of time or at a faster pace will cause the loan balance to reach the home's value sooner. To compensate for this risk to the lender, the homeowner begins with a lower loan amount—or in other words, they receive fewer proceeds or benefits as shown in Figure 10.5.

FHA Home Equity Conversion Mortgage

As the U.S. population began aging in the 1980s, lenders became more interested in reverse mortgages. A common version of a reverse mortgage was an equity share loan, where the lender shared in the growth of

FIGURE **10.5** Home Equity Conversion Mortgage Loan Comparison

REVERSE MORTGAGE LOAN COMPARISON

Est Property Value: $300,000.00

Borrower Age(s): 75

	HECM 1 MO LIBOR 300	HECM 1 MO LIBOR 325	HECM FIX ClosedEnd
Initial Interest Rate Index	0.273 %	0.273 %	5.56 %
Lender's Margin	3 %	3.25 %	
Initial Interest Rate	3.273 %	3.523 %	5.56 %
Mortgage Insurance Premium	0.5 %	0.5 %	0.5 %
Initial Effective Loan Rate	**3.773 %**	**4.023 %**	**6.06 %**
Effective Loan Rate Cap	13.273 %	13.523 %	5.56 %
HECM Expected Rate	6.95 %	7.2 %	5.56 %
Creditline Growth Rate	3.773 %	4.023 %	6.06 %
Monthly Service Fee	$30.00	$30.00	$30.00
Plan Adjusted Home Value	**$300,000.00**	**$300,000.00**	**$300,000.00**
Total Principal Limit	**$182,700.00**	**$177,000.00**	**$219,600.00**
Financed Origination Fee	$-5,000.00	$-5,000.00	$-5,000.00
Other Financed Costs	$-2,308.71	$-2,308.71	$-2,308.71
Initial Mortgage Insurance	$-6,000.00	$-6,000.00	$-6,000.00
Left after Fees and Costs	**$169,391.29**	**$163,691.29**	**$206,291.29**
Loan Service Set-Aside	$-4,102.83	$-4,014.70	$-4,653.20
Repairs Set-Aside	$0.00	$0.00	$0.00
First Year Property Expenses	$0.00	$0.00	$0.00
Left after Set-Asides	**$165,288.46**	**$159,676.59**	**$201,638.09**
Liens and Disbursements	$0.00	$0.00	$0.00

The key drivers for determining the principal benefits of a HECM are property value, the age of the youngest borrower on the application, the "Expected Rate," which is the expected long term rate for the particular product (not the note rate), and the servicing fee. Usually the closing costs are financed into the loan, which subtracts from immediate benefits. Set-asides reduce how much can be borrowed today in order to create a cushion for other expenses to be paid later. For example, a repair set-aside saves some of the borrowing power in order to cover estimated repairs that must be completed as a condition of the loan. A servicing set-aside reduces what can be borrowed today in order to create a cushion for financing the monthly servicing fee in the future months in which they are incurred. In this example, note the closing costs. The FHA up-front insurance is 2% of the appraised value of $300,000; the origination fee is 2% of the first $200,000 of value, and 1% of the remaining amount up to the "Adjusted Home Value" or FHA Maximum Claim Amount.

Source: Reprinted with permission of Mark A. Burton and Associates
© 2010 REMOC Associates, LLC

the home's value over the period of the loan. In some circumstances, this resulted in large windfalls to the lender, exposing the lender to charges of predatory practices.

In 1989, the Federal Housing Administration piloted what has now become the staple reverse mortgage program in the industry, the FHA-insured Home Equity Conversion Mortgage (HECM). HECMs have the important feature of being fully guaranteed by the U.S. government. This guarantee protects the lender or servicer against loan default or value home depreciation. HUD is a secured lender of record (in second position behind the mortgage lender); this guarantees the homeowner will receive payments irrespective of the condition of the lender.

The federal guarantee also covers the borrower in several ways. The homeowner is guaranteed to receive benefits as stipulated at loan origination, even if home values depreciate. The loan is non-recourse to the borrower. This means that if the loan balance exceeds the value of the home, the borrower or heirs may satisfy the loan in full by selling the home at fair market value in an arm's length transaction—even if the net proceeds of the sale are less than what is owed on the HECM.

The federal guarantee comes at a price. The FHA mortgage insurance is two percent of the value of the home at origination, and one-half percent annual rate on the outstanding monthly loan balance. The insurance, plus a loan origination fee that is based on the home value, plus traditional settlement costs, can add up to an expensive closing. Closing costs typically range from $10,000 on smaller loans to around $23,000 for larger loans, depending on the property location and product options.

Additionally, because of the federal guarantees involved, the FHA must obtain credit subsidy appropriations from Congress to operate the program. Like other government agency programs sponsored by the USDA and HUD, the need for periodic approval—especially in different economic, federal budget, and political climates—adds a level of uncertainty to the program. Presently, Congress allocated $150 million for the HECM program, which always has a chance of being modified.

In October 2010, FHA introduced the HECM Saver program with significantly lower closing fees and maximum payout, compared to the standard HECM program. The upfront premium is 0.1 percent, and payout is 10–18 percent lower than the standard HECM program. If the program generates enough loan volume, it will produce approximately 1.25 percent annual income to the FHA and enable the program to operate without the need for uncertain congressionally-approved credit subsidies.

FHA HECMs may be sold to Fannie Mae or securitized as Ginnie Mae HMBSs (HECM mortgage backed securities), or even held in a lender's portfolio if they have a means of servicing them. In the 1990s, Fannie Mae introduced its own product for loan amounts that exceeded FHA limits, and Wall Street designed jumbo products for reverse mortgage amounts exceeding the Fannie Mae loan limit. The mortgage market meltdown of the late 2000s ended (for the time being) private securitization of jumbo loans, and regulatory changes that made the HECM more competitive caused Fannie Mae to discontinue its own product line. Currently, FHA HECM programs comprise essentially 100 percent of the reverse mortgage market.

Consumer Protection for Reverse Mortgages

Because of the upfront expense—which is typically rolled into the initial loan balance—and the erosion of home equity due to negative amortization, product suitability is a critical concern surrounding HECMs and other reverse mortgage products. Combine these suitability concerns with the fact that the client base for these products is senior citizens, some of whom may have declining faculties, and it is easy to see the potential for abuse.

HUD has done much to mitigate the potential for abuse. Mandatory third-party counseling is required. A list of approved, local counselors can be found at HUD's website. These counselors must be trained and approved by HUD, and local jurisdictions may have their own regulations in addition to HUD's as shown in Figure 10.6.

The application documents and disclosures of an HECM (Figure 10.7) are designed to disclose to the borrower not only the financial mechanics of reverse mortgages, but some of the areas in which seniors have been abused

FIGURE **10.6** Home Equity Conversion Mortgage Counseling Requirements

- All borrowers on an FHA HECM must received certified counseling from a HUD-approved HECM counselor. Any quality reverse mortgage program will have similar counseling requirements.
- Counseling must be arm's length – the lender may not contact the counseling agency or otherwise discuss the borrower's personal information or any aspect of the counseling itself.
- Borrower must initiate contact with the counselor – lender may not be involved.
- HUD's Mortgagee Letter 2009-10 says that borrowers must be provided the names of at least 10 approved counselors, five of which must be within the state or local area, and five of which are national counseling agencies.
- Some states – like Massachusetts – may have their own counseling requirements in addition to HUD's.
- HECM counselors are required to perform a budget analysis to evaluate the client's financial situation.

Source: HUD, Reprinted with permission of Mark A. Burton and Associates
© 2010 REMOC Associates, LLC

FIGURE **10.7** Key Reverse Mortgage Application Documents

- See supplemental materials
- The 1009 – the reverse mortgage version of the 1003.
- Key disclosure not found in traditional applications:

  – Reverse Mortgage Loan Comparison – E-7

  – Amortization Schedule – E-8

  – Total Annual Loan Cost (TALC) – E-9

  – Request for Information...Intent to Purchase Annuity – E-13

  – HECM T-I-L/Important Terms Disclosure – E-16

  – Certification Regarding Third Party Fees – E-20

  – Ownership Interest Certification – E-26

  – Notice to Non-borrowing Spouse or Resident – E-27

Source: HUD, Reprinted with permission of Mark A. Burton and Associates
© 2010 REMOC Associates, LLC

in the past, both by lenders and "advisors." HUD has been so diligent about protecting senior citizens' rights and helping them be informed consumers that the FHA HECM program has become the gold standard by which other reverse mortgage programs and origination practices are measured. Some states have passed legislation that requires all programs except the HECM to be reviewed and approved by the state; other states or regulatory bodies have identified specific features of the HECM as required features or practices that lenders should follow in the development of new programs.

Reverse Mortgage Program Suitability

The question of program suitability and HUD's intent to manage it—or governments' intent to regulate it—must ultimately be answered by the senior homeowner and his or her family, along with the expert guidance of a qualified loan officer. The best loan officers in this field have in-depth knowledge and appreciation of the lives of seniors, and they have expertise in the alternatives to reverse mortgages that may be more cost-effective or otherwise better suited to the specific circumstances of the homeowner. Reverse mortgage proceeds are generally not considered income for federal tax purposes or entitlement programs like Social Security and Medicare, but they can have an impact on state or local assistance programs, like Medicaid, heating assistance, and tax rebate programs for the elderly. Similarly, for some homeowners, reverse mortgages can affect estate planning and general financial planning. As a whole, these issues can complicate the question of product suitability, and it is important for lenders to know their limitations in both the quality and appropriateness of advice they provide. It is always appropriate to have a network of professional colleagues who have expertise in these areas and who will work with homeowners in their best interests.

The outlook for the reverse mortgage market remains mixed. On the surface, it would seem that with baby boom generation reaching retirement age, the demand for reverse mortgages would be high. However, high closing costs will cause consumers to shop for alternatives. Indeed, to date, the penetration rate of reverse mortgages as a percentage of homeowners of eligible age is approximately two percent. The number of loan originations (Figure 10.8) in the last few years has leveled off in the 110,000–115,000 range, despite the fact that HECM loan limits were lifted from a maximum county limit of approximately $363,000 to a national limit of $625,500.

A number of factors have constrained the reverse mortgage market besides cost. In recent years, declines in home values have reduced proceeds; the general pullback on underwriting standards in the wake of the mortgage market meltdown has caused FHA to issue across-the-board benefit reductions on HECMs; and persistent media reports, which are either ill-informed about reverse mortgages or accurately report the abuses of a small minority of bad actors, create a skepticism about the product that keeps both consumers and lenders on the sidelines.

On the other hand, home equity remains the greatest source of wealth for the vast majority of older homeowners, and with the economic uncertainty of

FIGURE **10.8** Reverse Mortgage Origination Volume

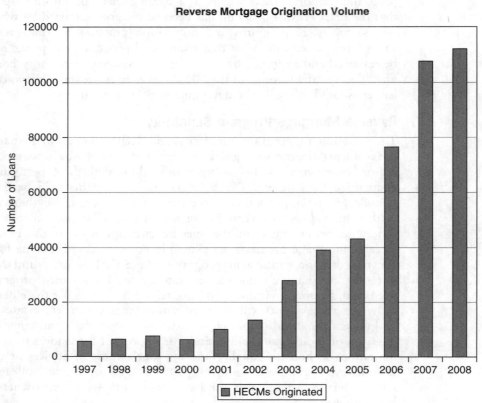

Source: HUD, Reprinted with permission of Mark A. Burton and Associates
© 2010 REMOC Associates, LLC

possible modifications to entitlement programs or impaired retirement funding, reverse mortgages should remain a significant alternative for seniors who need to tap home equity for financial support.

DISCUSSION POINTS

1. Why are home equity loans so popular with consumers?
2. Identify and discuss the keys for success from a mortgage lender's perceptive.
3. What are the important differences between a closed-end home equity loan and a home equity line of credit (HELOC)?
4. What is the most popular method of repaying a HELOC? Why is this payment method so popular?
5. What is the periodic statement that is used with a HELOC? What information is contained in this statement?
6. What factors determine the loan amount for reverse mortgages?
7. What are important differences in types of reverse mortgage programs?

CHAPTER 11

Compliance

INTRODUCTION

A consumer compliance regulation begins as an act of Congress, which also will direct one or more federal agencies to enforce the new law. Congress may select an agency that directly regulates depository institutions: Federal Reserve Board (FRB) of Governors, Federal Deposit Insurance Corporation (FDIC), Office of the Comptroller of the Currency (OCC), Office of Thrift Supervision (OTS), Farm Credit Administration (FCA), or the National Credit Union Administration (NCUA). Congress may instead appoint another agency: Housing and Urban Development (HUD), Federal Trade Commission (FTC), Department of Justice (DOJ), Federal Emergency Management Agency (FEMA), or an interagency body like the Federal Financial Institutions Examination Council (FFIEC).

Any reader can see this is a long list of federal departments and agencies involved in mortgage lending compliance. One goal of the 2010 Dodd-Frank Wall Street Reform and Consumer Protection Act (DFA) is to consolidate compliance and oversight responsibilities of fifteen different regulations into one agency, the Bureau of Consumer Financial Protection (CFPB). The discussion of DFA comes at the end of this chapter. *It is imperative that the reader of this chapter and student of mortgage lending review the impact of DFA on thirteen important federal regulations which precede it in this chapter.*

All mortgage originators, lenders, and servicers must be careful that they are aware of and follow the various requirements for more than a dozen federal regulations affecting residential mortgage lending. The goal is to lend legally, to avoid penalties for noncompliance, and, most importantly, to avoid discrimination against a protected class of consumers.

This chapter provides the mortgage professional with a practical overview of each major federal law or regulation (not legal advice or analysis). It organizes the rules in general categories consistent with their general purpose and includes the following:

FAIR LENDING REGULATIONS

- Fair Housing Act (FHA)
- Equal Credit Opportunity Act (ECOA)

Consumer Privacy Regulations

- Uniting and Strengthening America by Providing Appropriate Tools Required to Intercept and Obstruct Terrorism Act (USA PATRIOT)
- Fair Credit Reporting Act (FCRA)
  - Fair and Accurate Credit Transactions Act (FACT)
- Gramm-Leach-Bliley Financial Modernization Act of 1999 (GLBA)
  - Privacy of Consumer Financial Information (FTC Privacy Rule)
  - Standards for Insuring the Security, Integrity, and Protection of Customer Records and Information (FTC Safeguards Rule)
  - Telemarketing Sales Rule (FTC Do Not Call Registry)

Consumer Protection Regulations

- Truth in Lending Act (TILA)
  - Home Ownership and Equity Protection Act of 1994 (HOEPA)
  - Home Equity Consumer Loan Protection Act
- Real Estate Settlement Procedures Act (RESPA)
- Mortgage Disclosure Improvement Act (MDIA)
- Flood Disaster Protection Act (FDPA)
- Homeowners Protection Act of 1998 (HPA)
- Fair Debt Collection Practices Act (FDCPA)
- Home Mortgage Disclosure Act (HMDA)
- Community Reinvestment Act (CRA)
- Secure and Fair Enforcement for Mortgage Licensing Act of 2008 (SAFE)
- Dodd-Frank Wall Street Reform and Consumer Protection Act (DFA)

What may be a surprise to many readers is that only five of the fifteen or so major regulations involved in residential mortgage lending deal directly with the actual loan terms: TILA, RESPA, MDIA, HPA, FDPA. Most regulations limit or prescribe lender behavior or practices with respect to fair lending, consumer privacy, and consumer protection.

Complying with a regulation can be as complex as calculating the annual percentage rate or as simple as posting the correct sign in a lending office. Still, it is important that mortgage professionals have additional resources (compliance manuals, software references, or compliance experts on staff) to check the specifics of any compliance question or issue they may have.

Mortgage professionals must also comply with numerous state laws and regulations or court rulings for each state in which a lender is active. State-specific laws and regulations cannot be covered here, but they are a rapidly growing source of additional regulation.

Regulatory compliance has changed dramatically since 2007—at both the federal and state levels. The near future promises even more regulatory burdens for lenders and servicers: the federal government seeks to over-haul existing regulatory agencies and create new ones; states and even municipalities nationwide have added an additional layer of laws with which lenders and servicers must comply.

As a result, the compliance environment for all mortgage professionals is more confusing and complex. Almost all recent compliance changes are intended to increase consumer protection, which increases lender liability. They come in response to subprime lending abuses, fraud, and predatory lending. The recent changes impact the entire mortgage lending process at each stage of origination and servicing: before an application to payoff or foreclosure—and even property management after foreclosure.

Additionally, existing regulations like Truth in Lending and RESPA, and the new Secure and Fair Enforcement (SAFE) Act, now have a specific meaning for formerly generic industry terms like "lender" and "originator" and have added many new ones. These terms now have significant legal and compliance consequences, and so even the familiar language has changed. Other terms have been introduced without legal definition.

To attempt to clarify implementation issues, several agencies have added FAQ pages to their Web sites. HUD, immediately after its implementation, provided monthly updates on a special RESPA FAQ Web page to explain how it interprets its recent RESPA changes:

http://www.hud.gov/offices/hsg/ramh/res/respa_hm.cfm

Overall, this new method has assisted mortgage professionals tremendously, but at times results in conflicting or confusing directives that require *additional* clarification. The final update in April, 2010 is more than 60 pages long and contains more than 280 questions.

While it is responsive, this internal method bypasses the valuable cooperation and "due process" formerly present in establishing policy—where a regulator seeks input and formal commentary from the industry, consumer groups, judicial areas, and Congress *before* setting policy. Partly because this "due process" is lacking, HUD's interpretation of recent RESPA changes has been inconsistent. The "Web site FAQ update" method has real benefits, but sets a dangerous precedent for the regulatory process overall.

The past two years of RESPA and TILA implementation demonstrated that the practical impact of such unprecedented change in so short a time—and resolving problems via Web page updates—is an uncertain and severely constricted lending environment. Sadly, this dangerous trend of passing unfinished legislation continued with the Dodd-Frank Wall Street Reform and Consumer Protection Act, but on a much grander scale than occurred recently for TILA or RESPA.

A cautious and uncertain mortgage lending climate will remain until regulators provide satisfactory guidance developed with reasonable input from the industry. Only then can lenders implement appropriate adjustments. The consumer suffers in the meantime—at a time when the supply of mortgage funding is critical.

FAIR LENDING REGULATIONS

The first discussion of residential mortgage lending compliance should start with the concept of fair lending. While there is no "Fair Lending Act," two separate acts form the basis of fair lending:

- Fair Housing Act
- Equal Credit Opportunity Act

These fair lending laws as amended and as interpreted by the courts are designed to accomplish the following:

- Prohibit discrimination in housing-related transactions
- Prohibit discrimination against credit applicants
- Cover all mortgage, construction, and home improvement loans
- Apply to all lenders

Discrimination

Regulators identify three types of fair lending discrimination:

1. *Overt*—blatant or openly discriminatory policies or practices, based on a prohibited basis (SEE the ECOA section for a complete federal list)
2. *Disparate treatment*—treating some credit applicants differently than others based on a prohibitive basis; may not be overt or intentional
3. *Disparate impact*—policies or practices which appear nondiscriminatory, but in practice produce a disparate, adverse impact on persons who are protected under fair lending laws (unless the lender can demonstrate a business necessity for the policy and there is no less discriminatory alternative

Effects Test

The effects test is a term used to establish disparate impact. If it can be shown that a lending practice has a disparate impact on a protected class, then that practice might be discriminatory and may be investigated further.

These fair lending laws and regulations have penalties for noncompliance, including liability (fines and penalties) for the financial institution and for individuals, and the possibility of criminal charges. HUD can investigate individual complaints. Otherwise, in situations where a "pattern or practice" of discrimination is suspected, the regulatory agency must refer the lender to the Housing and Civil Enforcement Section of the Department of Justice (DOJ). Since the early 1990s, the DOJ has initiated more than six hundred actions nationwide for a variety of alleged fair lending violations. Settlement fines often range from hundreds of thousands to millions of dollars. Summaries of these actions can be found at:

http://www.justice.gov/crt/housing/fairhousing/caseslist.htm#lending

FAIR HOUSING ACT

The Fair Housing Act (FHA) was the first of the fair lending regulations, enacted as a part of the Civil Rights Act of 1968 and enforced by HUD and the Department of Justice. The primary purpose is to prohibit discrimination in all phases of housing sales, financing, or rental on the basis of race, color, national origin, religion, sex, disability, or familial status.

Redlining

Although not specifically mentioned in the act, other practices have been held by various courts to be covered by this act. Among these other practices is "redlining," a practice in which a mortgage lender states that it does not lend in certain geographic areas (drawing a red line around a particular

FIGURE **11.1** The Equal Housing Opportunity Logo

EQUAL HOUSING OPPORTUNITY

Source: www.HUD.gov

neighborhood or section of a city) primarily inhabited by a protected class (e.g., racial minorities).

The courts have ruled that other practices fall under the Fair Housing Act, including a prohibition against the use of excessively low appraisals. This occurs when a lender uses appraisers that undervalue real estate in a defined geographical area. Further, the FHA prohibits the setting of a minimum mortgage loan amount that exceeds purchase price of a meaningful amount of the housing stock in a defined geographical area. Additionally, using only one race or color in advertisements is illegal, as it can create the impression that the lender makes loans only to that group. Finally, this epic legislation prohibits the use of more onerous terms or conditions on members of one class, race, or group.

Equal Housing Opportunity Logo

All mortgage originators must post the Equal Housing Opportunity logo and poster in any branch where mortgage applications are taken. When advertising mortgage loan products, mortgage originators must use the Equal Housing Opportunity logo (Figure 11.1) in the advertisement or must use the term *"equal housing lender"* if the advertisement is played over the air (radio, television, or the Internet).

EQUAL CREDIT OPPORTUNITY ACT

The second of the fair lending laws is the Equal Credit Opportunity Act (ECOA). ECOA became federal law as part of the federal Consumer Protection Act when it became effective in 1974. ECOA is often referred to as Regulation B, and was issued by the Federal Reserve Bank Board of Governors but is enforced by many different agencies: FRB, FDIC, OCC, OTS, FCA, and NCUA for financial institutions; and by the FTC for all other creditors, such as retailers, finance companies, and most mortgage companies.

Like the FHA, ECOA is a "cradle to grave" regulation covering all phases of lending, including the following:

- Advertising
- Inquiries
- Taking and evaluating applications

- Discouragement
- Credit decisions and notification
- Administration of accounts
- Treatment of delinquent or slow accounts
- Collections and default remedies

The original ECOA was limited to prohibiting discrimination on the basis of sex or marital status. Through the years, various amendments to ECOA have expanded the act to include more prohibited bases. The prohibited bases (the so-called "Naughty Nine") include:

- Sex
- Marital status
- Age
- Race
- Color
- Religion
- National origin
- Receipt of income from a public assistance program
- Good faith exercise of any right the applicant has under the Consumer Credit Protection Act (or applicable state law)

(Note: The Fair Housing Act also adds to the preceding list disability and familial status. In some states, additional protected classes have been added, such as sexual orientation.)

Taking the Application

No mortgage lender may discourage any consumer from applying for a mortgage loan. In fact, the best approach for a mortgage lender is to always encourage consumers to apply. Note: ECOA applies to both written and oral applications. If a mortgage lender's policy is to accept only written applications for mortgage loans, the lender could be held to have made a credit decision based on an "oral" application *if* it gives an "opinion" (such as "you will not qualify") rather than "facts" ("our ratio for total debt is 40 percent").

It is important that mortgage lenders realize that ECOA does not prohibit a lender from considering information that is not barred by ECOA. For example, if a person does not have sufficient income to qualify for a loan, the lender is completely justified in declining the mortgage application. But the lender may not discount the following when making these decisions:

- Part-time income
- Pensions
- Welfare
- Alimony, child support, or separate maintenance (if voluntarily given after appropriate warning)

However, the mortgage lender *can* consider the likely duration of the income.

Marital Status

A mortgage lender needs to establish the marital status of the mortgage applicant(s). Many reasons exist for establishing the status, but the most important reason is identifying whether or not a non-applicant spouse will be required to sign the security agreement. For instance, if a woman qualifies for a mortgage loan, a lender must grant her the mortgage loan. But, if she is married, depending on the state (e.g., community property states), the lender may require her husband to sign the security agreement but not the promissory note. This is done so that the husband's ownership in the community property securing the mortgage loan is subject to the security interest of the lender. If the applicant defaults on the loan, the lender will be able to foreclose not only on the woman's interest but also on that of her husband, thus getting clear title to the real estate. On the other hand, by not signing the promissory note, the non-applicant spouse has no obligation to make any payments.

Therefore, mortgage lenders can ask about marital status, but may only ask: "Are you married, unmarried, or separated?" Further, a lender should not ask for courtesy titles (Mrs., Miss, Ms., Mr., Dr., or any other title).

Cosigner

A mortgage lender cannot require an applicant to get a cosigner or guarantor if the applicant qualifies independently. If a cosigner is required, a mortgage lender cannot stipulate who that person will be, but instead should say, "Anyone who qualifies is acceptable."

Mortgage lenders may not request information regarding the applicant's spouse, unless:

- Spouse will be a user of the account
- Applicants reside in a community property state
- Applicant relies on the spouse's income to support the credit
- Applicant relies on alimony, child support, or separate maintenance as a basis for repayment

As discussed, if real estate will be taken as collateral for a loan, the mortgage lender can require a non-applicant spouse to sign the security instrument (but not the promissory note). On the other hand, if a nonworking spouse wants to sign the note (to build up a credit history), a mortgage lender should not deny that request.

Copy of the Appraisal

ECOA requires that a mortgage lender must supply the mortgage applicant with a copy of the real estate appraisal if a copy is requested. Most lenders routinely provide a copy of the appraisal today, while other lenders do so only when requested (after the applicant is informed of right to the appraisal). A mortgage lender can charge a fee to copy the appraisal, but usually it does not.

Notice of Status of the Application

A mortgage lender must notify the applicant if the application is approved, incomplete, or denied—or a counteroffer is being made. Notification must occur within 30 calendar days after receiving a *complete application*. According to ECOA, a mortgage application is considered complete when all required information has been received by the lender. RESPA and HMDA definitions of a complete application are very different. If the application has multiple applicants, a lender needs to give notice to only one.

ECOA does not require a written notice if a lender approves an application, but this practice is common and highly recommended. All other actions require written notice.

Adverse Action

If the application is incomplete, a lender may send either a notice of incomplete application or adverse action within 30 days. The notice should state by what date information must be received and must also state that if the information is not received by that date, the lender will consider the application withdrawn. A lender must notify a consumer in writing of an *adverse action*. The form used to provide this information is called a Statement of Credit Denial, Termination, or Change, as shown in Figure 11.2.

Adverse action can mean either a straight denial by the lender of the terms applied for, or that the applicant does not accept a *counteroffer* by the lender. A **counteroffer** is a situation in which a lender does not accept the original application terms, but the lender does offer terms different than requested. In this situation, adverse action occurs if the applicant does not accept the lender's counteroffer.

If the adverse action taken is a result of information obtained from a credit report, the lender must disclose the name, address, and telephone number of the consumer reporting agency; in addition, the lender must provide the ECOA Notice. If the adverse action is a result of information from a third party, then the adverse action notice must disclose that.

Government Monitoring

Mortgage lenders are required (for the purpose of government monitoring of discrimination) to ask applicants to provide the following information:

- Ethnicity: Hispanic or Latino, or Not Hispanic or Latino
- Race or national origin: American Indian or Alaskan Native, Native Hawaiian or other Pacific Islander, Asian, White, Black or African American
- Sex: Male or Female

The mortgage lender must inform applicants that the federal government requires this information. Lenders can ask for this information only if it will be reported to the government (thus, lenders should be careful not to use a first mortgage application for a second mortgage unless the lender also reports on seconds). If an applicant decides not to provide this information, a lender must, to the best of its ability based on visual observation or surname, provide the information. If the mortgage application is mailed to a lender or received through the Internet and the applicant did not provide the required information, the lender is not in violation of this requirement if the completed application does not have this information.

Mortgage lenders must retain the mortgage application, monitoring information, and any notice of adverse action for at least 25 months.

Consumer Privacy Regulations

There are several federal regulations that involve—either directly or indirectly—the safety and privacy of consumers' information and their rights. Some of these

FIGURE **11.2** Notice of Action Taken

NOTICE OF ACTION TAKEN

The Federal Equal Credit Opportunity Act prohibits creditors from discriminating against credit applicants on the basis of race, color, religion, national origin, sex, marital status, age (provided that the applicant has the capacity to enter into a binding contract); because all or part of the applicant's income derives from any public assistance program; or because the applicant has in good faith exercised any right under the Consumer Credit Protection Act. The Federal Agency that administers compliance with this law concerning this creditor is:

National Credit Union Administration
9 Washington Square, Albany, NY 12205

THOMAS PINKOWISH,

ESSEX, CT 06426

Date:
American Eagle Federal Credit Union
417 Main Street
East Hartford, CT 06118-0128

Dear THOMAS PINKOWISH

Thank you for your Application for

Based upon your Application we must inform you that:

[X] We are unable to make a decision on your Application because it is missing the following information:

2009 and 2008 tax returns, complete, signed and all schedules attached

Please furnish this information to us on or before 12/21/2010 at the address listed above or we will be unable to give further consideration to your credit request.

[ ] We are unable to offer you credit on the terms that you requested, but can offer you credit on the following terms:

If this offer is acceptable to you, please notify us on or before _____ at the address listed above.

[ ] If checked, our principal reasons for denying your original request are indicated below.

[ ] We are regrettably unable to approve your request. Our principal reasons for this decision are indicated below.

Where applicable, the following are our principal reasons for taking adverse action:

[X] Credit Application Incomplete	[ ] Excessive Obligations in Relation to Income	[ ] Delinquent Past/Present Credit Obligations w/Others
[ ] Insufficient Number of Credit References Provided	[ ] Unable to Verify Income	[ ] Collection Action or Judgment
[ ] Unacceptable Type of Credit References Provided	[ ] Length of Residence	[ ] Garnishment or Attachment
[ ] Unable to Verify Credit References	[ ] Temporary Residence	[ ] Foreclosure or Repossession
[ ] Temporary or Irregular Employment	[ ] Unable to Verify Residence	[ ] Bankruptcy
[ ] Unable to Verify Employment	[ ] No Credit File	[ ] Number of Recent Inquiries on Credit Bureau Report
[ ] Length of Employment	[ ] Limited Credit Experience	[ ] Value or Type of Collateral not Sufficient
[ ] Income Insufficient for Amount of Credit Requested	[ ] Poor Credit Performance with Us	
[ ] Other, specify: _____		

If you have any questions regarding this notice, you should contact:

Creditor's Name: American Eagle Federal Credit Union
Creditor's Address: 417 Main Street
East Hartford, CT 06118-0128
Creditor's Telephone Number: 860-568-2020

DISCLOSURE OF USE OF INFORMATION OBTAINED FROM AN OUTSIDE SOURCE:

[ ] Our credit decision was based in whole or in part on information obtained in a report from the consumer reporting agency listed below. You have a right under the Fair Credit Reporting Act to know the information contained in your credit file at the consumer reporting agency. The reporting agency played no part in our decision and is unable to supply specific reasons why we have denied credit to you. You also have a right to a free copy of your report from the reporting agency, if you request it no later than 60 days after you receive this notice. In addition, if you find that any information contained in the report you receive is inaccurate or incomplete, you have the right to dispute the matter with the reporting agency.

Name: _____   Telephone Number: _____
Address: _____   or
                                 Toll Free Number: _____

[ ] Our credit decision was based in whole or in part on information obtained from an affiliate or from an outside source other than a consumer reporting agency. Under the Fair Credit Reporting Act, you have the right to make a written request, no later than 60 days after you receive this notice, for disclosure of the nature of this information.

You have the right to a copy of the appraisal report used in connection with your application for credit. If you wish a copy, please write to us at the mailing address we have provided. We must hear from you no later than 90 days after we notify you about the action taken on your credit application or you withdraw your application.

VMP -132 (0404)   VMP Mortgage Solutions, Inc. (800)521-7291   9/03

Source: REMOC Associates, LLC www.remoc.com

regulations impact our society way beyond commerce or financial products and services, and do not apply just to residential lending. However, as the residential lending environment changed with more technology and overall complexity, it has become more difficult for lenders to manage the double issues of (a) maintaining consumer privacy to avoid predatory lending practices, and (b) securing consumers' private information to avoid identity theft. In response, older, existing regulations have evolved, and new ones have been introduced in an attempt to keep up with technologies and practices in mortgage lending. These regulations heavily impact mortgage origination and lending operations, software, and procedures.

Uniting and Strengthening America by Providing Appropriate Tools Required to Intercept and Obstruct Terrorism Act (USA PATRIOT)

The USA PATRIOT Act was enacted into law just 45 days after the terrorist attacks on September 11, 2001. It helps fight the funding of terrorism and money laundering activities. Section 326 requires financial institutions to obtain, verify, and record information which identifies each person opening an account.

This applies to mortgage applications and all mortgage originators, who have three basic responsibilities under this act:

1. At application, obtain each applicant's name, address, date of birth, taxpayer ID (for U.S. persons), or other information that will help identify the applicant. Verification is most often made by a government-issued photo ID.
2. Compare the applicants' identification to government lists and report to the appropriate federal agency, if required.
3. Provide a Privacy Notice to applicants "not later than when the loan contract is executed," but most mortgage lenders and originators provide it at first contact/application.

FAIR CREDIT REPORTING ACT

The FCRA was enacted in 1970 and amended several times for specific purposes. Generally, it regulates the activities of consumer reporting agencies and users of consumer credit reports, and is enforced by the Federal Trade Commission. It also describes how a lender must communicate with a consumer if an application is denied or adversely affected because of information on a credit report or from another source.

A "consumer report" (credit report) can be written, oral, or other communication of information *from a consumer reporting agency* relating to credit, character, general reputation, personal characteristics, or mode of living. This does not include internal communications or that which bypasses the consumer reporting agency (such as information from a verification of mortgage, rent, etc.). The report cannot contain information regarding bankruptcies more than 10 years old. Credit reports cannot contain adverse information over seven years old unless it was in connection with a credit of $50,000 or more. Consumer reporting agencies must provide free of charge a credit report if a consumer was turned down for a loan because of a credit report.

A mortgage lender may share the contents of a credit report with a mortgage applicant. This, however, does not make the lender a consumer reporting agency.

Generally, lenders can obtain credit reports only to determine whether or not the applicant has acceptable credit for the loan requested. Lenders can also obtain reports to prescreen a list of customers to be solicited for credit services, as long as the lender meets certain conditions.

If a lender denies a loan because of information on a credit report, it must notify each consumer separately of that fact and disclose: (a) the name, street address, and telephone number of the consumer reporting agency supplying the report, (b) the consumer's right to dispute the accuracy of the credit report, and (c) the consumer's right to a free credit report. A similar notice is required if the information is from a third party source.

FAIR AND ACCURATE CREDIT TRANSACTIONS ACT

The FCRA was expanded with the FACT Act amendment in 2003. It provides consumers with additional rights in how their credit information is reported, and also requires all businesses (including mortgage originators, lenders, and servicers) to enact policies to help prevent identity theft.

The FACT Act entitles consumers to a free credit report annually from each of the three nationwide consumer reporting agencies in order to verify its accuracy and to help discover identity theft. It also allows consumers to have more control in or restrict the type and amount of marketing solicitations they receive.

The FACT Act requires lenders to disclose to the applicant that his or her credit score was used to evaluate a residential mortgage application. A lender must also notify the consumer within 30 days when the lender reports negative credit information for him/her to a consumer reporting agency.

Finally, the FTC issued the "Red Flags Rule" to assist originators, lenders, and servicers to establish an identity theft program. This program must include identifying what kinds of risk factors and red flags the business will likely encounter, procedures on how to detect them, steps taken to prevent and mitigate identity theft, and how the program will be monitored and updated. These two sources provide valuable information on this rule:

1. "Fighting Fraud with the Red Flags Rule: A How-to Guide for Business"
   www.ftc.gov/bcp/edu/pubs/business/idtheft/bus23.pdf
2. FTC Web site FAQ page
   www.ftc.gov/bcp/edu/microsites/redflagsrule/faqs.shtm

GRAMM-LEACH-BLILEY FINANCIAL MODERNIZATION ACT OF 1999

Congress enacted Gramm-Leach-Bliley Financial Modernization Act of 1999 (GLBA) to recognize the changing electronic and Internet communication environments in which businesses now operate. GLBA has many parts that govern business operation, but our focus is on the consumer financial privacy provisions.

The FTC issued two rules that help implement GLBA requirements:

1. **Privacy of Consumer Financial Information (Privacy Rule)**
   http://www.ftc.gov/bcp/edu/pubs/business/idtheft/bus67.pdf
2. **Standards for Insuring the Security, Integrity, and Protection of Customer Records and Information (Safeguards Rule)**
   http://www.ftc.gov/bcp/edu/pubs/business/idtheft/bus54.pdf

The FTC and seven other federal agencies are responsible for enacting these rules and enforcing their provisions. These rules require that *financial institutions* protect a *consumer's nonpublic personal information* (NPI) collected, and that they notify *consumers* of these practices (does not apply to businesses).

GLBA Definitions

The FTC Privacy and Safeguards rules have very specific terms and definitions that impact mortgage lending:

- A *financial institution* includes depositories, lenders, mortgage bankers, mortgage brokers, mortgage servicers, credit counseling agencies, real estate settlement service providers, debt collectors, etc.
- A *consumer* is an individual who obtains a financial product or service for non-business reasons.
- A *customer* is an individual who has a continuing (significant) relationship with that financial institution, and remains one until the relationship stops. A mortgage applicant is a customer of a mortgage broker or banker or lender.

Generally, *nonpublic personal information* (NPI) is all information that the financial institution obtains directly from the consumer. NPI includes information disclosed during loan application, which can be given verbally or electronically, or can be written documentation submitted (deposit or loan statements, IRS returns or W-2s, etc.). Even public information can be considered NPI if the financial institution obtains it directly from the consumer and not from the public source (i.e., existing mortgage lien info). It also includes information that the consumer authorizes the financial institution to obtain:

- A credit report
- Verification of deposit, loan, or employment
- Appraisal

Privacy Notice

These rules limit when a financial institution may disclose a consumer's NPI to nonaffiliated third parties, and require them to notify their customers via a clear, conspicuous, accurate, written Privacy Notice. This notice must detail how the financial institution collects, shares, protects, and safeguards the customers' NPI. Only a customer is entitled to receive a privacy notice automatically and annually, as long as the customer relationship lasts. The consumer must receive a privacy notice only if the financial institution shares his information with companies not affiliated with it, with some exceptions. The privacy notice applies to NPI, and must be mailed or hand-delivered prior to consummation of the business transaction. It can be delivered electronically if so authorized by the consumer, but most lenders provide the notice at first contact.

Consumer's Right to "Opt Out"

The financial institution's Privacy Notice also must inform the customer of his right to "opt-out"—not allow the financial institution to share NPI with nonaffiliated third parties—and explain how to do so. Even if the consumer or customer has not opted out, financial institutions cannot disclose account numbers for telemarketing, direct mail, or other marketing through e-mail, or engage in pretexting—the practice of obtaining customer information from financial institutions under false pretenses.

Finally, in a secondary market transaction where one or more mortgage brokers, bankers, lenders, and servicers may be involved for a single mortgage application, a special rule applies:

> How to Comply with the Privacy of Consumer Financial Information Rule of the Gramm-Leach-Bliley Act—A Guide for Small Businesses from the Federal Trade Commission July 2002

A Word About Customer Relationships and Loans

A special rule defines the customer relationship when several financial institutions participate in a loan transaction. A financial institution establishes a customer relationship with an individual when it originates a loan. If the financial institution sells the loan but maintains the servicing rights, it continues to have a customer relationship with the individual. If the financial institution transfers the servicing rights but retains an ownership interest in the loan, the individual is a "consumer" of that institution and a "customer" of the institution with the servicing rights. If other institutions hold an ownership interest in the loan (but not the servicing rights), the individual is their consumer, too.

Telemarketing Sales Rule

Another area of concern for consumer privacy deals with telemarketing sales and fraud. On January 29, 2003, the FTC enacted the Telemarketing Sales Rule, amending several prior rules (and the rule itself has been modified since its effective date of March 31, 2003).

http://www2.ftc.gov/os/2003/01/tsrfrn.pdf

The rule contains requirements concerning deceptive and abusive telemarketing acts or practices.

"Do Not Call" Registry

The rule establishes a national "do not call" registry maintained by the commission. The registry allows consumers to remove their telephone number(s) from telemarketing call lists (although certain calls from certain political organizations, charities, and telephone surveyors may still be permitted). Calls from companies with whom the consumer has an existing business relationship may still be permitted for up to 18 months after the relationship ends, unless the consumer asks the company not to call again. The consumer must give authorization for all other calls.

The rule prohibits sellers and telemarketers from calling the numbers in the registry. This includes any plan, program, or campaign to sell goods or services through interstate phone calls, and offers to provide goods or services, and it applies to for-profit telemarketers calling consumers on behalf of an *Exempt Organization*. Sellers and telemarketers must synchronize their call lists with the FTC Do Not Call Registry list every 31 days and remove those telephone numbers.

More detailed information for businesses and consumers is available at:

- Q&A for Telemarketers and Sellers About the Do Not Call Provisions of the FTC's Telemarketing Sales Rule (for businesses): http://www.ftc.gov/bcp/edu/pubs/business/alerts/alt129.pdf
- Q&A: The National Do Not Call Registry (for consumers): http://www.ftc.gov/bcp/edu/pubs/consumer/alerts/alt107.pdf

TRUTH IN LENDING ACT (TILA)

The Consumer Credit Protection Act of 1968 (as amended) contains Title I, known as the Truth in Lending Act (or as it is often called, Regulation Z). TILA is enforced by the Federal Reserve Board of Governors. The basic purpose of this legislation is to provide consumers with an easily understandable means of comparing the credit offerings of various lenders. The desired result is that consumers will then shop for the most favorable credit terms.

The FRB amended TILA periodically as the mortgage lending industry became more complex. The most recent and very extensive amendments came in 2008 from the FRB and from Congress via the Mortgage Disclosure Improvement Act. These changes affect RESPA, HMDA, and TILA. They broaden the scope of TILA significantly, with several dates effective in 2009 and 2010. Unfortunately, not all changes apply to the same situations, and at times use undefined terms. The result is that the affected regulations are more difficult to interpret and confusing to implement.

TILA is an evolving regulation, and the FRB has more proposed changes pending. It is another "cradle to grave" regulation like FHA and ECOA, with a broad range of requirements. Generally, lenders must comply with the following:

- Advertise first and second mortgage programs and terms in a manner consistent with guidelines and restrictions
- Calculate and disclose the Annual Percentage Rate, finance charges, and amount financed within three business days of application and again when appropriate
- Provide any applicable special disclosures for an adjustable rate mortgage or Home Equity Line of Credit when a consumer expresses interest in them

- Follow restrictions on collecting fees from applicants and waiting appropriate periods to close
- Notify consumers of their right of rescission and extend that right at closing, when applicable
- Avoid coercion of appraisers
- Report and offer appropriate *Higher Priced Mortgage Loans,* if required
- Report and offer appropriate *High Cost Mortgage Loans,* if required
- Design, disclose, and service home equity lines of credit as required
- Follow appropriate servicing practices for payment posting, late fees, and payoffs
- Notify consumers of certain billing rights

Scope

TILA covers consumer purpose loans in amounts less than or equal to $25,000, or any consumer purpose loan, regardless of size, if secured by a one- to four-family dwelling or real property (e.g., vacant land). Business loans are *not* included in this regulation. Agricultural or loans to "non-natural persons" are *not* included in this regulation.

Disclosures

TILA requires mortgage lenders to provide early disclosures to the consumer (see the TILA form in Figure 12.1 on p. 367) including the following required loan application information:

- *Annual Percentage Rate* (APR)
- *Amount financed*
- *Finance charges*
- Loan payment schedule(s)
- The following statement: "You are not required to complete this agreement merely because you have reviewed these disclosures or signed a loan application."

With today's origination software, many lenders provide this and other disclosures at the time of application. If a lender is not able to provide this disclosure at the application stage, it must be provided within three business days after receiving the mortgage loan application. Whenever the above terms are used, they must be more conspicuous than any other term.

Finance Charge

The finance charge that must be disclosed is the cost of consumer credit expressed as a dollar amount. Charges that are included in the finance charge are as follows:

- Interest adjustments (odd day's interest)
- Loan discounts
- Origination fee
- Mortgage insurance premiums
- Underwriting fee
- Fees for determining current tax lien status

- Fees for determining flood insurance requirements
- Borrower-paid mortgage broker fees
- Any other service, transaction, activity, or carrying charge

Typical charges not included (generally, third-party fees) are as follows:

- Appraisal fees
- Credit reports
- Title examination fees
- Loan document preparation fees
- Property survey fees
- Amounts required to be paid into escrow

TILA allows a finance charge error tolerance of $50 for mortgage loans involving regular transactions, and $100 for irregular transactions. However, recent changes to the Good Faith Estimate Form and the FRB's 2009 proposal to revise TILA indicate that finance charges and APR calculations may change drastically in upcoming years.

Annual Percentage Rate (APR)

Probably no other disclosure is as baffling to the average consumer as the Annual Percentage Rate. Few understand how the APR can be higher (or even lower) than the interest rate at closing. The APR is the finance charge expressed as a numerical percentage, which is an expression of the annualized finance charge. Thus, the APR includes the interest rate plus all of those items that are included in the finance charge.

Although few mortgage lenders actually do it, lenders are required to disclose the APR when inquiries are made orally. The APR disclosures also have error tolerances:

- For Regular Transactions—APR within one eighth percent
- For Irregular Transactions—APR within one quarter percent

If a lender discovers an error in the APR or Finance Charge, it has 60 days within which to make restitution, and if done in a timely manner, the lender has no penalty. *NOTE: this timeline is different than RESPA/MDIA requirements for GFE errors.*

Adjustable Rate Mortgage (ARM) Disclosures

If the mortgage loan requested is an ARM, the early disclosure described previously must include a composite APR that reflects the initial discount and full indexed rate for the remaining term. Additionally, whenever the consumer "expresses interest" in an ARM product (it may be even before completing an application) the mortgage lender must provide (a) the CHARM (*Consumer Handbook on Adjustable Rate Mortgages*) booklet, and (b) the ARM loan program disclosure, which explains how this particular type of ARM loan will adjust in the future, as well as other significant program features. It also includes a historical example of a $10,000 loan, illustrating how interest rate changes over the past 15 years affect payments and the loan balance. See Figure 11.3 for an example of an Adjustable Rate Mortgage Disclosure.

FIGURE **11.3** Advanced ARM Disclosure Form

FIVE / ONE ADJUSTABLE RATE MORTGAGE DISCLOSURE (CONVERTIBLE)

Interest Rate Caps 2/6

LIBOR Index

This disclosure describes features of the _____ adjustable rate mortgage (ARM) program you are considering. Information about our other ARM programs is available upon request.

The undersigned acknowledges receipt of this disclosure and a copy of the "Consumer Handbook on Adjustable Rate Mortgages".

How Your Interest Rate and Monthly Payment are Determined:

-Your interest rate will be adjusted based on an index plus a margin, rounded to the nearest 1/8th of 1%.

-Your interest rate will be adjusted based on the following index: the one-year London Interbank Offered Rate ("LIBOR") which is the average of interbank offered rates for one-year U.S. dollar-denominated deposits in the London market, as published in The *Wall Street Journal.* If this index is no longer available, we will choose a comparable index, which is based on comparable information. We will give you notice of this choice.

-Your interest rate will be adjusted to equal the index plus our margin, rounded to the nearest 1/8th of 1%, unless your interest rate "caps" limit the amount of change in the interest rate.

-Your initial interest rate is not based on the index used to make later adjustments. Your initial interest rate may be discounted or may include a premium. Ask us for our current initial rate and margin, and the amount of our current discount or premium.

-Your monthly payment of principal and interest ("monthly payment") will be adjusted based on the interest rate, loan balance, and remaining loan term.

How Your Interest Rate Can Change:

-Your interest rate can change after 5 years, and every 12 months thereafter.

-At each rate adjustment, your interest rate will not increase or decrease by more than 2 percentage points.

-Your interest rate will not increase or decrease more than 6 percentage points over the term of the loan. In addition, your interest rate will never be less than the margin.

How Your Monthly Payment Can Change:

-Your monthly payment can change after 5 years, and every 12 months thereafter, whenever the interest rate changes. Your monthly payment can increase or decrease substantially based on changes in the interest rate.

-For example, on a $10,000 loan with a **30-year Amortization Period** and an initial interest rate of 4.750%* in effect in July 2010, the maximum amount that the interest rate can rise under this program is 6%, to 10.750%. The monthly payment of principal and interest could rise from a first year payment of $52.16 to a maximum of $87.06 in the 8th year of the loan.

-To see what your payment would be, divide your mortgage amount by $10,000. Then multiply the result of this division by the monthly payment stated above. For example, the initial monthly payment for a mortgage amount of $60,000 would be: $60,000 divided by $10,000 equals 6; 6 multiplied by $52.16 equals $312.96 per month.

-For example, on a $10,000 loan with a **15-year Amortization Period** and an initial interest rate of 4.750%* in effect in July 2010, the maximum amount that the interest rate can rise under this program is 6%, to 10.750%. The monthly payment of principal and interest could rise from a first year payment of $77.78 to a maximum of $98.97 in the 8th year of the loan.

-To see what your payment would be, divide your mortgage amount by $10,000. Then multiply the result of this division by the monthly payment stated above. For example, the initial monthly payment for a mortgage amount of $60,000 would be: $60,000 divided by $10,000 equals 6; 6 multiplied by $77.78 equals $466.68 per month.

-You will be notified in writing at least 25 days before the monthly payment is adjusted. This notice will contain information about the index, your interest rate, monthly payment amount, and loan balance.

FIGURE **11.3** (*Continued*)

<u>Fixed Interest Rate Conversion Option:</u>

This ARM Program permits you to convert your loan to a fixed rate mortgage loan. You may exercise your option to convert to a fixed rate mortgage on a date(s) specified by the Note Holder during the period beginning on the first change date and ending on the fifth change date.

To exercise your conversion option, you must meet certain conditions. Those conditions are that: (I) you must give the Note Holder notice that you want to do so; (II) on the conversion date you must not be in default under the Note or Security Instrument; (III) by a date specified by the Note Holder, you must pay the Note Holder a conversion fee of $250.00; and (IV) you must sign and give the Note Holder any documents the Note Holder requires to effect the conversion.

<u>Calculation of Fixed Rate:</u>

Your new fixed interest rate will be equal to the Federal Home Loan Mortgage Corporation's required net yield as of a date and time specified by the Note Holder for: (I) if the original term of this Note is greater than 15 years, 30-year fixed rate mortgages covered by applicable 60-day mandatory delivery commitments, plus three-eighths of one percentage point (0.375%), rounded to the nearest one-eighth of one percentage point (0.125%); or if the original term of the Note is 15 years or less, 15-year fixed rate mortgages covered by applicable 60-day mandatory delivery commitments, plus three-eighths of one percentage point (0.375%), rounded to the nearest one-eighth of one percentage point (0.125%). If this required net yield cannot be determined because the applicable commitments are not available, the Note Holder will determine your interest rate by using comparable information. Your new rate calculated will not be greater than the maximum rate cap stated in your note.

<u>Disclaimer Notice:</u>

This disclosure is being given to you for information purposes only. In no event shall this disclosure be considered as a commitment by us to make the loan for which you are applying, or to extend any other form of credit to you whatsoever.

* In July 2010 this initial interest rate was equal to the index plus the margin, rounded to the nearest 1/8th of 1%, plus an initial interest rate premium of 1.125%. Your initial rate discount or premium, and also your initial interest rate, may be different.

Source: REMOC Associates, LLC

Adjustable-Rate Adjustment Notice

TILA requires that servicers of ARM loans provide the consumer with rate-adjustment notices 25 to 120 days before a payment at a new level is due. The notice must contain the current and prior interest rate, the index used to calculate the rate, and the new payment rate. The new payment rate is based on the new interest rate and the unpaid principal balance at the time of the adjustment.

Assumptions

A mortgage lender must give a new TIL disclosure if the lender expressly agrees to allow a subsequent mortgagor (who is assuming the existing mortgage) to become the primary obligor on an existing loan.

MDIA AND 2008 TILA REVISIONS/RESPA FINAL RULE

Since TILA and RESPA disclosures work in concert to explain loan terms and closing costs, changes to them needed to be coordinated. The Mortgage Disclosure Improvement Act (MDIA) helps unify the changes in disclosure forms and practices from the 2008 TILA and 2008 RESPA revisions. The MDIA is part of the Housing and Economic Recovery Act and amended TILA, along with the FRB's TILA Revision. HUD's Final Rule amended RESPA.

These changes became effective throughout 2009 and 2010, and were designed to protect consumers from predatory lending practices. They have some real value; however, in practice the changes also have disrupted the origination process significantly and inconvenienced thousands of consumers.

The following sections describe the many complex changes resulting from MDIA and 2008 TILA/RESPA revisions:

Disclosure Practices—for all *closed-end* mortgages secured by a consumer's principal *dwelling*

Now a *lender* (in this context includes a mortgage broker or mortgage banker):

- Must provide early disclosures to purchase *and refinance* transactions within three business days of the application.
- Is responsible for any disclosures previously given to consumers in the same application by mortgage brokers and bankers.
- Must provide the early TIL and GFE disclosures before it can collect any fees from consumers (except for credit report fees). Mailed disclosures are assumed to be received in three business days.
- Cannot close the mortgage loan until after seven business days from the date the consumer receives the TIL/GFE initial disclosures.
- Must provide revised TIL disclosures within three business days if loan terms change the APR beyond the accepted tolerance levels (1/8% regular; 1/4% irregular) or if a *changed circumstance* requires a revised GFE.

- Must delay the closing for three business days after providing revised/corrected/updated TIL/GFE disclosures.

Section 226.2 of the TILA defines a general business day as, "a day when the creditor's offices are open to the public for carrying on substantially all of its business functions." (*Note: Rescission follows a different definition.*)

The mortgage lending industry's "*3/7/3 Rule*" refers collectively to the:

- *Three (3)* business days from application required to disclose initially
- *Seven (7)* business days to wait from initial disclosure before closing
- *Three (3)* business days to wait before closing if revised disclosures are required because of a change in the application that results in either:
  a) a change in APR exceeding tolerance levels, or
  b) a *changed circumstance* affecting the *origination charge* or *other settlement charges* subject to tolerance levels (described later in this chapter's RESPA section)

Reg X&Z Revisions / MDIA
Disclosure / Closing Timeline
Creditor closed Sat/Sun

1 Sun	2 Mon	3 Tue	4 Wed	5 Thurs	6 Fri	7 Sat
				Application *Disc given Face2face Ok to collect Fees	Bus Day 1	
8 Sun	9 Mon	10 Tue	1 Wed	12 Thurs	13 Fri *Face2face Ok 2 close ^Mail Disclosure "Received"	14 Sat ^ok to collect Fees
		^Must mail Disclosure				
	Bus Day 2	Bus Day 3				
15 Sun	16 Mon	17 Tue	18 Wed	19 Thurs	20 Fri	21 Sat
			^Mail-ok to close			

REMOC Associates, LLC

Reg X&Z Revisions / MDIA
Corrected/Revised Disclosure Timeline
Creditor closed Sat/Sun

1 Sun	2 Mon	3 Tues	4 Wed	5 Thurs	6 Fri	7 Sat
				APR Error Discovered *Mail Disclosure*	Bus Day 1	
8 Sun	9 Mon	10 Tue	1 Wed	12 Thurs	13 Fri	14 Sat
		Mail Disclosure "Received"			*Ok to close*	
	Bus Day 2	Bus Day 3	Day 1	Day 2	Day 3	
15 Sun	16 Mon	17 Tue	18 Wed	19 Thurs	20 Fri	21 Sat

REMOC Associates, LLC

Required Lender Practices and Behavior

"*Lender*" in this context may include mortgage brokers and bankers, which are considered to be acting on behalf of the lender if they originate the loan, and the lender approves and funds the loan. In addition to the above disclosure practices, TILA requires *lenders* to follow or avoid the following practices when advertising, processing, and servicing mortgages:

Advertising Practices—for all *closed-end* mortgages secured by a *dwelling*

- Prominently and fully describe promotional terms for rate and payment in all advertisements to consumers.
- Prominently include "triggering terms" in all advertisements to consumers.
- Restrict certain statements in all advertisements to consumers about:
  - "fixed rate" loans, when the rate is fixed for only an initial period
  - government guarantees
  - debt elimination
  - soliciting in the name of the existing lender who holds a consumers' mortgage
- Disclose the annual percentage rate (APR) whenever providing interest rate information (both in oral or written communication with consumers).

- Inform the applicants of the right to rescission (when applicable).
- Disclose loan terms and disclosures in the same language.

Processing Practices—for all closed-end mortgages secured by a consumer's *principal dwelling*

- *Mortgage broker* definition revised—a mortgage broker is now considered to be a *counselor* for the consumer and no longer just an agent for the lender.
  - TILA does not define "*counselor*"

Appraiser definition revised to also include "persons who employ, refer, or manage appraisers and affiliates of such persons."

- Cannot improperly influence appraisers—meaning a lender cannot directly or indirectly coerce, influence, or otherwise encourage an appraiser to misstate or misrepresent the value
- Cannot use an appraisal if improper influence occurs, unless the lender can verify the value was not affected

Servicing Practices—for all closed-end loans secured by a consumer's *principal dwelling*

- Must credit regular payments when received
- Must provide payoff statements promptly
- Cannot "pyramid" late fees

Billing Rights

TILA requires that consumers be notified about their billing rights concerning mortgage loans. Basically, the consumer has 60 days after receiving a billing statement to give the creditor written notice of an error in the billing. The creditor must resolve any alleged billing errors within 90 days of the error notice.

Home Ownership and Equity Protection Act of 1994

TILA was amended by the Home Ownership and Equity Protection Act of 1994 to include special requirements for high-rate, high-fee mortgages (so-called Section 32 and 34 loans). These requirements apply to applications for closed-end loans secured by applicants' principal dwellings when either: (a) the APR is more than 10 percentage points above the yield on a Treasury security with a similar maturity (the HMDA Rate Spread Calculator to test for HOEPA loans is found at www.ffiec.gov/hmda), or (b) the total points and fees that the customer paid at or before closing exceed the greater of eight percent of the loan amount or $592 (the HOEPA fee limit for 2011, adjusted annually by the FRB).

The creditor of a HOEPA loan must provide the following disclosure at least three days before the transaction is consummated (in addition to APR and amount of payment): "You are not required to complete this agreement merely because you have received these disclosures or have signed a loan application. If you obtain this loan, the lender will have a mortgage on your home. You could lose your home, and any money you have put into it, if you do not meet your obligation under the loan."

Mortgage Loan Programs—3 TILA Categories (as of 2009)

A very significant result of MDIA/Reg Z revisions in 2008 impacts loan program, product design, and reporting (see Table 11.1). The recent change to TILA now establishes a third category of loans, *Higher Priced Mortgage Loans (HPML)*, in addition to HOEPA loans (established in 1994 and described above) and normal, *Prime* Mortgages.

Like HOEPA loans, a lender must report the HPML status for all applications on the HMDA Loan Application Register (LAR). Unlike HOEPA loans, there is only one test to determine if an application meets the HPML threshold. The lender must compare the application's APR to the Average Prime Offer Rate (APOR) weekly index determined by the Federal Reserve (there is no fee test or threshold). The FFIEC publishes both old and new rate spread calculators at:

http://www.ffiec.gov/ratespread/default.aspx

If the application's APR exceeds the APOR by 1.5% for a first lien or 3.5% for a subordinate lien, then the lender must report the application as a HPML and must make sure that the loan:

- Requires a tax and insurance escrow for the first year (may allow consumer to drop the escrows after the first year)
- Prohibits a prepayment penalty
- Verifies applicant income and calculates applicant ability to repay the mortgage

Home Equity Loan Consumer Protection Act

The Home Equity Loan Consumer Protection Act of 1988 (HELCPA) is a revision of the TILA, thus the Federal Reserve Board provides commentary and enforcement. This act further extends TILA into Home Equity Lines Of Credit (HELOCs). It covers open-end lines of credit, *not* closed-end seconds. It reinforces that the right of rescission applies to HELOCs. It also requires that lenders provide consumers at application with two documents: (a) the brochure "When Your Home Is On the Line," and (b) the early disclosure of the terms of the lender's HELOC (this disclosure is similar to an "early" TIL explaining how the lender's HELOC works).

The HELCPA also requires a lender to establish a draw and a repayment period. A *draw period* is the period during which the borrower may draw against the line. The *repayment period* is the period during which any balance at the end of the draw period is fully repaid. The combination of the two cannot exceed the maximum term for a mortgage loan in that state. A few lenders let the two periods run concurrently—this could result in a balloon payment, and is probably not competitive in today's market.

TABLE 11.1
Reg Z Revisions Functional Impact

Regulation Z Revision Checklist - Functional Impact on Bank and Lending Areas

Bank/Lending Area	Open-End Credit-Advertising Rules 226.16(d)	Closed-End Credit-General Disclosure Requirements 226.17	Closed-End Credit-Initial Disclosures/Fees 226.19(a)	Closed End Credit-Advertising Rules 226.24	Certain Home Mortgage Transactions-Prepayment Penalty Restrictions 226.32	Certain Home Mortgage Transactions-Underwriting Requirements 226.34	Certain Home Mortgage Transactions-APR Analysis 226.35(a)	Certain Home Mortgage Transactions-Underwriting Requirements 226.35(b)
Board of Directors	M	N	N	M	N	M	M	M
Compliance/Audit	Y	Y	Y	Y	Y	Y	Y	Y
Risk Management	M	M	M	M	M	M	M	M
Marketing/Advertising	Y	Y	Y	Y	Y	Y	Y	Y
Operations	Y	Y	Y	Y	Y	Y	Y	Y
Data Processing	Y	Y	Y	Y	Y	Y	Y	Y
Retail/Consumer Banking	Y	Y	Y	Y	Y	Y	Y	Y
Training	N	N	Y	Y	Y	Y	Y	Y
Loan Committee	N	N	N	Y	Y	Y	Y	Y
Mortgage Dept. Management	Y	Y	Y	Y	Y	Y	Y	Y
Loan Product Design	Y	Y	Y	Y	Y	Y	Y	Y
Loan Production								
Pre-Application	Y	Y	Y	Y	Y	Y	Y	Y
Application	Y	Y	Y	Y	Y	Y	Y	Y
Processing	N	Y	Y	Y	Y	Y	Y	Y
Underwriting	N	Y	Y	Y	Y	Y	Y	Y
Closing	N	Y	N	N	Y	N	N	N
Secondary Mktg./Investor Rel.	N	N	Y	N	Y	Y	Y	Y
Loan Servicing								
Customer Service	Y	Y	N	N	Y	N	N	N
Payment Processing	N	N	N	N	Y	N	N	N
Escrow Administration	N	N	N	N	N	N	N	N
Collections	N	N	N	N	Y	N	N	N
Payoffs	N	N	N	N	Y	N	N	N
Quality Assurance	Y	Y	Y	Y	Y	Y	Y	Y

Y = Direct Impact, N = No Impact, M = Monitors Procedure.

TABLE **11.1**
(Continued)

Regulation Z Revision Checklist - Functional Impact on Bank and Lending Areas

Bank/Lending Area	Regulation Section/General Proicedure							
	Certain Home Mortgage Transactions–Prepayment Penalties 226.35(b)	Certain Home Mortgage Transactions–Escrows 226.35(b)	Certain Home Mortgage Transactions–Mortgage Broker Definition 226.36(a)	Certain Home Mortgage Transactions–Appraisal Coercion 226.36(b)	Certain Home Mortgage Transactions–Payment Processing and Late Fees 226.36(c)	Certain Home Mortgage Transactions–Payoff Statement Practices 226.36(c)	Certain Home Mortgage Transactions–Irregular Payments 226.36(c)	Certain Home Mortgage Transactions–Valid Servicing Charges 226.36(c)
Board of Directors	M	M	M	M	M	M	M	M
Compliance/Audit	Y	Y	Y	Y	Y	Y	Y	Y
Risk Management	M	M	M	M	M	M	M	M
Marketing/Advertising	Y	Y	N	N	N	N	N	N
Operations	Y	Y	N	N	Y	Y	Y	Y
Data Processing	Y	Y	N	N	Y	Y	Y	Y
Retail/Consumer Banking	Y	Y	N	Y	Y	Y	Y	Y
Training	Y	Y	N	Y	Y	Y	Y	Y
Loan Committee	Y	Y	Y	Y	N	N	N	N
Mortgage Dept. Management	Y	Y	Y	Y	Y	Y	Y	Y
Loan Product Design	Y	Y	Y	N	Y	Y	Y	Y
Loan Production								
Pre-Application	Y	Y	N	Y	N	N	N	N
Application	Y	Y	N	Y	N	N	N	N
Processing	Y	Y	N	Y	N	N	N	N
Underwriting	Y	Y	Y	Y	N	N	N	N
Closing	N	N	N	N	N	N	N	N
Secondary Mktg./Investor Rel.	Y	NY	Y	Y	Y	Y	Y	Y
Loan Servicing								
Customer Service	Y	Y	N	Y	Y	Y	Y	Y
Payment Processing	Y	Y	N	N	Y	N	Y	Y
Escrow Administration	N	Y	N	N	Y	N	Y	Y
Collections	Y	Y	N	Y	Y	Y	Y	Y
Payoffs	Y	N	N	N	Y	Y	Y	Y
Quality Assurance	Y	Y	Y	Y	Y	Y	Y	Y

Y = Direct Impact, N = No Impact, M = Monitors Procedure.

Source: ABA, Community Lending Associates, LLC

In addition, TILA requires that a lender must mail at the end of each billing cycle a periodic statement for all HELOC loans. This requirement and other details about HELOC are examined extensively in Chapter 10—Home Equity Lending.

Right to Rescind

One of the most important consumer protection rights TILA grants to consumers is the right of rescission. This allows any consumer who has an ownership interest to cancel certain real estate financial transactions involving his primary residence as security for a debt. The owner occupant does not need to be on the application, note, or mortgage deed in order to have this right to cancel; however, the transaction must be a refinance either with a new lender or involve new funds (not a rate/term refinance with the same lender).

If it is a rescindable transaction, the mortgage lender must at closing give the Notice of Right to Cancel as shown in Figure 11.4, to all parties with a legal interest in the property and who occupy the property as their primary residence. The material disclosure must clearly state that the lender is taking a security interest in the applicant's principal residence (can be a mobile home or trailer), that the applicant has the right to cancel the transaction, how to cancel, the effects of canceling, and the date the right to cancel expires. Each consumer with this right to rescind must receive two copies of the written notice of the right to cancel and one copy of material disclosures.

The right of rescission applies to the following types of loans:

- Loans to purchase (or construct) new principal residence if that loan is secured by existing principal residence (otherwise, does not apply to purchase money mortgages)
- Any added principal as part of refinancing (otherwise, does not apply to refinancing)
- Closed-end seconds and HELOCs, and to all increases in the credit line (but does not apply to advances)

Canceling the Transaction

This right to cancel the transaction must be exercised within three business days of the closing of the loan. For example, if the loan closes on Monday, the clock for rescission begins at midnight on Monday, and the consumer has until midnight on Thursday to exercise the right to cancel the transaction. Sundays and legal holidays are not business days, but all other days are considered business days, whether or not the lender is open for business. (Note: the *rescission business day definition* differs from the *early disclosure business day definition* that applies to providing early disclosures and the applicable waiting periods for closing when issuing early or revised disclosures.)

Notice of cancellation may be given by mail, telegram, or other written communications (notice is considered given when mailed). Any one consumer can cancel, and that cancels the transaction for all parties.

FIGURE **11.4** Sample Notice of Right to Rescission or Cancel Statement

NOTICE OF RIGHT TO CANCEL

LENDER: American Eagle Federal Credit Union

DATE 01/31/2011
LOAN NO.
TYPE Conventional

BORROWERS/OWNERS THOMAS J. PINKOWISH,

ADDRESS
CITY/STATE/ZIP   ESSEX, CT 06426
PROPERTY
        ESSEX, CT 06426

YOUR RIGHT TO CANCEL

You are entering into a transaction that will result in a mortgage/lien/security interest on your home. You have a legal right under federal law to cancel this transaction, without cost, within THREE BUSINESS DAYS from whichever of the following events occurs last:

(1) The date of the transaction, which is January 31, 2011
        or
(2) The date you received your Truth In Lending disclosures;
        or
(3) The date you received this notice of your right to cancel.

If you cancel the transaction, the mortgage/lien/security interest is also cancelled. Within 20 CALENDAR DAYS after we receive your notice, we must take the steps necessary to reflect the fact that the mortgage/lien/security interest on your home has been cancelled, and we must return to you any money or property you have given to us or to anyone else in connection with this transaction.

You may keep any money or property we have given you until we have done the things mentioned above, but you must then offer to return the money or property. If it is impractical or unfair for you to return the property, you must offer its reasonable value. You may offer to return the property at your home or at the location of the property. Money must be returned to the address below. If we do not take possession of the money or property within 20 CALENDAR DAYS of your offer, you may keep it without further obligation.

HOW TO CANCEL

If you decide to cancel this transaction, you may do so by notifying us in writing, at:

American Eagle Federal Credit Union
417 Main Street
East Hartford, CT 06118-0128

You may use any written statement that is signed and dated by you and states your intention to cancel, or you may use this notice by dating and signing below. Keep one copy of this notice because it contains important information about your rights.

If you cancel by mail or telegram, you must send the notice no later than MIDNIGHT of February 03, 2011   (or MIDNIGHT of the THIRD BUSINESS DAY following the latest of the three events listed above). If you send or deliver your written notice to cancel some other way, it must be delivered to the above address no later than that time.

I WISH TO CANCEL

_____   _____
CONSUMER'S SIGNATURE   DATE

Each of the borrowers/owners in this transaction has the right to cancel. The exercise of this right by one borrower/owner shall be effective as to all borrowers/owners.

The undersigned each acknowledge receipt of two copies of NOTICE of RIGHT TO CANCEL

X_____   1/31/2011   X_____
BORROWER/OWNER THOMAS J. PINKOWISH   DATE   BORROWER/OWNER   DATE

X_____   X_____
BORROWER/OWNER   DATE   BORROWER/OWNER   DATE

CONFIRMATION CERTIFICATE

DO NOT SIGN UNTIL THREE BUSINESS DAYS HAVE ELAPSED

Three business days have elapsed since the undersigned have received two copies of this document. Each of the undersigned hereby certify and warrant that they have not exercised any right which they may have to rescind the transaction, that they do not desire to do so, and that they ratify and confirm the transaction in all respects.

                             2/4/2011
_____   _____
BORROWER/OWNER THOMAS J. PINKOWISH   DATE   BORROWER/OWNER   DATE

_____   _____
BORROWER/OWNER   DATE   BORROWER/OWNER   DATE

VMP -66 (0305).02
VMP Mortgage Solutions (800)521-7291   10/00

Source: REMOC Associates, LLC

Confirmation of Non-cancellation

Mortgage lenders should (but are not required to) use a Notice of Right to Rescission (or Cancel) form that has a section for the consumers to confirm that they have not exercised their right to cancel. A lender should not disburse any funds until consumers sign the form confirming that they have not exercised the right to cancel. If this form is not signed, a lender should wait a reasonable period of time for the mail to be delivered before disbursing any funds.

Until the three-day period expires, the creditor may not:

- Disburse any funds
- Permit any services to be performed
- Permit any materials to be delivered

If the transaction is rescinded, the creditor must:

- Cancel the transaction
- Not charge any interest or other finance charge
- Return any money received

In rare situations, the right of rescission can be waived so that monies can be disbursed immediately if any of the following conditions are met:

- A personally handwritten note is delivered to the lender explaining a bona fide, personal or financial emergency.
- A letter specifically waives the right to rescind.
- A letter containing the signatures of *all* persons having the right to rescind is delivered to the lender.
- Printed forms for these purposes are prohibited except when allowed by the Federal Reserve (e.g., natural disaster).

If the mortgagor is not given the proper right of rescission notice, the right to rescind shall extend to the earliest of the following times:

- Three years from closing
- Transfer of consumer's interest in the property
- Sale of the property

The TILA amendments of 1995 provided special rescission rules for borrowers in *foreclosure*:

- Mortgagor can rescind any time after foreclosure if mortgage broker fee is not included in finance charge.
- Rescission notice did not follow FRB's prescribed form.
- Three-year time limit still applies.

REAL ESTATE SETTLEMENT PROCEDURES ACT (REGULATION X)

RESPA was enacted in 1974 to ensure that consumers are provided with full disclosure of the costs involved in the real estate settlement process. Like TILA, RESPA expanded with subsequent amendments and is now a full "cradle to grave" regulation. RESPA is enforced by HUD.

Scope

RESPA applies to federally related mortgage loans, which basically means *all* residential mortgage loans. In 1994, coverage expanded to include subordinate liens. RESPA does not apply to the following transactions:

- Construction loans
- Loans on 25 acres or more
- Business purpose loans, unless security is residence
- Vacant land
- Bona fide secondary market transactions

RESPA also prohibits such practices as these:

- Illegal kickbacks
- Referral fees
- Excessive escrow requirements

Required Disclosures

Like TILA, RESPA can require various disclosures at different stages of the mortgage lending transaction as shown in Table 11.2. The exact rules for each disclosure listed below differ, depending on the transaction:

A) *Origination Disclosures*

- Special Information Booklet (HUD's Settlement Cost Booklet)
- Initial Servicing Disclosure Statement
- Affiliated Business Arrangement Disclosure
- Good Faith Estimate Form

B) *Closing Disclosures*

- HUD-1 or HUD-1A Settlement Statement
- Initial Escrow Statement

TABLE **11.2**
RESPA Disclosure Requirement Summary

Forms	First Liens	Equity (Closed)	Equity (Open-End)
Servicing Disclosure	Yes	No	No
Good Faith Estimate	Yes	Yes	No
Closing Cost Booklet	Yes—Purchase only	No—Unless to purchase	No
HUD-1 or HUD-1a	Yes	Yes	No
Initial / Annual Escrow Statement	Yes	Yes	Yes
Notice of Transfer of Servicing	Yes	No	No

Source: HUD

C) Servicing Disclosures

- Annual Escrow Statement
- Servicing Transfer Statement (transferor and transferee)

Special Information Booklet

For purchase transactions, RESPA requires that the lender provide an applicant with HUD's newly updated Special Information Booklet (now called *Shopping for your Home Loan*) at the time of application or within three business days. The recent March 2010 edition (see Figure 11.5) updates the information from the 1997 version (*Settlement Costs and You*). Through this publication, HUD provides consumers with advice through the entire home process as well as an overview of the process of purchasing real estate, including:

- A list of recommended steps that the consumer should take during this process
- An explanation of the various roles of the real estate broker, the lender, the appraiser, the attorney, and others
- A discussion of a buyer's rights, including the various compliance disclosures
- An explanation of the Good Faith Estimate Form and HUD-1 Settlement Statement, and the fees that are disclosed on these forms

    The updated booklet contains 48 pages. This version can be found at: http://www.hud.gov/offices/hsg/ramh/res/settlementmarch25revised.pdf

Servicing Disclosure Statement

RESPA, as amended in 1990 and 2008, requires mortgage lenders to provide applicants with a Servicing Disclosure Statement within three business days of application. The simplified disclosure declares the lender's ability to service loans as shown in Figure 11.6.

Affiliated Business Relationship Disclosure

If a business relationship exists between the lender and a particular provider or group of providers, the lender must disclose this to the consumer with the GFE using an *Affiliated Business Relationship Disclosure:* provider's name, type of service provided, and nature of relationship to lender.

MDIA and HUD's RESPA Final Rule November 2008

Overview

Similar to TILA, RESPA's most recent changes became effective in 2009 and 2010 through two sources: HUD's 2008 RESPA Final Rule and the MDIA. The changes impact the design and use of three RESPA disclosures: the Good Faith Estimate Form (extensively), the HUD-1 and -1A Settlement Statements (moderately), and the Servicing Disclosure (minimally). They include:

- Revising RESPA's two most comprehensive disclosures, the Good Faith Estimate Form (GFE) and Settlement Statement (HUD-1/HUD-1A)

FIGURE **11.5** Sample HUD Special Information Booklet

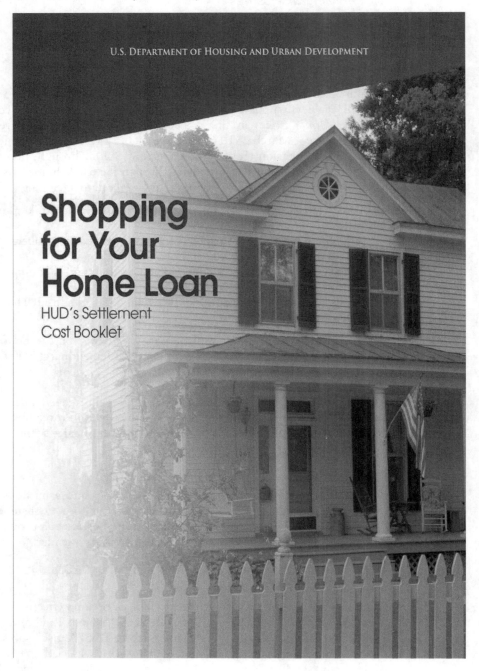

FIGURE **11.5** (*Continued*)

Table of Contents

I.   **Introduction**
                Purchasing Time-line
II.   **Before You Buy**
                Are You Ready to be a Homeowner?
III.   **Determining What You Can Afford**
IV.   **Shopping for a House**
                Role of the Real Estate Broker
                Role of an Attorney
                Terms of the Sales Agreement
                Affiliated Businesses
                Builders
V.   **Shopping for a Loan**
                Loan Originator
                Types of Loans and Programs
VI.   **Good Faith Estimate (GFE)**
                Page 1
                Page 2
                Page 3
VII.   **Shopping for Other Settlement Services**
VIII.   **Your Settlement and HUD-1**
                Page 1
                Page 2
                Page 3
IX.   **Your Loan after Settlement**
X.   **Home Equity and Refinances**
XI.   **Appendix**
        Additional Information
        Contact Information
        Glossary of Terms
                Types of Mortgage Loan Products
        HUD-1 Settlement Statement
        The Do List/The Don't List

2

Source: www.HUD.gov

FIGURE **11.6** Servicing Disclosure Statement

THE McCUE MORTGAGE COMPANY
ONE LIBERTY SQUARE
NEW BRITAIN, CT 06050

Date: **February 03, 2011**

SERVICING DISCLOSURE STATEMENT

**NOTICE TO FIRST LIEN MORTGAGE LOAN APPLICANTS: THE RIGHT TO COLLECT
YOUR MORTGAGE LOAN PAYMENTS MAY BE TRANSFERRED**

You are applying for a mortgage loan covered by the Real Estate Settlement Procedures Act (RESPA) (12 U.S.C. 2601 et seq.). RESPA gives you certain rights under Federal law. This statement describes whether the servicing for this loan may be transferred to a different loan servicer. "Servicing" refers to collecting your principal, interest, and escrow payments, if any, as well as sending any monthly or annual statements, tracking account balances, and handling other aspects of your loan. You will be given advance notice before a transfer occurs.

Servicing Transfer Information

[X] We may assign, sell, or transfer the servicing of your loan while the loan is outstanding.

[ ] We do not service mortgage loans of the type for which you applied. We intend to assign, sell, or transfer the servicing of your mortgage loan before the first payment is due.

[ ] The loan for which you have applied will be serviced at this financial institution and we do not intend to sell, transfer, or assign the servicing of the loan.

Applicant **NICKIE C. GREEN**	Date	Applicant	Date
Applicant	Date	Applicant	Date
Applicant	Date	Applicant	Date

© 2008 Harland Financial Solutions, Inc.
MULTISTATE
ITEM 7199L0 (120208)

GreatDocs®
(Page 1 of 1)

Source: Reprinted with permission of McCue Mortgage Co.

- Introducing new, and revising existing, terms and definitions that impact consumers and many participants in the real estate finance industry
- Implementing several other changes in lender practices and behavior, in addition to those consistent with the TILA/MDIA changes

NOTE: The Truth in Lending section of this chapter explains additional important changes in RESPA disclosure practices, as they apply to TIL disclosure as well. See the heading "MDIA and 2008 TILA Revisions/RESPA Final Rule" (pages 316–319)

These changes proved very disruptive for many parties involved in residential mortgage transactions, including mortgage brokers, lenders, closing agents, title companies, consumers, builders, and realtors. One major national trade association filed lawsuits against HUD over some particularly onerous proposals and changes.

In response to HUDs' unclear and at times contradictory interpretation of the 2008 RESPA Final Rule, many lenders restricted their operations for several months until more satisfactory regulatory guidance was provided. Such an uncertain lending climate increased lender liability significantly and adversely impacted consumers struggling in an economic recession. The negative effects of this situation were exaggerated by occurring during a critical period in the real estate market. This difficult situation culminated in November 2009, when HUD—in an unprecedented step to acknowledge the severity of unresolved issues for industry participants—announced that it would still proceed with its January 1, 2010, RESPA changes, but was going to "exercise restraint" in their enforcement under certain conditions for four months after the implementation date.

As discussed in the introduction to this chapter, HUD now maintains a FAQ Web page—started in August 2009 with updates every few months—in an attempt to resolve ongoing implementation issues. The long-term impact of this responsive but unsettling regulatory process is unknown. As a result, all mortgage and real estate professionals should periodically review the 60-plus pages of HUD commentary to keep abreast of HUD's most recent interpretation of RESPA changes:

http://www.hud.gov/offices/hsg/ramh/res/respa_hm.cfm

Definitions

Understanding the new and revised definitions from 2008 RESPA changes provides a key to understanding the new GFE and HUD-1 and -1A rules and forms. Most of the implementation difficulties stem from the innate complexity of the changes and the need for more complete information from HUD on how these new definitions and rules apply in the thousands of real estate lending and closing variations across the country, coupled with the thousands of specific scenarios that consumers encounter in real estate purchase and refinance transactions.

HUD's new and revised definitions are specific to RESPA. Often, one term is used to define another and at times a full definition becomes quite technical. Here is a list with basic, "informal" definitions:

Loan Originator—lender or *mortgage broker*.

Mortgage Broker—a person who renders *origination services* and serves as an *intermediary* between a borrower and a lender (HUD does not define *intermediary*); can include an entity that table funds a transaction or FHA-approved correspondent; not an employee of a lender.

Application—requires a minimum of six items: applicant name, income, social security number (or equivalent), loan amount, property address, property value, and any other information the loan originator deems necessary.

Origination Service—another very broad term that includes <u>any</u> and <u>all</u> *loan originator* services involved in the creation of a mortgage loan (the range of services from prior to taking an application to the mortgage closing, including processing and administrative services).

Origination Charge—*Block 1* on the GFE; the one reportable fee that equals the total of all *origination service* fees for all lenders and mortgage brokers involved in the transaction (these fees were itemized in the prior GFE). The *Origination Charge* may include finance charges, prepaid finance charges, and closing costs.

Interest Rate Related Charge—*Block 2* on the GFE; a single adjustment to the *Origination Charge* that equals the total of all interest rate related fees paid. May include finance charges and prepaid finance charges. No broker transactions use Box 1; brokered transactions use either Box 2 or Box 3, depending on if there is a net credit or charge, respectively, to the *Origination Charge*. These charges were itemized in the prior GFE.

Other Settlement Charges/Services—*Blocks 3-11* on the GFE; all other charges/services involved in the mortgage transaction that are not considered an origination service. These charges were itemized in the prior GFE.

Title Service—*Blocks 4 and 5* on the GFE; a very broad term that includes <u>any</u> service involved in the provision of lender's or owner's title insurance (including processing and administrative services).

Changed Circumstance—applies to GFE and includes several categories:

- Acts of God, war, disaster, or other emergency
- New information for borrower or the transaction not known when the lender issues the initial disclosure
- Changed or inaccurate information for borrower or the transaction not known when the lender issues the initial disclosure
- Does NOT include market price fluctuations, lender errors, or situations where the lender had knowledge before issuing the disclosure
- Borrower-initiated changes that impact rate and/or fees

Average Pricing—charging all borrowers in a class of transactions the same amount for one or more settlement services. The charge is based on the average cost of providing the service(s), developed over a one- to six-month period.

Mortgage professionals are strongly encouraged to study the exact definitions and periodically revisit the HUD RESPA FAQ Web site for more information and direction in how these terms are interpreted by HUD.

Good Faith Estimate Form

RESPA requires that mortgage lenders provide to the applicant a Good Faith Estimate form (GFE) within three business days of application. The GFE provides a complete and accurate estimate of settlement charges that the applicant is expected to incur as is shown in Figure 11.7.

HUD's 2008 RESPA Final Rule extensively revised the GFE form, its required use, and the manner in which it is completed. HUD's main stated objective for the changes was to simplify the GFE for the consumer. The result of HUD's simplification project is a totally new GFE form expanding from one to three pages, containing thirteen new categories of fees, requiring several new and modified definitions for its understanding and completion, requiring several rules governing redisclosure, and instituting waiting period restrictions on closing. These GFE-related changes are by far the most controversial area of HUD's recent RESPA changes and the most difficult to implement.

Highlights of the 2008 GFE-related changes and their impact on the mortgage origination process include:

- Summary vs. Itemization
  The GFE no longer provides consumers with an itemized list of the various charges they may incur. Instead, the GFE summarizes all fees on page two into *Origination Charges (*Officially, *Blocks 1 and 2, including Boxes 1–3)* and *Other Settlement Services* (Officially, *Blocks 3–11)*. This new organization makes it impossible to identify individual finance charges which affect the loan's APR. It also allows for more unidentified "junk fees" to filter into different sections of the form, increasing costs to the consumer. Some individual charges instead will now "show up" for the first time on the HUD-1 or -1A, and can create more confusion at closing.
- Key Loan Information
  Pages one and three of the GFE contain effective summaries of the consumer's specific loan and payment terms, including higher risk features. Consumers should find this useful and should better understand potentially risky features of the loan applied for.
- Tradeoff Table and Shopping Chart
  The Tradeoff Table allows consumers to see how a lower and higher interest rate for the loan applied for will increase or lower settlement charges. The lender must complete the first column of this table. The Shopping Chart allows consumers to compare loan terms from different lenders. The lender is not required to complete this section. Both Table and Chart are on page 3 of the GFE.
- Closing Delays
  All consumers must now wait seven business days from when they receive the GFE (and TIL) before they can close on their transactions. This impacts consumers applying for second mortgages more than first mortgages, as they tend to close more quickly. Changes during application also require a three-day closing delay, which often will adversely impact consumers in purchase transaction and rate lock expiration situations.

FIGURE **11.7** Sample Good Faith Estimate Form

OMB Approval No. 2502-0265

Good Faith Estimate (GFE)

Name of Originator	Brokerworld	Borrower	Bob Borrower
Originator Address	123 Main Street Somewhere, USA 00001		
Originator Phone Number	123-456-7890	Property Address	124 Main Street Somewhere, USA 00001
Originator Email	bradbroker@brokerworld.com	Date of GFE	June 3, 2010

Purpose
This GFE gives you an estimate of your settlement charges and loan terms if you are approved for this loan. For more information, see HUD's *Special Information Booklet* on settlement charges, your *Truth-in-Lending Disclosures*, and other consumer information at www.hud.gov/respa. If you decide you would like to proceed with this loan, contact us.

Shopping for your loan
Only you can shop for the best loan for you. Compare this GFE with other loan offers, so you can find the best loan. Use the shopping chart on page 3 to compare all the offers you receive.

Important dates
1. The interest rate for this GFE is available through 07/02/10 @ 4 pm EST . After this time, the interest rate, some of your loan Origination Charges, and the monthly payment shown below can change until you lock your interest rate.
2. This estimate for all other settlement charges is available through 06/16/10
3. After you lock your interest rate, you must go to settlement within 30 days days (your rate lock period) to receive the locked interest rate.
4. You must lock the interest rate at least 15 days before settlement.

Summary of your loan

Your initial loan amount is	$ 294,566.00
Your loan term is	30 years
Your initial interest rate is	5.0 %
Your initial monthly amount owed for principal, interest, and any mortgage insurance is	$ 1,713.98 per month
Can your interest rate rise?	☒ No ☐ Yes, it can rise to a maximum of %. The first change will be in
Even if you make payments on time, can your loan balance rise?	☒ No ☐ Yes, it can rise to a maximum of $
Even if you make payments on time, can your monthly amount owed for principal, interest, and any mortgage insurance rise?	☒ No ☐ Yes, the first increase can be in and the monthly amount owed can rise to $. The maximum it can ever rise to is $
Does your loan have a prepayment penalty?	☒ No ☐ Yes, your maximum prepayment penalty is $
Does your loan have a balloon payment?	☒ No ☐ Yes, you have a balloon payment of $ due in years.

Escrow account information
Some lenders require an escrow account to hold funds for paying property taxes or other property-related charges in addition to your monthly amount owed of $ 1,713.98 .
Do we require you to have an escrow account for your loan?
☐ No, you do not have an escrow account. You must pay these charges directly when due.
☒ Yes, you have an escrow account. It may or may not cover all of these charges. Ask us.

Summary of your settlement charges

A	Your Adjusted Origination Charges (See page 2.)	$3,750.00
B	Your Charges for All Other Settlement Services (See page 2.)	$9,751.44
A + **B**	Total Estimated Settlement Charges	$ 13,501.44

Good Faith Estimate (HUD-GFE) 1

- **Fee Collection**
  Lenders (and all loan originators) cannot collect any fees (except a credit report fee) from applicants until they receive the GFE. This makes it easier for the consumer to inquire elsewhere and compare loan terms

FIGURE **11.7** (*Continued*)

Understanding your estimated settlement charges

Your Adjusted Origination Charges

1.	**Our origination charge** This charge is for getting this loan for you.	$6,750.00
2.	**Your credit or charge (points) for the specific interest rate chosen** ☐ The credit or charge for the interest rate of [＿＿＿＿＿] % is included in "Our origination charge." (See item 1 above.) ☒ You receive a credit of $ [3,000.00] for this interest rate of [5.0]%. This credit **reduces** your settlement charges. ☐ You pay a charge of $ [＿＿＿＿] for this interest rate of [＿＿＿＿]%. This charge (points) **increases** your total settlement charges. The tradeoff table on page 3 shows that you can change your total settlement charges by choosing a different interest rate for this loan.	-$3,000.00
A	Your Adjusted Origination Charges	**$ 3,750.00**

Some of these charges can change at settlement. See the top of page 3 for more information.

Your Charges for All Other Settlement Services

3.	**Required services that we select** These charges are for services we require to complete your settlement. We will choose the providers of these services. Service — Charge Appraisal / Credit Report — $220 / $40 Tax Service / Flood Certification — $65 / $12 Upfront MortgageInsurance Premium — $5055.25	$5,392.25
4.	**Title services and lender's title insurance** This charge includes the services of a title or settlement agent, for example, and title insurance to protect the lender, if required.	$925.00
5.	**Owner's title insurance** You may purchase an owner's title insurance policy to protect your interest in the property.	$725.00
6.	**Required services that you can shop for** These charges are for other services that are required to complete your settlement. We can identify providers of these services or you can shop for them yourself. Our estimates for providing these services are below. Service — Charge Survey — $250 Pest Inspection — $45	$295.00
7.	**Government recording charges** These charges are for state and local fees to record your loan and title documents.	$50.00
8.	**Transfer taxes** These charges are for state and local fees on mortgages and home sales.	$1,368.00
9.	**Initial deposit for your escrow account** This charge is held in an escrow account to pay future recurring charges on your property and includes ☒ all property taxes, ☒ all insurance, and ☐ other [＿＿＿＿] .	$306.60
10.	**Daily interest charges** This charge is for the daily interest on your loan from the day of your settlement until the first day of the next month or the first day of your normal mortgage payment cycle. This amount is $ [39.59] per day for [1] days (if your settlement is [10/31/09]).	$39.59
11.	**Homeowner's insurance** This charge is for the insurance you must buy for the property to protect from a loss, such as fire. Policy — Charge Insure-U — $650	$650.00
B	Your Charges for All Other Settlement Services	**$ 9,751.44**
A + **B**	Total Estimated Settlement Charges	**$ 13,501.44**

 Good Faith Estimate (HUD-GFE) 2

and fees. It also delays processing for every consumer, as few lenders will initiate any processing steps before they collect a fee.

- Fee Liability

  Lenders now are responsible for the amounts initially disclosed on an initial GFE, including charges beyond their control and for services

FIGURE **11.7** (*Continued*)

Instructions

Understanding which charges can change at settlement

This GFE estimates your settlement charges. At your settlement, you will receive a HUD-1, a form that lists your actual costs. Compare the charges on the HUD-1 with the charges on this GFE. Charges can change if you select your own provider and do not use the companies we identify. (See below for details.)

These charges **cannot increase** at settlement:	The total of these charges **can increase up to 10%** at settlement:	These charges **can change** at settlement:
• Our origination charge • Your credit or charge (points) for the specific interest rate chosen (*after you lock in your interest rate*) • Your adjusted origination charges (*after you lock in your interest rate*) • Transfer taxes	• Required services that we select • Title services and lender's title insurance (*if we select them or you use companies we identify*) • Owner's title insurance (*if you use companies we identify*) • Required services that you can shop for (*if you use companies we identify*) • Government recording charges	• Required services that you can shop for (if you do not use companies we identify) • Title services and lender's title insurance (if you do not use companies we identify) • Owner's title insurance (if you do not use companies we identify) • Initial deposit for your escrow account • Daily interest charges • Homeowner's insurance

Using the tradeoff table

In this GFE, we offered you this loan with a particular interest rate and estimated settlement charges. However:
- If you want to choose this same loan with **lower settlement charges,** then you will have a **higher interest rate.**
- If you want to choose this same loan with a **lower interest rate,** then you will have **higher settlement charges.**

If you would like to choose an available option, you must ask us for a new GFE.

Loan originators have the option to complete this table. Please ask for additional information if the table is not completed.

	The loan in this GFE	The same loan with lower settlement charges	The same loan with a lower interest rate
Your initial loan amount	$ 296,566.00	$ 294,566.00	$ 294,566.00
Your initial interest rate [1]	5.0 %	6.0 %	4.5 %
Your initial monthly amount owed	$ 1,713.98	$ 1,898.66	$ 1,652.11
Change in the monthly amount owed from this GFE	No change	You will pay $ 184.78 **more** every month	You will pay $ 88.77 **less** every month
Change in the amount you will pay at settlement with this interest rate	No change	Your settlement charges will be **reduced** by $ 1,500.00	Your settlement charges will **increase** by $ 1,500.00
How much your total estimated settlement charges will be	$ 13,501.44	$ 12,051.44	$ 15,051.44

[1] *For an adjustable rate loan, the comparisons above are for the initial interest rate before adjustments are made.*

Using the shopping chart

Use this chart to compare GFEs from different loan originators. Fill in the information by using a different column for each GFE you receive. By comparing loan offers, you can shop for the best loan.

	This loan	Loan 2	Loan 3	Loan 4
Loan originator name	Brokerworld			
Initial loan amount	$294,566.00			
Loan term	30 years			
Initial interest rate	5.0			
Initial monthly amount owed	$1,713.98			
Rate lock period	30 days			
Can interest rate rise?	no			
Can loan balance rise?	no			
Can monthly amount owed rise?	no			
Prepayment penalty?	no			
Balloon payment?	no			
Total Estimated Settlement Charges	$13,051.44			

If your loan is sold in the future

Some lenders may sell your loan after settlement. Any fees lenders receive in the future cannot change the loan you receive or the charges you paid at settlement.

 Good Faith Estimate (HUD-GFE) 3

Source: © 2010 Community Lending Associates, LLC www.communitylendassoc.com

provided by others. Additionally, lenders are now responsible for GFE information provided by mortgage brokers and bankers. The resulting effect is that now lenders "overdisclose" fees. Lenders include more fees than necessary and/or estimate high in other areas to avoid paying out of pocket for an unanticipated fee. The aggregate effect is that now many consumers have less accurate GFE information than before and will base their selection for financing on overinflated GFEs.

- Fee Categories and Tolerances

  Lenders are now responsible for evaluating every fee involved in the lending process and reporting it on the GFE in the correct tolerance category. If a fee increases from the GFE to settlement and exceeds the tolerance level, the lender must refund the borrower at settlement or within thirty days. Page three of the GFE organizes the three tolerance categories of fees based on their tolerance levels:

  - *These charges cannot increase at settlement:*
    - *Block 1—Our origination charge*
    - *Block 2—Your credit or charge (points) for the specific interest rate chosen (after you lock in your interest rate)*
    - *Line A—Your adjusted origination charges (after you lock in your interest rate)*
    - *Block 8—Transfer taxes*

  Note that no block in this category can increase at settlement (decreases are permitted).

  - *The total of these charges can increase up to 10% at settlement:*
    - *Block 3—Required services that we select*
    - *Block 4—Title services and lender's title insurance (if we select them or you use companies we identify)*
    - *Block 5—Owner's title insurance (if you use companies we identify)*
    - *Block 6—Required services that you can shop for (if you use companies we identify)*
    - *Block 7—Government recording charges*

  Note that this category refers to the total of charges in these blocks, not each individual Block or charge. An individual charge or an entire Block can increase more than 10 percent and the lender will still be within tolerance if the total of all the increases remains less than 10 percent of the overall total charges in this category.

  - *These charges can change at settlement:*
    - *Block 6—Required services that you can shop for (if you do not use companies we identify)*
    - *Block 4—Title services and lender's title insurance (if you do not use the companies we select)*
    - *Block 5—Owners title insurance (if you do not use companies we select)*
    - *Initial deposit for your escrow account*
    - *Block 12—Daily interest charges*
    - *Block 13—Homeowner's insurance*

  Note that the exact same settlement service reported in Blocks 4, 5, and 6 can be included in one of two fee tolerance categories, depending on the status of the provider. Which category depends on whether the lender requires that the borrower use a particular service provider, if the borrower selects a provider that the lender identifies, or if the borrower does not use a provider that the lender identifies.

- *Changed Circumstance*
  Fees can increase beyond tolerance levels without requiring the lender to refund the borrower, but only if there is a permitted *Changed Circumstance*, another source of decision making. Lenders must document the reason(s) for the change, and only change applicable charge(s) related to that change. Lenders must redisclose within three business days if there is a changed circumstance. Determining and evaluating this can delay processing. The added complexity and difficulty to manage this process increases lender liability and costs. Some consumers may benefit from these changes.

HUD-1 Uniform Settlement Statement (HUD-1 or HUD-1A)

The Settlement Statement itemizes all charges involved in the mortgage loan transaction. RESPA requires that the lender complete a HUD-1 form if a buyer and seller are involved, and allows the lender to use either a HUD-1 or a HUD-1A if only a mortgagor is involved (refinance). The mortgage lender (or other organization that will conduct the loan closing: closing attorney, title company, escrow agent) prepares the Settlement Statement. If a mortgage applicant requests it, the lender must provide the borrower with a Settlement Statement for review at least 24 hours before settlement. RESPA prohibits charging a specific fee for the preparation of the Settlement Statement.

HUD revised the Settlement Statement forms extensively in 2008 to work in concert with the new GFE. The biggest change includes more specific line-to-section references to the corresponding GFE Box/Block sections on page two of the HUD-1 and HUD-1A. This change makes it easier to identify where GFE fees appear on the HUD-1 and HUD-1A fees. Page two also expands reporting of Realtor® commission and title charges. See Figure 11.8 for sample of what this form looks like.

More importantly, a new page three on the Settlement Statement provides consumers with a detailed comparison of each estimated GFE charge to the final settlement cost. It also includes a summary of significant loan terms similar to page one of the new GFE. Page three also organizes all costs into the same three GFE tolerance level categories:

- Charges That Cannot Increase
- Charges That In Total Cannot Increase More Than 10%
- Charges That Can Change

Note: Since the mortgage servicer may be a different entity than the mortgage lender, the following RESPA sections use the terms lender and servicer interchangeably.

Servicing Transfer Statement

RESPA servicing requirements apply to both mortgage lenders and servicers. As discussed more extensively in Chapter 16—Loan Administration, a lender can service its own loans, hire a subservicer to perform this function, or sell the right to service the loans to a third party. The existing servicer must give

FIGURE **11.8** Sample HUD-1 Settlement Statement

OMB Approval No. 2502-0265

A. **Settlement Statement (HUD-1)**

B. Type of Loan		

1. ☒ FHA 2. ☐ RHS 3. ☐ Conv. Unins.	6. File Number:	7. Loan Number:	8. Mortgage Insurance Case Number:
4. ☐ VA 5. ☐ Conv. Ins.	11111	222222222	249-00000000

C. **Note:** This form is furnished to give you a statement of actual settlement costs. Amounts paid to and by the settlement agent are shown. Items marked "(p.o.c.)" were paid outside the closing; they are shown here for informational purposes and are not included in the totals.

D. Name & Address of Borrower:	E. Name & Address of Seller:	F. Name & Address of Lender:
Bob Borrower 124 Main Street Somewhere, USA 00001	Samantha Seller 456 Home Place Anywhere, USA 00002	Your Lender 1 Main Street Somewhere, USA 00001

G. Property Location:	H. Settlement Agent:	I. Settlement Date:
456 Home Place Anywhere, USA 00002	Title Town USA	July 8, 2010
	Place of Settlement: 222 Your Corner, Anywhere, USA 00002	

J. Summary of Borrower's Transaction		**K. Summary of Seller's Transaction**	
100. Gross Amount Due from Borrower		**400. Gross Amount Due to Seller**	
101. Contract sales price	$305,250.00	401. Contract sales price	$305,250.00
102. Personal property		402. Personal property	
103. Settlement charges to borrower (line 1400)	$14,358.85	403.	
104.		404.	
105.		405.	
Adjustment for items paid by seller in advance		**Adjustment for items paid by seller in advance**	
106. City/town taxes to		406. City/town taxes to	
107. County taxes to		407. County taxes to	
108. Assessments to		408. Assessments to	
109.		409.	
110.		410.	
111.		411.	
112.		412.	
120. Gross Amount Due from Borrower	$319,608.85	**420. Gross Amount Due to Seller**	$305,250.00
200. Amount Paid by or in Behalf of Borrower		**500. Reductions In Amount Due to seller**	
201. Deposit or earnest money	$2,000.00	501. Excess deposit (see instructions)	
202. Principal amount of new loan(s)	$294,566.00	502. Settlement charges to seller (line 1400)	$18,228.00
203. Existing loan(s) taken subject to		503. Existing loan(s) taken subject to	
204.		504. Payoff of first mortgage loan	$247,000.00
205.		505. Payoff of second mortgage loan	
206. Seller credit for transfer taxes	$1,368.00	506. Earnest money deposit	$2,000.00
207.		507. Seller credit for transfer taxes	$1,368.00
208.		508.	
209.		509.	
Adjustments for items unpaid by seller		**Adjustments for items unpaid by seller**	
210. City/town taxes to		510. City/town taxes to	
211. County taxes to		511. County taxes to	
212. Assessments to		512. Assessments to	
213.		513.	
214.		514.	
215.		515.	
216.		516.	
217.		517.	
218.		518.	
219.		519.	
220. Total Paid by/for Borrower		**520. Total Reduction Amount Due Seller**	
300. Cash at Settlement from/to Borrower		**600. Cash at Settlement to/from Seller**	
301. Gross amount due from borrower (line 120)	$319,608.85	601. Gross amount due to seller (line 420)	$305,250.00
302. Less amounts paid by/for borrower (line 220)	($297,934.00)	602. Less reductions in amounts due seller (line 520)	($266,596.00)
303. Cash ☒ From ☐ To Borrower	$21,674.85	**603. Cash ☒ To ☐ From Seller**	$38,654.00

The Public Reporting Burden for this collection of information is estimated at 35 minutes per response for collecting, reviewing, and reporting the data. This agency may not collect this information, and you are not required to complete this form, unless it displays a currently valid OMB control number. No confidentiality is assured; this disclosure is mandatory. This is designed to provide the parties to a RESPA covered transaction with information during the settlement process.

FIGURE **11.8** (*Continued*)

L. Settlement Charges

700. Total Real Estate Broker Fees			Paid From Borrower's Funds at Settlement	Paid From Seller's Funds at Settlement
Division of commission (line 700) as follows :				
701. $ 9,360.00	to Stella Sella			
702. $ 9,360.00	to Marty Mover			
703. Commission paid at settlement				$16,720.00
704. Earnest money deposit held by RE #2	$2,000. P.O. C.			

800. Items Payable in Connection with Loan			
801. Our origination charge Brokerworld / Your Lender	$ 6,250.00 (from GFE #1)		
802. Your credit or charge (points) for the specific interest rate chosen	$ 3,000.00 (from GFE #2)		
803. Your adjusted origination charges	(from GFE #A)	$3,250.00	
804. Appraisal fee to MAI Appraisal	(from GFE #3)	$250.00	
805. Credit report to Credit U Want Company	(from GFE #3)	$40.00	
806. Tax service to Tom's Tax Service Company	(from GFE #3)	$76.00	
807. Flood certification to Water-tight Flood Certification Company	(from GFE #3)	$12.00	
808.			
809.			
810.			
811.			

900. Items Required by Lender to be Paid in Advance			
901. Daily interest charges from 07/08/10 to 07/31/10 @ $ 39.59 /day	(from GFE #10)	$516.03	
902. Mortgage insurance premium for 12 months to FHA	(from GFE #3)	$5,066.25	
903. Homeowner's insurance for 1 years to Insure-It	(from GFE #11)	$600.00	
904.			

1000. Reserves Deposited with Lender				
1001. Initial deposit for your escrow account		(from GFE #9)	$516.03	
1002. Homeowner's insurance 1	months @ $ 50.00	per month $ 50.00		
1003. Mortgage insurance 1	months @ $ 132.69	per month $ 132.69		
1004. Property Taxes 3	months @ $ 166.67	per month $ 500.01		
1005.	months @ $	per month $		
1006.	months @ $	per month $		
1007. Aggregate Adjustment		-$ 166.67		

1100. Title Charges			
1101. Title services and lender's title insurance	(from GFE #4)	$925.00	
1102. Settlement or closing fee Title Town USA	$		$125.00
1103. Owner's title insurance Title Town USA / Title Underwriter	(from GFE #5)	$725.00	
1104. Lender's title insurance Title Town USA / Title Underwriter	$ 175.00		
1105. Lender's title policy limit $ 294,566.00			
1106. Owner's title policy limit $ 305,250.00			
1107. Agent's portion of the total title insurance premium to Title Town USA	$ 720.00		
1108. Underwriter's portion of the total title insurance premium to Title Underwriter	$ 180.00		
1109.			
1110.			
1111.			

1200. Government Recording and Transfer Charges			
1201. Government recording charges	(from GFE #7)	$50.00	
1202. Deed $ 25.00 Mortgage $ 25.00 Release $ 15.00			$15.00
1203. Transfer taxes	(from GFE #8)	$1,368.00	
1204. City/County tax/stamps Deed $ 684.00 Mortgage $ 684.00			
1205. State tax/stamps Deed $ 684.00 Mortgage $ 684.00			
1206. Transfer taxes- seller portion			$1,368.00

1300. Additional Settlement Charges			
1301. Required services that you can shop for	(from GFE #6)	$270.00	
1302. Survey to Measure-It	$ 225.00		
1303. Pest Inspection to Rid-A-Bug	$ 45.00		
1304. Home Warranty to Home Warranty Company		$300.00	
1305.			

1400. Total Settlement Charges (enter on lines 103, Section J and 502, Section K)			$14,358.85	$18,228.00

FIGURE **11.8** (*Continued*)

Comparison of Good Faith Estimate (GFE) and HUD-1 Charrges		Good Faith Estimate	HUD-1
Charges That Cannot Increase	**HUD-1 Line Number**		
Our origination charge	# 801	$6,750.00	$6,250.00
Your credit or charge (points) for the specific interest rate chosen	# 802	-$3,000.00	-$3,000.00
Your adjusted origination charges	# 803	$3,750.00	$3,250.00
Transfer taxes	# 1203	$1,368.00	$1,368.00

Charges That In Total Cannot Increase More Than 10%		Good Faith Estimate	HUD-1
Government recording charges	# 1201	$50.00	$50.00
Appraisal	# 804	$220.00	$250.00
Credit Report	# 805	$40.00	$40.00
Tax Service Fee	# 806	$54.00	$76.00
Flood Certification	# 807	$12.00	$12.00
Up-front Mortgage Insurance Premium	# 902	$5,066.25	$5,066.25
Title services & lender's title insurance	# 1101	$925.00	$925.00
Owner's title insurance	# 1103	$725.00	$725.00
Total		$7,092.25	$7,144.25
Increase between GFE and HUD-1 Charges		$ 52 or	.8 %

Charges That Can Change		Good Faith Estimate	HUD-1
Initial deposit for your escrow account	# 1001	$306.60	$516.03
Daily interest charges $ 39.59 /day	# 901	$39.59	$910.57
Homeowner's insurance	# 903	$650.00	$600.00
Survey	# 1302	$250.00	$225.00
Pest Inspection	# 1303	$45.00	$45.00
	#		

Loan Terms

Your initial loan amount is	$ 294,566.00
Your loan term is	30 years
Your initial interest rate is	5.0 %
Your initial monthly amount owed for principal, interest, and any mortgage insurance is	$ 1713.98 includes [X] Principal [X] Interest [X] Mortgage Insurance
Can your interest rate rise?	[X] No [ ] Yes, it can rise to a maximum of %. The first change will be on and can change again every after . Every change date, your interest rate can increase or decrease by %. Over the life of the loan, your interest rate is guaranteed to never be **lower** than % or **higher** than %.
Even if you make payments on time, can your loan balance rise?	[X] No [ ] Yes, it can rise to a maximum of $
Even if you make payments on time, can your monthly amount owed for principal, interest, and mortgage insurance rise?	[X] No [ ] Yes, the first increase can be on and the monthly amount owed can rise to $. The maximum it can ever rise to is $
Does your loan have a prepayment penalty?	[X] No [ ] Yes, your maximum prepayment penalty is $
Does your loan have a balloon payment?	[X] No [ ] Yes, you have a balloon payment of $ due in years on
Total monthly amount owed including escrow account payments	[ ] You do not have a monthly escrow payment for items, such as property taxes and homeowner's insurance. You must pay these items directly yourself. [X] You have an additional monthly escrow payment of $ 216.67 that results in a total initial monthly amount owed of $ 1930.65 . This includes principal, interest, any mortgage insurance and any items checked below: [X] Property taxes [X] Homeowner's insurance [ ] Flood insurance [ ] [ ] [ ]

Note: If you have any questions about the Settlement Charges and Loan Terms listed on this form, please contact your lender.

Source: © 2010 Community Lending Associates, LLC www.communitylendassoc.com

this notice to the borrower 15 days before any sale or transfer of servicing occurs. The borrower cannot be penalized if he makes a payment to the old servicer within 60 days of the transfer. The Servicing Transfer Statement must include the new servicer's contact information, including a toll-free telephone number.

Initial and Annual Escrow Statements

For loans with escrows, a lender must provide a borrower with an initial escrow statement at closing (or within 45 calendar days for accounts that are established as a condition of the loan), itemizing payments and projected disbursements. The lender must also provide an annual escrow account statement within 30 days of the end of the computation year. This statement must itemize all deposits and payments made to the escrow account(s), and explain shortages or surpluses.

Escrow Rules and Requirements

RESPA escrow rules and requirements apply to the mortgage lender as well as the servicer. In addition to providing the above mentioned Escrow Statements to borrowers, RESPA requires that all mortgage lenders and servicers follow specific rules for a loan with an escrow account (or impound). *Escrow account* means any account that a servicer establishes or controls on behalf of a borrower to pay any of the following:

- Property taxes
- Mortgage-related insurance (FHA or private)
- Property-related insurance (hazard, flood, earthquake, or property repair)
- Borrower-related insurance (credit life, disability, or unemployment)
- Homeowner association fees
- Special assessments
- Partial payments
- Other charges

The intent of the RESPA escrow rules amendment limits abusive escrow servicing practices. Abusive servicing practices include: keeping excess consumer funds in escrow accounts to invest for profit, requiring a much higher escrow payment to build a "payment cushion" in case of delinquency, not disbursing required payments promptly or at all—resulting in tax liens and other liability for the consumer and lender.

To curb these practices, RESPA escrow rules require lenders and servicers to:

- Limit the charges to the borrower when a lender creates an escrow account.
- Disburse all required escrow payments timely.
- Analyze the escrow account when it is established and at least annually thereafter.
- Use a standard accounting method known as aggregate accounting. *Aggregate accounting* means reviewing the escrow account as a whole in analyzing sufficiency of escrow funds for multiple payments.

- Limit the cushion permitted to build up in the escrow account to one sixth (thus, a two-month cushion) of the total annual payments from the account (but excludes monthly charges, such as for private mortgage insurance). A mortgage servicer may charge a monthly sum equal to one twelfth of total annual escrow payments anticipated (plus the cushion).
- Maintain records on escrow account activity for five years after loan payoff.

Escrow Surplus, Shortage, and Deficit

RESPA escrow rules require that the servicer monitor the amount(s) held in escrow and modify the escrow payment(s) or escrow balance(s) accordingly, depending on whether the escrow has a surplus, shortage, or deficit, or if the mortgage is delinquent:

- If an analysis discloses a surplus, the servicer must do one of the following:
  - For a surplus of at least $50, refund it to the borrower within 30 days.
  - For a surplus of less than $50, either refund it to the borrower or credit it to the escrow account.
  - If the loan is more than 30 days delinquent, the servicer may apply the surplus in accordance with the repayment terms of the loan.
- If an analysis discloses a shortage, the servicer must do one of the following:
  - Change nothing and allow the shortage to exist.
  - For a shortage of less than one monthly escrow payment, allow the borrower up to 30 days to pay.
  - For a shortage of more than one monthly escrow payment, allow the borrower up to a 12-month period to pay.
- If an analysis discloses a deficit (not a shortage—an actual negative balance), the servicer must do one of the following:
  - For a deficit of less than one monthly escrow payment, the servicer may collect in 30 days.
  - For a deficit of more than one monthly escrow payment, the servicer may collect in 2 to 12 months (lender's choice).

FLOOD DISASTER PROTECTION ACT (FDPA)

The National Flood Insurance Act of 1968, as amended in 1973 and 1994, was passed to reduce flood relief assistance expenditures made by the federal government. The Federal Emergency Management Agency (FEMA) enforces the FDPA. FDPA applies to all mortgage lenders and all mortgage loans (first or junior liens) *made, increased, renewed, or extended* (regardless of purpose) that are secured by improved real property (this includes manufactured homes, condominiums, and cooperatives).

A mortgage lender must determine whether or not the proposed real estate collateral is located in a community that participates in the National Flood Insurance Program (NFIP). The lender also must determine whether or not any portion of that improved real property is located in a special flood hazard area. Mortgage lenders can complete this determination using FEMA flood zone maps or by using vendors or appraisers. The use of an outside vendor does *not* release the lender from responsibility for any errors committed by the vendor.

If property is in a special flood hazard area, a lender must require the borrower to purchase flood insurance. A lender must notify the applicant at least 10 days prior to closing whether or not flood insurance is available, and must require the applicant to acknowledge in writing that the applicant realizes the property is in a flood hazard area.

The amount of flood insurance required is the loan principal minus the value of the land or the maximum available amount (under the program).

This flood insurance requirement is in effect for the *life of the loan*. If the property is later classified as existing in a special flood hazard area, the lender must notify the mortgagor of that fact and require flood insurance to be purchased within 45 days. If the consumer does not do so, then lender must force-place it. See Figure 11.9 for an example of Flood Hazard Determination Form.

HOMEOWNERS PROTECTION ACT (HPA) OF 1998

The HPA outlines conditions under which mortgage insurance must or can be cancelled on an outstanding mortgage. HPA is enforced by the various federal financial institution regulatory agencies. The HPA's cancellation/termination provisions apply to loans originated on or after July 29, 1999, with borrower-paid mortgage insurance (MI). Mortgage loans entered into before that date may also have the mortgage insurance cancelled, but the process is different. Both situations are discussed in the following sections. HPA applies to owner-occupied, residential mortgage loans regardless of lien priority, but excludes FHA insurance. The disclosure provisions of HPA depend on the type of loan (i.e., when it was originated, whether the loan is high risk, and whether MI is borrower- or lender-paid).

Automatic Cancellation of Mortgage Insurance

A mortgage lender must automatically terminate MI when a borrower is current on payments and LTV is first scheduled (based on an amortization schedule) to reach 78 percent. Equity based on property appreciation is not a factor. Automatic termination is not limited by decline in property value or existence of a subordinate lien.

Borrower Cancellation of Mortgage Insurance

A borrower can request that a lender cancel MI when the principal balance of the loan reaches 80 percent of the mortgaged property's original value (lesser of sales price or appraised value). A lender does not need to take into account increases in property value in determining when a borrower may cancel. The LTV calculation may be based on either the initial amortization schedule of the loan or actual loan payments. Upon reaching 80 percent, the borrower must do the following:

FIGURE **11.9** Sample Flood Hazard Determination Form

FEDERAL EMERGENCY MANAGEMENT AGENCY STANDARD FLOOD HAZARD DETERMINATION	O.M.B. No. 30670264 Expires October 31, 2001

SECTION I – LOAN INFORMATION

1. LENDER NAME AND ADDRESS

ACME Investments
123 Anystreet
 STE 100
Anytown, CT 10000

Phone: 999-999-9999

Contact: Susan Smith

2. COLLATERAL (Building/Mobile Home/Personal Property)
 PROPERTY ADDRESS (Legal Description may be attached)

Certified Location:
51 GOODNOW LN
FRAMINGHAM, MA 017025575
Originally Submitted (or AKA) Address:
51 GOODNOW LANE
FRAMINGHAM, MA 01702
Borrower(s) Names:
John Doe

APN:

3. LENDER ID. NO. 29950	4. LOAN IDENTIFIER	5. AMOUNT OF FLOOD INSURANCE REQUIRED

SECTION II

A. NATIONAL FLOOD INSURANCE PROGRAM (NFIP) COMMUNITY JURISDICTION

NFIP Community Name	County	State	NFIP Community Number
Framingham, Town	MIDDLESEX COUNTY	MA	250193

B. NATIONAL FLOOD INSURANCE PROGRAM (NFIP) DATA AFFECTING BUILDING/MOBILE HOME

NFIP Map Number/Community-Panel Number (Community name, if not the same as "A")	NFIP Map Panel Effective/Revised Date	LOMA/LOMR	Flood Zone	No NFIP Map
250193-0007B	2/3/82		C	

C. NATIONAL FLOOD INSURANCE AVAILABILITY *(Check all that apply)*

[X] Federal Flood Insurance is available (community participates in NFIP)   [X] Regular Program   [ ] Emergency Program of NFIP
 Date: 2/3/82

[ ] Federal Flood Insurance is NOT available because community is not participating in the NFIP

[ ] Building/Mobile Home is in a Coastal Barrier Resources Area (CBRA), Federal Flood Insurance may not be available.
 CBRA Designation Date:

D. DETERMINATION

IS BUILDING/MOBILE HOME IN SPECIAL FLOOD HAZARD AREA (ZONED BEGINNING WITH LETTERS "A" OR "V")?

If yes, flood insurance is required by the Flood Disaster Protection Act of 1973.
If no, flood insurance is not required by the Flood Disaster Protection Act of 1973.

[ ] Yes   [X] No

E. COMMENTS   LIFE OF LOAN DETERMINATION

HMDA CENSUS - State: 25 County: 017 MSA: 1120 Tract/Group: 3840.00-3

This determination is based on examining the NFIP map, and Federal Emergency Management Agency revisions to it, and any other information needed to locate the building/mobile home on the NFIP map.

F. PREPARER'S INFORMATION

NAME, ADDRESS, TELEPHONE NUMBER Integrated Loan Services 31 Inwood Rd Rocky Hill, CT 06067 Phone: (800)842-8423	DATE OF DETERMINATION 6/7/02 10:42:39 AM CERTIFICATE NUMBER 253014

FEMA Form 81-93, OCT 98

Source: REMOC Associates, LLC www.remoc.com

- Request cancellation in writing from the servicer.
- Have a good payment history, which means no 60-day late payments within 24 months of reaching 80 percent and no 30-day late payments within 12 months prior to that time.
- Satisfy any lender requirements for proof that property values have not declined below the original value and/or there is not a subordinate lien.

FIGURE **11.9** (*Continued*)

NOTICE TO BORROWER

Notice Is Given To: John Doe
Subject Property: 51 GOODNOW LN
FRAMINGHAM, MA 017025575
NFIP Community: 250193 - Framingham, Town

Date: 6/7/02 10:42:39 AM
Certificate #: 253014
Loan #:

THE LEGAL REQUIREMENT: The Flood Disaster Protection Act of 1973, and amendments, state that Federally regulated lending institutions shall not make, increase, extend, or renew any loan secured by improved real estate, or a mobile home located or to be located, in an area that has been identified by the Director of the Federal Emergency Management Agency (FEMA) as an area having special flood hazards and in which flood insurance has been made available under the National Flood Insurance Act of 1968, through the National Flood Insurance Program (NFIP), unless the building or mobile home and any personal property securing such loan is covered for the term of the loan by flood insurance in an amount at least equal to the outstanding principal balance of the loan or the maximum limit of coverage made available under the Act with respect to the particular type of property, whichever is less.

NOTICE OF SPECIAL FLOOD HAZARD AREA STATUS

[ ] **Notice of Property in Special Flood Hazard Area (SFHA)**
The building or mobile home securing the loan for which you have applied is or will be located in an area with special flood hazards. The area has been identified by the Director of FEMA as a SFHA using FEMA's Flood Insurance Rate Map or the Flood Hazard Boundary Map. This area has at least a one percent (1%) chance of a flood equal to or exceeding the base flood elevation (a 100-year flood) in any given year. During the life of a 30-year mortgage loan, the risk of a 100-year flood in a SFHA is 26 percent (26%). Federal law allows a lender and borrower to jointly request the Director of FEMA to review the determination of whether the property securing the loan is located in a SFHA. If you would like to make such a request, please contact us for further information.

[x] **Notice of Property Not in Special Flood Hazard Area (SFHA)**
The building or mobile home securing the loan for which you have applied is not currently located in an area designated by the Director of FEMA as a SFHA. NFIP flood insurance is not required; however, a preferred rate (lower hazard risk) policy is available if your community "participates" (see below). During the term of this loan, if the subject property is identified as being in a SFHA, you may be required to purchase and maintain flood insurance at your expense.

NOTICE REGARDING FEDERAL FLOOD DISASTER ASSISTANCE

[x] **Notice in Participating Communities**
The community in which the property securing the loan is located participates in the NFIP. If the property is or will be located in a SFHA (see section above), federal law will not allow us to make you the loan that you have applied for unless you purchase flood insurance. The flood insurance must be maintained for the life of the loan. If you fail to purchase or renew flood insurance on the property, Federal law authorizes and requires us to purchase the flood insurance at your expense.

Flood insurance coverage under the NFIP may be purchased through an insurance agent who will obtain the policy either directly through the NFIP or through an insurance company that participates in the NFIP. Flood insurance also may be available from private insurers that do not participate in the NFIP. At a minimum, flood insurance purchased must cover the lesser of:

1. The outstanding principal balance of the loan; or
2. The maximum amount of coverage allowed for the type of property under the NFIP.

Flood insurance coverage under the NFIP is limited to the overall value of the property securing the loan minus the value of the land on which the property is located. Federal disaster relief assistance (usually in the form of a low-interest loan) may be available for damages incurred in excess of your flood insurance if your community's participation in the NFIP is in accordance with NFIP requirements.

[ ] **Notice in Non-Participating Communities**
Flood insurance coverage under the NFIP is not available for the property securing the loan because the community in which the property is located does not participate in the NFIP. In addition, if the non-participating community has been identified for at least one year as containing a SFHA, properties located in the community will not be eligible for Federal disaster relief assistance in the event of a Federally-declared flood disaster.

John Doe _____ 6/10/02		_____	
Borrower's Signature **Date**		**Co-Borrower's Signature** **Date**	
_____		*J. L. Smith* 6/10/02	
Lending Institution *ACME INVESTMENTS*		**Lending Institution Authorized Signature** **Date**	

Other Termination

If the borrower is current on payments, a lender may not require MI beyond the midpoint date of the amortization period of the loan (e.g., 15 years on a 30-year loan). In all situations, any unearned premiums must be returned to the borrower within 45 days.

Disclosure Requirements

If the lender is paying for the MI at the time of commitment, that lender must disclose to the applicant information comparing lender- and borrower-paid MI. If the borrower pays for the MI (and the loan is not a high-risk loan), the lender must disclose at consummation of the transaction that the borrower has the following rights:

- For a fixed-rate mortgage—to request MI cancellation once the LTV reaches 80 percent and to request MI automatic termination once the LTV reaches 78 percent.
- For an adjustable-rate mortgage—to request MI cancellation once the LTV reaches 80 percent and that the lender notify the borrower when that date is reached and to request automatic termination once the LTV reaches 78 percent.

Annual Notice

If the borrower paid for the MI for loans made on or after July 29, 1999, the lender must advise the borrower of cancellation rights and provide the address and telephone number of the servicer. For loans made prior to July 29, 1999, the lender must advise the borrower that MI may, under certain circumstances, be canceled by the borrower and must provide the address and telephone number of the servicer.

The servicer must notify the borrower of termination or cancellation of MI within 30 days. Upon determination that the borrower does not meet the requirements for cancellation or termination, the servicer must inform the borrower of grounds for its determination.

HOME MORTGAGE DISCLOSURE ACT (HMDA)

The Home Mortgage Disclosure Act (Regulation C) is enforced by the Federal Financial Institutions Examination Council (FFIEC), and requires that certain lenders collect and report specific data for each loan application. Regulators and the public can review HMDA-reported information to determine whether or not a depository institution or non-depository institution (i.e., a mortgage company) is meeting the housing needs of their communities and to help identify discriminatory practices.

This information is available at FFIEC's HMDA Web site:

http://www.ffiec.gov/hmda/default.htm

HMDA reporting criteria for mortgage lenders changes annually. Criteria for a depository lender include:

- Assets of $39 million or more (for 2009 lending activity)
- Federally insured or regulated
- Operate a home or branch office in a Metropolitan Statistical Area (MSA)
- Made at least one one- to four-family first mortgage in the calendar year reported

- Have mortgage loan(s) that involve a federal agency insurance, guarantee, or supplement, <u>or</u> are intended for sale by Fannie Mae or Freddie Mac

Requirements for a non-depository mortgage lender include:

- A for-profit institution
- Operate a home or branch office in an MSA, <u>or</u> make at least five one- to four-family mortgage loans in the calendar year reported
- Originate home purchase loans (including refinance of home purchase loans) that represent either at least 10 percent of the total amount of loan originations <u>or</u> at least $25 million in the calendar year reported
- Assets of at least $10 million <u>or</u> make at least 100 home purchase loans (including refinance of home purchase loans) in the calendar year reported

In order to determine whether these lenders are servicing their communities, they are required to collect data on applicants, including the following:

- Gross annual income of applicants
- Race or national origin of applicants
- Sex of loan applicants
- Both approved and denied applications

Mortgage lenders are also required to collect data on the property, including the following:

- Property location by census tract number, MSA, and state and county codes
- Whether owner-occupied as principal residence

Additionally, starting in January 2003, mortgage lenders must also report the spread between the loan Annual Percentage Rate and the yield on the comparable Treasury security when the APR exceeds the Treasury yield by a certain amount:

- Three percentage points for first liens
- Five percentage points for subordinate liens

HMDA Loan Activity Register (HMDA-LAR)

The data must be maintained in a log or register of all applications for home loans. This register is sent to the lender's regulator by March 1 of the year following the calendar year of data collection. Types of loans included in the register are as follows:

- Home purchase
- Home improvement
- Refinancing
- Subordinate financing
- Purchased, broker, or correspondent loans (if approved and subsequently acquired according to a pre-closing arrangement)

Mortgage applications for loans not covered include these:

- Loans on unimproved land
- Construction loans
- Purchase of an interest in a pool of mortgages or purchase of servicing rights

In addition to the information mentioned here, the following information must be reported on the HMDA-LAR:

- Identifying number
- Date the application was received
- Type of loan (conventional, government insured, etc.)
- Purpose of loan
- Action taken and date
- Loan amount
- Type of entity that purchased loan if it was originated, or purchased and then sold within same calendar year
- Reason for denial (optional)

FAIR DEBT COLLECTION PRACTICES ACT

The Fair Debt Collection Practices Act was enacted to eliminate abusive, deceptive, and unfair debt collection practices. It is enforced by the Federal Trade Commission and applies only to the collection of consumer debt (including real estate). Any person (or financial institution) who regularly collects or attempts to collect consumer debts for another person or institution is classified as a debt collector. A financial institution that collects only its own debts is not a debt collector.

COMMUNITY REINVESTMENT ACT (CRA)

The purpose of CRA is to encourage commercial banks, savings banks, and saving associations to meet the borrowing needs of their local community (but it does not apply to credit unions). Like HMDA, it is administered by the FFIEC, which works with the data supplied by HMDA LARs. The FFIEC's CRA Web site is:

http://www.ffiec.gov/cra/default.htm

Regulators of those depository institutions covered by CRA will review the lending records of that institution to determine whether it is meeting the credit needs of the community, and will grade that lender accordingly. CRA requires each institution to have available to the general public a CRA statement, which delineates the characteristics of the local community, lists the types of credit the institution is prepared to extend in that community, and includes a copy of the CRA notice. The statement must be readily available for public inspection at the institution's main office and all its branches within the community.

Detailed instructions from the FFIEC for collecting and reporting CRA data is online at "A Guide to CRA Data Collection and Reporting": http://www.ffiec.gov/cra/guide.htm

SECURE AND FAIR ENFORCEMENT FOR MORTGAGE LICENSING ACT OF 2008

The SAFE Act is part of the Housing and Economic Recovery Act of 2008 (HERA), which has several key components related to housing finance. Enforced by and interpreted by HUD, its objectives are to enhance consumer protection and to reduce mortgage fraud.

To meet these goals, the SAFE Act directs the Conference of State Banking Supervisors (CSBS) and the American Association of Residential Mortgage Regulators (AARMR) to develop a national registry database—the National Mortgage Licensing System and Registry (NMLSR)—for tracking all mortgage loan originator (MLO) licensing and registration information. The NMLSR will establish one record for each company and each MLO, regardless of where each operates nationwide, and is used by the different jurisdictions that license and regulate MLOs. The NMLS Resource Center provides information for companies, licensees, and course providers:

http://mortgage.nationwidelicensingsystem.org/Pages/default.aspx

The SAFE Act allows consumers to review a company's or MLO's individual NMLSR record for employment history and for any information on "publicly adjudicated disciplinary and enforcement actions." Consumers can access the NMLS information at:

http://www.nmlsconsumeraccess.org/

The SAFE Act encourages each state to pass legislation to implement its MLO requirements for licensing and registration. Only a "state loan originator supervisory authority" (typically, the department of banking or equivalent) can license an MLO—not HUD or NMLS. Each state determines the exact timing and any *additional* licensing requirements beyond SAFE Act requirements. HUD will implement and administer a system for each state that does not pass such legislation (or make a good faith effort to do so) within one to two years.

The SAFE Act also sets minimum licensing standards for all MLOs and creates two classes of MLOs:

1. Federally Registered MLOs—employees of agency-regulated financial institutions. These MLOs are regulated by their respective federal agency (FDIC, OCC, OTS, NCUA, FCA), depending on the financial institution for which they work. The Agency Registry became active February 1, 2011.
2. State Licensed MLOs—employees (or 1099 contractors) of mortgage brokers, mortgage bankers, and Credit Union Service Organizations (CUSOs). These MLOs are regulated by their appropriate state department. There are still implementation issues in many states.

Federally Registered MLO Requirements

Specific requirements for Federal Registration of MLOs include:

1. Register with NMLSR online:
   http://mortgage.nationwidelicensingsystem.org/Pages/default.aspx

2. Furnish fingerprints for criminal history background check
3. Provide personal history and experience
4. Authorize NMLSR to obtain credit report

State Licensed MLO Requirements

Specific requirements for State Licensed MLOs include:

1. Steps 1–4 listed above for Federally Registered MLOs, *PLUS*
2. Complete a total of 20 hours of NMLS-approved pre-licensing education (PE), which can be taken in different combinations. NMLS-approved course topics include:

   a. PE Federal Law   3 hours

   b. PE Ethics   3 hours

   c. PE Nontraditional Mortgage   2 hours

   d. PE Elective (mortgage origination)   12 hours

3. Pass a federal test at an NMLS-approved test center, consisting of:

   a. A national component (100 questions)

   b. A state component (55–65 questions) for each state in which the MLO wants to be licensed.

4. On an annual basis, take eight hours of NMLS-approved Continuing Education (CE) programs, which can be taken in different combinations. NMLS-approved course topics include:

   a. CE Federal Law   3 hours

   b. CE Ethics   2 hours

   c. CE Nontraditional Mortgage   2 hours

   d. CE Elective (Mortgage Origination)   1 hour

   e. Cannot take the same course in successive years

In all cases, an MLO must still meet any *additional* state requirements for licensing and/or registration for each state in which the MLO originates. The NMLS Resource Center has a tremendous amount of information for these SAFE Act licensing requirements, as well as state requirements, education courses, and testing.

DODD-FRANK WALL STREET REFORM AND CONSUMER PROTECTION ACT

Like the Gramm-Leach-Bliley Act, the Dodd-Frank Wall Street Reform and Consumer Protection Act originated in Congress as the result of a financial crisis. Also like the GLBA, the Dodd-Frank Reform Act (DFA), enacted on July 21, 2010, is enormous in scope (over 2,300 pages). It is a large and complex law that extends far beyond mortgage lending, but impacts mortgage lending in dozens of areas.

Unlike the GLBA and other consumer compliance laws, the DFA contains many provisions that are general in nature and leaves the actual writing of most of the regulations to the agency involved in its implementation. The rule writing feature of DFA will create even more regulatory rules—several times that of the original DFA. Many critical rules are yet to be written and this important step takes place outside of Congress—over 300 rulemaking requirements remain, along with over 140 study and reporting provisions.

Additionally, the actual dates of implementation for the hundreds of new rules will vary greatly from provision to provision, depending on when final regulations are issued or the designated transfer date. The end result of the DFA is a series of complex regulatory changes over approximately a two- to three-year period. Congress established a similar regulatory format with recent RESPA reforms—passing comprehensive regulation with somewhat distant effective dates and leaving much of its interpretation to an agency.

The DFA is likely to follow a similar pattern, resulting in substantial confusion and uncertainty in the industry for a long period. It is likely that some of the yet-to-be-written rules will become effective during a completely different market for real estate and a mortgage finance market in which the fundamental dynamics have already changed. *As a result of this process, the DFA represents a tremendous source of compliance risk and liability to mortgage originators and lenders—arguably greater than any other single element in the history of U.S. mortgage lending.*

This chapter outlines the two sections of DFA that impact mortgage lending: Title X and Title XIV. Describing in detail the proposed changes is beyond the scope of this chapter, especially since many major rules and details are not yet known. For example, just one of the over 300 pending rules is incredibly controversial—the Loan Originator Compensation Rule, located in Section 1403 (See page 353). It was interpreted by the Federal Reserve and is effective April 1, 2011. It fundamentally changes loan originator compensation, which includes mortgage brokers and all other commission-based originators. Lawsuits have been filed against its implementation and Congressional leaders have become involved in the debate.

Title X

Title X governs the creation and authority of a new federal agency, the Bureau of Consumer Financial Protection (BCFP). The BCFP will have broad authority and assume regulatory responsibility from other federal agencies for many existing regulations for all lenders—depository and non-depository. It can write rules for all consumer financial products, not just mortgages, and will become the primary regulatory authority for all depositories with assets over $10 billion. Presently, the BCFP is under the Treasury department but will become completely independent as it develops.

Section 1002, 1022—General Rulemaking Authority

The BCFP will become the primary federal rulemaking authority for the following consumer compliance laws directly related to mortgage financing:

- Equal Credit Opportunity Act
- Fair Credit Billing Act / Fair Credit Reporting Acts
- Homeowner's Protection Act of 1998
- Fair Debt Collection Practices Act
- Home Mortgage Disclosure Act

- Home Ownership and Equity Protection Act of 1994
- Real Estate Settlement Procedures Act
- SAFE Mortgage Licensing Act
- Truth in Lending Act

Sections 1025, 1026, 1042—Supervision and Enforcement of Depositories

BCFP will be the primary authority to examine consumer compliance for depositories with over $10 billion in assets, will conduct joint or coordinated examinations with state-chartered depositories. Enforcement remains with existing regulatory bodies.

Section 1024—Supervision of Non-Depositories

BCFP will conduct risk-based supervision and examinations of mortgage-related businesses, regardless of size and coordinate with state or other regulators for enforcement.

Section 1032, 1094—Mortgage Regulation

BCFP will develop model combined RESP-TILA disclosure within one year from transfer date; may require NMLS MLO unique identifiers for HMDA data.

Section 1100—SAFE Act

BCFP assumes HUD's role in oversight for registered and licensed MLOs.

Title XIV

Title XIV has many provisions affecting the four major areas of mortgage lending: program design, origination, servicing, and secondary marketing. They are far-reaching in nature. Over the next two or three years, the DFA provisions will become new rules. As of now, the existing DFA provisions will: add new and change existing disclosures, affect loan program features and underwriting guidelines, govern origination and servicing practices, restrict compensation, change oversight of different mortgage lenders and originators, and increase liability and responsibility of different lending and servicing entities.

Sections 1400, 1401, 1405—Regulatory Authority, Rulemaking, Definitions

BCFP to assume federal responsibility for mortgage origination standards, programs, servicing, and high cost mortgage programs. Revises MLO definition to exclude workout and servicing personnel and secondary market creditors.

Section 1402—Residential Mortgage Loan Origination

Transfers oversight of depository MLOs from different agencies to CFPB.

Section 1403, 1404—Anti-Steering Prohibitions and Liability

CFPB to define illegal steering activities; prohibits several origination practices:

- Steering applicant to a loan with predatory characteristics or one an applicant lacks reasonable ability to repay
- Compensating originator based on anything other than size of loan or volume of loans (yield-spread premiums no longer permitted)
- Mischaracterizing an applicant's credit history

- Coercing or influencing appraisers in their assignment
- Discouraging applicants from seeking other loan terms from other originators
- Makes MLOs liable for steering violations.

Section 1411—Ability to Repay

CFPB to develop regulations to prohibit loans that consumers cannot repay by requiring certain minimum underwriting standards verifying income and/or assets. Lender must:

- make reasonable determination and verification of applicant's income and assets;
- establish credit history and future housing payment based on a fully amortizing schedule;
- meet minimum underwriting standards for ARM, interest only, and negative amortization loans

Section 1412—Safe Harbor for Qualified Mortgage Rebuttable Presumptions

Defines "Qualified mortgage" as a loan with the following features:

- no negative amortization,
- fully verified and documented,
- total points and fees at or below 3% of loan amount
- underwritten based on
  - fully amortizing PITI payment for fixed rate loan
  - same as above, but at maximum interest rate permitted for first five years for ARM loans
  - maximum debt-to-income ratio (to be established)
- Special rules for Balloon loans
- Establishes rebuttable presumption that a consumer has the ability to repay if the loan meets certain "qualified mortgage" standards.

Section 1413—Defense to Foreclosure

Lenders violating sections 1411 and 1412 may provide consumers with a defense to foreclosure without statute of limitations.

Section 1414—Additional Standards and Requirements

Establishes a series of restrictions on prepayment penalties for qualified and non-qualified loans, according to different phase-out schedules depending on interest rate. Negative amortization loans allowed only if applicant provided certain disclosures and counseling (if first-time homebuyer).

Sections 1418—420—Required Disclosures

Expands TILA requirements for disclosures and for monthly statements for: hybrid ARMs, ARMs with escrows

Section 1431—High Cost Mortgages

Expands high-cost mortgages to include purchases and reduces triggers for interest rate and fees.

Section 1432—Amendments to existing requirements for certain mortgages

Prohibits prepayment penalties and balloon payments for high-cost mortgages.

Section 1433—Additional requirements for certain mortgages

Adds several servicing requirements for high-cost mortgages for: late fees, counseling

Section 1442—Office of Housing Counseling

Establishes Office of Housing Counseling within HUD for homeownership and rental.

Section 1461—Escrow and Impound Accounts for Certain Consumer Credit Transactions

Establishes when escrow loans must be required and maintained on certain loans, requires disclosures.

Section 1462—Disclosures for consumers who waive escrow services

Requires disclosure regarding consumers' responsibilities for non-payment.

Section 1463—RESPA Amendments

Increases penalties and servicer requirements for force-placed insurance, charging fees, responding to certain borrower customer service requests, and crediting payments.

Section 1471—Property Appraisal Requirements

Expands USPAP appraisal requirements, requires advance disclosure/copy of appraisal to consumer, requires second appraisals for certain loans.

Section 1472—Appraisal Independence Requirements

Restricts actions that would violate appraisal independence, establishes penalties.

Sections 1481 through 1484—Mortgage Resolution and Modification

Increases assistance to single- and multi-family and rental programs, revises HAMP.

Timing

As stated previously, most changes have yet to be written and implementation dates not yet determined. DFA is so complicated and cumbersome, one national trade association, the ABA, maintains a link to its Web site dedicated exclusively to the status and dates of the over 1,000 pages of regulatory proposals in play and 360 pages of final rules written within six months of DFA's enactment.

ABA Dodd-Frank Tracker: http://regreformtracker.aba.com/p/dodd-frank-calendar.html

In general, DFA provisions are effective July 22, 2010 (the date of its enactment), unless final regulations need to be written. Final regulations must be issued within eighteen months after the "designated transfer date" of July 21, 2011. The effective date must occur within twelve months after final regulations are issued. For those sections of FDA without regulations, the effective date must be within eighteen months after the designated transfer date (see Figure 11.10).

FIGURE **11.10** Summary of Disclosure Requirements

REQUIRED FEDERAL DISCLOSURES FOR PRIMARY RESIDENCE ONLY!

Disclosure	Regulation	1st Mtg Pur/Ref	2nd Mtg-Closed Pur/Ref/1st	2nd Mtg-HELOC Pur/Ref/1st
Good Faith Estimate/ABA Notice	RESPA	Y	Y	N
Preliminary TIL	Truth In Lending	Y	Y	N
Servicing Disclosure	RESPA	Y	N	N
Fair Lending Notice	Fair Housing	ALL CONSUMER/MORTGAGE LOANS SECURED BY REAL ESTATE		
Right to Appraisal Notice	ECOA	ALL CONSUMER/MORTGAGE LOANS SECURED BY REAL ESTATE		
Privacy Notice	USAPATRIOT	ALL CONSUMER/MORTGAGE LOANS SECURED BY REAL ESTATE		
Credit Report Notice	FACT	ALL CONSUMER/MORTGAGE LOANS SECURED BY REAL ESTATE		
Flood Certification	Flood Disaster Protection	ALL CONSUMER/MORTGAGE LOANS SECURED BY REAL ESTATE		
HUD-1 or HUD-1A	RESPA	Y	Y	Y
HUD-1 REQUIRED IN ALL TRANSACTIONS WHERE PROPERTY IS TRANSFERRED				
Settlement Costs Booklet	RESPA	Y	Y	N
Right of Rescission	Truth In Lending	N	Y	Y
RESCISSION TO OWNER-OCCUPANTS ONLY FOR NEW MONEY REFINANCES.				
Initial HELOC Disclosure	Truth In Lending	N	N	Y
Home is on the Line	Truth In Lending	N	N	Y
Periodic Statement	Truth In Lending	N	N	Y
Initial & Periodic ARM Disclosure	Truth In Lending	Y*	Y*	N
CHARM Booklet	Truth In Lending	Y*	Y*	N
*only if an ARM loan (not Fixed)				
Initial Escrow Statement	RESPA	Y^	Y^	Y^
Annual Escrow Statement	RESPA	Y^	Y^	Y^
^only if escrow required				
Private Mortgage Insurance	Homeowners Protection	Y~	Y~	Y~
Annual PMI Statement	Homeowners Protection	Y~	Y~	Y~
~only if PMI required				

Source: © 2010 Community Lending Associates, LLC
Consulting Services for Community Lenders
www.communitylendassoc.com

SUMMARY

The mortgage lending compliance arena is complex and now very fluid. It promises to become even more complex and uncertain. Hopefully for consumers and lenders, the contentious dynamic during implementation of the HUD's RESPA rules and the Federal Reserve's Dodd-Frank loan originator compensation rule will not be the new "norm" for the industry.

The following summary of current disclosure requirements will help the student of mortgage compliance review the scope of existing disclosure requirements throughout the lending and servicing process. It is but a snapshot of rapidly occurring compliance changes not only in disclosures, but also in lending practices, loan program requirements, underwriting guidelines, servicing practices, and oversight. Perhaps the biggest challenge in mortgage lending today is staying current with these evolving compliance responsibilities and avoiding the potential liability created by imprecise and at times confusing enforcement of these evolving laws.

DISCUSSION POINTS

1. ECOA (Regulation B) prohibits discrimination based on which factors?
2. If a mortgage lender declines an application for a mortgage loan, what must the lender do? How is it done?
3. Are business loans covered by Truth In Lending? What is covered?
4. What items are included in the annual percentage rate? What is excluded?
5. What is the Right of Rescission (Right to Cancel)? What is required of a mortgage lender?
6. What does "life of loan coverage" mean? Why is this important to a mortgage lender?
7. What three categories of fees does the revised RESPA rule create?
8. List three important areas of mortgage lending that the Dodd-Frank Act impacts and how.
9. How has the process of creating and enforcing a consumer compliance regulation evolved? What is the impact on mortgage originators, lenders, and consumers?

CHAPTER 12

Residential Mortgage Loan Origination and Processing

INTRODUCTION

The residential mortgage loan origination and processing functions include all actions and procedures that occur from the time a potential applicant has contact with the lender through the time the underwriter reviews the application for a decision to approve, deny, or counteroffer (explained in Chapter 13—Underwriting the Residential Mortgage Loan). The speedy, professional completion of this function, along with the quality of loans originated, is a large determining factor in the success and profitability of the residential mortgage lending operation.

Major changes in the solicitation and creation of mortgage applications started even before the collapse of the mortgage industry in 2008. Some changes include: more origination players overall, increased use of the correspondent channel for originations by large lenders, more loan products and programs, improved marketing tools, and expanded use of technology in general, and the Internet in particular. All mortgage originators and lenders therefore revised their origination and processing procedures tremendously. As in many aspects of residential lending, the secondary market giants, Fannie Mae and Freddie Mac, set the industry standards. Most lenders nationwide follow their guidelines and use their forms, regardless of whether they sell [or place in portfolio] loan production.

Despite many changes and improved efficiencies, the processing stage remains the lengthiest step involved in mortgage origination. Technology shortened the process, reducing turnaround time to 48 hours for straightforward, automated transactions. However, recent compliance requirements enacted in 2008 have had the polar opposite effect—reversing these industry gains—and pushing normal processing times back to 30–45 days from application to closing. All parties involved in a transaction, including sellers and realtors, must understand the impact that these changes may have on different aspects of mortgage processing: loan commitment, property inspections, title work, closing dates, even scheduling the moving truck. The mortgage loan officer must clearly present the timeline, from application through closing, to the client—the applicant—and continuously aid all parties through the process.

One important change since 2008 is in the approach to processing itself. New compliance and disclosure guidelines make processing more arduous for the applicant and the lender. Truth in Lending (TIL), RESPA, appraisal requirements, and guidelines created in response to these regulations add time and cost to loan processing. All those involved need additional communication to complete each step within the required calendar dates.

A final, but equally significant, difference one sees today in the mortgage origination and processing area is a blurring of lines traditionally separating these functions. Prior to banking deregulation in 1978, mortgage loan officers were "order takers"—essentially they completed the forms for a mortgage product and gave the documents to the processor, who handled the application until closing.

This passive role has evolved over the past 20 years, along with the mortgage marketplace. Today, the best mortgage loan officers have complete product knowledge, act as an advisor to the client, and counsel the consumer on the different loan products available. While taking a loan application, they complete a significant amount of the processing at application and perform basic underwriting, then maintain contact with the applicant(s) until loan closing. Mortgage loan officers need additional skills and knowledge to perform these roles effectively. Although this approach can increase the lender's compliance risk, both consumer and lender benefit from the expertise offered by well-educated and well-trained mortgage loan officers.

A negative feature of this more aggressive, advisory approach in mortgage origination is the presence of fraud, abuse, and predatory lending practices. These elements always were present in the origination area, but became more prominent during the recent "mortgage meltdown crisis". As a result, regulatory changes now provide further restrictions for origination behavior beyond traditional fair lending and discrimination that are addressed in Fair Housing Act and ECOA. Revisions to Truth in Lending, RESPA, and the new SAFE and Dodd-Frank Acts form a framework of originator do's and don'ts. Any person involved in mortgage loan origination must know these important changes or risk fines, imprisonment, or a lifetime ban from the industry.

TECHNOLOGY

The impact of technology on the mortgage industry cannot be overstated—an entire chapter and even a book can be devoted to this topic alone. Because the mortgage lending industry relies so heavily on data management and cost efficiencies, significant improvements in technology have far-reaching effects (both good and bad) and transform the way in which the industry operates.

Web-based computer software programs designed for mortgage origination enable mortgage loan officers to work virtually and improve time management. A mortgage loan officer can take a loan application on the road using a laptop, send pre-application documents virtually to clients for signing, received signed and supporting documents back from the client, order credit reports, obtain automated underwriting system (AUS) decisions from Fannie Mae or Freddie Mac, and e-mail a complete file to a processor, all within a few hours. The processor can then "open" the file, create lender disclosures to send to clients, order an appraisal, and move the file along, all without printing a single page. This allows processors to accomplish work faster and manage more loans efficiently. They can handle more functions, perform many calculations, accommodate more loan programs, save computer keystrokes, produce reports, and operate efficiently.

The downside of this automation is the lender must ensure that the mortgage loan officer and processor are properly educated and trained to complete functions that were previously handled only by underwriters. One increased risk is that the mortgage loan officers might operate too much as underwriters—making decisions they should not be making. This, unfortunately, occurred far too frequently during peak volume levels recently. Another growing concern is customer privacy—protecting sensitive application data. Technology and mobility make the process more convenient, but less secure. Lenders must take equal steps to protect all nonpublic customer information, or face severe compliance and legal penalties.

As a result of increased computing capacity and speed, lenders now link one software program to others that handle underwriting, closing, secondary marketing, and servicing functions. Technology allows lenders to close, package, grade for risk, and sell within a few weeks entire pools of mortgages in the global secondary market. Unfortunately, this phenomenon played a big part in the global financial crash, as speed and capacity outstripped management's ability to control the process effectively.

On an individual loan level, the Internet, improved technology, and proprietary software programs also allow secondary market investors to provide lenders with immediate confirmation of a loan's eligibility and approval for sale—complete with a list of *commitment conditions* (the processing documentation and underwriting conditions that lenders must obtain to complete the sale). Typically, the processor reviews the application, issues the proper disclosures, and inputs the data into the AUS. The processor receives the AUS report (within minutes), including any conditions and documentation needed prior to and at closing.

Mortgage Loan Originator—SAFE Act

Under the new Secure and Fair Enforcement for Mortgage Licensing Act (SAFE Act) a **mortgage loan originator** (MLO) is defined as an "individual"—a natural person, *not* an organization or entity—who takes a mortgage loan application or offers or negotiates terms of a mortgage loan for, or in the expectation of, compensation or gain, either directly or indirectly for another individual. This applies to educating the client on mortgage products, interest rates, and fees.

Any person who *acts* in this capacity—regardless of their work title—is considered an MLO *and* must adhere to all the applicable federal and state licensing requirements. Thus, a mortgage loan officer, mortgage originator, vice president, processor, underwriter, office/department assistant, or *any* company employee who offers mortgage guidance to a consumer may first need to be licensed by a state or registered with NMLS. It is important for lenders, MLOs, mortgage loan officers, and other employees to understand the specific regulations that apply to their services for each state in which they work.

For purposes of clarity in this book, we refer only to the loan officer, as opposed to the special designation *mortgage loan originator* or *MLO* described above.

INTERVIEW

The first step in mortgage loan origination is the initial interview. The initial contact with the potential applicant(s) defines the entire process and is arguably the most important step. This contact will establish early on whether or not the potential applicant(s) can qualify for a mortgage loan. If handled correctly, the interview saves both the consumer and mortgage lender considerable time and money.

The person conducting this interview is typically the mortgage loan officer. The mortgage loan officer plays a key role in guiding consumers through the complicated process of mortgage finance. It is a huge responsibility in what will be the biggest financial and quality of life decision for many consumers. Consumers place their trust in the mortgage loan officer and act on the information and advice that he or she provides. It is critical to remember that *any* employee, regardless of title, who interacts in this capacity with the consumer, formally or informally, intentionally or unintentionally, makes the lender responsible (and liable) for the completion of these functions in compliance with state and federal regulations.

Many initial interviews result in completed (formal) applications. However, the initial interview can have several different outcomes:

- Counseling
- Prequalification (different from pre-approval)
- Application (and possibly a pre-approval)

These potential outcomes reflect an increasing level of information exchanged between the potential applicant(s) and loan officer. Here is a general description of what can happen:

Counseling: The loan officer describes to potential applicants the various programs available, explains the general nature of the application process and the financial obligations inherent in a mortgage loan, and may recommend steps they must take to prepare for a formal application. The loan officer may provide them with a list of necessary documents needed to complete an application, along with a worksheet for them to calculate their monthly housing expenses.

Prequalification: This process is mostly the same as counseling, but in addition, the loan officer may "run the numbers" in more detail—apply the information to the potential applicants' specific situation *but not convey an opinion on credit approval or denial.* Again, it is a fine line between conversation and advice.

Formal application: Usually contains the preceding steps, but is defined as when the potential applicant(s) actually completes a written application, receives and signs pre-application disclosures, and is prepared to pay an application fee and order an appraisal.

During counseling and prequalification, the loan officer does not complete a formal application or issue a pre-approval. Still, the loan officer provides a valuable service by giving the potential applicant(s) specific information to help decide which of many loan products is best, or whether to apply at all. These types of initial interviews are common and useful for consumers to compare loan programs and shop around for rates from several different lenders.

Unfortunately, recent RESPA changes can actually impede this process. The revised Good Faith Estimate form (GFE) makes it easier for consumers to shop and compare rates and total costs. Page 3 of the GFE form presents a tradeoff table and shopping chart for consumers to compare rates and fees. However, two issues work against the consumer in keeping this valuable information from them:

1. HUD's interpretation of RESPA holds the lender responsible for most cost estimates in the GFE, so originators are very reluctant to provide a "draft" GFE with incomplete information at the counseling or prequalification stages.

2. HUD has ruled that if an originator issues a GFE, then it assumes there is enough information exchanged to require a formal application. The end result is the RESPA changes effectively force the consumer to apply with each lender in order to shop and compare their fees.

When counseling and prequalifying the potential client, the lender *does not* make a formal credit decision—no approval, denial, or counteroffer—and the mortgage loan officer must consciously and carefully avoid giving the consumer the impression that a credit decision was made. Under the new RESPA guidelines, if a mortgage loan officer gives any indication of loan advice, then it may be considered the first step of a loan application, so pre-application disclosures must be provided.

A **pre-approval** is an outcome that may result from an initial interview. This may occur at the end of the initial interview if the lender has sufficient information to make a credit decision. Under the new RESPA guidelines, a mortgage loan officer must be able to complete a loan application, run a credit report, and issue at a minimum an initial good faith estimate worksheet. It is important to note that *all* initial interviews can be completed in the following ways: face to face, by mail, by telephone, by fax, or electronically. Regardless of the outcome, each method of conducting the initial interview poses significant consumer compliance challenges for the lender and loan officer.

FORMAL APPLICATION

The following sections describe the formal application process.

Be Careful Not to Discourage a Formal Application

According to Regulation B of the Equal Credit Opportunity Act (ECOA—See Chapter 11—Compliance), lenders cannot discourage consumers from applying for credit. After having the financial obligations of a mortgage loan explained to them in counseling or prequalification, most individuals will not apply for a mortgage loan if they realize that they will not qualify. Regardless of the circumstances, a loan officer must be careful not to discourage potential applicant(s) from applying for a mortgage loan if they so desire.

Further, as mentioned, mortgage lenders must be careful that this initial interview does not imply a credit decision, and it must not be explicitly represented as one. If a lender—even at this stage of the process—tells a potential applicant that, based upon the applicant's income, he or she does or does not qualify, the lender has made a credit decision. This requires a formal application, several disclosures and reporting requirements, and (depending on the situation) a commitment letter or a notice of adverse action. There are serious consumer compliance issues if the lender improperly handles this situation.

Other Application Compliance Issues

Chapter 11—Compliance details the many compliance issues and requirements which arise at application and during processing. However, it is important to emphasize a few here. Mortgage originators must not collect any fees before the applicant has received the initial disclosures (Good Faith Estimate and Truth in Lending Disclosure (See Figure 12.1, pages 366–372)). An exception may be made for the credit report fee. Other initial federal disclosures include ones for privacy, fair housing, servicing, and others if applicable (ARM program disclosure, HOEPA loans, flood insurance, etc.)

The mortgage originator's compensation must not be based on any factor outside of the loan amount or aggregate volume. The industry-standard yield spread premium—compensation based on other loan risk factors—is no longer allowed.

Once an application is fully processed, the lender has thirty days in which to make a decision. This does not mean thirty days from application. The thirty days start from the day the originator receives the last document necessary to make a credit decision.

The Uniform Residential Loan Application and Uniform Documentation

The mortgage application form is the most important document in the residential mortgage lending process. Every step that follows is based on the information provided in the application. Numerous compliance and regulatory issues depend on its accurate completion. It is important to emphasize that all lenders should use the Fannie Mae/Freddie Mac Uniform Residential Loan Application (Fannie Mae Form 1003 or 1003[S] and Freddie Mac Form 65) and all other uniform processing and closing documentation—*regardless* of whether the lender intends to keep the loan in its portfolio or sell it on the secondary market to an investor. *Not* using this uniform documentation (also called standard or conforming documentation) makes selling those mortgages much more difficult and expensive.

Additionally, the use of a lender's own forms may place a lender (and subsequent investors, if the loan is sold) in violation of the various consumer protection laws if the forms are not drafted correctly. The Fannie Mae/Freddie Mac Uniform Application form in Figure 12.1 along with additional uniform processing and closing documentation, have been accepted as meeting all consumer protection requirements. (There is still a risk that uniform documentation may have an issue at the state level, but it is more likely that any potential problems have already been identified and addressed with these

FIGURE **12.1** Sample Uniform Residential Loan Application, Truth in Lending Disclosure, and Good Faith Estimate

Uniform Residential Loan Application

This application is designed to be completed by the applicant(s) with the Lender's assistance. Applicants should complete this form as "Borrower" or "Co-Borrower," as applicable. Co-Borrower information must also be provided (and the appropriate box checked) when ☐ the income or assets of a person other than the Borrower (including the Borrower's spouse) will be used as a basis for loan qualification or ☐ the income or assets of the Borrower's spouse or other person who has community property rights pursuant to state law will not be used as a basis for loan qualification, but his or her liabilities must be considered because the spouse or other person has community property rights pursuant to applicable law and Borrower resides in a community property state, the security property is located in a community property state, or the Borrower is relying on other property located in a community property state as a basis for repayment of the loan.

If this is an application for joint credit, Borrower and Co-Borrower each agree that we intend to apply for joint credit (sign below):

Borrower NICKIE C. GREEN | Co-Borrower

I. TYPE OF MORTGAGE AND TERMS OF LOAN

| Mortgage Applied for: | VA ☐   [X] Conventional   ☐ Other (explain): | | Agency Case Number | Lender Case Number |
| | FHA ☐   ☐ USDA/Rural Housing Service | | | 00125224 |

| Amount | Interest Rate | No. of Months | Amortization Type: | Fixed Rate ☐   Other (explain): |
| $180,000.00 | 3.7500% | 360 | | GPM ☐   [X] ARM (type): |

II. PROPERTY INFORMATION AND PURPOSE OF LOAN

Subject Property Address (street, city, state & ZIP) — No. of Units

1144 REEF ROAD, FAIRFIELD, CT 06824 — 1

Legal Description of Subject Property (attach description if necessary) — Year Built
See attached legal description — 2000

| Purpose of Loan | [X] Purchase   ☐ Construction   ☐ Other (explain): | Property will be: |
| | ☐ Refinance   ☐ Construction-Permanent | [X] Primary Residence   ☐ Secondary Residence   ☐ Investment |

Complete this line if construction or construction-permanent loan.

| Year Lot Acquired | Original Cost | Amount Existing Liens | (a) Present Value of Lot | (b) Cost of Improvements | Total (a + b) |
| | $ | $ | $ | $ | $ |

Complete this line if this is a refinance loan.

| Year Acquired | Original Cost | Amount Existing Liens | Purpose of Refinance | Describe Improvements | ☐ made   ☐ to be made |
| | $ | $ | | Cost: $ | |

Title will be held in what Name(s)
NICKIE C GREEN

Manner in which Title will be held
SOLE OWNERSHIP

Estate will be held in:
[X] Fee Simple
☐ Leasehold (show expiration date)

Source of Down Payment, Settlement Charges, and/or Subordinate Financing (explain)
Bank accts

III. BORROWER INFORMATION

| | Borrower | | | | Co-Borrower | | | |

Borrower's Name (include Jr. or Sr. if applicable)
NICKIE C. GREEN

Co-Borrower's Name (include Jr. or Sr. if applicable)

| Social Security Number | Home Phone (incl. area code) | DOB (mm/dd/yyyy) | Yrs. School | Social Security Number | Home Phone (incl. area code) | DOB (mm/dd/yyyy) | Yrs. School |
| 123-00-3333 | 203-767-1234 | 07/24/1978 | 14.0 | | | | |

| [X] Married   ☐ Unmarried (include single, divorced, widowed)   ☐ Separated | Dependents (not listed by Co-Borrower) no. 1   ages 16 | ☐ Married   ☐ Unmarried (include single, divorced, widowed)   ☐ Separated | Dependents (not listed by Borrower) no.   ages |

Present Address (street, city, state, ZIP)   [X] Own   ☐ Rent   3.00 No. Yrs.
100 TERRACE STREET
WEST HAVEN, CT 06516

Present Address (street, city, state, ZIP)   ☐ Own   ☐ Rent   No. Yrs.

Mailing Address, if different from Present Address | Mailing Address, if different from Present Address

If residing at present address for less than two years, complete the following:

Former Address (street, city, state, ZIP)   ☐ Own   ☐ Rent   No. Yrs. | Former Address (street, city, state, ZIP)   ☐ Own   ☐ Rent   No. Yrs.

IV. EMPLOYMENT INFORMATION

| | Borrower | | | | Co-Borrower | | |

Name & Address of Employer	☐ Self Employed	Yrs. on this job
CENTES PACKAGE STORE		8.00
123 MAIN STREET		Yrs. employed in this line of work/profession
BRIDGEPORT, CT 06111		8.00

Name & Address of Employer	☐ Self Employed	Yrs. on this job
		Yrs. employed in this line of work/profession

Position/Title/Type of Business
MANAGER

Business Phone (incl. area code)
203-374-2121

Position/Title/Type of Business | Business Phone (incl. area code)

If employed in current position for less than two years or if currently employed in more than one position, complete the following:

| Name & Address of Employer | ☐ Self Employed | Dates (from - to) | Name & Address of Employer | ☐ Self Employed | Dates (from - to) |
| | | Monthly Income $ | | | Monthly Income $ |

| Position/Title/Type of Business | Business Phone (incl. area code) | Position/Title/Type of Business | Business Phone (incl. area code) |

| Name & Address of Employer | ☐ Self Employed | Dates (from - to) | Name & Address of Employer | ☐ Self Employed | Dates (from - to) |
| | | Monthly Income $ | | | Monthly Income $ |

| Position/Title/Type of Business | Business Phone (incl. area code) | Position/Title/Type of Business | Business Phone (incl. area code) |

Freddie Mac Form 65 6/09

MULTISTATE
ITEM 1138L1 (072009)

Fannie Mae Form 1003 6/09

GreatDocs®
(Page 1 of 4)
Ap#: 00125224

FIGURE **12.1** (*Continued*)

V. MONTHLY INCOME AND COMBINED HOUSING EXPENSE INFORMATION

Gross Monthly Income	Borrower	Co-Borrower	Total	Combined Monthly Housing Expense	Present	Proposed
Base Empl. Income*	$ 5,833.00	$	$ 5,833.00	Rent	$	
Overtime			0.00	First Mortgage (P&I)	920.00	$ 833.61
Bonuses			0.00	Other Financing (P&I)		
Commissions			0.00	Hazard Insurance	100.00	50.00
Dividends/Interest				Real Estate Taxes	850.00	445.00
Net Rental Income			0.00	Mortgage Insurance	45.00	
Other (before completing, see the notice in "describe other income," below)			0.00	Homeowner Assn. Dues		
			0.00	Other:		
Total	$ 5,833.00	$ 0.00	$ 5,833.00	Total	$ 1,915.00	$ 1,328.61

* Self Employed Borrower(s) may be required to provide additional documentation such as tax returns and financial statements.

Describe Other Income   *Notice:* Alimony, child support, or separate maintenance income need not be revealed if the Borrower (B) or Co-Borrower (C) does not choose to have it considered for repaying this loan.

B/C		Monthly Amount
		$

VI. ASSETS AND LIABILITIES

This Statement and any applicable supporting schedules may be completed jointly by both married and unmarried Co-Borrowers if their assets and liabilities are sufficiently joined so that the Statement can be meaningfully and fairly presented on a combined basis; otherwise, separate Statements and Schedules are required. If the Co-Borrower section was completed about a non-applicant spouse or other person, this Statement and supporting schedules must be completed about that spouse or other person also.   Completed ☐ Jointly ☒ Not Jointly

ASSETS	Cash or Market Value	Liabilities and Pledged Assets. List the creditor's name, address, and account number for all outstanding debts, including automobile loans, revolving charge accounts, real estate loans, alimony, child support, stock pledges, etc. Use continuation sheet, if necessary. Indicate by (*) those liabilities, which will be satisfied upon sale of real estate owned or upon refinancing of the subject property.		
Description				
Cash deposit toward purchase held by: ATTORNEY	$ 500.00			
		LIABILITIES	Monthly Payment & Months Left to Pay	Unpaid Balance
List checking and savings accounts below				
Name and address of Bank, S&L, or Credit Union LIBERTY BANK MIDDLETOWN CT		Name and address of Company AMEX	$ Payment/Months 294.00 20	$ 5,883.00
Acct. no. XXXXX13579	$ 17,900.00	Acct. no. 186581359125413993		
Name and address of Bank, S&L, or Credit Union PEOPLE UNITED BANK BRIDGEPORT CT		Name and address of Company BK OF AMER	$ Payment/Months 25.00 55	$ 1,377.00
Acct. no. XXXXX-2468	$ 1,600.00	Acct. no. 599971422963		
Name and address of Bank, S&L, or Credit Union PEOPLE UNITED BANK BRIDGEPORT CT		Name and address of Company BOA/MBNA	$ Payment/Months 15.00 198	$ 2,969.00
Acct. no. XXXX-9876	$ 10,000.00	Acct. no. 4681		
Name and address of Bank, S&L, or Credit Union		Name and address of Company CHASE	$ Payment/Months 107.00 50	$ 5,389.00
Acct. no.	$			
Stocks & Bonds (Company name/number & description) ESSEX FINANCIAL SVC	$ 19,500.00	Acct. no. 525831313543 Name and address of Company FORD MOTOR CO	$ Payment/Months 244.00 38	$ 9,430.00
Life insurance net cash value	$			
Face amount: $				
Subtotal Liquid Assets	$ 49,500.00	Acct. no. 40300611		
Real estate owned (enter market value from schedule of real estate owned)	$ 200,000.00	Name and address of Company * OPTION ONE	$ Payment/Months 920.00	$ 162,975.00
Vested interest in retirement fund	$ 3,500.00			
Net worth of business(es) owned (attach financial statement)	$	Acct. no. 7581128319409		
Automobiles owned (make and year) FORD EDGE	$ 15,000.00	Name and address of Company	$ Payment/Months	$
		Acct. no.		
Other Assets (itemize)	$	Alimony/Child Support/Separate Maintenance Payments Owed to:	$	
		Job-Related Expense (child care, union dues, etc.)	$	
		Total Monthly Payments	$ 1,605.00	
Total Assets a.	$ 268,000.00	Net Worth (a minus b) ▶ $ 79,977.00	Total Liabilities b.	$ 188,023.00

Freddie Mac Form 65 6/09

MULTISTATE
ITEM 1138L2 (072009)

Fannie Mae Form 1003 6/09

GreatDocs®
(Page 2 of 4)
App#: 00125224

FIGURE **12.1** (*Continued*)

VI. ASSETS AND LIABILITIES (cont'd)

Schedule of Real Estate Owned (If additional properties are owned, use continuation sheet.)

Property Address (enter S if sold, PS if pending sale or R if rental being held for income) ▼	Type of Property	Present Market Value	Amount of Mortgages & Liens	Gross Rental Income	Mortgage Payments	Insurance, Maintenance, Taxes & Misc.	Net Rental Income
100 TERRACE STREET WEST HAVEN, CT S	1-FAMILY	$ 200,000.00	$ 162,975.00	$	$ 920.00	$ 1,990.00	$
Totals		$ 200,000.00	$ 162,975.00	$	$ 920.00	$ 1,990.00	$

List any additional names under which credit has previously been received and indicate appropriate creditor name(s) and account number(s):

Alternate Name	Creditor Name	Account Number

VII. DETAILS OF TRANSACTION

a. Purchase price	$ 225,000.00
b. Alterations, improvements, repairs	
c. Land (if acquired separately)	
d. Refinance (incl. debts to be paid off)	
e. Estimated prepaid items	1,376.25
f. Estimated closing costs	3,032.50
g. PMI, MIP, Funding Fee	
h. Discount (if Borrower will pay)	2,700.00
i. Total costs (add items a through h)	232,108.75
j. Subordinate financing	
k. Borrower's closing costs paid by Seller	
l. Other Credits (explain) Escrow Deposit	500.00
m. Loan amount (exclude PMI, MIP, Funding Fee financed)	180,000.00
n. PMI, MIP, Funding Fee financed	
o. Loan amount (add m & n)	180,000.00
p. Cash from/to Borrower (subtract j, k, l & o from i)	51,608.75

VIII. DECLARATIONS

If you answer "Yes" to any questions a through i, please use continuation sheet for explanation.

	Borrower Yes	Borrower No	Co-Borrower Yes	Co-Borrower No
a. Are there any outstanding judgments against you?		X		
b. Have you been declared bankrupt within the past 7 years?		X		
c. Have you had property foreclosed upon or given title or deed in lieu thereof in the last 7 years?		X		
d. Are you a party to a lawsuit?		X		
e. Have you directly or indirectly been obligated on any loan which resulted in foreclosure, transfer of title in lieu of foreclosure, or judgment? (This would include such loans as home mortgage loans, SBA loans, home improvement loans, educational loans, manufactured (mobile) home loans, any mortgage, financial obligation, bond, or loan guarantee. If "Yes," provide details, including date, name, and address of Lender, FHA or VA case number, if any, and reasons for the action.)		X		
f. Are you presently delinquent or in default on any Federal debt or any other loan, mortgage, financial obligation, bond, or loan guarantee?		X		
g. Are you obligated to pay alimony, child support, or separate maintenance?		X		
h. Is any part of the down payment borrowed?		X		
i. Are you a co-maker or endorser on a note?		X		
j. Are you a U.S. citizen?	X			
k. Are you a permanent resident alien?		X		
l. Do you intend to occupy the property as your primary residence? If "Yes," complete question m below.	X			
m. Have you had an ownership interest in a property in the last three years?	X			
(1) What type of property did you own—principal residence (PR), second home (SH), or investment property (IP)?	PR			
(2) How did you hold title to the home—by yourself (S), jointly with your spouse or jointly with another person (O)?	S			

IX. ACKNOWLEDGEMENT AND AGREEMENT

Each of the undersigned specifically represents to Lender and to Lender's actual or potential agents, brokers, processors, attorneys, insurers, servicers, successors and assigns and agrees and acknowledges that: (1) the information provided in this application is true and correct as of the date set forth opposite my signature and that any intentional or negligent misrepresentation of this information contained in this application may result in civil liability, including monetary damages, to any person who may suffer any loss due to reliance upon any misrepresentation that I have made on this application, and/or in criminal penalties including, but not limited to, fine or imprisonment or both under the provisions of Title 18, United States Code, Sec. 1001, et seq.; (2) the loan requested pursuant to this application (the "Loan") will be secured by a mortgage or deed of trust on the property described in this application; (3) the property will not be used for any illegal or prohibited purpose or use; (4) all statements made in this application are made for the purpose of obtaining a residential mortgage loan; (5) the property will be occupied as indicated in this application; (6) the Lender, its servicers, successors or assigns may retain the original and/or an electronic record of this application, whether or not the Loan is approved; (7) the Lender and its agents, brokers, insurers, servicers, successors, and assigns may continuously rely on the information contained in the application, and I am obligated to amend and/or supplement the information provided in this application if any of the material facts that I have represented herein should change prior to closing of the Loan; (8) in the event that my payments on the Loan become delinquent, the Lender, its servicers, successors or assigns may, in addition to any other rights and remedies that it may have relating to such delinquency, report my name and account information to one or more consumer reporting agencies; (9) ownership of the Loan and/or administration of the Loan account may be transferred with such notice as may be required by law; (10) neither Lender nor its agents, brokers, insurers, servicers, successors or assigns has made any representation or warranty, express or implied, to me regarding the property or the condition or value of the property; and (11) my transmission of this application as an "electronic record" containing my "electronic signature," as those terms are defined in applicable federal and/or state laws (excluding audio and video recordings), or my facsimile transmission of this application containing a facsimile of my signature, shall be as effective, enforceable and valid as if a paper version of this application were delivered containing my original written signature.

Acknowledgement. Each of the undersigned hereby acknowledges that any owner of the Loan, its servicers, successors and assigns, may verify or reverify any information contained in this application or obtain any information or data relating to the Loan, for any legitimate business purpose through any source, including a source named in this application or a consumer reporting agency.

Borrower's Signature X *Nickie C Green*	Date 2/01/11	Co-Borrower's Signature X	Date
NICKIE C. GREEN			

X. INFORMATION FOR GOVERNMENT MONITORING PURPOSES

The following information is requested by the Federal Government for certain types of loans related to a dwelling in order to monitor the lender's compliance with equal credit opportunity, fair housing and home mortgage disclosure laws. You are not required to furnish this information, but are encouraged to do so. The law provides that a lender may not discriminate either on the basis of this information, or on whether you choose to furnish it. If you furnish the information, please provide both ethnicity and race. For race, you may check more than one designation. If you do not furnish ethnicity, race, or sex, under Federal regulations, this lender is required to note the information on the basis of visual observation and surname if you have made this application in person. If you do not wish to furnish the information, please check the box below. (Lender must review the above material to assure that the disclosures satisfy all requirements to which the lender is subject under applicable state law for the particular type of loan applied for.)

BORROWER	[ ] I do not wish to furnish this information		CO-BORROWER	[ ] I do not wish to furnish this information	
Ethnicity: [ ] Hispanic or Latino	[ ] Not Hispanic or Latino		**Ethnicity:** [ ] Hispanic or Latino	[ ] Not Hispanic or Latino	
Race: [ ] American Indian or Alaska Native [ ] Asian [ ] Black or African American [ ] Native Hawaiian or Other Pacific Islander [X] White			**Race:** [ ] American Indian or Alaska Native [ ] Asian [ ] Black or African American [ ] Native Hawaiian or Other Pacific Islander [ ] White		
Sex: [X] Female [ ] Male			**Sex:** [ ] Female [ ] Male		

To be Completed by Loan Originator:

This information was provided: [X] In a face-to-face interview [ ] In a telephone interview [ ] By the applicant and submitted by fax or mail [ ] By the applicant and submitted via e-mail or the Internet

Loan Originator's Signature X *Tes Trep*		Date 02/01/11
Loan Originator's Name (print or type) TESTREP	Loan Originator Identifier 59555	Loan Originator's Phone Number (including area code) (800) 382-0017
Loan Origination Company's Name THE McCUE MORTGAGE COMPANY	Loan Origination Company Identifier 71717	Loan Origination Company's Address ONE LIBERTY SQUARE NEW BRITAIN, CT 06050

Freddie Mac Form 65 6/09   Fannie Mae Form 1003 6/09

MULTISTATE
ITEM 1138L3 (072009)

GreatDocs®
(Page 3 of 4)
Ap#: 00125224

FIGURE **12.1** (*Continued*)

FEDERAL TRUTH-IN-LENDING DISCLOSURE STATEMENT

Borrower:
NICKIE C. GREEN
100 TERRACE STREET
WEST HAVEN, CT 06516

Creditor:
THE McCUE MORTGAGE COMPANY
ONE LIBERTY SQUARE
NEW BRITAIN, CT 06050

Loan Number: 00125224

Date: 02/04/2011

ANNUAL PERCENTAGE RATE	FINANCE CHARGE	Amount Financed	Total of Payments
The cost of your credit as a yearly rate.	The dollar amount the credit will cost you.	The amount of credit provided to you or on your behalf.	The amount you will have paid after you have made all payments as scheduled.
3.4482%	$105,037.66	$175,643.75	$280,681.41

INTEREST RATE AND PAYMENT SUMMARY

	INTRODUCTORY Rate & Monthly Payment (for first 60 months)	MAXIMUM During FIRST FIVE YEARS April 01, 2016	MAXIMUM EVER (as early as April 01, 2016)
Interest Rate	3.7500 %	8.7500 %	8.7500 %
Principal + Interest Payment	$833.61	$1,333.02	$1,333.02
Estimate Taxes + Insurance (Escrow) ☐ Includes Private Mortgage Insurance ☐ Includes Mortgage Insurance	$495.00	$495.00	$495.00
Total Estimated Monthly Payment	$1,328.61	$1,828.02	$1,828.02

☐ **Introductory Rate Notice.**
You have a discounted introductory rate of   % that ends after
In the   even if market rates do not change, this rate will increase to   %

VARIABLE RATE: Your loan contains a variable-rate feature. Disclosures about the variable-rate feature have been provided to you earlier.

INSURANCE: The following insurance is required to obtain credit: *Property
   You may obtain the insurance from anyone that is acceptable to creditor.

SECURITY: You are giving a security interest in the real property being purchased.
    Property address: 1144 REEF ROAD, FAIRFIELD, CT 06824

LATE CHARGE: If a payment is more than 15 days late, you will be charged 5.0000% of the payment.

PREPAYMENT: If you pay off your loan early, * You will not have to pay a penalty.
    * You may be entitled to a refund of part of the finance charge.

ASSUMPTION: Someone buying your property may assume the remainder of your loan on the original terms.

NO GUARANTEE TO REFINANCE: There is no guarantee that you will be able to refinance to lower your rate and payments.

All dates and numerical disclosures except the late payment disclosure are estimates.

See your contract documents for any additional information about nonpayment, default, any required repayment in full before the scheduled date, and prepayment refunds and penalties.

You are not required to complete this agreement merely because you have received these disclosures or signed a loan application.

_____

NICKIE C. GREEN   DATE

FIGURE **12.1** (*Continued*)

Good Faith Estimate (GFE)

OMB Approval No. 2502-0265

Name of Originator	Borrower
THE McCUE MORTGAGE COMPANY	NICKIE C GREEN

Originator Address	Property Address
ONE LIBERTY SQUARE NEW BRITAIN, CT 06050	1144 REEF ROAD FAIRFIELD, CT 06824

Originator Phone Number (800) 382-0017	
Originator Email	Date of GFE February 04, 2011

Purpose

This GFE gives you an estimate of your settlement charges and loan terms if you are approved for this loan. For more information, see HUD's *Special Information Booklet* on settlement charges, your *Truth-in-Lending Disclosures*, and other consumer information at www.hud.gov/respa. If you decide you would like to proceed with this loan, contact us.

Shopping for your loan

Only you can shop for the best loan for you. Compare this GFE with other loan offers, so you can find the best loan. Use the shopping chart on page 3 to compare all the offers you receive.

Important dates

1. The interest rate for this GFE is available through ☐ March 30, 2011 12:00 AM ☐. After this time, the interest rate, some of your loan Origination Charges, and the monthly payment shown below can change until you lock your interest rate.

2. This estimate for all other settlement charges is available through ☐ February 18, 2011 ☐

3. After you lock your interest rate, you must go to settlement within ☐ 55 ☐ days (your rate lock period) to receive the locked interest rate.

4. You must lock the interest rate at least ☐ NA ☐ days before settlement.

Summary of your loan

Your initial loan amount is	$ 180,000.00
Your loan term is	30 years
Your initial interest rate is	3.7500 %
Your initial monthly amount owed for principal, interest, and any mortgage insurance is	$833.61 per month
Can your interest rate rise?	☐ No ☒ Yes, it can rise to a maximum of 8.7500 %. The first change will be in 60 months
Even if you make payments on time, can your loan balance rise?	☒ No ☐ Yes, it can rise to a maximum of $
Even if you make payments on time, can your monthly amount owed for principal, interest, and any mortgage insurance rise?	☐ No ☒ Yes, the first increase can be in 61 months and the monthly amount owed can rise to $1,333.02 . The maximum it can ever rise to is $1,333.02 .
Does your loan have a prepayment penalty?	☒ No ☐ Yes, your maximum prepayment penalty is $.
Does your loan have a balloon payment?	☒ No ☐ Yes, you have a balloon payment of $ due in years.

Escrow account information

Some lenders require an escrow account to hold funds for paying property taxes or other property-related charges in addition to your monthly amount owed of $ 833.61 ☐

Do we require you to have an escrow account for your loan?

☐ No, you do not have an escrow account. You must pay these charges directly when due.

☒ Yes, you have an escrow account. It may or may not cover all of these charges. Ask us.

Summary of your settlement charges

A	Your Adjusted Origination Charges (*See page 2.*)	$	3,350.00
B	Your Charges for All Other Settlement Services (*See page 2.*)	$	3,658.75
A + B	TOTAL ESTIMATED SETTLEMENT CHARGES	$	7,008.75

FIGURE **12.1** (*Continued*)

Understanding your estimated settlement charges

Some of these charges can change at settlement. See the top of page 3 for more information.

YOUR ADJUSTED ORIGINATION CHARGES

1. Our origination charge
This charge is for getting this loan for you. — **650.00**

2. Your credit or charge (points) for the specific interest rate chosen
☐ The credit or charge for the interest rate of ☐% is included in "Our origination charge." (See item 1 above.)
☐ You receive a credit of $☐ for this interest rate of ☐%. This credit **reduces** your settlement charges.
☒ You pay a charge of $|2,700.00| for this interest rate of |3.7500|%. This charge (points) **increases** your total settlement charges.
The tradeoff table on page 3 shows that you can change your total settlement charges by choosing a different interest rate for this loan. — **2,700.00**

| **A** | **Your Adjusted Origination Charges** | **$ 3,350.00** |

YOUR CHARGES FOR ALL OTHER SETTLEMENT SERVICES

3. Required services that we select
These charges are for services we require to complete your settlement. We will choose the providers of these services.

Service	Charge
Appraisal fee	375.00
Credit report	25.00
	400.00

4. Title services and lender's title insurance
This charge includes the services of a title or settlement agent, for example, and title insurance to protect the lender, if required. — **1,440.00**

5. Owner's title insurance
You may purchase an owner's title insurance policy to protect your interest in the property. — **267.50**

6. Required services that you can shop for
These charges are for other services that are required to complete your settlement. We can identify providers of these services or you can shop for them yourself. Our estimates for providing these services are below.

Service	Charge
TERMITE INSPECTION	75.00
	75.00

7. Government recording charges
These charges are for state and local fees to record your loan and title documents. — **200.00**

8. Transfer taxes
These charges are for state and local fees on mortgages and home sales.

9. Initial deposit for your escrow account
This charge is held in an escrow account to pay future recurring charges on your property and includes ☒ all property taxes, ☒ all insurance, and ☐ other ☐ — **495.00**

10. Daily interest charges
This charge is for the daily interest on your loan from the day of your settlement until the first day of the next month or the first day of your normal mortgage payment cycle. This amount is $|18.7500| per day for |15| days (if your settlement is |03/17/2011|). — **281.25**

11. Homeowner's insurance
This charge is for the insurance you must buy for the property to protect from a loss, such as fire.

Policy	Charge
Hazard ins. premium	600.00
	600.00

| **B** | **Your Charges for All Other Settlement Services** | **$ 3,658.75** |
| **A** + **B** | **TOTAL ESTIMATED SETTLEMENT CHARGES** | **$ 7,008.75** |

MULTISTATE
ITEM 73308L2 (C3093L) (100209)

Good Faith Estimate (HUD-GFE)
GreatDocs®
(Page 2 of 3)
00125224

FIGURE **12.1** (*Continued*)

INSTRUCTIONS

Understanding which charges can change at settlement

This GFE estimates your settlement charges. At your settlement, you will receive a HUD-1, a form that lists your actual costs. Compare the charges on the HUD-1 with the charges on this GFE. Charges can change if you select your own provider and do not use the companies we identify. (See below for details.)

These charges cannot increase at settlement	The total of these charges can increase up to 10% at settlement	These charges can change at settlement
• Our origination charge • Your credit or charge (points) for the specific interest rate chosen *(after you lock in your interest rate)* • Your adjusted origination charges *(after you lock in your interest rate)* • Transfer taxes	• Required services that we select • Title services and lender's title insurance *(if we select them or you use companies we identify)* • Owner's title insurance *(if you use companies we identify)* • Required services that you can shop for *(if you use companies we identify)* • Government recording charges	• Required services that you can shop for *(if you do not use companies we identify)* • Title services and lender's title insurance *(if you do not use companies we identify)* • Owner's title insurance *(if you do not use companies we identify)* • Initial deposit for your escrow account • Daily interest charges • Homeowner's insurance

Using the tradeoff table

In this GFE, we offered you this loan with a particular interest rate and estimated settlement charges. However:

• If you want to choose this same loan with **lower settlement charges**, then you will have a **higher interest rate**.

• If you want to choose this same loan with a **lower interest rate**, then you will have **higher settlement charges**.

If you would like to choose an available option, you must ask us for a new GFE.

Loan originators have the option to complete this table. Please ask for additional information if the table is not completed.

	The loan in this GFE	The same loan with lower settlement charges	The same loan with a lower interest rate
Your initial loan amount	$180,000.00	$	$
Your initial interest rate[1]	3.7500 %	%	%
Your initial monthly amount owed	$833.61	$	$
Change in the monthly amount owed from this GFE	No change	You will pay $ **more** every month	You will pay $ **less** every month
Change in the amount you will pay at settlement with this interest rate	No change	Your settlement charges will be **reduced** by $	Your settlement charges will **increase** by $
How much your total estimated settlement charges will be	$7,008.75	$	$

[1] For an adjustable rate loan, the comparisons above are for the initial interest rate before adjustments are made.

Using the shopping chart

Use this chart to compare GFEs from different loan originators. Fill in the information by using a different column for each GFE you receive. By comparing loan offers, you can shop for the best loan.

	THIS LOAN	LOAN 2	LOAN 3	LOAN 4
Loan originator name	THE McCUE MORTGAGE COMPANY			
Initial loan amount	$180,000.00			
Loan term	30 years			
Initial interest rate	3.7500			
Initial monthly amount owed	$833.61			
Rate lock period	55 days			
Can interest rate rise?	YES			
Can loan balance rise?	NO			
Can monthly amount owed rise?	YES			
Prepayment penalty?	NO			
Balloon payment?	NO			
TOTAL ESTIMATED SETTLEMENT CHARGES	$7,008.75			

If your loan is sold in the future

Some lenders may sell your loan after settlement. Any fees lenders receive in the future cannot change the loan you receive or the charges you paid at settlement.

MULTISTATE
ITEM 73306L3 (C3093L) (100209)

Good Faith Estimate (HUD-GFE)
GreatDocs®
(Page 3 of 3)
00125224

Source: © REMOC Associates, LLC
Reprinted with permission of the McCue Mortgage Company.

forms rather than with lender-produced forms.) There is so much risk with compliance these days that it is wise to use the forms provided by either the computer processing software, which are updated frequently, or the forms from the direct lender. Mortgage brokers and other third party lenders are typically required to use the end lenders' forms now when submitting a file. This is good practice because it will reduce risk and liability if any of the disclosures are not in proper format.

Once completed and signed by the applicant(s), the lender should not alter or discard the original application form. If the application is approved and the loan is closing, the mortgage lender will generate a final application form for the borrower to sign at closing. This final application form contains the updated or verified information as a result of the lender's processing activities. The lender should always keep both the original and final application forms in the loan file.

Information that Applicants Must Bring to Application

Most applicants, unless they have applied for mortgage loans before, have no idea of the amount of information they will be asked to provide a mortgage lender. In order to speed up processing, a lender should distribute to real estate brokers and/or applicants a brochure listing the information that applicants should bring to the application meeting. Many lenders and loan officers place this information on their Web sites or on the back of their business cards to assist potential applicants. Regardless, the information requested includes the following:

Nonfinancial information (for *all* applicants):

- Names in which title will be held and how title will be held (e.g., joint tenants) for the property being financed.
- Address of property to be financed and, if available, its legal description (if the property is being purchased, include a fully executed, *clear* copy of the contract of sale).
- Copy of a government-issued, active photo ID (driver's license or passport is ideal). For non-U.S. citizens, a copy of both sides of a visa will also be required.
- Principal residence address history of applicant(s) for previous two years, whether owned or rented.

Financial information (for *all* applicants):

- Income history for the prior two years (verified in the form of paycheck stubs covering the most recent 30 days and copies of W-2s for the prior two years).
- Additional or supplemental income history (verified same as preceding).
- If self-employed, the most recent two years of signed, complete federal income tax returns (with all schedules) along with a balance sheet and income statement for the latest quarter of the current year. These items may or may not need to be prepared by an accountant, but must be signed and dated by the applicant.

- Creditor information: credit cards, revolving charges, 401(k) loans, leases, installment or automobile loans, current and past mortgages, and so forth (a simple list would be sufficient because the mortgage loan officer will obtain the actual creditor and account information directly from the credit report).
- Employment history, for the two most recent years, including all names and addresses of employers.
- A list of liquid and non-liquid assets is important to have at the outset. The applicant should bring copies of the last two months statements (all pages) for each of these accounts. If quarterly, the last quarter will suffice. The lenders will also verify directly with the depositor the most current balances on the accounts.)
- List of all other investments that may be used for reserves or closing costs.

Please note that a lender should not discourage completing an application even if the applicants do not provide all of the preceding information at application. A follow-up list of missing documents will allow the process to start without excessive delay. Most additional documents may be either faxed, or scanned and e-mailed afterwards. Sometimes it is impossible or less convenient for applicant(s) to apply in a face-to-face interview. Lending practices have become more customer sensitive, so additional options exist for consumers who wish to apply for a mortgage but cannot meet with a loan officer: mail, telephone, and electronic applications. Each method of taking a loan application has its own compliance guidelines to follow as far as providing original documents to the client. In some states, these compliance issues override any federal regulations; so the mortgage loan officer should ask his or her manager for the most recent requirements for mailing hard copy originals and keeping copies of documents in the loan file.

Applications Received by Mail

Circumstances sometimes require that an application be completed through the mail, usually when out-of-town applicants cannot meet for a face-to-face interview. In these situations, the lender mails an application package containing an original and copy of the loan application, required pre-application disclosures along with a cover letter containing instructions. The instructional letter should include an explanation of the application process and provide specific instructions on the following:

- Completing the actual application
- Requesting additional information and list of supporting documents
- Clearly marked signature locations on each document
- Schedule of payment of application fee, appraisal, and any other required costs
- Returning the completed documentation (a self-addressed stamped envelope must be provided)
- Contacting the lender with questions via a toll-free number or e-mail address

Upon receipt of the signed Authorization to Verify Information form, contained in the completed package, the lender mails out the Verification forms along with a copy of the Authorization form to the employers, depositories, and others identified on the application.

As with face-to-face applications, all of the federally mandated consumer compliance and protection regulations apply to mail-in applications. Even though the applicant completes the documentation, the lender is still responsible for compliance with regulations and should review these applications quickly and carefully.

Telephone Applications

If an application is completed by a mortgage loan officer over the telephone, two original copies of the application and disclosures need to be sent via mail, *typically* within ten business days, to each applicant. This must accompany an instructional letter informing the persons to sign one copy and ensure that the other copy is signed, dated, and returned to the lender. A self-addressed stamped envelope must also be included in the package. This may vary state by state, so be sure to check with management about the individual state guidelines.

Electronic Applications

With the ease of technology, paired with applicants' busy schedules, the Internet has become a useful tool for taking loan applications and transmitting documents for signature. Many applicants are tech-savvy enough to complete a loan application electronically, and are able to send the required supporting documents directly to the lender. In fact, some people prefer and appreciate this method over face-to-face meetings or snail mail.

However, an application may not be taken electronically unless the applicant can either digitally sign the pre-application disclosures he or she has received electronically or acknowledges electronic receipt of the pre-application disclosures through the use of a "required confirm button." Without such a confirmation, the transaction may not proceed.

In addition, if any of the applicants indicate that they do not have the capacity to print a copy of the documents transmitted electronically, then a hard copy must be sent out to them within three business days of the electronic transmission of same. The lender and any third party originator must either keep a copy of the pre-application disclosures that were digitally signed by the applicant or provide proof that the applicant did not proceed with the mortgage application after they were sent. Where a hard copy of the pre-application disclosures is not mailed to the applicant(s), the mortgage broker must be able to demonstrate that information was obtained as to the applicant's computer capacity to download and print such disclosures. Proof of the same should be maintained in the file. (i.e., electronic acknowledgment from the applicants that they were able to download and print in e-mail form will suffice).

While this method of origination may provide more business for the lender and additional convenience for the applicant, it also raises a number of security and compliance issues for the lender. Lenders must ensure that this form of origination is consistent with their lending practices and policies, and that it does not create compliance issues. For example, certain lenders have Community Reinvestment Act responsibilities, or may be restricted by charter (state, federal, or regulatory) and may lend only within a geographic area or to certain applicants (e.g., credit unions can lend only to their members). If electronic applications are not managed properly, the lender may lose control over who applies, what credit terms are requested, and actual loan volume. Keeping track of loan applications taken is important for compliance with banking department volumes reports. Thus, monitoring and recording system applications taken, credit decisions, and compliance of same, is imperative. In addition, the lender must ensure that their system complies with the guidelines of the Gramm-Leach-Bliley Act of 1999 to "design, implement, and safeguard the customers' finance information in their possession" (See Chapter 11—Compliance).

QUALIFYING AN APPLICANT

The purpose of initially qualifying applicants is to provide them with the best information possible at that time (see Figure 12.2). The loan officer must ask the consumer a number of general and specific follow-up questions to clarify the information disclosed and convert it into mortgage lending use. At this stage, the purpose is not to make a credit decision, but to help the consumer and lender decide how to proceed with the application process, if at all.

Although this is a preliminary stage, it still requires that the loan officer be familiar with all loan programs, policies and underwriting guidelines, and steps in the application process. The loan officer must then apply this information to the applicants' financial situation. When qualifying applicants, the mortgage loan officer wears three hats: business developer, processor, and underwriter. The loan officer must view each situation creatively for its potential, request from the applicants the proper documentation needed to complete the transaction, and keep in mind the loan policy guidelines.

Many lenders structure their programs and policies to conform to secondary market standards created by Fannie Mae and Freddie Mac. Portfolio lenders may have additional programs that provide the mortgage loan officer with more flexibility and alternatives for the applicants. Secondary market agencies describe these transactions or programs as *conforming/nonconforming* or *eligible/ineligible* for the secondary market.

Areas of consideration when qualifying a mortgage applicant include loan transaction and program, debt/income ratios, credit history, assets, collateral, and other compensating factors. This process by necessity involves a certain amount of what is traditionally called "underwriting," but the information is not verified and, therefore, not final.

Qualifying an applicant involves many specific guidelines for a lender, but in its simplest form it involves addressing three main concerns: Does the proposed transaction conform to the lender's loan policy? Have the

FIGURE **12.2** Sample Qualification Worksheet

FAIRFIELD SAVINGS ASSOCIATION
FIRST MORTGAGE LOAN INFORMATION

QUALIFICATION WORKSHEET

BORROWER(S)			SOC. SEC. #
Joseph F. Lynch			123-45-6789
Margaret J. Lynch			987-65-4321

INCOME EVALUATION:		PER MONTH	
BORROWER'S INCOME		$	5000.00
COBORROWER'S INCOME		$	4000.00
BONUS OR COMMISSION		$	
INVESTMENT INCOME		$	
OVERTIME		$	
OTHER INCOME		$	
TOTAL INCOME		$	9250.00

CREDIT EVALUATION:			
INTEREST RATE		6.000	%
TERM (YEARS)		30	
POINTS		2.000%	
AMOUNT		$	189000.00
PRINCIPAL & INTEREST		$	1133.16
REAL ESTATE TAXES		$	250.00
INSURANCE		$	75.00
OTHER		$	39.38
TOTAL HOUSING EXP		$	1497.54

INSTALLMENT DEBT	Incl	Mos		Balance
Peoples Bank	N	345		234255.00
Chase Auto Finance	Y	12		3000.00
Fleet Bank	Y	7		600.00
OTHER MONTHLY DEBT		$	$	
TOTAL DEBT PAYMENTS			$	365.91
CASH REQUIRED FOR CLOSING			$	28310.76
CASH AVAILABLE FOR CLOSING			$	22600.00
CASH RESERVE AFTER CLOSING			$	-5710.76

PROPERTY EVALUATION:			
LOAN AMOUNT		$	189000.00
SALES PRICE		$	210000.00
APPRAISED PRICE		$	210000.00
LOAN TO VALUE			90.00%

HOUSING STANDARDS:		
HOUSING TO INCOME RATIO		16.19%
DEBT TO INCOME RATIO		20.15%

Source: © REMOC Associates, LLC
Reprinted with permission of the McCue Mortgage Company.

applicants demonstrated the ability and willingness to repay the proposed mortgage? Is the collateral sufficient to secure the proposed mortgage loan?

In contrast, underwriters have several points of concern when analyzing a file, sometimes known as the **four C's.** They review the **collateral** (the real estate value and condition) credit (FICO® score and debt ratios of the applicant), **capacity** (the ability to pay the mortgage and all other debts), **character** (job and income stability and post closing reserves), and **condition** (health of the overall market and the applicants' place in it). Manual underwriting is a combination of professional training and the art of experience. Each underwriter may analyze and treat each file a little differently than another, depending on his or her personal background. Chapter 13—Underwriting describes the underwriting function in more detail, but loan originators must be familiar with the guidelines and process in order to explain this clearly and accurately to the consumer.

Lenders must qualify applicants fairly and in a consistent manner from loan application to loan application, including pricing and interest rates. Although a challenging task for lenders, the development of clear loan policies assists them in this step. These objective guidelines govern the lender's mortgage activities. They should explain how to handle the most common scenarios and should provide direction in more unusual circumstances.

The secondary market provides recommended guidelines detailing how to qualify an applicant. These industry standards develop from an ongoing statistical review of millions of loan applications across the nation, and are incredibly predictive from a national perspective.

Portfolio lenders may be more familiar with the special circumstances in their region or in a particular applicant's situation. They often deviate from secondary market standards in their general policies or make exceptions in individual cases when, in their opinion, the industry standard is not the most appropriate guideline for their local lending area and prevents them from making an acceptable mortgage loan.

Sample Qualification Worksheet

Historically, qualifying applicants for the secondary market meant following a single, specific formula into which the applicants needed to fit. This chapter describes the most conventional, traditional, or standard secondary market processing guidelines. Keep in mind that portfolio lenders and smaller regional institutions that service their own loans may have special guidelines to meet the needs of their own applicants.

Today, some lenders still have alternative-, streamlined-, limited-, and even no-documentation programs, although these programs and guidelines change frequently. Separate sections in this chapter and in Chapter 13—Underwriting the Residential Mortgage Loan, explain in further detail these and other programs. Unless otherwise noted, for clarity this chapter describes standard secondary market guidelines.

It is important to note that qualifying an applicant is a totally different issue than whether or not the lender will make a *profit* on the proposed loan. While this is a very important concern (especially for the lender), it is a separate consideration from how to qualify an applicant.

Loan Transaction and Program

Often, the first thing a loan officer discusses with the applicants is what their mortgage needs entail. A lender must obtain information about the real estate transaction and loan request. Once this information is developed, the loan officer must evaluate whether the lender's loan programs and policies can meet these needs. For example, an applicant might need a loan amount of $445,000 to complete a purchase, but the lender's loan limit is $417,000 (secondary market limit for single-family homes in the continental 48 states for 2011). The applicants may qualify in all other aspects, but the lender does not offer a loan program for that amount.

Another example might be a refinance request in which the applicants need $110,000 to consolidate their consumer debt, but know this amount is 95 percent of the value of their property. In this case, the lender's loan policies might limit refinance transactions to a maximum of 80 percent of the value of the collateral (the secondary market limit for refinance transactions that take equity out of the collateral).

Mortgage bankers usually have less flexibility in this regard, so the mortgage loan officer must approve only those applications that are eligible for secondary market purchase. Lenders willing to hold loans in their portfolios may have more flexibility in accepting applications that the secondary market deems nonconforming. Chapter 13—Underwriting the Residential Mortgage Loan, contains more specific information on secondary market loan programs and transactions.

Debt/Income Ratios

After discussing the proposed loan transaction and program, the next qualifying area the loan officer must address is whether the applicant has the financial ability and willingness to repay the debt. A loan officer first conducts a comprehensive review of the applicant's income, debts, and credit history. This information is used to develop debt/income ratios for housing and total debt. These objective measures help evaluate the applicant's financial capacity.

Lenders calculate the housing ratio by dividing the total monthly housing expense (principal, interest, real estate taxes, insurance, PMI, and any other monthly expense for the home) by total gross (before taxes) monthly income. Currently, the standard secondary market guideline for this ratio is 28 percent and higher for some programs.. The total debt ratio is total monthly debt payments divided by total gross monthly income. The standard secondary market guideline for this ratio is 36 percent. Some programs go as high as 50 percent, depending on the loan to value, FICO® score, and loan purpose. Most large lenders will get the loan approved by Fannie Mae Desktop Underwriter® (DU®) and use the ratios that the approval requests. Lenders no longer think in terms of "compensating factors," but rather create a matrix weighing one factor with another. Evaluating and verifying an applicant's qualifying income can be a complex process, depending on the circumstances. Since the loan officer may not have complete information at this time, these initial numbers are treated as estimates. Once the lender verifies all information, an underwriter determines the final figures.

Income of Applicant(s)

An applicant's income provides the means for repayment of the mortgage debt, along with the applicant's other debts and everyday expenses. Lenders must evaluate the *amount* and the likely *continuation* of the income. Lenders must consider several sources of income in this analysis, but most income is received from the following sources:

- Wage or salary
- Self-employment
- Bonus or commissions
- Rental property
- Interest, dividends, investments, or trust
- Child support, alimony, or separate maintenance
- Retirement, pension, or disability
- Unemployment, welfare, or other sources

These sources of income have different characteristics. Lenders must consider the following questions: How long has the income been received? How regularly will it be received? Will the amount be consistent? How timely will it be paid? How reliable is the source? How long will it continue? In addition, underwriters now take job history, probability of continued employment, and average income changes into consideration for wage earners. For commissioned, bonus, and self-employed applicants, past history, future potential, and yearly averages, are reviewed with greater scrutiny. (This will be discussed in greater detail later in this chapter.) As a result, how a lender will verify and use income to qualify an applicant varies dramatically according to its source. A precise evaluation can be difficult because applicants receive income from many sources, and the factors affecting receipt of income are different with each application.

As is discussed later, certain regulations, particularly the Equal Credit Opportunity Act, limit the manner in which a lender can inquire about these sources of income, and privacy rules can affect what information a lender obtains and how an employer discloses it.

Lenders typically begin the income analysis by converting the applicant's disclosed income from all sources into a gross monthly amount, then comparing this figure with the most recent two years of income.

Wage or salary income is the most common form of income disclosed on mortgage applications. Lenders often qualify applicants using the current salary or wage level disclosed, as it is the most stable form of income. Wage or salary income is consistent and paid weekly, biweekly, semimonthly, or monthly. Total income from these payments should be consistent year over year (lenders expect to see variations of less than 15 percent); however, if there are great variations, additional documentation will be required.

The standard form developed by the secondary market to verify wage or salary income is the Request for Verification of Employment (Fannie Mae Form 1005, commonly called the VOE as shown in Figure 12.3). If applicable, lenders also use this form to verify previous employment in the two-year history. Among other things, the VOE requests the following information from an employer:

- Date of employment
- Present position
- Breakdown of income (base, overtime, commissions, bonus, military)

FIGURE **12.3** Sample Request for Verification of Employment (VOE)

FannieMae **Request for Verification of Employment**

Privacy Act Notice: This information is to be used by the agency collecting it or its assignees in determining whether you qualify as a prospective mortgagor under its program. It will not be disclosed outside the agency except as required and permitted by law. You do not have to provide this information, but if you do not your application for approval as a prospective mortgagor or borrower may be delayed or rejected. The information requested in this form is authorized by Title 38, USC, Chapter 37 (if VA); by 12 USC, Section 1701 et. seq. (if HUD/FHA); by 42 USC, Section 1452b (if HUD/CPD); and Title 42 USC, 1471 et. seq., or 7 USC, 1921 et. seq. (if USDA/FmHA).

Instructions: Lender – Complete items 1 through 7. Have applicant complete item 8. Forward directly to employer, named in item 1.
Employer – Please complete either Part II or Part III as applicable. Complete Part IV and return directly to lender named in item 2.
The form is to be transmitted directly to the lender and is not to be transmitted through the applicant or any other party.

Part I – Request

1. To (Name and address of employer)	2. From (Name and address of lender)
Centes Package Store 123 Main Street Bridgeport, CT 06111 Attn: Personnel	THE McCUE MORTGAGE COMPANY One Liberty Square New Britain, CT 06050 Phone: (800) 382-0017

I certify that this verification has been sent directly to the employer and has not passed through the hands of the applicant or any other interested party.

3. Signature of Lender	4. Title	5. Date	6. Lender's Number (Optional)
Pete Processor	Mtg Processor	02/03/2011	00125224

I have applied for a mortgage loan and stated that I am now or was formerly employed by you. My signature below authorizes verification of this information.

7. Name and Address of Applicant (include employee or badge number)	8. Signature of Applicant
NICKIE C. GREEN 123-00-3333 100 TERRACE STREET WEST HAVEN, CT 06516	See Attached

Part II – Verification of Present Employment

9. Applicant's Date of Employment	10. Present Position	11. Probability of Continued Employment
June 2000	Manager	Good

12A. Current Gross Base Pay (Enter Amount and Check Period): [X] Annual [ ] Monthly [ ] Weekly [ ] Hourly [ ] Other (Specify) $

12B. Gross Earnings

Type	Year To Date	Past Year	Past Year
Base Pay	Thru $ 4167	$ 48,927	$ 47,122
Overtime	$	$	$
Commissions	$	$	$
Bonus	$	$ 500	$
Total	$	$	$

13. For Military Personnel Only

Pay Grade	
Type	Monthly Amount
Base Pay	$
Rations	$
Flight or Hazard	$
Clothing	$
Quarters	$
Pro Pay	$
Overseas or Combat	$
Variable Housing Allowance	$

14. If Overtime or Bonus is Applicable, is Its Continuance Likely?
Overtime [ ] Yes [ ] No
Bonus [X] Yes [ ] No

15. If paid hourly - average hours per week

16. Date of applicant's next pay increase: January 2012

17. Projected amount of next pay increase: Unk.

18. Date of applicant's last pay increase: January 2011

19. Amount of last pay increase: 3%

20. Remarks (If employee was off work for any length of time, please indicate time period and reason)

Part III – Verification of Previous Employment

21. Date Hired
22. Date Terminated
23. Salary/Wage at Termination Per (Year) (Month) (Week)
Base Overtime Commissions Bonus
24. Reason for Leaving
25. Position Held

Part IV – Authorized Signature – Federal statutes provide severe penalties for any fraud, intentional misrepresentation, or criminal connivance or conspiracy purposed to influence the issuance of any guaranty or insurance by the VA Secretary, the U.S.D.A., FmHA/FHA Commissioner, or the HUD/CPD Assistant Secretary.

26. Signature of Employer	27. Title (Please print or type)	28. Date
Barb Beener	Owner	2/7/11
29. Print or type name signed in item 26	30. Phone No.	
BARB BEENER		Ap#: 00125224

[001252241011]

ITEM 7041L0 (0609) Fannie Mae Form 1005 Jul 96 GreatDocs™ (Page 1 of 1)

Source: © REMOC Associates, LLC
Reprinted with permission of the McCue Mortgage Company.

- Current (year to date) and past two years' income
- Probability of continued employment, bonus, or overtime

To maintain the integrity of the information, the VOE must travel directly from the lender to the employer and back—not through a third party (such as the applicant or real estate broker). The lender will review the VOE for consistencies, looking at overtime, bonuses, and commission in detail. If there are decreases in current years, the lender may choose to average the bonus, overtime, or commissions, or eliminate it altogether if there is a chance that it will continue to decrease. Some lenders require a third party verification of employment/income performed from an outside service company. In addition, most lenders will do a verbal verification of employment within 48 hours prior to the closing to make sure the applicant is still employed before becoming a borrower.

SUPPORTING DOCUMENTATION AND TAX RETURNS

For salaried employees, the lender will want to see the last 30 days of pay stubs and the previous two years' IRS W-2 forms. If more than 25 percent of the employee's income is in the form of overtime, bonuses, or commissions, the lender will also require the last two years' federal Tax returns (1040s with all schedules attached). The lender will want to see if there appear to be any unreimbursed business expenses taken on the personal tax returns, if all income is reported, and if there are any inconsistencies. If any of the listed income is needed to qualify for the mortgage, the lender might ask for additional information from the employee as proof that that income will likely continue in the future years. If the lender is not satisfied that it will continue, it might be disqualified altogether.

Whether the applicant is salaried or self-employed, the lender will send an IRS Form 4506 (see Figure 12.4) to the IRS to verify that the income included in the loan application matches that which was submitted for tax purposes. Any inconsistencies might disqualify the loan altogether. In addition, the underwriter is required to report unsubstantiated income tax inconsistencies as fraud, which will cause bigger problems for the applicant.

Self-Employment

Self-employed applicants represent the highest risk category for default. An applicant who owns 25 percent or more of a company is considered to be self-employed. Self-employment income is considered stable income if the applicant has been self-employed for two or more years, during which time the net income is stable or increasing.

Qualifying income is calculated using the average of two years of net income from the business. Depending on the business, a lender may add back to net income the amount deducted for depreciation or other paper losses.

In addition to the most recent two years of personal Federal IRS returns, the loan officer should obtain a year-to-date profit and loss statement and a balance sheet for the business, which must be signed and dated by the applicant, although not necessarily prepared by an accountant. The underwriter may request the corporate Federal IRS returns, depending on the type of company, income, and simplicity of personal income reported by the applicant. If the applicant is self-employed and takes a combination of W-2 and K-1 income, those forms might suffice as proof of income. If the applicant is a partner in a larger firm and the income is drawn through a combination of K-1 and profit sharing, the lender may request the business IRS returns, which could pose a problem for

FIGURE **12.4** Sample IRS Form 4506T

Form **4506-T**	Request for Transcript of Tax Return	
(Rev. January 2010)		
Department of the Treasury Internal Revenue Service	▶ Request may be rejected if the form is incomplete or illegible.	OMB No. 1545-1872

Tip. Use Form 4506-T to order a transcript or other return information free of charge. See the product list below. You can also call 1-800-829-1040 to order a transcript. If you need a copy of your return, use Form 4506, Request for Copy of Tax Return. There is a fee to get a copy of your return.

1a Name shown on tax return. If a joint return, enter the name shown first.	1b First social security number on tax return or employer identification number (see instructions)
NICKIE C. GREEN	123-00-3333
2a If a joint return, enter spouse's name shown on tax return.	2b Second social security number if joint tax return

3 Current name, address (including apt., room, or suite no.), city, state, and ZIP code
NICKIE C. GREEN
100 TERRACE STREET WEST HAVEN, CT 06516

4 Previous address shown on the last return filed if different from line 3

5 If the transcript or tax information is to be mailed to a third party (such as a mortgage company), enter the third party's name, address, and telephone number. The IRS has no control over what the third party does with the tax information.
McCue Mortgage Company AOISAAATIMA
One Liberty Square, New Britain, CT 06050   800-382-0017

Caution. *If the transcript is being mailed to a third party, ensure that you have filled in line 6 and line 9 before signing. Sign and date the form once you have filled in these lines. Completing these steps helps to protect your privacy.*

6 **Transcript requested.** Enter the tax form number here (1040, 1065, 1120, etc.) and check the appropriate box below. Enter only one tax form number per request. ▶ _____

a **Return Transcript,** which includes most of the line items of a tax return as filed with the IRS. A tax return transcript does not reflect changes made to the account after the return is processed. Transcripts are only available for the following returns: Form 1040 series, Form 1065, Form 1120, Form 1120A, Form 1120H, Form 1120L, and Form 1120S. Return transcripts are available for the current year and returns processed during the prior 3 processing years. Most requests will be processed within 10 business days. . . . . □

b **Account Transcript,** which contains information on the financial status of the account, such as payments made on the account, penalty assessments, and adjustments made by you or the IRS after the return was filed. Return information is limited to items such as tax liability and estimated tax payments. Account transcripts are available for most returns. Most requests will be processed within 30 calendar days . . □

c **Record of Account,** which is a combination of line item information and later adjustments to the account. Available for current year and 3 prior tax years. Most requests will be processed within 30 calendar days . . . . ☒

7 **Verification of Nonfiling,** which is proof from the IRS that you **did not** file a return for the year. Current year requests are only available after June 15th. There are no availability restrictions on prior year requests. Most requests will be processed within 10 business days. . . . . . . □

8 **Form W-2, Form 1099 series, Form 1098 series, or Form 5498 series transcript.** The IRS can provide a transcript that includes data from these information returns. State or local information is not included with the Form W-2 information. The IRS may be able to provide this transcript information for up to 10 years. Information for the current year is generally not available until the year after it is filed with the IRS. For example, W-2 information for 2007, filed in 2008, will not be available from the IRS until 2009. If you need W-2 information for retirement purposes, you should contact the Social Security Administration at 1-800-772-1213. Most requests will be processed within 45 days. . . . . . □

Caution. *If you need a copy of Form W-2 or Form 1099, you should first contact the payer. To get a copy of the Form W-2 or Form 1099 filed with your return, you must use Form 4506 and request a copy of your return, which includes all attachments.*

9 **Year or period requested.** Enter the ending date of the year or period, using the mm/dd/yyyy format. If you are requesting more than four years or periods, you must attach another Form 4506-T. For requests relating to quarterly tax returns, such as Form 941, you must enter each quarter or tax period separately.
12/31/2009   12/31/2008

Signature of taxpayer(s). I declare that I am either the taxpayer whose name is shown on line 1a or 2a, or a person authorized to obtain the tax return information requested. If the request applies to a joint return, **either** husband or wife must sign. If signed by a corporate officer, partner, guardian, tax matters partner, executor, receiver, administrator, trustee, or party other than the taxpayer, I certify that I have the authority to execute Form 4506-T on behalf of the taxpayer. **Note.** *For transcripts being sent to a third party, this form must be received within 120 days of signature date.*

Telephone number of taxpayer on line 1a or 2a

Sign Here
▶ Signature (see instructions)   Date
Title (if line 1a above is a corporation, partnership, estate, or trust)
▶ Spouse's signature   Date

For Privacy Act and Paperwork Reduction Act Notice, see page 2.   Form **4506-T** (Rev. 1-2010)

ITEM 9470L1 (042610)
MFCD2100   00126224

Source: © REMOC Associates, LLC
Reprinted with permission of the McCue Mortgage Company.

the applicant. Regardless, the mortgage loan officer should discuss this with the applicant and obtain as much documentation upfront as is possible.

Interest, Dividends, Investments, and Trusts

Lenders calculate this income by averaging the past two years' income reported on the IRS returns. They may also accept as alternative documentation for the brokerage statements, interest/dividend checks, or other account statements to verify this income. Trust income may require additional verification via the trust agreement or letter from the trust administrator.

The lender must consider whether the same assets generating this income will be available. For example, in purchase or home improvement transactions, the mortgage loan officer should determine whether the applicants will use any of these funds to complete the proposed purchase or home improvements. In these situations, those assets used for down payment, moving, or construction will not be available to generate future interest or dividend income and therefore cannot be included in qualifying income.

Rental Income

Applicants may rely upon rental income from either the subject property or other investment property. If current rental income is to be used to qualify for a mortgage, the applicant must produce the last two years' federal IRS returns, along with the IRS Schedule E. Lenders will no longer rely on leases to calculate income, and might not accept them for the file at all. The underwriter will normally use only 75 percent of the gross reported income, and will average the last two years' rental income with certain amounts added back to the net income figure if they are duplicated in the proposed housing expenses or elsewhere on the application. If there are significant differences from year to year, the underwriter will require an explanation as to why. If the subject property is a purchase and will produce rental income, 75 percent of the proposed rental income as stated in the Rental Analysis Form of the appraisal will be used.

Additionally, if the applicant will be moving from his or her current house and plans to rent it out, the proposed rental income might not be acceptable income to be used to qualify for the new loan. If the proposed rental income of the current primary home is needed to qualify, it is best to find out what the program requires as documentation. Typically, a fully executed proposed lease, canceled security checks, and possibly an appraisal to show market rents, will be required. Again, it depends on the lender, program and underwriter, so it would be best for the mortgage loan officer to speak to the underwriter in advance.

Child Support, Alimony, or Separate Maintenance

Child support, alimony, or separate maintenance is a significant source of income for many loan applicants. Payment is mandated by a court order, divorce decree, separation, or other written agreement. Unfortunately, actual receipt of this income is typically dependent on another individual and may be inconsistent.

Lenders will use this income to qualify if verified by a review of the complete legal agreement or a letter from an attorney, and payment is made in a regular manner. The lender will want to see a payment history as well as commitment to receive the income for a minimum of two to three years in the future. Thus, if the applicant is in the process of or just completed the divorce, the income might not be allowed to qualify for the mortgage.

The loan officer must be mindful of the ECOA requirements with regard to alimony, child support, and maintenance. Applicants are not required to disclose this income unless they choose to use it to qualify for the mortgage loan. In turn, the mortgage loan officer is not allowed to inquire if this income exists. Once it is disclosed, the lender may ask for required supporting documents to verify its receipt.

Pension, Retirement, and Social Security

Pension, retirement, and social security income is usually a fixed amount or adjusted annually. The lender must verify this income by obtaining a letter from the company or organization providing the income, or by obtaining a copy of the checks received. The lender must then compare this income to the level received in prior years for consistency and duration.

Public Assistance

The ECOA states emphatically that lenders cannot discriminate against income from public assistance when an applicant is trying to qualify for a mortgage loan. That includes income from unemployment, welfare payments, state assistance, or aid to dependent children. As with all other income, the lender must verify the amount received and establish its consistency and duration when determining whether it should be used to qualify applicants. If the income from these sources is recurring and reliable enough to meet the lender's requirements, then the lender cannot discriminate on income based on public assistance being its source.

Assets

In addition to verifying the income of the applicants, the lender will verify the assets of those applicants as shown in Figure 12.5. The applicant must show enough assets for the down payment, closing costs, prepaid interest, taxes and insurance and required reserves. It is best to show all assets, and not just liquid accounts. Now, more is better than less, and lenders are looking for higher levels of post-closing reserves than ever before. The mortgage loan officer should ask the applicant to send the last two months' bank statements, including all pages for all bank accounts, and the last quarter for retirement and other accounts that do not show monthly. The lender may request updated statements or verifications of current balances if the applicant is short funds or if the statements are too old prior to closing. In addition to checking balances, the underwriter will be looking for large deposits (anything out of the ordinary) into the accounts and will request paper trails and explanations for all of them. The mortgage loan officer should review the statements for anything unusual and request supporting documents from the applicant in anticipation of this.

A gift of funds that is not required to be paid back is also considered an asset, but must be documented properly. The mortgage loan officer should provide the applicants with a standard gift letter form, to be completed by the donor. A copy of the canceled check or transfer from the donor to the applicant's account and the corresponding deposit should be

FIGURE **12.5** Sample Request for Verification of Deposit (VOD)

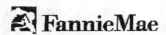 **FannieMae**

Request for Verification of Deposit

Privacy Act Notice: This information is to be used by the agency collecting it or its assignees in determining whether you qualify as a prospective mortgagor under its program. It will not be disclosed outside the agency except as required and permitted by law. You do not have to provide this information, but if you do not your application for approval as a prospective mortgagor or borrower may be delayed or rejected. The information requested in this form is authorized by Title 38, USC, Chapter 37 (if VA); by 12 USC, Section 1701 et.seq. (if HUD/FHA); by 42 USC, Section 1452b (if HUD/CPD); and Title 42 USC, 1471 et.seq. or 7 USC, 1921 et.seq. (if USDA/FmHA).

Instructions: Lender – Complete Items 1 through 8. Have applicant(s) complete Item 9. Forward directly to depository named in Item 1.
Depository – Please complete Items 10 through 18 and return DIRECTLY to lender named in Item 2.
The form is to be transmitted directly to the lender and is not to be transmitted through the applicant(s) or any other party.

Part I – Request

1. To (Name and address of depository)	2. From (Name and address of lender)
LIBERTY BANK MIDDLETOWN CT	THE McCUE MORTGAGE COMPANY One Liberty Square New Britain, CT 06050 Phone: (800) 382-0017

I certify that this verification has been sent directly to the bank or depository and has not passed through the hands of the applicant or any other party.

3. Signature of lender	4. Title	5. Date	6. Lender's No. (Optional)
		02/03/2011	00125224

7. Information To Be Verified

Type of Account	Account in Name of	Account Number	Balance
Other	NICKIE C. GREEN	None Given	$ 17,900.00
			$
			$

To Depository: I/We have applied for a mortgage loan and stated in my financial statement that the balance on deposit with you is as shown above. You are authorized to verify this information and to supply the lender identified above with the information requested in Items 10 through 13. Your response is solely a matter of courtesy for which no responsibility is attached to your institution or any of your officers.

8. Name and Address of Applicant(s)	9. Signature of Applicant(s)
NICKIE C. GREEN 100 TERRACE STREET WEST HAVEN, CT 06516	**See Attached**

To Be Completed by Depository
Part II – Verification of Depository

10. Deposit Accounts of Applicant(s)

Type of Account	Account Number	Current Balance	Average Balance For Previous Two Months	Date Opened
Money Market	XXXXX 13579	$ 17,993.21	$ 17,700	03/12/02
		$	$	
		$	$	

11. Loans Outstanding To Applicant(s)

Loan Number	Date of Loan	Original Amount	Current Balance	Installments (Monthly/Quarterly)		Secured By	Number of Late Payments
		$	$	$	per		
		$	$	$	per		
		$	$	$	per		

12. Please include any additional information which may be of assistance in determination of credit worthiness. (Please include information on loans paid-in-full in Item 11 above.)

13. If the name(s) on the account(s) differ from those listed in Item 7, please supply the name(s) on the account(s) as reflected by your records.

Part III – Authorized Signature
Federal statutes provide severe penalties for any fraud, intentional misrepresentation, or criminal connivance or conspiracy purposed to influence the issuance of any guaranty or insurance by the VA Secretary, the U.S.D.A., FmHA/FHA Commissioner, or the HUD/CPD Assistant Secretary.

14. Signature of Depository Representative	15. Title (Please print or type)	16. Date
	SR	2/9/11
17. Please print or type name signed in item 14	18. Phone No.	
Cheri Johnson		

Fannie Mae
Form 1006 July 96
Ap#: 00125224
GreatDocs™ *(Page 1 of 1)*

[001252241012]
ITEM 7042L0 (0609)

Source: © REMOC Associates, LLC
Reprinted with permission of the McCue Mortgage Company.

returned with the completed form. The lender may also require a copy of the donor's bank statement to document the source of funds at time of transfer. A loan from the applicant's retirement account is also considered an asset, and must be appropriately documented. A copy of the loan agreement along with the transfer of money must be provided. In addition, the monthly repayment amount must be included in the applicant liability section when calculating the debt/income ratios. It is imperative to document this loan in the beginning of the process so as not to trigger any problems before the closing.

Applicants' ability to accumulate substantial financial assets can be an indication of how well they manage their fiscal responsibilities. For self-employed applicants, it should be consistent with the income earned. An underwriter might not use substantial post-closing reserves as a compensating factor for other weaknesses, but it does make a file stronger.

CREDIT HISTORY

Of utmost importance to any mortgage lender is how the applicant handles his or her credit responsibilities. Many lenders would argue that this is the most significant element of the mortgage application, which dictates not only the applicant's interest rate, but also additional fees and the down payment required. Lenders use a credit report to help evaluate the applicant's credit history—their outstanding and paid debts and the payment histories on active and prior obligations. A basic credit report must be issued by an independent credit reporting agency (or credit bureau), and should list the information it has for all of the applicant's debts, not just the ones disclosed on the application. This type of credit report is known as a tri-merge, because the information shown is based on the three main credit bureaus. The credit reporting agency relies on its own files, various national repositories of credit information, and public records. This may include the following information: name of creditor, loan type, account number, open or closed status and dates, highest and current balance, and monthly payment.

The lender needs the full name, current address, date of birth, and Social Security number for each applicant. Married applicants are reported jointly, as many credit accounts are jointly held. If the applicants are not married to each other and wish to be co-applicants, then the lender must order separate credit reports for each applicant.

The credit report (see Figure 12.6) lists only the debt that is reported to the three major bureaus, so the applicant must disclose other obligations such as 401(k) loans, child support payments, alimony, and any other debt obligations that need to be calculated into the debt ratios.

An applicant may not be aware of some of the information contained in a credit report, especially if the information is old, incorrect, or a duplicate entry. The mortgage loan officer should review with the applicants the creditors, total owed, and monthly payments as soon as the credit report is obtained. Any errors, judgments, or liens must be addressed early on in the process. Credit reporting agencies encounter many difficulties in trying to

FIGURE **12.6** Sample Credit Report

Prepared By:
Avantus
600 Saw Mill Road
West Haven, CT 06516
800-530-8008 Fax: 203-931-2055

Prepared For:
AVANTUS TEST ACCOUNT
600 Saw Mill Road
West Haven, CT 06516

Report ID
62709
Customer Code
M1234
Requested By
mfsadmin

Ordered	Released	Reissued	Repositories Requested
01/21/2011	01/21/2011		TransUnion, Experian, Equifax

Applicant / **Co-Applicant**

Name	Social Security Number	Name	Social Security Number
Nickie Green	123-00-3333		

Current Address	Current Address
100 Terrace West Haven, CT 06516	

TransUnion	Experian	Equifax	TransUnion	Experian	Equifax
FICO Risk Score, Classic (04)	Fair Isaac (v2)	Beacon 5.0			
730	**732**	**734**			
Credit Assure™	Credit Assure™	Credit Assure™			
+6	**OK**	**OK**			
We found opportunities to raise your credit score by 6 points with the default settings.	We did not find opportunities to raise your credit score with the default settings.	We did not find opportunities to raise your credit score with the default settings.			

* **Available cash is set at $3,500. Timeframe: Rapid Rescore mode.** CreditXpert(R) products are based on information derived from credit reports produced by the major credit reporting agencies. CreditXpert Inc. is not responsible for inaccurate results due to incorrect, missing, or outdated credit report information. CreditXpert Inc. does not represent that CreditXpert Credit Scores(TM) are identical or similar to credit scores produced by any other company. CreditXpert Inc. is not associated with Fair Isaac Corporation. Score changes predicted by CreditXpert products are only estimates and are not guaranteed. CreditXpert Inc. is not a credit counseling or a credit repair organization. THE FOREGOING IS NOT INTENDED TO PROVIDE OR IMPLY WARRANTIES OF ANY KIND. CREDITXPERT PRODUCTS ARE PROVIDED ON AN "AS IS" BASIS, AND CREDITXPERT INC. AND ITS DISTRIBUTORS DISCLAIM ANY AND ALL WARRANTIES, EITHER EXPRESS OR IMPLIED, INCLUDING BUT NOT LIMITED TO ANY WARRANTY OF MERCHANTABILITY, FITNESS FOR A PARTICULAR PURPOSE, NON-INFRINGEMENT, SYSTEM INTEGRATION, NON-INTERFERENCE AND/OR ACCURACY OF INFORMATIONAL CONTENT. Copyright (c) 2000-2007, CreditXpert Inc. All rights reserved. CreditXpert(R) is a registered trademark of CreditXpert Inc.

SCANNED BY
CREDIT ASSURE

Credit Summary

Account Type	Number of Accounts	Open Accounts	Accounts Currently Past Due	Past Due	Payment	Balance	Accounts	30 Days	60 Days	90+ Days
								Historical Late Payments		
Mortgage	1	1	0	$0	$1,915	$162,975	0	0	0	0
Installment	2	1	0	$0	$244	$9,430	2	8	5	0
Revolving/Credit Line	8	7	0	$0	$441	$15,608	2	3	1	0
Totals	11	9	0	$0	$2,600	$188,013	4	11	6	0

Number of Public Records: 0
Number of Collections/Charge-offs: 0
Bankruptcy: No

Available Credit: $25,721
Revolving/Credit Line Used: 38%
Number of Inquiries: 5
Number of Authorized User Accounts: 0

Late Payment History

1	Current	4	90-119 Days Late	8	Repossession
2	30-59 Days Late	5	120-149 Days Late	9	Charged Off / Collection
3	60-89 Days Late	6	150+ Days Late	X	No Data Available

Trade	Type	2006 O N D	2007 J F M A M J J A S O N D	2008 J F M A M J J A S O N D	2009 J F M A M J J A S O N D	2010 J F M A M J J A S
FORD MOTOR (0611)	Inst			X X X X X X X X X X X X X X	X X X X X X X X X X 1 1	1 1 1 1 1 1 2 2
FST USA BK B (0931)	Rev	2 2 3	1 1 1 1 1 1 1 1 1 1 1 1			

coordinate information into one format from the different computer systems of hundreds of thousands of creditors nationwide. Errors occur from name changes, common names (i.e., Smith or Jr.), Social Security numbers, and unreported information.

On a monthly basis, credit reporting agencies receive and store an enormous amount of confidential and sensitive information in the regular monthly reporting by creditors. As a result, the bureaus are held to strict standards by federal and state regulations, such as the Fair Credit Reporting Act, which entitles consumers access to the same information that the lenders get, as well as affords them additional protection in cases of identity theft. Internet reporting raises additional privacy concerns, which the Gramm-Leach-Bliley Act addresses, restricting in what circumstances lenders may disclose personal financial information to nonaffiliated third parties. As these privacy laws develop, lenders are responsible for ensuring that the credit bureaus they use—acting as agents for the lenders—are currently and always will be in compliance with these increasingly complex regulations. In addition, the trend is moving toward the lenders themselves being subjected to physical

FIGURE **12.6** (*Continued*)

MergePlus(3)		Page 1 of 5

Prepared By:
Avantus
600 Saw Mill Road
West Haven, CT 06516
800-530-8008 Fax: 203-931-2055

Prepared For:
AVANTUS TEST ACCOUNT
600 Saw Mill Road
West Haven, CT 06516

Report ID
62709
Customer Code
M1234
Requested By
mfsadmin

Ordered	Released	Reissued	Repositories Requested
01/21/2011	01/21/2011		TransUnion, Experian, Equifax

Applicant / Co-Applicant

Name	Social Security Number	Age	Dependants	Marital Status	Name	Social Security Number	Age	Dependants	Marital Status
Nickie Green	123-00-3333								

Current Address	Former Address	Current Address	Former Address
100 Terrace West Haven, CT 06516			

Employer	Former Employer	Employer	Former Employer
Centes Package Store Bridgeport, CT			

Repository Files

Name	Social Security Number	Repository	Score(s)	Pulled	File ID
Nickie C. Green	123-00-3333	TransUnion	730	09/20/2010	TUC-A1
Nickie C. Green	123-00-3333	Experian	732	09/20/2010	EXP-A1
Nickie C. Green	123-00-3333	Equifax	734	09/20/2010	EQX-A1

Credit Score Information

Score	Name	Repository	Model	Developed By	Range	Calculated	Reported On
730	Nickie C. Green	TransUnion	FICO Risk Score, Classic (04)	Fair Isaac	250-900	09/20/2010	TUC-A1

Factors (018, 030, 012, 010)
• Number of accounts with delinquency
• Time since most recent account opening is too short
• Length of time revolving accounts have been established
• Proportion of balances to credit limits is too high on bank revolving or other revolving accounts
• Score value was adversely affected by credit inquiries present in the credit file.

Score	Name	Repository	Model	Developed By	Range	Calculated	Reported On
732	Nickie C. Green	Experian	Fair Isaac (v2)	Fair Isaac	300-850	09/20/2010	EXP-A1

Factors (18, 10, 08, 05)
• Number of accounts delinquent.
• Proportion of balance to high credit on bank revolving or all revolving accounts.
• Number of recent inquiries.
• Number of accounts with balances.

Score	Name	Repository	Model	Developed By	Range	Calculated	Reported On
734	Nickie C. Green	Equifax	Beacon 5.0	Fair Isaac	300-850	09/20/2010	EQX-A1

Factors (30, 18, 23, 5)
• Time since most recent account opening is too short
• Number of accounts with delinquency
• Number of bank or national revolving accounts with balances
• Too many accounts with balances
• Score value was adversely affected by credit inquiries present in the credit file.

File Summary

Account Type	Number of Accounts	Open Accounts	Accounts Currently Past Due	Past Due	Payment	Balance	Accounts	Historical Late Payments 30 Days	60 Days	90+ Days
Mortgage	1	1	0	$0	$1,915	$162,975	0	0	0	0
Installment	2	1	0	$0	$244	$9,430	2	8	5	0
Revolving/Credit Line	8	7	0	$0	$441	$15,608	2	3	1	0
Totals	11	9	0	$0	$2,600	$188,013	4	11	6	0

Number of Public Records: 0
Number of Collections/Charge-offs: 0
Bankruptcy: No

Available Credit: $25,721
Revolving/Credit Line Used: 38%
Number of Inquiries: 5
Number of Authorized User Accounts: 0

Credit History

Summary

Number of Accounts	Number of Open Accounts	Number of Delinquent Accounts	Credit Limit	High Credit	Past Due	Payment	Balance
11	9	0	$39,330	$208,222	$0	$2,600	$188,013

and virtual inspections to make sure that both office space and computer systems are secure.

The secondary mortgage market requires a certain kind of credit report (see Figure 12.6) that includes more than just the computer-generated information that a simpler, standard factual credit report provides. The Residential Mortgage Credit Report (RMCR) provides the following additional information:

FIGURE **12.6** (*Continued*)

MergePlus(3)								Page 2 of 5
Applicant **Nickie Green**	Applicant's SSN **123-00-3333**	Co-Applicant			Co-Applicant's SSN	Loan Number		Report ID **62709**
Credit History (continued)								

OPTION ONE
Account Number: 7581128319409
Months Reviewed: 12

ECOA Individual	Opened 11/2007	Last Activity 01/2011	Closed	Reported 01/2011A	Credit Limit	High Credit $165,000		
Account Type **Mortgage**	Collateral **Conventional**	Terms **360 Months**	Reported On **Applicant**		Manner of Payment **Current (M01)**			
30-59 Days Late **0 Times**		60-89 Days Late **0 Times**		90-119 Days Late **0 Times**		Past Due **$0**	Payment **$1,915**	Balance **$162,975**
120-149 Days Late **0 Times**		150+ Days Late **0 Times**						
Payment Pattern Start Date **01/2011**	Payment Pattern **111111111111**							

FORD MOTOR
Account Number: 40300611
Months Reviewed: 14

ECOA Individual	Opened 11/2007	Last Activity 12/2010	Closed	Reported 01/2011A	Credit Limit	High Credit $11,109		*
Account Type **Installment**	Collateral	Terms **62 Months**	Reported On **Applicant**		Manner of Payment **Current (I01)**			
30-59 Days Late **3 Times** 11/2010, 09/2010, 08/2010		60-89 Days Late **0 Times**		90-119 Days Late **0 Times**		Past Due **$0**	Payment **$244**	Balance **$9,430**
120-149 Days Late **0 Times**		150+ Days Late **0 Times**						
Payment Pattern Start Date **12/2010**	Payment Pattern **121221111111-11**							

AMEX
Account Number: 186581359125413993
Months Reviewed: 48

ECOA Individual	Opened 09/2005	Last Activity 04/2010	Closed	Reported 04/2010A	Credit Limit $14,500	High Credit $5,883		
Account Type **Revolving**	Collateral **Credit Card**	Terms	Reported On **TUC-A1, EXP-A1, EQX-A1**		Manner of Payment **Current (R01)**			
30-59 Days Late **0 Times**		60-89 Days Late **0 Times**		90-119 Days Late **0 Times**		Past Due **$0**	Payment (Est.) **$294**	Balance **$5,883**
120-149 Days Late **0 Times**		150+ Days Late **0 Times**						
Payment Pattern Start Date **03/2010**	Payment Pattern **111111111111-111111111111-111111111111-111111111111**							

CHASE
Account Number: 525831313543
Months Reviewed: 1

ECOA Individual	Opened 02/2010	Last Activity 04/2010	Closed	Reported 04/2010A	Credit Limit	High Credit $5,499		
Account Type **Open**	Collateral **Credit Card**	Terms	Reported On **TUC-A1, EXP-A1, EQX-A1**		Manner of Payment **Current (O01)**			
30-59 Days Late **0 Times**		60-89 Days Late **0 Times**		90-119 Days Late **0 Times**		Past Due **$0**	Payment (Min.) **$107**	Balance **$5,379**
120-149 Days Late **0 Times**		150+ Days Late **0 Times**						
Payment Pattern Start Date **03/2010**	Payment Pattern **1**							

BOA MBNA
Account Number: 4681
Months Reviewed: 12

ECOA Individual	Opened 04/2009	Last Activity 04/2010	Closed	Reported 04/2010A	Credit Limit $6,000	High Credit $3,502		
Account Type **Revolving**	Collateral **Credit Card**	Terms	Reported On **TUC-A1, EXP-A1, EQX-A1**		Manner of Payment **Current (R01)**			
30-59 Days Late **0 Times**		60-89 Days Late **0 Times**		90-119 Days Late **0 Times**		Past Due **$0**	Payment (Min.) **$15**	Balance **$2,969**
120-149 Days Late **0 Times**		150+ Days Late **0 Times**						
Payment Pattern Start Date **03/2010**	Payment Pattern **111111111111**							

- Credit information from three national credit repositories
- Check of public records for divorce, liens, judgments, etc.
- Verification (if possible) of current employment and address of employer
- List of credit inquiries within previous 24 months
- Credit score from each of the three bureaus

RMCRs must be dated within 60–90 days of the mortgage closing date to be valid, and must also contain a certification that they meet the standards of Fannie Mae, Freddie Mac, the VA, and HUD. Each lender may individually choose to run another credit report right before the closing, so it is important that the applicant maintain stable debt and current payments.

FIGURE **12.6** (*Continued*)

MergePlus(3) Page 3 of 5

Applicant	Applicant's SSN	Co-Applicant	Co-Applicant's SSN	Loan Number	Report ID
Nickie Green	123-00-3333				62709

Credit History (continued)

BK OF AMER

Field	Value
Account Number	599971422963
ECOA	Individual
Opened	06/2008
Last Activity	04/2010
Closed	
Reported	04/2010A
Credit Limit	$11,000
High Credit	$5,428
Account Type	Revolving
Collateral	Credit Card
Terms	
Reported On	TUC-A1, EXP-A1, EQX-A1
Manner of Payment	Current (R01)
Months Reviewed	21
30-59 Days Late	0 Times
60-89 Days Late	0 Times
90-119 Days Late	0 Times
120-149 Days Late	0 Times
150+ Days Late	0 Times
Payment Pattern Start Date	03/2010
Payment Pattern	111111111111-111111111
Past Due	$0
Payment (Min.)	$25
Balance	$1,377

AHM *

Field	Value
Account Number	2210-75105931112
ECOA	Individual
Opened	11/2005
Last Activity	10/2006
Closed	
Reported	08/2007A
Credit Limit	
High Credit	$5,182
Account Type	Installment
Collateral	
Terms	
Reported On	EQX-A1, TUC-A1, EXP-A1
Maximum Delinquency	09/2006, 60-89 Days Late
Manner of Payment	Current (I01)
Months Reviewed	21
30-59 Days Late	5 Times 07/2006, 06/2006, 05/2006, 03/2006, 01/2006
60-89 Days Late	5 Times 09/2006, 08/2006, 04/2006, 02/2006, 12/2005
90-119 Days Late	0 Times
120-149 Days Late	0 Times
150+ Days Late	0 Times
Payment Pattern Start Date	07/2007
Payment Pattern	XXXXXXXXXX33-22232323X
Past Due	$0
Payment	$128
Balance	$0

FST USA BK B *

Field	Value
Account Number	652822780931
ECOA	Individual
Opened	04/2002
Last Activity	08/2007
Closed	12/2006
Reported	12/2007A
Credit Limit	$3,500
High Credit	$3,871
Account Type	Revolving
Collateral	Credit Card
Terms	
Reported On	TUC-A1, EXP-A1, EQX-A1
Maximum Delinquency	05/2003, 60-89 Days Late
Manner of Payment	Current (R01)
Months Reviewed	48
30-59 Days Late	2 Times 11/2006, 10/2006
60-89 Days Late	1 Time 12/2006
90-119 Days Late	0 Times
120-149 Days Late	0 Times
150+ Days Late	0 Times
Payment Pattern Start Date	11/2007
Payment Pattern	111111111113-221111111111-111111111111-11111111
Comment	ACCOUNT CLOSED BY CREDIT GRANTOR
Past Due	$0
Payment	
Balance	$0

MCYDSNB

Field	Value
Account Number	523155269
ECOA	Individual
Opened	03/2002
Last Activity	04/2010
Closed	
Reported	04/2010A
Credit Limit	$1,750
High Credit	$560
Account Type	Revolving
Collateral	Revolving Charge Account
Terms	
Reported On	EXP-A1, EQX-A1
Manner of Payment	Current (R01)
Months Reviewed	1
30-59 Days Late	0 Times
60-89 Days Late	0 Times
90-119 Days Late	0 Times
120-149 Days Late	0 Times
150+ Days Late	0 Times
Payment Pattern Start Date	04/2010
Payment Pattern	1
Comment	Curr Acct
Past Due	$0
Payment	
Balance	$0

RBS NB CC

Field	Value
Account Number	665625211
ECOA	Joint
Opened	05/2001
Last Activity	10/2009
Paid	10/2009
Reported	04/2010A
Credit Limit	$1,900
High Credit	$1,895
Account Type	Revolving
Collateral	Credit Card
Terms	
Reported On	TUC-A1, EXP-A1, EQX-A1
Manner of Payment	Current (R01)
Months Reviewed	48
30-59 Days Late	0 Times
60-89 Days Late	0 Times
90-119 Days Late	0 Times
120-149 Days Late	0 Times
150+ Days Late	0 Times
Payment Pattern Start Date	03/2010
Payment Pattern	111111111111-111111111111-111111111111-111111111111
Past Due	$0
Payment	
Balance	$0

Credit Scores

Most credit reports today include at least one **credit score**—a numeric rating of the applicant's overall credit history. A credit score considers a person's long-term and short-term use of credit and repayment history. The computer program creates a numerical *score* within a range of 350 and 850; 850 being the highest and 350 being the lowest.

FIGURE **12.6** (*Continued*)

MergePlus(3)										Page 4 of 5
Applicant **Nickie Green**	Applicant's SSN **123-00-3333**	Co-Applicant				Co-Applicant's SSN	Loan Number			Report ID **62709**

Credit History (continued)

WFNNB/EXPRESS	ECOA **Individual**	Opened **05/2003**	Last Activity **04/2010**	Closed	Reported **04/2010A**	Credit Limit **$680**	High Credit **$293**			*
Account Number **50789**	Account Type **Revolving**	Collateral **Revolving Charge Account**	Terms	Reported On **EXP-A1, TUC-A1, EQX-A1**	Maximum Delinquency **01/2007, 30-59 Days Late**	Manner of Payment **Current (R01)**				
	Months Reviewed **83**	30-59 Days Late **1 Time**		60-89 Days Late **0 Times**		90-119 Days Late **0 Times**		Past Due **$0**	Payment	Balance **$0**
		120-149 Days Late **0 Times**		150+ Days Late **0 Times**						
	Payment Pattern Start Date **04/2010**	Payment Pattern **111111111111-111111111XXX-X**								
	Comment **Cur Was 30**									

Public Records

THE REPORTING BUREAU CERTIFIES THAT: public records have been checked for judgements, foreclosures, bankruptcies, tax liens, and other legal actions involving the subject(s) were obtained directly through the repositories used, or by direct searches, or a public records search firm other than the repository, or by all methods with the following results:
PUBLIC RECORDS LEARNED: NONE

Inquiries

Date	Name	Subscriber Code	Reported On	ECOA
05/02/2010	CIBMS	Z 419063	TUC-A1	Individual
04/19/2010	CBD	Z 49997	TUC-A1	Participant
04/19/2010	CBOFDELMAR	243ZB00420	EQX-A1	
04/19/2010	CREDIT PLUS	1971155	EXP-A1	
02/19/2010	FIRST USA,NA	1203600	EXP-A1	

Fraud Messages

OFAC Statement: In compliance with section 326 of the Patriot Act, your credit provider has checked the applicant(s) name(s) supplied by the borrower against the Office of Foreign Asset Control (OFAC) data base maintained by the Department of the Treasury. Any messages returned by your credit provider are located in this section of this credit report.

Date	Reported On	Comment
01/21/2011	Applicant	OFAC (UltraAMPS) clear. SDN list published on 01/06/2011.

Repository Files Returned

File ID **TransUnion / TUC-A1** Pulled **09/20/2010** Infile Date **07/01/1997**	Name **Nickie C. Green** Social Security Number **123-00-3333** Age / DOB **07/24/1978**	Current Address, Reported: 12/01/2005 **100 Terrace St** **West Haven, CT 06516** Former Address, Reported: 01/01/2001 **45 Maple St** **N Haven, CT 06511**	Current Employer **Centes Package Store, Reported:2002, Bridgeport, Ct**
File ID **Experian / EXP-A1** Pulled **09/20/2010**	Name **Nickie C. Green** Social Security Number **123-00-3333** Age / DOB **1978**	Current Address, Reported: 09/1997 **100 Terrac St** **West Haven, CT 06516** Former Address, Reported: 04/2002 **45 Maple Ave** **N Haven, CT 06484** Second Former Address, Reported: 02/2001 **1400 Madison Ave** **New York, NY 02222**	Current Employer **Connecticut Distributor, Reported:0304** Former Employer **Ct Distributors, Reported:1103**
File ID **Equifax / EQX-A1** Pulled **09/20/2010** Infile Date **07/30/1997**	Name **Nickie C. Green** Social Security Number **123-00-3333** Age / DOB **07/24/1978**	Current Address, Reported: 02/2001 **100 Terrace St** **West Haven, CT 06516** Former Address, Reported: 11/2005 **45 Maple Ave** **N Haven, CT 06511**	Current Employer **Conn Dist,**

A credit score is popularly known as a "FICO® Score", named after Fair Isaac & Company, the self-proclaimed creator of the scoring system. Several companies produce credit scores, each with its own proprietary formula for calculating its score. Experian, Trans Union, and Beacon are the most common.

Many factors are considered in arriving at a score. The general breakdown is as follows:

- What is their payment history? Roughly 35 percent of score
- Do they owe too much? 30 percent of score

FIGURE **12.6** (*Continued*)

MergePlus(3)					Page 5 of 5
Applicant **Nickie Green**	Applicant's SSN **123-00-3333**	Co-Applicant	Co-Applicant's SSN	Loan Number	Report ID **62709**

Credit Repositories

TransUnion **P. O. Box 1000** **Chester, PA 19022** **800-888-4213** **www.transunion.com**	**Experian** **P. O. Box 2002** **Allen, TX 75013** **888-397-3742** **www.experian.com**	**Equifax** **P. O. Box 740241** **Atlanta, GA 30374** **800-685-1111** **www.equifax.com/fcra**

This merged report can be used for lending purposes but does not meet the requirements of a Residential Mortgage Credit Report (RMCR). This report contains information which is supported by the repositories listed above and may also contain duplicate information.

This completed Credit Report includes all applicable Legislative Cost Recovery Fees from the respective credit repositories associated with the federal Fair and Accurate Credit Transactions Act of 2003 (FACT Act).

End of Report

Credit Score Disclosure

AVANTUS TEST ACCOUNT **600 Saw Mill Road** **West Haven, CT 06516**	Applicant **Nickie Green** **100 Terrace** **West Haven, CT 06516**	Report ID **62709**	Date **01/21/2011** Repositories Requested **TransUnion, Experian, Equifax**

"NOTICE TO THE HOME LOAN APPLICANT"

"In connection with your application for a home loan, the lender must disclose to you the score that a consumer reporting agency distributed to users and the lender used in connection with your home loan, and the key factors affecting your credit scores.

The credit score is a computer generated summary calculated at the time of the request and based on information that a consumer reporting agency or lender has on file. The scores are based on data about your credit history and payment patterns. Credit scores are important because they are used to assist the lender in determining whether you will obtain a loan. They may also be used to determine what interest rate you may be offered on the mortgage. Credit scores can change over time, depending on your conduct, how your credit history and payment patterns change, and how credit scoring technologies change.

Because the score is based on information in your credit history, it is very important that you review the credit-related information that is being furnished to make sure it is accurate. Credit records may vary from one company to another.

If you have questions about your credit score or the credit information that is furnished to you, contact the consumer reporting agency at the address and telephone number provided with this notice, or contact the lender, if the lender developed or generated the credit score. The consumer reporting agency plays no part in the decision to take any action on the loan application and is unable to provide you with specific reasons for the decision on a loan application.

If you have any questions concerning the terms of the loan, contact the lender."

For information on FICO scores, please contact the developer, Fair Isaac Corporation, at www.myfico.com or 1-800-777-2066.

Questions regarding your credit report should be directed to TRANSUNION, EXPERIAN or EQUIFAX. You will find their contact information below:

TransUnion **P. O. Box 1000** **Chester, PA 19022** **800-888-4213** **www.transunion.com**	**Experian** **P. O. Box 2002** **Allen, TX 75013** **888-397-3742** **www.experian.com**	**Equifax** **P. O. Box 740241** **Atlanta, GA 30374** **800-685-1111** **www.equifax.com/fcra**

Score	Name	Repository	Model	Developed By	Range	Calculated	Reported On
	Nickie C. Green	**TransUnion**	**FICO Risk Score, Classic (04)**	**Fair Isaac**	**250-900**	**09/20/2010**	**TUC-A1**
730	Factors (018, 030, 012, 010) • Number of accounts with delinquency • Time since most recent account opening is too short • Length of time revolving accounts have been established • Proportion of balances to credit limits is too high on bank revolving or other revolving accounts • Score value was adversely affected by credit inquiries present in the credit file.						
Score	Name **Nickie C. Green**	Repository **Experian**	Model **Fair Isaac (v2)**	Developed By **Fair Isaac**	Range **300-850**	Calculated **09/20/2010**	Reported On **EXP-A1**
732	Factors (18, 10, 08, 05) • Number of accounts delinquent. • Proportion of balance to high credit on bank revolving or all revolving accounts. • Number of recent inquiries. • Number of accounts with balances.						
Score	Name **Nickie C. Green**	Repository **Equifax**	Model **Beacon 5.0**	Developed By **Fair Isaac**	Range **300-850**	Calculated **09/20/2010**	Reported On **EQX-A1**
734	Factors (30, 18, 23, 5) • Time since most recent account opening is too short • Number of accounts with delinquency • Number of bank or national revolving accounts with balances • Too many accounts with balances • Score value was adversely affected by credit inquiries present in the credit file.						

I have received a copy of this disclosure.

_____   _____
Nickie Green   Date

FIGURE **12.6** (*Continued*)

AVANTUS TEST ACCOUNT 600 Saw Mill Road West Haven, CT 06516	Applicant Nickie Green 100 Terrace West Haven, CT 06516	Report ID 62709	Date 01/21/2011

AVANTUS TEST ACCOUNT
Your Credit Score and the Price You Pay for Credit

Your Credit Score	
Your credit score	732
	Source: **Experian** Date: **09-20-2010**

Understanding Your Credit Score	
What you should know about credit scores	Your credit score is a number that reflects the information in your credit report.
	Your credit report is a record of your credit history. It includes information about whether you pay your bills on time and how much you owe to creditors.
	Your credit score can change, depending on how your credit history changes.
How we use your credit score	Your credit score can affect whether you can get a loan and how much you will have to pay for that loan.
The range of scores	Scores range from a low of 300 to a high of 850.
	Generally, the higher your score, the more likely you are to be offered better credit terms.
How your score compares to the scores of other consumers	Your credit score ranks higher than 53 percent of U.S. consumers.
Key factors that adversely affected your credit score	Number of accounts delinquent. Proportion of balance to high credit on bank revolving or all revolving accounts. Number of recent inquiries. Number of accounts with balances.

Checking Your Credit Report	
What if there are mistakes in your credit report?	You have a right to dispute any inaccurate information in your credit report. If you find mistakes on your credit report, contact the consumer reporting agency.
	It is a good idea to check your credit report to make sure the information it contains is accurate.
How can you obtain a copy of your credit report?	Under federal law, you have the right to obtain a free copy of your credit report from each of the nationwide consumer reporting agencies once a year.
	To order your free annual credit report -
	By telephone: Call toll-free: 1-877-322-8228
	On the web: Visit www.annualcreditreport.com
	By mail: Mail your completed Annual Credit Report Request Form (which you can obtain from the Federal Trade Commission's web site at http://www.ftc.gov/bcp/conline/include/requestformfinal.pdf) to:
	Annual Credit Report Request Service P.O. Box 105281 Atlanta, GA 30348-5281
How can you get more information?	For more information about credit reports and your rights under federal law, visit the Federal Reserve Board's web site at www.federalreserve.gov, or the Federal Trade Commission's web site at www.ftc.gov.

Source: © 2010 REMOC Associates, LLC
Reprinted with permission of Advantus

- How established is their credit? 15 percent of score
- Do they have a "healthy" mix of credit? 10 percent of score
- Are they taking on more debt? 10 percent of score

A person's score also may be affected by repeated applications for credit, though the model states that it treats multiple inquiries in a short period of time as a single inquiry, to avoid penalizing consumers for shopping for the best rate. It is recommended that an applicant not have too many credit checks while shopping, as this may impact their score overall.

Secondary market programs have different guidelines for the use of credit scores, with many programs establishing a minimum value required for that loan program and pricing adjustments for different credit score ranges. Automated origination and underwriting systems may issue their own credit reports or may simply provide the lender with a summary evaluation of the credit history and account information.

Derogatory Items

When qualifying applicants, the loan officer should also explain how the lender defines an "acceptable credit history" in its loan policy or for that particular program. Most lenders consider only the FICO® score, but will also consider the following items, which will adversely affect the credit decision:

- Late payments
- Past due and/or collection accounts
- Lawsuits
- Judgments
- Bankruptcy
- Concealed liabilities
- Numerous recent inquiries

Regardless of the applicants' FICO® score, the lender may reject a loan if late payments on a current mortgage, income tax liens, or judgments exist that cannot be rectified. Foreclosures, deed in lieu, short sales, and bankruptcies will greatly restrict a person's ability to obtain a new mortgage within a certain time afterwards and without strong reestablished credit.

Most lenders will now base their loan approval and pricing on the Fannie Mae credit scoring requirements and the chart that shows the loan-to-value and pricing adjustments that lenders should impose based on the applicants' credit scores. Most lenders will simply follow those guidelines to ensure that they can sell the loans and get the best pricing on the secondary market. Therefore, some applicants, although strong in other areas, get rejected merely because they "don't fit into the matrix." In all situations, applicants should be advised that if the loan is turned down because of adverse credit information, they may contact the credit bureau that furnished the derogatory information.

A mortgage lender must be aware of the Fair Credit Reporting Act and the limitations that are placed on credit information gathering. That law, as mentioned earlier in Chapter 11—Compliance, governs the fair and accurate reporting of information regarding consumer credit. A mortgage lender seeking credit information from a consumer reporting agency must certify the purpose for which the information is sought and use it for no other purpose. This act prohibits investigative reports, which are based on interviews with non-creditors relating to character, general reputation, mode of living, and other subjective areas.

COLLATERAL

At qualification, mortgage loan officers should clarify the collateral and appraisal requirements for the mortgage loan. This means that they should inquire about the house the applicant(s) will be financing and explain how the lender will appraise it. New federal regulations based on the HVCC (Home Valuation Code of Conduct) guidelines but now outlined in Truth In Lending and the Dodd-Frank Act (see Chapters 11—Compliance and 14—Appraisal) require that all lenders adhere to the rules and timing of ordering appraisals, interacting with appraisers, and taking fees from the applicant. Mortgage loan officers should explain these details during the initial interview because industry changes greatly affect the applicant (See Chapter 14—The Appraisal Process).

Housing standards vary tremendously from community to community across the country. Lenders develop fairly specific standards for property types they will finance based on local housing characteristics. These standards may specify property types (single-family or multifamily, condominium, Planned Unit Development (PUD), vacation/seasonal, construction, land, etc.) and other features such as minimum square footage, heating and electrical, acreage, zoning restrictions, and flood insurance. Depending on the lender's charter, additional regulatory appraisal requirements may shape the appraisal policy and how it impacts mortgage applicants.

A lender obtains an appraisal for the subject property to establish whether the condition and value of the property is sufficient for the loan amount and product requested. The appraisal also establishes the market value by the sales comparison approach, and gives additional information on the salability in case of default. Most lenders use a standard appraisal form for all loan applications, to comply with sale in the secondary market. The appraisal can be ordered anytime after four business days of the lender receiving the application packet. A fee from the client for the appraisal may not be taken prior to this time.

Additionally, prior to application, the lender should make the applicants—especially first-time homebuyers—aware of the responsibilities and obligations a mortgage lien entails for both lender and borrower. The mortgage document that the applicants sign at closing includes many covenants regarding lender's and borrower's rights and obligations regarding the property, including maintenance, access, defense of title, hazard insurance, taxes, and so forth.

Finally, the loan officer should explain the mortgage closing and lien process along with other legal requirements. The loan officer should provide useful information, but should not attempt to act as a legal counsel. Instead, the loan officer should recommend that the applicants engage an attorney for professional legal advice and counsel. Since a mortgage lien is a legal transaction recorded in public records, it involves a number of legal issues. In many states, attorneys or other legal representatives such as title companies handle the mortgage transaction.

Again, the secondary market provides industry standards for both the appraisal process and for the mortgage (or deed of trust). It is highly recommended that lenders use the uniform documentation established by Fannie Mae and Freddie Mac for appraisals and legal forms—mortgages, riders, assignments, and so forth.

OTHER COMPENSATING FACTORS

Loan officers, in their discussion with potential applicants at qualification, may discover an event that significantly impacts the applicants' financial situation. If this event was unique or unusual and nonrecurring, the negative impact may be compensated for by another strength in the loan application. For example, the loan officer notices that last year's W-2 earnings were much lower than the current salary, but finds out that the applicant was injured in a car accident and out of work for several months. Other strengths, like high year-to-date earnings or large cash reserves may compensate for this negative feature, even with a high loan-to-value loan. An effective mortgage loan officer must develop a sense for discovering the reasons behind the events that negatively impact applicants' chances for loan approval. Regardless of extenuating circumstances and compensating factors, the applicant must still meet the minimum requirements of credit score, ratios, and down payments. Again, no mortgage personnel may discourage a consumer from applying, but qualified personnel may explain program and underwriting guidelines so a consumer can make an informed decision about applying for mortgage finance.

FINAL CHECK

Before sending a residential mortgage loan file on to an underwriter, a loan processor should review the file to ascertain that all required documents (Figure 12.7) are present and properly prepared. Mortgage processing software often includes date and document tracking reports which help processors and management reduce processing time and improve efficiency.

A processed file ready for underwriting should include at a minimum the following items:

- Application—both updated typed and preliminary applications
- Sufficient verification of employment, credit, and deposits, and supporting documentation
- Residential Mortgage Credit Report
- Appraisal report
- Compliance review to confirm that all federally mandated consumer protection requirements have been followed for:

  1. ECOA
  2. RESPA
  3. Truth in Lending
  4. Flood insurance
  5. Fair housing
  6. Servicing
  7. State rate lock or other disclosures
  8. Others (if applicable)

- Proper fees collected for:

  1. Credit report
  2. Appraisal

FIGURE **12.7** First Mortgage Loan Documentation

Mortgage Origination Documentation

Preliminary Analysis

    Loan Products/Rate Sheet
    Pre-Qualification Worksheet
    Applicant Documentation List (what to bring to application)

Application

    Processing Checklist/Member Contact Sheet
    Original Application
    Verifications of Employment, Deposit, Loan
    IRS Form 4506
    Application Fee Itemization
    HUD Booklet/CHARM Booklet
    Initial ARM Disclosure
    Truth-In-Lending Disclosure
    Good Faith Estimate
    Servicing Transfer Disclosure
    Fair Lending Notice
    ECOA Notice (Appraisal)
    FACT Act Notice (Credit Scores)
    Privacy Notice (USAPATRIOT Act)
    Applicant Certification & Authorization/Appraisal Request Form
    Rate Lock-In Agreement
    Escrow Waiver
    Loan Origination System Printout

Processing

    Copy of Original Application
    Credit Report
    Appraisal Order Form
    Appraisal
    Flood Zone Determination/Certification/Notification
    Sales Agreement
    Additional Documentation Request Form
    Other:

Underwriting

    Underwriting Worksheet
    Underwriting Conditions/Summary Sheet
    Commitment Letter/Adverse Action Notice
    Underwriting Transmittal Summary

Pre-Closing Package

    Closing Documentation Checklist
    Insured Closing Letter
    Instructions to Closing Agent
    Copy of Commitment Letter/Conditions Needed

FIGURE **12.7** (*Continued*)

> Preliminary Title Search/Policy
> Final Application
> Final Truth-In-Lending/Revised Good Faith Estimate
> Preliminary HUD-1/1-A Settlement Statement
> Escrow Waiver Agreement/Initial Escrow Statement
> Closing Disbursement Funds
> Initial Payment Letter

Final Closing Package

> Executed Note
> Certified Copy of Mortgage/Riders
> Recorded Mortgage/Riders
> Final Title Insurance Policy/Schedules/Endorsements
> HUD-1/1-A Settlement Statement
> Hazard Insurance Binder/Policy
> Flood Insurance Binder/Policy
> Survey / Endorsement/Affidavit
> Notice To Borrower
> Errors and Omissions/Compliance Agreement
> W-9(s)
> Name Affidavit/Notarization
> Tax Registration/Certification
> Occupancy Agreement
> Other:

Additional Documentation:

Source: Community Lending Associates, LLC www.communitylendassoc.com

The processor should forward to the underwriter a complete mortgage file as expeditiously as possible. It is not recommended that the person who processed a loan be the same person who underwrites the loan. The chances for error or fraud in this situation are too great. If a lending institution is too small for a full-time, qualified underwriter, it should use an independent underwriting service, one of the private mortgage insurance companies, or a secondary market automated underwriting service.

DISCUSSION POINTS

1. In what three general ways have mortgage origination and processing changed in the last 20 years?
2. How has technology impacted mortgage origination and processing (discuss the benefits and drawbacks)?
3. What documentation should a consumer bring to a mortgage lender when applying for a loan?
4. What special challenges do Internet applications present?
5. What three issues must a lender identify when qualifying an applicant, and why are they important?
6. Discuss the benefits and risks of using alternative documentation loan programs.
7. What recent compliance changes affect origination behavior and fees?

CHAPTER 13

Underwriting the Residential Mortgage Loan

INTRODUCTION

Different segments in the American economy use the term *underwriting* to describe the process of analyzing information relating to risk and making the decision whether or not to accept that risk. Insurance underwriting—life, hazard, and medical—are examples of this risk analysis. In mortgage lending, the purpose of an underwriting review is to:

- Analyze the features of a mortgage application
- Determine whether the cumulative risk is acceptable to the lender and falls within its lending guidelines
- Establish the final conditions and terms (price) under which the lender will approve, deny, or make a counteroffer to the application
- Identify and investigate "red flags" which may indicate mortgage fraud

Underwriting is an integral part of the mortgage lending process, regardless of the type of transaction, loan product, borrower, or property involved. It follows a similar process for all applications. For many programs, differences are more procedural and not of great significance; many other programs require specialized knowledge and conditions.

This chapter examines the underlying issues and risks involved in underwriting a residential mortgage loan, explains the procedural steps, and reviews how underwriting has evolved and is practiced today. It is not intended to train the reader to underwrite for Fannie or Freddie or for a particular program, as specific guidelines change regularly. However, this chapter will present fundamental underwriting concepts and prudent guidelines which have formed the basis of mortgage lending for several years.

Until 1995, mortgage underwriting was performed only by individuals. Today, many lenders use an automated underwriting system (AUS) in their underwriting decision. An AUS, such as Fannie Mae's Desktop Underwriter or Freddie Mac's Loan Prospector, is a computer software program that empirically assesses individual and overall risks of an application. These complex software programs rely on an enormous loan performance database for their calculations and statistical analysis. In the initial years of AUS usage, results were very promising; however, over time, problems with how AUSs are used, how much money these systems actually save lenders, and how predictive they really are has come into question. AUSs are discussed later in this chapter.

UNDERWRITING BY A MORTGAGE LENDER

Regulations do not provide complete underwriting guidelines and do not require that a residential mortgage lender make a particular loan. Regulations do make it clear, however, that mortgage lenders have a responsibility to attempt to satisfy mortgage loan requests, *as long as the risk is analyzed fully and deemed acceptable.* The desire to make loans must be balanced by a mortgage lender's fiduciary responsibility to protect whoever provides funds for those loans: depositors, shareholders, government agencies, or secondary market investors.

All lenders, servicers, investors, and insurers share the danger that even properly underwritten mortgages may become delinquent. The expense incurred in collecting these funds can exceed the income generated from originating and servicing the loan—that is how costly the collection process is. If several defaults occur, the costs involved in either curing the defaults or from foreclosing may result in severe losses, to the point where it jeopardizes the solvency of the lender or the return to an investor in a mortgage-backed security.

Mortgage brokers and mortgage bankers have a unique problem: no margin for error. They underwrite each loan knowing that it must be sold to a permanent investor. If a poorly underwritten loan is not secondary marketable at a reasonable price, it may result in considerable loss to a mortgage banker or broker. Because a deposit-based mortgage lender has the option of placing a mortgage into its own portfolio (instead of selling it to an investor), its loss potential for a poorly processed/underwritten mortgage is less than that of a mortgage banker.

In any event, the underwriting phase has significant, lasting financial effects. It is imperative that all mortgage lenders adopt prudent guidelines, maintain an objective reporting structure, develop and maintain professional underwriting expertise, and review underwriting performance through quality control.

Analyzing Risk

All mortgage loans involve the risk of possible financial loss to a mortgage lender, servicer, investor, or insurer. The underwriting analysis quantifies the risk factors present and measures these against other strengths in the file to determine whether the strengths offset the weaknesses.

It is important to understand that risks in mortgage lending are never eliminated completely—risks can only be managed. Mortgage lending is a risk business, and each party must assume some risk in order to earn a fee or make a profit. The questions are how much risk and for how much reward?

The following kinds of risks are present in a typical residential mortgage loan:

- Credit—based on the credit history of the applicant
- Collateral—the condition and value of the property being secured
- Default—the repayment of the debt
- Fraud—approval and pricing based on intentional deception
- Compliance—failure to follow all state and federal regulations involved
- Interest rate—changes in market interest rates vs. loan interest rate
- Price and market—changes in the value of the loan before it is sold
- Liquidity—either lack of funding for a loan or prepayment of an existing loan
- Secondary market—several risks, including losing an investor or program
- Portfolio—changes in market value due to internal or external conditions
- Servicing—changes in market value or failure to meet servicing requirements

Depending on its circumstances, a single mortgage application may undergo five separate underwriting reviews at various stages by the following parties:

Stage 1. Lender: The loan originator and/or processor initially review the application to determine whether or not it warrants full processing or an immediate credit decision.

Stage 2. Lender: After processing, the underwriter analyzes the application to determine whether or not to lend funds and under what terms and conditions.

Stage 3. Insurer/Guarantor: Before closing, a mortgage insurer or guarantor determines whether or not the submitted application is eligible for mortgage insurance or a guarantee.

Stage 4. Investor: Before or after closing, an investor determines whether or not it will purchase the mortgage or mortgages and at what price.

Stage 5. Credit Rating Agency: Before or after sale to an investor, the mortgages in a mortgage-backed security must be evaluated for quality and risk to help determine the rating and price of the security.

Each underwriter analyzes the loan package, estimates the risk to its organization, and determines whether the benefits are sufficient to balance the risk. An AUS analysis may be performed at any stage.

A lender's underwriter is concerned mostly with determining credit, collateral, compliance, fraud, and possibly secondary market risk, as they all relate to default risk. The other areas of risk are more toward management, operations, and finance—equally important, but typically not within the direct scope of the underwriter's file review.

The delivery price of the mortgage—the interest rate, points, and fees paid by the borrower to the lender or investor—rises *incrementally* with the number and extent of risk factors present in the loan. Although the price of the mortgage increases, the risk of default—and financial loss to the lender, insurer, guarantor, or investor—rises *exponentially* with each additional high-risk factor in the loan. Underwriters use the term *risk layering* or *risk stacking* to describe this situation.

UNDERWRITING GUIDELINES

The need for underwriting guidelines to address areas of risk in mortgage lending is evident. In addition, regulations—and sound business practice—require lenders to qualify applicants fairly and in a consistent manner from loan application to loan application. Clear loan policies and objective underwriting guidelines assist lenders in this challenging task. Such guidelines should explain how lenders must handle the most common scenarios and provide direction in more unusual circumstances.

Before the development and dominance of the secondary market, mortgage lending and underwriting was not standardized. Each lender developed unique policies, programs, and procedures as a result of its charter, state/local laws, local economy, and financial situation. Each lender employed different underwriting rules and formulas.

Today, it is still the case that no single method of underwriting exists for all residential mortgage loans. In fact, no single uniform set of underwriting guidelines exists. However, most lenders follow the *standard* underwriting guidelines of Fannie Mae and Freddie Mac as delineated in their separate *Seller/Servicer Guides*, or of *standard* government programs (such as FHA or VA). These guidelines are available online through links on their Web sites:

Fannie Mae https://www.efanniemae.com/sf/guides/ssg/index.jsp

Freddie Mac http://www.freddiemac.com/sell/guide/

FHA http://www.fhaoutreach.gov/FHAHandbook/prod/index.asp

VA http://www.warms.vba.va.gov/pam26_7.html

It is critical to point out the reference to the "standard" guidelines of Fannie, Freddie, FHA, and VA programs. These major agencies have dozens of mortgage products and programs (Fannie and Freddie number well over a hundred in total). These *standard* (or "traditional") programs should not be confused with the many specialty or subprime programs developed by these agencies. Standard guidelines have performed fairly well even in the recent economic recession. The many specialty or subprime guidelines (including "Alt A") have performed as poorly as private label programs. The development of many programs—and underwriting guidelines—by these agencies has caused some confusion within the lending community, in the media, and as a result, with regulators and Congress and the general public. Too often they incorrectly make a blanket reference to a Fannie or Freddie programs without specifying which one(s) they are including.

Accordingly, the comments in this chapter refer to Fannie's and Freddie's *standard* (or "traditional") underwriting guidelines. Today, similarities in underwriting guidelines for either conventional or government loans far outweigh their differences. Even lenders that don't intend to sell loans in the secondary mortgage market follow these well-conceived underwriting guidelines. They provide the industry with much needed uniformity and ease of use, and have proved effective in avoiding delinquency in all economic climates.

Finally, it is important to stress that only *guidelines* exist—not specific, precise formulas to apply to every applicant. This illustrates the scope of diversity and complexity involved in underwriting mortgage loans on a national basis. It also emphasizes that lenders need some flexibility to adapt these national standards to local or regional conditions and practices. Over time, underwriting guidelines will move back and forth on spectrum—often described as "looser" or "tighter" standards.

Use of Technology for Underwriting

Although advances in technology have not resulted in one uniform set of underwriting guidelines, they have inspired an equally fundamental change. Expanded data management over the last decade now enables investors, secondary market players, and large lenders and servicers to perform ongoing statistical analyses on an unprecedented amount of loan data—millions of loans nationwide! They compare loan performance and identify more precisely what specific loan application feature(s) affect repayment, default, and loan loss. These analyses have proven incredibly predictive from a national perspective—again, for *standard* underwriting guidelines.

As a result, there is a shift to base national underwriting guidelines and risk pricing on empirical results derived from this data. The theory is that this approach is more objective, fairer to consumers overall, and accurate in assessing risk pricing. Two positive results of this shift to technology for loan product design and pricing are:

- An expanded number of loan programs offered to the consumer
- Statistical measurement and pricing of various risk features

Negative results are:

- Lender and consumer confusion caused by these numerous loan programs
- Managing the complexity in determining different rates, points, and fees that apply to each loan program and each application

Risk-based Pricing Adjustments

Now standard underwriting guidelines include loan level risk-based pricing adjustments for dozens of features in an individual application: LTV, credit score, type of employment, debt to income ratios, cash reserves, property type, loan product, documentation, and more. Complicated underwriting matrices detail all of these adjustments.

The two most widely used matrices are from Fannie and Freddie; they are several pages long, and are very similar in categories, amounts, and their use. Most individual risk adjustments are 0.25 percent or 0.5 percent, but can range up to 1.5 percent. The consumer pays each fee to the lender who pays Fannie or Freddie. Automated underwriting systems (AUS) automatically include these adjustments, but manually underwritten applications require manual calculations. They are updated regularly and change with market conditions.

> Freddie Mac (Post-Settlement Delivery Fees)
> http://www.freddiemac.com/singlefamily/pdf/ex19.pdf
>
> Fannie Mae (Loan Level Pricing Adjustments)
> https://www.efanniemae.com/sf/refmaterials/llpa/pdf/llpamatrix.pdf

Figures 13.1 and 13.2 show the scope and complexity of these Fannie and Freddie pricing adjustments and a few examples of how to calculate them.

Conflicting Objectives?

The use of statistical analyses and their resulting impact on program guidelines and pricing adjustments places underwriting at the focal point of two seemingly conflicting objectives:

- Regulator/consumer trend toward equal treatment of and uniformity for each application.
- Investor/lender trend toward risk-based pricing of each application and, along with it, underwriting guidelines that reflect its unique risk profile.

Although today's underwriter has access to sophisticated automated underwriting systems, credit scores, and mortgage scores, the time-honored industry saying still rings true: "underwriting is an art, not a science." A successful underwriter's greatest asset is not these powerful analytic tools, but the ability to apply common sense and creativity to the many situations that arise when qualifying mortgage applicants. More important than which underwriting guidelines a lender selects is how skillfully the underwriter follows them.

In the past, secondary market underwriting meant following a single, specific formula into which the applicants needed to fit, and underwriters were perceived as those people who found ways to say, "No." Today, there is more flexibility, and more often the underwriters say, "It depends."

FIGURE **13.1** Pricing Adjustment Matrix

FannieMae

SELLING GUIDE

Loan-Level Price Adjustment (LLPA) Matrix and Adverse Market Delivery Charge (AMDC) Information

This document provides the LLPAs applicable to loans delivered to Fannie Mae and provides details of the AMDC. LLPAs are assessed based upon certain eligibility or other loan features, such as credit score, loan purpose, occupancy, number of units, product type, etc. Special feature codes (SFCs) that are required when delivering loans with these features are listed next to the applicable LLPAs. Not all loans will be eligible for the features described in this Matrix and unless otherwise noted, FHA, VA, Rural Development (RD) Section 502 Mortgages, HUD 184 Native American Mortgages, matured balloon mortgages (refinanced or modified, per *Servicing Guide* requirements) redelivered as fixed-rate mortgages (FRMs) (effective June 1, 2010), and reverse mortgages are excluded from these LLPAs. **Refer to the *Selling Guide* and your contracts with Fannie Mae to determine loan eligibility.**

Pricing Guidelines for LLPAs and AMDC (AMDCs are drafted in the same way as LLPAs):

□ All LLPAs and AMDC are cumulative. The LLPAs apply to all loans that meet the stated criteria for the LLPA, unless otherwise noted or excluded. The AMDC applies to all loans.

□ Credit score requirements are based on the "representative" score as defined in the *Selling Guide*. Loans delivered without a credit score will be charged under the lowest credit score range shown in each of the applicable LLPA tables (however, Fannie Mae does not waive any rights by accepting such loans and charging the applicable LLPA).

□ All applicable LLPAs and the AMDC for MBS transactions will be drafted from the lender's account. All applicable LLPAs and the AMDC for whole loan transactions will be deducted from the loan net proceeds, as set forth in the *Selling Guide*. For certain whole loan deliveries, including interest-only loans and loans with 40-year terms, the product-specific LLPAs are reflected in the commitment price available via eCommitting™ and eCommitOne™; any additional LLPAs applicable to loan features will be deducted from purchase proceeds.

□ Footnotes and expiration/effective dates are important guides to the correct application and accumulation of LLPAs. □

Mortgages are subject to all applicable SFCs, in addition to any that may be indicated below.

□ For loans with financed mortgage insurance, applicable LLPAs are applied based on gross LTV, which is calculated after the inclusion of financed mortgage insurance.

Table of Contents

Table 1: Adverse Market Delivery Charge		Page 2
Table 2: All Eligible Mortgages: LLPA by Credit Score/LTV		Page 2
Table 3: All Eligible Mortgages: LLPA by Product Feature		Pages 2-3
□ ARM □ 7-Year Balloon Mortgage	□ Investment Property □ Multiple-Unit Properties	
□ 40-year Term (MBS only) □ Manufactured Home	□ Cash-Out Refinance	
□ Interest-Only (IO) □ Condominiums and Cooperatives	□ High-Balance Mortgage Loans	
Table 4: Mortgages with Subordinate Financing (Excluding MCM)		Page 4
Table 5: Minimum Mortgage Insurance Option		Page 4
Table 6: Flexible Mortgages		Page 4
Table 7: Expanded Approval® (EA)		Page 5
Table 8: MyCommunityMortgage® (MCM®)		Page 5
Examples of Loan Transactions showing total LLPAs and AMDC		Page 6
LLPA Matrix and AMDC Information 2009 Change Tracking Log		Pages 7-8

1

April 30, 2010

This Matrix is incorporated by reference into the Fannie Mae *Selling Guide*, and supersedes any inconsistent information in the *Selling Guide* or earlier dated version of the Matrix.

Source: http://www.freddiemac.com/singlefamily/pdf/ex19.pdf

407

FIGURE **13.1** (*Continued*)

Examples of Loan Transactions Showing Total LLPAs and AMDC

The examples below are for illustrative purposes only and are not intended to imply actual DU recommendations (assumes 1-unit, primary residence)

Example 1a: 30-YR FRM, COR, Credit Score = 680, LTV = 85%

- ☐ From Table 1: AMDC = 0.250%
- ☐ From Table 2: Representative Credit Score LLPA = 1.000%
- ☐ From Table 3: COR LLPA = 2.500%
- **Total: 3.750%**

Example 1b: -YR FRM, COR, Credit Score = 680, LTV = 85%, Minimum MI

- ☐ From Table 1: AMDC = 0.250%
- ☐ From Table 2: Representative Credit Score LLPA = 1.000%
- ☐ From Table 3: COR LLPA = 2.500%
- ☐ From Table 5b: Minimum Mortgage Insurance = 0.125%
- **Total: 3.875%**

Example 2: 30-YR FRM, Purchase, Subordinate Financing, Credit Score = 670, LTV = 80%, CLTV = 95%

- ☐ From Table 1: AMDC = 0.250%
- ☐ From Table 2: Representative Credit Score LLPA = 2.500%
- ☐ From Table 4: Mortgage with Subordinate Financing = 0.500%
- **Total: 3.250%**

Example 3: Matured balloon mortgages (refinanced or modified, per *Servicing Guide* requirements) redelivered as FRM, Credit Score = 690, LTV = 80%, Investment Property

- ☐ From Table 1: AMDC = 0.250%
- ☐ From Table 3: Investment property - matured balloon mortgages (refinanced or modified) redelivered as FRM = 1.750% **Total: 2.000%**

Example 4: 10/1 ARM, COR, High-Balance Mortgage Loans, Credit Score =690, LTV = 75%

- ☐ From Table 1: AMDC = 0.250%
- ☐ From Table 2: Representative Credit Score LLPA = 1.000%
- ☐ From Table 3: COR LLPA = 0.750%
- ☐ From Table 3: High-Bal Mtg ARM LTV/CLTV = 0.750%
- ☐ From Table 3: High-Bal Mtg COR LLPA = 1.000%
- **Total: 3.750%**

April 30, 2010

FIGURE **13.2** Postsettlement Delivery Fees

Exhibit 19—Postsettlement Delivery Fees

MORTGAGES WITH SECONDARY FINANCING[11, 15,16]
Effective for Settlements on or before February 28, 2011

Product	LTV Ratios	TLTV Ratios	Credit Score < 720	Credit Score ≥ 720
All Eligible Product	> 65% & ≤ 75%	> 90% & ≤ 95%	0.50%	0.25%
	> 75% & ≤ 80%	> 76% & ≤ 90%	0.25%	0.00%
	> 75% & ≤ 80%	> 90% & ≤ 95%	0.50%	0.25%
	> 80% & ≤ 90%	> 81% & ≤ 95%	1.00%	0.50%
	> 90% & ≤ 95%[29]	> 90% & ≤ 95%[29]	0.50%	0.25%
	ALL[29]	> 95%[29]	1.50%	1.50%

MORTGAGES WITH SECONDARY FINANCING[11, 15,16]
Effective for Settlements on or after March 01, 2011

Product	LTV Ratios	TLTV Ratios	Credit Score < 720	Credit Score ≥ 720
All Eligible Product	≤ 65%	> 80% & ≤ 95%	0.50%	0.25%
	> 65% & ≤ 75%	> 80% & ≤ 95%	0.75%	0.50%
	> 75% & ≤ 80%	> 76% & ≤ 90%	1.00%	0.75%
	> 75% & ≤ 80%	> 90% & ≤ 95%	1.00%	0.75%
	> 80% & ≤ 90%	> 81% & ≤ 95%	1.00%	0.75%
	> 90% & ≤ 95%[29]	> 90% & ≤ 95%[29]	0.50%	0.25%
	ALL[29]	> 95%[29]	1.50%	1.50%

11 Secondary financing fees apply to both purchase and refinance transactions.
15 A secondary financing delivery fee will not be assessed on a Mortgage with a HELOC balance of zero at loan closing.
16 A secondary financing delivery fee will not be assessed on a Mortgage with an Affordable Second meeting the requirements of Section 25.1(g).
29 Applies to Freddie Mac Relief Refinance Mortgages only.

Volume 1
Bulletin 2010-30

Single-Family Seller/Servicer Guide

Page E19-10
11/22/2010

Source: Freddie Mac

As our society has evolved culturally, ethnically, and demographically, so has the approach to qualifying mortgage applicants. Secondary market guidelines still provide structure (and with good reason), but today's underwriting flexibilities allow an underwriter to review each situation individually instead of viewing it mechanically, as in the past. In this way, the underwriter works as a team with the loan officer, for many marginal loan applications require additional documentation and verifications, or require changes in the loan offered (counteroffer).

Additionally, portfolio lenders often develop special loan programs that reflect their unique knowledge of special circumstances in their region. They create niche products that deviate from standard secondary market underwriting guidelines. When properly crafted, these programs provide the local lender a competitive advantage when competing with larger, national mortgage bankers who may offer better pricing but are limited to traditional underwriting guidelines.

Another conflicting issue is the fairness of a specific underwriting guideline and/or associated risk pricing adjustment that is applied to all loans nationally when the underlying condition is not present equally throughout the nation. While the condition and pricing might reflect the lender's activity, is it fair to penalize a consumer from a region which never experienced that level of risk?

For example, recent housing market conditions ("excesses", some would say) in California, Florida, Nevada, and other key markets resulted in massive losses to national lenders involved in lending there. So why should a consumer in, say, Montana or Iowa housing markets—areas which never shared the same high risk conditions or level of home price depreciation or foreclosure activity—have to pay the same risk premium? When housing prices remain relatively stable in a region (0-5 percent price decline), why is an "adverse market" risk premium of 0.25 percent charged universally to each consumer in that region, regardless of LTV, property type, etc.? When applied in this manner, risk pricing adjustments have the effect of punishing future borrowers for past consumer and lender mistakes—they do not accurately reflect the real risk factors in the current application or borrower.

UNDERWRITING AREAS OF REVIEW

The areas of review set by a lender's underwriting guidelines should address the many different risks inherent in mortgage lending (listed previously in this chapter). What does an underwriter review when making a loan decision? Which issues are significant and to what extent?

No discussion of loan underwriting would be complete without referencing the traditional areas of a loan application the underwriter must consider, the three Cs of lending: *capacity*, *credit*, and *collateral*.

- *Capacity*—do the applicants have the financial resources to repay existing and proposed debts? Do they have adequate assets to complete the transaction?

- *Credit*—do the applicants have an acceptable credit history? Have they used credit responsibly?
- *Collateral*—is the property sufficient collateral to secure the loan?

These three areas are very important risk factors. Historically, lenders and secondary market investors view capacity, credit, and collateral risks differently, depending on the economic and lending environment. From 2000–2005, they were more expansive when considering delinquent credit history, debt/income ratios, and property. In the recent recession, they have become significantly more restrictive. As economic conditions stabilize and loan demand increases, they will move toward the more expansive range in this continuum.

Lenders also look at a fourth "C"—that of *character*. Today, residential mortgage lenders consider this area in different ways—formally and informally—or fold it into other areas of review because it is subjective. **Character** is traditionally defined as the "willingness" to repay the debt—something very difficult to measure objectively. Lenders evaluate this from a review of the other "C's" listed above, considered within the context of the real estate transaction for which the applicant seeks financing.

While this area is difficult to define objectively, many lenders argue it may be the most influential factor in evaluating an application. Some borrowers with sufficient capacity elect not to repay their obligations. Others with "blemished" credit histories and low FICO scores are willing to make significant sacrifices and change their behavior to keep their mortgage current. The art of lending is developing the skill to distinguish which situation you have in front of you when making the credit decision. Local lenders tied more closely to their communities and their customers may argue that they are better able to develop this history and skill than statistically-based automated underwriting systems or distant underwriters who have no experience and no other connection to their applicants.

Recently, lenders often speak of a fifth "C"—Compliance. Even before the massive regulatory changes starting in 2008 and continuing through 2011, compliance risk was rising in importance. Today it is an even larger consideration for all parties involved in mortgage loan origination and servicing.

Prequalification of Applicants

The underwriting review in many ways mirrors the criteria that loan originators consider when they prequalify applicants at application: loan transaction and program, debt/income ratios, credit history, collateral, and other compensating factors. The difference here is that the underwriter now has verified information and can review the file to see whether "the whole picture" fits together. If it does not, the underwriter must consider under what terms a marginal application can be approved.

Loan Policy and Eligibility Issues

An underwriter first must determine whether or not the general terms of the application are allowed in the lender's loan policy. Additionally, the underwriter may need to review the application for general *eligibility* requirements for government programs or secondary market programs. Eligibility and general loan policy factors include the transaction type, loan product, loan amount, loan-to-value ratios, number of units, and credit score. A **nonconforming loan** is one that does not meet Fannie Mae or Freddie Mac general eligibility and specific underwriting requirements (but may still be allowed by a lender's loan policy or be approved by a private investor).

Some common eligibility issues that are revealed at underwriting and can make a loan nonconforming or ineligible include:

- What was thought to be a purchase may now be a refinance
- A second mortgage appears when the applicants thought a particular loan for which they are obligated was unsecured
- The property "under appraised" from the original estimate
- Change in request from an ARM to fixed-rate loan
- Applicants request an increase in loan amount above loan limits

Industry studies rank default risk by loan transaction. Of highest risk are:

- Investment property
- Construction loans
- Land loans

In the next tier of risk is:

- Cash-out refinances
- Purchases
- No cash-out refinances (rate/term refinances)

Other industry studies rank loan product in a similar fashion (highest risk to lowest):

- ARMs
- Interest-only mortgages
- Balloon mortgages
- Fixed-rate mortgages

The underwriter considers the performance and inherent risk in these general loan policy and eligibility features—loan transaction and product type—as a starting point in the file analysis. Within this context, the underwriter then reviews the individual application's specific features and associated risk.

LOAN-TO-VALUE RATIOS

The loan-to-value ratio (LTV) measures the amount of collateral risk that the lender takes and, conversely, the amount of equity the borrower risks losing. Industry studies find the LTV is the most significant risk factor affecting loan delinquency, default, and loss. It is arguably the most important underwriting ratio and has the greatest single impact on the other underwriting guidelines for an application.

The LTV may be calculated as (rounding up to the next whole number) LTV = Mortgage Amount ÷ Lesser of Sales Price or Appraised Value

According to various studies, the following may be true:

- A 90 percent LTV loan is twice as likely to default as an 80 percent LTV loan.
- A 95 percent LTV loan is nearly three times the default risk as an 80 percent LTV loan.
- A 97 percent LTV loan is nearly six times the default risk as an 80 percent LTV loan.

Ninety-five percent and higher LTV loans are especially vulnerable, as there is no equity in the property if the loan defaults shortly after closing. According to Mortgage Guaranty Insurance Corporation, "Once default occurs, there is a better than 50 percent chance of foreclosure, largely because of the borrower's inability to sell the property at a price high enough to cover the remaining loan balance plus selling costs and delinquent interest."

There are two reasons for this strong correlation between a high LTV ratio (greater than 80 percent) and default:

- Borrower has a low equity investment in the property and has less total dollars at risk for loss.
- Borrower quickly loses all equity in the property and then has less incentive to keep paying the mortgage.

This situation is riskier if the property is located in a real estate market where property values decline and do not recover for several years, such as Texas in the early 1980s, California or New England during the early 1990s, and most of the United States from 2008 through 2010.

On the other hand, a low LTV (less than 70 percent) may be an indication of the borrower's ability to handle his or her finances and accumulate wealth. This adds strength to the application and may offset a weakness, such as high income/debt ratios or low cash reserves.

A common industry practice and secondary market requirement is that any loan with an LTV greater than 80 percent be supported by mortgage insurance (discussed in detail in Chapter 8—Government Insurance and Guaranty Programs, and Chapter 9—Private Mortgage Insurance). Additional underwriting guidelines change substantially as LTV rises. They usually become more stringent as LTV climbs above 80 percent and at each breakpoint above that important divide: 85, 90, 95 (and 97, 100, or 103 percent when available). Expect to see more stringent income/debt ratios, credit scores, cash reserves, restrictions on gift or seller contributions, and property or loan types as the LTV increases.

Combined LTV

As the mortgage marketplace became more complex in the 1980s, the secondary market players developed two additional LTV ratios acknowledging these changes:

- Combined LTV (CLTV for Fannie Mae; TLTV for Freddie Mac)
- Home equity LTV (HCLTV for Fannie Mae; HTLTV for Freddie Mac)

CLTV or TLTV will equal the LTV, unless the property has *subordinate financing*—any secured lien from borrowing that is junior to the proposed first mortgage. Subordinate financing can include a second mortgage or home equity line of credit, regardless of its source (lender, relative, employer, or builder). This ratio recognizes all mortgage debt on the property and the resulting amount of real equity the applicants have. CLTV or TLTV may be calculated as CLTV or TLTV = First Mortgage Amount + Second Mortgage Amount ÷ Lesser of Sales Price or Appraised Value.

Calculating the HCLTV or HTLTV includes several conditions which differ from each other, but thankfully both apply only to specific situations. This ratio increases normal CLTV limits for applicants with good credit scores. It was developed as a convenience to those applicants who have demonstrated that their Home Equity Line of Credit (HELOC) is not active, but who might have a CLTV issue because of their proposed loan amount.

CAPACITY

Down Payment (Equity)

Down payment, or equity, is related to LTV, but represents the collateral risk that the applicant takes in the transaction. Typically, purchase transactions refer to *down payment*; refinances refer to *equity*. The down payment in a purchase transaction may be calculated by simply subtracting the proposed mortgage amount and all other secondary financing from either the sales price (or total acquisition cost for a construction loan; see Chapter 9—Construction Lending) or the appraised value, whichever is lower. The equity in a refinance transaction may be calculated by subtracting the proposed mortgage amount and all other secondary financing from the appraised value.

As with LTV, industry studies show the amount of down payment (or equity) the applicants put into the property is a very significant factor in default and loss. A larger down payment/equity generally reduces lender default/loss risk; however, it may not be the result of applicant savings. For this reason, underwriters examine not only the amount of down payment, but also its source.

Why is the source of down payment of concern? It gives underwriters a clearer picture of how the applicant acquired this equity—was it developed through savings or housing price appreciation, received as a gift, or obtained through other borrowing?

Down payment from accumulated savings, investments, retirement funds, or equity in another home sold is generally earned over time. It provides a good indication of an applicant's ability to handle debt and manage income. As a general rule, the secondary mortgage market is interested in establishing that an applicant either saved or obtained through housing price appreciation at least five percent of the down payment for the mortgage loan. Secondary market players, other investors, and mortgage insurance (MI) companies place restrictions on gift funds, contributions from the builder or seller, and other down payment borrowing for applications with at least 80 percent LTV.

Exceptions to this general rule do exist, such as under certain "affordable housing" programs that allow for a three/two split, whereby the borrower has to produce only three percent of the purchase price from savings while the remaining two percent can come from another source, such as an employer. In all situations, the borrower is expected to be able to establish how the required money had been saved.

As mentioned, some or all of the down payment may come from a gift, but it is essential that a true gift has been made and that there is no expectation of that money being repaid. The grantor of gift funds must sign a legally binding gift letter and verify the source and transfer of the gifted funds to the applicants.

To establish the source of down payment/equity, the underwriter reviews a Verification of Deposits (VOD) or the most recent sixty days of deposit statements if using alternative documentation (alt doc). The underwriter looks for the following data:

- When was the account opened?
- How long have the funds been there?
- What is the current balance versus average balance?
- What kind of deposit/withdrawal activity occurred?
- In whose name(s) are the funds held?

Recent substantial deposits in joint accounts, recently opened new accounts, and recent name changes on accounts often hide loans from family members, but not necessarily; a common practice when purchasing a home is to consolidate savings into one liquid account to complete the transaction, which confuses this analysis. Underwriters must use common sense in evaluating whether the applicants' activity and total amount of liquid or investment assets matches their income and debt levels, general spending and debt repayment habits, or any other significant features.

Income of Applicant(s)

As with the credit history, underwriters must evaluate the applicant's level and type of income. Of most concern are the applicant's income stability and the probability that income will continue. Industry studies indicate that, over time, the risk of default is not impacted by the applicant's specific position, industry, salary versus hourly rate, and similar factors. Of most importance is whether the borrower maintains the same level of income, regardless of its source.

Chapter 12—Residential Mortgage Loan Origination and Processing, details much of the documentation and treatment of the different sources of income. Because applicants bring most of this information to the loan interview, the loan originator completes the basic analysis. The underwriter's main objective when verifying income is to confirm whether or not: a) sources of income are documented appropriately and b) a complete two-year income/employment history is verified, and to determine which information needs updating.

Economic events in the 1980s and 1990s changed the approach to reviewing employment history and income. "Job stability" now means consistent income level and employment in related lines of work, instead of having the exact same job. Moving from one job to another, especially if it is for an increase in pay and is in the same field of endeavor, is a positive characteristic. On the other hand, extensive job changes without advancement or pay increases may be indicative of future financial instability. Gaps in employment may indicate possible future employment problems and should be adequately explained.

For several successive years, underwriters would see applications with consistent bonus, overtime, and commission income. The national recession starting in 2008 now requires that underwriters more closely scrutinize the stability of these sources of income.

Because most applicants rely on employment income to repay the mortgage loan, the underwriter should review carefully the Verification of Employment (VOE) or alt docs (pay stubs and W-2s) for the following:

- Salary/wage corresponds with the application, and is reasonable.
- Probability of continued employment is acceptable.
- Overtime/bonus income is likely to continue.
- Dates of employment correspond with the application.
- Appropriate name and signature of employer on the form.

IRS and Sources of Income

A residential mortgage loan underwriter will review in detail IRS returns for applicants who rely on the sources of income listed in Table 13.1. Each source listed can have very different characteristics. It can be relatively simple, like a guaranteed pension income from a 1099-R, or very complex, like partnership income from a Schedule E. To qualify an applicant, an underwriter normally uses a two-year average of net income for the income source, as long as that source can be relied upon in the future. Certain deductions from

TABLE **13.1**

IRS Forms Documenting Income

Source	Personal IRS Form 1040	Others IRS Forms
Commission/bonus/OT		W-2/1099
Pension/retirement		1099-R
Interest/dividend	Schedule B	1099-INT/DIV
Self-employment	Schedule C/C-EZ	1099-MISC
Investment	Schedule D	1099-DIV
Rental real estate/trust/royalty	Schedule E	1099-MISC
Partnership/S corporation	Schedule E/K-1	1065/1120
Farm	Schedule F	

Source: © 2010 REMOC Associates, LLC. www.remoc.com

the net income reported may be added back to reported income and included in qualifying income. These deductions typically include depreciation of five or more years in duration; nonrecurring, discretionary expenses; and housing expenses accounted for elsewhere in the application.

Financial statement analysis can be simple or very complex. Fannie Mae/ Freddie Mac, private investors, and mortgage insurance companies provide specific guidelines and forms for completing this analysis, but in the end, the underwriter must rely on common sense to interpret the numbers, their relevancy, and the reliability of the documentation. Once the underwriter has established the income to be used for qualifying, the next step is debt/income ratio analysis.

Repayment and default risks rise as debt/income ratios exceed these standards. The presence of offsetting strengths may justify higher debt/income ratios. Underwriters should think of ratios in terms of ranges, not specific numbers. The difference in default risk for a loan with a 36.3 percent versus 36.4 percent total debt ratio is insignificant, but is substantially higher than loans with 21 to 24 percent total debt ratio. It is also important for underwriters to examine what kind of debt makes up the ratios—mortgage, installment, revolving, or other obligations.

Housing Ratio

The housing ratio (or front-end ratio, as it is sometimes called) measures the percentage of monthly income necessary to meet the monthly housing expense. Most lenders calculate the proposed monthly housing expense in a similar manner, but the maximum ratio allowed may differ for investor, loan product, and LTV. When computing the proposed monthly housing expense on a conventional loan, the following monthly charges or monthly share of annual expenses must be added:

- Principal
- Interest
- Hazard insurance premium
- Flood insurance premium (if required)
- Real estate tax
- Mortgage insurance premium (if required)
- Homeowners' association fee (if required)
- Ground rents (if required)
- Any payment on an existing or proposed second mortgage

Divide the proposed monthly housing expense by the verified gross monthly income. (*Gross monthly income* includes income before deductions of any type.) Generally, the ratio should not exceed 28 percent without compensating factors.

Total Debt Ratio

Individuals often have other monthly contractual debt obligations in addition to mortgage payments. Underwriters use the verified information from the credit report to determine other debt. The total debt ratio may be calculated using the following verified payments divided by the gross monthly income:

- Proposed monthly housing expenses (from housing ratio)
- Revolving charges
- Installment debts with more than 10 payments remaining
- Any alimony or child support payments
- Other legal obligations such as cosigned or endorsed loans, unless satisfactory repayment is documented for the other party

Higher ratios above 36 percent may be justified by compensating factors, such as the following:

- Demonstrated ability of an applicant to allocate a higher percentage of gross income to housing expenses
- Larger down payment than normal
- Demonstrated ability of an applicant to accumulate savings and maintain a good credit rating
- Large net worth
- Potential for increased earnings because of education or profession

FIGURE **13.3** Calculation of the Total Debt Ratio

Example: Ed and Jane Smith want to borrow $120,000 in order to purchase a single-family detached house appraised at $150,000. He earns $35,000 a year as a brick-layer, and she earns $40,000 as an assistant professor of English. Their current debts include these monthly payments: car, $400; truck, $300 (both vehicles with 25 months remaining); credit cards, $100; child support, $400. Calculations are as follows:

Verified income:

Gross monthly income (borrower)	$2,917
Gross monthly income (co-borrower)	**3,333**
Total Monthly Income	$6,250

Projected monthly housing expense:

Principal and interest (7.5% for 30 years)	$838.80
Insurance escrow	35.00
Tax escrow	**255.00**
Total Projected Housing Expense	$1,128.80

Current long-term debts:

Car payments	$400.00
Truck payments	300.00
Child support	400.00
Credit cards	**100.00**
Total Long-Term Debts	$1,200.00

Total of All Monthly Payments	$2,328.80

Housing Expense Ratio: $1,128.80/$6,250 = 18 percent

Total Debt Ratio: $2,328.80/$6,250 = 37 percent

Source: © 2010 REMOC Associates, LLC. www.remoc.com

Equally important is for the underwriter to look beyond the total debt ratio number—to review the *type* of debt used and to identify the repayment risks involved. For example, an underwriter calculates other debt and comes up with a total of $300 per month, which represents a total debt ratio of 35 percent (just within the guideline maximum). The underwriter should review this situation differently if the $300 payments were all charge accounts versus all installment debt. A $300 car loan payment is constant, so the underwriter knows the total debt ratio is constant. If the $300 is the total of four charge accounts in active use and with balances of more than $1,000 each, then monthly payment is variable and more likely to change from month to month. This means that the total debt ratio would also change and, depending on the month chosen, may exceed the recommended guideline for that loan scenario.

CREDIT

Credit History

The total debt ratio measures only the current level of other debt—a snapshot of the applicants' financial picture. Studying the credit report completely reveals the applicants' history of credit use and provides a longer-term view of their use of debt. In addition to analyzing the current amounts outstanding and the repayment history, the underwriter should also consider the type of credit used, highest balances, and open accounts with no balances. Although the credit report includes the past seven years of history, an underwriter must not make a personal judgment on how consumers spend their money or use debt. The underwriter's concern is only with how the applicants' documented use of debt and credit repayment history may impact the repayment of the proposed mortgage.

Use of Debt

Installment debt payments amortize the underlying principal amount over time, and the balance declines each month. Total repayment of this kind of debt "manages itself"—all the consumer has to do is make the same payment each month, and the loan gets paid off.

In contrast, revolving debt payments and balances can change dramatically from one month to the next. Additionally, the minimum payment required only slightly pays down the underlying principal. Consumers can easily accumulate charge debt that will take several years to pay off with their current level of income. As a result, active users of revolving debt tend to stay active and carry the balance and payment. This debt is by its nature more difficult for consumers to budget and manage—it does not "manage itself" like installment debt. This variability presents a higher credit and repayment risk than does the structure of installment debt. If the applicants rely on income that is variable as well, this increases their risk of cash flow problems.

Repayment History

How well an applicant has repaid credit in the past is an additional key factor in underwriting an application. If an underwriter verifies that an applicant always pays debt obligations "as agreed" (according to contract terms), then that application should be considered in a positive manner. If, on the other hand, the credit history includes debt repayment problems ranging from delinquent or past due payments, to collection accounts, judgments, foreclosures, or bankruptcy, then an underwriter needs to analyze the credit history very carefully and may need to obtain additional documentation in order to make an informed loan decision. Credit reports measure delinquent or past due payments in terms of months (1 × 30, 2 × 60, etc.). It is important to review date(s), the frequency, and the extent of the problem(s). In the loan policy or underwriting guideline, lenders should establish specific credit standards so underwriters can complete this review consistently from application to application.

Minor Delinquency

One or two isolated 30-day delinquencies reported in the past two years, with several other "as agreed" accounts are considered to be minor or incidental delinquency. Example: a credit history with a single 30-day past due payment in the past five years is not a serious matter, especially if several other accounts were handled satisfactorily since that incident. The underwriter should not consider this application negatively or request an explanation.

Situational Delinquency

Delinquency that shows up on the credit report as a result of an event, not a pattern, is considered situational. Example: a credit history shows three consecutive 30-day and one 60-day delinquencies, but at all other times repayment on all accounts was excellent; this might then be a case of situational delinquency. If the delinquency was the result of nonrecurring circumstances beyond the control of the applicant, then the information should not be viewed negatively. To verify this situation, the underwriter should request a satisfactory written explanation from the applicants with verification of the cause of the delinquency. Some common examples are unemployment, an accident or illness and time out of work, extensive medical bills, divorce, or other nonrecurring events.

Chronic Delinquency

These are unexplained delinquencies that are very serious in either frequency or severity (days past due). Example: a credit history that lists several accounts with 30-day delinquencies, three 60-day delinquencies, and a collection account spread out over different periods of the past five years is an indication of chronic delinquency. No one event or situation can explain the delinquent payment history. This kind of information normally is a reason for denial.

Bankruptcy

A bankruptcy in an applicant's credit history does not in itself mean a denial of the application. As with the preceding example, the reasons for the bankruptcy and the type of filing are the most important factors for an underwriter to consider. If the circumstances are nonrecurring and beyond the applicants' control (such as a serious illness with no insurance), the bankruptcy may not be the reason for a credit denial. If a Chapter 7 or 11 bankruptcy exists in the credit history, secondary market guidelines generally require a four-year "waiting period" with excellent credit history has been maintained since the discharge or dismissal (or as little as two years with documented extenuating circumstances).

A form of bankruptcy that has become common is a wage earner's petition. A *wage earner's petition* under Chapter 13 of the Bankruptcy Law provides for partial or full repayment of debts over a period of time, usually two to five years. When all payments have been satisfactorily made, underwriters should consider that accomplishment as reestablishing credit. Secondary market guidelines allow for a two-year "waiting period" since its discharge. Occasionally, applicants apply for a mortgage loan before full discharge of bankruptcy. In such a situation, the approval of the bankruptcy judge may be required. Certain other bankruptcies, such as those over seven years old, should not be given excessive consideration.

Past Foreclosures or Deed in Lieu

A past foreclosure or an agreement for a deed in lieu of foreclosure is evidence that the applicant had a problem handling credit. The secondary mortgage market requires that these applicants have five years of excellent credit history since the foreclosure or deed in lieu (or as few as three years with documented extenuating circumstances). This type of credit problem is serious because it involves a mortgage loan—the same type of loan the applicants are requesting.

Credit Scores

A **credit score** is a numeric rating of applicants' use of debt and credit repayment history. Although the use of credit scores for consumer loan underwriting was common in the 1980s, their use in mortgage lending was not widespread until the proliferation of automated underwriting systems in the mid-1990s. Scores range from the mid-800s (excellent) to below 400 (extremely poor). More than 90 percent of the population has a score above 680. See Table 13.2 for a complete list of Credit Scores.

TABLE **13.2**

Credit Score and Underwriting Review Levels

Credit Score	Level of Underwriting
720 and above	Streamlined or minimal review
660–719	Basic or Full review
620–659	Full review
619 and below	Caution, full review

Source: © 2010 REMOC Associates, LLC. www.remoc.com

Secondary market guidelines set minimum credit score levels for different loan programs and manual vs. automated underwriting. These guidelines tailor the risk pricing and level of underwriting review to these "threshold" levels. Some recent examples are listed in the table, but exact numbers vary by lender, program, LTV, and constant refinement of the historical data from which they are derived.

Underwriters must be careful to not place too much emphasis on the credit score number alone—it is only as good as the information on which it is based, and an applicant's situation can change quickly. Incorrect reporting of delinquent and excessive credit or credit disputes eventually won by the consumer may negatively affect the credit score unfairly. Debts not reported to the credit bureaus would result in an artificially high credit score. Additionally, underwriters should also review carefully the credit scores reported on credit histories with recent, substantial changes in use of debt. These recent events may be very serious and of most significance, but their impact on the credit score may be "diluted" by a strong prior history.

Collateral

Although the lender relies primarily on the applicants' income and assets to fulfill the mortgage obligation, the mortgage lender must protect both its own position and that of any investor by having adequate security. The lender obtains an appraisal report to assist with this step (see Chapter 14—Residential Real Estate Appraisal).

An **appraisal** is an opinion or estimate of market value made by a licensed or certified appraiser who is either an independent fee appraiser or employed by a mortgage lender. The appraiser has separate "underwriting" guidelines and standards to follow: the Uniform Standards of Professional Appraisal Practice (USPAP). The standard appraisal form that satisfies regulatory and secondary mortgage market requirements is the Uniform Residential Appraisal Report (URAR), Fannie Mae 1004/Freddie Mac 70. Underwriters review this report to determine whether the subject property is sufficient collateral for the mortgage loan. The property must conform to the lender's property standards, provide sufficient value, and be in marketable condition.

Property and Appraisal Standards

Regulatory agencies have similar requirements for lenders regarding appraisals and their use. The lenders should include the particular requirements for both appraisals and property standards. Underwriters should be familiar with these requirements, as they review appraisals daily. It is recommended that either the underwriter or another qualified person review appraisals regularly for violations in policy or unacceptable appraisal practices, such as redlining. **Redlining** is the withdrawal of mortgage funds from an area due to perceived risks in that area based on racial, social, religious, or ethnic factors. It is similar to property discrimination. The lender must not designate any area or neighborhood as being unacceptable—nor allow any appraiser to do so—for illegally discriminatory reasons.

TABLE **13.3**
Collateral-related Characteristics of Property

Property Type	Location	Property Value
Investment	Rural	Decreasing
Construction/land	Urban	Stable
Vacation/second home	Suburban	Increasing
Cooperative		
Condominium		
PUD		
Single family		

Source: © 2010 REMOC Associates, LLC. www.remoc.com

When reviewing the appraisal, an underwriter is concerned with risks that the property represents to the lender in the event of foreclosure and subsequent sale by the lender. The collateral-related characteristics listed in Table 13.3 may affect loan repayment, property value, and marketing time (listed from highest risk to lowest).

Descriptive information from the front page of the appraisal describes the overall market conditions, neighborhood, site, improvements, and condition of the subject property. Information on this page details the condition of the subject property and identifies any legal or flood zone issues.

The descriptive information on the first page must support the market conditions, comparable selections, and adjustments to value found on the second page of the appraisal. This page details the analysis the appraiser performs to establish market value.

Throughout the appraisal form are comment sections that should contain explanations for any unusual or significant conditions, characteristics, or adjustments. The processor and underwriter should establish an effective relationship with the appraiser to resolve quickly any issues, questions, or requests for additional documentation or an addendum.

Underwriter's Review of Appraisal

The underwriter's review should include the previously mentioned items and the following additional property considerations for their impact on value, marketability, and property eligibility:

1. *Location/Site.* This is always the most critical of all evaluating factors.
   a. Property must be residential in nature, not agricultural or commercial.
   b. Adequate sewage and water facilities and other utilities are present.
   c. Property is readily accessible by an all-weather road.
   d. No danger is posed to health and safety from immediate surroundings (including environmental hazards).
2. *Physical security.* The age, equipment, architectural design, quality of construction, floor plan, and site features are considered when establishing the adequacy and future value of the physical security.

     a. Evidence of compliance with local codes should be in the file for underwriter's review.

     b. Topography, shape, size, and drainage of a lot are equally important.

     c. View, amenities, easements, and other encroachments may have either a positive or negative influence on market value.

3. *Local government.*

     a. The amount of property tax can have a great effect on future marketability.

     b. Building codes, deed restrictions, and zoning ordinances help to maintain housing standards and promote a high degree of homogeneity.

4. *Comparable sales.* This is a critical section for residential real estate loans.

     a. The comparables are truly similar to the subject in regards to location, type of real estate, and time of sale.

     b. The adjustments exceed 10 percent for any line item.

     c. The total of all adjustments, disregarding plus and minus signs, exceeds 25 percent.

     d. Adjusted sales prices "bracket" the market value of the subject property.

In the overwhelming majority of appraisals, the sales comparison approach to value is the greatest determination of the property's market value. Comparable selection is the most subjective step in the appraisal process and has the greatest impact on market value. Analyzing comparable selection is one of the most difficult and important skills for an underwriter to develop.

The underwriter must use common sense to evaluate whether all the technical data, market assumptions, and sales comparable selections realistically support the market value. More detail on the appraisal report is in Chapter 14—Appraisals. Often, an underwriter will use a checklist to assist in his or her review (See Figure 14.3—Sample Appraisal Review Checklist)

AUTOMATED UNDERWRITING SYSTEMS

As discussed earlier, two systems exist for evaluating the creditworthiness of an applicant: judgmental (manual) and empirical (automated). Historically, mortgage lenders used the judgmental system, which relies on trained underwriters to evaluate each application on a case-by-case basis. The same standards are applied to each application in the same manner. Exceptions are allowed, but the reason must be clearly demonstrable. For example, if a larger-than-normal down payment is made, then an increased total debt ratio of 40 percent of gross monthly income may be acceptable. This system attempts to be objective, but people (who are subjective by nature) perform the analysis. Lending policies and guidelines provide structure and consistency.

The second system—automated underwriting system (**AUS**)—determines the creditworthiness of an applicant by having a computer software program assign values to certain attributes and facts for each application. To analyze and calculate these values, the AUSs use as their database enormous loan portfolios, which track the performance of millions of loans over several years. AUSs evaluate and score each application, much like the credit-scoring systems discussed earlier. ECOA regulations state that these systems must be "demonstrably and statistically sound and empirically derived."

When these systems were first introduced, lenders were wary of using them because of the complexities of lending and potential for unintended discrimination. Information on how these AU systems work is proprietary (as are credit-scoring systems), but since the late 1990s, most lenders either own or have access to AU systems. Fannie Mae/Freddie Mac, FHA/VA, MI companies, and large private lenders rely on AUSs for much of their originations.

Fannie Mae and Freddie Mac developed the most widely used systems. Practically all loans purchased by them today are reviewed by Desktop Underwriter and Loan Prospector. Government loans (FHA, VA) can also be submitted through these systems, as well as subprime loans that these agencies offer.

All AUSs operate in a similar manner. The lender logs on to the system, inputs and submits the completed loan application information, then receives within a few minutes what is formally called an underwriting recommendation from the AUS. The basic recommendations are to "accept/approve" or "refer/caution" (technically this is not a denial, but realistically it means there is very little chance the loan as submitted will be purchased by the investor).

It is important to recognize that the accuracy and soundness of AUS recommendations depend totally on the knowledge, skill, and ability of the person inputting the information. Lenders retain liability for the accuracy of what is submitted. If the secondary market player later determines (in a "post closing review" performed by a human underwriter) that the information upon which its recommendation was based is inaccurate, then the lender is subject to repurchase of the loan.

AUSs provide the potential for enormous cost savings, and faster approval and closings. As they develop, the capacities and services of these AUSs go way beyond providing a credit decision. Now lenders can manage their mortgage pipelines; sell loans to investors; and order credit reports, appraisals, flood and tax determinations, and so forth, with AUSs.

AUSs provide important benefits in the processing area as well. An "accept" recommendation includes a list of exactly which processing documentation is needed for closing. This minimizes the time and extent of processing.

STANDARD VS. LIMITED/STREAMLINED DOCUMENTATIONS

Fannie Mae/Freddie Mac, private investors, and large lenders offer several additional loan programs that reduce even further the amount and extent of processing. They may allow even more flexible underwriting guidelines or may eliminate the verification process altogether. The secondary market players and other investors who developed these programs could not have done so without the analytical horsepower that advanced technology now offers. Their AUSs recognize and automatically rate an application that qualifies for these special programs. Manual guidelines also define when an application is eligible for streamlined processing. Although traditional under-writers believe some guidelines are too lax, these streamline guidelines are based on national statistical data for loan repayment, default, and loss.

Fannie Mae and Freddie Mac use such terms as *streamlined* or *accept plus* to signify applications that qualify for limited documentation programs. Limited documentation expedites the processing and closing of applications identified as "low risk" (remember—risk is never eliminated, just managed). AUSs recognize the low-risk profiles for these applications, such as LTV below 50 percent, credit scores greater than 720, or cash reserves in excess of 10 months of total debt obligations.

Fannie Mae/Freddie Mac and large lenders use the same statistical analysis to develop the other extreme of the risk scale, "subprime" mortgage loan programs. These applications have higher risk profiles than "prime" or standard secondary market guidelines permit. Rather than denying the application under standard programs, the AUS identifies them as eligible for these "Alt-A" or "A–" or "Expanded Approval" guidelines. Higher risk profiles might include high debt/income ratios over 50 percent, credit scores below 660, or no income verification.

Applicants in these programs pay a 0.25–0.50 percent risk-based pricing fee to compensate for the higher risk vs. the standard documentation program. Lenders expect higher delinquency in these loans, and price them accordingly. But again, all of this depends on proper data input into the AUS and effective controls in place for detecting fraud and other errors.

Comprehensive Risk Assessment

Clearly, the development and implementation of AUSs provide the mortgage-lending industry with many benefits as described. In recent years, secondary market players invested heavily in developing AUSs, and placed a strong emphasis on cultivating the market of lenders who use them, as this is the most efficient way for Fannie Mae and Freddie Mac to receive and sell mortgages on a flow basis.

A significant number of lenders choose not to use an AUS system exclusively. Many lenders use AUS *and* manual underwriting; some use manual underwriting only. One drawback to using AUS is that some feel the guidelines are not appropriate for their markets; others find it either economically or operationally impractical. To avoid alienating this segment of the mortgage origination market, in 2002, Fannie Mae and Freddie Mac updated their *Selling Guide* to include manual review guidelines for lenders who do not submit loans through an AUS. Fannie and Freddie call this review a *Comprehensive Risk Assessment*. It is similar to the risk analysis format described at the beginning of this chapter, but it adds risk pricing adjustments as well. The assessment guidelines are based on the analysis of millions of GSE mortgage loans. The GSEs recommend that a lender complete the following steps in this assessment:

- Evaluate primary risk factors
- Evaluate each contributory risk factor
- Use information from both evaluations to make a comprehensive risk assessment of the application

Fannie Mae outlines in more detail their assessment, so the following information is based on their example. The assessment differentiates between "primary" and "contributory" risk factors. Fannie Mae identifies two primary risk factors that most significantly impact default risk: equity investment (LTV and CLTV) and credit history. The two factors may not impact equally the default risk of a particular loan, but the overall dynamic is similar. Loans with the same LTV have different repayment histories, depending on the credit history. Loans with the same credit scores have different repayment histories, depending on the LTV.

The lender must consider the *combined impact* of these factors on mortgage default and identify it as low, moderate, or high primary risk. Fannie Mae lists three representative combinations of primary risk factors (Figure 13.4) that it considers moderate risk:

- Generally, LTV/CLTV ratio of 91 to 100 percent and a representative credit score of mid-600 to low 700
- Generally, LTV/CLTV ratio of 81 to 90 percent and a representative credit score of low 600 to mid-600
- Generally, LTV/CLTV ratio of 80 percent or less and a representative credit score in the low 600 range

Once the lender completes its primary risk assessment, it next assesses contributory risk factors. These factors individually are insufficient to form an underwriting decision, but when combined may significantly affect mortgage default risk (and therefore, a lender's underwriting decision). Fannie Mae identifies the following contributory risk factors (the categories are added in parentheses to help organize them):

1. **(Financial)**
   - Liquid financial reserves
   - Total debt/income ratio
   - Employment classification

FIGURE **13.4** Primary Risk Assessment

Primary Risk Assessment					
LTV/CLTV	Representative Credit Score for the Mortgage				
	>740	700	660	620	<600
>95%				High Primary Risk	
95%					
90%					
80%		Moderate Primary Risk			
70%					
60%					
<50%	Low Primary Risk				

Source: Fannie Mae

2. **(Transactional)**
   - Mortgage term
   - Mortgage product type
   - Transaction type
   - Property type
3. **(Credit)**
   - Previous mortgage delinquency
   - Prior bankruptcy and/or foreclosure

To complete risk assessment in this step, the lender categorizes in the following manner the impact each contributory risk factor has on default risk:

- Significantly decreases risk
- Decreases risk
- Risk-Neutral (Satisfies basic risk tolerances)
- Increases risk
- Significantly increases risk (Table 13.4)

In its *Selling Guide*, Fannie Mae provides more detail on how to assess and document each contributory risk factor using the preceding categories. For example:

- two months of principal, interest, taxes, and insurance (PITI) reserves is considered "risk-neutral" and would satisfy the basic risk tolerance for liquid financial reserves, six-plus months of reserves would decrease risk, and no reserves would significantly increase risk;
- a debt-to-income ratio in the 30-40 percent range is considered risk-neutral, a ratio of 45 percent or greater significantly increases risk, a ratio of 10 percent or less significantly decreases risk.

Once the lender completes this step for each contributory risk factor, it then considers the cumulative effect of its primary and contributory assessments to form a Comprehensive Risk Assessment. This final assessment should document the application's strengths, weaknesses, layering of risk factors, and offsetting factors. This assessment determines whether the application is eligible for sale to Fannie Mae:

- *Low Comprehensive Risk*—low probability of default.
- *Moderate Comprehensive Risk*—moderate probability of default.
- *High Comprehensive Risk*—high probability of default. The lender should not deliver this loan to Fannie Mae (unless it has access to DU and Expanded Approval programs).

It is important to note the evolution in terms and language used here. This recent format focuses on the assessment and evaluation of the loan application's risk factors, not on cultural or subjective issues. Additionally, Fannie Mae stresses that assessments are on a gradient. Each factor may have a different weight in the overall loan decision, and again may differ from one application to the next. The Comprehensive Risk Assessment attempts to quantify in objective terms the underwriting review process, but

TABLE **13.4**

Assess Contributory Risk Factors

Contributory Risk Factor	Significantly Decreases Risk	Decreases Risk	Risk-Neutral	Increases Risk	Significantly Increases Risk
Mortgage Term	≤15 years	>15 and ≤25 years	≥25 years	N/A	
Total DTI Ratio	≤10%	>10% and ≤30%	>30% and ≤40%	>40% and ≤45%	>45%
Liquid Reserves	≥24 months	<24 and ≥6 months	<6 and ≥2 months	<2 and ≥1 months	<1 month
Previous Mortgage Payment History		0 × 30 days late within 24 months	0 × 30 days late within 12 months	1 × 30 days late within 12 months	2 × 30 days late or 1 × 60 days late within 13–24 months
Prior Bankruptcy (BK)			None	Any history of BK	Any BK within 5 years* OR repeat filer
Prior Foreclosure (FC), Deed-in-lieu (DIL), or Preforeclosure Sale			None	Any history of FC, DIL, or preforeclosure sale	1. FC within 6 years* 2. DIL within 5 years* 3. Preforeclosure sale within 3 years*
Presence of Co-Borrower		Co-borrower with applicable credit score ≥700			

*Refer to the *Selling Guide* for minimum elapsed time requirements since BK or FC, etc., and for guidance on identifying and documenting extenuating circumstances that may apply.

Read the following notes before using the chart above:

- Property type, occupancy type, transaction (purpose) type, and product type are all contributory risk factors already taken into consideration as part of Fannie Mae's eligibility criteria for standard products and special products. The items listed below are those contributory risk factors not already incorporated into our eligibility criteria.
- For each row on the chart, circle the box that includes the characteristic that applies to the mortgage loan under review. For example, if the mortgage loan has a total debt-to-income (DTI) ratio of 36%, circle the middle box (>30% and ≤40%) under the Risk-Neutral heading. Continue until you have circled one box per row, or determined that it is not applicable.
- Areas shaded and marked with an "N/A" do not apply. For example, the lack of a prior bankruptcy does not decrease risk and mortgage terms greater than 25 years do not increase risk.
- If the specific mortgage loan being requested must meet a higher minimum eligibility requirement (e.g., 6 months' reserves for an investment property), that minimum eligibility requirement must be viewed as risk-neutral rather than a factor that decreases the risk of the mortgage loan.

Source: Fannie Mae

still allows for individual circumstances (not so easily quantifiable) to have an impact on the loan decision.

Like AUSs, the Comprehensive Risk Assessment mainly (if not exclusively) relies on past history and may not adequately incorporate recent economic events or other factors specific to a local geographic area. The basis for AUSs and Comprehensive Risk Assessment is a blend of national data over a long period of time, a method that may distort the real impact of a positive or negative factor in a particular area of lending.

Underwriting Worksheet and Summary

It is of vital importance for the lender to document the analysis and conclusions of the underwriting review. Normally, the underwriter completes a worksheet showing the calculations supporting the analysis and a summary form itemizing the conditions under which the loan will be approved and can close. There are several benefits to adhering to this practice:

- Highlights the key issues in the credit decision
- Ensures a consistent underwriting review process
- Explains the methodology used for income and other calculations
- Enables secondary market investors to understand the decision
- Allows faster review during processing
- Summarizes commitment or denial conditions in one place

Conditions on the underwriting worksheet or summary as shown in Figures 13.5 and 13.6 should be included on the commitment letter to the applicants (and later forwarded to the closing agent). This consistency in communication minimizes confusion between the many parties involved: lender, applicant, underwriter, processor, closing agent, loan committee, loan review/quality control, and private investor.

THE UNDERWRITING DECISION

When the lender has a fully processed mortgage loan application, the lender makes a credit decision that either accepts, rejects, or modifies the mortgage loan application. According to ECOA (See Compliance—Chapter 11), the lender must notify the applicant of this decision within 30 days of the date of a "completed" loan application. In this context, *completed* means fully processed—when the lender has obtained all the documentation normally needed to make a decision.

If the application is approved, a mortgage lender sends a commitment letter to the approved applicants and explains the procedures for loan closing. If the application is modified by any action, such as offering less credit or credit at different terms, and the applicants accept the counteroffer terms, the loan application proceeds as with a normal loan acceptance. If the lender denies an application or the applicants reject the counteroffer terms, the lender must notify the applicants of that adverse action in writing, include the reason for denial, and provide the ECOA notice of nondiscrimination. A Statement of Credit Denial usually accomplishes this requirement.

FIGURE **13.5** Sample Underwriting Worksheet

REMOC Associates, LLC - Underwriting Worksheet
35 Pratt Street   Suite 104   PO Box 115   Essex, CT 06426
TEL: (860) 767-6844   FAX: (860) 767 6843   EMAIL: tpink@remoc.com

CLIENT: Your Lender		**Applicant:** XXXX	
Originator: Brad Broker		**Co-Applicant:** XXXX	
Processor: XXXX			
Applic. Number: XXXX		**Subject Property:** XXXX	

LOAN TERMS **TRANSACTION** **DEBT / INCOME RATIOS**

Amount:	$174,400	**Transaction:** Pruchase		**Housing:**	22%
Type:	Fixed Rate	**Occupancy:** Owner occupied		**Total:**	37%
Rate:	5.000	**Property Type:** Single Family			
Term (months):	360			**CREDIT HISTORY**	
Lien Position:	1st	**LTV:** 80.00%		**Applicant:**	777
Subord. Financing:	$0.00	**CLTV:** 80.00%		**Co-Applicant1:**	719

SECONDARY MARKET ASSESSEMENT

X   Standard / Manually-Underwritten and eligible for immediate sale.
         Expanded Approval and eligible for immediate sale, but would require a Loan Level Pricing Adjustment (LLPA)
         May be eligible for sale in 12 months with no late payments. Additional conditions may apply.
         May be eligible for sale in 36 months with no late payments. Additional conditions may apply.
         Not eligible for sale. Portfolio loan only.

COMPREHENSIVE RISK ASSESSMENT

Comprehensive Risk Assessment: Moderate

Primary Risk Factors: Low   Credit History/ Equity (Downpayment)

Contributory Risk Factors: Increase   Risk

Increases	Financial Liquid Reserves
Satisfies	Employment Classification
Satisfies	Transaction Type
Satisfies	Mortgage Term
Satisfies	Product Type
Satisfies	Property Type
Decreases	Presence of Co-Borrowers
Increases	Total Deb-to-Income Ratio
Satisfies	Previous Mortgage Delinquency
Satisfies	Prior Bankruptcy or Foreclosure

UNDERWRITING SUMMARY COMMENTS AND CONDITIONS:

Purchase of primary residence.
Overall excellent credit history.
 Satisfactory employment/income stability; low liquid assets disclosed.
Company relocation. Total debt ratio reflects new salary level, no bonus.
Need current paystubs at new salary level , current deposit statements, current market data.

LLPA for: adverse market, credit score, total debt/income ratio.

Thomas Pinkowish   **07/01/10**
Underwriter   **Date**

CONSULTING SERVICES FOR COMMUNITY LENDERS

www.remoc.com

FIGURE **13.5** (*Continued*)

MONTHLY INCOME / SOURCE				MONTHLY DEBTS / TYPE	
	Type	Amount	Length	Present Housing:	$1,475
Applicant1:	Base	$5,833	3 yrs	Proposed Housing:	$1,285
Applicant2:		$0	yrs		
Co-Applicant1:		$0	yrs	Total Revolving:	$162
Co-Applicant2:		$0		Installment:	$715
Other1:		$0		Other:	$0
Other2:		$0		Other:	$0
				Total Rev/Inst/Other:	$877
Total Income:		**$5,833**		**Total Monthly Obligations:**	**$2,162**

Income Comments:

Income verified by VOE, YTD paystubs, W-2s.
Company relocation.

Debts Comments:

Several charges recently
paid . Included in debt ratio.

FINANICAL INFORMATION

ASSETS			CASH NEEDED TO CLOSE	
Purchase Deposit:	$0		Downpayment:	$43,600
Deposits:	$54,331		Required Payoffs:	$0
Retirement:	$0		Prepaid Costs:	$2,537
Other:	$0		Closing Costs:	$3,538
Other:	$0		PITI Reserves:	$2,570
Total:	$54,331		Total Needed To Close:	$52,245

Need 60-day history of deposits

Loan Proceeds:

Comments:

Required Payoffs Detail:	$0	1st mtg
	$0	2nd mtg

PROPERTY

Appraisal Information			Housing Trends	
Appraiser:			Property Location:	Suburban
Sales Price/Acquisition Cost:	$219,000		Property Values:	Stable
Appraised Value:	$218,000		Marketing Time:	3 to 6 months
Land Value:	$35,000	16%		
Appraisal Made:	As Is		Housing Price Range	
			Low:	$50,000
Subject Property Description			High:	$1,000,000
Age	11	yrs	Predominate:	$225,000
Type:	PUD - Detached			
Special Flood Hazard Area:	No	Zone: X	Sales Comparables	
Water Source:	Public		Overall:	Average
Sewer:	Sewer		Date:	Below average
Zoning:	Residential		Proximity:	Above Average
Overall Condition:	Average		Adjustments:	Above Average

Appraisal Comments:

Fannie Mae Form 1004 Interior/Exterior.
XXXX PUD Association. Per appraisal, PUD project appears to meet Lender-Delegated
Expedited Approval guidelines. Per appraisal no further documentation is required for
secondary market sale, but lender warranties still apply.
Most recent sales comparable is 5 months old and range up to 12 months old.
Need more current real estate market data.

CONSULTING SERVICES FOR COMMUNITY LENDERS

www.remoc.com

FIGURE **13.6** Sample Underwriting Summary

REMOC ASSOCIATES, LLC
LOAN UNDERWRITING SUMMARY

Review Date: 07/01/10

XXXXX
Vice President, Mortgage Lending
Your Lender
1 Main Street
Somewhere, USA 00001

Application #: 1-
Name: XXXXXX
Property Address: XXXX
          XXXXX
Loan Amount: $ 174,400.
Loan Program: Fixed Rate

REMOC ASSOCIATES, LLC has reviewed the application for the following mortgage loan and recommends approval, subject to the following conditions listed below:

UNDERWRITING CONDITIONS:

Underwriter Review Recommended [*]

[X] This loan must close by 09/15/10 for the current documents to be valid. **Rate lock EXPIRES 07/31/10.**

[X] The maximum allowed interest rate for this loan is: 5.250%

[X] Final corrected, typed Loan Application and all other revised documents to be signed at loan closing.

[X] Recent, original paystubs covering 30-days verifying disclosed level of income prior to closing.

[X] Recent, complete, original deposit statements verifying disclosed level of liquid/retirement assets prior to closing.

[X] Lender should obtain more current market data prior to closing.

NOTE: The following condition(s) are recommended to meet secondary market guidelines:

[X] Lender to certify all title, flood insurance, deposit, loan, and credit documentation to secondary market standard
[X] Subject property/PUD project must meet Fannie Mae Limited Project Review standards.

[X] This loan application may not meet standard secondary market guidelines. This loan application may require significant Loan Level Pricing Adjustments (LLPA) for: adverse market, credit score.

Please review the conditions to this recommendation detailed above. If you have any questions regarding this recommendation, please do not hesitate to contact me.

Sincerely,

Thomas Pinkowish
REMOC ASSOCIATES, LLC

Source: © 2010 REMOC Associates, LLC. www.remoc.com

MANAGING THE UNDERWRITING FUNCTION

Fraud and Quality Control

Throughout the underwriting review, an experienced underwriter must be aware of and investigate "red flags" that may indicate that the application contains mortgage fraud. The FTC's "Red Flags Rule" mandates that lenders establish a policy for identifying identity theft (See Compliance—Chapter 11). Secondary market agreements normally contain clauses that the lender report incidents of fraud, and clauses that require immediate repurchase of loans containing mortgage fraud. Secondary market investors now require more quality control auditing, both before and immediately after loan closing. This quality control/audit function operates separately from the loan origination area (where the underwriting function is).

The mortgage underwriter generally is the person responsible for detecting fraud in each application during the approval process. They should have immediate access to quality control and audit information, and regular training to help prevent fraud from occurring, to detect it before closing, and to maintain consistent quality in all underwriting reviews.

AUS and Comprehensive Risk Assessments

Unfortunately, several implementation problems for AUS and comprehensive risk assessments soon became evident and grew virtually unchecked, helping contribute to the "mortgage meltdown" crisis that surfaced in 2008. These problems accelerated because secondary market agencies and private investors required the use of AUS (by penalizing those applications not submitted by AUS with a 0.25% manual underwriting fee).

First, the accuracy of information submitted into AUSs was not adequately monitored by the GSEs and private investors. This resulted in inaccurate pricing and risk assessment for many loans sold in the secondary market. Additionally, these systems had inadequate controls for detecting fraud before loan closing. GSEs and private investors intended to control these implementation issues with the threat of repurchase, but that proved to be not effective and, on a grand scale, impossible to enforce.

Another implementation issue is really an inherent drawback to any AUS or Comprehensive Risk Assessment based on a national scale. As is stated in advertisements for financial investments, "Past performance is no guarantee of future results." It is dangerous for a local or regional lender, or one that portfolios loans regularly, to rely exclusively on the findings of AUSs or Comprehensive Risk Assessments without taking into account current or local conditions that may impact mortgage repayment—essentially adding a "judgment factor" to these objective pricing and risk assessment schemes.

Additionally, it is important for local or regional lenders to realize that underwriting guidelines developed by Fannie Mae/Freddie Mac, large lenders, or other private investors are tailored to a very different—and at times, inappropriate—level of risk tolerance. For a variety of reasons, this level is not necessarily the same for a local or regional lender, or one that portfolios most of its mortgage loans.

All lenders must take into account the validity and applicability of any externally developed underwriting guidelines to their lending operation and business objectives. As the recent "mortgage meltdown" has demonstrated, these pricing matrices and AUS can become less appropriate when (a) national real estate and lending markets vary significantly from region to region, and (b) when the GSE, private investor, or large bank uses its risk based pricing schemes to reflect profit motives in addition to assessing the various credit, capacity, and collateral risks involved in mortgage lending.

UNDERWRITING GUIDELINES AND LOAN APPLICATION REGISTER

The lender's underwriting standards should be clearly written, nondiscriminatory, and available for review by the general public. These standards should be reviewed periodically to assure continuing compliance with evolving legislation and good business practices. All mortgage lenders (excluding credit unions) also need to be concerned with the Community Reinvestment Act (CRA). This regulation establishes guidelines for taking care of the credit needs of the community.

DISCRIMINATION AND THE FEDERAL GOVERNMENT

Unfortunately, discrimination in residential mortgage lending is not a new issue. Chapter 11—Compliance, describes three types of discrimination and details several regulations involving civil rights issues that shape the federal government's policy and role regarding discrimination in lending. These regulations were drafted in the 1960s and 1970s in part because of actual and perceived inequities in the way mortgage applicants were handled. Their objectives are to ensure that each individual receives equal treatment when applying for a mortgage loan and to eliminate all discriminatory lending practices.

Through these regulations, the federal government actively monitors the fairness of underwriting guidelines. This shift in the underwriting concept makes a mortgage lender liable for civil and/or criminal penalties for violating the letter and spirit of the various antidiscrimination laws. In essence, the burden shifted from the applicant, who had to demonstrate that he or she was qualified for a mortgage loan, to the lender, who must establish that the applicant is not so qualified.

Regrettably, this issue still challenges mortgage lenders. Data collected from lenders (required by the Home Mortgage Disclosure Act) in 1990 revealed that denial rates for minorities were still much higher than denial rates for whites. (The *denial rate* for a particular category—white, black, Hispanic, male, female, and so forth—is the number of denied applications divided by the total number of applications.) The data indicates that, although a bit different than in the past, inequities in mortgage lending still exist.

As a result of this data, the federal government renewed its emphasis on determining why the same pattern of declinations continues even after the enactment of many consumer and discrimination safeguards. The 1992 Housing and Community Development Act requires GSEs to promote nondiscriminatory lending practices in their underwriting. It also requires these secondary market players to discourage discrimination by loan originators, and it authorized HUD to call upon these two players to help monitor originators for signs of discrimination.

In response, secondary market players developed affordable housing and community outreach programs targeting minority applicants and low- to moderate-income census tracts. These programs offer different underwriting guidelines that recognize cultural and economic differences between minority and nonminority applicants and low/moderate-income and higher-income census tracts. The secondary market players actively market and encourage lenders to participate in these programs, but with limited success. Often these transactions require substantial time and effort, and present unique underwriting challenges that are difficult to resolve.

Another part of the federal government's strategy to encourage lending to minorities is the Community Reinvestment Act (CRA), which requires lenders to serve their local communities. Mortgage lenders found not serving the local community's borrowing needs receive "poor" or "needs to improve" CRA ratings. In some of these situations, federal regulators denied their requests for charter revisions. In other situations, federal regulators denied lenders with poor CRA results the opportunity to purchase other lending institutions or change branch structure.

Despite these numerous initiatives, the problem still exists. Department of Justice discrimination and fair lending cases appear regularly. As recently as March 2010, the DOJ entered into a consent order with a lender who must pay more than $6 million in damages to consumers for alleged unfair loan pricing to African American applicants.

All mortgage lenders have an obligation to review their mortgage-lending underwriting standards and the effects of their lending policies to avoid overt discrimination and disparate impact on protected classes of applicants.

DISCUSSION POINTS

1. Identify the types of risks present in residential mortgage lending. Which of these does an underwriter evaluate?

2. How do underwriting guidelines mitigate the risks in mortgage lending?

3. What are the pros and cons of automated underwriting systems?

4. How do the LTV and CLTV affect the way the underwriter reviews a mortgage application? Why are these ratios so important?

5. What compensating factors might offset a total debt ratio that exceeds a lender's guideline?

6. What are credit scores? How does the secondary market use credit scores, and how are they different from mortgage scores?

7. In what ways does a Comprehensive Risk Assessment differ from other underwriting reviews?

CHAPTER 14

Residential Real Estate Appraisal

INTRODUCTION

Appraising residential real estate requires extensive reading, course work, and field experience for a complete understanding of the technical processes and requirements. This chapter provides an overview of residential real estate appraisals, defines the standard terminology used, and explains the common methodology of estimating value. It then explains briefly how lenders use and underwrite appraisals in mortgage lending.

THE RESIDENTIAL REAL ESTATE APPRAISAL PROCESS

Purpose of the Appraisal

The primary purpose in obtaining an appraisal report is to help the lender determine whether the collateral is sufficient security for the loan. The secondary purpose of obtaining an appraisal report is to meet the requirements of state and federal laws and regulations, and to sell the loan in the secondary mortgage market.

Prudent mortgage underwriting requires that the lender consider the collateral pledged as security for the loan requested. This involves two main issues, and the most commonly used appraisal forms can be divided into two sections to address them:

- What is the condition of the property?
- What is the value of the property?

Evaluating the condition of the property involves more than a simple inspection. It is an assessment of factual data about the land, buildings, and immediate area around the property. The condition of some properties can be relatively straightforward to assess, but many others require years of experience in order to evaluate the condition accurately. After ascertaining the condition of the property, estimating its market value is an even more complex skill for the appraiser to master.

Value

A residential appraisal report should describe clearly its estimate of value and the method(s) used to arrive at that value. **Value** is generally defined as the relationship between an object desired and the person desiring it. Translating the value of this object into a more universal commodity, usually money, results in a clearer estimate of value. Value, stated as a price, is that point at which supply and demand coincide or intersect. Value is also quite subjective. Two individuals might not pay the same price for the same object; thus, its value is different to each of them.

Lenders must always remember this underlying subjectivity of value when reviewing an appraisal report and relying on its value for a loan decision. Although an appraiser uses objective methods, details factual information, and performs empirical calculations in producing an appraisal report, the appraiser makes certain (subjective) judgments based on years of experience and training to select the most appropriate information and methods. The lender relies on the skill of the appraiser to complete the report as objectively as possible and to minimize subjectivity. Although completed in a totally professional manner, at its essence, the appraisal report's estimate of value contains a certain amount of subjectivity.

Uniform Residential Appraisal Report

Appraisers and the appraisal process were under intense scrutiny in the mid- to late-1980s because of the extremely high residential delinquency rates, wide swings in market value of real estate, and the resulting losses to the mortgage industry. Lenders, investors, and mortgage insurance companies all experienced terrible losses because of higher than anticipated real estate delinquency and foreclosures. Many consumers lost all the equity in their homes when they either sold or lost their homes.

Some important players in the real estate lending business blamed the high losses on inflated and poorly prepared appraisals. Fannie Mae and several private mortgage insurance companies were among the more vocal in their criticism of the current level of appraisal practices. As a result of this criticism and a desire to improve their profession, the various appraisal organizations worked with the five government agencies involved in residential real estate to develop a single form acceptable to all agencies.

The result was the Uniform Residential Appraisal Report (URAR) in 1986. Freddie Mac Form 70/Fannie Mae Form 1004 allows appraisers to produce professional reports that are self-contained and that logically support the final value estimate given. The URAR has been revised periodically since its introduction, most recently in March 2005. Use of a new addendum, the Market Conditions Addendum to the Appraisal Report (Freddie Mac Form 71/ Fannie Mae Form 1004MC) started in April 2009.

The first page of the URAR contains extensive descriptive information about the property, its condition, the neighborhood in which it is located, and the market conditions at the time of the appraisal. The form provides descriptive information in the following major areas:

- *Subject*: address, ownership rights, legal description, occupancy
- *Contract*: price, date, seller, sales concessions
- *Neighborhood*: market conditions, price ranges, land use, boundaries
- *Site*: dimensions, zoning, off-site improvements, utilities, flood zone
- *Description of improvements*: exterior, foundation, room count, interior, heating and venting and air conditioning (HVAC), kitchen, amenities

The second page of the URAR develops the three approaches to value (described later) and overall estimate of market value for the property:

- *Cost approach*: site value, reproduction cost, depreciation
- *Sales comparison analysis and value*: three or more comparable sales, detailed value adjustments, sources, prior sales data
- *Income approach*: estimated market rent, gross rent multiplier
- *Reconciliation*: final reconciliation, estimate of market value, appraiser signature(s)

Completion of the URAR is part of the appraisal process (described later). The appraiser delivers this report directly to the client—the lender. Regulation B (ECOA) requires that the lender offer a copy to the applicant if requested; however, most lenders provide one automatically.

Uniform Standards of Professional Appraisal Practice

The **Uniform Standards of Professional Appraisal Practice** sets the guidelines by which the appraiser completes this or any other appraisal form and makes an estimate of market value. In 1986, the various appraisal organizations also developed a set of professional practice standards that govern appraisers in preparing the URAR (and subsequent forms). The practice standards are called the Uniform Standards of Professional Appraisal Practice, or *USPAP*. These standards were an important step forward for the profession, since they were the first uniform standards ever adopted by the appraisal industry as a whole. Although the specific forms have changed since 1986, these standards remain as the basis for the objective practice of appraising real estate.

In 1993, the Financial Institutions Reform, Recovery and Enforcement Act (FIRREA) legislation addressed the issue of appraisals as a part of the real estate lending process, and formally adopted the USPAP. The nonprofit body known as the Appraisal Foundation facilitated this step.

The FIRREA legislation also required that beginning on January 1, 1993, all real estate transactions needing an appraisal must include one performed by either a state-licensed or certified appraiser. A licensed appraiser is one who possesses a basic level of skills and education in real estate appraising sufficient to prepare a "noncomplex" residential assignment. A certified residential appraiser is one whose experience and education level is such that the appraiser is qualified to handle all residential properties, in particular those deemed complex or above a certain transaction level (currently $1 million).

Principles of Real Estate Value

Lenders may need an estimate of value at different stages of a real estate transaction or activity. A lender may need a real estate appraisal for any of the following:

- Market value for mortgage-lending purposes
- Assessed value for taxation purposes
- Insurance value
- Market value for sale or exchange purposes
- Compensation for condemnation/municipal acquisition
- Investment value for rental income purposes

The value determined for the same piece of real estate can vary according to the ultimate purpose of the appraisal assignment. For example, the estimated value for insurance purposes may be much different than the value estimated for condemnation purposes. Most mortgage lenders are regulated by law to lend according to a certain percentage of market value, the focus of this discussion.

Market Value

Market value is defined by the Appraisal Foundation and the Uniform Standards of Professional Appraisal Practice as "the most probable price which a property should bring in a competitive and open market under all conditions requisite to a fair sale, the buyer and seller, each acting prudently and knowledgeably, and assuming the price is not affected by undue stimulus." Implicit in this definition is the consummation of sale as of a specific date and the passing of title from seller to buyer under conditions whereby:

- Buyer and seller are typically motivated.
- Both parties are well informed and well advised, and acting in what they consider to be their best interests.
- A reasonable time is allowed for exposure in the open market.
- Payment is in terms of cash in U.S. dollars or in terms of financial arrangements comparable thereto.
- The price represents the normal consideration for the property sold, unaffected by special or creative financing or sales concessions granted by anyone associated with the sale.

Market Price

The **market price** is that price for which the real estate actually sells. In theory, market value and price should be the same, but they rarely are. For example, a seller may decide to accept less (market price) than asked (presumed market value) in order to facilitate the sale if the seller believes that time is more valuable than the difference in money.

Factors Affecting Market Value

For almost 30 years, from 1950 to 1980, residential real estate appreciated steadily across the country, increasing at an average rate of three to six percent per year. This stability reinforced the commonly-held perception that investment in residential real estate was a no-risk investment.

But the value of a particular piece of real estate may not remain constant. It may change over time, because of economics, governmental intervention, and the changing tastes of consumers. Value does not constantly go up, as mortgage lenders and consumers in the Southwest learned during the early 1980s and in New England during the late 1980s. For example, in 1986–1987, it was not uncommon in some areas of Texas, notably Houston, for real estate values to drop 30 to 40 percent in a year. And during the recent housing crisis, home values declined almost 24 percent nationally from 2007–1Q2010, according to the National Association of REALTORS®.

Here is a general list of factors that affect the value of real estate:

- Population growth or decline
- Economic developments
  - micro or local changes
  - macro or national changes
- Financial factors
  - the rate of inflation
  - cost of financing
  - type of financing available
- Shifts in consumer preference
- Governmental regulations
  - zoning
  - building codes
  - taxation
- Shifts in traffic patterns or public transportation
- Physical forces
  - water supply
  - soil contamination
  - location on an earthquake fault

Even if these factors remain constant, market value may still change as a result of the most basic of value determinants: supply and demand. Like all other marketable commodities, real estate value will increase or decrease based on its supply and demand. Supply conditions result from the number of housing units available in the market at any given time—the number of new units being constructed, the number of building permits issued, as well as the number of units lost or destroyed. Demand conditions depend on the level of employment, the level of income, inflation rates, family size, and savings rates, along with other economic factors of this type.

In addition to the preceding factors, other economic principles of value influence the appraisal of real estate:

- Highest and best use
- Diminishing returns
- Substitution

Market value of real estate is influenced to a great extent by whether or not the real estate is put to its *highest and best use,* defined as the use that creates the highest present value. The Uniform Standards state, "Two separate highest and best uses exist for each property site: one for the site as though it were vacant, and one for the site as though it were improved. The first looks through the existing building as though it did not exist and estimates the best use of the site as if it were vacant. The second estimates the best use of the site and building(s) with all improvements together."

Four important considerations must be present to determine highest and best use for a property:

- Physical possibility
- Legal permissibility
- Appropriate support
- Financial feasibility

The principle of diminishing returns recognizes that, after a certain point, additional improvements to the property will not continue to increase its total value by the amount of new improvements. For example, if we add a second bathroom to a house, the property might increase in value by an amount equal to the cost of the new bathroom. But if we add a third, fourth, or fifth bathroom, the value will increase by an amount greatly less than the cost of the additional bathrooms.

Finally, the principle of substitution demonstrates that the upper range of value for a property tends to be established by the cost of acquiring an equally desirable substitute property, or the cost of building a similar structure.

As with mortgage underwriting, no single formula applies to all properties and situations. An experienced appraiser must consider and blend these various principles and factors to produce a professional estimate of market value for the proposed collateral.

COMPLETING THE RESIDENTIAL APPRAISAL REPORT

The first step in the appraisal process is to plan the appraisal (Figure 14.1). Since the appraisal is intended to solve a problem—to estimate value of a particular property—it must be clearly stated as to what type of value is being sought. The process required to produce this estimate of value necessitates identification of the following:

- Real estate to be appraised
- Type of value sought
- Effective date of the appraisal
- Character of the property

FIGURE **14.1** Completing the Residential Appraisal Report

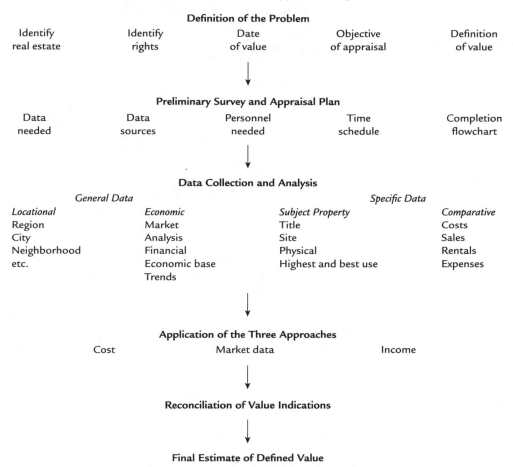

Definition of the Problem

| Identify real estate | Identify rights | Date of value | Objective of appraisal | Definition of value |

Preliminary Survey and Appraisal Plan

| Data needed | Data sources | Personnel needed | Time schedule | Completion flowchart |

Data Collection and Analysis

General Data   *Specific Data*

Locational   *Economic*   *Subject Property*   *Comparative*
Region   Market   Title   Costs
City   Analysis   Site   Sales
Neighborhood   Financial   Physical   Rentals
etc.   Economic base   Highest and best use   Expenses
                     Trends

Application of the Three Approaches

Cost   Market data   Income

Reconciliation of Value Indications

Final Estimate of Defined Value

Source: © 2010 REMOC Associates, LLC www.remoc.com

- Property rights
- Character of the market in which the property is located

The next step in the appraisal process is to identify the data that the appraiser needs. The data required by the appraiser can be found in the public records and obtained from mortgage lenders, other appraisers, or real estate agents. Other sources include the local chamber of commerce, planning and zoning authorities, and even local homebuilders. Finally, the appraiser has the professional dual responsibilities of keeping this data current and relying only on accurate data.

Alternative Approaches to Value

Appraisers use three very specific appraisal techniques when developing a real estate appraisal: the direct sales comparison approach, the cost approach, and the income approach. Although one of these "approaches," or techniques, may be more appropriate under certain circumstances, the combination of the three is intended to provide the most complete solution to the appraisal problem.

Direct Sales Comparison Approach

The direct sales comparison approach is considered to be the most reliable determinant of market value for most residential properties. This approach assumes that an informed and rational purchaser will pay no more for a property than the price or cost of a substitute property with the same characteristics and utility. As a result, this approach relies on the ability of the appraiser to locate similar, or "comparable," properties that have recently sold in that neighborhood. Although no two properties are identical, nevertheless the two homes can be compared and a reasonable value established using an appropriate adjustment process. The principle of substitution is evident with this approach because the value of a property similar to the subject property should closely approximate the value of the subject property.

An appraiser will use as many recent sales of similar or comparable properties as possible; the more used, the more accurate the estimate. The URAR requires the use of at least three comparable sales, or "sales comps." The market prices of the comparables are adjusted for the physical differences between the comparable and the subject property. Appraisers adjust the features of the sales comp to the subject property. If the sales comp has a feature missing in the subject property, the appraiser calculates a negative adjustment to that sales comp equal to the market value of that feature. If the sales comparable lacks a feature present in the subject property, the appraiser makes a positive adjustment to that sales comp. The basic formula is as follows:

Sales Price of the Comparable ± Adjustment = Value of the Subject

Financing Concessions

Seller-paid financing concessions complicate the effectiveness of the direct sales comparable approach. The seller, for example, may pay all of the buyer's closing costs, pay something to buy down the interest rate, or pay some other concession to facilitate the sale. This increases the speed of selling the property and increases the number of buyers capable of buying the property. The net result of these actions is an increase in the sales price to cover the cost of providing these concessions.

 EXAMPLE

Sales comp 1 (SC1), which has a finished basement worth $15,000, recently sold for $115,000. Except for the finished basement, this property is otherwise comparable to the subject property (SP), so the estimate of value for the SP would be $100,000.

SC1 value – Value of Basement = SP Value
$115,000 – $15,000 = $100,000

The appraiser recognizes the impact of sales concessions when preparing an appraisal that relies on comparables with these characteristics. This is important to a mortgage lender because the mortgage should be secured by the value of the real estate alone, not by real estate plus some concession. To assist the appraiser in these situations, the Uniform Standards require that the appraiser request a copy of the sales contract during the information-gathering phase of the appraisal. A mortgage lender is required to provide the appraiser with a copy of the sales contract and as much information on the sale as possible.

Cost Approach

The cost approach is the second most important method used for estimating the market value for residential real estate. It relies on the appraiser's ability to calculate an estimate of the current cost of production, which is defined as the reproduction cost, or the cost to build an exact replica of the improvements. More specifically, the cost approach can be explained using the following formula:

Cost of Reproduction − Depreciation + Land Value = Value of Subject Property

When figuring costs, the appraiser includes both direct costs and indirect costs. Direct costs include building materials and supplies, labor, and profits. Indirect costs include various fees, taxes, and financing costs.

Next, the appraiser recognizes that a newly reproduced structure will not be *exactly* the same value or condition as the subject property because of its effective economic age. Every physical thing of economic use eventually wears out or its condition deteriorates with age. Think of the value of a new car versus last year's model with less than 100 miles on it, or the value of a new computer versus one that is a year old but never been used. All comparables have effectively the same usefulness and may have the same features, but the new car and computer appeal to more buyers and are easier to sell, so they are more expensive. In real estate, the older subject property has depreciated in value from when it was new—some features of the subject experience wear or are not as valuable as new ones with improved features. Although the subject may appear to be in the same condition with no noticeable deterioration, it has, by virtue of time, a shorter economic life. The appraiser adjusts the reproduction cost to reflect depreciation in value from three possible forms:

1. *Physical deterioration*: A loss in value from the cost of a new structure is equal to the loss of economic life in the subject property caused by wear and tear. Physical deterioration may be "curable" or "incurable," meaning it may or may never be brought to current standards (such as a roof that is 15 years old that can be replaced, versus a termite-infested wood frame that is rotted and cannot be fixed so that the entire structure must be razed).

2. *Functional obsolescence*: A loss in value resulting from structural components that are outmoded or inefficient, as judged by current

standards (such as bathrooms or the overall design or layout of the structure).

3. *Economic obsolescence*: A loss in value resulting from changes external to the property (such as changes in zoning classifications, traffic patterns, or environmental hazards).

Finally, the appraiser includes the value of the land upon which the structure stands, plus any improvements to it such as landscaping, stone walls, or public sewer and water connections.

 EXAMPLE

> Assume the appraisal assignment is to estimate the value of a 10-year-old Cape Cod that has depreciated 15 percent. The cost of building a comparable structure is $185,000. The estimate of value is made in this way:
>
> Cost of Reproduction − Depreciation = Adjusted Value + Land Value
> = Value of Subject Property
> $185,000 − $27,750 = $157,250 + Land Value = Value of the Subject Property

The idea of the cost approach starts to break down with older improvements. Generally, properties older than 25 years cannot be reliably appraised with the cost approach because there is too much depreciation to estimate, and the changing skills and techniques in home construction make it too speculative.

Generally, the cost approach sets the upper limit to value, because a house will not be worth more than a house built new. Again, this method of value becomes less accurate as the property ages. At some point, a house's value has dropped so low because of disrepair and a lack of maintenance that the land is worth more than the improved property. This is because it costs more to demolish the house than the improvements are worth.

Income Approach

The income approach to estimating market value uses the net operating income of the property, but is similar to the cost and direct market approaches. The income approach assumes that there is a strong relationship between the rental income that a property earns and the price someone would prudently pay for that property. This method also reflects the choice that the buyer has in the marketplace between renting and buying a similar unit or property (from the buyer's standpoint, "Why should I pay more for a property when I can rent a similar property for less?"). The appraiser developing the income approach selects sales comparables with rental unit(s) similar to those in the subject property, then reviews both the rents for similar units and the sales prices for similar properties.

Obviously, this approach makes the most sense for those properties that have or can produce rental income. Generally, the sales comparison approach and the cost approach apply more to residential real estate, and the income approach is more suitable to income-producing properties, such as offices or apartment buildings. But a special technique called the gross rent multiplier (GRM) can be used to either estimate value for a single-family residence or to serve as a check against the other approaches. The theory behind the GRM is that the same economic influences affect both sales prices and rents. This relationship can be expressed as a ratio:

$$\frac{\text{Sales Price}}{\text{Gross Monthly Rental Income}} = \text{GRM}$$

 ### EXAMPLE

If a house recently sold for $125,000 and was rented for $750 per month, the GRM would be the following:

$$\frac{\$115,000}{\$750} = 153.33, \text{ rounded to } 153$$

Thus, if the appraisal assignment is to estimate the value of another similar property that is being rented for $675 per month, the result would be $675 × 153 = $103,275, rounded to $103,000 (value of the subject house using the income approach).

Reconciliation and Final Value Estimate

Although most appraisal problems call for a single final estimate of market value, the Uniform Standards require that appraisers consider all three approaches on their way to the final estimate of value. While each method can serve as a check against the other approaches, it is true that certain types of properties lend themselves more to one method than another. For example, the cost approach lends itself to a property currently under construction, and the income approach applies best to a duplex rental property.

In most situations, the estimates of value using all three approaches should be fairly similar. If the estimates are widely divergent, the data-gathering method and analysis for each approach should be carefully reviewed. If the estimates remain far apart, the appraiser must consider the purpose of the appraisal. If the appraisal (Figure 14.2) is to estimate market value for mortgage-lending purposes, the sales comparison approach is most important. For insurance claim purposes, the cost approach may be most important. If, on the other hand, the subject property is a residential rental property, then the income approach will be the most applicable.

It is in the correlation of value that an appraiser's skill and experience comes to the forefront and the problem of estimating market value is resolved. This reconciliation process and final value estimate is not simply a mathematical exercise. It is, however, a process of judgment, analysis, and reason that results in a professional, logical, and supportable estimate of market value.

FIGURE **14.2** Sample Uniform Residential Appraisal Report

Uniform Residential Appraisal Report   File No.

The purpose of this summary appraisal report is to provide the lender/client with an accurate, and adequately supported, opinion of the market value of the subject property.

Property Address	City Port St Joe	State FL Zip Code 32456-7757
Borrower	Owner of Public Record	County Gulf
Legal Description		
Assessor's Parcel # 03180	Tax Year 2009	R.E. Taxes $ 3,838.50
Neighborhood Name Treasure Shores Subdivision	Map Reference SMSA	Census Tract 9603.00

Occupant ☐ Owner [X] Tenant ☐ Vacant   Special Assessments $ N/A   ☐ PUD   HOA $ N/A   ☐ per year ☐ per month

Property Rights Appraised [X] Fee Simple ☐ Leasehold ☐ Other (describe)

Assignment Type [X] Purchase Transaction ☐ Refinance Transaction ☐ Other (describe)

Lender/Client   Address

Is the subject property currently offered for sale or has it been offered for sale in the twelve months prior to the effective date of this appraisal?   [X] Yes ☐ No

Report data source(s) used, offering price(s), and date(s).   Public Record / MLS. The subject is currently offered for sale in MLS as a short sale. The subject was listed on 05/08/2008 and is currently listed at $250,000.

I [X] did ☐ did not analyze the contract for sale for the subject purchase transaction. Explain the results of the analysis of the contract for sale or why the analysis was not performed. I received a contract containing 11 pages. The contract is an "As-is" contract with a short sale addendum. The contract contained no seller concessions, but did include some personal property that will not be considered in the opinion of value.

Contract Price $ 250,000   Date of Contract 02/27/2010   Is the property seller the owner of public record? [X] Yes ☐ No Data Source(s) Public Record

Is there any financial assistance (loan charges, sale concessions, gift or downpayment assistance, etc.) to be paid by any party on behalf of the borrower? ☐ Yes [X] No

If Yes, report the total dollar amount and describe the items to be paid.   N/A   None per contract

Note: Race and the racial composition of the neighborhood are not appraisal factors.

Neighborhood Characteristics	One-Unit Housing Trends	One-Unit Housing		Present Land Use %	
Location ☐ Urban [X] Suburban ☐ Rural	Property Values ☐ Increasing [X] Stable ☐ Declining	PRICE	AGE	One-Unit	60 %
Built-Up ☐ Over 75% [X] 25-75% ☐ Under 25%	Demand/Supply ☐ Shortage [X] In Balance ☐ Over Supply	$(000)	(yrs)	2-4 Unit	%
Growth ☐ Rapid [X] Stable ☐ Slow	Marketing Time ☐ Under 3 mths ☐ 3-6 mths [X] Over 6 mths	180 Low	0	Multi-Family	%
Neighborhood Boundaries The neighborhood boundaries for the subject are considered to be the		450 High	60	Commercial	10 %
areas along the coast ranging from Port St Joe to Apalachicola.		284 Pred.	20	Other Vac/ag	30 %

Neighborhood Description   There appear to be no adverse conditions affecting the marketability of properties in the subject neighborhood.

Market Conditions (including support for the above conclusions)   According to local MLS data, there is 14 active listings. Average Days On Market are 365. There is currently 26 months of inventory. In the last 12 months there have been 6 sales. Median sales price for the last 12 months is $283,500.

Dimensions Survey not provided	Area 0.25 Acres +/-	Shape Rectangular	View Gulf of Mexico
Specific Zoning Classification Residential	Zoning Description Residential		

Zoning Compliance [X] Legal ☐ Legal Nonconforming (Grandfathered Use) ☐ No Zoning ☐ Illegal (describe)

Is the highest and best use of the subject property as improved (or as proposed per plans and specifications) the present use? [X] Yes ☐ No If No, describe.

Utilities	Public	Other (describe)		Public	Other (describe)	Off-site Improvements—Type	Public	Private
Electricity	[X]		Water	[X]		Street Asphalt	[X]	☐
Gas	☐	[X] None	Sanitary Sewer	☐	[X] Septic Tank	Alley None	☐	☐

FEMA Special Flood Hazard Area [X] Yes ☐ No   FEMA Flood Zone AE   FEMA Map # 12045C0442E   FEMA Map Date 09/28/2007

Are the utilities and off-site improvements typical for the market area? [X] Yes ☐ No If No, describe. Septic tanks Are Typical as public sewer is not avail.

Are there any adverse site conditions or external factors (easements, encroachments, environmental conditions, land uses, etc.)? ☐ Yes [X] No If Yes, describe. None Apparent. The subject is located on the first tier of the gulf of Mexico, which could be affected by the current BP oil spill. The homes compared to the subject will also have the same vulnerability to the oil spill, but will not have sold during the spill.

GENERAL DESCRIPTION	FOUNDATION	EXTERIOR DESCRIPTION materials/condition	INTERIOR materials/condition
Units [X] One ☐ One with Accessory Unit	☐ Concrete Slab [X] Crawl Space	Foundation Walls Wood pilings / Av	Floors Carpt-Ctile / Avg
# of Stories 1 Story	☐ Full Basement ☐ Partial Basement	Exterior Walls Vinyl Siding / Avg	Walls Drywall / Avg
Type [X] Det ☐ Att ☐ S-Det/End Unit	Basement Area 0 sq.ft.	Roof Surface Comp Shingle /Gd	Trim/Finish Wood / Average
[X] Existing ☐ Proposed ☐ Under Const.	Basement Finish %	Gutters & Downspouts Aluminum / Avg	Bath Floor Ceramic Tile/A
Design (Style) Elevated 1 Story	☐ Outside Entry/Exit ☐ Sump Pump	Window Type Metal-Insul-Sh /Av	Bath Wainscot Ceramic Tile/A
Year Built 1996	Evidence of ☐ Infestation	Storm Sash/Insulated None	Car Storage ☐ None
Effective Age (Yrs) 7	☐ Dampness ☐ Settlement	Screens Yes / Average	[X] Driveway # of Cars 2
Attic ☐ None	Heating [X] FWA ☐ HWBB ☐ Radiant	Amenities ☐ WoodStove/s #No	Driveway Surface Unpaved
☐ Drop Stair ☐ Stairs	☐ Other Fuel Electric	Fireplace(s) # No ☐ Fence None	☐ Garage # of Cars
☐ Floor [X] Scuttle	Cooling [X] Central Air Conditioning	[X] Patio/Deck None [X] Porch	[X] Carport # of Cars
☐ Finished ☐ Heated	☐ Individual ☐ Other	☐ Pool None [X] Other Stg Bldg	☐ Att. ☐ Det. [X] Built-in

Appliances [X] Refrigerator [X] Range/Oven [X] Dishwasher ☐ Disposal ☐ Microwave ☐ Washer/Dryer ☐ Other (describe)

Finished area above grade contains: 6 Rooms   3 Bedrooms   2 Bath(s)   1,482 Square Feet of Gross Living Area Above Grade

Additional features (special energy efficient items, etc.).   Insulated Windows, Ceiling fans and Heat Pump

Describe the condition of the property (including needed repairs, deterioration, renovations, remodeling, etc.).   No physical or functional inadequacies noted at the time of inspection.

Are there any physical deficiencies or adverse conditions that affect the livability, soundness, or structural integrity of the property? ☐ Yes [X] No If Yes, describe.

Does the property generally conform to the neighborhood (functional utility, style, condition, use, construction, etc.)? [X] Yes ☐ No If No, describe. The subject is surrounded by homes of equal quality.

FIGURE **14.2** (*Continued*)

Uniform Residential Appraisal Report   File No.

There are   0   comparable properties currently offered for sale in the subject neighborhood ranging in price from $ 0   to $ 0
There are   1   comparable sales in the subject neighborhood within the past twelve months ranging in sale price from $ 439,000   to $ 439,000

FEATURE	SUBJECT	COMPARABLE SALE NO. 1		COMPARABLE SALE NO. 2		COMPARABLE SALE NO. 3	
Address	Port St Joe	Port St Joe, FL 32456		Port St Joe, FL 32456		Cape San Blas, FL 32456	
Proximity to Subject		2.22 Miles		0.86 Miles		0.25 Miles	
Sale Price	$ 250,000		$ 194,000		$ 270,000		$ 297,000
Sale Price/Gross Liv. Area	$ 168.69 sq. ft.	$ 154.09 sq. ft.		$ 300.00 sq. ft.		$ 330.00 sq. ft.	
Data Source(s)		MLS 108574 DOM 1482		MLS 238077 DOM 43		MLS 236030 DOM 256	
Verification Source(s)	Public Records	Public Records		Public Records		Public Records	
VALUE ADJUSTMENTS	DESCRIPTION	DESCRIPTION	+(-) $ Adjustment	DESCRIPTION	+(-) $ Adjustment	DESCRIPTION	+(-) $ Adjustment
Sale or Financing	N/A	Cash		Cash		New Conv	
Concessions	None Known	None Known		None Known		None Known	
Date of Sale/Time	02/27/2010	11/18/2009	No Adj	01/29/2010	No Adj	02/08/2010	No Adj
Location	Suburban	First Tier Gulf		First Tier Gulf		First Tier Gulf	
Leasehold/Fee Simple	Fee Simple	Fee Simple		Fee Simple		Fee Simple	
Site	0.25 Acres +/-	0.05 Acres +/-	15,000	0.33 Acres +/-	No Adj	0.06 Acres +/-	15,000
View	Gulf of Mexico	Gulf of Mexico		Gulf of Mexico		Gulf of Mexico	
Design (Style)	Elevated 1 Story	1 Story w pilings		1 Story w pilings		1.5 Story w piling	
Quality of Construction	Average	Average		Average		Average	
Actual Age	1996 / Eff 7	2001 / Eff 4	-3,000	1995 / Eff 7	No Adj	2002 / Eff 4	-3,000
Condition	Average	Average		Average		Average	
Above Grade	Total Bdrms Baths	Total Bdrms Baths		Total Bdrms Baths		Total Bdrms Baths	
Room Count	6 3 2	6 3 2	No Adj	5 2 2	3,500	5 2 2.5	No Adj
Gross Living Area 25.00	1,482 sq. ft.	1,259 sq. ft.	5,575	900 sq. ft.	14,550	900 sq. ft.	14,550
Basement & Finished	None	None		None		None	
Rooms Below Grade	None	None		None		None	
Functional Utility	Average	Average		Average		Average	
Heating/Cooling	Central	Central		Central		Central	
Energy Efficient Items	Standard	Standard		Standard		Standard	
Garage/Carport	4 Carport under	4 Carport under	No Adj	2 Carport under	1,800	2 Car Garage	-2,500
Porch/Patio/Deck	Porch & Deck	Wood Decks	1,500	Wood Decks	1,500	Porch & Deck	No Adj
Fireplace	None	None	No Adj	None	No Adj	None	No Adj
Fence / Pool	Stg Bldg	Stg Bldg	No Adj	Stg Bldg	No Adj	Stg Bldg	No Adj
Kitchen	Equipped	Equipped	No Adj	Equipped	No Adj	Equipped	No Adj
Net Adjustment (Total)		☒+ ☐- $	19,075	☒+ ☐- $	21,350	☒+ ☐- $	24,050
Adjusted Sale Price		Net Adj. 9.8%		Net Adj. 7.9%		Net Adj. 8.1%	
of Comparables		Gross Adj. 12.9% $	213,075	Gross Adj. 7.9% $	291,350	Gross Adj. 11.8% $	321,050

I ☒did ☐did not research the sale or transfer history of the subject property and comparable sales. If not, explain.

My research ☐did ☒did not reveal any prior sales or transfers of the subject property for the three years prior to the effective date of this appraisal.
Data source(s)   Public Record / Property Appraiser's Web Site
My research ☐did ☒did not reveal any prior sales or transfers of the comparable sales for the year prior to the date of sale of the comparable sale.
Data source(s)   Public Record / Property Appraiser's Web Site
Report the results of the research and analysis of the prior sale or transfer history of the subject property and comparable sales (report additional prior sales on page 3).

ITEM	SUBJECT	COMPARABLE SALE NO. 1	COMPARABLE SALE NO. 2	COMPARABLE SALE NO. 3
Date of Prior Sale/Transfer	No sales within 36months	No sales within 12months	No sales within 12months	No sales within 12months
Price of Prior Sale/Transfer				
Data Source(s)	Public Record	Public Record	Public Record	Public Record
Effective Date of Data Source(s)	05/07/2010	05/07/2010	05/07/2010	05/07/2010

Analysis of prior sale or transfer history of the subject property and comparable sales   The date used for effective date for data sources is the last time the
public records web-site was updated.   The date the information was pulled from the site is 05/27/2010.

Summary of Sales Comparison Approach.   Due to the coastal nature of the market the search appears to exceed normal guidelines, however the
market area for the subject is based on the Gulf of Mexico which requires a lineal search instead of the typical radius search. This
makes it necessary to search further along the coast in order to find good indicators of the subject's value. All comparables were
equally considered good indicators of value even though there was a wide range of adjusted values, this is typical in rural markets
where trends are not as stable as in a subdivision. An adjustment for market conditions and age of sale were not required due to the
market appears to be stabilizing and the sales took place within 4 months of the contract date. The site value ratio is above the lender's 30%
guideline, but this does not have a negative effect on appraised value, because this is typical in markets with large acreage or
have water influence, as the subject.

Indicated Value by Sales Comparison Approach $ 275,000   Comp 1: 33.33%,   Comp 2: 33.33%,   Comp 3: 33.33%,   Comp 4: 0%,   Comp 5: 0%
Indicated Value by: Sales Comparison Approach $ 275,000   Cost Approach (if developed) $ 257,600   Income Approach (if developed) $ N/A
All Assumptions and limiting conditions attached hereto apply.   This is a Summary appraisal report.   This appraisal is for financing
purposes. The sales comparison approach, the current sales contract, and the subject's listing history were considered when
developing the final opinion of value.

This appraisal is made ☒"as is," ☐subject to completion per plans and specifications on the basis of a hypothetical condition that the improvements have been completed,
☐subject to the following repairs or alterations on the basis of a hypothetical condition that the repairs or alterations have been completed, or ☐subject to the following required
inspection based on the extraordinary assumption that the condition or deficiency does not require alteration or repair: None

Based on a complete visual inspection of the interior and exterior areas of the subject property, defined scope of work, statement of assumptions and limiting
conditions, and appraiser's certification, my (our) opinion of the market value, as defined, of the real property that is the subject of this report is $ 275,000
as of   05/28/2010   , which is the date of inspection and the effective date of this appraisal.

FIGURE **14.2** (*Continued*)

Uniform Residential Appraisal Report   File No.

COMPLETE VISUAL INSPECTION (CVI):
A CVI INCLUDES READILY OBSERVABLE FEATURES INCLUDING FLOORPLAN, AMENITIES, ETC. A CVI DOES NOT INCLUDE
INSPECTIONS OF ANY INACCESSIBLE AREA, SUCH AS ATTICS, CRAWL SPACES, OVERGROWN AREAS, ETC. A CVI DOES NOT
INCLUDE ACTIVATION OR TESTING OF MECHANICAL SYSTEMS INCLUDING, BUT NOT LIMITED TO: HVAC, PLUMBING,
ELECTRICAL, PRIVATE WATER AND/OR SEWER SYSTEMS, ETC. A CVI DOES NOT INCLUDE PERSONAL PROPERTY, CODE
COMPLIANCE, ZONING VIOLATIONS, PERMITS, ETC. THE APPRAISER IS NOT A TERMITE, WDO, OR HOME INSPECTOR. THIS
APPRAISAL IS NOT INTENDED TO REVEAL ANY DEFECTS.

COST APPROACH:
REPLACEMENT COST FIGURES USED IN COST APPROACH ARE FOR VALUATION PURPOSES ONLY, NO ONE, CLIENT OR
THIRD PARTY, SHOULD RELY ON THESE FIGURES FOR ANY OTHER PURPOSE, INCLUDING BUT NOT LIMITED TO ,
INSURANCE PURPOSES.

THE INTENDED USER OF THIS APPRAISAL REPORT IS THE LENDER/CLIENT. THE INTENDED USE IS TO EVALUATE THE
PROPERTY THAT IS THE SUBJECT OF THIS APPRAISAL FOR A MORTGAGE FINANCE TRANSACTION, SUBJECT TO THE
STATE SCOPE OF WORK, PURPOSE OF THE APPRAISAL, REPORTIN
DEFINITION OF MARKET VALUE. NO ADDITIONAL INTENDED USERS ARE IDENTIFIED BY THE APPRAISER.

COST APPROACH TO VALUE (not required by Fannie Mae)

Provide adequate information for the lender/client to replicate the below cost figures and calculations.

Support for the opinion of site value (summary of comparable land sales or other methods for estimating site value)	Site value was estimated from similar land sales

within the subjects market area. Four land sales were used to determine land value. All were 1st tier lots. Two were either short sales or
REO's. MLS 238457 0.23 Ac. $100,000. MLS 237925 0.53 Ac. $115,000. MLS 238161 0.33 Ac. $131,000. MLS 238584 0.25 Ac.
$135,000.

ESTIMATED	☐ REPRODUCTION OR	☒ REPLACEMENT COST NEW	OPINION OF SITE VALUE	= $	120,000
Source of cost data Marshall & Swift			Dwelling 1,482 Sq. Ft. @ $ 81.33	= $	120,531
Quality rating from cost service Average Effective date of cost data 06/2007			Porch & Deck 758 Sq. Ft. @ $ 17.95	= $	13,606
Comments on Cost Approach (gross living area calculations, depreciation, etc.)			Flooring,Appliances,Heatpump,Stg Bldg		11,115
Marshall & Swift Residential Cost Handbook was used in			Garage/Carport 1,342 Sq. Ft. @ $ Included	= $	0
preparing the Cost Approach.			Total Estimate of Cost-New	= $	145,252
Est Remaining Econ. Life = 58 Years.			Less 65 Physical Functional External		
The property appears to meet the HUD/VA standards.			Depreciation $15,642	= $(	15,642)
See Attached Building Sketch			Depreciated Cost of Improvements	= $	129,610
Marshall & Swift, Special studies, Elevated homes.Page Spec-21			"As-is" Value of Site Improvements Utilities,landscaping,etc	= $	8,000
Estimated Remaining Economic Life (HUD and VA only) 58 Years			INDICATED VALUE BY COST APPROACH	= $	257,600

INCOME APPROACH TO VALUE (not required by Fannie Mae)

Estimated Monthly Market Rent $ N/A   X Gross Rent Multiplier   = $ N/A Indicated Value by Income Approach
Summary of Income Approach (including support for market rent and GRM)   N/A

PROJECT INFORMATION FOR PUDs (if applicable)

Is the developer/builder in control of the Homeowners' Association (HOA)?	☐ Yes	☐ No Unit type(s)	☐ Detached	☐ Attached

Provide the following information for PUDs ONLY if the developer/builder is in control of the HOA and the subject property is an attached dwelling unit.

Legal name of project		
Total number of phases	Total number of units	Total number of units sold
Total number of units rented	Total number of units for sale	Data source(s)

Was the project created by the conversion of an existing building(s) into a PUD? ☐ Yes   ☐ No If Yes, date of conversion.
Does the project contain any multi-dwelling units? ☐ Yes ☐ No Data source(s)
Are the units, common elements, and recreation facilities complete? ☐ Yes ☐ No If No, describe the status of completion.

Are the common elements leased to or by the Homeowners' Association? ☐ Yes ☐ No If Yes, describe the rental terms and options.

Describe common elements and recreational facilities.

FIGURE **14.2** (*Continued*)

Market Conditions Addendum to the Appraisal Report

File No. _____

The purpose of this addendum is to provide the lender/client with a clear and accurate understanding of the market trends and conditions prevalent in the subject neighborhood. This is a required addendum for all appraisal reports with an effective date on or after April 1, 2009.

Property Address _____ City **Port St Joe** State **FL** Zip Code **32456-7757**

Borrower _____

Instructions: The appraiser must use the information required on this form as the basis for his/her conclusions, and must provide support for those conclusions, regarding housing trends and overall market conditions as reported in the Neighborhood section of the appraisal report form. The appraiser must fill in all the information to the extent it is available and reliable and must provide analysis as indicated below. If any required data is unavailable or is considered unreliable, the appraiser must provide an explanation. It is recognized that not all data sources will be able to provide data for the shaded areas below; if it is available, however, the appraiser must include the data in the analysis. If data sources provide the required information as an average instead of the median, the appraiser should report the available figure and identify it as an average. Sales and listings must be properties that compete with the subject property, determined by applying the criteria that would be used by a prospective buyer of the subject property. The appraiser must explain any anomalies in the data, such as seasonal markets, new construction, foreclosures, etc.

Inventory Analysis	Prior 7-12 Months	Prior 4-6 Months	Current - 3 Months	Overall Trend		
Total # of Comparable Sales (Settled)	4	2	0	☐ Increasing	☐ Stable	☒ Declining
Absorption Rate (Total Sales/Months)	0.67	0.67	0.00	☐ Increasing	☐ Stable	☒ Declining
Total # of Comparable Active Listings	16	17	14	☒ Declining	☐ Stable	☐ Increasing
Months of Housing Supply (Total Listings/Ab.Rate)	23.88	25.37		☐ Declining	☐ Stable	☒ Increasing
Median Sale & List Price, DOM, Sale/List %	Prior 7-12 Months	Prior 4-6 Months	Current - 3 Months	Overall Trend		
Median Comparable Sale Price	361,557	283,500		☐ Increasing	☐ Stable	☒ Declining
Median Comparable Sales Days on Market	73	150		☐ Declining	☐ Stable	☒ Increasing
Median Comparable List Price	307,000	300,000	379,900	☒ Increasing	☐ Stable	☐ Declining
Median Comparable Listings Days on Market	367	365	222	☒ Declining	☐ Stable	☐ Increasing
Median Sale Price as % of List Price	95.70%	92.29%		☐ Increasing	☐ Stable	☒ Declining
Seller-(developer, builder, etc.)paid financial assistance prevalent?	☒ Yes	☐ No		☐ Declining	☐ Stable	☒ Increasing

Explain in detail the seller concessions trends for the past 12 months (e.g., seller contributions increased from 3% to 5%, increasing use of buydowns, closing costs, condo fees, options, etc.).
In this market it is typical for the seller to pay up to 6% of the buyer's closing costs. Many buyer's in this market use either USDA rural housing or FHA backed loans. This has remained the same during the last 12 months.

Are foreclosure sales (REO sales) a factor in the market? ☒ Yes ☐ No If yes, explain (including the trends in listings and sales of foreclosed properties).
There are several REO and short sale properties listed in local MLS that compete with conventional properties. These lower priced properties drive down values and increase marketing times on conventional properties.

Cite data sources for above information. All information gathered from local MLS statistics. Search parameters are not flexible enough to search for sales which are similar to the subject's quality and lot size. Statistics are from single family detached homes in the subject's market area only. Information would be more accurate and reliable if search parameters were more tailored to the subject's features.

Summarize the above information as support for your conclusions in the Neighborhood section of the appraisal report form. If you used any additional information, such as an analysis of pending sales and/or expired and withdrawn listings, to formulate your conclusions, provide both an explanation and support for your conclusions.
The information above does not portray the actual market conditions. The information above does not accurately provide for seasonal differences in this market. This market also is very rural and statistical information is sorted only by type of housing such as detached single family, this does not allow for the difference of quality such as a low quality older home vs. a high quality new construction home which is commonly found in the same market & neighborhood.

If the subject is a unit in a condominium or cooperative project , complete the following: Project Name: _____

Subject Project Data	Prior 7-12 Months	Prior 4-6 Months	Current - 3 Months	Overall Trend		
Total # of Comparable Sales (Settled)				☐ Increasing	☐ Stable	☐ Declining
Absorption Rate (Total Sales/Months)				☐ Increasing	☐ Stable	☐ Declining
Total # of Active Comparable Listings				☐ Declining	☐ Stable	☐ Increasing
Months of Unit Supply (Total Listings/Ab. Rate)				☐ Declining	☐ Stable	☐ Increasing

Are foreclosure sales (REO sales) a factor in the project? ☐ Yes ☐ No If yes, indicate the number of REO listings and explain the trends in listings and sales of foreclosed properties.

Summarize the above trends and address the impact on the subject unit and project.

APPRAISER	SUPERVISORY APPRAISER (ONLY IF REQUIRED)
Signature _____	Signature _____
Name _____	Name _____
Company Name _____	Company Name _____
Company Address _____	Company Address _____
State License/Certification # _____	State License/Certification # _____ State _____
Email Address _____	Email Address _____

Freddie Mac Form 71 March 2009

Produced using ACI software, 800.234.8727 www.aciweb.com
Page 1 of 1

Fannie Mae Form 1004MC March 2009
1004MC_2009-090909

FIGURE **14.2** (*Continued*)

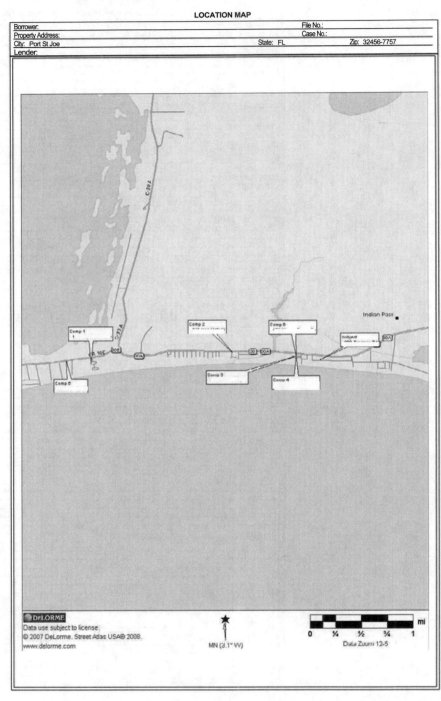

FIGURE **14.2** (*Continued*)

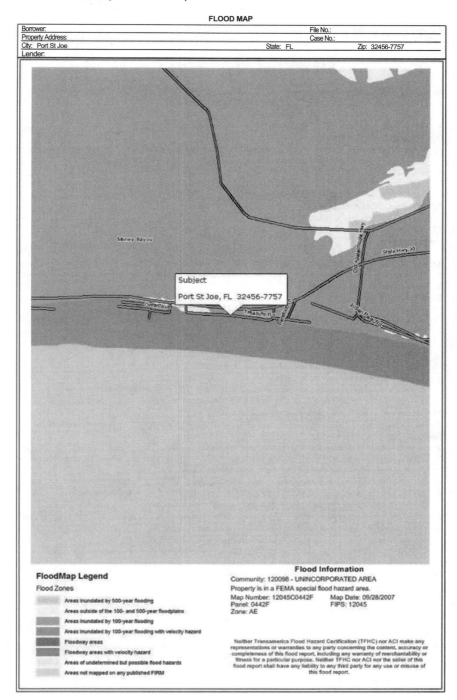

Source: © 2010 REMOC Associates, LLC www.remoc.com

FIGURE **14.3** Sample Appraisal Review Checklist

Genworth Financial ※.

APPRAISAL REVIEW CHECKLIST

Property Identified As_____

Subject (PURCHASE ONLY):

1. Do the property address and legal description match the sales contract?.. ☐ yes ☐ no
2. Does current owner of public record = seller? .... ☐ yes ☐ no
3. Is occupancy status noted (compare to 1003) and does it make sense?... ☐ yes ☐ no

Contract (PURCHASE ONLY):

4. Did appraiser analyze the contract for sale and address any financial assistance to be paid by any party on behalf of the borrower? If any financial assistance is being paid on behalf of borrower, the amount must be disclosed. .... ☐ yes ☐ no

Subject (REFI ONLY):

5. Do the property address and legal description match the application? .... ☐ yes ☐ no
6. Does current owner of public record = borrower? .... ☐ yes ☐ no

Subject (ALL TRANSACTIONS):

7. Are property rights appraised as Fee Simple? .... ☐ yes ☐ no
8. Is subject currently offered for sale or has it been offered in the past 12 months? .... ☐ yes ☐ no

Neighborhood:

9. Is location type consistent with the location map and neighborhood description?....................................... ☐ yes ☐ no
10. Does built up % reflect location type? (If built up < 25%, location should be rural) .... ☐ yes ☐ no
11. Is value between low and high ranges? (If value > 10% of predominant value, appraiser should have addressed) .... ☐ yes ☐ no
12. Does present land use add up to 100%?... ☐ yes ☐ no

Site:

13. Are dimensions listed or survey attached? .... ☐ yes ☐ no
14. Is Zoning Classification indicated as well as Zoning Description? (i.e. R1-Residential SF or Residential 1- to 4-family) .... a. ☐ yes ☐ no
    If zoning is "legal/non-conforming", has appraiser addressed whether subject can be rebuilt if destroyed? Must b. ☐ yes ☐ no
    provide source of opinion, and if other than "legal," did appraiser indicate any marketability impact?............... c. ☐ yes ☐ no
    Is highest and best use the present use? .... d. ☐ yes ☐ no
15. If shared well, has appraiser validated shared well agreement?.. ☐ yes ☐ no
16. Does appraiser address non-public utilities and offsite improvements?... ☐ yes ☐ no
17. If offsite access is private, does appraiser provide road condition? Must be at least average condition. .... ☐ yes ☐ no
18. If under- or above-ground tank, does appraiser provide location and condition? .... ☐ yes ☐ no
19. Does appraiser address flood zone? Cannot be left blank... ☐ yes ☐ no
20. Are there any adverse site conditions, external factors or land use changes? If yes, appraiser must explain. .... ☐ yes ☐ no

Description of Improvements:

21. Is general description consistent with property photographs? .... ☐ yes ☐ no
22. Is there a large difference between effective age & year built? If yes, did appraiser provide the recent renovation or a. ☐ yes ☐ no
    extent of improvements when describing the condition of the property?... b. ☐ yes ☐ no
23. Are interior photos needed to support the age/renovation adjustments? .... ☐ yes ☐ no
24. If manufactured home, is appraisal done on Fannie Mae Form 1004C or Freddie Mac Form 70C? .... ☐ yes ☐ no
    (Note: Modular homes can be compared to "similar quality" stick built homes.)
25. If appraiser indicated evidence of infestation, dampness or settlement, is a full description provided in the "Condition
    of the property"? Note: Underwriter may need to condition for an inspection. ☐ yes ☐ no
26. Is anything rated less than average? If yes, has appraiser addressed properly? .... a. ☐ yes ☐ no
27. Is there a permanent heat source? (Space heater, kerosene and wood burning stoves are not acceptable.) .... ☐ yes ☐ no
28. Do amenities include a pool or pier/dock access? If yes, is a photo included with appraisal? .... ☐ yes ☐ no
29. Does room count/square footage agree with room count/square footage in sales comparison
    and cost approach, if completed? .... ☐ yes ☐ no
30. Did appraiser list any deficiencies or adverse conditions that affect the livability, soundness or structural integrity of
    the property? .... ☐ yes ☐ no
31. Does property conform to the neighborhood? If no, did appraiser properly describe? .... ☐ yes ☐ no

Sales Comparison Approach:

32. Did appraiser provide # comparable listings and # of closed sales in subject neighborhood along with a price range? .... ☐ yes ☐ no
33. Did appraiser provide address, city and proximity of each comparable, including data verification source? .... ☐ yes ☐ no
34. Are sales within the required time frames or addressed with support? Six months in most cases would be typical............ ☐ yes ☐ no
35. Do comparables look similar in appeal/condition to the subject? .... ☐ yes ☐ no
36. If time adjustments made, did appraiser provide commentary / proper support? .... ☐ yes ☐ no
    (Consistent with Neighborhood section / Demand & Supply)
37. Are site sizes for subject / comps provided? Has to be actual size, not "typical". .... ☐ yes ☐ no
38. Are all major aspects/ amenities of subject "bracketed" as required (site size, age and square footage)? .... ☐ yes ☐ no
39. Do at least two or all comps have same bedroom count? If no, is subject bedroom count bracketed? .... ☐ yes ☐ no

FIGURE **14.3** (*Continued*)

40. Are adjustments appropriate for the market area and supported by the sales price and price per square footage ranges? .... ☐ yes ☐ no
41. Are Gross (25) /Net (15) /Line (10) adjustments within guidelines and/or addressed? .... ☐ yes ☐ no
42. Are adjustments done in "proper direction" (+/-) and is all math correct?.. ☐ yes ☐ no
43. Are adjustments being made consistently for the same item descriptions? .... ☐ yes ☐ no
44. Are all adjustments above square footage section addressed and supported with details? .... ☐ yes ☐ no
45. Are all three comparables closed sales? Additional comps over three can be listings or pending sales. .... ☐ yes ☐ no
46. If comp is a listing, ensure list date is provided. Should be consistent with Neighborhood section.
    Are the distances between comps reasonable with the neighborhood / location? .... ☐ yes ☐ no
47. Did appraiser use the same per-square-foot adjustment for each comparable sale? .... ☐ yes ☐ no
48. Did appraiser research the sale or transfer history of the subject and comparable sales? .... ☐ yes ☐ no
49. Did appraiser's research reveal any prior sales or transfers for the subject in the past three years from the effective date of the appraisal? .... ☐ yes ☐ no
50. Did appraiser's research reveal any prior sales or transfers for the comparables in the past year from the effective date of the appraisal? .... ☐ yes ☐ no
51. Purchases: Did appraiser provide list price, time on market & verify arms length transaction? If no, have appraiser provide. ☐ yes ☐ no
52. Did appraiser provide a summary of the sales comparison approach? .... ☐ yes ☐ no

Reconciliation:
53. Is a value indicated by the Sales Comparison Approach? Cost and Income approach are optional in most cases. .... ☐ yes ☐ no
54. Is appraisal marked appropriately "as is" or "subject to repairs, completion or an inspection" ? .... a. ☐ yes ☐ no
55. If "subject to", are conditions present? .... b. ☐ yes ☐ no
56. If "subject to" are the conditions/inspection reports attached? If missing, underwriter must obtain and review. .... c. ☐ yes ☐ no
57. Is appraisal properly signed and dated? If older than four months, does it have required Appraisal Update? .... ☐ yes ☐ no

Additional Items:
58. Are there sufficient comments regarding items such as second kitchens, in-law suites, commercial influence and condition adjustments and do they make sense? .... ☐ yes ☐ no
59. Does subject sketch include dimensions and room layout? Is layout consistent with appraisal adjustments? .... ☐ yes ☐ no
60. Do maps identify subject and comparables? .... ☐ yes ☐ no
61. Does map show subject/comps in proximity to external obsolescence (R/R tracks, highways, main arterial, etc)? .... ☐ yes ☐ no
62. Are subject and comparable photos included and legible? .... ☐ yes ☐ no
63. Are there any inconsistencies/abnormalities between photos and descriptions? If yes, has appraiser addressed properly? .... a. ☐ yes ☐ no
                                                                                                                                               b. ☐ yes ☐ no
64. Are addendums referenced present? .... ☐ yes ☐ no
65. For rural or large acreage properties, is there commercial farming or large outbuildings? .... ☐ yes ☐ no
66. Have the subject or any of the comparables been sold multiple times in the past year? If yes, this is a Red Flag that value may be inflated. a. ☐ yes ☐ no
67. If no similar or good comparables available, did appraiser state to what extent the market was searched? .... b. ☐ yes ☐ no

Cost Approach: Not required as of November 1, 2005. If completed:
68. Is the land value greater than 30% of total value? If yes, has appraiser addressed properly? .... ☐ yes ☐ no
69. Do sales support land-to-value ratio? .... ☐ yes ☐ no
70. Did appraiser indicate if data supports either reproduction cost or replacement cost? .... ☐ yes ☐ no
71. Did appraiser provide the source of his data for the cost approach? .... ☐ yes ☐ no

Income Approach: Not required as of November 1, 2005, unless property is for investment purposes
PUD Information: Only required if project is under control of the builder AND is an attached property
72. If required, did appraiser provide HOA fees on page one? .... ☐ yes ☐ no
73. Is the legal name of the project provided and does it match the sales contract or title commitment? .... ☐ yes ☐ no
74. Are all questions regarding the project phase completed? If not, a project questionnaire will be required. .... ☐ yes ☐ no
75. Does the association own or lease the common elements? If leased, did appraiser provide rental terms? .... ☐ yes ☐ no
76. Did appraiser provide a description of the common elements and recreational facilities, if any? .... ☐ yes ☐ no

Market Condition Addendum 1004MC: Required as of April 1, 2009
77. Did appraiser complete the inventory analysis section for each time frame and calculate absorption rate? .... ☐ yes ☐ no
78. Did appraiser provide median sale and list price and days on market?... ☐ yes ☐ no
79. Did appraiser address seller concession trends for the past 12 months? .... ☐ yes ☐ no
80. If foreclosures are a factor, did appraiser address trends and impact of value, and use as comparables?...................... ☐ yes ☐ no
81. Did appraiser provide data source for his conclusions and fully explain his analysis of the market and his value?............. ☐ yes ☐ no
82. Did appraiser provide details or comments when information was not completed or average was used in lieu of median?... ☐ yes ☐ no

Condominium Market Condition Information
83. Did appraiser complete the subject property absorption rate and housing supply inventory?... ☐ yes ☐ no
84. Did appraiser address any trends for the project?.. ☐ yes ☐ no

Updated 12/2008

Required Forms

The secondary market has developed several standardized appraisal forms for residential mortgage lending. Their use depends on the type of property appraised. They include the following:

- *For single-family property*: URAR (Fannie Mae Form 1004/Freddie Mac Form 70)
- *For two- to four-family property*: Small Residential Income Property Form (Fannie Mae Form 1025/Freddie Mac Form 72)
- *For condominium or cooperatives*: Individual Condominium Form (Fannie Mae Form 1073/Freddie Mac Form 465)
- *Planned Unit Development (PUD) properties*: URAR Form or Individual Condominium Form
- *For all appraisal forms:* Market Conditions Addendum (Fannie Mae Form 1004MC/Freddie Mac Form 71)

The following attachments must be a part of each appraisal report:

- Original photos of the subject property (front, rear, and street)
- Original photos of the comparable sales (front)
- Location map showing the subject and the comparable sales
- Exterior sketch of the subject dwelling, with measurements
- Certification and Statement of Limiting Conditions (Fannie Mae Form 1004B)
- Addendum warranting compliance with all pertinent FIRREA requirements

STREAMLINED APPRAISALS AND AUTOMATED VALUATION MODELS

In the mid-1990s, Fannie Mae and Freddie Mac adopted new appraisal requirements and developed new appraisal forms as part of their automated underwriting systems (AUSs)—Desktop Underwriter (DU) for Fannie Mae and Loan Prospector (LP) for Freddie Mac. Driven by the desire of large lenders and investors for faster decision making and delivery in secondary market transactions, in 1996, Fannie Mae and Freddie Mac developed shorter "abbreviated" appraisal forms to expedite the underwriting process in their proprietary AUSs.

Lenders who submit loans to either DU or LP have several options for appraisals in addition to what is now considered the "full" appraisal using the URAR Fannie Mae Form 1004/Freddie Mac Form 70. The new appraisal standards and options include streamlined appraisals and automated valuations (AVs). These abbreviated forms provide less descriptive and market information and require less time to complete than the industry standard URAR Fannie Mae Form 1004/Freddie Mac Form 70. In some cases, Fannie Mae and Freddie Mac require only a "drive-by" inspection of the property. The following sections describe the forms most commonly used.

Streamlined Appraisals

1. *DU or LP Quantitative Analysis Appraisal Report (Fannie Mae Form 2055)—Exterior Inspection and/or Interior Inspectio*n: This form

differs from the standard URAR Fannie Mae Form 1004/Freddie Mac Form 70 in several areas:

- Fewer areas for comments
- Less descriptive neighborhood, site, improvement, and sales comparison sections
- Elimination of income and cost approaches
- Only an exterior, drive-by inspection required, depending on the recommendation from the AUS

2. *DU Qualitative Analysis Appraisal Report (Fannie Mae Form 2065)— Interior Inspection Only*: This form differs from the standard URAR Fannie Mae 1004/Freddie Mac 70 Form in all the same areas as detailed for the Fannie Mae Form 2055, in addition to the following areas:

- Sales comparison adjustments do not contain dollar values, only a +, –, or = value when compared to the subject property.
- Only an exterior drive-by inspection is required—no internal inspection.

Note that the Desktop Underwriter® Property Inspection Report (Fannie Mae Form 2075) and Loan Prospector® Condition and Marketability Report (Form 2070) do not meet USPAP standards and are not appraisal reports.

Uniform Appraisal Dataset and Uniform Collateral Data Portal

In an attempt to improve the quality of appraisal reports nationwide, the FHFA initiated the Uniform Mortgage Data Program (UMDP) for loans sold to Fannie Mae and Freddie Mac. The above appraisal reports must be completed using the Uniform Appraisal Dataset (UAD) if they have a date of inspection on or after September 2011. Beginning in March 2012, these appraisal reports must be submitted to the Uniform Collateral Data Portal (UCDP).

Automated Valuation Models (AVMs)

The process for developing AVMs differs substantially from the normal appraisal process. AVMs use high-powered econometric models designed to emulate the marketplace and predict the value of a property based on the surrounding actions within the property's marketplace. The statistical model, not the appraiser, develops the estimate of market value. Sources of information that are compared to the subject property or methods used to produce an estimate of value include the following:

- Repeat sales in the subject property's area
- "Hedonic models," which focus on property characteristics
- Property tax and assessments
- Prior lending information
- Economic, cost-of-living, and home price appreciation statistics

Recent housing and economic conditions highlight the challenges for AVM methodologies. Advances in AVM data collection and analysis hope to recognize accurately the volatility in the market overall and variances in local real estate markets.

Both Fannie Mae's and Freddie Mac's AUS use AVM methodology to estimate market value and determine property valuation documentation. Both Fannie Mae and Freddie Mac AUS at times will recommend an AVM as the minimum report needed for purchase. However, traditional lender reps and warranties with the GSEs will still hold the lender responsible for the condition and marketability of the property. While Fannie Mae does not endorse any specific AVM product, Freddie Mac does. It's AUS and Home Value Suite recommends and endorses two AVM-type products: Home Value Explorer® and Home Value Calibrator®.

Other companies involved in real estate lending have also developed AVMs. Lenders can now select from private companies, credit bureaus, title companies, and other large lenders or investors.

Use of Streamlined Appraisals and AVMs

Although Fannie Mae and Freddie Mac would like the streamlined appraisals and AVM valuation process to replace the industry standard URAR form, not all loans submitted through AUS can use them. Lenders and appraisers, always ultimately responsible for all information submitted to the GSE, must pay particular attention to the condition of the property, its conformity to the neighborhood characteristics, and its overall marketability. If adverse or uncertain factors exist, then the appraiser must recommend a more complete analysis.

Only loans with other strong factors to offset this increased collateral risk may be approved by the GSE for this limited documentation. An ideal loan application for AVM would include features such as a no-cash-out refinance with an LTV of less than 50 percent, a home located in a clearly defined and uniform neighborhood with a high level of maintenance, and applicants who have lived in the house for five or more years and have excellent credit and cash reserves. Properties in declining markets or neighborhoods with deferred maintenance, where real estate price stability and property condition are variable, may require a more comprehensive valuation method such as the URAR.

Initially, these changes met with mixed reception in the lending and appraising communities. Both appraisers and lenders were concerned with the less stringent standards and quality that would result from these appraisals, but most realized how these changes were a part of the evolution in technology in mortgage lending.

These changes, without question, provide lenders and secondary market investors with benefits: faster processing and turnaround time, less work and time needed for appraisers, fewer documents and steps for many loans. The changes may also bring some drawbacks: less accurate reporting of property condition and value, more fraudulent information used in completing appraisal reports, and an increase in delinquency and/or foreclosure as a result of inaccurate appraisal valuation. MI company studies indicate that fraudulent appraisals are on the increase, but no clear information has emerged to confirm an increase in delinquency as a result of these new appraisal requirements and forms.

Since streamlined appraisals and AVMs require less work and time to complete, and do not apply to complex properties or real estate markets, they cost less than the standard URAR. Depending on the type of property appraised and the general cost of living in the area of the country in which the appraisal is performed, typical appraisal price ranges are as follows:

- *Standard URAR*—$200.00 to $550.00
- *Streamlined appraisals*—$125.00 to $275.00
- *AVMs, drive-bys, and other limited appraisals*—$35.00 to $175.00

In many cases, the savings on appraisal costs are now replaced with AUS fees or other items that lenders now charge in addition to the application fee. Proponents of the changes explain that these changes apply to only those loan applications with low overall risk factors or to applications where collateral risk is low—*not* to high-risk applications or to applications where collateral risk is high.

Development and adoption of streamlined and automated valuation guidelines come after research on millions of loan applications with years of repayment history, and these AUSs have a predictive ability for delinquency at least 10 times better than conventional underwriting. Applying these less-stringent appraisal requirements to loan applications selected by AUSs does not affect their investment quality or likelihood of delinquency or loss in any significant way.

Finally, the streamlined and AVM guidelines state that the appraiser should recommend and follow a more comprehensive analysis (such as the URAR) if, in the appraiser's opinion, these reports cannot establish satisfactorily the condition and marketability of the property. In this way, streamlined and AVM appraisal and property inspection forms represent additional tools for the appraiser to use when appropriate.

Critics of these changes liken the new appraisal process to valuing a car by riding by it on a bicycle and taking a snapshot of it—never seeing the other side of the vehicle or finding out whether it starts or runs. An external, drive-by inspection or assimilation of property tax and home sale information does not reveal reliable information about the condition of the property structure or interior and its effect on marketability. In other words, the appraiser doesn't know what he or she is missing, so accuracy suffers.

Age of Appraisal Report

The appraisal report must be signed and dated within 120 days of the date the mortgage loan is closed. If an appraisal is older than that, it can be "recertified"—updated by the original appraiser certifying that the value has not declined since the original appraisal was prepared. (Fannie Mae and Freddie Mac allow the appraisal to be up to 180 days old from the date the loan closes, if the property is considered new construction.) If the appraisal report is older than one year, the GSEs require a new appraisal.

Hiring the Appraiser

All mortgage lenders should clearly understand that it is their responsibility to order the residential mortgage loan appraisal. In no situation should a mortgage lender allow applicants or a third party to select the appraiser or supply an appraisal report for a mortgage loan. The reason for this is obvious: another party with an interest in the transaction may simply shop for an appraiser who will produce the highest appraised value.

The lender should consider the best appraiser available from a list of approved (by the lender) appraisers. If a mortgage lender hires the best appraiser available, that lender will get the best results. One of the premier attributes that a lender should look for is the ability of the appraiser to accurately communicate information about the property that will secure the mortgage loan. The narrative on an appraisal report is equally as important as the value listed on the back of the appraisal report.

This has always been a prudent business approach in lending. Because of the recent explosion in appraisal fraud—mostly in third party originations—now there are extensive secondary market requirements and federal regulations that provide detailed direction in this area.

HVCC and Federal Reserve Final Rule—TILA Section 129E

In March 2008, pressured by the New York Attorney General's office, Fannie Mae and Freddie Mac via their regulator (the FHFA) adopted the Home Valuation Code of Conduct (HVCC). This highly unusual and controversial process resulted in a temporary change in the ordering of and payment for single-family appraisals involving third-party originations of conforming loan applications. Although this rule applied only to loans originated for sale to Fannie Mae and Freddie Mac, it had a profound impact on the mortgage origination process. Among other things, HVCC restricted:

- Who could order appraisals
- Who could communicate with appraisal companies
- The content of communications with appraisal companies

In effect, HVCC removed the mortgage broker and many processing/underwriting experts from the appraisal selection process, and encouraged the use of appraisal management companies (AMCs) over independent appraisers.

These requirements highlighted the debate amongst industry professionals of the benefits of an AMC vs. the experience of local appraisers. Local appraisers often draw on their own direct experience and inspections when appraising local properties. They also have long-term knowledge of and experience in the local real estate market and neighborhood trends.

An AMC often may charge less for an appraisal and, being more regionally-oriented than local, in theory may be more independent than a local appraiser. But an AMC will not have a similar database or experience with as many local properties as a local appraiser. AMCs rely more on MLS and tax records data. Some industry experts feel that AMC appraisers will have only cursory knowledge of the local real estate market and are too distant to have a grasp on neighborhood dynamics in different economic times.

Regulatory Changes Affecting Appraisals

The Dodd-Frank Act required the HVCC agreement to expire in October 2010, and for the Federal Reserve to issue new regulations to preserve the integrity of the appraisal process. Like many other provisions in the Dodd-Frank Act, the provisions provide general guidance only and lack details. In some cases there is no exact date of implementation.

In 2008, the Federal Reserve amended appraisal practices in Regulation Z (see Chapter 11—Compliance); however, compliance with the Fed's new Interim Final Rule is mandatory in April 2011. Highlights of these regulations include:

- Prohibits coercive behavior and communication with the appraiser by lenders and their agents.
- Prohibits appraisers and appraisal management companies from having a financial interest in the real estate transaction involved.
- Requires lenders to report violations by appraisers to appropriate state licensing agencies.
- Outlines guidelines for payments for appraisal services.

Other regulatory changes contained in Subtitle F of Title XIV in the Dodd-Frank Act include:

- Expanded requirements for USPAP appraisals and requires a second appraisal in certain situations involving a property with an active resale activity.
- An advanced appraisal disclosure to the consumer.
- Requirement to provide a copy of the appraisal to the consumer.
- Prohibits behaviors which would adversely impact appraiser independence.
- Protect appraisers in reporting fraud or illegal influence during the appraisal process.
- Establishes significant civil penalties for violations.

As stated above, the Dodd-Frank Act provides no details for many of its provisions. It directs different agencies to write the new rules. The implementation date can vary, depending on when the rules are finalized, however a likely date is January 21, 2013.

Inappropriate or illegal appraisal practices, inflated values, and property misinformation still comprise a large percentage of quality control and fraud issues (See Chapter 15 - Closing and Delivery; Quality Control and Fraud). These often lead to repurchase orders from secondary market investors to selling lenders.

Appraisers are state-regulated. On a national basis, three organizations work to regulate appraiser activity: The Association of Appraiser Regulatory Officials, The Appraisal Foundation, and the Appraisal Subcommittee. They operate not unlike the CSBS in assisting state regulators regulate state-licensed mortgage lenders and originators. Some industry experts feel that setting up an appraisal licensing system (similar to the NMLS for mortgage loan officers) would help reduce fraud and inappropriate appraisal practices.

DISCUSSION POINTS

1. What two main areas of consideration does an appraisal report help a lender evaluate? How does the appraisal report do this?

2. Explain the appraisal process that an appraiser would follow in developing a traditional appraisal report.

3. What three approaches to value are used in developing an appraisal? When is each approach most appropriate?

4. What factors can affect the market value of the subject property?

5. Why are sales comparable adjustments necessary to estimate the value of the subject property?

6. How do other appraisal forms differ from the Uniform Residential Appraisal Report (URAR)? Why are these differences significant?

7. Discuss the benefits and drawbacks to a lender using streamlined appraisals and automated valuation models (compared to traditional appraisals).

8. Explain the impact of the HVCC on the mortgage origination process.

CHAPTER 15

Closing and Delivery; Quality Control and Fraud

INTRODUCTION

Applications approved by the lender and accepted by the applicant(s) then move to the closing or settlement stage. The industry phrase, "It's going to closing" means different things with different lenders. Closing departments handle various functions and follow real estate law customs that can vary greatly by county and state. Most applications at this point still have plenty of work to do: meeting underwriting conditions, completing title work, obtaining title insurance, coordinating several settlement service providers, securing funding and applicable credit enhancements (insurances, endorsements, or guarantees), finalizing sales contract conditions (for a purchase), and setting an actual closing date for all of this to happen.

If the lender closes the loan for portfolio, then the above items represent most of the outstanding work for that application. If, however, the loan will be a secondary market transaction, then the closing starts a new phase for that application: loan delivery, funding, and quality control.

Some lenders start the closing process when the applicant returns a signed commitment letter. Many lenders will not schedule a closing date until all approval conditions are met and/or the subject property title search receives a favorable review. The closing of a mortgage loan should not be interpreted to mean the end of the mortgage-lending process, but only the end of the production phase. The mortgage loan may exist for 30 years or longer. During that time it requires servicing.

A residential mortgage transaction is closed by (a) the proper execution and delivery of a mortgage (or deed of trust), note, and other loan application documents to the mortgage lender and (b) the disbursement of the mortgage funds to the mortgagor pursuant to the mortgagor's direction and all other funds to other parties involved in the real estate transaction. The term *loan closing* as used in residential mortgage lending refers to the process with the following characteristics:

- Formulating, executing, and delivering all documents required to create an obligation to repay a debt and to create a valid security instrument

- Disbursing the mortgage funds

- Protecting the security interest of the lender or investor (e.g., *recording*)

- Establishing the rights and responsibilities of the mortgagor

- Formally complying with all state and federal settlement procedures and regulations

A clear distinction should be drawn between this type of closing and a real estate sales closing, which requires a different set of documents such as a purchase agreement, deed, sales contract, and a closing statement, among others. A closing for sale of real estate that also involves financing requires both sets of documents or a combination of the two.

State law governs most of the steps necessary to close a mortgage loan and create a valid security interest in the real estate. As a result, this text cannot establish the exact requirements for closing any residential mortgage loan. Mortgage lenders must be careful to understand the requirements of their state, and the best way to understand these requirements is to have a competent closing agent. Finally, secondary market investors and conduits may add an additional layer of policies and procedures for lenders to follow for those transactions not remaining in portfolio.

FEDERALLY RELATED MORTGAGE LOANS

As mentioned previously in Chapter 11—Compliance, Regulation X (RESPA) governs many settlement procedures when closing federally related mortgage loans. Practically all residential mortgage loans today are federally related. Thus, the act requires lenders to provide the following:

- Good Faith Estimate form, containing settlement service charges (provided within three business days of application)
- Notice of Servicing Disclosure (provided during application)
- The HUD booklet, *Shopping for your Home Loan*
- Use of a HUD-1 or HUD-1A settlement sheet
- Initial Escrow Statement describing funds collected for escrow accounts

Closing Costs (Settlement Services—GFE)

Recent RESPA changes on the Good Faith Estimate (GFE) now define all closing costs as "settlement charges" require accurate disclosure at application of all fees involved in the mortgage financing transactions (See Chapter 11—Compliance). RESPA also restricts changes in fees from the initial GFE—some fees cannot increase at settlement; some fees can increase up to ten percent only; and some can change. See Figure 15.1.

RESPA will permit restricted fees to change only under certain conditions (typically in situations beyond the lender's control). If this happens, RESPA requires redisclosure to the consumer and a delay in closing for at least three business days. This new rule has adversely impacted the closing process dramatically, adding time and cost to the process. In some situations, federally-mandated delays have caused consumers to lose a rate lock or even lose a sale or purchase of a property. Lenders concerned with penalties for "under-disclosing" fees will simply overdisclose. A recent study by Bankrate showed a significant increase in fees nationally—over 36% on average from 2009 to 2010—since this new rule became effective. (See Figure 15.2 for closing cost averages by state.)

FIGURE **15.1** RESPA Fee Restrictions at Closing

These charges cannot increase at settlement:	The total of these charges can increase up to 10% at settlement:	These charges can change at settlement:
<ul><li>Our origination charge</li><li>Your credit or charge (points) for the specific interest rate chosen *(after you lock in your interest rate)*</li><li>Your adjusted origination charges *(after you lock in your interest rate)*</li><li>Transfer taxes</li></ul>	<ul><li>Required services that we select</li><li>Title services and lender's title insurance *(if we select them or you use companies we identify)*</li><li>Owner's title insurance *(if you use companies we identify)*</li><li>Required services that you can shop for *(if you use companies we identify)*</li><li>Government recording charges</li></ul>	<ul><li>Required services that you can shop for (if you do not use companies we identify)</li><li>Title services and lender's title insurance (if you do not use companies we identify)</li><li>Owner's title insurance (if you do not use companies we identify)</li><li>Initial deposit for your escrow account</li><li>Daily interest charges</li><li>Homeowner's insurance</li></ul>

Source: HUD Good Faith Estimate

FIGURE **15.2** Closing Costs By State, 2009–2010

Bankrate Survey–2010 Closing Costs					
2010 rank	**2009 rank**	**State or city**	**Origination**	**Title and closing**	**2010 Total**
1	2	New York	$2,015	$3,608	$5,623
2	1	Texas	$1,539	$3,169	$4,708
3	16	Utah	$1,431	$3,174	$4,605
4	4	California–San Francisco	$1,386	$3,181	$4,566
5	14	California–Los Angeles	$1,419	$2,987	$4,406
6	6	Alaska	$1,936	$2,391	$4,327
7	8	Oklahoma	$1,352	$2,902	$4,254
8	7	Pennsylvania	$1,340	$2,897	$4,236
9	28	New Jersey	$1,338	$2,772	$4,110
10	27	Idaho	$1,365	$2,711	$4,077
11	18	Massachusetts	$1,548	$2,477	$4,025
12	3	Florida	$1,237	$2,751	$3,987
13	9	Ohio	$1,446	$2,540	$3,985
14	42	Rhode Island	$1,989	$1,983	$3,972
15	39	Arizona	$1,437	$2,514	$3,950
16	34	Wyoming	$1,460	$2,462	$3,922
17	38	Minnesota	$1,403	$2,517	$3,920
18	23	Louisiana	$1,491	$2,406	$3,897
19	15	Virginia	$1,528	$2,355	$3,883
20	19	Michigan	$1,424	$2,380	$3,804
21	11	North Dakota	$1,515	$2,285	$3,800
22	41	District of Columbia	$1,363	$2,322	$3,685
23	35	Delaware	$1,401	$2,248	$3,649
24	20	West Virginia	$1,421	$2,216	$3,637
25	51	Kansas	$1,453	$2,161	$3,615
26	45	Nebraska	$1,529	$2,079	$3,608
27	10	Washington	$1,452	$2,154	$3,607
28	31	Georgia	$1,402	$2,201	$3,604
29	26	South Carolina	$1,366	$2,155	$3,522
30	30	Alabama	$1,529	$1,983	$3,512
31	43	Illinois	$1,422	$2,083	$3,505
32	12	Tennessee	$1,450	$2,033	$3,483
33	13	New Mexico	$1,401	$2,079	$3,480
34	52	Nevada	$1,248	$2,223	$3,471
35	50	Indiana	$1,452	$2,013	$3,465
36	21	Hawaii	$1,303	$2,139	$3,442
37	49	Maine	$1,456	$1,976	$3,432
38	40	Maryland	$1,481	$1,921	$3,402
39	24	Connecticut	$1,408	$1,983	$3,391
40	48	Vermont	$1,483	$1,889	$3,372
41	29	Colorado	$1,449	$1,917	$3,366
42	32	South Dakota	$1,458	$1,905	$3,363
43	36	New Hampshire	$1,533	$1,825	$3,358
44	47	Missouri	$1,344	$2,012	$3,356
45	44	Kentucky	$1,488	$1,893	$3,341
46	25	Mississippi	$1,480	$1,855	$3,335

FIGURE **15.2** (*Continued*)

Bankrate Survey–2010 Closing Costs					
2010 rank	2009 rank	State or city	Origination	Title and closing	2010 Total
47	5	Oregon	$1,450	$1,883	$3,333
48	22	Wisconsin	$1,491	$1,812	$3,303
49	33	Montana	$1,409	$1,890	$3,298
50	37	Iowa	$1,477	$1,784	$3,261
51	46	North Carolina	$1,476	$1,779	$3,255
52	17	Arkansas	$1,466	$1,542	$3,007
		Average	**$1,463**	**$2,277**	**$3,741**

Researchers requested a good faith estimate for a $200,000 loan, assuming a 20 percent down payment and good credit.

Read more: Closing costs: State by state http://www.bankrate.com/finance/mortgages/2010-closing-costs/state-ranking-chart.aspx#ixzz1CQzUSVpq

Source: Bankrate.com

Income Tax Reporting

If the mortgage transaction is a purchase money mortgage, the Internal Revenue Code requires real estate brokers (defined as the person or company responsible for closing the transaction) to file an informational return showing the gross sales proceeds of the transaction in which they are involved. The return (IRS 1099-B) is sent to the IRS, and a copy is provided for the seller. If the seller does not provide the necessary Social Security or taxpayer identification number, the broker is required to deduct and withhold 20 percent of the amount of money due the seller.

Process of Mortgage Loan Closing

The process of loan closing begins with issuing a commitment letter to the applicant and concludes with the execution of documents, the exchange of funds, and the recording of all pertinent instruments. As mentioned, it is important to realize that a loan closing is not the end of the mortgage-lending cycle. It continues through servicing until the loan is finally repaid or refinanced.

Who Handles Mortgage Loan Closings

Any of the following professionals will handle residential mortgage loan closings in the United States, depending on the law or custom in the jurisdiction:

- Outside attorney for either the seller or buyer
- Escrow agent
- Title insurance company
- Qualified mortgage lender staff

Regardless of who performs it, the purpose of a loan closing is to ensure that the loan closes according to all laws of that state, meets any applicable lender and investor requirements, and disburses the correct amount of funds to all the proper parties involved. The expected result, of course, is a valid first lien on the property.

This chapter explains closing requirements for a basic, permanent residential mortgage loan. Specialized loan closings include those for: construction, land, government, higher priced, high cost, home equity, reverse, portfolio, secondary market, and warehouse. Each loan program has different closing requirements.

Insured Closings

Most secondary market investors require an insured closing. Anyone approved and accepted by a title company, such as an attorney, can act as an insured closing agent. The title company in effect insures that the loan closes according to the lender's directions as well as the title company's requirements, and insures against any fraud or dishonesty on the part of the loan closer.

Historically, outside attorneys and title or escrow companies handle most closings. Many still do, but more and more mortgage lenders use qualified staff members, especially for home equity loans (see Chapter 10—Home Equity Lending). When a lender closes its own loan, it typically has a centralized closing department prepare and analyze all necessary closing documents and, as a general rule, can do it more inexpensively than an outside attorney or other closing agent. Then branch or retail personnel meet with the new borrower to perform the actual closing functions. Lenders must first ascertain whether or not state law requires a licensed attorney to close a loan.

STEPS IN CLOSING A RESIDENTIAL MORTGAGE LOAN

When an underwriter approves a loan application, the lender must complete several steps to close the loan. These steps include the following:

1. Advise applicant of loan acceptance with a commitment letter (and, if applicable, set rate, terms, etc.).
2. Order final title report (and survey, if separate) and any other documents or verifications still outstanding.
3. Schedule closing and prepare closing documents.
4. If applicable, obtain appropriate IRS Form 1099-B information (and report to the IRS) or withhold appropriate funds at closing.
5. Conduct closing, obtain all required signatures, and disburse funds.
6. Record mortgage.
7. Return all closing documents to mortgage lender for inclusion in loan file.
8. Review closing and file documents for post-closing quality control.
9. If applicable, deliver required documentation to investor.
10. If applicable, receive funding from investor.

Commitment Letter

Most residential mortgage lenders use a commitment letter to inform applicants that their applications have been approved and the conditions of the loan; some lenders do not. Although a written commitment letter is not required by federal law, lenders should review that policy with a view toward using one. The commitment letter serves as the lender's acceptance of the mortgagor's application as submitted. If the lender makes a counteroffer, the applicant must accept that offer. The commitment letter creates the contractual right of the borrower to receive a mortgage loan. It also helps to establish clearly in the borrower's mind what is expected and required in order for the loan to close.

Besides the legal implications of a commitment letter, lenders must acknowledge the marketing or public relations benefits of using a commitment letter. The letter can start off by congratulating the applicants on their approval for a mortgage loan. The letter can then spell out the specifics of the loan for which they have been approved by listing the amount of the loan, term of the loan, interest rate, and so forth. This letter can also tell applicants that they must have a hazard insurance policy or binder at closing, and how the mortgagee payable clause should read. In addition, in the commitment letter a lender can inform the applicant of a need for flood insurance, what the closing fees will be, the date of closing, and other items. The issuance of a commitment letter should be the policy for all residential mortgage lenders.

Contents of a Commitment Letter

Most loan-processing systems contain a commitment letter (Figure 15.3). If a lender does not have one on its system, it can easily develop one. Most lenders require the borrowers to sign the commitment letter indicating that they accept the terms of the loan.

The contents of a commitment letter should be consistent from application to application and cover the following subjects:

- For whom the loan is approved
- The real estate that will secure the loan
- Loan program (conventional, FHA/VA/USDA, other)
- Type of loan (fixed rate, adjustable rate, balloon, or construction)
- Loan amount
- Interest rate and rate lock expiration date
- Term of the loan
- Any escrow provisions
- Payment amount (initial payment if an ARM loan)
- Requirements for insurance:
  - Hazard
  - Flood
  - Mortgage insurance
- Date by which the loan must close
- Other provisions:
  - Pest inspections
  - Certificate of occupancy

Reviewing Title and Title Insurance

A mortgage lender must establish with certainty that the mortgagor has good title to the real estate that will secure the mortgage debt. The obvious reason

FIGURE **15.3** Sample Commitment Letter

One Liberty Square - New Britain, CT - 06051

(800) 382-0017 - www.mccuemortgage.com

THE M^cCUE MORTGAGE COMPANY

MORTGAGE APPROVAL

Date: February 9, 2011   Application #:   00125224

Dear NICKIE C. GREEN

Congratulations!   The McCue Mortgage Company is pleased to inform you that your mortgage loan application has been approved! **We look forward to helping you complete the mortgage process. We are committed to doing our best to make this process happen as smoothly as possible and to answer any questions that you have along the way.**

Hello, my name is   **and I will be the Closing Administrator for your loan. My e-mail address is**   . **You can reach me by phone at and by fax at**   . **You may submit any of the documents needed to my attention via postal mail, fax or e-mail.**

Please note: Although our regular business hours are 8:30 a.m. to 4:30 p.m., my e-mail and fax machine are available 24 hours a day / 7 days a week.   In the event you are unable to get through on my fax, the alternate closing department fax number is (860) 223-2060.

Please read this letter completely.

The terms of your loan are as follows:

Property Address: 1144 REEF ROAD FAIRFIELD, CT 06824

Loan Amount: $ 180,000.00   Interest Rate: 3.750 %

Loan Type: CONF 5/1 LIBOR ARM   Term: 360 months

Points: 1.500 % $ 2,700.00   Date Rate Lock Expires: March 30, 2011

Monthly Principal and Interest: $ 833.61   Must Close On or Before:
(This does not include real estate taxes or insurance costs.)

The attorney representing The McCue Mortgage Company is   ANY LAW FIRM OF CT
Address: ANY STREET, FAIRFIELD CT 06824
Phone #: (999) 999-9999   Fax #: (999) 999-9999

If you choose to have our attorney represent you at the closing, you should contact the attorney's office upon receipt of this commitment to expedite the closing of your loan.

The attorney representing your interests will contact you with the final closing costs.

The closing of this mortgage loan is subject to our receipt and approval of all the conditions in this letter.

NOTE: Any change in the facts or information that led to the approval of this loan gives the Lender the right to void or revise the terms, the conditions and/or loan approval. Any and all reasonable future conditions placed on this loan by the Lender will become a part of this Commitment and must be fulfilled prior to closing.

We MUST receive an insurance binder/policy and a paid receipt for the first year's premium prior to closing. (Not applicable for condominiums.)

If you are refinancing your current loan, **please forward a copy of your current policy with a paid receipt for the existing policy period.   If your current policy expires within 60 days from closing, we require that the next year's policy period be paid in full. Please have your insurance agent contact me if there are any questions.**

The maximum allowable deductible on your insurance policy is $1000.

The loss payee/mortgagee clause is as follows:

"The McCue Mortgage Company and/or its successors and assigns as their interest may appear, One Liberty Square, P.O. Box 1000 New Britain, CT 06050"

00125224
rev Dec-03

FIGURE **15.3** (*Continued*)

The following conditions must be forwarded to my attention prior to closing.   In some matters, conditions must be reviewed and approved before your closing date can be scheduled.   It would be to your advantage to forward the information requested as soon as possible.

1. SATISFACTORY BANK STATEMENT FOR: ESSEX FINANCIAL VERFIYING DISCLOSED LEVEL OF ASSETS PRIOR TO CLOSING
2. PROVIDE 2009 AND 2010 W2S VERIFYING DISCLOSED LEVEL OF INCOME PRIOR TO CLOSING
3. THE MAXIMUM ALLOWED INTEREST RATE FOR THIS LOAN IS 4.00%

ITEMS NEEDED AT CLOSING AND RETURNED WITH THE CLOSING PACKAGE. THE CLOSING ATTORNEY IS RESPONSIBLE FOR THE COMPLETION AND ACCURACY OF THESE CONDITIONS.

4. THE FOLLOWING DISCLOSURES TO BE SIGNED AT CLOSING: FINAL CORRECTED, TYPED LOAN APPLICATION AND ALL OTHER REVISED DOCUMENTS

ITEMS NEEDED BEFORE FUNDS CAN BE DISBURSED AT THE CLOSING.

5. HUD-1 SETTLEMENT STATEMENT FOR PRESENT HOME NETTING AT LEAST $20000 AT CLOSING

The file documents expire on   .
If documents (such as bank statements, paystubs etc.) are due to expire prior to the closing date, please contact me to arrange for the update of those documents.

FAILURE TO SATISFACTORILY MEET THE ABOVE CONDITIONS LISTED WILL RENDER THIS COMMITMENT NULL AND VOID.

Thank you again for the opportunity to serve you!

Borrower:	NICKIE C. GREEN	Co-borrower:	
Home Phone:	(203) 767-1234	Home Phone:	
Work Phone:	(203) 374-2121	Work Phone:	

Borrower:	Co-borrower:	
Home Phone:	Home Phone:	
Work Phone:	Work Phone:	

8806

00125224
rev Mar-03

is that if another person has a superior interest in the real estate securing the mortgage loan and exercises that interest, the mortgage lender can have an unsecured personal loan.

A mortgage lender therefore demands that all questions pertaining to ownership rights and property boundaries be resolved before the loan is closed. Questions of ownership can be raised by misfiled legal documents, undisclosed heirs, mistaken interpretations of wills or intestate statutes, confusions about marital status, or other legal problems. Questions of property rights and boundaries arise in deeds, attachments, easements, and encroachments.

The manner in which the lender ascertains that the borrower will have good title can vary greatly from state to state. The most common method to review legal title is through a title search; the most common method to provide protection to mortgage lenders is through the purchase of *title insurance*. In some states, title insurance is unavailable or is available only in certain areas. Those states use an attorney's opinion based on an abstract of title. Other states, such as New York, employ a registration system of land title (referred to as the Torrens system of land registration).

Ordering Title Insurance

Today, with the emphasis placed on getting a loan approved as fast as possible, some lenders will order title insurance at approval or earlier (right after reviewing the credit report). Obviously, some of the loans for which title insurance has been ordered do not close for other reasons (for example, the appraisal is not sufficient). In these situations, some title insurance companies will not charge for the work they have put into reviewing the title. They provide this courtesy to solidify their relationship with that lender, who is trying to be timely in loan closing for competitive reasons. A lender should ask a title insurance company if it follows this policy.

Content of the Title Commitment

The lender must review the title commitment from the title insurance company. The items reviewed should include the following:

- Name(s) of the seller (if a sale) or the name(s) of the applicants (if a refinance) in the title commitment are the same as on the loan application.
- Legal description in the title commitment is the same as the real estate that was appraised and is being offered as security for the loan.
- Which liens or encumbrances on the property will remain or be removed with this loan.
- Whether or not any mechanics liens, lis pendens, tax liens, or any other title issues need resolution.

Depending on state law, the title insurance policy may contain a clause covering survey matters and, thus, eliminates the need for a separate survey. In some states, the lender will need a survey either for all mortgage loans or only if the loan is a purchase money mortgage. See Figure 15.4 for an example of a Title Insurance Policy.

FIGURE **15.4** Sample Title Insurance Policy

C A T I C ®

101 Corporate Place, Rocky Hill, CT 06067 • (860) 257-0606

MP

Mortgagee Title Insurance Policy
ALTA Loan Policy of Title Insurance (6-17-06)

Any notice of claim and any other notice or statement in writing required to be given to the Company under this Policy must be given to the Company at the address shown in Section 17 of the Conditions.

COVERED RISKS

SUBJECT TO THE EXCLUSIONS FROM COVERAGE, THE EXCEPTIONS FROM COVERAGE CONTAINED IN SCHEDULE B, AND THE CONDITIONS, CONNECTICUT ATTORNEYS TITLE INSURANCE COMPANY, a Connecticut corporation (the "Company") insures as of Date of Policy and, to the extent stated in Covered Risks 11, 13, and 14, after Date of Policy, against loss or damage, not exceeding the Amount of Insurance, sustained or incurred by the Insured by reason of:

1. Title being vested other than as stated in Schedule A.
2. Any defect in or lien or encumbrance on the Title. This Covered Risk includes but is not limited to insurance against loss from
    (a) A defect in the Title caused by
    　(i)　forgery, fraud, undue influence, duress, incompetency, incapacity, or impersonation;
    　(ii)　failure of any person or Entity to have authorized a transfer or conveyance;
    　(iii) a document affecting Title not properly created, executed, witnessed, sealed, acknowledged, notarized, or delivered;
    　(iv) failure to perform those acts necessary to create a document by electronic means authorized by law;
    　(v)　a document executed under a falsified, expired, or otherwise invalid power of attorney;
    　(vi) a document not properly filed, recorded, or indexed in the Public Records including failure to perform those acts by electronic means authorized by law; or
    　(vii)a defective judicial or administrative proceeding.
    (b) The lien of real estate taxes or assessments imposed on the Title by a governmental authority due or payable, but unpaid.
    (c) Any encroachment, encumbrance, violation, variation, or adverse circumstance affecting the Title that would be disclosed by an accurate and complete land survey of the Land. The term "encroachment" includes encroachments of existing improvements located on the Land onto adjoining land, and encroachments onto the Land of existing improvements located on adjoining land.
3. Unmarketable Title.
4. No right of access to and from the Land.
5. The violation or enforcement of any law, ordinance, permit, or governmental regulation (including those relating to building and zoning) restricting, regulating, prohibiting, or relating to
    (a) the occupancy, use, or enjoyment of the Land;
    (b) the character, dimensions, or location of any improvement erected on the Land;
    (c) the subdivision of land; or
    (d) environmental protection
    if a notice, describing any part of the Land, is recorded in the Public Records setting forth the violation or intention to enforce, but only to the extent of the violation or enforcement referred to in that notice.
6. An enforcement action based on the exercise of a governmental police power not covered by Covered Risk 5 if a notice of the enforcement action, describing any part of the Land, is recorded in the Public Records, but only to the extent of the enforcement referred to in that notice.
7. The exercise of the rights of eminent domain if a notice of the exercise, describing any part of the Land, is recorded in the Public Records.
8. Any taking by a governmental body that has occurred and is binding on the rights of a purchaser for value without Knowledge.

FIGURE **15.4** (*Continued*)

9. The invalidity or unenforceability of the lien of the Insured Mortgage upon the Title. This Covered Risk includes but is not limited to insurance against loss from any of the following impairing the lien of the Insured Mortgage
    (a) forgery, fraud, undue influence, duress, incompetency, incapacity, or impersonation;
    (b) failure of any person or Entity to have authorized a transfer or conveyance;
    (c) the Insured Mortgage not being properly created, executed, witnessed, sealed, acknowledged, notarized, or delivered;
    (d) failure to perform those acts necessary to create a document by electronic means authorized by law;
    (e) a document executed under a falsified, expired, or otherwise invalid power of attorney;
    (f) a document not properly filed, recorded, or indexed in the Public Records including failure to perform those acts by electronic means authorized by law; or
    (g) a defective judicial or administrative proceeding.
10. The lack of priority of the lien of the Insured Mortgage upon the Title over any other lien or encumbrance.
11. The lack of priority of the lien of the Insured Mortgage upon the Title
    (a) as security for each and every advance of proceeds of the loan secured by the Insured Mortgage over any statutory lien for services, labor, or material arising from construction of an improvement or work related to the Land when the improvement or work is either
        (i) contracted for or commenced on or before Date of Policy; or
        (ii) contracted for, commenced, or continued after Date of Policy if the construction is financed, in whole or in part, by proceeds of the loan secured by the Insured Mortgage that the Insured has advanced or is obligated on Date of Policy to advance; and
    (b) over the lien of any assessments for street improvements under construction or completed at Date of Policy.
12. The invalidity or unenforceability of any assignment of the Insured Mortgage, provided the assignment is shown in Schedule A, or the failure of the assignment shown in Schedule A to vest title to the Insured Mortgage in the named Insured assignee free and clear of all liens.
13. The invalidity, unenforceability, lack of priority, or avoidance of the lien of the Insured Mortgage upon the Title
    (a) resulting from the avoidance in whole or in part, or from a court order providing an alternative remedy, of any transfer of all or any part of the title to or any interest in the Land occurring prior to the transaction creating the lien of the Insured Mortgage because that prior transfer constituted a fraudulent or preferential transfer under federal bankruptcy, state insolvency, or similar creditors' rights laws; or
    (b) because the Insured Mortgage constitutes a preferential transfer under federal bankruptcy, state insolvency, or similar creditors' rights laws by reason of the failure of its recording in the Public Records
        (i) to be timely, or
        (ii) to impart notice of its existence to a purchaser for value or to a judgment or lien creditor.
14. Any defect in or lien or encumbrance on the Title or other matter included in Covered Risks 1 through 13 that has been created or attached or has been filed or recorded in the Public Records subsequent to Date of Policy and prior to the recording of the Insured Mortgage in the Public Records.
The Company will also pay the costs, attorneys' fees, and expenses incurred in defense of any matter insured against by this Policy, but only to the extent provided in the Conditions.

CATIC

SEAL

Richard J. Patterson

RICHARD J. PATTERSON
PRESIDENT

FIGURE 15.4 (*Continued*)

EXCLUSIONS FROM COVERAGE

The following matters are expressly excluded from the coverage of this policy, and the Company will not pay loss or damage, costs, attorneys' fees, or expenses that arise by reason of:

1. (a) Any law, ordinance, permit, or governmental regulation (including those relating to building and zoning) restricting, regulating, prohibiting, or relating to
    (i) the occupancy, use, or enjoyment of the Land;
    (ii) the character, dimensions, or location of any improvement erected on the Land;
    (iii) the subdivision of land; or
    (iv) environmental protection; or the effect of any violation of these laws, ordinances, or governmental regulations. This Exclusion 1(a) does not modify or limit the coverage provided under Covered Risk 5.
    (b) Any governmental police power. This Exclusion 1(b) does not modify or limit the coverage provided under Covered Risk 6.
2. Rights of eminent domain. This Exclusion does not modify or limit the coverage provided under Covered Risk 7 or 8.
3. Defects, liens, encumbrances, adverse claims, or other matters
    (a) created, suffered, assumed, or agreed to by the Insured Claimant;
    (b) not Known to the Company, not recorded in the Public Records at Date of Policy, but Known to the Insured Claimant and not disclosed in writing to the Company by the Insured Claimant prior to the date the Insured Claimant became an Insured under this policy;
    (c) resulting in no loss or damage to the Insured Claimant;
    (d) attaching or created subsequent to Date of Policy (however, this does not modify or limit the coverage provided under Covered Risk 11, 13, or 14); or
    (e) resulting in loss or damage that would not have been sustained if the Insured Claimant had paid value for the Insured Mortgage.
4. Unenforceability of the lien of the Insured Mortgage because of the inability or failure of an Insured to comply with applicable doing-business laws of the state where the Land is situated.
5. Invalidity or unenforceability in whole or in part of the lien of the Insured Mortgage that arises out of the transaction evidenced by the Insured Mortgage and is based upon usury or any consumer credit protection or truth-in-lending law.
6. Any claim, by reason of the operation of federal bankruptcy, state insolvency, or similar creditors' rights laws, that the transaction creating the lien of the Insured Mortgage, is
    (a) a fraudulent conveyance or fraudulent transfer, or
    (b) a preferential transfer for any reason not stated in Covered Risk 13(b) of this policy.

7. Any lien on the Title for real estate taxes or assessments imposed by governmental authority and created or attaching between Date of Policy and the date of recording of the Insured Mortgage in the Public Records. This Exclusion does not modify or limit the coverage provided under Covered Risk 11(b).

CONDITIONS

1. DEFINITION OF TERMS
    The following terms when used in this policy mean:
    (a) "Amount of Insurance": The amount stated in Schedule A, as may be increased or decreased by endorsement to this policy, increased by Section 8(b) or decreased by Section 10 of these Conditions.
    (b) "Date of Policy": The date designated as "Date of Policy" in Schedule A.
    (c) "Entity": A corporation, partnership, trust, limited liability company, or other similar legal entity.
    (d) "Indebtedness": The obligation secured by the Insured Mortgage including one evidenced by electronic means authorized by law, and if that obligation is the payment of a debt, the Indebtedness is the sum of
    (i) the amount of the principal disbursed as of Date of Policy;
    (ii) the amount of the principal disbursed subsequent to Date of Policy;
    (iii) the construction loan advances made subsequent to Date of Policy for the purpose of financing in whole or in part the construction of an improvement to the Land or related to the Land that the Insured was and continued to be obligated to advance at Date of Policy and at the date of the advance;
    (iv) interest on the loan;
    (v) the prepayment premiums, exit fees, and other similar fees or penalties allowed by law;
    (vi) the expenses of foreclosure and any other costs of enforcement;
    (vii) the amounts advanced to assure compliance with laws or to protect the lien or the priority of the lien of the Insured Mortgage before the acquisition of the estate or interest in the Title;
    (viii) the amounts to pay taxes and insurance; and
    (ix) the reasonable amounts expended to prevent deterioration of improvements; but the Indebtedness is reduced by the total of all payments and by any amount forgiven by an Insured.
    (e) "Insured": The Insured named in Schedule A.
    (i) The term "Insured" also includes
    (A) the owner of the Indebtedness and each successor in ownership of the Indebtedness, whether the owner or successor owns the Indebtedness for its own account or as a trustee or other fiduciary, except a successor who is an obligor under the provisions of Section 12(c) of these Conditions;

Source: Reprinted with permission of CATIC Financial, Inc.

Mortgagor's Policy

Mortgagors must understand that they are not protected against any defects in their title to the real estate under the lender's policy. The lender's policy protects only the lender's interests, even though the borrowers must pay for it. The policy should be an American Land Title Association's standard policy, equal to the original loan amount.

Borrowers can purchase a separate borrower's title insurance policy to protect their interest (usually from the same insurer as issued the lender's policy). This is a decision made solely by the mortgagor, as mortgage lenders do not require that mortgagors purchase this insurance.

DOCUMENTS REQUIRED FOR A PROPERLY CLOSED FIRST-MORTGAGE LOAN

Essential documents in a complete residential first-mortgage file vary by state as well as by loan type, product, or purpose. A lender's or investor's requirements can also add to the list. As in any discussion involving legal documents, lenders should consult with competent counsel on all the state laws in which they lend for both documents, and closing policies and procedures. State law or custom can require additional documents to those listed here. Mortgage lenders should realize that the required documentation for home equity loans (see Chapter 10—Home Equity Lending)—especially a home equity line of credit—differs from first-mortgage loans.

The process of gathering, producing, and preparing the necessary documents, and the careful checking of all forms, is often referred to as a pre-closing procedure. Mortgage loan documents need not appear in any particular order in a loan file; however, many secondary mortgage market transactions do require file documents to be arranged in a specified order. Lenders often print on the inside cover of their loan files the order of required documents that should be in each file. In that way, lenders efficiently check that all required documents are present.

CONFORMING DOCUMENTATION

Most residential mortgage lenders understand the necessity of creating conforming mortgage loans and are aware of general requirements of the secondary mortgage market in regard to closing documentation. Uniform closing documents have several benefits, including making the mortgage note, deed, and riders more liquid (able to be sold if desired), consistent, and compliant. The same argument applies to other documents required for a closed loan. Conforming documents have both Fannie Mae and Freddie Mac form numbers. Lenders should use the latest versions, as they are readily available to all lenders and have passed numerous federal and state compliance and legal examinations.

FIGURE **15.5** First Mortgage Document Checklist

APPLICANT:_____ APPLIC #_____ DATE_____

PURCHASE____ REFINANCE____ LOAN AMT:_____ TERM_____ RATE_____ PAYMENT_____

SECONDARY FINANCING AMT:_____ TERM_____ RATE_____ PAYMENT_____

PROPERTY ADDRESS: _____

SINGLE FAMILY ____ PUD ____ CONDO ____ OTHER: _____ PROJECT NAME: _____

APPRAISED AMT:_____ NEW CONSTRUCTION? _____

LTV _____ CLTV _____ HOUSING RATIO _____ TOTAL DEBT RATIO _____

APPLICATION

_____Application Form

_____ Privacy Notice

_____USAPATRIOT Act Notice

_____RESPA Servicing Disclosure

_____ECOA/Occupancy/Appraisal/Employment Certification

_____Fair Lending Notice

_____ FACT Act Notice (Credit Score)

_____Borrowers Certification & Authorization

_____IRS Form 4506 – Request for Copy of Tax Return

_____IRS W-9

_____Good Faith Estimate/Good Faith Addendum/Truth in Lending

_____HUD Booklet

_____ ARM Disclosure

_____ PMI Disclosure

_____Application Fee Itemization

_____Verification of Employment (W-2s or tax returns – 2 years tax returns if self-employed)

_____ Rate Lock Disclosure / Fee

_____ Other: _____

PROCESSING/ORDERING

_____Credit Report

_____Flood Certification

_____Appraisal Type: ____ Automated Valuation ____ Streamlined (Interior / Exterior Only) ____ Full Appraisal

_____Appraisal Received and Reviewed

_____Title Insurance

_____Title Insurance Received and Reviewed

_____ Income Verification: ____ VOE ____ Paystubs ____ W-2s ____ IRS Returns ____ Other:_____

_____ Asset Verification: ____ VOD ____ Statements ____ Other:_____

_____ Loan Verification: _____ VOL ____ Statements

_____ Other: ____ Sales Contract ____ Divorce Decree ____ Gift Letter

_____ Other: _____

UNDERWRITING

_____Underwriting Worksheet

_____Underwriting Conditions/Summary Sheet

_____Commitment Letter/Adverse Action Notice

_____Underwriting Transmittal Summary

_____Preliminary Title Search/Policy

_____ Other: _____

_____Approving Officer Conditions Received

FIGURE **15.5** (*Continued*)

_____Denying Officer / Reasons:_____

_____

_____

_____Date Notice Sent

CLOSING

_____Closing Instruction Sheet
_____Note
_____Mortgage / Riders: ____ 1-4 Family ____ ARM ____ PUD ____ Condo ____ Construction
_____Hazard Certificate/Insurance With Paid Receipt
_____Hazard Insurance Binder / Policy
_____Flood Insurance Binder (if applicable)
_____HUD-1/1A Settlement statement
_____Final Truth in Lending
_____Rescission Notices (if applicable)
_____Final Typed Application
_____Initial Escrow Account Disclosure Statement _____ Escrow Waiver Agreement
_____Closing Disbursement Funds
_____Occupancy Affidavit
_____Consumer Privacy Information Notice
_____Error and Omissions
_____ Payoff information
_____ Other: _____

POST CLOSING

_____COPY: Mortgage or Trust Deed Executed for Note & Wire Transfer Dollar Amount
_____RECORDED ORIGINAL MORTGAGE: If Applicable: Riders: _____1-4 Family Rider
_____Recorded:_____   _____Condominium Rider
_____Title Policy: $ Amount_____ (MUST MATCH MORTGAGE)
_____Notice of Right to Cancel (Refinance Only)
_____HMDA REPORTING: Enter information on P.C. Data Sheet for HMDA reporting
_____Letter To Borrower
_____ Other: _____

SECONDARY MARKETING/DELIVERY

_____ AU Underwriting Sheet
_____ Pricing Date/Confirmation
_____ Delivery Date/Confirmation
_____ Investor Receipt Date/Confirmation
_____ Investor Funding Confirmation
_____ Investor Q/C Feedback/Report
_____
_____
_____ Other: _____

I verify that this mortgage loan file is complete:
_____Posted
_____All pertinent documents accounted   Dated_____ Loan Officer_____

Source: ©2011 REMOC Associates, LLC www.remoc.com

First-Mortgage Closing Checklist

This checklist (Figure 15.5) is an important mortgage-lending tool for each of the following loan types:

- First-mortgage loan:
  - Conventional program:
    - Fixed-rate mortgage
    - Adjustable-rate mortgage
    - Balloon mortgage
  - Government program:
    - FHA
    - VA
    - USDA
  - Other:
    - Construction
    - Special/Portfolio program
    - Higher Cost/HOEPA loan
- Equity loan:
  - Closed-end second
  - Line of credit

A closing document checklist reminds the loan processor, closing personnel, servicers, and loan quality review personnel what should be in a properly closed loan file. The following documents are listed in alphabetical order and include a discussion of the reason for their requirement in the loan file.

Adjustable rate rider: If the mortgage is an adjustable-rate mortgage, this rider amends certain sections of a standard mortgage document and is recorded. It is signed by the borrower who, among other things, acknowledges that he or she understands that the interest rate and payment may increase. See Figure 15.6.

ARM disclosure: ARM applicants must receive a separate disclosure explaining each ARM program offered, plus the booklet *Consumer Handbook on Adjustable-Rate Mortgages (CHARM)*.

Application: A closed loan file must contain both the original and the typed final application. All areas must be completed with information consistent with the commitment letter and must have all required signatures. Lenders should never alter the original application.

Appraisal: A recent appraisal (or valuation) is strongly recommended for all real estate loans (some regulators do not require one if the loan amount is for less than $250,000). If the loan is a single-family detached conventional mortgage and is to be sold to the secondary mortgage market, lenders should use the Uniform Residential Appraisal Report (Fannie Mae Form 1004 / Freddie Mac Form 70) which conforms to secondary market standards for typical single family residences. If the loan collateral is another type of residential real estate, the lender should use the correct appraisal form (e.g., condominium, 2-4 family).

FIGURE **15.6** Fixed Adjustable Rate Rider

FIXED/ADJUSTABLE RATE RIDER
(LIBOR One-Year Index (As Published In *The Wall Street Journal*)—Rate Caps)

THIS FIXED/ADJUSTABLE RATE RIDER is made this ___ **28th** day ___ of _____**March 2011** _____, and is incorporated into and shall be deemed to amend and supplement the Mortgage, Deed of Trust, or Security Deed (the "Security Instrument") of the same date given by the undersigned ("Borrower") to secure Borrower's Fixed/Adjustable Rate Note (the "Note") to **THE McCUE MORTGAGE COMPANY**

("Lender") of the same date and covering the property described in the Security Instrument and located at:

**1144 REEF ROAD
FAIRFIELD, CT 06824**

[Property Address]

THE NOTE PROVIDES FOR A CHANGE IN BORROWER'S FIXED INTEREST RATE TO AN ADJUSTABLE INTEREST RATE. THE NOTE LIMITS THE AMOUNT BORROWER'S ADJUSTABLE INTEREST RATE CAN CHANGE AT ANY ONE TIME AND THE MAXIMUM RATE BORROWER MUST PAY.

ADDITIONAL COVENANTS. In addition to the covenants and agreements made in the Security Instrument, Borrower and Lender further covenant and agree as follows:

A.   ADJUSTABLE RATE AND MONTHLY PAYMENT CHANGES

The Note provides for an initial fixed interest rate of ___ **3.7500** %. The Note also provides for a change in the initial fixed rate to an adjustable interest rate, as follows:

4.   ADJUSTABLE INTEREST RATE AND MONTHLY PAYMENT CHANGES

(A) Change Dates

The initial fixed interest rate I will pay will change to an adjustable interest rate on the first day of **April 2016** _____, and the adjustable interest rate I will pay may change on that day every 12th month thereafter. The date on which my initial fixed interest rate changes to an adjustable interest rate, and each date on which my adjustable interest rate could change, is called a "Change Date."

(B) The Index

Beginning with the first Change Date, my adjustable interest rate will be based on an Index. The "Index" is the average of interbank offered rates for one-year U.S. dollar-denominated deposits in the London market ("LIBOR"), as published in *The Wall Street Journal.* The most recent Index figure available as of the date 45 days before each Change Date is called the "Current Index."

If the Index is no longer available, the Note Holder will choose a new index that is based upon comparable information. The Note Holder will give me notice of this choice.

MULTISTATE FIXED/ADJUSTABLE RATE RIDER—WSJ One-Year LIBOR—Single Family—
Fannie Mae Uniform Instrument

Form 3187 6/01

MULTISTATE
ITEM 7577L1
(042909)   MFCD7577
MFCD7577

00125224

GreatDocs®
(Page 1 of 4)
00125224

Assignment of mortgage: A loan sold in the secondary market requires a recorded assignment from the original lender to the investor. The assignment transfers the rights and obligations of the original mortgagee to an investor who buys the note from the lender.

Building restrictions: The loan file should contain a statement as to whether or not the collateral property meets local building restrictions. A lawyer's opinion may address this concern. Many jurisdictions issue an occupancy permit or certificate of occupancy as evidence that a newly constructed property meets all applicable building codes and restrictions.

Cancelled mortgage: Refinance transactions that satisfy a prior lien require a recorded release of mortgage for that prior lien. If the prior lien is with the same lender, a copy of the refinanced mortgage and note (the original is returned to the consumer, unless the existing loan is a modification) should remain in the file.

Certificate of occupancy: For mortgages on all new construction and refurbishing projects that require it, the lender should obtain a certificate issued by the local authorities declaring that the building is habitable and meets all current building codes and restrictions.

Chattel lien: Personal property serving as security for the note (in addition to the real estate) requires a financing statement or other document creating the lien or pledging that collateral as well.

Closing instructions: These instructions to the closing agent inform him or her of what to do and how. Instructions later help establish whether or not the closing was executed correctly.

Closing statement: The closing statement for a mortgage closing (like a closing statement for a real estate sale) determines how the proceeds are to be apportioned to the parties. The statement itemizes: purchase price; adjustments to the purchase price; prorations of rents, taxes, and other revenue and expense items related to the property; the allocation of the costs of the transaction between the buyer and the seller; payment for all settlement services. A receipt signed by the mortgagor is required, indicating that loan proceeds have been disbursed according to instructions.

Commitment letter: A commitment letter should be examined closely because it establishes the contractual rights and obligations between the lender and the borrower. Lenders should compare the closing documents to the commitment letter and the application in order to determine whether the applicant is receiving everything required. Files with mortgage insurance, guarantees, endorsements, or sold to a third party should contain those commitment letters as well.

Contract of sale: Mortgages for the purchase of an existing property should contain the contract of sale and all amendments in the loan file to verify an actual sale and to assist later in verifying the appraisal of the property.

Credit report: Most secondary market investors require a Residential Mortgage Credit Report provided by a local credit bureau with a tie-in to a national repository of credit information. Some portfolio lenders require only a consumer credit report. Loans approved using an AUS may have that investor's credit report information.

Deed: Mortgage loans where an interest in the subject property is transferred during the transaction should have a copy of the recorded deed used in the loan file.

Disclosures, federal: In addition to federally-mandated disclosures already listed, other required disclosures include: fair lending notice, notice of right to a copy of the appraisal, servicing disclosure, disclosure of a business relationship with a required service provider. See Chapter 11—Compliance.

Disbursement papers: Instructions are required on how funds are to be delivered to the mortgagor or other involved parties.

Escrow: If the transaction involved has been closed in escrow, a copy of the escrow agreement should be in the loan file. When the term *escrow* or *impounded* describes the monthly payments of taxes or insurances, this agreement should also be in the loan file.

FHA/VA/USDA: All agency-specific mortgage origination documents required by an FHA, VA, USDA program (e.g., credit report, verification of employment, building certificate, certificate of occupancy, flood insurance) should be in the loan file.

Flood certification: A statement from a qualified entity that the property is or is not in a special flood hazard area is required. If it is, the file should include a statement of whether or not flood insurance is available. Life of loan coverage is strongly recommended, whereby a third party continually monitors the flood determination status of the property securing the mortgage loan.

Good Faith Estimate: Lender must provide a loan applicant with a written estimate of charges payable at settlement within three business days of application. A signed, dated receipt of this Good Faith Estimate should be in the file. This estimate may also be combined with the Truth-In-Lending loan cost and APR disclosure. In addition, the lender must provide the HUD booklet *Shopping for your Home Loan* (formerly, *Settlement Costs and You*) within three business days of application. If loan terms change significantly from the original application, then the lender must provide a revised GFE. Copies of original and all revised GFEs should remain in file.

Home Owners Association agreement: If the property is a condominium, the file should contain a satisfactory review of the association documents. Many secondary market investors publish an approved list certifying an association's acceptability.

Insurance (hazard) policies: Mortgage loans require that borrowers maintain a hazard insurance policy (probably a homeowners policy)—covering losses for fire, liability, and any other hazard that should exist—with a mortgagee loss payable clause. Evidence of coverage should remain in the file. The borrower selects the hazard insurance policy provider. The amount of insurance should be equal to the *lesser* of 100 percent of the insurance value of the improvements or the unpaid principal balance of the mortgage as long as it equals the minimum amount (80 percent) required to compensate for damages on a replacement cost basis.

FIGURE **15.7** Sample Open-End Mortgage Deed

After Recording Return To:
McCue Mortgage Co
One Liberty Square, Post Office Box 1000
New Britain, CT 06050

———————————————— [Space Above This Line For Recording Data] ————————————————

OPEN-END MORTGAGE DEED

MIN: 100017000000112614

DEFINITIONS

Words used in multiple sections of this document are defined below and other words are defined in Sections 3, 11, 13, 18, 20 and 21. Certain rules regarding the usage of words used in this document are also provided in Section 16.

(A) "Security Instrument" means this document, which is dated   **March 28, 2011**   , together with all Riders to this document.

(B) "Borrower" is **NICKIE C GREEN**

Borrower is the mortgagor under this Security Instrument.

(C) "MERS" is Mortgage Electronic Registration Systems, Inc. MERS is a separate corporation that is acting solely as a nominee for Lender and Lender's successors and assigns. **MERS is the mortgagee under this Security Instrument.** MERS is organized and existing under the laws of Delaware, and has an address and telephone number of P.O. Box 2026, Flint, MI 48501-2026, tel. (888) 679-MERS.

(D) "Lender" is **THE McCUE MORTGAGE COMPANY**
Lender is a **COMPANY**   organized and existing under
the laws of **CONNECTICUT**   . Lender's address is
ONE LIBERTY SQUARE, NEW BRITAIN, Connecticut 06050

(E) "Note" means the promissory note signed by Borrower and dated   **March 28, 2011**   . The Note states that Borrower owes Lender **One Hundred Eighty Thousand and no/100**
                                                                                  Dollars (U.S. $**180,000.00**   )
plus interest. Borrower has promised to pay this debt in regular Periodic Payments and to pay the debt in full not later than   **April 01, 2041**   .

(F) "Property" means the property that is described below under the heading "Transfer of Rights in the Property."

CONNECTICUT—Single Family—**Fannie Mae/Freddie Mac UNIFORM INSTRUMENT**   Form 3007 1/01

CONNECTICUT-MERS
ITEM 2632L1 (051309)   GreatDocs®
MFCT3115   (Page 1 of 14)
                                                                                                             00125224

Internal Revenue Service reporting form: IRS form 1009-B reports the gross proceeds of the sale.

Mortgage or deed of trust: A copy of the recorded mortgage or deed of trust creating the security interest must appear in the loan file, including all riders. Any chattel liens on personal property or any financing statements

FIGURE **15.7** (*Continued*)

(G) "**Loan**" means the debt evidenced by the Note, plus interest, any prepayment charges and late charges due under the Note, and all sums due under this Security Instrument, plus interest.

(H) "**Riders**" means all Riders to this Security Instrument that are executed by Borrower. The following Riders are to be executed by Borrower [check box as applicable]:

- [X] Adjustable Rate Rider
- [ ] Condominium Rider
- [ ] Second Home Rider
- [ ] Balloon Rider
- [ ] Planned Unit Development Rider
- [ ] VA Rider
- [ ] 1-4 Family Rider
- [ ] Biweekly Payment Rider
- [ ] Other(s) [specify]

(I) "**Applicable Law**" means all controlling applicable federal, state and local statutes, regulations, ordinances and administrative rules and orders (that have the effect of law) as well as all applicable final, non-appealable judicial opinions.

(J) "**Community Association Dues, Fees, and Assessments**" means all dues, fees, assessments and other charges that are imposed on Borrower or the Property by a condominium association, homeowners association or similar organization.

(K) "**Electronic Funds Transfer**" means any transfer of funds, other than a transaction originated by check, draft, or similar paper instrument, which is initiated through an electronic terminal, telephonic instrument, computer, or magnetic tape so as to order, instruct, or authorize a financial institution to debit or credit an account. Such term includes, but is not limited to, point-of-sale transfers, automated teller machine transactions, transfers initiated by telephone, wire transfers, and automated clearinghouse transfers.

(L) "**Escrow Items**" means those items that are described in Section 3.

(M) "**Miscellaneous Proceeds**" means any compensation, settlement, award of damages, or proceeds paid by any third party (other than insurance proceeds paid under the coverages described in Section 5) for: (i) damage to, or destruction of, the Property; (ii) condemnation or other taking of all or any part of the Property; (iii) conveyance in lieu of condemnation; or (iv) misrepresentations of, or omissions as to, the value and/or condition of the Property.

(N) "**Mortgage Insurance**" means insurance protecting Lender against the nonpayment of, or default on, the Loan.

(O) "**Periodic Payment**" means the regularly scheduled amount due for (i) principal and interest under the Note, plus (ii) any amounts under Section 3 of this Security Instrument.

(P) "**RESPA**" means the Real Estate Settlement Procedures Act (12 U.S.C. § 2601 et seq.) and its implementing regulation, Regulation X (24 C.F.R. Part 3500), as they might be amended from time to time, or any additional or successor legislation or regulation that governs the same subject matter. As used in this Security Instrument, "RESPA" refers to all requirements and restrictions that are imposed in regard to a "federally related mortgage loan" even if the Loan does not qualify as a "federally related mortgage loan" under RESPA.

(Q) "**Successor in Interest of Borrower**" means any party that has taken title to the Property, whether or not that party has assumed Borrower's obligations under the Note and/or this Security Instrument.

CONNECTICUT—Single Family—**Fannie Mae/Freddie Mac UNIFORM INSTRUMENT**

CONNECTICUT-MERS
ITEM 2632L2 (051309)
MFCT3115

Form 3007 1/01

GreatDocs®
(Page 2 of 14)
00125224

should also appear. Recording instructions are required to protect all parties. See the sample Open-End Mortgage Deed in Figure 15.7.

Mortgagor's affidavit: Signed affidavits attesting to the mortgagor's current position regarding divorce proceedings, judgments or liens, or any recent improvement on the real estate or other pertinent facts that would affect the mortgage loan.

FIGURE **15.7** (*Continued*)

TRANSFER OF RIGHTS IN THE PROPERTY

This Security Instrument secures to Lender: (i) the repayment of the Loan, and all renewals, extensions and modifications of the Note; and (ii) the performance of Borrower's covenants and agreements under this Security Instrument and the Note. For this purpose, Borrower in consideration of this debt does hereby grant and convey to MERS (solely as nominee for Lender and Lender's successors and assigns) and to the successors and assigns of MERS, the following described property located in the **CITY** of

FAIRFIELD :
[Name of Recording Jurisdiction]   [Type of Recording Jurisdiction]

SEE LEGAL DESCRIPTION ATTACHED HERETO AND MADE A PART THEREOF

which currently has the address of   **1144 REEF ROAD**
[Street]

FAIRFIELD   , Connecticut   **06824**   ("Property Address"):
[City]   [Zip Code]

TO HAVE AND TO HOLD this property unto Lender and Lender's successors and assigns, forever, together with all the improvements now or hereafter erected on the property, and all easements, appurtenances, and fixtures now or hereafter a part of the property. All replacements and additions shall also be covered by this Security Instrument. All of the foregoing is referred to in this Security Instrument as the "Property." Borrower understands and agrees that MERS holds only legal title to the interests granted by Borrower in this Security Instrument, but, if necessary to comply with law or custom, MERS (as nominee for Lender and Lender's successors and assigns) has the right: to exercise any or all of those interests, including, but not limited to, the right to foreclose and sell the Property; and to take any action required of Lender including, but not limited to, releasing and canceling this Security Instrument.

BORROWER COVENANTS that Borrower is lawfully seised of the estate hereby conveyed and has the right to mortgage, grant and convey the Property and that the Property is unencumbered, except for encumbrances of record. Borrower warrants and will defend generally the title to the Property against all claims and demands, subject to any encumbrances of record.

THIS SECURITY INSTRUMENT combines uniform covenants for national use and non-uniform covenants with limited variations by jurisdiction to constitute a uniform security instrument covering real property.

UNIFORM COVENANTS. Borrower and Lender covenant and agree as follows:
     1. **Payment of Principal, Interest, Escrow Items, Prepayment Charges, and Late Charges.** Borrower shall pay when due the principal of, and interest on, the debt evidenced by the Note and any prepayment charges and late charges due under the Note. Borrower shall also pay funds for Escrow Items pursuant to Section 3. Payments due under the Note and this Security Instrument shall be made in U.S. currency. However, if any check or other instrument received by Lender as payment under the Note or this Security Instrument is returned to Lender unpaid, Lender may require that any or all subsequent payments due under the Note and this Security Instrument be made in

CONNECTICUT—Single Family—**Fannie Mae/Freddie Mac UNIFORM INSTRUMENT**   Form 3007 1/01

CONNECTICUT-MERS   GreatDocs®
ITEM 2632L3 (051309)   (Page 3 of 14)
MFCT3115   00125224

Source: Reprinted with permission of The McCue Mortgage Co.

Note: It is essential to include a properly executed promissory note. This note creates the obligation to repay the debt that is secured by the mortgage; it should state the amount of the loan, the term, the interest rate, and any other pertinent conditions as shown in Figure 15.8.

Payoff statement: This form itemizes the encumbrance(s) or other obligation(s) to be paid off and released at the closing.

Perc test: This test may be required if the property has or will need a septic tank. If so, the result of a percolation test must be in the loan file.

Pest control report: This test may be required for evidence of termites and other destructive insects. If so, the report must be in the loan file.

Private mortgage insurance documents: All documents required by the mortgage insurance company to issue its insurance, as well as a copy of its commitment, should appear in the loan file.

Real estate taxes: In some states a form showing that all past due taxes have been paid is required. In most states, unpaid real estate taxes and other liens appear in the title report.

Right to Cancel notice: Whenever a mortgagor puts up a primary residence as security, the notice of a three-day right of rescission is required. Not required for a purchase money mortgage.

Survey: It is in the mortgagee's interest to obtain a survey to identify the collateral property correctly and determine whether or not any encroachments exist. Many states do not require a separate survey, as the title insurance covers this area. There are several survey standards. The most exacting and universally accepted are those adopted by the American Land Title Association (ALTA) and the American Congress of Surveying and Mapping (ACSM), revised most recently in 2005.

Title insurance or examination: In all cases, it is essential for the lender to maintain a copy of an approved American Land Title Association (ALTA) title insurance policy or title examination from a qualified provider. A title examination establishes who has right to the real estate and, therefore, who must execute the mortgage to encumber it. It also discloses all prior encumbrances, tax liens, or other interests. (Some states use a Torrens certificate.)

Truth in Lending Disclosure: The loan file must contain a Truth In Lending Loan Disclosure statement that discloses both the Annual Percentage Rate (APR) and the total finance charge. Copies of original and all revised TILs should also remain in the file.

Uniform Settlement Statement (HUD-1 or HUD-1A): The Real Estate Settlement Procedures Act of 1974 (RESPA) requires the use of this statement for all federally related mortgage loans. The statement provides the borrower and seller a full itemization of all settlement costs. The HUD-1A can be used when there is no transfer of interest in the property, such as in a refinance as shown in Figure 15.8.

USA PATRIOT Act: The closing agent must document that it verified via government-issue photo identification the identity of all parties involved in the closing (property owners, borrowers, sellers, etc.) to comply with the USA PATRIOT Act (see Chapter 11—Compliance). Most secondary market investors also require identity verification to prevent fraud.

Verification reports: The mortgage lender should verify all relevant statements made on the loan application by obtaining verifying documentation. The most commonly used verification forms are those for income, employment, and deposits.

FIGURE **15.8** Sample Uniform Settlement Statement (HUD-1)

 A. **Settlement Statement (HUD-1)**

OMB Approval No. 2502-0265

B. TYPE OF LOAN				
1. ☐ FHA 2. ☐ RHS 3. ☒ Conv. Unins.	6. File Number:	7. Loan Number:		8. Mortgage Insurance Case Number:
4. ☐ VA 5. ☐ Conv. Ins.		00125224		

C. **Note:** This form is furnished to give you a statement of actual settlement costs. Amounts paid to and by the settlement agent are shown. Items marked "(p.o.c.)" were paid outside the closing; they are shown here for informational purposes and are not included in the totals.

D. Name & Address of Borrower:	E. Name & Address of Seller:	F. Name & Address of Lender:
NICKIE C. GREEN 100 TERRACE STREET WEST HAVEN, CT 06516		THE McCUE MORTGAGE COMPANY ONE LIBERTY SQUARE NEW BRITAIN, CT 06050
G. Property Location: 1144 REEF ROAD FAIRFIELD, CT 06824	H. Settlement Agent: ANY LAW FIRM OF CT	I. Settlement Date: March 28, 2011
		Place of Settlement: ANY STREET FAIRFIELD, CT 06824

J. SUMMARY OF BORROWER'S TRANSACTION		K. SUMMARY OF SELLER'S TRANSACTION	
100. Gross Amount Due from Borrower		**400. Gross Amount Due to Seller**	
101. Contract sales price	225,000.00	401. Contract sales price	225,000.00
102. Personal property		402. Personal property	
103. Settlement charges to borrower (line 1400)	6,508.75	403.	
104.		404.	
105.		405.	
Adjustment for items paid by seller in advance		Adjustments for items paid by seller in advance	
106. City/town taxes to		406. City/town taxes to	
107. County taxes to		407. County taxes to	
108. Assessments to		408. Assessments to	
109.		409.	
110.		410.	
111.		411.	
112.		412.	
120. Gross Amount Due from Borrower	231,508.75	**420. Gross Amount Due to Seller**	225,000.00
200. Amounts Paid by or in Behalf of Borrower		**500. Reductions In Amount Due to Seller**	
201. Deposit or earnest money	500.00	501. Excess deposit (see instructions)	
202. Principal amount of new loan(s)	180,000.00	502. Settlement charges to seller (line 1400)	
203. Existing loan(s) taken subject to		503. Existing loan(s) taken subject to	
204. Seller Paid Fees		504. Payoff of first mortgage loan	
205.		505. Payoff of second mortgage loan	
206.		506. Fees Paid for Borrow	
207.		507.	
208.		508.	
209.		509.	
Adjustments for items unpaid by seller		Adjustments for items unpaid by seller	
210. City/town taxes to		510. City/town taxes to	
211. County taxes to		511. County taxes to	
212. Assessments to		512. Assessments to	
213.		513.	
214.		514.	
215.		515.	
216.		516.	
217.		517.	
218.		518.	
219.		519.	
220. Total Paid by/for Borrower	180,500.00	**520. Total Reduction Amount Due Seller**	0.00
300. Cash at Settlement from/to Borrower		**600. Cash at Settlement to/from Seller**	
301. Gross amount due from borrower (line 120)	231,508.75	601. Gross amount due to seller (line 420)	225,000.00
302. Less amounts paid by/for borrower (line 220)	(180,500.00)	602. Less reductions in amount due seller (line 520)	(0.00)
303. Cash ☒ From ☐ To Borrower	51,008.75	**603. Cash** ☒ To ☐ From Seller	225,000.00

The Public Reporting Burden for this collection of information is estimated at 35 minutes per response for collecting, reviewing, and reporting the data. This agency may not collect this information, and you are not required to complete this form, unless it displays a currently valid OMB control number. No confidentiality is assured; this disclosure is mandatory. This is designed to provide the parties to a RESPA covered transaction with information during the settlement process.

Previous editions are obsolete

FIGURE **15.8** (*Continued*)

L. SETTLEMENT CHARGES			Paid From Borrower's Funds at Settlement	Paid From Seller's Funds at Settlement
700. Total Real Estate Broker Fees				
Division of commission (line 700) as follows:				
701. $ to				
702. $ to				
703. Commission paid at settlement				
704.				
800. Items Payable in Connection with Loan		From		
801. Our origination charge **(Includes Origination Point % or $)**	$650.00	(GFE #1)		
802. Your credit or charge (points) for the specific interest rate chosen	$2,700.00	(GFE #2)		
803. Your adjusted origination charges		(GFE A)	3,350.00	
804. Appraisal fee to		(GFE #3)	375.00	
805. Credit report to **AVANTUS**		(GFE #3)	25.00	
806. Tax service to		(GFE #3)		
807. Flood certification to		(GFE #3)		
808.				
809.				
810.				
811.				
812.				
813. **Reinspection Paid to Appraiser**				
814.				
815.				
816.				
817.				
900. Items Required by Lender to Be Paid in Advance		From		
901. Daily interest charges from 03/17/2011 to 04/01/2011 @ $18.7500 /day		(GFE #10)	281.25	
902. Mortgage insurance premium		(GFE #3)		
903. Homeowner's insurance for 1 years to	600.00 P.O.C.(B*)	(GFE #11)		
904. **Flood Ins. Premium**				
905. **Town Tax Installment**				
1000. Reserves Deposited with Lender		From		
1001. Initial deposit for your escrow account		(GFE #9)	495.00	
1002. Homeowner's insurance 2 months @ $ 50.00 per month	$100.00			
1003. Mortgage insurance months @ $ per month	$			
1004. Property taxes 1 months @ $ 445.00 per month	$445.00			
1005. months @ $ per month	$			
1006. **Flood Insurance** months @ $ per month	$			
1007. months @ $ per month	$			
1008. months @ $ per month	$			
1009. months @ $ per month	$			
1010. Aggregate Adjustment	– $-50.00			
1100. Title Charges		From		
1101. Title services and lender's title insurance		(GFE #4)	1,440.00	
1102. Settlement or closing fee	$700.00			
1103. Owner's title insurance	267.50	(GFE #5)		267.50
1104. Lender's title insurance	$640.00			
1105. Lender's title policy limit $				
1106. Owner's title policy limit $				
1107. Agent's portion of the total title insurance premium	$			
1108. Underwriter's portion of the total title insurance premium	$			
1109.				
1110. **Borr. Atty. Representation Retail**	$100.00			
1200. Government Recording and Transfer Charges		From		
1201. Government recording charges		(GFE #7)	200.00	
1202. Deed $ Mortgage $200.00 Releases $				
1203. Transfer taxes		(GFE #8)		
1204. City/County tax/stamps Deed $ Mortgage $				
1205. State tax/stamps Deed $ Mortgage $				
1206.				
1300. Additional Settlement Charges		From		
1301. Required services that you can shop for		(GFE #6)	75.00	
1302. **TERMITE INSPECTION**	$75.00			
1303. Inspections (other than by App	$			
1304.				
1305.				
1306.				
1307.				
1308.				
1400. TOTAL SETTLEMENT CHARGES (enter on lines 103, Section J and 502, Section K)			6,508.75	

*P.O.C.= Paid Outside of Closing
    B = Borrower
    S = Seller
    L = Lender
    T = Third Party

Previous editions are obsolete

MULTISTATE
ITEM 73131L2 (C3094L) (081310)
MFCD8840

HUD-1
GreatDocs®
(Page 2 of 3)
00125224

FIGURE **15.8** (*Continued*)

Comparison of Good Faith Estimate (GFE) and HUD-1 Charges		Good Faith Estimate	HUD-1
Charges That Cannot Increase	HUD-1 Line Number		
Our origination charge	# 801	650.00	650.00
Your credit or charge (points) for the specific interest rate chosen	# 802	2,700.00	2,700.00
Your adjusted origination charges	# 803	3,350.00	3,350.00
Transfer taxes	# 1203		

Charges That in Total Cannot Increase More Than 10%		Good Faith Estimate	HUD-1
Government recording charges	# 1201	200.00	200.00
Appraisal fee	# 804	375.00	375.00
Title services and lender title insurance	# 1101	1,440.00	1,440.00
	#		
	#		
	#		
	#		
	#		
	#		
	#		
	#		
	#		
	#		
	#		
	#		
	#		
	#		
	#		
	#		
	#		
	#		
	TOTAL	2,015.00	2,015.00
	INCREASE BETWEEN GFE AND HUD-1 CHARGES	$ 0.00 or	0.0000 %

Charges That Can Change		Good Faith Estimate	HUD-1
Initial deposit for your escrow account	# 1001	495.00	495.00
Daily interest charges	# 901 $18.7500 /day	281.25	281.25
Homeowner's insurance	# 903	600.00	600.00
Owner's title insurance	# 1103	267.50	267.50
	#		
	#		
	#		
	#		
	#		

Loan Terms

Your initial loan amount is	$180,000.00
Your loan term is	30 years
Your initial interest rate is	3.7500%
Your initial monthly amount owed for principal, interest, and any mortgage insurance is	$833.61 includes [X] Principal [X] Interest [ ] Mortgage Insurance
Can your interest rate rise?	[ ] No. [X] Yes, it can rise to a maximum of 8.7500%. The first change will be on 04/01/2016 and can change again every 12 months after 04/01/2016. Every change date, your interest rate can increase or decrease by 2.0000-5.0000 %. Over the life of the loan, your interest rate is guaranteed to never be **lower** than 2.2500% or **higher** than 8.7500%.
Even if you make payments on time, can your loan balance rise?	[X] No. [ ] Yes, it can rise to a maximum of $.
Even if you make payments on time, can your monthly amount owed for principal, interest, and mortgage insurance rise?	[ ] No. [X] Yes, the first increase can be on 05/01/2016 and the monthly amount owed can rise to $1,333.02. The maximum it can ever rise to is $1,333.02.
Does your loan have a prepayment penalty?	[X] No. [ ] Yes, your maximum prepayment penalty is $.
Does your loan have a balloon payment?	[X] No. [ ] Yes, you have a balloon payment of $ due in years on .
Total monthly amount owed including escrow account payments.	[ ] You do not have a monthly escrow payment for items, such as property taxes and homeowner's insurance. You must pay these items directly yourself. [X] You have an additional monthly escrow payment of $495.00 that results in a total initial monthly amount owed of $1,328.61. This includes principal, interest, any mortgage insurance and any items checked below: [X] Property Taxes [X] Homeowner's Insurance

Note: If you have any questions about the Settlement Charges and Loan Terms listed on this form, please contact your lender.

Previous editions are obsolete

MULTISTATE
ITEM 73131L3 (C3094L) (081310)
MFCD8840

HUD-1
GreatDocs®
(Page 3 of 3)
00125224

Source: Reprinted with permission of The McCue Mortgage Co.

Final Requirements

The note and mortgage are the most important documents in the first-mortgage package. As such, they require special attention and care in completion. Some of these requirements include the following:

- All blanks on uniform instruments must be completed.
- All corrections on forms must be initialed by the borrowers.
- No correction fluid or tape can be used on the documents.
- Documents should contain original signatures.
- Names of signers must be consistent through all documents, and signatures should be the same as name.
- Legal description and property address should be consistent throughout and agree with title policy.
- Note and security instrument should be signed on same date.
- Signatures should be notarized according to state requirements.

FUNDING AND LOAN DELIVERY

Chapter 4—Mortgage Lenders, describes the sources of funding for the different originators involved in mortgage lending. Chapter 17—Selling, describes various loan delivery options and requirements.

For a portfolio mortgage loan, the lender is the source of permanent funding so it is immediate. Most often deposits are the source of funds for a portfolio loan, although a FHLB advance or other borrowed funds can serve this role, too. Errors that occur during closing need resolution, of course, but do not pose the same funding problems as with secondary market transactions.

In secondary market transactions the loan is sold at or soon after closing. This type of transaction actually involves two sources of funding:

1. Interim or temporary funding by the originating lender. For mortgage bankers and some mortgage brokers, this means accessing a line of credit for closing funds and for the time it takes to deliver an acceptable closed loan package to the mortgage investor (or its inclusion in an issued mortgage-backed security).
2. Permanent funding when the loan is actually sold from an originating lender to an investor or part of an issued mortgage-backed security. The funding sources vary widely, depending on the type of investor purchasing the loan.

For whole loan sales, permanent funding occurs when the investor wires the net amount to the lender, who pays down its line of credit accordingly. Delivery issues cost mortgage bankers for each day they remain unresolved, because the investor will wire these funds only after it receives and reviews a satisfactory loan package with no outstanding underwriting or closing issues.

Correcting outstanding documentation issues quickly is critical to this aspect of the operation. Profitable mortgage banking operations will minimize the time it takes from closing to funding. Using quality closing agents, clear instructions and procedures, and effective documentation review all help to make this part of the process more efficient and less costly.

QUALITY CONTROL AND FRAUD PREVENTION

A common perception is that the mortgage production process ends with the loan closing and funding; however, a lender's quality control area is an integral part of loan production. Failure to implement and maintain a strong quality control program will eventually result in a lender suffering from loan losses, regulator action, and suspension from any major secondary market investor relationship. While errors can occur at any time in the origination process, closing errors directly impact funding and often become the most problematic to resolve, so we discuss QC and fraud issues in this chapter.

Quality control programs have two main objectives:

1. Detect and help minimize production and closing errors.
2. Detect and help minimize mortgage fraud.

Both production errors and mortgage fraud can have serious consequences for lenders and consumers.

Production errors are typically a result of either personnel not following lending policies and procedures or poor or incorrect documentation in the mortgage file. Depending on the error, it can cripple a mortgage lender in several ways:

- Invalidate the lien
- Jeopardize repayment of the note
- Suffer financial loss by delaying or canceling sale of the loan
- Incur higher post-closing settlement fees/loan level pricing adjustments
- Result in regulatory consumer compliance violations, fines, and/or penalties
- Cause regulatory licensing suspension and/or termination of mortgage-lending activities
- Expose the lender and its personnel to lawsuits and civil money penalties

It is imperative that the mortgage lender perform a structured quality control review of the loan file to evaluate: compliance with policies and procedures, documentation quality, underwriting decisions, compliance requirements, and service to the applicants. Many lenders perform a quality control review immediately after the loan has closed. The primary reasons for performing this important step immediately after loan closing is that the transaction is still recent in the parties' memories and, normally, it is easiest to correct any production errors at this time. (Consumers should be required to sign a compliance agreement at closing in which they agree to correct any errors in the mortgage transaction whenever they are discovered.)

Fannie Mae, Freddie Mac, other investors, and government agencies require that approved sellers institute a quality control program separate from and not reporting to the mortgage production department. Regulators strongly recommended such a program, too. To comply with these requirements, lenders will set up a separate department, use their existing auditing area, or hire outside vendors to manage the QC program. If done properly, lenders find these programs valuable and review the results to improve efficiency and workflow, minimize pricing errors that the lender must absorb, evaluate (and reward) employee performance, and benchmark service standards for mortgage applicants.

Mortgage Fraud

The other objective for a quality control program is to detect and prevent fraud. Contrary to media headlines, presently there is no specific federal "mortgage fraud" law. However, the Acknowledgement and Agreement—Section IX on page four of the Uniform Residential Loan Application (Fannie Mae 1003/ Freddie Mac 65)—lists several applicant representations and warranties, including a notice that making false statements on the application is a violation of Title 18 of the United States Code.

Sections 1001-1040 of Title 18 of the United States Code prohibit lying to or concealing information from a federal government official. Different sections of Title 18 and Title 42 specify various federal agencies and practices which may be involved when applicants make false statements or submit falsified information during a federally related mortgage application. The Fraud Enforcement and Recovery Act of 2009 strengthened enforcement against fraudulent activities involving mortgage lending and established a commission to study financial fraud (see Figure 15.9—FBI Mortgage Fraud Warning).

The FBI publishes a comprehensive Mortgage Fraud Report and maintains a comprehensive Web site with information on mortgage fraud (http:// www.fbi.gov/hq/mortgage_fraud.htm). According to the FBI, mortgage fraud schemes include "material misstatement, misrepresentation, or omission relating to the property or potential mortgage relied on by an underwriter or lender to fund, purchase, or insure a loan." Several states now have enacted their own mortgage fraud laws.

Another common belief is that mortgage fraud is confined to certain geographic areas, type of application or originator, or is a sporadic event that has subsided with the decline in mortgage lending activity. Mortgage fraud is present in all fifty United States, in all loan programs, and involves all types of applicants. It impacts: urban, suburban, and rural areas; low, moderate, and high incomes; credit scores in the 800s, 700s, 600s, and 500s; salaried and self-employed; purchase, refinance, and construction loans; fixed, ARM, and government (FHA/VA/USDA); prime, higher priced, and subprime mortgage programs; portfolio, secondary market, and brokered transactions. Industry losses are in the billions of dollars annually, and the most recent FBI mortgage fraud study indicates that it is still increasing. The Department of Justice also actively investigates mortgage fraud. In 2009 it initiated a joint state/federal Maryland Mortgage Fraud Task Force to make investigations by state and federal officials more effective and efficient, and to better inform the public to help prevent more people from becoming mortgage fraud victims. The IRS, USPS, and HUD also may handle reports of mortgage fraud activity.

In addition to the FBI Web site, several companies publish indices to attempt to track mortgage fraud activity: interthinx (used by the National Associations of Mortgage Brokers) and Mortgage Asset Research Institute (used by the Mortgage Bankers Association). While the studies differ, they both track incidents of fraud involving loan purpose, property valuation,

FIGURE **15.9** FBI Mortgage Fraud Warning

MORTGAGE FRAUD IS INVESTIGATED BY THE FBI

Mortgage Fraud is investigated by the Federal Bureau of Investigation and is punishable by up to 30 years in federal prison or $1,000,000 fine, or both. It is illegal for a person to make any false statement regarding income, assets, debt, or matters of identification, or to willfully overvalue any land or property, in a loan and credit application for the purpose of influencing in any way the action of a financial institution.

Some of the applicable Federal criminal statutes which may be charged in connection with Mortgage Fraud include:

    18 U.S.C. § 1001 - Statements or entries generally
    18 U.S.C. § 1010 - HUD and Federal Housing Administration Transactions
    18 U.S.C. § 1014 - Loan and credit applications generally
    18 U.S.C. § 1028 - Fraud and related activity in connection with identification documents
    18 U.S.C. § 1341 - Frauds and swindles by Mail
    18 U.S.C. § 1342 - Fictitious name or address
    18 U.S.C. § 1343 - Fraud by wire
    18 U.S.C. § 1344 - Bank Fraud
    42 U.S.C. § 408(a) - False Social Security Number

Unauthorized use of the FBI seal, name, and initials is subject to prosecution under Sections 701, 709, and 712 of Title 18 of the United States Code. This advisement may not be changed or altered without the specific written consent of the Federal Bureau of Investigation, and is not an endorsement of any product or service.

Source: www.fbi.gov

statements made on the application, verification of applicant information, and closing irregularities.

Mortgage Fraud Types

The mortgage industry classifies fraud into two large categories: fraud for profit and fraud for property. In general, fraud for profit occurs less frequently than fraud for property, but results in a higher loss each time.

Fraudsters conspire to acquire and keep mortgage funds and not repay them, using different common schemes:

- Using a "straw buyer" (a fictitious person) to purchase a house
- Selling a house to several people at once
- Falsifying the existence or condition or value of the mortgage property
- Obtaining several mortgages simultaneously for the same property

Each scheme can involve one or several people in different mortgage production areas and result in losses exceeding several million dollars. Realtors, loan originators/processors/underwriters/closers, builders, appraisers, attorneys, title companies, rating companies, and secondary market investors have all been involved. Because of its limited resources, the FBI states that it will focus its investigations mainly on this type of mortgage fraud.

Fraud for property has very different characteristics. The fraudster intends to repay the debt without delinquency and maintain ownership of the property. But they commit fraud either by obtaining a higher loan amount than they legitimately qualify for or by obtaining more favorable credit terms (i.e., a lower rate and point structure) than the transaction truly reflects. Common scenarios include:

- Falsifying income, asset, or credit information to qualify or for better loan terms or a higher loan amount.
- Concealing an investment property as owner-occupied for better loan terms.

Generally, fraud for property involves the applicants, possibly the originator, or a person who helps the borrower/originator obtain the falsified documentation. As a result, lenders and investors do not suffer the large losses as in fraud for profit, but are "cheated" out of a higher rate or higher fees. It often remains undetected if the borrower never becomes delinquent.

As discussed in Chapter 11—Compliance, lenders and mortgage loan originators have the responsibility to establish policies and procedures to identify "Red Flags" that detect identity fraud, as well as safeguard the non-public personal information they collect from applicants. Fannie Mae provides an excellent summary of different industry "Red Flags" (this term is different from the identity theft term) to help identify mortgage application misrepresentations as shown in Figure 15.10: https://www.efanniemae.com/utility/legal/pdf/commonredflags.pdf

Despite extensive secondary market quality control requirements, mortgage fraud increased significantly over the past ten to fifteen years. Private investor, brokered, and subprime mortgage programs led the increase—especially stated income and no income programs, as well as interest only products. The quality of these programs and all third party originations deteriorated steadily until 2006/2007, when many lenders suspended these types of programs as a result of investors demanding that they repurchase more and more fraudulent loans. However Fannie Mae and Freddie Mac also experienced a dramatic increase in mortgage fraud in their standard programs, but especially in their "Expanded Approval" and "Alt A" programs (see Chapter 6—Conventional Lending). Although Expanded Approval programs contain higher risk factors overall, the Alt A program represented higher levels of fraud and delinquency for these GSEs.

FIGURE **15.10** Fannie Mae Common Red Flags

 FannieMae   Mortgage Fraud Program

Your Partner in Fighting Mortgage Fraud™

Common Red Flags
Resources to Help You Combat Mortgage Fraud

Fannie Mae is committed to working with our industry partners to help combat fraud by offering you the following list of Common Red Flags that may indicate mortgage fraud.

Inconsistencies in the loan file are often a tip off that the file contains misrepresentations. The presence of one or more of these red flags in a file does not necessarily mean that there was fraudulent intent. However, several red flags in a file may signal a fraudulent transaction.

High-level Red Flags
- Social Security number discrepancies within the loan file
- Address discrepancies within the loan file
- Verifications addressed to a specific party's attention
- Verifications completed on the same day they were ordered
- Verifications completed on weekend or holiday
- Documentation includes deletions, correction fluid, or other alteration
- Numbers on the documentation appear to be "squeezed" due to alteration
- Different handwriting or type styles within a document
- Excessive number of AUS submissions

Mortgage Application
- Significant or contradictory changes from handwritten to typed application
- Unsigned or undated application
- Employer's address shown only as a post office box
- Loan purpose is cash-out refinance on a recently acquired property
- Buyer currently resides in subject property
- Same telephone number for applicant and employer
- Extreme payment shock may signal straw buyer and/or inflated income
- Purchaser of investment property doesn't own residence

Sales Contract
- Non arms-length transaction: seller is real estate broker, relative, employer, etc.
- Seller is not currently reflected on title
- Purchaser is not the applicant
- Purchaser(s) deleted from/added to sales contract
- No real estate agent is involved
- Power of Attorney is used
- Second mortgage is indicated, but not disclosed on the application
- Earnest money deposit equals the entire down payment, or is an odd amount
- Multiple deposit checks have inconsistent dates, i.e., #303 dated 10/1, #299 dated 11/1
- Name and/or address on earnest money deposit check differ from buyer
- Real estate commission is excessive
- Contract dated after credit documents
- Contract is "boiler plate" with limited fill-in-the-blank terms, not reflective of a true negotiation

In addition to the FBI Web site and DOJ Web sites, Fannie, Freddie, HUD, and several private mortgage insurance companies now have extensive on-line resources to help consumers and lenders identify, prevent, and report mortgage fraud:

Fannie Mae https://www.efanniemae.com/utility/legal/antifraud.jsp

Freddie Mac http://www.freddiemac.com/avoidfraud/

FIGURE **15.10** (*Continued*)

Credit Report
- No credit history or "thin" credit files
- Invalid Social Security number or variance from that on other documents
- Duplicate Social Security number or additional user of Social Security number
- Recently issued Social Security number
- Liabilities shown on credit report that are not on mortgage application
- Length of established credit is not consistent with applicant's age
- Credit patterns are inconsistent with income & lifestyle
- All tradelines opened at the same time
- Authorized user accounts have superior payment histories
- Significant differences between original and new or supplemental credit reports
- Also Known As (AKA) or Doing Business As (DBA) indicated
- Numerous recent inquiries
- Missing pages and/or supplements
- Employment discrepancies
- Social Security alerts

Employment and Income Documentation
- Applicant's job title is generic, e.g., "manager," "Vice President"
- Employer's address is a post office box, the property address, or applicant's current residence
- Applicant's residence is (will be) in location remote from employer
- Employer name is similar to a party to the transaction, e.g., utilizes applicant's initials
- Employer unable to be contacted
- Year-to-date or past-year earnings are even dollar amounts
- Withholding not calculated correctly (check FICA tables)
- Withholding totals don't foot from pay advice to pay advice
- Pay period dates overlap and/or don't correspond with other documentation
- Abnormalities in paycheck numbering
- Handwritten VOE, pay stubs, or W-2 forms
- W-2 form presented is not the employee's copy
- Employer's identification number has a format other than 12-3456789
- Income appears to be out of line with type of employment
- Self-employed applicant does not make estimated tax payments
- Real estate taxes or mortgage interest claimed, but no ownership of real property disclosed
- Tax returns not signed or dated
- High income applicant without paid preparer
- Paid preparer signs taxpayer's copy of tax returns
- Interest and dividend income don't substantiate assets
- Applicant reports substantial income but has no cash in bank
- Large increase in housing expense
- Reasonableness test: income appears to be out of line with type of employment, applicant age, education and/or lifestyle

HUD http://www.hud.gov/offices/hsg/sfh/buying/loanfraud.cfm

Genworth Financial http://www.genworth.com/content/genworth/ca/en/tools/resources/mortgage_fraud.html

PMI Mortgage Insurance http://www.pmi-us.com/media/pdf/brochures/pmi_fraudpreventn0207.pdf

FIGURE **15.10** (*Continued*)

Asset Documentation
- Down payment source is other than deposits (gift, sale of personal property)
- Applicant's salary doesn't support savings on deposit
- Applicant doesn't utilize traditional banking institutions
- Pattern of loyalty to financial institutions other than the subject lender
- Balances are greater than the FDIC, SIPC insured limits
- High asset applicant's investments are not diversified
- Excessive balance maintained in checking account
- Dates of bank statements are unusual or out of sequence
- Recently deposited paper-trail funds without a plausible paper-trail or explanation
- Bank account ownership includes unknown parties
- Balances verified as even dollar amounts
- Two-month average balance is equal to present balance
- Source of earnest money is not apparent
- Earnest money isn't reflected in account withdrawals
- Earnest money is from a bank or account with no relationship to the applicant
- Bank statements do not reflect deposits consistent with income
- Reasonableness Test: Assets appear to be out of line with type of employment, applicant age, education and/or lifestyle

Appraisal
- Appraisal ordered by a party to the transaction
- Occupant shown to be tenant or unknown
- Owner is someone other than seller shown on sales contract
- Appraisal indicates transaction is a refinance, but other documentation relects a purchase
- Purchase price is substantially higher than predominant market value
- Purchase price is substantially lower than predominant market value
- Subject property obsolescence is minimized
- Large positive adjustments made to comparable properties
- Comparables' sales prices don't bracket the subject's value
- Comparable sales are not similar in style, size and amenity
- Dated sales used as comparable sales
- New construction / Condo conversion: All comparable sales located in subject development
- Comparable properties are a significant distance from the subject, or located across neighborhood boundaries (main arteries, waterways, etc.)
- Map scale distorts distance of comparable properties
- "For Rent" sign appears in photographs
- Photos appear to be taken from an awkward or unusual standpoint
- Address reflected in photos does not match property address
- Weather conditions in photos inconsistent with average marketing time, date of appraisal
- Appraisal dated before sales contract
- Significant appreciation in short period of time
- Prior sales are listed for subject and/or comparables without adequate explanation

Quality Control Programs Today

Clearly, quality control programs and standards throughout the mortgage industry were woefully inadequate and failed to achieve their purpose during the expansion of third-party mortgage originations from 2000 onward.

However, it can be argued that these standards were inadequate for an even longer period, and fraud was present at high levels throughout the

FIGURE **15.10** (*Continued*)

Title
- Prepared for and/or mailed to a party other than the lender
- Evidence of financial strain may indicate a compromised sale transaction (flip, foreclosure rescue, straw buyer refinance, etc.), or might suggest undisclosed credit problems in the case of a refinance
  - Income tax, judgements or similar liens recorded
  - Delinquent property taxes
  - Notice of default or modification agreement recorded
- Seller not on title
- Seller owned property for short time
- Buyer has pre-existing financial interest in the property
- Date and amount of existing encumbrances don't make sense
- Chain of title includes an interested party such as realtor or appraiser
- Buyer and seller have similar names (property flips often utilize family members as straw buyers)

Owner Occupancy
Purchase Transactions:
- Real estate listed on application, yet applicant is a renter
- Applicant intends to lease current residence
- Significant or unrealistic commute distance
- Applicant is downgrading from a larger or more expensive house
- Sales contract is subject to an existing lease
- Occupancy affidavits reflect applicant does *not* intend to occupy
- New homeowner's insurance is a rental policy (declarations page)
Refinance Transactions:
- Rental property listed on application is more expensive than subject property
- Different mailing address on applicant's bank statements, pay advices, etc.
- Different address reported on credit report
- Significant or unrealistic commute distance
- Appraisal reflects vacant or tenant occupancy
- Occupancy affidavits reflect applicant does *not* intend to occupy
- Homeowner's insurance is a rental policy (declarations page)
- Reverse directory does not disclose subject property address

HUD-1 Settlement Statement
- Borrower or seller name is different than on sales contract and title
- Sales price is inconsistent with contract, loan approval and/or appraisal
- Excessive earnest money or builder deposit
- Earnest money deposit is inconsistent with sales contract and/or application
- Payouts to unknown parties
- Refinance pays off previously undisclosed liens
- Excessive sales commissions
- Excessive fees and/or points
- Seller-paid closing costs, especially for purchaser with sufficient assets for down payment
- Cash proceeds to borrower are inconsistent with final application and loan approval

4

industry. The long-term economic expansion starting in the 1990s—with favorable employment conditions, increasing real estate values, and loose underwriting standards—masked the true level of fraud for property present in mortgage and MBS portfolios. To avoid delinquency, fraudulent borrowers could easily either sell the property for a profit or refinance it for more money to make payments until they were ready to sell. One cause of the mortgage meltdown crisis

FIGURE **15.10** (*Continued*)

Foreclosure Rescue Red Flags

- The borrower was advised by a foreclosure assistance consultant that they should avoid contact with their servicer
- The borrower has paid someone to negotiate with the servicer on their behalf
- The borrower states that they are sending their mortgage payments to a third party
- Borrower receives a purchase offer that is greater than the asking price
- Borrower states that they will be renting back from new owner
- Cash-back at closing to the delinquent borrower, or disbursements that have not been expressly approved by the servicer
- The borrower has quit claimed title to a third party at the advice of a foreclosure assistance consultant

Short Sale Fraud Red Flags

- Sudden default, no workout discussions, and immediate offer at short sale price
- Ambiguous or conflicting reasons for default
- Short sale offer is from a related party

5

Source: www.fanniemae.com

was a result of a "no harm, no foul" attitude that production-driven companies and securitization companies adopted: since delinquency remained low throughout this period, lenders ignored warning signs in quality control programs, and risk rating agencies were lax in their due diligence efforts.

Mortgage fraud and quality control issues persist even after the mortgage meltdown crisis in 2007, despite all the media publicity, numerous legal actions, and increased due diligence. Additionally, material differences persist between loan application data submitted to the GSEs for sale prior to closing and the closed loan file documentation. In response, Fannie and Freddie quality control program guidelines were thoroughly revised early in 2010 and revised throughout the year. Fannie Mae's version, Loan Quality Initiative (LQI), adds several requirements to their already extensive guidelines and increases lender liability through more reps and warranties.

> Fannie Mae (Part D, Ensuring Quality Control) https://www.efanniemae.com/sf/guides/ssg/sg/pdf/sel081210.pdf

> Freddie Mac (Discover Gold through Quality Control) http://www.freddiemac.com/dgtq/

Secondary market quality control programs require a seller conduct post closing QC reviews that sample either a random ten percent or a statistical sample of its mortgage production. This sample must be representative of all sources of origination and all loan products, and be completed on selected loans within sixty days of closing. The quality control program should test all areas of the origination process, from application to closing.

Of this sample, a certain percentage of loan applications need to be totally re-verified, including a review or new appraisal, with an attempt to verify owner occupancy. A borrower-executed IRS Form 4506 authorizes the lender to obtain a copy of federal tax returns directly from the IRS to verify self-employed and other income.

The GSEs now also require lenders to establish a prefunding QC review process to reduce the number of closed loans with misrepresentations, inaccurate data, or inadequate documentation. Many private investors and some portfolio lenders require this step for third-party originations and other types of mortgage transactions. GSE AUSs now issue "Potential Red Flag" messages to assist lenders in investigating potential fraud areas *before* closing to avoid buybacks and other losses. AUSs also provide tracking reports for management to assist them in evaluating the effectiveness of their policies and procedures. In summary, both of these initiatives (pre-closing QC reviews and AUS reporting) highlight the recent trend to minimize production and closing errors and mortgage fraud before the mortgage transaction occurs.

DISCUSSION POINTS

1. Identify the reasons why residential loan closings are so important to the parties involved.
2. What are the steps in closing a residential mortgage loan? Who normally handles the closing?
3. Why is a commitment letter so important to proper mortgage lending?
4. What is the purpose of title insurance? Who is protected by title insurance?
5. Why does the Internal Revenue Service need to be informed about a loan closing?
6. Describe the different types of mortgage fraud.
7. What federal areas investigate mortgage fraud?
8. Why is quality control an important aspect of mortgage loan production?
9. What recent steps are lenders taking to improve quality control?

CHAPTER **16**

Mortgage Loan Servicing and Administration

INTRODUCTION

After closing a mortgage loan, the next step in the residential lending process involves servicing (or as it is sometimes known, loan administration). All residential mortgage loans require servicing. **Loan servicing** includes the responsibilities, functions, and day-to-day operations that an organization performs after the closing and over the term or repayment of that loan. These must be completed in accordance with:

- Federal, state, and local laws and regulations

- The terms of the loan documents: the commitment letter, note, mortgage or deed of trust, mortgage riders, and other closing documents (Many forget that both the borrower and the lender make several covenants and have ongoing fiduciary responsibilities, as itemized in these documents.)

- Investor or agency (FHA, VA) guidelines if the mortgage is sold or originated as part of a specific program

One negative result of the consolidation of servicing that has occurred in the past twenty years is many more borrowers are affected when a servicer for whatever reason fails to meet any of the legal, fiduciary, and contractual responsibilities outlined above. Recently, the servicing practices of mega-servicers have come under increased scrutiny. Regulatory and investor examinations have found small- and large-scale violations by servicers with respect to laws and regulations, loan documents, and secondary market requirements. Typically, investigations found smaller servicers made errors while attempting to follow complex rules; larger servicers chose intentionally to violate their responsibilities because of profitability or efficiency goals. As with recent changes on the origination side of the mortgage business, the result is now the servicing side also has new regulations to follow as a result of these abusive or predatory servicing practices. Truth in Lending, RESPA, and the Dodd-Frank Act all include new rules, behaviors, and practices for mortgage servicers (See Chapter 11—Compliance). The new Consumer Financial Protection Bureau has stated that investigating servicing abuses is at the top of its list for enforcement actions.

LOAN SERVICING VS. LOAN ADMINISTRATION

All residential mortgage loans require servicing, which involves several functions. Performing them can be quite complex and expensive. Servicing departments are organized differently, depending on a number of factors, including the types of mortgages serviced. Typically, all handle the following activities for mortgage loans:

- Borrower inquiries
- Billing and repayment
- Tax and insurance escrows
- Adjustments and changes
- Delinquency and collections
- Pay-off and release
- Internal accounting and management reporting

In contrast to loan servicing, **loan administration** describes a servicing department that plays a larger, more sophisticated role in the lender's overall strategy—one that includes servicing loans for secondary market investors or government agencies. This could be a passive role, in which the lender handles only those loans it originates and sells, or it could be an active role in which the lender sells and buys servicing portfolios to and from mortgage lenders.

Loan administration includes the typical servicing department activities just described, but may also add the following functions:

- Investor accounting and management reporting
- Servicing portfolio pricing, selling, and acquisition
- Delivery and quality control

If performed correctly, loan administration should result in the following:

- Rendering of all required services to the mortgagor
- Protecting the security interest of the mortgagee (or an investor)
- Producing a profit for the servicer

An originating lender is not required to service the mortgage, regardless of whether the particular loan is sold to an investor or held in portfolio. Lenders can hire another entity to service loans for their portfolio or service the loans they sell to secondary market investors, the terms of which is formalized in a *servicing contract*. The issue of who will service the loans is generally more significant for depository institutions, which rely more on a relationship business strategy than a transactional one. Fannie Mae and Freddie Mac set the standards by which the loan servicer agrees to perform this function. They purchase more loans than any other investor but *never* service loans. Mortgage bankers usually sell all their loans, but will retain their servicing if part of their business model is to generate servicing income and/or cross-sell other products.

Loan administration can be the most difficult of all the steps to perform in the residential lending process. On the other hand, it can also be the most profitable. The difficulty in performing this function stems from two general areas: the broad scope of operations it entails and its duration. A myriad of problems can develop when dealing with the different tasks performed in-house or outsourced, computers, servicing systems, communications, and people and their problems. The longer the servicing relationship, the more likely an issue can develop as the result of human error, implementation of new procedures and technology, change in operation or ownership, or cyclical changes in the economy. These problems are discussed in greater detail in the following sections.

If an organization handles these problems correctly and maintains sufficient loan volume, servicing produces meaningful revenue. Servicing revenue may be the primary business reason that the lender is in residential mortgage lending, since it can offset other production-related losses to make a profit.

Organization of a Mortgage-Servicing Department

The organization of the mortgage-servicing department varies. It must support the overall strategy of that institution and the manner in which other departments operate. The department's organization depends on a combination of its size, scope, and complexity, as measured by the number of loans (volume), loan programs and investor(s) (scope), and responsibilities (complexity). As these elements change, so can the department structure. A change in operation, or addition of technology, or the election to outsource a function can impact some or all areas of servicing.

Most departments use either the *function system* or the *unit system*. The *function system* assigns each employee to a specific servicing function, such as real estate taxes, payments, or assumptions. This system allows for task specialization, a higher level of customer service, and speed of operation. The main drawback is that that function will not be performed when that person is absent. The *unit system* assigns small teams of employees to a group of loans for which they perform all of the related tasks. All employees can perform each function to cover for each other when one is absent. The benefit is a more consistent operation. The drawback is that no one person is an expert on any one function.

TABLE **16.1**

Organization of Mortgage-servicing Departments

Functional	Unit
Payment processing	ARM
Escrow administration	Fixed
Rate/payment adjustments	FHA/VA
Customer service	Delinquency/Collections
Delinquency/Collections	Fannie Mae/Freddie Mac
Investor Relations	
Payoff and release	

Source: © 2010 REMOC Associates, LLC www.remoc.com

Most large servicers use the function system because speed, accuracy, and efficiency are critical to their economies of scale. Their loan volume requires several people to perform the same function, which alleviates the negative effects of absenteeism. Smaller servicers with limited resources use the unit system in order to have more coverage of all functions at all times to maintain high customer service levels.

The actual loan programs serviced and/or the investor for whom the loans are serviced in large part influences the servicing department organization and functions (see Table 16.1). For example, a servicer with adjustable-rate loans requires a function for rate review and notification, whereas a servicer dealing with only fixed-rate loans does not; a servicer with tax or insurance escrows requires an escrow administration function, whereas a servicer of loans without escrows does not. A medium-sized servicer with few functions may need to reorganize from the unit to function system if a change in loan programs requires specialized functions.

SERVICING RESPONSIBILITIES AND FUNCTIONS

Similarly, the *servicing responsibilities* and *functions* performed are a result of the loan programs, investor requirements, and legal regulations for that servicer. **Servicing responsibilities** refers to the more global fiduciary responsibility that the servicer assumes as agent for the following parties:

- Borrower
- Lender/investor
- Insurer/guarantor
- Regulator

Servicing functions refers to the operations involved in meeting these responsibilities. A small servicer with 2,000 mortgage loans may be complex as a result of different loan programs, each requiring several different functions. A large servicer with 400,000 loans may service only fixed-rate, non-escrow loans for its own portfolio, requiring only four functions.

Setting Up the Loan File

The first step in mortgage servicing is to establish a servicing file. The objective is to put all the right documents in all the right places, following a similar format so anyone reviewing the file can quickly find the needed information. The servicer then adds the new loan to its servicing software system, based on the specific features of the mortgage. Care must be exercised in this effort to ensure that the loan is inputted correctly. This will prevent mistakes in the future. The servicer should perform the loan setup function immediately after closing for two reasons: quality control and customer service.

Post-closing Review

Most lenders use the loan setup step as a type of quality control. During a normal post-closing review, the servicer compares the list of required documents to the list of documents actually in the loan file, as well as reviewing the documents for errors and omissions. Loan setup is probably the last convenient time for the lender to cure any defects, such as missing documents or other financial or documentation errors. Resolving these defects may take time, especially if the error involves the legal documents, but it should not delay the servicer from performing the customer service aspect of loan setup.

Welcoming Letter

The next step is to mail a welcoming letter to establish a correct relationship with a borrower. Think of it this way: this is the start of what is potentially a 30-year relationship with the borrower, involving what is for most people their largest financial commitment and their most important asset—their home. Few services can be more important to a consumer, so it is critical that the servicer begin this relationship properly. The welcoming letter is the servicer's first contact with the borrower. It should be mailed soon after closing—the sooner the better! It should clearly explain three areas: servicing contacts and assistance, borrower obligations, and repayment.

The welcoming letter should introduce the servicing people and provide contact information, such as locations, telephone numbers, e-mail and regular mail addresses, and hours of operation. It should also explain what is expected of the borrower as a mortgagor and restate the significant covenants contained in the closing documents regarding insurance, taxes, property damage, and so forth. Finally, the letter should provide clear instruction for the first and subsequent payments by the borrower, and should help the borrower realize how important it is to make the mortgage payments on time.

Mortgage Payment Methods

Most mortgages are paid monthly, some biweekly. The billing method varies according to the mortgage product and lender, but the most common are these:

- *Coupons*: Provided in one-year supply; mortgagor submits one with each payment. The coupon includes the loan number, due date, and payment amount (often, this information can be encoded on the coupon for rapid and efficient processing).
- *Monthly statement billing*: Servicer mails a statement (bill) to the borrower each month. Its main advantage is as a reminder that the payment

is due, but the drawback is the mailing cost. Cross-selling other services by including advertising on the bill can offset this drawback. Providing loan information also helps to reduce customer inquiries (and servicing personnel to answer them.)

Mortgage payment methods differ as well. Servicers strive for efficiency and accuracy when processing payments. Manual payment processing involves personnel, training, and daily balancing and auditing issues. Technology offers borrowers more payment options, but comes at a higher infrastructure cost, specialized maintenance, and its own balancing, privacy and security, and regular auditing issues.

- *Regular USPS or express mail:* The traditional manner in which the borrower writes a check and sends it with either the coupon or bill. Mega-servicers use lock-box facilities to process the payments and apply to the loan account. Smaller servicers open their own mail and process it within the same servicing facility that the borrowers can visit for other business (i.e., the main office).
- *Preauthorized automatic payment:* Mortgage payment is automatically deducted from the mortgagor's depository account. This method assures prompt payments on the due date. This is a requirement for biweekly mortgages.
- *Pay-by-phone:* The borrower calls an 800 number and authorizes a certain amount from a certain depository account. Funds are transferred in batch processing from one institution to the other and applied automatically to the loan account.
- *Online payment:* The borrower visits the servicer's Web site, logs into his secure account, and authorizes a certain amount from a certain depository account. Funds are transferred in batch processing from one institution to the other and applied automatically to the loan account. Once online, the borrower can access other loan data and even submit inquiries.

For many borrowers, payment notification is the only correspondence they receive from the servicer. Depending on the mortgage terms, the servicer may notify the borrower for these other common, functional, events as well:

- An annual escrow statement
- An increase (decrease) in taxes or insurance
- A notice of interest rate and monthly payment change
- A late notice or other delinquency status
- Annual tax-related reporting for: interest paid/escrow interest received, real estate taxes, mortgage insurance premiums

Servicing Functions

To fulfill these responsibilities successfully, a mortgage loan servicer must have either well-trained people or separate departments to perform five essential functions:

1. The *payment processing department* has the daily responsibility of applying all payments received and balancing the accounts. It receives

payments and deposits, applies them to the individual mortgage loans, and transmits this information to loan accounting. Depending on the size of the servicer, this area may also produce and screen bills sent to borrowers and, on the other end, handle payoff requests from other lenders or their closing agents and send mortgage releases once the loan is paid off.

Activity in this area is cyclical and can be frenetic, depending on the situation. For example, most mortgages are due on the first of the month, so most payments arrive at the beginning of each month. Changes in payments from tax escrows or adjustable-rate mortgages result in many payment issues. In times of heavy refinancing waves, payoff and release requests explode, even if the lender is refinancing its own mortgages.

2. The *loan accounting department* reconciles loan payments to funds received, notifies investors of deposits made to their account, and draws a check (if funds are not paid through a custodial account) to distribute principal and interest less the servicing fee.

Depending on the size and composition of the servicing portfolio, this area can be fairly straightforward or very complex. Today, many investors require that all funds due them (principal and interest) be collected by the investor debiting a "P&I custodial account" established for their benefit, separate from funds for tax and insurance payments which are placed in a "T&I custodial account." Some investors also require that excess reserves be deposited with them and not in the custodial account. This area also produces management reports to assist with investor accounting and portfolio management.

Activity in this area somewhat mirrors the payment-processing area but is one step away from individual mortgage loan accounts, instead dealing with the summary of activity. Loan accounting must balance investor loans daily, complete monthly reporting diligently, and remit payment according to each investors' specific schedules.

3. The *escrow administration department* ensures the protection of the security interest by determining whether adequate coverage is in place and is current with a mortgagee-payable clause for required insurances or credit guarantees. This may include the following: hazard, flood, private mortgage, FHA, VA, or other state/federal housing agency insurance or credit guarantee. It monitors in a similar manner the status of real estate tax payments for all towns in which the servicer has loans.

The escrow administration accomplishes this in one of three ways: it either collects funds from the borrower and disburses payments for all required taxes and policies; it monitors the status of tax payments and required policies, "force-placing" them if it receives notification of cancellation; or, a less common approach is to takes out a blanket or umbrella insurance policy—a mortgage impairment policy—to cover any losses sustained as a result of individual loan tax liens or insurance lapses of coverage. This department may also inspect property repairs (if the damage was large and affects the actual structure of the security) before releasing an insurance claim payment to the mortgagor, adhering to lender or investor requirements.

4. The *customer service department* handles all borrower inquiries and requests, resolves errors and disputes, and processes other changes that may occur. This area may also handle assumptions, payoffs, modifications, any cross-selling of other products, and any other services offered by the company.

Activity in this area is cyclical as well. Customer service must field numerous telephone calls, e-mails, and chat sessions. It handles requests for information at year-end as well as responses after any mass mailing to borrowers, such as escrow analyses, operational changes, or transfers of loan servicing. To alleviate these waves of inquiries, many servicers now provide information online, allowing borrowers to access their loan account anytime over the Internet. The most effective loan servicing Web sites allow borrowers to view loan history and escrow activity, change payment amount, date, and method, and obtain year-end/tax-related information.

5. The *delinquency and collection department* handles past-due loan accounts. In many ways, this is the most difficult function, but it is also the most essential for a successful servicing operation. Those involved in this function must be familiar with the Fair Debt Collection Practices Act that prohibits certain collection practices. When attempts at collection fail, then this function often is also responsible for initiating foreclosure proceedings.

Ideally, this area is not as active as other departments and traditionally handles fewer loan accounts (approximately eight percent of all loans), but the complexity and level of knowledge is substantial and requires an enormous amount of time for each loan account. Activity in this area involves legal issues and court proceedings as well as specific investor guidelines, so most servicers will restrict borrower communication with other areas once a loan becomes delinquent. Any activity in either the payment processing, escrow, or customer service areas can void or otherwise disrupt collection or foreclosure efforts. Often one collector handles all communications and issues regarding a delinquent loan because of this concern.

Most servicers hire outside attorneys to manage each loan that becomes severely delinquent. It is critical for this area to minimize the substantial expenses and losses that occur when a loan goes to foreclosure. Normally, it is most active in the worst economic times. Depending on the number or severity of delinquencies in a servicing portfolio, a separate department related to collections, a real estate owned (REO) department, may be required to handle foreclosed property.

Servicing Contract

A servicing contract establishes the servicing relationship when a mortgage loan is sold to an investor with the servicing retained by the loan originator. This contractual relationship continues for the life of the mortgage loans sold to that investor, but it can be terminated. Termination can be either for cause (some failure to perform on the part of the servicer) or, in some cases, without cause. If servicing is withdrawn without cause, then it is common for an investor to pay a fee, typically one or two percent of the amount serviced, as compensation.

The servicing contract or the servicing manual supplied by an investor describes in detail the servicing responsibilities. These responsibilities typically include the following:

- Monthly collection and allocation of principal and interest
- Disbursement of funds to the investor
- Collection and periodic payment of real estate taxes and insurance premiums
- Handling of assumption, partial release, and modification of lien requests
- Annual review of loans involving, among other tasks, ARM adjustments, current insurance policy, taxes paid, and escrow analysis
- Any other activity necessary to protect the investor's security interest, including, if necessary, collection activity and foreclosure proceedings

Although servicing contracts can vary and are negotiated between parties, GSEs require certain policies, procedures, and capabilities for a company to earn an approved seller or servicer status. Fannie and Freddie requirements set the bar for other areas of the mortgage industry, and most servicing contracts include these. FHA and VA also require similar servicing standards and contracts.

MANAGING DELINQUENCIES AND FORECLOSURES

Of all of the functions performed by the loan administration department, the most important is managing delinquencies (defaults). Default occurs when a mortgagor breaches any of the covenants in a mortgage. Mortgage default may result from a failure to pay taxes, provide hazard insurance, or maintain the premises, but most commonly it is the result of nonpayment of principal and interest.

A residential mortgage loan is generally classified as delinquent if it is 30 days past due. (Technically, a residential loan is delinquent after the first of the month since that is when the payment is due.) Uniform instruments allow for payment until the 15th of the month with no late fee added and, of course, no additional interest due. If the payment is received on the 16th or later, the lender may impose a late fee of up to 5 percent of the payment due.

Successful delinquency management can keep servicing expenses under control and therefore enhance servicing profits. For sold loans, the investor or servicing contract outlines the steps required of servicers in managing delinquencies, especially when a loan is seriously delinquent. For portfolio loans, the lender may have more flexibility.

Serious mortgage delinquency (90 days or more past due) for all types of loans rose dramatically throughout 2007 to the end of 2009, reaching levels not seen since the Great Depression. Overall serious mortgage delinquency

FIGURE **16.1** Serious Delinquency Rates, 1998–2009

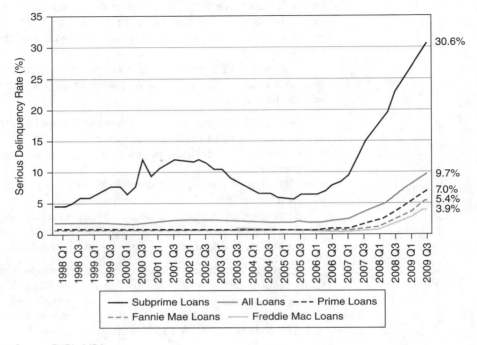

Source: FHFA, MBA

peaked at approximately 9.7 percent, but varied widely by loan program (subprime over 30 percent; Freddie Mac loans 4 percent). See Figure 16.1.

Technology has assisted servicers manage loan delinquency, which employ the use of automated calling to remind borrowers of payments, loan software programs to help track new and recurring delinquency by geographic location, loan product type, originator, credit score, employment, etc. See Figure 16.2.

Mortgagee Options

The mortgagee usually has certain options in the event of a default. One option (provided by the mortgage instrument) is to accelerate all future payments immediately, but seldom does the instrument require immediate acceleration. Accelerating the entire debt may not be the best choice for a mortgagee and is certainly not the best alternative for a mortgagor.

Accelerating the entire debt and suing for the total most likely will lead to foreclosure, since most consumers do not have the funds on hand to pay off their mortgage. For a discussion of the various methods of foreclosure and the right of redemption, see Chapter 15—Real Estate Law and Security Instruments.

In practically all situations, a mortgagee does not want to proceed to foreclosure if it can be prevented. Although the average consumer may not believe it, mortgagees not only dislike foreclosure, but generally lose money if they must foreclose. Most mortgagees are in the business of lending

FIGURE **16.2** Mortgage Delinquency Analyses

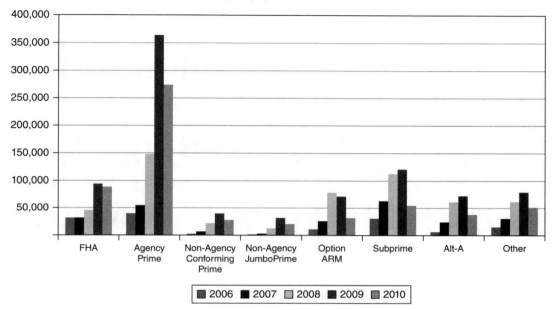

Estimated number of loans that were current at the beginning of the year and 60+ or in Foreclosure in May by Calendar Year across the investor

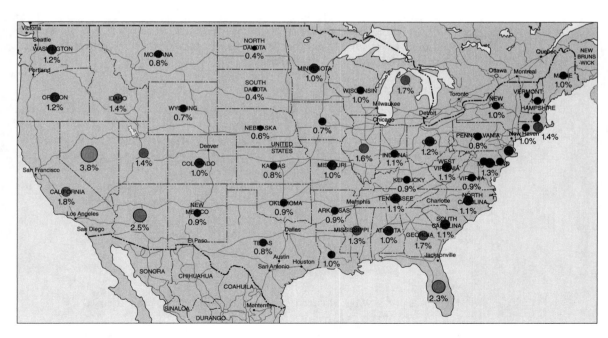

In 2010, newly delinquent loans were still at elevated levels in NV, AZ, CA, FL

FIGURE **16.2** (*Continued*)

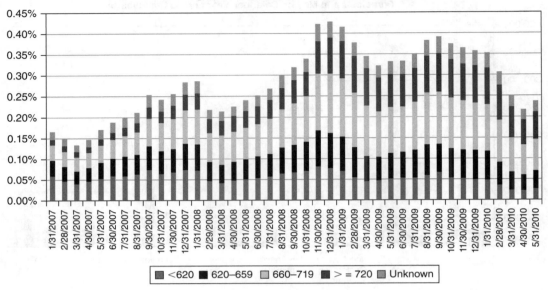

Source: Reprinted with permission from Lender Processing Services

money, not owning or managing real property. The mortgagee may have other options, depending on the reasons for the default and "work-out" possibilities. GSEs and other private investors have developed loss mitigation techniques (described later) that enable the borrower to work out of the delinquent situation and avoid foreclosure.

Reasons for Default

Mortgagors default on mortgage obligations for different reasons. They mirror the different categories of delinquent credit discussed in Chapter 13—Underwriting the Residential Mortgage Loan. Some delinquencies are purely honest oversights on the part of mortgagors. People occasionally miss a mortgage payment because of vacation, forgetfulness, or some other logical, nonrecurring reason. On the other hand, the more common reasons for residential mortgage defaults read like a list of personal tragedies:

- Financial problems
- Loss of employment
- Layoff or strike
- Death of a wage earner
- Credit overextension or bankruptcy
- Illness of a wage earner or mounting family medical expenses
- Loss of wage as a result of accident
- Marital issues

- Mortgage payment changes due to ARM rate/payment or escrow payment increases
- Strategic foreclosures due to the borrower(s) losing all home equity

Collection Procedures

The collection activity should bring the delinquent mortgage current as quickly as possible for the benefit of both the mortgagor and mortgagee. The lender's servicing system must quickly identify a loan as delinquent. Time is of the essence when dealing with delinquent borrowers. The sooner the contact, the sooner it can be resolved or a repayment plan put in place.

The first step is usually a payment reminder notice sent to the borrower seven to ten days after the payment was due. This notice simply reminds the mortgagor that the payment was due on the first, and that if not paid by the 15th, a late fee will be assessed. If payment is not received by the 16th, the servicer sends a second notice informing the mortgagor that a late fee is now due in addition to the scheduled payment. Some coupons may already have this information printed on them.

Telephone Contact

Telephone calling is a very effective and inexpensive method for contacting delinquent mortgagors. Often it is the first contact. Some lenders use it for habitually delinquent borrowers who, once reminded, pay by the seventh or tenth day after the due date. Other lenders use the telephone to contact a mortgagor if the scheduled payment and late fee are not received by the 20th of the first month. Of course, if a lender prefers, a personalized letter sent around the 20th of the first month could be a very effective way of explaining the difficulties caused by not bringing the loan current.

Larger servicers employ auto-dialing systems to remind borrowers or help collection clerks be more efficient. Typically, they are used earlier in the collections process (before 30 days).

Two Months Delinquent

The critical point is when a mortgage loan reaches two payments past due. The chances of the loan going to foreclosure increase dramatically if the delinquency is not cured during this second month. Shortly after 30 days delinquent (the first of the second month past due), the lender should perform one or all of the following actions:

- Have an extended telephone conversation with the borrower with a plan for repayment (no voicemail or auto-dial) and to determine the condition and occupancy of the mortgaged property.
- Schedule and conduct a face-to-face meeting with the borrowers.
- Send a strongly worded letter informing the mortgagor that unless the loan is brought current, the mortgagor may be seriously jeopardizing his/her credit rating. The letter should include required compliance notifications regarding reporting the delinquency to a credit bureau and any other required disclosures.

Once a loan is 60 days past due, the lender should insist on a face-to-face interview with the mortgagor. While this is not practical for the mega-servicers, it is for local and even regional ones. At this critical stage of repayment, it is very important for the servicer to establish the best connection possible with the borrower. As stated before, lending is a trust business. Making a personal, physical connection with the borrower reinforces this partnership between the two parties better than telephone or written correspondence. The 60-day meeting should clearly establish the reason for delinquency and what the mortgagor intends to do about it. Based on the reason or reasons for the default, the lender may be able to suggest ways to cure the default.

Mortgage lenders should report delinquent mortgagors to credit bureaus. They are required by the secondary market players to report all 90-day delinquencies. Most lenders report 30- and 60-day delinquencies as well. At this point, investor guidelines govern the collection process, with any violations by the servicer exposing it to a repurchase order.

Curing Delinquencies

The important concept to realize is that most mortgage delinquencies are cured. Historically, only a small percentage of delinquent mortgages reach foreclosure. Often a mortgagee and mortgagor resolve the problem that led to the delinquency. In assessing a delinquency, a lender should determine why the loan became delinquent, whether the delinquency reflects a temporary or permanent situation, and the mortgagor's attitude toward the mortgage debt. The lender should also realize the manner in which a delinquency is cured today will impact the borrower's long-term relationship and how he repays the debt going forward for the remaining term of the loan.

LOSS MITIGATION

The recent mortgage crisis is still unfolding for servicing areas and, more specifically, the delinquency and collection area. This latest wave of mortgage delinquency reaches five percent nationally, exceeding 30 percent for some subprime loan programs and geographic areas—levels unseen since the Great Depression. The increase in foreclosures stalled somewhat in 2010, but many experts forecast that 2011 will see an increase in foreclosures as the resolution for many loans which at present are seriously delinquent.

As a result, managing mortgage default has taken on a dramatically different role and approach. No longer is it a "dial for dollars" effort. The concept or strategy of *loss mitigation*—minimizing financial loss to investor/lender, borrower, and servicer—dominates most collection efforts today. Foreclosure remains the last option desired by all parties involved, so servicers and lenders will try to employ any of several other options first.

Loss mitigation options available to mortgage lenders for handling delinquencies include the following:

- Payment relief:
  - Accepting partial payments
  - Providing temporary indulgence
  - Collecting just a portion of the past-due amount immediately

- Making a second mortgage to bring the loan current:
- Modifying the existing loan terms:
  - Extending the term
  - Lowering the rate and/or payment
  - Re-advancing principal to the original amount
  - Federally-sponsored modification programs
- Forebearance:
  - Deed-in-lieu
  - Cash for keys
  - Short sale
  - Looking to other solutions tailored to the needs of both parties that will rectify the problem: lender- or federally-sponsored modification or refinance programs

The servicer/lender may need investor approval of one of these options if the loan has been sold. Since all parties lose in the event of foreclosure, the secondary market has become more open to avoiding this and exploring the previously listed options. To help manage severe delinquency, servicers today will use third-party vendors in loss mitigation and property preservation.

The federal government has stepped in and provided default directives—as have state and local governments. In 2009, the Making Home Affordable plan was announced to provide relief to homeowners with difficulties making mortgage payments. The plan included several programs with different objectives and restrictions:

- Home Affordable Modification Program (HAMP) and Second Lien Modification Program (2MP)

  - allows borrowers to modify the interest rate on their existing mortgage if they meet certain income, asset, and LTV guidelines

- Home Affordable Refinance Program

  - allows borrowers with existing Fannie Mae or Freddie Mac mortgages to refinance into more affordable monthly payments

- Home Affordable Foreclosure Alternatives Program

  - allows borrowers to utilize short sales or deed-in-lieu options to avoid foreclosure.

Sadly, these formal federal programs have been very disappointing. Few borrowers able to qualify because of the program guidelines and servicers have been very slow to implement and support them. However, investors, and particularly the GSEs, have demanded increased efforts, placing immense pressure on mortgage servicers. Default management no longer is a passive role where the servicer mails some notices and automatically sends the loan file to the foreclosure attorney. Servicers, working in concert with investors and lenders, develop complex strategies for each of the above loss mitigation techniques as shown in Table 16.2.

TABLE **16.2**
GSE Loss Mitigation Actions, 2008–2010

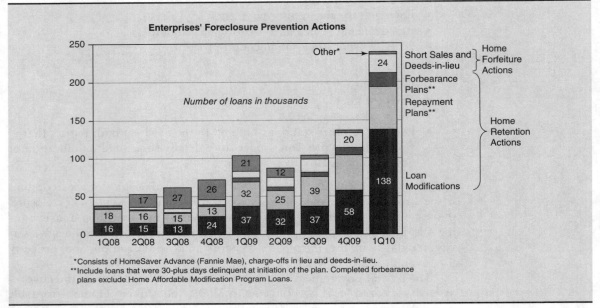

*Consists of HomeSaver Advance (Fannie Mae), charge-offs in lieu and deeds-in-lieu.
**Include loans that were 30-plus days delinquent at initiation of the plan. Completed forbearance plans exclude Home Affordable Modification Program Loans.

Source: Federal Housing Finance Agency

PORTFOLIO MANAGEMENT AND LOAN ADMINISTRATION

The following sections describe loan servicing and portfolio management for lenders.

Evolution of Loan Servicing

Historically, the servicing department was considered a cost center for a depository lender. Performing these functions was a necessary expense to get back the lender's money from the borrowers. More progressive depository lenders realized that servicing provides an opportunity to strengthen their customer relationship, and they implemented strategies to capitalize on that, but servicing was still accepted as an operational cost.

An even more sophisticated view of mortgage servicing developed with the expansion of the secondary market. Both investors and GSEs realize the crucial role a properly run servicing department plays in maintaining the marketability and value of the MBS and their underlying loans. Reliable and regular collection and transfer of money from borrower to investor is the basic foundation on which the secondary market rests. GSEs led the way in establishing servicing standards and developing quicker, more efficient methods of funds transfer from servicer to investor.

Since the GSEs and many investors who purchase loans do not want the responsibility of servicing them, they pay others a servicing fee to do it. The GSEs require that investors pay a servicer a minimum of 25 basis points

(0.25 percent) of the outstanding loan balances, which the servicer retains each month before forwarding the payments collected to the investor. This represents substantial servicing income for a large servicing portfolio, enabling the servicing function to transition from a cost center to a profit center if the servicer can manage expenses.

As discussed in Chapter 5—Secondary Mortgage Markets, the mega-servicing strategy developed over time. In the 1980s, the technology was not available to manage large portfolios; however, as computer capacity grew and software programs handled more functions, servicing portfolios grew 10-fold in size during the 1990s. In the early 2000s, the largest single servicing portfolio was almost $500 billion, with four million mortgage loans. The 10 largest servicers (Table 16.3) handled almost 60 percent of all mortgages serviced in the United States—double the percentage that the largest 10 handled in 1995.

Today, the largest single servicing portfolio is more than $2.1 trillion, with almost 14 million mortgage loans! Equally staggering, the 10 largest servicers handle more than 80 percent of all mortgages serviced in the United States, triple the percentage of the largest 10 handled in 1995. The top 20 servicers now handle 90 percent of all outstanding mortgage debt.

Improved computer and software technology enabled this dramatic increase in market share concentration, but the underlying explanation is a change in loan administration business strategy adopted by larger firms—both financial institutions and private mortgage companies. These firms want to service as many loans as possible to maximize their operational efficiency. Proper use of this technology lowers the cost per loan serviced. This strategy and the activities of just 20 companies have a dominating effect on the entire mortgage industry.

Mortgage Servicing Abuses

As mentioned early in this chapter, the result of mass consolidation also has negative effects on the industry and millions of borrowers. Mega-servicers set up for operational efficiencies often cannot handle the periodic rush of customer inquiries, such as

- requests for payoffs or loan terms when rates decline

- explanations of escrow analyses when tax payments change

- requests for loan modifications during difficult economic periods

Abuses in how larger servicers handled escrow account funds (i.e., keeping high reserves to increase float income) resulted in extensive regulatory changes in RESPA for aggregate accounting and annual analysis of the escrowed funds. Recently, Congressional committees and administration agencies publically criticized servicers for very slow implementation of the several federal modification and refinance programs designed to assist homeowners under the Making Home Affordable plan.

When a large servicer makes a mistake, often thousands, even millions of borrowers are affected. For example, several large servicers allegedly mishandled the foreclosure process for their delinquent borrowers via "robo-signing"—automated signing of foreclosure documents. For just one servicer, this meant over 50,000 foreclosure actions in 23 states were halted. Several states attorney offices, federal regulators, and a Congressional committee have initiated investigations into the practices of the large servicers. The Consumer Financial Protection Bureau, state attorney generals, and large mortgage servicers (most of whom received TARP fund via their bank parent) negotiated a controversial proposed settlement for the numerous lawsuits involved in this practice.

In addition, in April, 2011 the Federal Reserve issued formal enforcement actions against ten of the nation's largest mortgage servicers and two industry vendors, alleging a pattern of misconduct and negligence in servicing and foreclosure practices. Collectively, these servicers handle over $6.8 trillion in mortgage loans.

The result of these management errors and abuses impact borrowers in almost every state in the country and brought on additional regulatory changes. The 2008 revisions to RESPA and Truth in Lending and Title XIV of the 2010 Dodd-Frank Act include rules and proposals governing servicing practices for:

- valid customer requests and inquiries
- timely action to resolve errors and to prevent foreclosure
- prepayment penalty restrictions
- payment processing and posting
- irregular payments
- late fees
- valid servicing charges
- collection activities
- payoff requests

Going forward, the new Bureau of Consumer Financial Protection will be writing more rules governing the behavior of servicers and conducting studies of default and foreclosure activities. For a list of the largest residential mortgage services in the United States, please review Table 16.3.

FASB Rules

In addition to the role of technology, several major accounting changes have shaped today's mortgage-servicing industry. Because of these Financial Accounting Standards Board (FASB) rulings, many servicers calculate the value of their portfolios differently than before. This process began with the adoption of FAS 65 in 1982, followed with FAS 122 in 1995, FAS 125 in 1996, FAS 133 in 1998, and finally, FAS 157 in 2007 (see http://www.fasb.org).

Each accounting change fundamentally impacted the profitability and financial structure of all mortgage servicers. They impact the manner in which a servicer values its portfolio, how it categorizes the loan for sale or to be held in portfolio, and how it can offset the interest rate and value risk present as a result of these changes. The value of a servicing portfolio is no longer "fixed" (based on what it cost a lender to obtain it). Instead, the value changes with market interest rates, as well as the market's perception of borrower and economic behavior. And a servicer must decide at origination if it intends to keep the loan or sell it.

For example, the exact same portfolio would be valued higher if interest rates rose overnight from 5.0 percent to 5.5 percent. Why? Fewer loans refinance when rates rise, so the loans in this portfolio will generate servicing income for a longer period of time than if rates fell (or remained unchanged).

TABLE **16.3**
Largest Residential Mortgage Servicers, 2010–2001–1993 ($ in millions)

Company Name	Location	2010Q2 Total Volume (dollar)	2010Q2 Total Number of Loans Serviced (number)
Bank of America	NC	$2,197,662	14,204,957
Wells Fargo & Company	CA	$1,811,969	12,004,659
Chase	NJ	$1,353,566	9,434,133
CitiMortgage, Inc.	MO	$677,815	4,859,304
Ally Bank/Residential Capital, LLC (GMAC)	MN	$398,355	2,618,872
U.S. Bank Home Mortgage	MN	$199,575	1,338,154
SunTrust Bank	VA	$175,970	994,025
PHH Mortgage	NJ	$155,967	968,669
PNC Mortgage/National City	OH	$149,945	989,228
OneWest Bank/IndyMac	CA	$110,000	517,504
	Totals	$7,230,824	47,929,505
	Ave. Loan Amount		$150,863.73

Source: mortgagestats.com

	2001 Total Volume (dollar)
Washington Mutual	$497
Wells Fargo Mortgage	$488
Chase Manhattan Mortgage	$430
Countrywide	$337
Bank of America	$321

Source: National Mortgage News

	1993 Total Volume (dollar)
Countrywide	$80
Fleet Mortgage	$70
Prudential Home Mortgage	$68
General Electric Capital	$64
Citibank	$47

Source: American Banker

Since the servicer will receive more income in this interest rate environment, the value of this portfolio increases. In this way, the day-to-day value of the servicing portfolio is more volatile and subject to factors beyond the servicer's control. This offers the potential for significant economic gains when rates rise, although the gains may not be reflected on the company's financial statements. Price volatility also means increased risk from potential losses when rates drop (which ordinarily *are* reflected on the company's financial statements). In any event, the result of these related FASB rulings is a strategic change in how servicers manage their portfolios.

Servicing Strategies

Today, medium to large servicers view their servicing portfolios much like a stockbroker views a stock portfolio. Some servicers buy and trade parts of their larger portfolio in different economic climates. Others specialize in certain types of loans to service, similar to stockbrokers who trade and specialize in certain stocks. This active management of the servicing portfolio led to the development and more common use of the term *loan administration*. Since servicing is an asset that can provide income to an organization that specializes in this business, a lender must answer the following question: who will service the loan?

As discussed in Chapter 5—Secondary Mortgage Market, several options exist for mortgage loan originators. There is an active market for buyers and sellers of servicing, and for subservicers; conventional, government, and non-conventional loans; for fixed vs. ARM programs; for conforming and non-conforming and subprime loans; for performing and non-performing loans. The point is the valuing and selling of mortgage servicing—either as a *servicing-released premium (SRP)* or the price to acquire MSRs for a pool of seasoned loans—have grown to where these aspects of mortgage lending are more significant sources of income than the original sale of the loan.

Servicing: The Reason Some Lenders Are in Residential Lending

For some mortgage lenders, such as mortgage bankers, servicing profits are the primary reason for engaging in mortgage lending. Other mortgage lenders, who were almost exclusively portfolio lenders in the past (such as thrifts or credit unions), now sell a major portion of their originations and place a greater emphasis on loan administration. This shift in emphasis adds to the concentration of the servicing we see today, as larger organizations attempt to maximize operational efficiencies.

Servicing also plays a major role in the recent emergence of the so-called non-traditional mortgage lenders. Many of these players, such as General Motors Acceptance Corporation (GMAC), enter the residential mortgage-lending competition by buying large servicing portfolios. These large servicing portfolios give new entrants immediate economies of scale and thus enhance profit potential. GMAC bought two servicing portfolios totaling nearly $19 billion. Overnight, GMAC became one of the largest servicers of mortgage debt in the world.

Servicing Income

As stated previously, originating lenders earn a fee from the investor/servicer to whom they sell servicing. This fee, called a servicing release fee or premium, recognizes the value of that servicing operation. The servicing release premium provides practically all of the mortgage originator's revenue. Additional sources of income may include interest rate spread, origination fees, possible warehousing and marketing profits, late charges, and escrow float.

Collection of monthly mortgage payments generates the servicing income that a servicer retains. The servicing fee is earned only when the payment is collected, and it is based on the agreed-upon percentage of loan principal outstanding. After receiving the monthly payment of principal and interest, a servicer forwards that amount less the servicing fee to the investor. Today, the servicing fee ranges from 0.25 percent to 0.50 percent of the outstanding balance of the loan. The amount varies depending on volume of loans serviced and also by the type of mortgage (e.g., typically, ARMs pay 35 basis points, and GNMAs 44 basis points). The average for all residential mortgage loans today is probably closer to 25 basis points.

In the current mortgage market, many mortgage lenders are unable to generate a profit from the origination function. These mortgage lenders must look to servicing income to offset origination losses, and sometimes marketing losses, to produce a net profit from mortgage lending. With mortgage delinquency at a record level, servicing profitability is equally difficult to achieve.

Servicing Profitability

In the early 1980s, a period of such high inflation caused the wisdom of servicing profitability to come into serious question. Servicing expense was expected to increase each year with overall inflation, while the servicing income from a mortgage loan was expected to decrease each year over the life of the loan (as the loan balance amortizes). Two fundamental factors prevented this scenario:

1. Costs remained stable, as the overall level of interest rates and inflation declined to then-record lows.
2. Operational efficiency increased, as dramatic improvements in technology enabled larger servicing portfolios with existing resources.

The overall result was more net income per loan.

A Profitability Squeeze with Each Refinancing Wave

Unfortunately, in the 1990s the sustained decline in the overall level of interest rates presented an entirely different challenge to the profitability of mortgage servicing. With each significant decline in mortgage interest rates, wary consumers (still reeling from 18 percent fixed rate loans in the late 1980s) felt, "This was it!"—the bottom of the interest rate trough. Other consumers simply realized that the rate was low enough to recoup the expense of refinancing quickly. The combination was literally termed a "refinance wave" by industry professionals, as a record number of borrowers refinanced at the same time.

The effect was devastating to many servicers, who saw their portfolios evaporate in just a few months. So many borrowers refinanced during these waves that lenders were unable to service the old loans long enough to make a profit on servicing. Regrettably, from the servicers' viewpoint, many mortgagors refinanced their mortgage with another lender; thus, the servicing was lost to the other lender. For those lenders that counted on the servicing income to offset initial and ongoing lending expenses, the impact of the lost servicing income was painful—and even more severe for those servicers who purchased servicing rights from other lenders. These servicers not only didn't make a profit on the servicing they purchased, they did not recoup their purchase price. As a result of these losses, several medium to large servicers went out of business.

Despite these challenges, many mortgage servicers earn record profits. As with most lines of business, profitability depends more on how well a servicer executes its plan, rather than the plan itself. The annual *Cost of Servicing Study* by the Mortgage Bankers Association of America (http://mbaa.org) analyzes a variety of servicing organizations and several important areas that impact mortgage servicing: the cost of servicing and the characteristics of profitable and unprofitable servicers. Lenders and servicers eagerly await the results to find out what the average per loan servicing cost is and what organizations and strategies were successful in the previous year.

Industry pundits assume that the largest servicers are always the most profitable, but the study shows how significant profitability in recent years depends in large part on the economic activity and interest rate behavior for that time period. Refinance waves affect profitability by not allowing acquirers of servicing enough time to recoup their acquisition costs, as discussed earlier.

A surprising result that emerged during the 1990s was the success of "niche" servicers—organizations that specialize in a particular loan product or type. Studies show that those that do well in their specialty are very profitable, regardless of size. Some examples of niche servicers include FHA/VA loans, subprime or B and C credit loans, adjustable-rate loans, jumbo loans, and construction/permanent loans. Although these servicers are not the lowest-cost providers, they offset their additional expense either by earning a higher servicing fee or by successfully generating income from other areas.

The trend for many borrowers to jump on the "refinance wave" continued past the turn of the century, with the same impact as established in the 1980s. Rates dropped 1/2 percent or more, refinance activity surged, and shortly thereafter, several servicers posted significant losses and merged or went out of business. Because of massive prepayments, some servicers are unable to recoup the price paid for the MSR for these loans.

Other Income

A servicing company benefits from float income. Float exists as a result of the unequal timing between loan payment collections and remittance of those payments to the investors. The float depends on the date a mortgage servicer receives payment and when it is required to remit to the investor. The float period can last up to four or six weeks and it can involve millions of dollars. Other remittance plans, such as Fannie Mae's actual/actual option, require remittance whenever the servicer has collected $2,500, which shortens float time tremendously.

Often overlooked by institutions just beginning servicing is the importance of other fee income generated by the loan administration department. These fees include the following, among others:

- Late charges
- Processing an assumption or novation

- Preparation of discharge and release
- Reinstatement after default (if different from late fees)
- Substitution of hazard insurance policies other than on the renewal or annual premium rate
- Insurance commissions from accident, health, mortgagor life, and other casualty policies
- Prepayment penalty fees
- Bad check fees and other miscellaneous fees

Escrow Administration

Another important source of servicing income is derived from the value of funds held in escrow for the payment of real estate taxes, hazard insurance, or other insurance. (In certain parts of the country, these monthly payments are called impounds.) Many lenders require that mortgagors escrow one-twelfth of the annual real estate taxes and hazard insurance each month, while paying their mortgage principal and interest. The secondary mortgage market requires escrows when a mortgage has a loan-to-value ratio greater than 80 percent. Federal regulations require escrows for certain high-cost and HOEPA mortgages as well.

Requiring a tax or insurance escrow assures the lender that no loss will occur. If property damage occurs on the real estate securing the loan and the insurance premium is not paid, the lender could suffer a loss because its security, the real estate, was not insured and now is in need of repair. If real estate taxes are not paid, the local government may have a superior claim in the real estate that is securing the mortgage debt. It can eventually sell the real estate for the back taxes. Some lenders will advance funds to pay real estate taxes to avoid this situation, recovering the amount at the next escrow analysis or by adding that amount to the principal.

Use of Escrow Funds

Escrows as shown in Figure 16.3, can serve, if needed by the servicer, as the compensating balance required for a line of credit from a commercial bank. These funds "secure" the line of credit and keep the interest rate on that line lower than it would be without the compensating balances.

As mentioned earlier, mortgage servicers benefit from the float period on these funds because they are collected monthly but are only disbursed semiannually or annually. Servicers can invest these funds during the interim, which can be a meaningful source of low-or no-cost funds.

During the 1980s, many states passed laws requiring lenders to pay interest on escrows. The federal government has also considered whether a federal law is needed that would require all lenders to pay interest on escrowed funds. The amount of interest that must be paid varies from state to state. Currently, in the thirteen states requiring interest on escrow, the minimum rates generally require passbook-equivalent rates (between two percent and four percent per annum). Even when lenders must pay interest on escrow, these funds are still low-cost funds and enhance profitability.

FIGURE **16.3** Sample Initial Escrow Account Disclosure Statement

INITIAL ESCROW ACCOUNT DISCLOSURE STATEMENT   Date:

BORROWER(S) NAME AND ADDRESS	LENDER / SERVICER NAME AND ADDRESS
NICKIE C. GREEN 1144 REEF ROAD FAIRFIELD, CT 06824	THE McCUE MORTGAGE COMPANY ONE LIBERTY SQUARE NEW BRITAIN, CT 06050

LOAN NO. 00125224	TOLL FREE NO. MORTGAGE INSURANCE / CASE NUMBER

[ ] Your   [ ] monthly   [ ] biweekly   mortgage payment for the coming year will be $ _____ of which $ _____ will be for **principal and interest** $ _____ will go into your escrow account, and $ _____ will be for discretionary items (such as life insurance, disability insurance) that you chose to be included with your monthly payment.

[X] Your first   [X] monthly   [ ] biweekly   mortgage payment for the coming year will be $ **1,328.61** of which **$833.61** will be for **principal and interest** $**495.00** will go into your escrow account, and $ _____ will be for discretionary items (such as life insurance, disability insurance) that you chose to be included with your monthly payment. The terms of your loan may result in changes to the principal and interest payments during the year.

This is an estimate of activity in your escrow account during the coming year based on payments anticipated to be made from your account.

MONTH/ PAYMENT NO.	PAYMENTS TO ESCROW ACCT.	PAYMENTS FROM ESCROW ACCT.	DESCRIPTION	ESCROW ACCT. BALANCE
Starting balance:				$ 495.00
05/01/2011	495.00			990.00
06/01/2011	495.00			1,485.00
07/01/2011	495.00	1,335.00	Prop tax(1335.00)	645.00
08/01/2011	495.00			1,140.00
09/01/2011	495.00			1,635.00
10/01/2011	495.00	1,335.00	Prop tax(1335.00)	795.00
11/01/2011	495.00			1,290.00
12/01/2011	495.00			1,785.00
01/01/2012	495.00	1,335.00	Prop tax(1335.00)	945.00
02/01/2012	495.00			1,440.00
03/01/2012	495.00	600.00	Hom Ins(600.00)	1,335.00
04/01/2012	495.00	1,335.00	Prop tax(1335.00)	495.00

(Please keep this statement for comparison with the actual activity in your account at the end of the escrow accounting computation year.)

Cushion selected by servicer: $**495.00**

By signing below, borrower acknowledges receipt of this Initial Escrow Account Disclosure Statement.

Borrower **NICKIE C. GREEN**	Date	Borrower	Date

Borrower	Date	Borrower	Date

© 1993 Harland Financial Solutions, Inc.
ITEM 7197L0 (0609)

GreatDocs™
(Page 1 of 1)

MFCD2733

00125224

Source: Reprinted with permission of The McCue Mortgage Co.

A few lenders, usually thrifts and credit unions, decide not to escrow funds for taxes and insurance because they do not believe that they benefit enough from these funds after factoring in the administration costs of collecting and disbursing the funds. Normally this occurs when the servicing volume is low and the cost of additional personnel outweighs the investment income that would be earned.

When viewed from the mortgagors' side, many prefer the convenience of budgeting these expenses on a monthly basis. The additional income received from the interest paid on escrows is a benefit, but generally is not very important, especially because mortgagors must pay income taxes on the interest paid on escrows.

Limits on Escrows

Many lenders believe that escrows help lower the number of delinquencies and foreclosures. Most consumers recognize that an escrow account helps them to budget their insurance and tax payments. In the past, some lenders abused the purpose of escrowing funds to profit on the float. They required much more money in the escrow account than was needed.

RESPA changes in the 1990s required that servicers analyze the escrow payment amounts annually, and limit the payment amount to sufficient funds to pay the next annual installment plus a two-month cushion. Further, RESPA requires servicers to send an analysis of the escrows collected over the past year to mortgagors within 30 days of the conclusion of each escrow account year. The servicer must also make payments for taxes and insurance from the escrow account in a timely manner.

Cost of Servicing

For several years it was generally assumed that in today's market a mortgage lender must service about $50 million of secondary market loans to generate net servicing income (approximately 400 loans with an average size of $150,000). This threshold is down from the $100 million level of the late 1980s, due to better operational efficiency from technology and increase in per-loan income from a higher average loan size. This "break-even point" certainly varies for different lenders and regions. But as a general rule, it still appears to be a sound assumption based upon the annual *Cost of Servicing Study* produced by the Mortgage Bankers Association of America.

As the servicing portfolio of a mortgage lender increases, economies of scale develop. One measurement of efficiency is the number of loans per full-time employee. Better technology helps increase how many accounts each servicing employee can handle, all other things being equal. Personnel expenses represent the highest servicing cost, so reducing this cost for a given servicing portfolio will lower costs quickly (i.e., three employees versus five for a $50 million servicing portfolio; 45 employees versus 50 for the identical portfolio, etc.). Servicing productivity reflects improved technology overall, but "dips" in years 2002 reflect adverse market conditions—a large refinance period—and "peaks" reflect favorable market conditions—active purchase markets and loan growth. See Table 16.4.

A common measure used to determine profitability for a servicing department is the average cost per loan per year. Basically, this measure takes all the

TABLE **16.4**
Mortgage Servicing Productivity

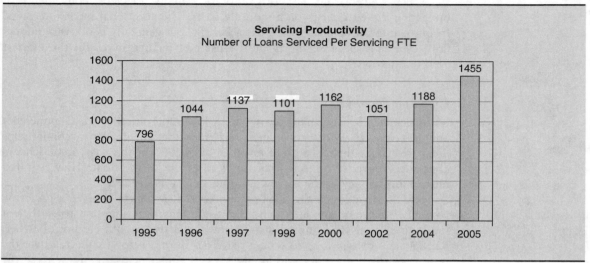

Source: MBA's Cost of Servicing Studies

servicing department expenses and divides it by the number of loans. For example:

Cost of Servicing—Expenses

Expenses	Dollars Per Loan
Total Personnel Expense	35.38
Occupancy & Depreciation	4.80
EDP & Depreciation	8.07
Communication, Delivery, Stationary & Supplies	9.45
Foreclosure & REO Expenses	6.77
Custodial & Safekeeping	2.21
Advertising, Prof. Fees, Travel, Seminars & Dues	2.30
Lockbox	.93
Outsourcing Expenses	2.12
Other	5.62
Total Direct Expenses	77.55

Source: MBA Cost of Servicing Study

The average annual cost can drop to approximately $100 per loan when the portfolio reaches $1 billion (or about 10,000 loans), and may get as low as $50 when the portfolio reaches $2 billion or $3 billion. The largest servicers of residential debt exceed those levels by a factor of five hundred to two thousand.

Since the mortgage crisis, servicing costs have increased significantly. Increasing regulatory burdens from federal, state, and local governments translate into ongoing compliance costs and additional training. High loan delinquency means higher collection costs and added staffing. Increased loss mitigation efforts and modifications also increase costs to service the same loan.

Purchasing Servicing

At certain points in the economic cycle and when a mega-servicer reaches a certain size, it becomes cheaper to grow the servicing portfolio by purchasing servicing than by increasing retail originations. Mortgage servicers buy servicing from other lenders, other originators, or other servicers. The price paid for servicing varies, but can range from less than 50 basis points to 250 basis points of the loan amount serviced. Thus, if one servicer desires to purchase $100 million of servicing from another, the price, depending on the market, could be in the $500,000 to $2.5 million range.

A servicing portfolio price is calculated by the projected cash flow generated by the portfolio. For example, all other aspects being equal, a servicer would pay less for a cash flow generated by a 25-basis-point servicing fee than one generated by a 37.5-basis-point fee. However, the big question is: how long will the loans at the higher servicing fee remain outstanding (which generates income) versus the loans at the lower fee? The duration of the servicing fee income is an important consideration in determining overall price. Finally, the purchasing servicer must determine if these loans are more expensive to service than others (i.e., ARM loans versus 30-year fixed-rate as shown in Figure 16.4) and adjust its offering price accordingly.

In summary, the purchasing servicer reviews many of the following items to determine the price of a servicing portfolio:

- Average loan balance
- Weighted-average servicing fee
- Weighted-average remaining maturity
- Weighted-average coupon rate
- Type of loan
- Fixed rate
- Adjustable rate
- Biweekly
- Average escrow amounts
- Interest to be paid on reserves
- Delinquency and foreclosure experience
- Geographic makeup of the loans
- Investors (determines float)
- Assumption and prepayment provisions
- Remaining life expectations of the loans
- Ancillary income and other miscellaneous items

FIGURE **16.4** Mortgage Servicing Values—Sample Servicing Released Premiums—November, 2010

COMPARISON BY LENDER

All loans: Loan Amount $300,000; NY State; 720 FICO minimum; LTV 80%; Full Doc

	Conv 30 yr	Conv 15 yr	Govt 30 yr	5/1 ARM
Lender 1	1.617	1.451	2.909	1.436
Lender 2	1.796	1.693	1.670	1.040
Lender 3	1.600	1.410	2.330	
Lender 4	0.984	0.695	1.528	0.326
Lender 5	2.130	1.770	2.550	0.033

COMPARISION BY LOCATION

Lender 5	Loan Amount	
	Low	High
AZ	0.900	1.450
CA	0.800	1.350
FL	1.250	1.800
MA	0.800	1.350
MD	1.100	1.650
NV	1.000	1.550
NY	1.150	1.700

Source: Level 1 Loans

©2011 Community Lending Associates, LLC www.communitylendassoc.com

Selling Servicing

When a mortgage lender sells servicing, the selling servicer—called the transferor—must (according to RESPA) provide the mortgagor with at least 15 days before the effective date of the transfer of a Notice of Assignment, Sale, or Transfer of Servicing Rights. This notice from the transferor (sometimes called a "goodbye letter") informs the mortgagor of the effective date of the transfer, provides a toll-free or collect phone number of the transferee, and provides the name of someone at the transferor's place of business who can answer questions. The purchasing servicer—called the transferee—must send a similar notice (a "hello letter") to the mortgagor within 15 days of the transfer. This notice states that no late fee will be charged for 60 days after the servicing is transferred if the borrower sends the payment to the wrong servicer. Also, at application the applicants receive a Servicing Disclosure that explains the lender's servicing transfer practices and may include its actual transfer history over the past three years.

Before it purchases a servicing portfolio, the lender/servicer should first establish its own cost of servicing. Additionally, the purchasing servicer will incur one-time expenses such as: data conversion, due diligence, file transfers, and assignments.

ALTERNATIVES TO SERVICING RESIDENTIAL MORTGAGE LOANS

For various reasons, many residential mortgage lenders decide not to service the loans they originate. Often it is an issue of whether a lender can service profitably; others realize they simply don't have the talent to do servicing well. These mortgage lenders can either sell the mortgage loans servicing released or enter into a subservicing arrangement.

Servicing Released

As has been mentioned, lenders have the option to sell a mortgage loan and either keep or sell the servicing (selling servicing-retained or servicing-released). The buyer acquires the servicing rights by purchasing a mortgage loan or loans for a premium, and then selling (normally, but not always) the mortgage loans into the secondary mortgage market, while retaining the servicing. The amount of servicing released premium paid to originating lenders depends on a number of factors including the volume of mortgages sold, where interest rates are, prepayment assumptions, and so forth. For example, if one lender can sell $5 million of mortgages per month, the acquiring lender may pay as much as 100 basis points as a premium for the servicing. The acquiring lender/servicer is simply buying the right to the future stream of income associated with servicing that loan for a number of years. If the loan prepays early, the servicer loses. This situation is exactly what happened to many purchasers of servicing in the early 1990s and 2000s as refinance waves lowered the average life of loan.

Subservicing

In order to make residential mortgage lending profitable as soon as possible, some new mortgage lenders, such as credit unions, opt not to establish a servicing department. Others lenders may have established servicing areas, but want to add a specialized loan program like FHA or VA. Either way the lender may not have sufficient volume to perform the function profitably or don't have a staff that is qualified. Other mortgage lenders do not want to sell loans servicing released (as described earlier) because they do not want another financial institution in contact with their customers. The solution for these mortgage lenders is to contract with another mortgage lender or servicing company to conduct all of the servicing responsibilities for them.

These lenders pay the subservicer a servicing fee (usually between $80 and $125 per loan per year) based on the total number of loans serviced. The originating lender is still responsible to ensure that the loans are serviced properly, but by using another qualified servicer, the originating lender can have the servicing function performed profitably. For example, if one of these lenders sells a $100,000 mortgage to Fannie Mae and receives a 25-basis-point servicing fee ($250 a year), it can contract with a subservicer to service the loan for, say, $125. The difference between the two fees is profit to the originating lender. Many of these originating lenders will put into the servicing contract with the subservicer the right to pull servicing when sufficient volume is reached to make the function profitable.

Subservicers have the ability to provide a "private label" arrangement. In this situation the subservicer acts as if it were a department for the lender, answering the phone in the lender's name, using its letterhead for statements and correspondence, etc. Private label servicing maintains the presence of the lender throughout the life of the loan.

DISCUSSION POINTS

1. Discuss the difference between mortgage loan servicing and mortgage loan administration and how this difference impacts the lender.
2. Explain the benefits and drawbacks to a unit versus functional form of organization for a loan servicing/administration department.
3. What are the various mortgage-servicing strategies implemented by lenders?
4. List and explain mortgage-servicing functions and responsibilities.
5. How do refinance waves affect servicing departments (and lenders)?
6. How does a lender determine its cost of servicing, and why is this important?
7. How are servicing fees calculated? When does a servicer earn these fees?
8. Explain the differences between servicing retained, servicing released, and subservicing.

CHAPTER 17

Selling Residential Mortgage Loans

INTRODUCTION

This chapter focuses on the practice of selling mortgage loans and not the broader industry issues discussed in Chapter 5—Secondary Mortgage Market. Here we describe the following functions, skills, and process involved in selling residential mortgage loans, often handled by the secondary marketing department at larger lenders:

- Loan sale options and secondary market math
- Loan sale strategies
- Investor approval and commitments
- Loan delivery—preparing, shipping, and funding
- Mortgage pipeline management

Also, in this chapter the term *"mortgage lenders"* includes those mortgage bankers who may keep loans in portfolio for a while, funding them with a line of credit, as well as all financial institutions that fund loans with deposits (or borrowing). Finally, Chapter 16—Loan Servicing and Administration—discusses the "other" asset created upon sale of a mortgage—the *mortgage servicing right*.

Today, the vast majority of all classifications of mortgage lenders sell some or all of their current loan production. Secondary mortgage market growth over the past 30 years bears witness to that importance, with annual secondary market transactions exceeding $1 trillion per year, since 2000—over $2 trillion at its peak in 2003—before fraud, delinquency, inadequate quality control, and MBS-rating issues shook investor confidence and caused the entire system to unravel.

Today, obtaining commitments and funding mortgage loans quickly and accurately are crucial to profitability, risk management, and market share for most lenders. From the 1980s to the present, advances in technology, communications, and security have eliminated most of the logistical issues of selling one or many loans. What was once performed manually is now done electronically. The speed and capacity of transferring commitments, documents, pricing, funding, etc., has increased dramatically and arguably outstripped the ability to manage them effectively. Currently, the main issues in selling loans successfully involve pricing, production, and quality: correctly implementing complex risk-based pricing matrices, successfully fulfilling loan commitments, and avoiding post-closing pricing adjustments or buybacks.

Since 2007, the variety of loan product sold has declined, as has the number of investors to which a lender can sell loans. Lenders now need to manage the growing risk that an investor cannot fund a loan without interruption or reliably support the loan programs it offers.

LOAN SALE OPTIONS

When Is A Mortgage Loan Sold?

Technically, the actual sale of a mortgage loan is completed when a lender closes a loan in its own name, then endorses its note and assigns its mortgage to another entity, delivers all the required documentation to the investor, and then receives investor funding for the loan. Endorsement and assignment may be at, or well after, closing. Funding can be immediate, or take several days to weeks if due diligence uncovers documentation or other issues in perfecting a lien or in following underwriting guidelines.

Prior to completing all the above, all participants involved in this process are really dealing with different kinds of commitments (described later in this chapter), not an actual sale. So in a strict sense, a loan is not "sold" until the investor finally wires funds to the seller, but one can see that funding occurs only after the seller completes the many steps involved in the process. Figures 17.1 and 17.2 compare portfolio vs. secondary market transactions.

FIGURE **17.1** Mortgage Application Lifecycle—Portfolio Loan

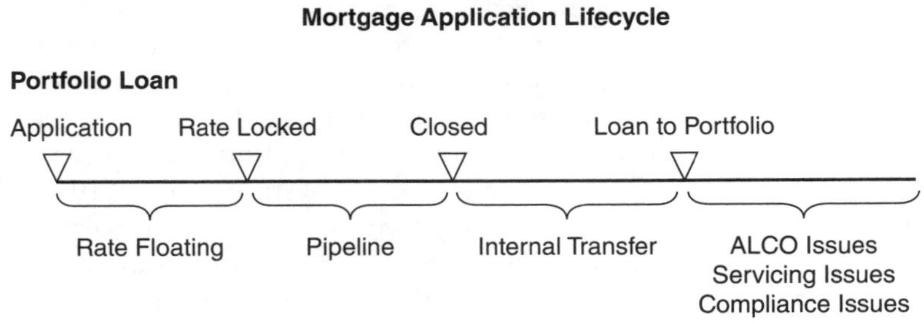

Mortgage Application Lifecycle

Portfolio Loan

| Application | Rate Locked | Closed | Loan to Portfolio |

Rate Floating   Pipeline   Internal Transfer   ALCO Issues / Servicing Issues / Compliance Issues

Source: Reprinted with permission of Peter Taglia, FTN Financial ©2010 Community Lending Associates, LLC www.communitylendassoc.com

FIGURE **17.2** Mortgage Application Lifecycle—Secondary Market Loan

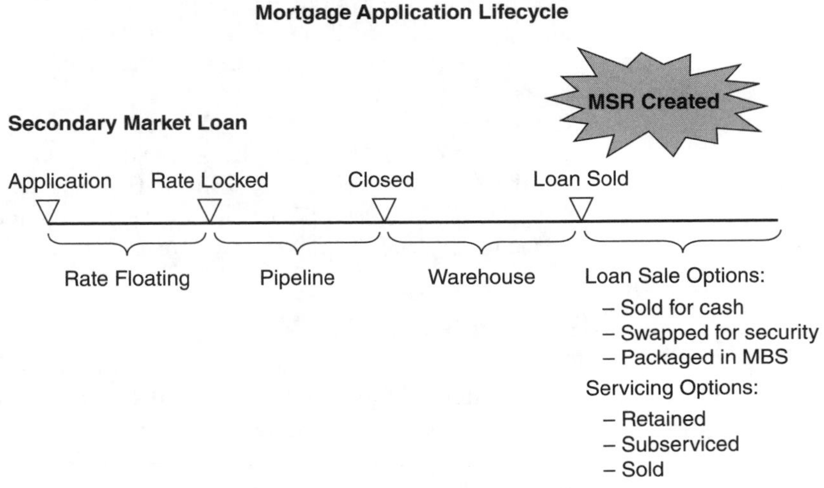

Mortgage Application Lifecycle

MSR Created

Secondary Market Loan

| Application | Rate Locked | Closed | Loan Sold |

Rate Floating   Pipeline   Warehouse   Loan Sale Options:
- Sold for cash
- Swapped for security
- Packaged in MBS

Servicing Options:
- Retained
- Subserviced
- Sold

Source: Reprinted with permission of Peter Taglia, FTN Financial ©2010 Community Lending Associates, LLC www.communitylendassoc.com

Flow Basis or Pooling

When a mortgage lender originates an application and takes steps to sell it at loan closing, it is selling loans on a *flow basis*. This method of loan sale involves one sale to (and one commitment with) an investor for each loan sold. It may not involve every loan that the lender originates and closes.

When a lender originates several applications and takes steps to sell them together at the same time to one investor (under one commitment), the lender sells its loan on a *pool basis*. Again, this may not involve every loan the lender originates and closes.

Whole Loans or Participations

Secondary market investors can purchase a *whole loan* or a *participation interest* in a pool of mortgages. A whole loan sale is the sale of a 100 percent interest in a loan or group of loans (a pool). A participation interest sale involves a percentage of ownership—a partial interest in a loan or a pool of loans. Both parties share the risks involved in those loans. The percentage is negotiated between investor and mortgage lender in five percent increments between 50 and 95 percent. The most common transaction is the sale of a 90 percent interest in a pool of mortgages to an investor, with the mortgage lender retaining a 10 percent interest.

Many lenders and investors favor participation sales because the actual sale requires only two documents—the participation agreement and the participation certificate—but in these transactions the mortgage lender never completely clears these assets off its books, and must maintain reserves, monitor balances, default ratios, etc.

 EXAMPLE

> A mortgage lender pools $1 million of interest-only loans, each with a note rate of 10 percent, so the entire pool earns $100,000 interest income annually. ($1,000,000 × 10% = $100,000.)
>
> The lender sells a 90 percent participation interest on these loans to an investor, and negotiates to pay the investor a rate of 9.75 percent. ($900,000 × 9.75% = $87,750.)
>
> The lender's return on the retained 10 percent participation interest will be $12,250 ($100,000 − $87,750 = $12,250), or 12.25 percent ($12,250 / $100,000). From this amount the lender may also have to cover servicing or other administrative costs.

Qualified Residential Mortgage

The Dodd-Frank Act impacts secondary market sales in several ways. Section 1412 creates a "Qualified Residential Mortgage" class of loans with several parameters. Section 941 states that *non-QRM* loans in mortgage-backed securities require that the lender must retain at least five percent of the loan balance on reserve for the life of the loan for credit risk.

Recourse

Unlike a participation arrangement, the whole loan (or pool) is sold, but part or all of the transaction can be reversed under certain conditions. **Recourse** can be defined as the contingent liability a seller has to repurchase the loan (or pool of loans) if the sale breaches one of the representations or warranties the seller made when the loan (or pool) was sold. A mortgage lender has three recourse options when selling a mortgage loan:

- *Full recourse.* Seller must repurchase the loan if loan becomes delinquent for any reason or there is a violation of the loan sale agreement. This arrangement contains great risk for the seller, who could be forced to repurchase many mortgages that defaulted (possibly because of economic events, such as a factory closing) and could put that seller out of business.
- *Normal recourse.* Seller must repurchase after delinquency, but only if seller did not process or underwrite the loan according to the investor's requirements *and* that was the reason for the default. Note that *both* conditions must be present.

- *No recourse*. Seller is not obligated to repurchase any loans (with the exception of fraud), even if delinquent, but gives up yield to the investor (net yield is 10 to 15 basis points higher). Therefore, the seller must decide whether or not to give up yield to avoid a contingent liability to repurchase mortgages.

For example, a seller of a mortgage loan warrants to Fannie Mae that a loan sold was originated according to Fannie Mae's Seller/Servicer Guide. If it is later discovered that the loan was not originated according to the Guide, then the investor (in this example, Fannie Mae) may require the seller to repurchase the loan (normal recourse).

Typically, an investor's quality control review identifies a deficiency and, if severe enough, the investor requires the seller immediately to repurchase the loan. In less severe situations, the investor may inform the seller that the loan is deficient, but may require an immediate repurchase *only if* the loan becomes delinquent *for any reason*. In even less severe situations, there must be a causal connection drawn between the delinquency and breach of warranty in order for the investor to require the seller repurchase the loan.

Most loans sold into the secondary mortgage market are with normal recourse. Although investors don't want to disclose how many loans are forced back on sellers, it has been suggested that the typical percentage of delinquent loans repurchased by sellers is approximately eight to ten percent. This definitely varies by lender and program involved. Some lenders produce higher-quality loans than other lenders, and thus have fewer delinquencies.

The recent increase in mortgage defaults and the subsequent fraud detected saw the repurchase rate soar to approximately 30 percent. In response, proposed legislation includes a requirement that issuers of certain mortgage-backed securities with higher risk features must maintain five percent of the credit risk.

WHICH MORTGAGE LOANS ARE SOLD?

Today, the vast majority of mortgage loans produced by mortgage lenders conform to "standard" secondary market programs and guidelines (sometimes referred to as *conforming loans*) established by Fannie Mae and Freddie Mac, and are run through their Automated Underwriting Systems (AUS). (See Underwriting—Chapter 13.) The term *conforming mortgage* is also used to describe the maximum original principal balance that Fannie Mae or Freddie Mac can purchase.

Approved lenders sell conforming loans to GSEs directly, or to private investors for their portfolios, or aggregate them to sell more efficiently. These loans are sold most frequently, partly because of their established marketability and price stability compared to non-conforming loans (see below).

Non-conforming Mortgages

Simply put, *non-conforming mortgages* are those that do not meet standard (or conforming) guidelines. This can occur in two ways: (1) the application follows standard Fannie or Freddie program parameters, but the property or applicant(s) do not qualify; or (2) the applicant(s), property, documentation, or loan terms differ from standard program parameters to the extent that they are ineligible for purchase by Fannie or Freddie. By definition, Fannie and Freddie cannot purchase these loans; private investors do (See Chapter 5—Secondary Mortgage Markets). Non-conforming mortgage loans include:

- Unusual ARM types
- Low- and no-documentation loans
- High LTV or high debt/income ratios
- So-called subprime loans—Grade B or lower
- Loans secured by unique, seasonal, or in need of repair properties

Mortgage lenders, especially portfolio lenders, understand that originating some non-standard/non-conforming mortgages can assist them in meeting the housing finance needs and goals of their communities. These loans are very important to some borrowers, especially for low-income borrowers or first-time homebuyers. Lenders should limit their portfolio exposure of these mortgages to a level supported by their experience and capital level—or have an investor who will purchase them.

Non-conforming loans are sold in the secondary market, but they are much riskier than conforming product for a few reasons: fewer investors want to purchase them, more volatile pricing, and higher rates of delinquency. As should be obvious, mortgage lenders who keep these loans in portfolio face the possibility of disaster when interest rates move up and they need liquidity quickly, or economic conditions deteriorate significantly. Many portfolio lenders review these applications using Fannie or Freddie AUS described above to see how the credit history and income/asset information compares. This analysis helps them assess the additional risk and value that these loans bring to their portfolios or if they are to be relied upon for sale later.

"Seasoning" Cures All?

In the years with strong investor demand for MBS product, many non-conforming loan issues were "cured" by loan *seasoning*—the strategy of placing the loan in portfolio for at least one year with no delinquency—and sold very easily and very close to a conforming loan price. This approach worked well from the 1980s and into the mid-2000s. But, as events in 2007 and after have shown, now the discounted price for these loans may be so low that a sale may not be a viable option, and both lender and investor may suffer devastating losses.

In all situations, a mortgage lender should require a sound legal foundation (correct security agreement, note, title insurance, etc.). While many other underwriting deficiencies can be overcome by seasoning, a deficiency in legal documentation can still prevent the sale of a loan to any investor.

SECONDARY MARKET MATH

Although automated programs can calculate most financial information needed to sell mortgage loans, secondary market participants must understand the concepts behind pricing and valuation. In general, the concepts involved with selling a mortgage loan are similar to the concepts for bonds: both involve interest income, principal, amortization, and maturity. In order to establish the value of the loan sold (its price), both seller and investor must calculate its yield.

Yield Calculations

Yield is defined as the return on an investment over a specified period of time, usually expressed as a percentage of the original investment amount. Mortgage loans are generally sold based on the yield of the mortgage or loan package to the investor (often called the *net yield*). The establishment of some yields (e.g., yield to maturity) is neither an easy nor exact task. Yield to maturity, for example, is impacted by defaults, foreclosures, and principal prepayments. When investors have a large enough package, they can establish to a degree the impact of these events. Mortgage-backed securities are marketed to investors based on certain assumptions regarding yield to maturity.

Our concern in this chapter is determining *current yield*. Yield is determined by dividing the annualized income by the money invested; for example:

$$\$90,000 \text{ annualized income} \div \$1,000,000 = 9 \text{ percent yield}$$

Put another way, what would an investor pay to receive $90,000 annually when the investor is looking for a nine percent yield?

$$\$90,000 \div 9 \text{ percent} = \$1,000,000$$

If the investor, with the same amount of annual income, wanted a 10 percent yield, the calculation would be as follows:

$$\$90,000 \div 10 \text{ percent} = \$900,000$$

Thus, if an investor paid $900,000 for a $90,000 annualized income, the yield to the investor would be 10 percent.

Net Yield

As a general rule, when yield to an investor is being negotiated, it refers to *a net yield* to that investor (sometimes called *required net yield*). Therefore, if a mortgage lender originates a package of mortgages at nine percent note rate to the consumer and wants to retain 25 basis points servicing, the net yield to an investor would be 8.75 percent.

Put another way, if the net yield requirement for an investor with delivery in 60 days is currently 8.75 percent, the originating lender will want to originate mortgages with an average coupon rate of nine percent. If the investor is charging a commitment fee, the fee must also be subtracted in order to correctly establish the yield for the lender. Yield conversion tables are required to arrive at exact yields, but as a general rule, a one percent commitment fee equals 14 basis points.

When loans go into a mortgage-backed security, the issuer (for example, Fannie or Freddie issuing a MBS or PC to investors) will charge an additional guaranty fee as well for their services, usually another 25 basis points. So a complete transaction from the note rate that the borrower pays to the investor receiving a mortgage-backed security would look something like this:

5.800%	Weighted Average Yield (or Coupon) = Note rate average
− 0.250%	Servicing Fee
5.550%	Net Yield to Investor (for Cash transactions)
	OR
− 0.250%	Guaranty Fee (if pooled into a security: MBS or PC)
5.300%	MBS Coupon (yield to investor)

Weighted-Average Yield (Coupon)

Seldom does the mortgage market rate remain constant long enough for a lender to originate a package of loans with the same coupon (interest) rate. If a lender has mortgages with varying interest rates, the yield to an investor will be calculated on a weighted-average basis *(weighted average yield* or *weighted average coupon*). For example, assume a lender has an outstanding commitment requiring delivery of $10 million in mortgages with a net yield to the investor of nine percent. The following calculations will occur:

1. Lender determines which loans in the pipeline will be used to fulfill commitment. Assume:

   $5 million at 9.50 percent
   $3 million at 9.25 percent
   $2 million at 9.00 percent
   $10 million

2. Yields are then converted into annualized income:

   $5 million × 9.50 percent = $475,000
   $3 million × 9.25 percent = $277,500
   $2 million × 9.00 percent = $180,000
   $932,500 annual income

3. Divide annualized income by loan package to establish weighted-average yield:

$$\frac{\$932,500}{\$10,000,000} = 9.325 \text{ percent}$$

In this example, minus the 25-basis-point servicing fee, the weighted-average yield of 0.09075 is more than the commitment of 0.09 net yield to the lender. When an originator is faced with this situation, it can do one of the following:

- Keep the difference as excess servicing
- Sell the loans at a slight premium
- Substitute a few more nine percent mortgages to bring the yield down

Price for a Package

Once a package of loans has been put together, the yield can be adjusted by the price paid by the investor for the package. Assume an originator has put together a $10 million package of fixed-rate mortgages for sale to an investor with a weighted-average yield of 8.75 percent. Further, assume that the originating lender predicts rates will remain steady so does not obtain a *forward delivery* commitment. As a result, now that the package is ready for delivery, the market requires an 8.75 net yield. The package of mortgages must be discounted to produce the required net yield to the investor. (With an 8.75 percent weighted-average yield on the underlying mortgages, minus the 25-basis-point servicing fee, the mortgages deliver a net yield to the investor of 8.50.) In this case, minus the servicing fee, the annualized income would be $850,000; thus, the calculation would be as follows:

$$\frac{850,000}{0.0875} = 0.9714$$

Thus, the package will be sold at a discounted price of 0.9714, or

$$\frac{850,000}{0.9714} = 8.75 \text{ yield}$$

Occasionally, a mortgage lender will sell mortgages (probably from portfolio) with coupon rates higher than those required in the secondary market. In those situations, the loans could be sold at a premium. Assume the investor's required net yield is 8.5, and the lender wants to sell $10 million in mortgages with a weighted-average yield of nine percent. After subtracting the 25-basis-point servicing fee, the net yield would be 8.75 percent, or $875,000:

$$\frac{\$875,000}{0.0850} = \$10,294.177, \text{ or a price of } \$102.94$$

PRICING

The *price* an investor will pay for a mortgage loan (i.e., the yield on the mortgage) determines the value of that loan in the secondary market. Put another way, the secondary mortgage market players (meaning, in this context, Fannie Mae and Freddie Mac), through posted yields, establish the price they will pay for a net yield (or *pass-through rate*) on a residential mortgage. Investors will buy mortgage loans at one of the following:

- *Par* (which means the mortgage loan is worth 100 percent of face value)
  Example: A $100,000 mortgage with a nine percent interest rate would produce $100,000 in cash to the seller and at that price would produce a yield of nine percent to the investor.
- *Discount* (which means that the mortgage is worth less than 100 percent of face value)
  Example: A $100,000 mortgage with a nine percent interest rate sold at 98 (98 percent of face value) would produce $98,000 in cash to the seller and deliver a yield of 9.184 percent to the investor.

- *Premium* (which means the mortgage loan is worth more than 100 percent of face value)

  Example: A $100,000 mortgage with a nine percent interest rate sold at a price of 102 (102 percent of face value) would produce $102,000 in cash to the seller and deliver a yield of 8.823 percent to the investor.

Pricing information for GESs is available either directly from the private investor or from a number of sources.

Risk-Based Pricing Adjustments

In addition to the calculations above for the price of the mortgage loan or pool of loans based on the note yields, investors now also charge the mortgage lender additional fees based on the risk characteristics in each loan being sold. These fees (pricing adjustments) become part of the total amount that the mortgage lender gives to the investor. Chapter 16—Underwriting—discusses the various types of risk-based pricing adjustments in detail. The lender typically collects these fees from the borrowers and passes them along to the investor. If the mortgage lender fails to properly identify and/or collect these fees, the investor may charge the lender for them. In the past few years, the scope and amount of these fees has increased significantly. AUSs help lenders manage this complex aspect of pricing, but it still is a source of difficulty and errors for many lenders.

Remittance Options

In addition to the net yield on a mortgage, the price paid by investors for a residential mortgage loan is also affected by the remittance option selected by the servicer. Once a loan has been sold to an investor, the principal and interest payments (minus any servicing fee) belong to the investor. How and when the principal and interest (P&I) collected by the servicer is remitted to the investor obviously impacts the price that the investor will pay for the loan. The options a servicer has for remittance include remitting P&I to the investor:

- As collected
- When a certain dollar level is reached
- At some date in the future (e.g., 15th of month after collected)

The longer it takes for an investor to receive the principal and interest, the lower the price the investor is willing to pay for a loan. Some mortgage lenders are willing to take a slightly lower price for their mortgages when they sell (i.e., they have selected a longer period to remit the payments) because they believe they can make more money on the use of the P&I before it is remitted.

Another option a seller needs to determine is which remittance option to select for principal and interest. This decision concerns whether to select one of the following:

- *Actual/Actual (A/A):* A type of remittance requiring the lender to remit to the investor only the principal and interest payments actually collected from borrowers.

- *Scheduled/Actual (S/A):* A type of remittance requiring the lender to remit to the investor the scheduled interest due (whether or not it is collected from borrowers) and the actual principal payments collected.
- *Scheduled/Scheduled (S/S):* A type of remittance used with mortgage-backed securities that requires the servicer to remit to the issuer the scheduled interest due and the scheduled principal due (whether or not payments are collected from borrowers).

Strategic Options in Selling Mortgage Loans

In today's sophisticated mortgage market, all classifications of mortgage lenders have the same strategic options for placement of their loan production. These choices include:

1. Retain some or all loan production in the lender's own portfolio.
2. Sell whole loans or participations to government-sponsored enterprises—Fannie Mae/Freddie Mac or Federal Home Loan Banks.
3. Sell whole loans or participations to private secondary market entities.
4. Directly issue mortgage-backed securities (MBSs).
5. Sell loans to conduits for packaging into MBSs.

These selling alternatives are available, conceptually, to all mortgage lenders. Most depositories (thrifts, credit unions, or commercial banks) opt for the portfolio alternative some or most of the time. Mortgage bankers rarely retain production in portfolio, since they do not have a low-cost funding source like a depository institution and therefore must sell all loans originated either at or soon after closing. Mortgage brokers technically are not lenders at all, but work with all lenders and provide valuable origination services to both lenders and applicants. (See Chapter 4—The Mortgage Lenders.)

Mortgage brokers can act like mortgage bankers or lenders through a method of financing called **table funding**. In this scenario, the broker originates, processes, closes, and records a mortgage in its own name so that it technically "funds" the loan. But the new loan is immediately assigned to the investor at the closing table. Because the investor underwrites and approves the application terms prior to closing, the investor can provide the broker with funds to complete the closing.

A mortgage lender should consider all alternatives before selecting the most advantageous loan sale option for that period of time. The process is called "Best Execution" (See Loan Commitments in this chapter). The lender compares the different ways in which a particular loan can be sold to the various investors who have approved that lender. Part of this strategic decision should be deciding how to handle the servicing issues inherent in selling loans. The various servicing alternatives are discussed in Chapter 16—Loan Administration.

Mortgage Banking Business Model

Sound modern asset and liability management dictates that all mortgage lenders involved in residential lending also be engaged in what is generically called the *mortgage banking business model*. The term **mortgage banking** in this sense refers to the process of originating mortgages that are saleable (even if not actually sold) in the secondary mortgage market.

Mortgage lenders who can place loans in portfolio should follow this prudent approach to origination, even if current economic conditions and investment philosophy dictate retaining some or all loans. Mortgage bankers typically sell all of their loans at or soon after closing.

SELLING LOAN PRODUCTION TO INVESTORS

All mortgage lenders are now authorized (by regulation) to sell residential mortgage loans to either Fannie Mae or Freddie Mac (both are referred to as government-sponsored entities, or GSEs) or to private investors. Both GSE investors and most private players buy whole loans or participations, conventional or FHA/VA, and fixed-rate or adjustable-rate mortgages. An extensive review of the programs, fees, and commitment requirements of Fannie Mae and Freddie Mac is made in Chapter 5—Secondary Mortgage Market.

For a residential mortgage lender, the advantage gained from selling loans to these major secondary market players or other participants is based on the following factors:

- No portfolio risk from changing interest rates
- Increased ability to meet local housing demand
- Instant liquidity
- Increased servicing volume and income
- Potential for marketing profit
- Participation leverage
- No portfolio risk from changing credit dynamics (other than repurchase risk)

As previously discussed, mortgage bankers must sell all their loan production to an investor. Although they can choose from many investors, they often sell to Fannie Mae or Freddie Mac, or to a private investor if the loan is non-conforming.

Other residential originators, on the other hand, can sell to either of these agencies or other investors, or can retain loan production in their portfolios. The deciding factors include type of loan, price, servicing fees, underwriting requirements, and commitments outstanding.

Direct Sales to Private Secondary Mortgage Market Entities

Ironically, this option pre-dates the establishment of the GSEs. The direct sale by mortgage bankers to private investors of mortgage loans originated in one part of the country and sold in another was the only alternative to portfolio lending until the start of Fannie Mae in 1938. Mortgage companies in the late 1890s were originating farm mortgages in the Ohio Valley and selling those loans to wealthy individuals or life insurance companies located in the northeastern states. This activity started the loan correspondent system and produced the first use of commitments in mortgage lending.

Mortgage bankers, at times, also purchase mortgages originated by other lenders, but not for their own portfolios. Brokers utilized this strategy to fill an outstanding commitment or to issue a Ginnie Mae or private mortgage-backed security (MBS). All mortgage lenders, including mortgage bankers, periodically purchase mortgages from other lenders *servicing released* (see discussion in Chapter 16—Loan Administration).

These mortgage lenders in turn sell the loans to the government-related agencies with the servicing rights retained. In this way, mortgage lenders are able to grow their servicing portfolio without the expense of origination. Some mortgage lenders purchase mortgage loans from other lenders because of a permanent or temporary imbalance of deposits and loan production.

Directly Issuing Mortgage-Backed Securities

Until 1977, the mortgage-backed securities (MBSs) field was the exclusive turf of government and government-related agencies. This changed in 1977 when the Bank of America issued the first private MBS. Since then, many other private concerns, including many different types of mortgage lenders, have issued MBSs. This entire subject is covered extensively in Chapter 5—Secondary Mortgage Market.

Even though mortgage bankers do not have the problem of securing existing portfolios, they have been very active in direct-issue MBSs. Practically all of the Ginnie Mae MBSs that have been issued to date are backed by FHA/VA loans originated or purchased from other lenders by mortgage bankers. Today, all types of mortgage lenders have directly issued mortgage-backed securities.

Selling Loan Production to Conduits for Packaging into MBSs

Private *conduits* in the marketplace are entities that buy loans from mortgage lenders and then package those mortgages with other mortgages from other lenders. One example, CUNA Mortgage Corporation, buys mortgages only from credit unions and in turn sells those mortgages to Fannie Mae or Freddie Mac or private investors, who then issue MBSs. Wall Street companies and mortgage insurance companies also purchase mortgages from many lenders and then directly issue MBSs themselves. The number and volume of these private-label securities (PLS) transactions grew steadily since the 1980s, until the collapse of the major investment banks on Wall Street in 2007–2008.

INVESTOR APPROVAL AND LOAN COMMITMENTS

Becoming an Approved Seller/Servicer

Before any mortgage lender can sell mortgage loans to any investor, it must become an approved lender with that investor. Fannie Mae and Freddie Mac refer to approved lenders as *Approved Seller/Servicers*. (Ginnie Mae refers to them as *approved program participants*). Many mortgage lenders are approved to be both a seller of loans and servicer of loans, but in many cases it is not required. In some circumstances, an approved seller can sell loans to its investor and transfer the servicing to another approved servicer.

The process of becoming an Approved Seller/Servicer requires a mortgage lender to apply for approval from the investor. The first step is stipulating the type(s) of loans to be sold, for example:

1. One- to four-family first mortgages
2. One- to four-family second mortgages
3. Reverse mortgages
4. Rural housing mortgages
5. Cooperative mortgages
6. Rehabilitation loans
7. Multifamily mortgages

The approval process includes the following steps:

1. Applicant submitting application for approval
2. Applicant paying nonrefundable fee
3. Examination of applicant's financial condition
   a. Fannie Mae requires:
      i. a minimum net worth of $2.5 million
      ii. 0.25 percent of the outstanding loan portfolio serviced for the GSE
      iii. a minimum Capital Ratio from six percent to ten percent, based on type of institution
   b. Freddie Mac makes reference to having an "acceptable" net worth based on the proposed duties and obligations with Freddie Mac
4. Reviewing mortgage-lending experience of lender in:
   a. Origination
   b. Secondary market operations
   c. Servicing
5. Establishing whether applicant is properly licensed in jurisdiction
6. Establishing whether staff has sufficient experience in:
   a. Originating investment quality mortgage loans
   b. Servicing loans for investors
7. Reviewing fidelity bond and errors and omissions coverage
8. Reviewing acceptability of:
   a. Quality control plan
   b. Loan-servicing systems in place

The approval letter telling a mortgage lender that it is an approved seller/ servicer will also make reference to the investor's seller/servicer guides. By agreeing to become an approved seller or servicer, the mortgage lender will agree to follow all of the investor guidelines. The new seller/servicer represents and warrants that all loans delivered for sale or servicing conform to these guidelines. If not, the investor may require that the seller/servicer repurchase the loan (or servicing).

The "reps and warrants" section may differ from investor to investor, but much is similar and it is a very powerful tool that the investor uses selectively. Sadly, in recent years investors more frequently have issued repurchase orders for loans or for an entire pool, most often after discovering incorrectly submitted or fraudulent loans. In other situations, it is the result of an early payment default (delinquency within the first three, six, or twelve months).

Once a mortgage lender receives investor approval, the next step is obtaining secondary market commitments.

SECONDARY MORTGAGE MARKET COMMITMENTS

Commitments are critical to successful mortgage lending for those lenders that sell mortgages. Mortgage lenders issue them to applicants for specific loan terms, and investors issue them to mortgage lenders for specific loan purchase terms. A commitment is legally binding as a contract if it agrees completely with the loan application or the purchase offer. If a commitment varies the terms of an application or purchase offer, then it becomes a counteroffer and must be accepted by the applicant or lender before a binding contract can result.

Commitments from investors to buy mortgage production are essential for successful marketing. During the early 1970s, a few mortgage lenders originated mortgages for later sale without a commitment from a permanent investor to purchase those loans. Because interest rates moved so slowly during that period, the interest rate exposure of an originator was limited. But practices changed later in that decade as interest rates became more volatile. Several mortgage bankers were forced out of business because of severe losses occasioned by not having their production covered. For all practical purposes, that was the end of the practice of not covering loan originations by either a firm (mandatory) or standby commitment.

An investor issues commitments to the mortgage lender only after it becomes an approved seller or seller/servicer. Similar commitments are used with the sale of mortgage servicing, too.

Details of Sale

The direct sales of loans to GSEs or private secondary mortgage market players can be either on a continuous basis supported by an outstanding commitment or on a case-by-case, negotiated basis and individual loan sale commitment. The details of a commitment can include the following items:

1. Type of mortgage loans to be delivered:
   a. FHA/VA or conventional
   b. Whole loan or participation
   c. Fixed-rate or variable-rate
2. Total dollar amount of this sale (plus or minus any amount?)
3. Type of pricing (discount/par/premium)
4. Yield (net) to the investor
5. Servicing requirements and fees:
   a. Amount of servicing fee
   b. Whether released or retained
6. **Commitment fees** (if any) charged to seller:
   a. How much
   b. Refundable or not

7. Delivery requirements to purchaser:
   a. Immediate delivery
   b. Future delivery and date
8. Underwriting standards to be used:
   a. Fannie Mae/Freddie Mac standards
   b. Other standards (investor, government, lender, etc.)
9. Type of loan documentation to be used
10. Recourse to seller:
    a. Whether for mortgage default
    b. Whether for breach of warranties
11. Method of monthly reporting and remittance to investor
12. Loan characteristics of mortgages to be delivered:
    a. Type of properties, for example:
       i. single-family detached
       ii. condominiums
       iii. second homes
    b. Location (geographic)
    c. Maximum loan amount per mortgage loan
    d. Coupon rates of loans
    e. Loan-to-value maximums
    f. Whether mortgage insurance is required
13. Other requirements to be negotiated

Master Commitments

Most mortgage lenders who sell to Fannie Mae, Freddie Mac, the FHLB, or private investors negotiate a master commitment with the secondary market investor. A master commitment locks in the program, product availability, volume agreement, and specific credit and documentation terms. In addition, a master commitment can establish price arrangements or leave those terms to be negotiated and included with each loan sale commitment.

Mandatory Delivery Commitments

The most common secondary market commitment is a **mandatory delivery**, under which a lender agrees to sell to an investor a specified dollar amount of specific loan product at an agreed-upon price to be delivered (not just closed) within a specific period of time. A mandatory commitment will specify the required net yield to the investor (not the note rate paid by the borrower(s). This type of commitment is used to sell loans for cash or to swap loans for securities. Typically, mandatory commitments are the most inclusive, as all the terms of sale (or swap) have been finalized. As a result, the pricing for the lender tends to be better than the other types of commitments that follow.

For example, Fannie and Freddie offer 5-, 10-, 30-, 60-, and 90-day commitments for many loan products. The required net yield to them (which does not include the required servicing by a servicer) is quoted over the telephone or is available through various financial information systems (such as MOR-NET or Bloomberg). The servicing fee, which Fannie and Freddie require a lender to collect, ranges from 25 to 50 basis points, depending on the type of mortgage and the volume and experience of the mortgage lender.

If the lender fails to meet all of the terms of the contract, it may have to pay a penalty or, as it is called, a pair-off fee. (Making a good delivery to Fannie or Freddie, for example, means that a lender must deliver at least 95 percent up to a maximum of 105 percent of the original commitment amount—or come within $10,000 of the original commitment, whichever is greater.) In some situations, a lender may request a 30-day extension on delivery of loans under the commitment.

Pair-Off

Before a commitment expires, a lender may request a full or partial **pair-off** (repurchase) of the outstanding amount of the commitment. The fee will always be at least one-eighth of one percent of the commitment, and could be more, based on the amount of the commitment, type of loan, and the direction of interest rates. If a lender did not request a pair-off and still does not fulfill the commitment, an investor will automatically pair off the remaining unfulfilled commitment.

Best Efforts

In the typical best-effort transaction, a mortgage lender agrees to sell a specific whole loan to a buyer (usually a mortgage wholesaler) at a specific price. In this transaction, both the loan and the servicing rights are often included. These transactions are referred to as **best efforts** because only those mortgage loans that actually close are obligated to be delivered. The benefit of this transaction is that there is no penalty if a loan does not close, as there would be in a mandatory delivery commitment. The disadvantage of this transaction is that the lender receives a lower price for its loans compared to a mandatory delivery. Typically, the pricing gets less favorable for the lender as the percentage of delivery/commitment falls.

Standby Commitments

A **standby commitment** obligates the issuer to purchase mortgages at a certain yield for a certain period of time, but it does not obligate the originator to whom it is issued to deliver any loans. Both parties recognize the likelihood

FIGURE **17.3** Hedge Cost

Hedge Cost **Best Efforts vs. Mandatory Cash**				
$300,000 loan amount, 30-Yr Fixed, 45-Day Rate Lock, 0.25 Servicing Fee, 5.75% Note Rate				
Serv. Retained	**Best Efforts**	**Mand. Cash**	**Hedge Cost**	**Cost to Hedge**
Jan. 2008	100.356	100.518	16.2 BP	$486.00

Source: Reprinted with permission of Sharon Whitaker, Lake Sunapee Bank ©2010 Community Lending Associates, LLC www.communitylendassoc.com

that the mortgage loans may not be delivered and that the standby is a type of insurance for the mortgage lender. This process is valuable to an issuer because it is a fee generator. The fees required for both types of commitments are, as a general rule, established by the marketplace. **Standby fees** are usually twice as much as those required for mandatory delivery because an investor must be compensated for holding funds at the ready to purchase loans, which may or may not be delivered.

LOAN DELIVERY

Documents Delivered to Secondary Market Investors

After agreeing to purchase a mortgage, neither Freddie Mac nor Fannie Mae wants to keep all the documents that a mortgage lender finds necessary to have when processing a mortgage loan. As a general rule, they only want the original mortgage, note, assignment of the mortgage, and a loan schedule whereby the characteristics of the mortgage(s) sold are listed. The mortgage lender, on the other hand, must keep these documents either in their original form or recorded on microfilm. These documents must be available at all times if an investor wants to perform its own quality control audit or if the loan becomes delinquent.

With the increase in mortgage fraud nationally, GSEs and government agencies now continually revise their quality control and document delivery requirements. More stringent standards require mortgage lenders to re-verify credit, employment, income, or assets immediately before and/or soon after closing. Each policy change expands lenders' representations and warranties in each loan sale, increasing lender liability and adding to the cost of delivery.

Establishing Custodial Accounts

In order to do business with an investor in the secondary mortgage market, a mortgage lender must set up a **custodial account** that allows for collecting payments from the borrower and passing those funds through to the investor. For example, if a lender sells loans to Fannie Mae, the lender must deposit borrowers' monthly payments into two specific accounts: one for principal and interest, and another for any tax and insurance escrow funds that must be collected. Further, the lender must establish a "drafting" arrangement that authorizes Fannie Mae to draft commitment and other fees.

Uniform Documentation

In order for mortgages to be readily saleable in the secondary market, a degree of uniformity must exist. Before Freddie Mac joined Fannie Mae in the secondary market, the required uniformity existed because all mortgages sold in the secondary market were either FHA insured or VA guaranteed. After 1970, conventional mortgages were eligible for secondary market sale, so the need developed for uniform documentation.

Both Fannie Mae and Freddie Mac have worked diligently to produce the state-by-state uniform documents that all mortgage lenders should use for all originations. Ginnie Mae has also adopted these forms, which include the following, among others:

- Mortgage note
- Deed of trust
- Mortgage
- Loan application
- Appraisal form
- Verification documents

VA-guaranteed mortgages can also use these forms if a VA-guaranteed loan rider is added to the mortgage or deed of trust to make the mortgage instrument conform to special VA requirements. These forms regrettably cannot be used for FHA-insured loans; FHA-approved forms must be used, but this may change in the future. These uniform forms may contain some minor variations to comply with different state laws.

FIGURE **17.4** Secondary Mortgage Market and Trading Mortgage for Cash

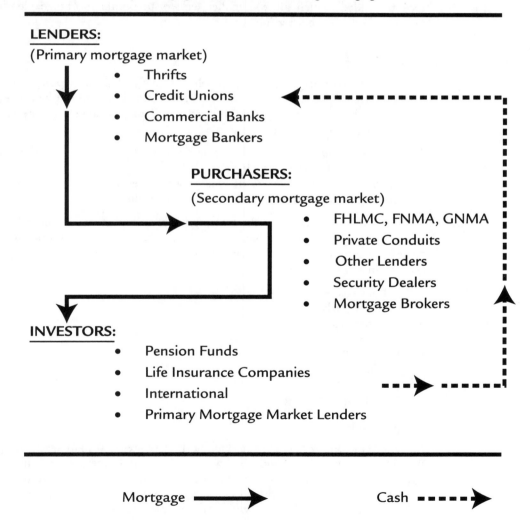

LENDERS:
(Primary mortgage market)
- Thrifts
- Credit Unions
- Commercial Banks
- Mortgage Bankers

PURCHASERS:
(Secondary mortgage market)
- FHLMC, FNMA, GNMA
- Private Conduits
- Other Lenders
- Security Dealers
- Mortgage Brokers

INVESTORS:
- Pension Funds
- Life Insurance Companies
- International
- Primary Mortgage Market Lenders

Mortgage ⟶   Cash ⇢

Mortgage Electronic Registration System (MERS)

MERS, modeled after the electronic system for tracking ownership of securities, allows mortgage lenders to register new mortgage loans and to record ownership transfers of mortgage loans and servicing in a similar fashion. At the end of 2001, about one out of three newly originated mortgage loans were being registered on this electronic registry. Projections are that one out of two newly originated mortgage loans will be registered in the future. The reason that MERS has become so successful is that lenders do not have to go to the local courthouse or recorder to register ownership changes. These ownership changes normally cost at least $25 per loan. The cost of registering on MERS is currently less than $4. The MERS system was tested and proved its worth during the massive refinancing boom in 2001. Lenders saved considerable time and money by not having to record every assignment or new mortgage loan at the courthouse. A new Web-enabled, turnkey system was recently added, which allows smaller lenders to obtain mortgage identification numbers and register loans on the system.

MORTGAGE PIPELINE MANAGEMENT

The residential mortgage-lending pipeline is defined as that period of time between when an applicant applies for a mortgage loan and the loan is either funded by the investor or placed in portfolio. This pipeline should be viewed as consisting of two segments:

1. *Production segment*: Period of time between the acceptance of the loan application and the loan closing
2. *Inventory segment*: Period of time between the loan closing and the sale/funding of the loan or its placement in portfolio

The distinction between the two segments is important. A lender has different risks in a loan that has not and may not close versus one that has closed. A secondary market manager must consider the following types of risks in managing the pipeline:

- Fallout Risk
- Delivery Risk
- Investor Risk
- Program Risk
- Funding Risk
- Repurchase Risk
- Liquidity Risk
- Price/Interest Rate Risk

Fallout Risk

At first glance, it would appear that the best strategy to manage a mortgage pipeline is to simply provide an interest rate commitment to the mortgage applicant and obtain a commitment to deliver a net yield to an investor at the same time. The problem with this strategy is that the applicant may not close, either because he or she is unwilling or unable to (i.e., the applicant doesn't qualify, or the loan amount or product changes, or interest rates drop and the applicant doesn't want to close at the rate quoted at application). The risk of an application not closing under the terms originally applied for by a date originally agreed to is a broad definition of **fallout risk**. The negative effect of fallout risk is a lender finds it can no longer fulfill a commitment to deliver a loan or loans at a certain net yield or product type by a certain date.

Some lenders manage their pipeline risk by estimating what percentage of their applications will always close—no matter what happens to interest rates—and obtaining commitments to sell those loans at the same time they commit to the applicants. If the lender's history is that 50 percent of applicants will always close, while 10 percent never close, that lender has an easier problem in having to manage only 40 percent of the pipeline and not 100 percent. As the loans flow through the pipeline and get closer to closing without falling out, the lender can increase the amount of coverage on those loans by obtaining investor commitments so that by the time the loans close, the lender has nearly 100 percent coverage.

Delivery Risk

Delivery risk broadly refers to any of the possible issues that the mortgage lender may have after closing and before funding a loan. An improper closing, resolution of title issues, or discovery of a missing underwriting condition after closing may result in a long delay until all the parties are brought together to correct them. During this time the loan file cannot be delivered to or funded by the investor.

Investor Risk

The risk of an application not being funded under the terms originally committed to by the investor is a broad definition of **investor risk**. This can occur before or after loan closing, and it results in the mortgage originator having to find funding for the consumer's application. Sadly, in 2007/2008, many mortgage bankers and mortgage brokers issued loan commitments to consumers but could not close them when private capital and investors disappeared almost overnight.

Program Risk

A type of investor risk is program risk. **Program risk** occurs when a lender originates and commits to a consumer for a loan program (e.g., six month ARM or no-income verification program), but the investor stops funding that program. The mortgage lender must either find a different investor or negotiate different loan terms (often at below market rates).

Funding Risk

Similar to delivery risk, but in this situation the mortgage lender has closed a loan, and the investor for whatever reason cannot fund the loan as agreed. While the source of the problem may be the investor's financial condition or a legal injunction, the lender may need to find permanent or interim funding.

Repurchase Risk

Repurchase risk occurs when an investor's post-closing audit discovers either mortgage fraud or significant enough error(s) to require the mortgage lender to repurchase the loan. This can also occur as late as six months after closing if the loan becomes delinquent, depending on the master or loan commitment.

Liquidity Risk

When a mortgage lender commits to an applicant but later finds that it cannot sell the loan as originally planned, it is referred to as illiquid in the sense that the mortgage loan cannot be converted into cash quickly. Now the lender must fund that loan for the time it takes to re-negotiate the sale. If this happens to a pool of loans—and the sale now is at a discount—then the lender may run out of available cash. The reason the loan cannot be sold may be because of an underwriting mistake or because the investor is no longer able to complete the transaction.

Price/Interest Rate Risk

All lenders active in the secondary market must be concerned about their interest rate risk. In this context, **interest rate risk** refers to the difference in price an investor will pay for the exact same mortgage loan when interest rates change. This interest rate risk occurs between the time a lender commits an interest rate to the applicant(s) and the time that lender receives a commitment from an investor to sell that loan at a certain yield to that investor. The length of time of the interest rate risk could be zero (if the lender immediately gets a commitment to sell the mortgage loan) or it could be months (if the lender holds the loan[s] in the warehouse for a period before obtaining a commitment to sell).

Mortgage lenders often manage this interest rate risk by *hedging*—purchasing another financial instrument that increases in value to negate the loss the lender would suffer on the mortgage loan being hedged. If rates rise and the investor's price for an uncommitted mortgage loan drops $1,500, then a good hedge would result in the other financial instrument increasing at least $1,500 in value (plus the cost to purchase the hedge). Like obtaining insurance, the purpose of hedging is not to make money but to avoid losses.

Locking Rates at Application

In a perfect world, a mortgage lender would only commit on interest rates to a loan applicant at or very near closing the mortgage loan, so it would not have a mismatch between rates committed first to the applicant and then to investors. But, if one lender is willing to lock in rates at application, other lenders will normally be forced by market pressures to do the same thing, even though they would prefer not to do so.

Many lenders face the problem of what to do if market rates drop after the lender has committed a rate to the applicant. Legally, the lender can require the applicant to close at the agreed-upon rate. What happens if the applicant refuses and goes to another lender with lower rates? If the transaction is a purchase money mortgage, an applicant may not have the time to shop for another mortgage and wait for the loan to be processed. If the mortgage is to refinance an existing mortgage, the applicant is not under any time constraints and may look for another lender with lower rates. In this situation the lender risks not meeting its investor commitment.

Many lenders have decided that the better business practice is to negotiate with the applicant. If they don't, and the applicant goes to another lender, the first lender will be forced to replace the lost loan with one at the lower rate anyway. Some lenders manage this situation by charging a rate lock-in fee at application. This strategy works only if other lenders follow the same practice.

Interest Rate Volatility

Even during periods of relative interest rate stability as existed in the United States during the 1990s and into the first decade of the new century, mortgage interest rates rose and fell marginally over short periods of time (0.0–1.5 percent annually). Sudden changes within this relatively small range can be significant enough to painfully hurt a lender without proper coverage on its pipeline. For example, between January 15 and February 15, 1992 (volatility result of Desert Storm), mortgage rates increased 110 basis points.

To illustrate this risk, assume that a lender committed to an applicant at a certain interest rate on January 15 and closed that loan four weeks later without having protected itself from interest rate movements. If that lender had to sell the mortgage loan, the price that the lender would receive from an investor would have to be discounted to make up for the difference in yield. This risk can be better understood by examining Figure 17.6. Note that the change in interest rate is 0.5% above and below the 5.50% interest rate at which the mortgage package was originated. However the price and value of the package does not change by an equal amount. This lack of convexity is a result of prepayment projections in pricing models when interest rates move.

Pipeline Reports

Before a lender can manage the pipeline risk successfully, management must have the necessary tools, and the most important tool is information. The loan-processing system should contain a module that allows for the preparation of reports that management can use to track the following information:

FIGURE **17.5** Impact of Interest Rate Movement

Impact of Interest Rate Movement

- On Closed Loans
  - Rates up, value goes down   (below market yield)
  - Rates down, value goes up   (better price)
- On Rate Locks
  Same effects as above on the underlying instrument, but with an additional dynamic:
  - Rates up, value goes down   (close more loans)
  - Rates down, value goes up   (close fewer loans)
- On Servicing Portfolios
  - Rates up, value up   (extended life of loan)
  - Rates down, value down   (refinance wave)

Source: ©2010 Community Lending Associates, LLC www.communitylendassoc.com

FIGURE **17.6** Interest Rate and Price Risk

Assume a $1 million package of 30-year, fixed-rate mortgage originated at 5.50%. The following chart shows the effect on its price and value when required yields in the secondary market increase or decrease.

Yield Required	Price	Package Value
5.00%	103.42	$1,034,200
5.50%	100.00	$1,000,000
6.00%	96.31	$ 963,100

Source: ©2010 REMOC Associates, LLC www.remoc.com

- Dollar amount of loans in the pipeline
- Types of loans
- Interest rates committed to applicants
- When loans are expected to close
- Outstanding commitments to investors
- Loans closed and funded/not funded
- Loans with post-closing pricing adjustments or repurchase requests

Once management has the appropriate pipeline reports, it will be able to manage the risks inherent with the mortgage loans in the pipeline. There are two basic methods for managing the price and product risk inherent in mortgages in the pipeline. The most obvious is to obtain from investors commitments to buy the loans at a certain yield sometime in the future—a *forward sale*. Most lenders use this method to protect themselves. A few of the large originators use substitute sales to protect themselves. Substitute sales are accomplished with debt market instruments, such as futures contracts, which are sold at an agreed-upon price for delivery on a specified future date. Before the contract expires, the lender purchases an equivalent security to offset the existing position. The normal result is a loss in one market offset by a gain in the other market, thus protecting the original transaction. These transactions can be expensive and don't always work. For that reason, few lenders use substitute sales. The vast majority is served well by obtaining commitments for forward sales.

DISCUSSION POINTS

1. Describe the business strategy of selling mortgage loans. Why is it the most popular residential mortgage loan strategy today?
2. What alternatives does a mortgage lender have for the residential mortgage loans that have been originated? What are the pros and cons of each?
3. Identify and discuss the inherent risk of residential mortgage origination.
4. What are the major benefits that a mortgage lender derives from selling loans into the secondary mortgage market?
5. What steps must a mortgage lender go through before it can sell loans into the secondary market?
6. What are loan commitments and why are they so important in secondary mortgage market transactions?
7. Explain the pricing options that a lender has when selling loans into the secondary mortgage market.

CHAPTER 18

Strategies for Generating Residential Loans

INTRODUCTION

Practically all mortgage lenders perform the origination function to one degree or another. They may use different methods or employ alternative strategies to originate loans according to their own unique sources of funds, portfolio possibilities, fee income needs, staff resources, origination channels, lending area, or other considerations, but they all perform some or all of the origination functions. In some situations, a mortgage originator may only take the application before turning the applicant over to another mortgage lender who completes the transaction. But in most situations the originating lender performs all of the origination functions. Mortgage investors, on the other hand, hold only mortgages that they have purchased from one of the many types of mortgage lenders or from other investors. This chapter focuses on those lenders involved in mortgage origination, and describes some of the issues and approaches involved in developing an effective mortgage lending operation.

THE FIRST STEP—FOCUS ON THE APPLICANT

The first step in originating a residential mortgage loan is getting an applicant in the door (either a real or a virtual one). With increased competition for mortgage loans, this first step can be a real hurdle for some lenders. All the other operational and financial activity which follows later in the lending process falls down if the lender does not connect with its targeted customer base in general, and its individual applicants in particular. In their strategic planning, lenders must identify who their customers are and establish how to attract them. While important, this is just the first part.

The next part is how the lender treats its customers. Treating mortgage applicants well is critical! When a lender establishes contact with a customer, the way he is treated at initial contact can determine whether that customer (potential soon-to-be applicant) will continue the origination process with the lender, will come back for another mortgage loan later, or will recommend the lender to another consumer. On the other hand, just one dissatisfied customer can turn away future business from the lender and, depending on the reason for dissatisfaction, involve other more damaging issues.

Measuring Customer Satisfaction

J. D. Power and Associates conducts an annual mortgage origination (Table 18.1) survey that measures several factors in the origination process to determine overall customer satisfaction. The survey measures more than twenty origination factors, organized into the following four general categories:

- Application/approval process
- Closing process
- Loan officer/representative or banker
- Problem resolution

The survey includes only customers of large, national mortgage originators. It does not include local or regional ones, which have different operational practices. Still, the survey information provides insight into overall satisfaction level, and best and worst practices.

Overall customer satisfaction varied by only five percent over five years and through vastly different mortgage markets. The "top" originator satisfaction rating varied only slightly more—seven percent, which, again, was measured over tremendous boom and bust years, during less restrictive and more restrictive lending conditions, under very difficult origination periods.

What is very significant is how important certain practices are in customer satisfaction. For example, one negative factor can drop overall ratings by 26 percent! Also important to note is that almost all of the factors identified as best and worst practices—as well as the most significant ones—are customer service oriented, not monetary (cost), logistical (closing date), or procedural (requesting additional documentation).

Not every application will be an approval or a smooth one. But at a minimum, a lender should communicate clearly with its customers throughout the application process and respond in a timely, professional manner.

At its essence, lending is a trust business. Effective customer service helps build that trust. A lending operation risks everything if it does not mandate certain customer service standards for all origination staff, or fails to develop

TABLE **18.1**
Mortgage Origination Satisfaction Surveys, 2005–2010

J.D. Power and Associates Mortgage Origination Satisfaction Survey				
	Overall Satisfaction	Top Originator Surveyed	Top Originator Satisfaction Rating	Number of Respondents
2005	69.90%	ABN AMRO	75.6%	4,498
2006	75.00%	SunTrust	78.2%	4,115
2007	75.00%	Wachovia	82.7%	4,378
2008	75.70%	SunTrust	79.0%	4,256
2009	73.90%	BB&T	78.3%	3,400
2010	73.40%	Quicken	82.6%	3,401

Best practices:

> Proactive updates on loan status
>
> Welcome acknowledgment immediately after application
>
> Request same information once
>
> Explain loan options and ensuring customer understands
>
> Explain entire origination process from application to approval
>
> Close on promised date

Worst practices:

> Failing to provide proactive updates   26.0% difference in satisfaction
>
> Not reviewing closing documents before   22.6% difference in satisfaction
>
> Failing to provide billing/servicing information   19.5% difference in satisfaction
>
> Closing costs higher than expected   18.4% difference in satisfaction

Note: Surveys involve customers of large, national lenders only

Source: J.D. Power and Associates Mortgage Origination Surveys 2005–2010

© Community Lending Associates, LLC

a real customer service culture throughout the origination process. Measuring performance in several areas helps improve department performance and overall success.

What Attracts Consumers?

The Mortgage Bankers Association of America (MBA) surveyed its membership to determine their opinion of what attracted consumers for a residential mortgage loan. The survey confirmed some old beliefs and introduced some new ideas. One of the old beliefs confirmed was the importance of the real estate agent for mortgage referrals, especially if a person is new to an area. Of course, for people purchasing a home locally or who are refinancing, the REALTOR® is less influential, and the most important element is referrals from friends.

The three attributes considered to be the most important by mortgage lenders in this survey in attracting consumers who are new to an area are as follows:

1. Referral by real estate sales agents
2. Low interest rates on loans
3. Good company reputation

The next five are of about equal importance:

4. Friendliness of loan officers
5. Previous experience with company/institution
6. Recognition of company/institution name
7. Availability of various loan products
8. Convenience of home or office application

Finally, this survey established the importance of attracting the potential applicant while the applicant is still "shopping around." Once an applicant has submitted an application elsewhere, it is extremely difficult to get him or her to drop that application and apply with another lender.

The Most Effective "Tool" in Attracting Mortgage Applications

At first blush, many mortgage people believe that mortgage loan advertisements or brochures are most important in attracting customers. Eye-catching mailers or posters are important (and recommended). Many mortgage lenders completely accept the conventional wisdom that Realtors steer most consumers to certain lenders, especially if the consumer has just moved into the area. But marketing pieces and REALTORS® are not the most important elements in attracting mortgage applicants.

As mentioned above, the importance of word-of-mouth between customers—recommendations from friends and family members—is the most important consideration in selecting a lender. If an applicant has a good experience with a lender, he or she will go to that lender again when the need arises for another loan. A 2005 J. D. Power and Associates survey determined that, on average, satisfied customers will recommend their lender to three other people. But provide a bad experience, and that person is gone forever and will tell everyone he or she knows just how bad the lender's service was.

Some lenders have the attitude that they are doing mortgage applicants a favor by considering them for a mortgage loan. Successful lenders recognize that a mortgage applicant is a customer and is entitled to be treated courteously and fairly. With so many residential mortgage originators in the marketplace today, treating customers courteously and fairly over time will positively impact a lender's market share.

Convenience for the Applicant

First impressions are very important to success in attracting and keeping the mortgage applicant. This includes making the mortgage loan process *convenient* for customers—coming to them if needed to establish contact. At least 50 percent of those borrowers surveyed obtained a loan from the first lender they contacted. The remaining borrowers talked to three or more mortgage providers before deciding on a lender. So if a lender is able to meet face-to-face with an applicant, it is likely that he will remain with them through the process.

Many mortgage lenders, especially mortgage bankers or brokers, meet with applicants at any time and place that is most convenient for the applicant. This often takes the form of an originator meeting at the applicant's home in the evening or at the applicant's workplace. Consumers greatly appreciate this accommodating approach. It also gets the attention of real estate salespeople, who often recommend lenders.

A related issue is whether or not a mortgage lender's origination personnel consider themselves "order takers" or "salespeople." Order takers merely respond to inquiries and instructions. Salespeople listen to consumers, recognize and anticipate needs, and find or suggest a solution to the issue or problem. Today's competitive residential lending market places a premium on salespeople, whereas order takers are a relic of the past.

Consumer Stress in Applying for a Mortgage Loan

Mortgage lenders must be sensitive to the stress that most applicants are under when they meet with them. After the stress of finally finding and negotiating successfully the purchase of their dream home, the applicants now must suffer the anxiety involved in applying for and waiting for mortgage approval. Lenders need to understand the sources of this stress: uncertainty, impatience, and being unfamiliar with the real estate process.

The process of applying for a residential loan is often an intimidating experience for many applicants. Consumers often look upon lenders as adversaries. If the origination function is neither smooth nor explained clearly and fully, it can further alienate applicants. Lenders should remember that most applicants have either never applied for a mortgage loan before or have done so only infrequently; they must be treated with care and understanding. Lenders should explain fully the reasons for the various verifications, appraisal, survey, insurance, other documentation, and closing procedures. In addition, lenders should provide applicants with the likely turnaround time for a decision on their application.

Application Information Booklet

In real estate transactions, time is usually of the essence; any delay can destroy the transaction. This is equally true for mortgage financing, where delay can cost money for the applicants or ruin their experience with the lender. Many lenders handle this timing issue by providing potential applicants with a marketing brochure that explains what information (e.g., W-2s, tax returns, divorce decree, credit card numbers, employment history) the lender needs to initiate or complete a mortgage application. Having the applicant bring all the required information ensures that both the lender and applicant use their time as efficiently as possible.

Lenders also provide a similar booklet (or Web page) to explain housing- and debt-to-income ratios, loan-to-value ratios, and other pertinent information that a potential applicant should be familiar with before completing an application. If the applicant has all or most of this information at application time, the process can move rapidly toward a decision—possibly immediately! A sample mortgage loan information form is shown in Figure 18.1.

FIGURE **18.1** Sample First Mortgage Loan Information Form

FAIRFIELD SAVINGS ASSOCIATION
FIRST MORTGAGE LOAN INFORMATION

What Happens After You Apply?

The time it takes to complete the loan process varies for each application. Here is a list of the stages required to process a mortgage. Remember that completing your application accurately and fully will help speed the process.

PROCESSING

After you apply, a loan processor will collect documents and verification to support your request for a loan. The time in processing will vary depending on the type of loan and how quickly the processor receives the documents needed. Much of processing involves help from other sources, such as:

Appraisal - An appraiser will judge the value of the property, generally based on the recent sales in your market. **Credit Verification** - We'll request a credit report through a credit reporting agency to verify your outstanding debts and payment history. **Income Verification** - In addition to the documents we request from you, we'll ask your employer to verify your income. **Asset Verification** - To confirm that you have the funds required to close your savings institution. **Previous Housing Verification** - We'll request the history of your rent or mortgage payments from your lender or landlord.

UNDERWRITING

Once the application is processed, your processor will submit the complete package for review. The Underwriter compares your loan request to the guidelines of the lender or its investors for the type of loan. Then the underwriter issues a decision on your application based on established investor guidelines.

CLOSING

Closing occurs when you sign the papers for your mortgage loan, and when the property is transferred, if your loan is for a home purchase. Most closings take place at a title company or real estate office, but the location procedures varies by state.

WHAT YOU NEED TO BRING!

Mortgage Application Checklist
Information required at application:

INCOME
- Signed copy of Agreement of Sale or copy of Deed - if refinance.
- Current pay stub & W2's for 2 years.
- Names & addresses of employers for past 2 years.
- Details of all other continuing income sources.

ASSETS
- Names, addresses, account numbers and balances for:
  - Checking Accts. - IRA's 401 & Keogh
  - Savings Accounts - Credit union
  - Investment & stock accounts.
- Gifts - complete details on all monetary gifts.

DEBTS
- Names, addresses, account numbers and balances for:
  - Charge Accounts - Personal Loans
  - Auto Loans - Student Loans
  - Current Mortgages
- Alimony and child support payment.

Self-Employed Borrowers

Additional information required for commissioned or self-employed persons:

- Signed copies of last 2 years Federal Tax Returns (1040's) - with all schedules.
- Copy of Partnership Return for 2 years. (if applicable)
- Copy of Corporate Return for 2 years. (if applicable)
- Current Balance Sheet
- Most recent Profit and Loss Statement (no more than 120 days old)

NOTE:
A Borrower who has an ownership interest of 25% or more in a business is considered to be self-employed.

Source: ©2010 REMOC Associates, LLC http://www.remoc.com

Tracking the Progress of the Application

Once he completes an application, the applicant soon wonders about its progress or has other questions during the process. Some mortgage lenders advise the applicant to talk only to the loan originator when questions develop; other lenders designate a loan processor as the contact person after loan application. Neither approach is inherently better than the other. Rather, it depends on how well the origination function is organized and which employees are best prepared and most effective at answering the applicant's questions courteously and knowledgeably. The customer contact person should have access to information similar to that in Figure 18.2.

How Loyal Are Mortgage Borrowers?

Over the past twenty years, the mortgage lending business has witnessed four major waves of refinancing activity (1992–1993, 2001–2003, and 2009–2010). For example, refinancing of existing loans produced 55 percent of all the loans processed in 2002. Normally, refinancing generates about 25 to 30 percent of loan originations. Another MBA survey found that homeowners had little loyalty when it came to mortgage refinancing. According to this survey, three out of five borrowers took their business elsewhere when they refinanced.

As a result of this survey and others like it, some mortgage lenders developed a strategy of sending a letter to all of their existing mortgagors asking them to "call us first" when the mortgagors began to consider refinancing their mortgage loan. Other mortgage lenders simply made sure that they were offering attractive interest rates, attentive service, and were doing effective marketing to let all potential borrowers—including existing borrowers—know their interest rates and programs.

To summarize the concepts for how a lender can successfully attract and retain mortgage consumers:

- Have the right mortgage product offered at an attractive rate
- Handle the application in a timely manner
- Give quality service

REQUIREMENTS FOR A SUCCESSFUL MORTGAGE LENDING OPERATION

Once a lender has taken steps to ensure a strong customer service culture exists, it should review other areas in its operation. For any residential mortgage lender to have a successful first-mortgage program, six elements must be in place:

- Trained personnel
- Program offerings
- Competitive pricing
- Targeted marketing
- Loan demand
- Effective origination channel(s)

FIGURE **18.2** Sample Loan Tracking Summary

LOAN TRACKING SUMMARY 03/15/04

AP NUMBER: 100101920
BORROWER: Joseph F. Lynch   Margaret J. Lynch   **PHONE**:   203-333-3990
LOAN TYPE: FIXED RATE PURCHASE

APP DATE: 02/13/04	**EST CLS DT**: 05/27/04	**APPROVED**:	
PMI ORDERED:	**FILE RECD**:	**TITLE REC**:	
LOAN STATUS:	**ACTION DT**:	**APPRAISAL**:	
AMOUNT: 189000.00	**ORIG CODE**: 123	**LTV RATIO**: 90.00	
RATE: 6.000	**PROC CODE**: 323	**DTI RATIO**: 20.15	
TERM: 360	**PROD CODE**: 001	**HTI RATIO**: 16.19	
RE AGENT: CENTURY 21		**PHONE**: 222-8976	
CLS AGENT: SEDENSKY & MYERS		**PHONE**: 315-366-8900	

VERIFICATIONS ORDERED	**REQ SENT**	**EXPECTED**	**REQ RECD**
* VOD Century 21	02/27/04	03/05/04	
* VOD Bank of Fairfield	02/27/04	03/19/04	
* VOD Bank of Fairfield	02/27/04	03/19/04	
* VOL Peoples Bank	02/27/04	03/12/04	
* VOL Chase Auto Finance	02/27/04	03/19/04	
* VOL Fleet Bank	02/27/04	03/19/04	
* VOE General Electric Corp.	02/27/04	03/19/04	
* VOE Town of Fairfield	02/27/04	03/12/04	
* VOE Fairfield University	02/27/04	03/12/04	
* VOR Jean Body	02/27/04	04/16/04	

OTHER CHECKLIST ITEMS:	**REQ SENT**	**EXPECTED**	**RECEIVED**
* APPRAISAL	02/27/04	03/12/04	
* TAX RETURNS	02/27/04	03/19/04	
* CURRENT PAY STUBS	02/27/04	03/18/04	
* SALES CONTRACT	02/27/04	03/19/04	
* TERMITE REPORT	02/27/04	03/19/04	
* DOWN PAYMENT SOURCE OF FUNDS	02/27/04	03/19/04	

APPLICATION NOTES:

Wants to close before school is out.

Source: ©2010 REMOC Associates, LLC www.remoc.com

Trained Personnel

Even during boom times in mortgage lending, some mortgage lenders fail. The reason is usually due to inexperienced or poorly trained personnel in key positions. These key positions are not just at the senior management level. They also include loan originators and processors. Poor decision making in pricing or selling loans can be very costly, but treating customers poorly or performing a function incorrectly can also lead to frustrated consumers, lost business, possible lawsuits, and often failure of the lender.

A successful mortgage lender understands this and attempts to hire qualified personnel for all functions. That seems simple and obvious. It often is easier said than done—especially during boom periods for originations. With the contraction in the mortgage industry since 2008, many qualified professionals are available for different positions. Lenders should review their credentials carefully.

The successful mortgage lender is the one that has an ongoing, productive training program for the origination staff. However, in the post-crisis environment, lenders will need to provide all mortgage personnel—new and experienced—with training in several areas: several compliance regulations, loan program and underwriting guidelines, customer privacy and security, mortgage fraud, and quality control.

Frequent, extensive changes in mortgage programs and compliance regulations requires that the lender make a significant commitment to keep its staff current and effective. Managers and supervisors must review operational procedures to ensure that all appropriate personnel have the skills needed to perform their functions successfully. Meeting this challenge poses the greatest risk to mortgage lenders for the next few years.

Program Offerings

Program offerings refer to the variety and scope of residential mortgage loans available. Chapters 6–10 describe a variety of conforming, non-conforming, and government programs offered today and a history of their development and activity during different markets. A crucial part of a successful residential mortgage lending operation is offering the right combination of products that consumers want during that particular economic market and that the lender can both offer and manage properly.

The most practical method for increasing the number of customers seeking a mortgage loan is to offer the loan program in which they have an interest, although customer appetites for mortgage loan products change constantly. Thus, a lender's mortgage offerings must also continue to change. A mortgage lender should not fall in love with its mortgage product offerings, but instead should constantly check the wind to see which way consumer sentiment is blowing for opportunities.

Although customer preference clearly is with fixed-rate mortgages (FRMs) during most interest rate environments (2002 is an example), in certain circumstances consumers become more interested in adjustable-rate mortgages (see Chapter 6—Conventional Lending). In 2002, 2009, and 2010, when mortgage rates hit 30- and 50-year lows, fixed-rate mortgages accounted for about 80 percent of all first mortgages originated. Some lenders believe that the ratio of fixed to variable will always be high because borrowers prefer fixed-rate loans.

Yet, there have been times over the past 15 years when ARMs accounted for nearly 70 percent of all home mortgages originated. The proportion of ARMs to total originations increases when mortgage rates are expected to rise for many months. Such conditions existed from 1984 to 1988, when ARM production was quite strong. In fact, in 1988 nearly 70 percent of all first mortgages originated were ARMs.

When mortgage rates are expected to fall for many months, and the spread narrows between initial ARM rates and FRM rates, then ARM production dwindles. Such conditions existed throughout most of the 1990s and 2000s. Hybrid ARMs also helped make these loans more desirable.

Lenders should always offer different types of ARM programs, including hybrid and discounted ones, to create an attractive spread between those and fixed rate programs. From a portfolio perspective, adjustable-rate mortgages (or ARMs) are important loan products to portfolio lenders because of their obvious asset/liability management value. However, ARMs also allow the lenders to serve the mortgage needs of more of their customers (e.g., first-time homebuyers, jumbos, relocations), so being known as an ARM lender is important, too.

Since the growth of the GSE conforming market, local and regional lenders often found success in offering "niche" or non-conforming mortgage programs. These programs historically served a very valuable purpose in the local economy. Local lenders who kept them in portfolio developed their programs prudently, based on local knowledge of the area and by identifying where conforming GSE or other federal government programs did not make sense.

Despite the recent legislative hysteria and attempt by Congress and the federal government to control much of mortgage lending, experienced lenders should still retain the power to identify those financial and credit risks that they are willing to take and provide consumers with reasonable lending options besides GSE and government agency programs. Most local, non-conforming portfolio programs perform extremely well compared to these national programs.

Competitive Pricing

Competitive pricing would appear to be an obvious strategy for a mortgage lender, but it is one of the most common mistakes that small lenders make. Often, they have no idea at what rates other mortgage lenders offer. The first decision a mortgage lender must make is whether or not it will sell originated loans in the secondary mortgage market or only place loans in portfolio. If the lender portfolios most or all of the loans it originates, pricing off the secondary market is not necessary; cost of funds or other strategic benchmarks become more important than the 60-day delivery price to Fannie Mae or Freddie Mac. On the other hand, if all or most of the loans will be sold, then being aware of secondary market prices is a necessity.

An important step for a lender that wants to be competitive is to price mortgage loans logically. For example, in 2002 and 2006–2009, secondary market pricing forced large mortgage banking companies to offer five- and seven-year ARMs at rates higher than for 15-year fixed-rate loans. This pricing makes no sense at all. Why do these sophisticated mortgage companies quote those rates? Because they must sell all their loans and must deliver the yields those investors want. Portfolio lenders need not follow that pricing, and can benefit from (a) identifying these opportunities and (b) exploiting them with pricing that is reasonable for their situation.

TABLE **18.2**

Example of Logical Pricing of Mortgage Rates (no-point option)

Loan Type	Interest Rate (%)
30-year fixed	4.750
15-year fixed	4.250
7-year ARM	3.875
5-year ARM	3.625
3-year ARM	3.500
1-year ARM	3.250

Source: ©2010 REMOC Associates, LLC www.remoc.com

The normal practice of pricing first-mortgage loans (Table 18.2) has the interest rate increase with the length of time that the rate is in effect—which is not necessarily the maturity date. For example, a five-year ARM with a 30-year term is priced based on the five-year period that the rate is in effect before adjustment, the 15-year fixed rate for 15 years, and so on.

This logical progression of rates assists customers in understanding the advantage of the various loan products. The advantage of an ARM loan is clear (lower rate), and the advantage of the fixed-rate is also clear (high initial rate but set for the life of the loan).

The pricing differential will vary between the different loan products, however, and is not so clear. The rate spread between loan products depends on several issues: overall level of interest rates, forecasts for interest rates, inflation, loan demand, etc., often mirroring the overall demand for money in the economy at different maturities. As a result, rate differences between loan products range between one quarter and five-eights of one percent. This is a wide range.

Mortgage lenders should offer their customers point and no-point options. Only quoting to customers a no-point option makes a competitor's one- or two-point option look better. Why? Most consumers see the interest rate, not the APR.

Most mortgage lenders review their first-mortgage loan rates daily. Reviewing mortgage rates daily does not necessarily mean that rates must be changed daily, but only that the lender should monitor what other local competitors, national players, and others offer in its market area.

Typical closing costs and origination fees are other elements of competitive pricing. Lenders should provide this information to customers inquiring about their programs. If a lender surveys its competition and finds that it has lower costs, then that should be a prominent feature in its marketing and advertising communications.

Targeted Marketing

Marketing mortgage loans is not the same as marketing other loans such as consumer loans. Mortgage loan marketing must be clear, consistent, and continuous. The biggest marketing mistake some mortgage lenders make is to do it only once or twice a year. It is hard to believe that a customer, seeking a mortgage loan, is going to remember an advertisement that the lender ran six months ago; instead, these important loans must be marketed continuously throughout the year.

Traditionally, for a local or regional lender this meant advertising with local newspapers, local radio, billboards, local television, and in-house presentations, as well as using different mailings (statement stuffers, postcards, coupons, etc.). To improve the effectiveness of these campaigns, the lender needs to match its products and services to the consumers' needs and select the avenue for communication to that common group of potential applicants. For example, marketing one-year discounted ARMs during a presentation at a senior citizens' center would not be a good match between loan features and consumer needs.

For today's market and into the future, it is absolutely critical to market mortgage loans on the Web. In the late 1990s, many lenders developed informational Web sites—where a consumer could browse the different loan programs and maybe calculate payments. This was a necessary first step in developing the Internet as a channel for business, but during that time it was not very productive.

Now the industry standard is having an interactive Web site where a consumer can obtain mortgage program information and complete an application. Many lenders still do not accept on-line applications. Some avoid this on purpose, as Internet applications can still attract many non-qualified applicants or those from outside a lender's area. So in terms of targeted marketing, an Internet-based presence can attract a certain segment of consumers who are more comfortable online. This spans all ages and includes people in urban, suburban, and rural areas. On the other hand, if not focused properly, the lender may incur a lot of work with little production from its Internet presence.

While not accepting online applications may not be a "mistake," it certainly can be a handicap. Those lenders must either recognize it as such or put in place other elements to reach their desired customers first and effectively. In a few years it will be critical that mortgage lenders be able to take mortgage applications over the Internet, as more and more potential applicants will demand this convenience and level of service.

Loan Demand

Loan demand is one of the most important elements for a successful mortgage-lending operation, and the one most affected by the local, state, and national economies. It is also the one factor that is predominately out of the control of mortgage lenders. Obviously, there is a direct correlation between residential mortgage originations and employment levels, interest rates, job creation, and consumer confidence. For example, when residential originations exceeded $3 trillion in 2003 and almost $4 trillion in 2005, the nation had the lowest unemployment rate since records began, interest rates were low, consumer confidence was high, and competition for employees was breathtaking. This strong correlation between the economy and mortgage originations occurred in the prior decade as well, during 1993–1994 and again in 1998 when originations hit what were record highs at the time.

When the economy turns down, originations fall off dramatically, as it did immediately after the Gulf War in the early 1990s and during 2005–2008. When originations drop nationally, the mortgage lender has two choices to maintain mortgage origination volume: (a) increase their lending areas, and/or (b) increase market share in their existing lending area.

Locally, lenders can review household demographic data, housing sales and prices, new construction permits and starts, and other employment data to help plan what loan demand may be in their areas over the next six months to two years.

Origination Channels

To maintain mortgage origination volume in the different economies that a lender will see over time, lenders utilize four strategies or methods of origination:

- Retail loan origination
- Wholesale loan origination (Broker and Correspondent Lender)
- Combination of retail and wholesale loan origination
- Online loan origination

Recent data indicate that most mortgage lenders continue to follow the traditional retail strategy, a growing minority uses the wholesale strategy, and a few larger lenders use a combination of the two. This does not suggest that the majority of loans are originated using the retail strategy; they are not, but the majority of lenders do use the retail strategy. With the proliferation of investors for non-conforming loans, the broker and correspondent channels increased during 2000–2006. Overall, mega-originators supplement their retail branch network with both broker and correspondent channels as shown in Figure 18.3. But since 2008, government agencies and GSEs have

FIGURE **18.3** Mortgage Origination Channels, 1993–2006

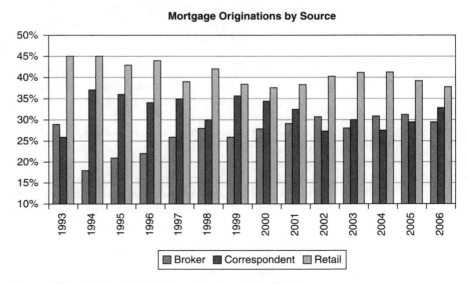

Source: Office of Federal Housing Enterprise Oversight (OFHEO)

either increased requirements or otherwise severely restricted broker originations.

The most recent method is the use of the Internet. Internet or online loan origination represents a growing percentage of mortgage loan applications annually.

The following sections discuss these four strategies in some detail, with particular emphasis placed on the advantages and disadvantages of each.

RETAIL LOAN ORIGINATION

The retail method of loan origination occurs when a mortgage lender performs directly all of the steps or functions of the origination process (no third party involved). Most consumers are familiar with retail loan origination. It is still the strategy or method used by most mortgage lenders today, especially smaller financial institutions. At times, the majority of mortgage loans, however, are not produced by this method; larger lenders tend to have a more diverse approach to maintain volume in different markets. See Figure 18.4 on page 574.

Purchase vs. Refinance Transactions

The broadest category for which one lends has to do with loan purpose. The vast majority of mortgage applications are for purchasing a home or to refinance an existing one. Lenders must consider how their operations deal with either situation effectively and develop appropriate strategies to reach their customers in either category.

Purchases—Importance of the Real Estate Agent

For purchase money mortgages, the principal customer or client of most mortgage lenders is the local real estate agent. Ultimately, of course, the lender's customer is the mortgage applicant. But initially the real estate agent is the one over time who directs many consumers to a mortgage lender. Good relations with real estate agents are essential for any retail mortgage lender. The National Association of REALTORS® and others estimate that 80 to 90 percent of homebuyers follow their real estate agent's recommendation for mortgage financing. New homebuyers seldom seek out or identify a lender on their own, except in small markets where they already have an established relationship in the area.

Real estate agents routinely advise consumers about current home-financing options and will recommend lenders, so it is essential that a lender maintain a good working relationship with them. Real estate agents usually recommend only those mortgage lenders who act promptly, who treat applicants in a courteous and timely manner, and who offer different programs to fit their client's needs. It is difficult for a mortgage lender to change a negative image within the real estate sales community and convince agents to send new applicants. Those mortgage lenders that provide quality service to the real estate agents, and ultimately to the consumer, are the lenders that will increase market share.

During periods of increased refinancing activity, real estate salespeople have a smaller impact on mortgage originations, but relationships must be maintained for the next cycle, when purchase money mortgages are important again.

Refinances—Rates, Reputation, and Convenience

Each major refinance wave was different in the last twenty years, mostly due to the massive changes in the industry as shown in Table 18.3. During 1993 and 2001–2003, interest rates and reputations of mortgage lenders attracted the most business. In the latest wave of refinancing (2008–2010), the Internet and economic conditions made rate information easily accessible to all consumers, so pricing was very similar among lenders. Instead, the element of convenience and service grew in importance. More homeowners used the Internet either for rate and program information or for completing the actual application. Others were intent on changing lenders based on an unsatisfactory loan servicing experience.

Commission Loan Agents

In today's age of mega-lenders and servicers, most large retail lenders employ commission-only loan officers or loan representatives to solicit business from real estate agents or, in some cases, builders. Mortgage bankers and brokers have traditionally used commission-only as the way to both compensate and motivate their originators. Many local and regional lenders began adopting this arrangement starting around the turn of the century. Some lenders will use a combination of salary and commissions. Other lenders, primarily smaller thrifts and credit unions, pay their originators a salary only.

A commission-based retail mortgage loan originator "normally" earns half of one percent of the loan amount (or, as normally stated, 50 basis points). This commission is payable, of course, only on closed loans (approved *and* closed). Some lenders may pay a smaller commission per loan until a certain quota has been reached, and then they increase the commission to a higher amount, say, 60 basis points. More recently, loan quality comes into play and often an originator must meet certain loan quality standards in order to receive full commission. Recent federal regulations from the Federal Reserve and final rules are mandated in the Dodd-Frank Act. These new laws, when finally written, will govern how commission-based originators can be paid, basically restricting compensation to volume-only criteria and making incentives based on interest rate or credit scores illegal (see Chapter 11—Compliance).

With the many nontraditional mortgage lenders (e.g., GMAC and Quicken) competing with traditional lenders in an already crowded marketplace, developing ways to meet the competition has become the backbone of all mortgage lenders' game plans. This concern for market share forced many lenders to change their lending philosophy from being simply order takers to being aggressive sellers of their mortgage products. Lenders with commissioned loan agents logically seem to be the lenders who will succeed in holding on to their market share and who will probably grow at the expense of lenders with only salaried loan officers. Increased compensation is still the

TABLE **18.3**
1–4 Family Mortgage Originations, 1990–2010 ($ in billions)

Year	Total Dollar Volume	Percentage of Total Refinances
1990	$458	13%
1991	562	30
1992	894	48
1993	1,020	55
1994	769	33
1995	640	25
1996	785	29
1997	840	31
1998	1,550	47
1999	1,214	36
2000	1,067	18
2001	2,067	57
2002	2,883	59
2003	3,860	65
2004	2,750	46
2005	3,034	50
2006	2,760	49
2007	2,631	50
2008	2,334	44
2009	1,995	68
2010	1,500 (e)	65 (e)

*Fannie Mae estimates.

Source: Fannie Mae, Freddie Mac, U.S. Department of Housing and Urban Development.

best reward for increased productivity and as an incentive for additional effort, but with newly-raised loan quality standards by GSE and investors, originator compensation structures now may include those considerations as well.

Functions Performed by Retail Lenders

The retail mortgage lender directly performs the following origination functions:

- Completes application with borrower
- Verifies all employment, income, and deposits
- Orders appraisal
- Obtains a credit report

- Prepares loan for underwriting/automated underwriting
- Underwrites the loan application
- Approves or rejects the loan application
- Closes and funds approved loan
- Portfolios or warehouses/sells loan

Historically, the majority of residential mortgage loans originate in this manner. A high percentage of local and regional financial institutions still use this method predominately. An obvious benefit to retail lenders in originating mortgage loans themselves is that they establish a long-term relationship with mortgage borrowers, which can prove profitable in future transactions. These future transactions can be either mortgage loans or other consumer loans.

Origination Income

Most retail mortgage lenders charge an application fee or an origination fee, or both, to offset some or all of the expenses incurred in performing the various origination functions. Overall, the local marketplace will determine which fees are charged and how much they are.

If the lender charges an application fee, it usually pays for the credit report, appraisal, and any other direct out-of-pocket expenses that a lender incurs in processing the loan application. Many lenders charge a one percent origination fee as well. This fee accomplishes the following:

- Offsets personnel and office expenses
- Increases yield on mortgages to secondary market requirements
- Produces current income

Estimates for the cost of processing a residential mortgage loan (not including the 50 basis points paid to a loan originator) range from 60 to 120 basis points. Keeping these costs as low as possible is the goal of all mortgage lenders. As a general rule, increasing loan volume helps to drive down the cost of processing.

Some mortgage lenders have concluded that they can put loans on the books more cheaply by buying individual residential mortgage loans from brokers rather than incurring the expense of processing the loans themselves, hence the wholesale and correspondent lender methods of origination.

FASB Statement No. 91

In Statement Number 91 of Financial Accounting Standards, the Financial Accounting Standards Board (FASB) ruled that any origination points that are not offset by actual expenses incurred in originating the loan must be amortized over the loan contract period or, if it can be clearly established, the expected life of the loan. (http://www.fasb.org/summary/stsum91.shtml)

This ruling changed the way many lenders look at origination points. Those lenders that sell loans immediately into the secondary mortgage market (e.g., mortgage bankers and others) are affected the least, since they can take any fee income into current income immediately after the sale of any loan. But portfolio lenders (e.g., thrifts and credit unions) must amortize much of that fee income over the expected life of the loan. This ruling affects smaller lenders most, as many often use these fees to boost current income.

Points and Interest Rate Trade-offs

The long-term result of the FASB ruling has been a return to the low- or no-point lending of the 1970s. No-point lending does not necessarily interfere with a lender's overall yield, since it can increase the interest rate to offset the loss of fee income. As a general rule, a one percent origination fee (or one point) equals an increase in yield of one-eighth of one percent; thus, a quote of five percent and two points is approximately the same to a borrower as a 5.25 percent quote with no points.

Retail Branch Offices

A retail mortgage lender is primarily interested in giving the best possible service to its customers—local REALTORS® and mortgage applicants. Even with growing online origination activity, having a convenient location for loan origination offices is probably the most basic "service" a lender can provide applicants. It can also be one of the most important rendered. Location is important to a retail lender in regard to walk-in business. Although the percentage of this type of business to total originations is generally small, walk-in business for a new mortgage and refinancing can be just the additional business that makes a branch profitable. Therefore, each branch origination office should be easily reached by automobile or public transportation, and should be in a highly visible location, preferably on a ground floor.

Depending on whether or not loan processing is centralized, a branch office houses the loan origination personnel and appropriate support staff. If loan processing is not centralized, loan processors are located at each branch office. The added convenience of processing and approving an application in the building must offset the economies and efficiencies of a central processing area.

Expected Mortgage Loan Volume

Mortgage loan volume per retail office varies widely, depending on many factors including what type of lender is involved (mortgage banker, credit union, etc.) and what loan programs it offers. But certain benchmarks exist for residential loan production. Many lenders believe a valid goal is to produce 70 to 80 loans per production employee (including originators, loan processors, underwriters, closing personnel, etc.) per year. While this number varies from lender to lender, it is most important for a lender to establish a useful process of measuring activity and setting goals for the branch involved.

For example, an office with a staff of nine—a branch manager who handles closing, a secretary, three loan originators, three loan processors, and one underwriter—should produce about 600 to 700 loans a year. At an average loan balance of $150,000, loan production for this office should be about $100 million. Some lenders will do more, others less, depending on loan demand, the economy, and personnel expertise.

WHOLESALE LOAN ORIGINATION

Over the past 30 years or so, a number of unpredictable factors have contributed to changes in the way many mortgage lenders approach residential mortgage origination. These factors include, among others, the following:

- Greater volatility in mortgage interest rates (e.g., fixed rates ranging from nine percent in 1979 to 18 percent in l982)
- Massive annual swings in one- to four-family mortgage originations from year to year, exceeding $1 trillion
- Increased geographical variations in real estate market and origination volume
- New, dynamic origination competition from traditional and nontraditional lenders
- Cheaper and more sophisticated technological support for mortgage lending
- Large variations in mortgage servicing right pricing

All of these factors contribute to the complexity and potential risk of originating mortgage loans. As a result, the wholesale origination strategy becomes a more viable option for loan production. This method of producing loans is sometimes referred to as "third-party origination," or TPO. The third-party originators are mortgage brokers and loan correspondents who sell the mortgages that they originate to acquiring mortgage lenders called wholesale lenders.

In recent years, as much as 40 to 60 percent of residential mortgage loans originate using this strategy. These third-party originators increased in numbers as the demand for their product has increased, then fell off sharply after the mortgage crisis occurred. Still, mega-originators with large servicing portfolios will rely on TPOs for maintaining these portfolios during refinance waves, and general market contraction as consumers pay down the staggering level of mortgage debt they accumulated throughout the 1990s and 2000s.

Advantages and Disadvantages of Wholesale Lending

As with most types of business strategies or methods of doing business, there are advantages and disadvantages for each. This is particularly true for the wholesale method of loan origination, which can provide a lender with several benefits:

- An inexpensive method of quickly originating a high volume of mortgage loans
- Fast entry into a geographical market or loan product market (i.e., FHA lending)
- More precise control over total volume or rate or product

Wholesale lending often is less expensive than retail lending for a number of reasons, including the ability to acquire loans without the need for a large loan-processing staff. Some experts indicate that from 60 to 70 percent of the

FIGURE **18.4** Largest Lender Origination Channel Production 2008–2009

Origination Channels for the Largest Residential Lenders 2008–2009

	Retail Production %	Retail Production $	Broker Production %	Broker Production $	Correspondent Production %	Correspondent Production $	*Online Production %	*Online Production $
2008	47%	$424,400	16%	$143,966	33%	$296,472	15%	$137,897
2009	45%	$602,142	12%	$164,748	42%	$566,047	14%	$187,134

*Incomplete data: missing 3 lender totals in 2009; 5 lender totals in 2008.

Lenders:

Wells Fargo	CA
Bank of America	NC
Chase	NJ
CitiMortgage, Inc.	MO
Ally Bank/Residential Capital	MN
U.S. Bank Home Mortgage	MN
SunTrust Bank	VA
Provident Funding Associates	CA
PHH Mortgage	NJ
LetLife Home Loans	TX

Source: Mortgagestats.com
© Community Lending Associates, LLC

cost of originating a mortgage loan involves personnel expenses. If the originating party performs some or all of the processing functions, the acquiring mortgage lender may further enhance its own profitability.

An important item to be considered in determining which approach is most appropriate for a particular lender is the expected number of loans produced per production employee. The rule of thumb for retail mortgage lending is yearly production of approximately 60 to 70 loans per production employee, as already discussed. A recent study suggests that the direct cost of producing a mortgage loan using the retail strategy is approximately $1,700 per loan. For nonretail production, the direct cost per loan averaged approximately $500 per loan. The nonretail production figure is approximately 100 to 110 loans per production employee. This major difference in productivity occurs because retail lenders must have more employees to perform all of the origination functions, while a mortgage broker or loan correspondent performs only certain functions.

Another important advantage a wholesale lender has is the ability to move quickly into and out of markets that are changing. Since a wholesale lender does not have to be concerned with brick-and-mortar expenses or with acquiring personnel for a new office, it can quickly move into a geographical area that is attractive even if it is on the other side of the country.

In addition, if a market deteriorates quickly, a wholesale lender can simply decide not to purchase any loans in that area; it does not have to be concerned with either selling its physical assets or relocating its personnel.

Unlike the retail lender, the wholesale lender does not have to be concerned with the attractiveness or the location of its offices. Not only will this lender need far fewer offices (each office can serve a very large geographical region), but none are needed for direct face-to-face contact with applicants. As a result, offices can be less visible and thus less costly.

Wholesale lenders are usually quite interested in rapid growth in their servicing portfolio. These institutions desire large portfolios in order to obtain the economies of scale that can produce profits approaching 40 percent of servicing revenue. To these lenders, the quickest way to increase their servicing portfolios is to acquire large blocks of loans through the wholesale approach, sell the loans immediately into the secondary mortgage market, and strip off the servicing rights.

Mortgage Brokers and Loan Correspondents

A third party originator from whom loans are purchased is normally either a mortgage broker or a loan correspondent. A mortgage broker usually does little application processing and no underwriting; a loan correspondent typically closes and (briefly) funds the loan.

Functions Performed

The extent of loan processing by a broker varies depending on the needs of the originating lender and the acquiring lender. In many situations, the broker completes the application with the borrower and orders the various verifications. The broker then ships the documentation to the acquiring lender (referred to as a wholesaler), who will then make the underwriting decision. The broker maintains contact with the applicants up to closing. The acquiring lender closes the loan in its own name and either puts the loan in its portfolio or sells it in the secondary mortgage market.

Table Funding

Loan correspondents, on the other hand, normally complete the loan processing and make an underwriting decision. The loan correspondent may or may not fund the loan. If the loan is funded by the acquiring lender, the transaction is called table funding. **Table funding** occurs when a broker closes a mortgage loan with funds belonging to an acquiring lender and immediately assigns the loan to that lender. This activity gives the originator the opportunity to say it is a direct lender, since it can close loans with its own funds. These originators believe that by funding the loan at closing, they acquire a marketing advantage over other brokers.

Upon purchase, the acquiring lender may re-underwrite the individual mortgage, or some or all of the mortgages if in a package. The extent of underwriting by the acquiring lender depends mainly on the amount of business it has previously done with the loan correspondent and the requirements of the ultimate investor in those loans.

If the loan is not closed before the correspondent sells the loan to the investor, the correspondent is most concerned with the turnaround time for an underwriting decision from the acquiring investor. The loan correspondent is normally looking for a 48-hour decision time. This is important to the originating lender because it may have to renegotiate with the applicant if the loan is declined as originally submitted. The ability of the wholesaler to fund quickly after the underwriting decision is also of great importance to the originating party.

Yield Spread Premiums

In the past, another tool that mortgage brokers used was to add a *yield premium* to the quoted yield requirement of an acquiring investor. For example, if an investor would buy conforming loans with a yield to the investor of six percent, the broker could close the loan to the consumer at 6.5 percent. This yield spread premium was not considered a violation of RESPA (Section 8, anti-kickback provisions) as long as the broker provided a service to the borrower, the fees were reasonable, and the broker disclosed this fee properly at the beginning of the application process. This practice has come under intense scrutiny recently, and new legislation from the Federal Reserve and pending from the Bureau of Consumer Financial Protection eliminates it as a form of originator compensation.

What Motivates the Third-party Originator?

The third-party originator is not interested in holding the loans or in selling them into the secondary mortgage market directly. This lender has determined that it can operate more profitably by originating loans for other lenders without the inherent interest rate risk associated with holding mortgages for a short or long period of time. This lender will almost always be originating against commitments that have been obtained from those lenders who rely on them for production.

Fees and Premiums

The mortgage broker or correspondent lender retains any application fee and will probably collect as large an origination fee as the market will bear. The TPO pays the mortgage originator the 50-basis-point commission and provides the staff necessary to process the loan. In addition to the fee income generated from the origination process, often an originating lender receives a fee called a **servicing release premium** from the acquiring lender. This fee is recognition that value (the value inherent in servicing a mortgage) is being transferred to the acquiring lender. Some lenders combine the fees into one amount paid to the TPO.

Affinity Groups

Another variation on the wholesale theme is the concept of one mortgage lender serving the mortgage lending needs of an *affinity group*. This arrangement involves a mortgage lender who links up with a large corporation or membership group (such as a credit union) as the preferred provider of mortgage loans. The benefits of this type of arrangement are mutual: the sponsor (credit union) endorses the mortgage lender, and applicants usually receive better treatment than they would with an inexperienced lender and may get more attractive deals. Mortgage lenders are also interested in arrangements of this type because the new business is usually in addition to their own business; thus, the economies of scale become even more attractive. As a general rule, the arrangement between the mortgage lender and the affinity group contains provisions that prevent the lender from selling the servicing rights to another lender.

A number of credit unions adopted this strategy with origination and servicing credit union service organizations (CUSOs) in earnest during the 2000s. However, massive losses due to fraud and poor management in several CUSOs, the most notable being losses totaling more than $125 million at U.S. Mortgage Corp., a CUSO in New Jersey, are sharp reminders of how ineffective this affinity "bond" can be at times. Lenders still should perform due diligence, quality control, and normal auditing functions, as these are still separate legal entities.

Quality Control

The strongest negative factor to wholesale lending is the issue of **quality control**. The mortgage lender does not process or underwrite a mortgage loan, so it greatly reduces the lender's ability to control the quality of the loan. Many wholesale lenders have addressed this issue by dealing only with well-established, reputable brokers or correspondents. Because the acquiring mortgage lender assumes responsibility for these quality control and compliance problems, these lenders generally have higher underwriting and quality control expenses than retail lenders. They face the need of increased spot-checking of appraisals and verifications in order to manage quality. Since these loans are probably sold in the secondary mortgage market, the wholesale lender could see its servicing profits greatly diminished with increased servicing expenses if quality controls are not in place and strictly followed.

Unlike a retail lender, an acquiring lender does not receive any application or processing fee, and normally receives none or just a small part of the origination points. This reduced fee is not a critical item to the wholesale lender because it does not have the expenses of a retail lender. The best example of an expense that an acquiring lender does not have to pay is the 50 basis points commission to an origination agent.

INTERNET LENDING

In this computer and Internet era, it should not be surprising that the use of the Internet for residential mortgage originations (Table 18.4) is rapidly growing. In addition to using the PC and Internet to underwrite, appraise, and obtain credit reports, many mortgage lenders are now using the Net to originate loans. Some major mortgage banking companies report as many as 30 percent of refinancing borrowers used the online services offered.

TABLE **18.4**

Online Mortgage Originations

Year	Share of Total New Mortgages (%)	Share of Total Refinanced Mortgages (%)	Share of Total Annual Originations (%)
2000	5.1%	10.8%	6.3%
2001	6.0	13.0	9.2
2002	7.1	15.6	9.6

Source: IDC Online Lending Consumer Survey, 2001.

Practically all mortgage lenders today have a Web site on which they advertise mortgage rates, and many allow the borrower to begin the application process online. Although the majority of consumers still prefer the face-to-face method of applying for a mortgage loan, many people feel no hesitancy about completing the mortgage-lending process online.

The 2010 J. D. Power and Associates survey of mortgage origination reveals that among large national lenders, 20 percent of applications were online, double the activity at the start of the decade. Additionally, at least 71 percent of customers surveyed initiated the application online by obtaining rate or loan program information. The top-rated lender in this survey, Quicken Loans, is the largest online lender and fifth largest retail lender in the country, further showing how far this method of origination has come in ten years.

The 18th Annual ABA Real Estate Lending Survey Report of 178 bank mortgage lenders conducted by the ABA in 2010 contained the following information about what bank web sites offer online: 86% of banks offer only general information; 51% offer current rate and product information; 47% will accept applications; 14% will make application decisions; 1% allow borrowers to close; and 11% have no web site.

The 2011 MORTECH annual survey of over 1,800 lenders with annual origination volume of over $50 million estimates the industry will spend over $4 billion on technology in 2011. This is a 15% increase over 2010, but much of this spending is just to keep compliant and will not be for new technology.

DISCUSSION POINTS

1. Discuss the six keys for a successful lending operation.
2. Identify the various methods of loan origination. Discuss the pros and cons of each method.
3. What functions are normally performed by a retail loan originator?
4. What features or attributes attract consumers to a particular mortgage lender?
5. Many mortgage lenders compensate their originators by commission. What is the typical commission for a loan officer and how is it calculated?
6. How do mortgage originators offset their expenses in producing a residential mortgage loan? What are the expenses in originating a residential loan?

A

Acceleration clause A clause in a security instrument that gives the lender the right to demand payment of the entire principal balance if a monthly payment is missed.

Acquisition cost In FHA lending, the total amount needed to complete the purchase of a home. It is calculated by adding the sales price to the allowable closing costs, as determined by FHA. In construction lending, it is the cost to construct plus the amount to purchase the land (instead of land value). *See* Cost to construct.

Actual/actual (A/A) A type of loan servicing remittance requiring the lender to remit to an investor only principal and interest payments actually collected from borrowers. *Compare with* Scheduled/Actual (S/A) and Scheduled/Scheduled (S/S).

Adjustment date The date on which the note interest rate changes for an ARM loan.

Adjustment period The period between interest rate adjustments for an ARM loan.

Advance commitment A written promise to make an investment or buy a loan or loans at some time in the future if specified conditions are met.

Adverse action Can mean either a straight denial by the lender of the terms applied for, or that the applicant does not accept a *counteroffer* by the lender.

Allodial System Owner of real estate has title irrespective of the sovereign and thus owes no duty, such as rent or the rendering of military service, to the sovereign.

Amortization Repayment of a debt in regular installments of principal and interest, rather than interest-only payments.

Amortization schedule A timetable for the payment of a mortgage loan that shows the amount of each payment that is applied to interest and to principal; shows the remaining principal balance after each payment.

Annual Percentage Rate (APR) The cost of a mortgage stated as a yearly rate. The APR includes interest, loan origination points, discount points, prepaid fees, mortgage insurance, and other fees that are required to be paid for credit to be granted. APR does not include appraisal fee, credit report costs, and some other third-party fees.

Application As defined by RESPA, it requires a minimum of six items: applicant name, income, social security number (or equivalent), loan amount, property address, property value, and any other information the loan originator deems necessary.

Appraisal A written report for a subject property which provides information on its condition and an estimate of its market value. The report must follow USPAP standards and be prepared by a qualified appraiser.

Assignment A legal document that transfers mortgage rights from one entity to another.

Assumable mortgage A mortgage that can be assumed (i.e., taken over) by a buyer when a home is purchased.

AUS Automated underwriting system.

Automated valuation (AV) A method for determining the value of a property that relies on a statistical model, which analyzes various data. Not a traditional appraisal, AVs do not use the income or sales comparable approach and do not meet USPAP standards. They are sometimes used in conjunction with a property inspection to verify the condition of the property.

Average Pricing An option under RESPA which permits a lender to charge all borrowers in a class of transactions the same amount for one or more settlement services. The charge is based on the average cost of providing the service(s), developed over a one- to six-month period.

B

Balloon mortgage A mortgage that has level monthly payments that amortize the loan over a stated term (e.g., 30 years), but has a shorter maturity date. Instead, the loan pays off with a lump sum payment due at the shorter maturity date (e.g., 5 years). This limits the lender's fixed interest rate risk to a five- or seven-year term and keeps the borrower's payment low by calculating the required payment based on a thirty-year amortization.

Balloon payment The final payment for a balloon mortgage.

Basis point A basis point is one-hundredth of 1 percent interest; thus, 50 basis points equal one-half of 1 percent.

Best efforts A secondary mortgage market transaction for which a seller is obligated to deliver only those loans that actually close according to the terms committed to in the best efforts agreement.

Biweekly payment mortgage A mortgage loan that requires a payment every two weeks that equals half of a regular monthly payment. The resulting 26 (or 27) payments a year produce the equivalent of an additional month's payment each year, which if amortizing will greatly speed the repayment of the loan.

Bridge loan A second mortgage that is secured by the borrower's present home (which is usually for sale) in a manner that allows the proceeds to be used for closing on a new house before the present home is sold.

Building permit A document issued by the local government housing authority that certifies that proposed construction is legally acceptable according to the plans and specifications submitted.

Buydown Money advanced by an individual (builder, seller, or borrower) to reduce the monthly payments for a home mortgage either during the entire term or for an initial period of years.

C

Cap A provision of an ARM loan that limits how much an interest rate or payment can increase or decrease.

Capacity An underwriting term referencing the applicant's ability to pay the mortgage and all other debts.

Capital market security A financial instrument, including both debt and equity securities, with a maturity greater than one year. Those instruments with maturities of less than a year are traded in the money markets.

Capital markets Markets in which long-term funds in the form of mortgages, stocks, and bonds are bought and sold. This includes informal markets as well as organized markets and exchanges.

Cash delivery The submission of a whole mortgage or a participation to an investor in exchange for cash rather than a mortgage-backed security.

Cash-out refinance A refinance transaction in which the borrower obtains a loan for more than the amount owed on the existing mortgage (including the mortgage, subordinate financing, closing costs, points, etc.). Some investors define a cash-out refinance transaction differently.

Certificate of Eligibility A document issued by the Veteran's Administration certifying a veteran's eligibility for a VA mortgage.

Certificate of Occupancy A document issued by the local government housing authority that certifies a dwelling has been built according to local housing code and is legally ready for residential occupancy.

Chain of title The history of all of the documents that transfer title to a specific piece of real property. A history starting with the earliest existing document and ending with the most recent.

Character An underwriting term referencing the applicant's willingness to repay a debt.

Charge-off The write-off of the portion of principal and interest due on a loan that is determined to be uncollectible.

Collateral The security for a loan. For mortgage loans, the property description contained in the recorded mortgage.

Commitment A written promise to make, insure, or buy a mortgage loan for a specified amount and on specified terms.

Commitment fee Any fee paid by an applicant to a lender for the lender's promise to lend money at a specified date in the future. The lender may or may not expect to fund the commitment. Or, a fee paid by a lender or an investor in a secondary market transaction.

Compensating balances Funds left on deposit with a lender as a condition for a loan.

Composite APR A method of APR calculation used for adjustable rate mortgages to reflect the interest rate changes over the life of the loan (*See* APR).

Condominium Real estate in which individual owners own title to a part of the whole (e.g., a unit in a building) and an undivided interest in the common areas. An association manages all the units and common areas according to association by-laws.

Conduits Entities that issue mortgage-backed securities backed by mortgages, which were originated by another, typically one or more of the traditional originators.

Conforming mortgage loan Mortgage that meet all the GSE eligibility and underwriting guidelines (Fannie Mae and Freddie Mac only).

Construction loan A short-term, interim loan for financing the cost of construction.

Construction loan advance A partial disbursement of mortgage loan funds by a lender to the borrower after verifying a portion of the home construction has been completed. Borrower and lender normally agree to an advance schedule beforehand to formalize the amounts and requirements for each advance.

Construction/permanent loan A type of mortgage loan that includes terms and conditions for both a construction phase (to build the proposed house) and a repayment phase (to amortize the loan by the maturity date).

Conventional loan A non-government mortgage loan neither insured by FHA nor guaranteed by VA or USDA.

Correspondent A mortgage banker who services mortgage loans as a representative or agent for the owner of the mortgage or for the investor. Also applies to the mortgage banker's role as originator of mortgage loans for an investor.

Cost of Funds Index An index that is used to determine interest rate changes for some ARMs. It represents the weighted-average cost of savings, borrowings, and advances of members of the 11th District of the Federal Home Loan Bank of San Francisco.

Cost to construct The amount needed to complete the construction of a home. Calculated by adding documented costs involved in the home's construction (land purchase, labor, materials, permits, fees, etc.)

Counteroffer A commitment offered by a lender to an application in which a lender does not accept the original application terms. Instead, the lender offers the applicant different loan terms than requested.

Coupon rate The annual interest rate on a debt. The coupon rate on a mortgage is the contract rate stated in the mortgage note. The coupon rate on a mortgage security is the rate stated on the face of the security, not the rate of the mortgages in the pool that backs the security.

Credit report A record of a person's open and repaid debts.

Credit score A numerical value that is assigned to a consumer. A credit score is calculated using statistical methods and evaluates a consumer's use and repayment of credit at a given point in time.

Custodial account An account required by an investor, borrower, or lender to hold funds and/or documents collected by an attorney or loan servicer on behalf of the lender, borrower, or investor.

Custodian Usually a commercial bank that holds for safekeeping funds and/or mortgages and related documents backing a loan or an MBS. A custodian may be required to examine and certify documents.

D

Debt/income ratios Underwriting ratios used to qualify mortgage applicants. Three common ratios used are for housing expense, total debt, and owner-occupant. These monthly payment amounts are divided by the monthly income used for qualification.

Deed A legal document that conveys title to real estate from one party to another. Different types of deeds are used in various states and legal situations.

Deed of trust A three-party mortgage instrument between a borrower, a lender, and a third party, called a trustee.

Default Failure to make mortgage payments when due or to comply with other covenants or requirements of a security agreement; can apply to the lender or the borrower.

Deficiency judgment A court determination that the mortgagor, who has lost property by foreclosure, is liable for the difference between the sales price of the property at foreclosure and the total amount of costs incurred by the lender (loan principal and interest, taxes, insurance, property maintenance and repair, legal and foreclosure costs, etc.).

Delinquency A situation in which borrower has not made the proper payment on a mortgage loan by its due date.

Delivery Sending the required application and loan documents to an investor after loan closing in order to obtain funding from the investor.

Delivery risk Broadly refers to any of the possible issues that the mortgage lender and investor may have after closing and before funding a loan.

Discount In loan obligations, an amount withheld from loan proceeds by a lender to lower the note interest rate. In secondary market sales, it is the amount by which the sale price of a note is less than its face value. In both instances, the purpose of a discount is to adjust the yield upward, either in lieu of interest or in addition to interest. The rate or amount of discount depends on money market conditions, the credit of the borrower, and the rate and terms of the note.

Discount point *See* Point.

Discounted rate The lower note rate as a result of paying a discount fee.

Disintermediation The systemic flow of funds out of one sector of the economy (e.g., the withdrawal of more money from financial intermediaries than incoming deposits).

Dower The rights of a widow in the property of her husband at his death.

Down payment The difference between the sales price of real estate and the mortgage amount. It can include savings and gift funds, but not borrowed funds.

Draw period That time within which a consumer can take advances from a line of credit. A draw period usually ranges from five to ten years, although it can be for any period up to the maximum period allowed for a mortgage loan in a particular state.

E

Easement A recorded, nonpossessory interest in the real estate of another, giving the holder the right to a limited use of that real estate.

Equity A homeowner's financial interest in real estate established by the difference between the market value of the property and the amount owed on its mortgage and other outstanding debts against the property.

Escrow account Funds held in a separate account by a legally agreed upon party that will be used to pay a third party at a later date. Mortgage lending uses escrow accounts for construction, property tax, and hazard, flood, or mortgage insurance.

Escrow analysis The periodic examination of escrow accounts to determine whether current monthly deposits will provide sufficient funds to pay taxes, insurance, and other bills when due. RESPA rules mandate how an account must be analyzed.

Escrow payment That portion of a mortgagor's monthly payment held by the lender or servicer to pay for taxes, hazard insurance, mortgage insurance, lease payments, and other items as they become due. Known as *impounds* or *reserves* in some states.

Estate An interest in real property that is measured by its potential duration.

F

Fallout Applications that fail to close under the original terms applied for because the applicant or lender changes them (applicant/lender fallout); also applications that fail to sell in the secondary market because an investor reneges on a commitment (investor fallout).

Fallout risk The risk incurred by the lender and investor that an application will not close and be delivered to the investor under the original terms committed to the investor.

Fannie Mae *See* Federal National Mortgage Association (FNMA).

Federal Home Loan Mortgage Corporation (FHLMC; Freddie Mac) A private corporation originally authorized by Congress as a government-sponsored enterprise to provide secondary mortgage market support for conventional mortgages. It can buy and can hold all types of loans in its portfolio and also sells participation certificates secured by pools of conventional mortgage loans. Popularly known as Freddie Mac, it incurred massive losses and in 2008 was placed under government conservatorship.

Federal Housing Administration (FHA) A division of HUD. Its main activity is the insuring of residential mortgage loans made by private lenders. Historically, it developed innovative standards for construction and underwriting. FHA rarely lends money directly or plans or constructs housing.

Federal National Mortgage Association (FNMA; Fannie Mae) A privately owned corporation created by Congress as a government-sponsored enterprise to support the secondary mortgage market. It purchases and sells residential mortgages insured by the FHA or guaranteed by the VA as well as conventional home mortgages; also issues mortgage-backed securities. Popularly known as Fannie Mae, it incurred massive losses and in 2008 was placed under government conservatorship.

Fee Tail An estate of potentially infinite duration, but is inheritable only by the grantee's lineal descendants, such as children or grandchildren. It was used in feudal times by nobility to ensure land stayed within the family.

Fee Tail General Property is inheritable by the issue of the grantee.

Fee Tail Special Property is inheritable only by the issue of the grantee and a specifically named spouse.

Fee option An option allowing lenders to pay a one-time commitment fee in exchange for a reduction in Fannie Mae's required yield. Also called *fee/yield tradeoff*.

Fee Simple or Fee Simple Absolute The highest form of real estate freehold ownership by non-government entities, giving the estate holder the most unrestricted rights to the property.

Fixed-rate mortgage A mortgage in which the interest rate does not change during the entire term of the loan.

Fixture Describes a piece of personal property permanently affixed to the real property and is now considered real property.

FHLMC *See* Federal Home Loan Mortgage Corporation (Freddie Mac).

Float The time between collection and disbursement of funds. In mortgage lending, it occurs between a lender's collection of payments from borrowers and the remittance of those funds to an investor.

FNMA *See* Federal National Mortgage Association (Fannie Mae).

Forbearance The act of refraining from taking legal action despite the fact that a mortgage is in arrears. It is usually granted only when a mortgagor makes a satisfactory arrangement by which the arrears will be paid at a future date.

Foreclosure An authorized procedure ... n by a mortgagee or lender under the terms of a mortgage or deed of trust for the purpose of having the property sold and the proceeds applied to the payment of a defaulted debt.

Forward delivery The delivery of mortgages or mortgage-backed securities to satisfy cash or future market transactions of an earlier date.

Forward sale An agreement in which a lender agrees to sell to an investor a specified amount of mortgages or securities at an agreed-upon price at a specified future date. Mandatory and best efforts delivery commitments are types of forward sale.

Freddie Mac *See* Federal Home Loan Mortgage Corporation (FHLMC).

Freehold estate Is the highest form of ownership interest possible in real property, as it involves all the rights in real property including use, passing the property to one's heirs, and selecting who is going to take it in a transfer.

Funding The disbursement of funds to complete a transaction. In mortgage finance, it occurs when the lender provides money to close a real estate sale or when an investor transfers funds to the lender to purchase a mortgage loan.

Futures contract A contract purchased on an organized market (e.g., Chicago Board of Trade) either for the purchase of a GNMA certificate at a specified price on a specified future date or for the sale of the certificate at a specified future date.

G

General contractor (GC) The person (or entity) legally responsible for the proposed construction on a residential property. Can perform all the work or use subcontractors to complete it.

General warranty deed The most common deed used to transfer interest in real estate. A grantor guarantees to a grantee that the title transferred is good and defendable from the time of the property's origin and against the whole world.

GNMA *See* Government National Mortgage Association (Ginnie Mae).

GNMA-backed bond A mortgage-backed bond using GNMA Certificates as the collateral rather than the individual mortgages.

GNMA Futures Market A regulated central market in which standardized contracts for the future delivery of GNMA securities are traded.

GNMA mortgage-backed securities Securities guaranteed by GNMA that are issued by mortgage bankers, commercial banks, savings and loan associations, savings banks, and other institutions. The GNMA security holder is protected by the "full faith and credit of the U.S. government." GNMA securities are backed by FHA, VA, or FmHA mortgages.

Government mortgage Mortgage intended for one of several federal or state government-sponsored programs —Federal Housing Agency (FHA), Veteran's Administration (VA), USDA/Rural Housing (RHS)/Farmer's Home Administration (FmHA), or one of a number of state agencies.

Government National Mortgage Association (GNMA; Ginnie Mae) On September 1, 1968, Congress enacted legislation to partition FNMA into two continuing corporate entities. GNMA assumed responsibility for the special assistance loan program and the management and liquidation function of the older FNMA. Also, GNMA administers the mortgage-backed securities program, which channels new sources of funds into residential financing through the sale of privately issued securities carrying a GNMA guaranty. Popularly known as Ginnie Mae.

GSEs Government-sponsored enterprises (e.g., Fannie Mae and Freddie Mac).

Guaranty fee A guarantor's fee for guaranteeing to an investor the timely payment of principal and interest from all mortgages underlying a mortgage-backed security.

H

Hazard insurance Insurance coverage on real estate that compensates the owner for physical damage to a property from fire, wind, or other hazards.

Home equity line of credit (HELOC) A mortgage loan, often in a second lien position, that allows the borrower to obtain multiple advances of funds up to an approved amount. As the funds are repaid, they can be advanced again during the draw period. Often contains a repayment period where no further draws are allowed.

I

Index A number used to compute the interest rate on a variable-rate mortgage (ARM loan or HELOC) that is based on a different financial instrument. The index is often based on the sale of U.S. Treasuries (T-bill), cost of funds (COFI), bank-to-bank lending (LIBOR), or business loans (prime rate). It is added to a margin to obtain the interest rate.

Initial interest rate The original interest rate on a variable-rate mortgage. Sometimes referred to as a *teaser rate* if discounted below the *fully indexed accrual rate.*

Insured risk Defined as the percentage share of each loan that is actually covered by the individual insurance policy.

Interest rate risk The risk of financial loss or gain resulting from changes in market rates compared to the mortgage note rate.

Inventory The loans a lender has closed but has not yet delivered to an investor.

Investor The holder of a mortgage or the permanent lender for whom a mortgage servicer services the loan. Any person or institution investing in mortgages.

Investor risk Risk of an application not being funded under the terms originally committed to by the investor.

Involuntary conveyance Occurs when a legal owner of real estate loses title contrary to the owner's intention.

J

Joint tenancy A form of real estate co-ownership that gives each tenant undivided and equal interest and rights in the property.

Judicial foreclosure A type of foreclosure proceeding used in some states that is handled as a civil lawsuit and goes through the court process.

Jumbo loan A loan that exceeds the secondary mortgage market's maximum mortgage amount limits. Also called a *nonconforming loan.*

L

Lease A type of estate that gives the tenant possession for a period of time through a contract establishing rights and duties for the parties.

Late charge The penalty a mortgagor must pay (usually 5 percent) when a payment is made a stated number of days after a due date (usually 10 or 15).

Legal description A legal property description recorded in government land records. It often appears on schedule "A" of a mortgage to locate and identify

real estate being secured as collateral for the loan.

LIBOR *See* London Interbank Offering Rate.

London Interbank Offering Rate (LIBOR) A base rate at which banks lend to each other and is based on dollar-denominated deposits (Eurodollars); used as an ARM index.

Lien A legally enforceable claim or encumbrance against real estate that must be paid when the property is sold.

Lien theory The legal approach where the mortgagor holds title while the debt is outstanding and not in default.

Life Estate Freehold estate like the fee simple absolute, but it is not inheritable and lasts for the entire life of the named party.

Loan A sum of money borrowed that is expected to be repaid at a stated rate of interest by a stated time.

Loan administration Describes a larger, more sophisticated loan servicing role in the lender's overall strategy. It includes a servicing department that handles the repayment of the loan with the borrower and a secondary market department that includes servicing and remittance responsibilities for loans sold to secondary market investors or government agencies.

Loan constant The yearly percentage of interest that remains the same over the life of an amortized loan based on the monthly payment in relation to the principal originally loaned.

Loan Originator Lender or mortgage broker. Also see "Mortgage Loan Originator" (MLO). Different regulations may have specific definitions.

Loan servicing The covenants, responsibilities, functions, and day-to-day operations that an organization performs after the closing and over the term or repayment of that loan until the loan is paid in full and released.

Loan submission A package of pertinent papers and documents regarding specific property or properties. It is derived from the application package and delivered to a prospective lender for review and consideration for the purpose of making or selling a mortgage loan.

Lock-in A written agreement between a lender and an applicant in which the lender guarantees the applicant a

specified interest rate if the loan closes within a specified period of time.

M

Mandatory delivery commitment A written agreement that a lender will deliver loans or securities to an investor by a certain date at an agreed-upon price and yield. *Compare with* Optional or best efforts commitment.

Margin The number of basis points a lender adds to an index to determine the interest rate of an adjustable-rate mortgage. The exact margin is contained in the mortgage note does not change over the life of the loan.

Marketable title A title that can transfer, but may not be completely clear. It may have only minor defects or objections that a well-informed and prudent seller would accept.

Market price That price for which the real estate or mortgage loan actually sells.

Market value for real estate Defined by the Appraisal Foundation and the Uniform Standards of Professional Appraisal Practice as "the most probable price which a property should bring in a competitive and open market under all conditions requisite to a fair sale, the buyer and seller, each acting prudently and knowledgeably, and assuming the price is not affected by undue stimulus."

Master commitment A written agreement between a lender and an investor which allows the lender to sell an agreed upon volume and type of mortgages under the same conditions over a specified period of time, typically six to 12 months.

Mechanic's lien A lien placed on the property by someone who has performed work on it and who has not been paid. Like a mortgage lien, it is recorded. In most states, this lien will take priority over a prior mortgage lien if recorded within a certain time from when the work was performed on the property.

Modification The act of formally changing any of the terms of a mortgage between the lender and borrower. It must be recorded in the land records.

MORNET Fannie Mae's communications network that enables customers to use a data terminal, personal computer, or mainframe to send and receive documents and reports electronically.

Mortgage A conveyance of an interest in real property given as security for the payment of a debt. The mortgage document must be recorded in land records to perfect the lien and security interest.

Mortgage-backed securities (MBSs) Bond- type investment securities representing an undivided interest in a pool of mortgages or trust deeds. Income from the underlying mortgage is used to pay off the securities. *See* GNMA mortgage-backed securities.

Mortgage banker A firm or individual active in the field of mortgage banking. Mortgage bankers, as local representatives of regional or national institutional lenders, act as correspondents between mortgage investors, lenders, and borrowers. Mortgage bankers typically sell all loan applications they receive. They need to borrow the funds they lend out temporarily before the investor funds them.

Mortgage banking The origination, sale, delivery, funding, and servicing of mortgage loans by a firm or individual. Loans are sold to a permanent investor, often with loan servicing performed for a fee. The investor-correspondent system is the foundation of the mortgage-banking industry.

Mortgage broker A firm or individual who solicits and takes a mortgage application then markets it to various lender/investors for a commission. A mortgage broker may also process the application, but does not approve, fund, or service loans.

Mortgage company A private corporation (sometimes called a mortgage banker) whose principal activity is the origination and servicing of mortgage loans that are sold to other financial institutions.

Mortgage discount The difference between the principal amount of a mortgage and the amount for which it actually sells. Sometimes called *points*, *loan brokerage fee*, or *new loan fee*. The discount is computed on the amount of the loan, not the sale price.

Mortgage instrument The document used to create a security interest in the real estate for the lender. It must be recorded to perfect the lien on the property and contains numerous covenants that both borrower and lender must follow.

Mortgage insurance (MI) Default insurance for the lender for a certain percentage of the original loan amount. Mortgage insurance premiums are usually paid by the borrower with monthly payments, although other arrangements are used. Most common forms are FHA, private mortgage insurance, and self-insurance by the lender.

Mortgage loan originator (MLO) As defined by the SAFE Act of 2008, an "individual"—a natural person, *not* an organization or entity—who takes a mortgage loan application or offers or negotiates terms of a mortgage loan for, or in the expectation of, compensation or gain, either directly or indirectly for another individual. Additional classes of people may be included if they advise the consumer or collect information on behalf of the consumer in order to obtain a mortgage loan.

Mortgage product Refers to the loan terms and instrument used.

Mortgage program Describes the entire package of loan product terms and restrictions and underwriting guidelines in addition to the instrument involved.

Mortgage Servicing Right (MSR) An asset created when a loan is sold in the secondary mortgage market. It consists of the right of a company to earn a servicing fee for servicing that sold loan. It includes the obligation to meet certain regulatory and investor requirements in the performance of those duties, outlined in a servicing agreement.

Mortgagee The lender in a transaction whereby real estate is being taken as security for the debt.

Mortgagors The borrower in a transaction whereby real estate is being taken as security for the debt.

N

Negative amortization An increase in mortgage debt that occurs when the required (monthly) payment is not sufficient to repay the accrued interest for that period and does not include a payment to principal. The amount of the shortfall (usually interest) is added to the remaining principal balance to create the negative amortization. *See* Amortization.

Negotiated transaction A secondary market transaction in which the terms and conditions are negotiated between the lender and the investor. These transactions do not fall under any of the investor's standard or formal loan programs.

Non-conforming mortgage loan A mortgage loan that does not meet GSE guidelines and is ineligible for sale to Fannie Mae or Freddie Mac. It typically includes government, jumbo, subprime, or portfolio loan programs.

Note Evidence of debt. In mortgage lending, a legal document that obligates a mortgagor to repay a mortgage loan at a stated interest rate during a specified period of time.

Notice of satisfaction A document that is executed and recorded when a judgment debt is paid (satisfied). The Notice provides evidence of such and must be recorded to release the obligation. Used in mortgage lending when a deficiency judgment exists after foreclosure.

O

Optional commitment A commitment that gives the lender the option to sell loans to an investor under specified terms. The lender pays a nonrefundable fee to obtain the commitment but, because delivery is not mandatory, suffers no penalty for not fulfilling the commitment. *Compare with* Mandatory delivery commitment.

Origination The process of marketing, advertising, taking, processing, underwriting, and closing mortgage applications. Solicitation may be from individual consumers, builders, or real estate brokers. Origination is the process by which the mortgage lender brings into being a mortgage secured by real property.

Origination fee A fee or charge for the work involved in the evaluation, preparation, and submission of a proposed mortgage loan. It is defined by Truth in Lending as a finance charge.

Originator A person who solicits consumers, builders, real estate brokers, and others to obtain applications for mortgage loans. *See* Loan Originator and Mortgage Loan Originator.

P

Pair-off A secondary market transaction whereby the lender cannot deliver the full amount of a mandatory forward commitment and negotiates a fee paid to the investor for non-delivery. The *pair-off fee* can be reduced or eliminated if a suitable substitute loan is accepted by the investor.

Par A sale price that equals the principal amount of a mortgage with no premium or discount.

Partial payment A payment that is less than the full amount of the scheduled monthly mortgage payment.

Participation certificate (PC) Mortgage-backed security issued by FHLMC (Freddie Mac) that consists of mortgages purchased from eligible sellers. Called a PC because seller retains some interest (5 or 10 percent) in the mortgages sold to FHLMC.

Participations A mortgage made by several lenders. One lender, known as the lead lender, and one or more other lenders, known as participants, own a part interest. Or, a mortgage originated by two or more lenders.

Pass-through rate The rate at which interest is paid to an investor for a mortgage. It is the lower of an investor's required yield or the mortgage interest rate after a minimum servicing fee has been deducted.

Pass-through security A form of mortgage-backed bond for which the monthly collections on the mortgage pool are "passed through" to the investor.

Piggyback loans A residential mortgage loan often used in a purchase transaction to complete the financing. Typically, it involves a 75 or 80 percent LTV first mortgage and a 10, 15, or 20 percent LTV second mortgage that are both closed at the same time. As a result of this structure, the down payment may be only 5 or 10 percent of the loan amount. Transactions structured this way do not require mortgage insurance.

Pipeline The aggregate of mortgage applications and loans in process for eventual sale in the secondary market. The term encompasses both applications that are in production and closed loans not yet delivered to and funded by an investor.

PITI An acronym for principal, interest, taxes, and insurance—items typically included in the monthly mortgage payment.

Point An amount equal to 1 percent of the principal amount of an investment or note. Loan discount points are a one-time charge assessed at closing by the lender to lower the borrower's interest rate and/or to increase the yield on the mortgage loan to a competitive position with other types of investments.

Pool insurance Mortgage insurance for the investor for a percentage of the original amount of a group (pool) of mortgage loans. The pool is usually securitized and sold in the secondary market.

Portfolio Investments (including mortgages and mortgage securities) held by an individual or institution. In mortgage lending, the term variously refers to mortgages held by a lender prior to their sale in the secondary market, to MBSs held by lenders for investment purposes, and to loans that a lender continues to service for investors.

Portfolio mortgage A loan that an originator places in its portfolio or that an investor purchases for cash and holds as an asset.

Pre-approval A formal commitment by a lender to an applicant for a period of time for a maximum loan amount. Usually provided to assist the applicant in searching for a property to purchase and may contain other conditions. Pre-approvals are subject to essentially the same compliance regulations as formal (written) applications.

Premium The amount, often stated as a percentage, paid in addition to the face value of a note or bond.

Prequalification An informal meeting during which a lender provides a consumer with information on mortgage loan products, procedures, and underwriting guidelines. The lender may do limited financial counseling as well, but does not discourage a formal application from being completed or make a credit decision on a specific loan request (or give such an impression to the consumer).

Prepayment penalty clause A covenant in the mortgage note that typically imposes the payment of a fee equal to a percentage of the principal balance if the borrower pays the note in full ahead of maturity, usually within the first two or three years.

Primary mortgage market The market in which lenders originate mortgages by making direct loans to homebuyers. *See also* Secondary mortgage market.

Principal The amount borrowed or remaining to be repaid.

Private mortgage insurance (PMI) Mortgage insurance provided by a private mortgage insurance company that protects the lender against loss if a borrower defaults. Usually obtained if the initial loan to value exceeds 80 percent. Required for GSE secondary market loans.

Program risk Occurs when a lender originates and commits to a consumer for a loan program (e.g., six month ARM or no-income verification program), but the investor stops funding that program. *See* also Investor risk.

Promissory note *See* Note.

Q

Quality control A system of safeguards to ensure that all applications taken and loans closed are originated, processed, underwritten, closed, and serviced according to the lender's and an investor's standards.

R

Rate lock *See* Lock-in.

Real Estate The ownership interest and rights associated with real property.

Real Property Land and everything permanently attached to it.

Recording The legal act of providing public notice in land records. In mortgage lending, the act of recording the details of a property transfer and/or financing at the registrar's office where the property is taken as security for the debt.

Recourse The right of a party to remedy a transaction if in default. In mortgage lending, an investor's right to seek compensation from or re-purchase by the lender for a loan sold and later determined to be in violation of the selling agreement or the terms of the loan sale commitment.

Redlining An illegal practice according to Regulation B in which the lender refuses to originate loans or lend mortgage funds in a certain geographic area based solely on perceived risks in that area from discriminatory factors, including racial, social, religious, or ethnic factors.

REMIC A security that represents a beneficial interest in a trust having multiple classes of securities. The classes of each class entitle investors to cash flows structured differently from the payments on the underlying mortgages.

Repayment period The agreed upon period of time outlined in the mortgage note by when the borrower must repay all money owed. It can be 5 to 20 years for home equity lines of credit or up to two years for construction loans.

Repurchase risk The risk of having the lender re-purchase a loan sold to an investor. It occurs when an investor's post-closing audit discovers significant mortgage fraud, violations of investor guidelines, or documentation or underwriting error(s) significant enough to require the mortgage lender to repurchase the loan.

Required yield The minimum yield return required by an investor in a particular secondary market transaction. It is quoted on a net basis—that is, it does not include the lender's servicing fee.

Reverse price risk Exposure to the risk of falling interest rates. It occurs when a lender makes a commitment to sell a loan to an investor before making a loan commitment to the borrower.

S

Seasoned loan A loan on which a borrower has made payments for more than one year, as compared to newly originated or current production loans. For some investors, a loan may require two or more years before it is considered seasoned.

Scheduled/Actual (S/A) A type of remittance requiring the lender to remit to Fannie Mae the scheduled interest due (whether or not it is collected from borrowers) and the actual principal payments collected.

Scheduled/Scheduled (S/S) A type of remittance requiring the lender to remit to Fannie Mae the scheduled interest due and the scheduled principal due (whether or not payments are collected from borrowers).

Secondary mortgage market A market in which existing or newly-originated mortgages are bought and sold between lenders and investors. It contrasts with the primary mortgage market, in which mortgages are originated between lender and borrower. *See also* Primary mortgage market.

Seller/servicer A term for a corporation that has been approved to sell and/or service mortgages for either FNMA or FHLMC.

Servicing The collection for an investor of payments, interest, principal, and trust items such as hazard insurance and taxes on a note by the borrower in accordance with the terms of the note. Servicing also consists of operational procedures covering accounting, bookkeeping, insurance, tax records, loan payment follow-up, delinquency loan follow-up, and loan analysis. For secondary market transactions, the duties of the mortgage servicer for an investor as specified in the servicing agreement for which a fee is received.

Servicing contract or servicing agreement A written contract between an investor of mortgages and an organization that will perform the servicing responsibilities for those loans for the investor.

Servicing fee The compensation a mortgage servicer receives from a lender or an investor each month for servicing loans on their behalf.

Servicing released premium The amount derived from the sale of the rights to service a loan (*See* MSR) when the loan is sold in the secondary market.

Servicing responsibilities Refers to the more global fiduciary responsibility that the servicer assumes as agent for the borrower, lender, insurer, or regulator.

Servicing retained Retention of the rights to service a loan when the loan is sold in the secondary market.

Spec home A proposed house built by a builder without a contract for sale with a consumer. Usually financed by a lender and built on the "speculation" by the builder that someone will purchase the property at a later date.

Special warranty deed Used in rare situations when a grantor wants to limit the guarantee. An executor of an estate would use this instrument to convey real estate to those specified in a will.

Standard commitment An agreement to sell or swap loans based on an investor's posted yields, rather than on negotiated terms.

Standby commitment A non-binding commitment by a secondary market investor to a lender to purchase a loan or loans with specified terms, when both parties understand that full delivery may not be likely unless circumstances warrant. It may be converted to a mandatory commitment before the standby commitment expires.

Standby fees The fees charged by an investor for a standby commitment. The fees are earned upon issuance and acceptance of the commitment.

Statutory right of redemption Certain states provide another form of redemption right that begins to accrue to a mortgagor (or those claiming through the mortgagor) after foreclosure and sale.

T

Table funding A financing technique that occurs when a mortgage broker or

mortgage banker closes a mortgage loan with funds belonging to an acquiring lender and immediately assigns the loan to that lender. This activity gives the mortgage broker the opportunity to say it is a direct lender since it can close loans with its own funds.

Takeout commitment A promise to make a loan at a future specified time. It is commonly used to designate a higher cost, shorter term, backup commitment as a support for construction financing until a suitable permanent loan can be secured.

Tenancy in common A concurrent estate with no right of survivorship. Tenants in common typically have the right to sell, gift, or will their ownership interest independently from the other tenants.

Teaser rate. *See* discount rate. The same concept as a discount rate, but sometimes defined by regulation as exceeding two percent points of the fully accrued interest rate.

Title A legal document evidencing a person's right to ownership in real estate.

Title insurance Insurance that protects the lender (or borrower, if separate policy) against loss arising from disputes over ownership of real estate.

Title Service A very broad RESPA term that includes *any* service involved in the provision of lender's or owner's title insurance (including processing and administrative services).

Title theory The legal concept that he mortgagee holds title while the debt is outstanding and not in default.

U

Underwriting The process of evaluating a loan application to determine the risk involved for the lender. Establishing whether the risk is worth taking.

Uniform Standards of Professional Appraisal Practice Sets the guidelines by which the appraiser completes this or any other appraisal form and makes an estimate of market value.

V

VA mortgage A mortgage that is guaranteed by the Department of Veterans Affairs (VA).

W

Warehousing The practice of holding of a mortgage on a short-term basis pending either a sale to an investor or other long-term financing. These mortgages may be used as collateral security with a bank to borrow additional funds. A builder warehouses mortgages when it takes back a mortgage from a homebuyer and holds the mortgage for a time period.

Whole loan A loan in which an investor purchases a 100 percent interest.

Y

Yield In real estate, the effective annual income accrued on an investment (i.e., for a lender, a mortgage note). Expressed as a percentage of the price originally paid.

Yield spread premium Compensation or incentives paid by lenders to mortgage originators for originating a mortgage application with either higher risk factors or an interest rate that differs from market rates at the time. Sometimes they are useful tools for borrowers to pay less closing costs upfront.

INDEX

A

ABA Real Estate Lending Survey, 576
abstracting, 37
adjustable-rate mortgages (ARMs). *See also* first-mortgage loan closing; loan, generation of
buydowns and, 168–69
comparison of fixed rated mortgages, 172–74
convertible mortgages and, 169–70
discounts and, 164
explanation of, 157, 159–60
fully-indexed accrual rate of, 164
graduated payment mortgages (GPMs), 170–71
index of, 161–63
interest rate caps of, 163–64
margin of, 163
spread of, 164–67
structure of, 161
two-step or reset, mortgages and, 170
uniform standards of professional appraisal practice and, 439–40
adjustable-rate mortgages (ARMs) programs, 168
adverse possession, 36
Affiliated business arrangement disclosure, 325
affinity groups, 576–77
allodial system, 28
America Community Bankers, 250
American Association of Residential Mortgage Regulators (AARMR), 350

American Credit Union Mortgage Association (ACUMA), 101
American Enterprise Institute for Public Policy (AEI), 55
amortization, 6–7
amortization schedule, 171
applicant, loan. *See* underwriting
and application information booklet, 559–61
attracting consumers, 557–58
consumer stress and, 559
convenience of, 558–59
focusing on, 555–56
measuring customer satisfaction, 556–57
tools for attracting, 558
applicant qualification worksheet, 377, 378
application information booklet, 559–61
appraisal
age of, 459
alternative approaches to value and, 443–44
automated valuation models (AVMs) and, 457–59
cost approach of, 445–46
direct sales comparsion approach of, 444–45
factors affecting market value of, 441–42
hiring the appraiser and, 460
HVCC and, 460–61
income approach of, 446–47
market price and, 440–41
market value and, 440
principals of real estate value and, 440

process of, 442–43
purpose of, 437–38
reconcilation and final value estimate of, 447
regulatory changes and, 461
required forms for, 456
streamlined appraisals, 456–57
uniform residential appraisal report and, 438–39
value of, 438
Appraisal Foundation, 440
ARMss, hybrid, 168. *See also* loan, generation of
asset/liability management (ALM), 109
assignment of mortgage, 50
assumption of mortgage, 49
automated underwriting system (AUS), 402, 424–25, 457–59
automated valuation models (AVMs), 457

B

balloon payment, 154, 156
Bank Insurance Fund (BIF), 93
Banking Act of 1933, 93
basis points, 71
biweekly mortgages, 171–72
bonds
builder, 75
mortgage credit certificates (MCCs), 74–75
mortgage revenue bonds (MRBs), 74
Bureau of Consumer Financial Protection (BCFP), 350
buydowns, 168–69

C

capital formation, 63–65
capital markets, 65–66
child support, 384–85
clause
  acceleration, 42
  default, 42–43
  due on sale, 49
  payment, 42
  prepayment, 42
  subordination, 43
closed-end second mortgages, 277–78
closing
  commitment letter and, 468, 469
  commitmentletter and, 472–76
  costs of, 465–67
  explanation of, 463–64
  first-mortgage loan. *See*
    first-mortgage loan closing
  funding and loan delivery for, 490
  handling of, 467
  income tax reporting, 467
  insured closings, 468
  mortgage fraud and, 491–96
  mortgagor's policy and, 476
  quality control and fraud prevention
    for, 490–91
  quality control programs and,
    496–500
  steps for residential property, 468
  title insurance and, 472
  title review and, 469–72
collateral, 395–96
combined loan to value (LTV) ratios
  (CLTV), 413–14
commercial banks
  federal reserve regulations of, 94–95
  historical development of, 92–93
  mortgage lending activity of, 94
  organization and regulation of, 93
commercial paper, sale of, 91
commitment letter, 468, 469
commitments, mortgage market
  best efforts and, 547
  details of sale and, 545–46
  loan delivery and, 548
  mandatory delivery of, 546–47
  master commitments of, 546
  pair-off and, 547
  standby commitments of, 547–48
community property, 35
Community Reinvestment Act (CRA),
  13, 298, 349, 376
  qualifying an applicant, 376–78
compensating balances, 91
Competitive Equality Banking Act
  (1987), 14
compliance
  acts relating to, 299–300
  discrimination and, 300–301
  fair lending regulations and, 300
  importance of, 298
Comprehensive Risk Assessment, 426–30

conditional fee simple, 29–30
conduits, 543
Conference of State Banking Supervisors
  (CSBS), 350
conforming loan, mortgage
  amount of, 175
  explanation of, 174–75
  Fannie Mae and Freddie Mac and,
    175–77
  insurance requirements of, 177
  loan to value (LTV)s ratio of, 177
Consolidated FARMsers Home
  Administration Act (1961), 12
construction lending
  administration and funding of, 267
  basics of, 251–52
  drawbacks of, 257–58
  economy and, 248–49
  management of, 258–59
  origination of, 249–51, 259–62
  permanant loans, differences from,
    252–54
  programs of, 255–57
  underwriting of, 262–67
Consumer Credit Protection
  Act (1968), 12
Consumer Financial Protection Bureau/
  Agency (CFPB) – *See* BCFP
consumer privacy regulations, 298
Consumer Protection Act (1968),
  10–11, 15, 122
consumer protection regulations,
  298–99
consumer protection, reverse mortgage,
  293–95
convertible mortgages, 169–70
conveyance (title transfer), 38
Cost of Servicing Study, 525
covenants, 33
credit
  countercyle nature of real estate,
    69, 72
  Federal Reserve bank system and,
    68–69
  line of and warehousing, 91
  users of, 66–68
Credit Alert Interactive Voice Response
  System (CAIVRS), 230
credit history, 391–95
  bankruptcy and, 420–21
  chronic delinquency and, 420
  collateral and, 422
  credit scores and, 421–22
  minor delinquency and, 420
  past foreclosures and, 421
  property and appraisal standards and,
    422–23
  reasons for mortage default, 512–13
  repayment history and, 419–20
  situational delinquency and, 420
  use of debt and, 419
Credit Union National Association
  (CUNA), 101

Credit Union Service Organizations
  (CUSOs), 105
credit unions
  description of, 100–102
  historical development of, 103
  mortgage-lending activity of, 104
  organization and regulation of, 103–4
CUNA. *See* Credit Union National
  Association (CUNA)
custodial accounts, 548

D

debt/income ratios, 379
decline and crisis of mortgage market.
  See mortgage market, secondary
deed
  general warranty and, 37
  quitclaim and, 37
  special warranty and, 37
  of trust, 41
deed in lieu, 47
defeasance clause, 38
defeasible fee simple, 29–30
deficiency judgments, 48
Deficit Reduction Act (1984), 14
delinquency, mortgage, 509–14
  2 month delinquencies and,
    513–14
  collection procedures for, 513
  curing delinquencies, 514
  loss mitigation and, 514–16
  mortgagee options and, 510–12
  reasons for default and, 512–13
  telephone contact and, 513
Delivery Options, 545
delivery risk, 551
Department of Housing and Urban
  Development (HUD)
  broker fees and, 85, 90
  Fannie Mae and, 127
  FHA and, 208–10, 292
  Good Faith Estimate and, 333
  GSE regulation and, 134
  introduction of, 10
  RESPA and, 316, 327–32
Deposit Insurance Fund (DIF), 93
Depository Institutions Deregulation
  and Monetary Control Act (1980),
  13, 137
Desktop Underwriter. *See* Fannie Mae
  Desktop Underwriter® (DU®)
discrimination
  acts pertaining to, 12–13, 361
  effects test for, 301
  explanation of, 300–301
  federal government and, 435–36
  government monitoring for, 305
  property and, 422
  underwriting and, 435–36
"Do Not Call Registry", 298, 310–11
documents, standard vs. streamlined,
  425–26

Dodd-Frank Act, 516, 567
Dodd-Frank Wall Street Reform and
    Financial Protection Act (DFA), 15,
    122, 298
    explanation of, 351–52
    timing of, 355
    Title X of, 352–53
    Title XIV of, 353–55
down payment, 414–15

E

easements, 33
economic stimulus of housing, 55–57
effects test, 301
Emergency Economic Stabilization Act
    (EESA), 93
Emergency Home Finance Act (1970),
    12–13, 185
eminent domain, 36
Energy Efficient Mortgages (EEMs), 211
English Common Law, 27–28
Equal Credit Opportunity Act (ECOA),
    13, 298
    adverse action and, 305
    application for, 303
    appraisal and, 304
    consumer privacy regulations and,
        305–7
    cosigner of, 304
    "cradle to grave regulation" of, 302–3
    government monitoring of, 305
    marriage status and, 303–4
    status of application, 304
    USA PATRIOT Act and, 307
equity, 4, 414–15
equity of redemption, 39
Escrow (administration; disclosures;
    rules and requirements; surplus,
    shortage, and deficit), 340, 480,
    521, 523–25

F

Fair and Accurate Credit Transactions
    Act (FACT), 308
Fair Credit Reporting Act (FCRA), 298,
    307–8
Fair Debt Collection Practices Act
    (FDCPA), 298, 349
Fair Housing Act (1968), 12, 298,
    301–2
fair lending practices regulations, 13,
    298
Fair Lending Practices Regulations,
    300–301
fallout risk, 550–51
Fannie Mae Desktop Underwriter®
    (DU®), 216, 233, 379, 425,
    456–57
Fannie Mae Fannie Mae Desktop
    Underwriter® (DU®),
    379, 402

Fannie Mae (Federal National Mortgage
    Association). *See also* automated
    underwriting system (AUS); gov-
    ernment lending; mortgage fraud;
    mortgage market, secondary
    description of, 125–27
    eligibility requirements matrix of, 178
    future needs and, 21
    history of, 89, 127
    issuance of MBSs and, 120
    programs of, 175–77
    URAR form 1004, 456
FDIC. *See* Federal Deposit Insurance
    Corporation (FDIC)
Federal Bureau of Investigation (FBI),
    150, 492–94
Federal Deposit Insurance Corporation
    (FDIC), 9, 93
Federal Deposit Insurance Reform Act
    (2006), 93
Federal FARMs Loan Act (1916), 11
Federal Financial Institutions
    Examination Council (FFIEC), 200
Federal Home Loan Bank (FHLBs), 8,
    11, 96, 128. *See also* mortgage
    market, secondary
Federal Home Loan Mortgage
    Corporation (FHLMC), 13
Federal Housing Administration (FHA).
    See also first-mortgage loan closing;
    mortgage market, secondary
    acts pertaining to, 14–15
    automated underwriting and, 216
    benefits to mortgage industry, 209
    created by Congress, 9, 89
    documented required, 217–27
    down payment and, 214–15
    eligibility for, 213–14
    green initiative of, 211
    history of, 208–9
    and HOPE, 210
    insurance type of, 212–13
    lender insurance (LI) and, 211
    loan limits of, 213
    loss mitigation tools, 209–10
    moderation of, 211–12
    modern considerations, 209–10
    qualifying ratios of, 216
Federal Housing Enterprise Financial
    Safety and Soundness Act
    (1992), 134
Federal Housing Finance Agency
    (FHFA), 14, 134
Federal Reserve Act (1913), 11, 93
Federal Reserve bank system, 68–69
Federal Savings and Loan Insurance
    Corporation (FSLIC), 9, 16, 96
fee simple absolute, 29
fee tail, 30
FHA. *See* Federal Housing
    Administration (FHA)
FHA-Home Affordable Modification
    Program (FHA-HAMP), 210

FHFA House Price Index (HPI), 182
FICO® Score, 392, 395
Financial Accounting Standards Board
    (FASB), 518–19, 571
Financial Institutions Reform, Recovery
    and Enforcement Act (FIRREA),
    14, 17, 96, 97
financial intermediaries, 70–71
first-mortgage loan closing
    closing checklist for, 476–78
    conforming documentation of, 476
    documentation for, 476–89
    final requirements for, 486–90
fixture, 28
float income, 522–23
Flood Disaster Protection Act (FDPA)
    1974, 13, 343–44, 345–46
flow basis, 533
foreclosure
    decree of, 46
    deed in lieu, 47
    deficiency judgements, 48
    entry and possession, 47
    judicial proceeding, 43–46
    power of sale, 46–47
    statutory right of redemption, 47–48
    strict, 43, 47
forward delivery commitment, 539
Fraud (mortgage), 306, 488–490, 561
Freddie Mac (Federal Home Loan Mort-
    gage Corporation). *See also* auto-
    mated underwriting system (AUS);
    government lending; mortgage
    fraud; mortgage market, secondary
    future needs and, 21
    history of, 127–28
    issuance of MBSs, 120
    programs of, 175–77
Freddie Mac Loan Prospector (LP),
    402, 456
free and clear, 49
freehold estate, 28
funding risk, 551

G

GAAP. *See* generally accepted account-
    ing principals (GAAP)
Garn-St. Germain Depository
    Institutions Act (1982), 14
generally accepted accounting principals
    (GAAP), 96
Ginnie Mae. *See* Government National
    Mortgage Association (GNMA)
GNMA. *See* Government National
    Mortgage Association (GNMA)
good faith estimates, RESPA, 333–38,
    370–72
government lending. *See also* first-
    mortgage loan closing
    vs. conventional lending, 158
    FHA and, 208–27. *See also* Federal
        Housing Administration (FHA)

identification of lenders, 206–7
U.S. Dept. of Agriculture and, 240–46. *See also* Rural Housing Services (RHS)
VA and, 227–39. *See also* Veterans Administration (VA)
Government National Mortgage Association (GNMA), 12, 118–19, 127, 134
government sponsored enterprise (GSE), 14, 19, 112–13. *See also* Fannie Mae (Federal National Mortgage Association); Freddie Mac (Federal Home Loan Mortgage Corporation)
graduated payment mortgages (GPMs), 170–71
Gramm-Leach-Biley Financial Modernization Act of 1999
  consumer's right to "opt out", 310
  definitions of, 309
  "Do Not Call Registry" and, 310–11
  explanation of, 308–9
  introduction, 298
  privacy notice and, 309–10
  telemarketing sales rule and, 310

H

Hedging, 550
Higher Priced Mortgage Loans (HPML), 320
HMDA. *See* Home Mortgage Disclosure Act (HMDA)
HMDA loan activity register (HMDA-LAR), 348–49
Home Affordable Foreclosure Alternatives Program, 513
Home Affordable Refinance Program, 513
Home Affordable Modification Program (HAMP), 513
home, ownership rates of, 60–61
Home Equity Consumer Loan Protection Act (HELCPA), 298, 320–23
home equity conversion mortgage, FHA (HEMC), 291–93
home equity line of credit (HELOC)
  adjustment periods and fees, 285
  loan to value (LTV), 280
  payment methods of, 284–85
  periodic statements of, 285–88
  rates, types of, 278–80
  terms of, 280–84
home equity loans
  amount of loan, 273
  appraisals for, 274
  closed-end second mortgages. *See* closed-end second mortgages
  closing of, 275
  as consumer loan, 270
  importance to consumers, 271–73
  importance to lenders, 271

line of credit programs. *See* home equity line of credit (HELOC)
  marketing of, 288–89
  nomenclature of, 269–70
  processing of, 274
  reverse annuity mortgages (RAMs). *See* reverse annuity mortgages (RAMs)
  security documentation, 276
home improvement loan, 269–70
Home Mortgage Disclosure Act (HMDA)
  as consumer protection regulation, 298
  explanation of, 347
  introduction of, 13
  loan activity register, 348–49
Home Owners Loan Act (HOLA), 8, 12
Home Owners Loan Corporation (HOLC), 8, 89
Home Ownership and Equity Protection Act (HOEPA) of 1994, 14, 298, 319–20
home sales, 58–59
Home Valuation Code of Conduct (HVCC), 460–61
Homeowners Protection Act (HPA) of 1998
  annual notice, 347
  automatic cancellation of mortgage insurance and, 344
  borrower cancellation of mortgage insurance and, 344–46
  disclosure requirements, 347
  introduction to, 14
  other terminations and, 346
HOPE (H4H). *See* Hope for Homeowners
Hope for Homeowners, 15, 210
housing
  demographic forces and, 62
  value of, 59–60
Housing Act (1949), 9–10, 12
Housing and Community Development Act (1987), 14
Housing and Community Development Amendments (1979), 13
Housing and Urban Development Act, 10
Housing and Urban Development Act (1965), 12
Housing Community Development Act (1965), 10
Housing Economic and Recovery Act (HERA), 14, 210, 211–13
Housing in America: the Next Decade, 62
housing ratio, 417
HUD. *See* Department of Housing and Urban Development (HUD)
HUD sample booklet, 328–31
HUD-1 Uniform Settlement Statement, 338
HVCC. *See* Home Valuation Code of Conduct (HVCC)

I

indices, interest rate, 161–63
Interagency Statement on Subprime Mortgage Lending (1999), 179
interest, security, 40
interest only payment, 156
Interest Rate Adjustment Act (1966), 12
interest rates
  discounts and ARMss, 164
  effect of low interest rate, 54–55
  fully-indexed accrual rate of, 164
  indices and, 161–63
  monetary policy and, 67–68
  rate cap of, 163–64
  spread of, 164–67
Internet lending, 577–78
Interstate Land Sales Full Disclosure Act (1968), 11, 12
interview, with MLO, 362–64
investor, 91
investor approval, 543–45
investor risk, 551
involuntary transfer, 36
issues, mortgage lending, 23

J

J. D. Powers and Associates, 578
joint tenancy, 33–34

L

land as security, 2–3
lease, 32
leasehold estate, 28–29, 32
legal life estate, 31–32
lien theory, 39
life estate, 30–31
liquidity risk
loan, generation of. *See also* retail loan origination; wholesale loan origination
  channels of, 567–68
  competitive pricing and, 564–65
  demand and, 566–67
  importance of trained personnel, 562–63
  programs for, 563–64
  requirements for success, 561–62
  and targeted marketing and, 565–66
  and tracking progress and, 561
loan, home equity. *See* home equity loans
loan administration
  escrow administration and, 523–25
  evolution of loan servicing, 516–18
  other income and, 522–23
  resident lending and, 520
  servicing income and, 520–21
  servicing profitability and, 521–22
  servicing strategies and, 520
loan correspondents, 575–76
loan delivery, 548

loan origination fee, 85
loan origination services, 85, 576
Loan Prospector (LP). *See* Freddie Mac
 Loan Prospector (LP)
loan servicing
 contract for, 508–9
 cost of, 525
 departmental organization of, 503–4
 evolution of, 516–18
 explanation of, 501–2
 vs. loan administration, 502–3
 managing delinquencies and
  foreclosures, 509–10
 mortgage payment methods of, 505–8
 and post closing review, 505
 purchasing of, 527
 responsibilities and functions of, 504
 selling of, 528
 setting up file, 505
 and welcoming letter, 505
loan servicing alternatives
 selling services, 529
 servicing released, 528
loan to value (LTV) ratios
 combined, 413–14
 explaination of, 412–13
loss mitigation, 514–16

M

Making Home Affordable plan, 513
Modifications, 515
modification of mortgage, 50–51
monetary policy, 67–68
moratorium, mortgage foreclosure, 7–8
MORTECH Annual survey, 576
mortgage
 conforming vs. nonconforming,
  158–59
 convention vs. govt. vs. other, 158
 instrument, 40
 nomenclature of, 158
 non-traditional, 159
 requirements, 41
 risk management of, 157
mortgage, adjustable rate (ARMs),
 108, 156
 buydowns and, 168–69
 comparison of types, 173–74
 convertible mortgage type, 169–70
 description of, 159–61
 hybrid types of, 168
 indices and, 161–63
 interest rate cap and, 163–64
 interest spread of, 164–67
 margin of, 163
 structure of, 161
mortgage, biweekly, 171–72
mortgage, graduated payment (GPMs),
 170–71
mortgage, standard fixed-rate, 157
 comparison of types, 172–73
mortgage, standard-fixed rate, 154–56

mortgage, two-step or reset, 170
mortgage bankers
 development of, 87–89
 financing and, 90–91
 history of, 85–87
 modern, 89–90, 92
 organization and regulation of, 90
 and portfolio lenders, 87
Mortgage Bankers Association (MBA),
 6, 140, 557
Mortgage Bankers Association National
 Delinquency Survey, 206
Mortgage Bankers Performance Report,
 140
mortgage borrowers, loyality, 561
mortgage brokers, 83–84, 575–77
Mortgage Disclosure Improvement Act
 (MDIA), 15, 298
Mortgage Electronic Registration
 System (MERS), 550
mortgage fraud, 491–96
Mortgage Guaranty Insurance
 Corporation (MGIC), 184–85
Mortgage Insurance Companies of
 American (MICA), 182–83, 185
mortgage insurance (MI), 9
 business of, 198
 financial requirements of, 201–2
 HPA and, 344–47
 loan quality and portfolio risk of,
  198–200
 piggy-back loans and, 202–3
 reserve types, 202
mortgage loan orgination, 359–61
mortgage loan origination agreement, 86
mortgage loan originator (MLO), 78,
 350–51. *See also* credit history
 applicant and public assistance, 385
 applicant assets and, 385–86
 applicant child support and, 384–85
 applicant collateral and, 395–96
 applicant credit history, 387–90
 applicant credit scores, 391–95
 applicant derogatory items and, 395
 applicant documentation and, 382
 applicant interest, dividends, investments and, 383–84
 applicant pension and, 385
 applicant rental income and, 384
 applicant self-employment and,
  382–83
 applicants information and, 373–74
 application compliance issues of, 365
 applications received by mail and,
  374–75
 debt/income ratios, 379
 electronic applications, 375–76
 final check (compliance) and, 397–99
 formal application and, 364–65
 income of applicant and, 379–82
 interview with, 362–64
 loan transaction and program and,
  378–79

compensating factors, 397
 SAFE Act and, 356
 standard qualification worksheet of,
  378
 telephone applications, 375
 uniform residential loan application
  and, 365–73
mortgage loan programs, TILA
 catagories, 320
mortgage market, primary
 collateral risk and, 107
 compliance risk and, 108
 interest rate risk and, 106
 liquidity risk and, 107
 and mortgage lenders, 71–73
 portfolio risks and, 108–9
 prepayment risk and, 106–7
 secondary markets, distinction of,
  112–13
mortgage market, secondary
 competition of, 130
 crisis of, 148–49
 economic functions of, 113–14
 Fannie Mae and Freddie Mac
  operations of, 129–30
 federal government and, 124
 FHLB financing and, 130–33
 fraud and, 149–51
 mega-servers and mega-originators of,
  138–40, 141–43
 operations of, 128–29
 participants in, 123–24
 period of growth, 1990, 137
 period of growth, 2000-2010, 140–43
 post-crisis issues of, 151–52
 and primary markets, distinction,
  112–13
 private markets of, 134–35
 rapid decline of, 2000-2009, 143–48
mortgage orgination documentation,
 398–99
Mortgage Partnership Finance program
 (MPF), 131–33
mortgage payment methods, 505–8
mortgage pipeline management, 550–55
mortgage product, comparison of,
 172–74
mortgage servicing right (MSR), 112–13
Mortgage Subsidy Bond Act (1981), 74

N

National Association of Home Builders
 (NAHB), 57
National Association of Mortgage
 Bankers, 85
National Association of Mortgage
 Brokers, 84. *See also* mortgage
 bankers; mortgage brokers
National Association of REALTORS,
 58
National Credit Union Administration
 (NCUA), 101, 103

National Credit Union Share Insurance Fund (NCUSIF), 103
National Environmental Policy Act (1969), 12
National Housing Act (1934), 9, 12, 208
National Mortgage Association of Washington (1938), 12
National Mortgage Licensing System and Reistry (NMLSR), 350
nature of real estate, countercyclical, 69, 72
"Naughty Nine", 303
Navy Federal Credit Union, 101
NCUA. *See* National Credit Union Administration (NCUA)
net interest margin (NIM), 71
non-conforming loan, mortgage, 177–79
  selling of, 535–36
non-prime loan, mortgage, 179–80
note
  mortgage debt, 40
  provisions, 40

O

Office of Federal Housing Enterprise Oversight (OFHEO), 134
Office of Thrift Supervision (OTS), 97
Omnibus Reconciliation Act (1980), 13
Origination charge/service, 330

P

Participating Financial Institutions (PFI), 131–33
participation interests, 533–34
"piggy-back" loans, 202–3, 269–70
Pipeline reports, 551
pool basis, 533
pool insurance, mortgage, 196–97
pooled loan sale, 112
portfolio management, 518–19. *See also* loan administration
power of sale, 46–47
prime rate, 16–17
primogeniture, doctrine of, 27–28
Privacy of Consumer Financial Information (FTC Privacy Rule), 298
private label security (PLS), 118, 120–21, 146, 541
Private Mortgage Insurance (PMI), 14
private mortgage insurance (PMI)
  claims to, 196
  contracting with, 194
  coverage amount of, 194–96
  history of, 183–89
  importance of, 182–83
  pool insurance and, 196–97
  sample plans and premiums of, 191–94
  workings of, 189–90
program risk, 551
"pull-through rates", 140

Q

Qualifying applicants, 374
quality control programs, 496–500

R

Real Estate Investment (REIT), 15
Real Estate Settlement Procedures Act (RESPA), 13, 14, 15, 84, 298–99
  business disclosure of, 327
  definitions of, 331–32
  escrow rules of, 342–43
  escrow surplus, shortage and deficit, 343
  good faith estimate form, 333–38
  HUD-1 and, 338–41
  initial and annual escrow statements of, 342
  MDIA and HUD overview, 327–31
  process of. *See also* closing
  required disclosures of, 326–27
  scope of, 325–27
  servicing disclosure statement of, 327
  servicing transfer statement of, 338, 342
  special information booklet of, 327
real property, 28
REALTORS®, 557–58, 572
Reconstruction Finance Act (1932), 8, 11
recording (of property transfer), 37–38
"Red Flags Rule", 308
redlining, 301–2
regulatory system, mortgage, 23
release of mortgage, 51
Remittance Schedules (Actual/Actual; Scheduled/Actual; Scheduled/Scheduled), 538
repurchase risk, 551–52
reserves, type, 202
residential debt, holders of, 78–82
RESPA. *See* Real Estate Settlement Procedures Act (RESPA)
retail loan origination
  branch offices and, 572
  commission loan agents and, 569–70
  expected volume and, 572–73
  FASB statement and, 571
  functions of retail lenders and, 570–71
  importance of purchase and, 568–69
  origination income and, 571
  refinances of, 569
  trade-off of points and interest of, 572
reverse annuity mortgages (RAMs)
  consumer protection and, 293–95
  FHA conversion mortgage of. *See* home equity conversion mortgage, FHA (HEMC)
  funding of, 291

program suitability, 295–96
  as supplemental income, 289–91
right of dower, 31–32
right of redemption
  equitable, 43
  statutory, 47–48
risks. *See also* asset/liability management (ALM); mortgage market, primary; mortgage pipeline management; underwriting
  of delivery, 551
  of fallout, 550
  of funding, 551
  interest rate and, 71, 106
  interest rate volatility and, 553
  of investor, 551
  investor and, 91
  of liquidity, 552
  locking rates and, 552–53
  pipeline reports of, 553–55
  of price/interest rate, 552
  of program, 551
Roman law, 2
Rural Housing Services (RHS)
  home loan guarantee program (SFHLGP) of, 241–46
  homeownership direct loan programs (HDLP) of, 241
  properties eligible for, 240–41
  single family programs of, 240

S

S&Ls. *See* thrift institutions
saving banks
  historical development of, 99
  mortgage lending activity of, 100
  organization and regulation of, 99–100
saving institutions. *See* thrift institutions
Savings Association Insurance Fund (SAIF), 93, 97
"seasoning" non-conforming loan, 535–36
second mortgage, 269–70
secondary market math, 536
Secondary Mortgage Markets, 21
Secure and Fair Enforcement for Mortgage Licensing Act (SAFE ACT)
  consumer protection regulations and, 298–99
  establishment of, 15
  MLO requirements, federal and, 350–51
  MLO requirements, state and, 351
  MLO's of, 78
  mortgage brokers and, 84–85
  non-traditional loans and, 159
  requirements of, 350
securities
  mortgage-backed (MBSs), 115–18
  private label type, 120–21

securities, mortgage-backed (MBSs)
conceptual problems with, 121–22
Ginnie Mae type, 118–19
importance in current market, 122–23
private issuers of (PLSs), 120–21
traditional type, 119–20
securitized loan, 112
seisin, 29, 32
Seller/Servicer, GSE-Approved, 128–29
selling loan production
advantages of, 542
conduits and, 543
direct issue of securities, 543
direct sales of, 542–43
uniform documentation and,
549–50
selling residential mortgages
loan sell options and, 532–35
managing mortgage pipeline, 550–54
MERS and, 550
mortgage banking business model for,
541–42
non-conforming mortgages and,
535–36
recourse for, 534–35
secondary market commitments and,
545–48
stragetic options for, 541
service release premium (yield speed
premium), 85
Servicemen's Readjustment Act (1944),
9, 12, 227
Settlement charge/service, 330
Settlement Costs and You, 327
Settlement statement (HUD-1), 485
Shopping for your Home Loan, 327,
465, 482
Standards for Insuring the Security,
Integrity, and Protection of Customer Records and Information
(FTC Safeguards Rule), 298
statute of frauds, 37
subprime lending, 21–22
sub-prime mortgage. *See* non-prime
loan, mortgage

T
table funding, 575–76
targeted marketing, 565–66
Tax Reform Act (1986), 14, 97
Taxpayer Relief Act (1997), 14
technology, 361–62, 405–506
Telemarketing Sales Rule (FTC Do Not
Call Registry), 298
tenancy by the entirety, 34
tenancy in partnership, 35
tenants in common, 34–35
Third party origination, 571
three C's of lending, 410–11
thrift institutions, 5, 6–7
historical development of, 95–96
modern, 98–99

organization and regulation of, 97–98
in trouble, 96–97
TILA. *See* Truth in Lending Act (TILA)
title insurance, 472
title review, 469–72
title theory, 39
Title X, 352–53
Title XIV, 353–55
"too big to fail", 82
total debt ratio, 417–19
transfers, real estate, 49–50
trends in mortgages, 73–74
Truth in Lending Act (TILA)
advertising practices by dwelling,
318–19
Annual Percentage Rate (APR) and, 315
ARMs disclosures and, 315–16
assumptions of mortgage and, 316
billing rights and, 319
canceling transaction and, 323–24
consumer protection regulations
and, 298
disclosure practices of, 316–18
disclosure statement of, 369
disclosures and, 312
explanation of, 311–12
FDPA and, 343–44
finances charges and, 312–15
HELCPA and, 320–23
HMDA and. *See* Home Mortgage
Disclosure Act (HMDA)
HOEPA and, 319–20
HPA and, 344–47
introduction of, 12, 15
mortgage loan programs and, 320
non-cancellation confirmation of, 325
processing practices by principal
dwelling, 319
required lender practices of, 318
RESPA and. *See* Real Estate Settlement Procedures Act (RESPA)
RESPA final rule and, 316
right to rescind and, 323
scope of, 312
two-step or reset, mortgages, 170

U
underwriting. *See also* credit history
analyzing risk of, 403–4
applicant credit history, 419–22
applicant income and, 415–17
applicant total debt ratio and, 417–18
areas of review and, 410–11
automated underwriting systems
(AUS) and, 425–26
combind loan to value (LTV) ratios
and, 413–14
comprehensive risk assessment and,
426–27
conflicting objectives of, 406–10
decision of, 430–33
definition of, 401–2

discrimination and federal government and, 435–36
documents, standard vs. streamlined
and, 425–26
downpayment, 414–15
guidelines for, 404–5
guidelines for application, 435
housing ratio, 417
loan policy and eligibility issues of,
411–12
loan to value (LTV) ratios, 412–13
by mortgage lender, 402–3
prequalifying applicants and, 411
reveiw of appraisal and, 423–24
risk-based price adjustments and,
406, 407–9
technology for, 405–6
worksheet and summary of, 430
underwriting function, managing
AUS and risk assessments, 434
fraud and quality control of, 434
unform residential appraisal report,
438–39
Uniform Appraisal Dataset (UAD), 457
uniform documentation, 549–50
Uniform Mortgage Data Program
(UMDP), 457
Uniform Partnership Act, 35
uniform residential appraisal report,
448–55
uniform residential loan application
forms. *See* mortgage loan originator
(MLO)
Uniform Stands of Professional
Appraisal Practice, 439–40
Uniting and Strengthening America by
Providing Appropriate Tools
Required to Intercept and Obstruct
Terrorism Act (USA PATRIOT).
See USA PATRIOT Act
URAR. *See* Fannie Mae (Federal
National Mortgage Association)
U.S. Department of Agriculture. *See*
Rural Housing Services (RHS)
USA PATRIOT Act, 298, 307. *See also*
first-mortgage loan closing

V
VA. *See* Veterans Administration (VA)
verification of employment (VOE),
380–82, 416
Veterans Administration (VA)
acts pertaining to, 13
authorized by Con
certificate of re
232–33
credit/liab
docum
do

no bids and, 236–39
qualifying ratios of, 232
restoration of, 228–29
underwriting of, 233–34
voluntary transfer, 36

W

warehousing, 91
weighted-average (coupon)
  yield, 538
whole loan sale, 112
wholesale loan orgination

advantages and disadvantages of,
  573–75
affinity groups and, 576–77
internet lending and, 577–78
quality control and, 578
by third party originators, 576
www.hud.gov/offices/hsg/ramn/res/
  respa_hm.cfm, 299

Y

yield calculations
  of net yield, 537–38

and package price, 539
pricing of loan, 539–40
remittance options of, 540–41
risk-based pricing adjustments and,
  540
of weighted-average (coupon) yield,
  538
yield speed premium (service release
  premium), 85
yield spread premiums, 576